Behavior Analysis and Learning

Behavior Analysis and Learning, Fifth Edition is an essential textbook covering the basic principles in the field of behavior analysis and learned behaviors, as pioneered by B. F. Skinner. The textbook provides an advanced introduction to operant conditioning from a very consistent Skinnerian perspective. It covers a range of principles from basic respondent and operant conditioning through applied behavior analysis into cultural design. Elaborating on Darwinian components and biological connections with behavior, the book treats the topic from a consistent worldview of selectionism. The functional relations between the organism and the environment are described, and their application in accounting for old behavior and generating new behavior is illustrated.

Expanding on concepts described in past editions, the fifth edition provides updated coverage of recent literature and the latest findings. There is increased inclusion of biological and neuroscience material, as well as more data correlating behavior with neurological and genetic factors. The chapter on verbal behavior has been expanded to include new research on stimulus equivalence and naming; there is also a more detailed and updated analysis of learning by imitation and its possible links to mirror neurons. In the chapter on applied behavior analysis (ABA), new emphasis is given to contingency management of addiction, applications to education, ABA and autism, and prevention and treatment of health-related problems.

The material presented in this book provides the reader with the best available foundation in behavior science, and is a valuable resource for advanced undergraduate and graduate students in psychology or other behavior-based disciplines. In addition, a website of supplemental resources for instructors and students makes this new edition even more accessible and student-friendly (www.psypress.com/cw/Pierce).

W. David Pierce is Professor, Emeritus, of Sociology at the University of Alberta, Canada. His main research concerns a biobehavioral analysis of activity anorexia, taste regulation of overeating, and exercise-induced taste aversion.

Carl D. Cheney is Professor, Emeritus, of Psychology at Utah State University, USA. He teaches behavior analysis and physiological psychology, and has published widely on the experimental analysis of behavior. His current research is focused on the management of diet selection in a variety of species.

Behavior Analysis and Learning

Fifth Edition

W. David Pierce and
Carl D. Cheney

Ψ Psychology Press
Taylor & Francis Group

NEW YORK AND LONDON

Please visit the Companion Website at www.psypress.com/cw/Pierce

This edition published 2013
by Psychology Press
711 Third Avenue, New York, NY 10017

Simultaneously published in the UK
by Psychology Press
27 Church Road, Hove, East Sussex BN3 2FA

Psychology Press is an imprint of the Taylor & Francis Group, an Informa business

First edition published by Prentice Hall 1995
Fourth edition published by Psychology Press 2008

Library of Congress Cataloging in Publication Data
  Behavior analysis and learning / edited by W. David Pierce and
  Carl D. Cheney.—5th ed.
    p. cm.
  Rev. ed. of: Behavior analysis and learning / W. David Pierce, Carl D. Cheney.
  4th ed. 2008.   1. Behaviorism (Psychology)   2. Learning, Psychology of.
  I. Cheney, Carl D.   II. Pierce, W. David. Behavior analysis and learning.
  BF199.P54 2013
  150.19'434—dc23   2012033081

ISBN: 978–1–84872–615–4 (hbk)
ISBN: 978–0–203–44181–7 (ebk)

Typeset in Times
by RefineCatch Limited, Bungay, Suffolk, UK

To B. F. Skinner

When an organism acts upon the environment in which it lives, it changes that environment in ways that often affect the organism itself. Some of these changes are what the layman calls rewards, or what are generally referred to technically as reinforcers: when they follow behavior in this way they increase the likelihood that the organism will behave in the same way again.

(Ferster & Skinner, 1957, p. 1)

Contents

Foreword

If one index of the vitality and longevity of a discipline is the number of editions of pertinent textbooks, the field of learning and behavior is going strong; there are several textbooks that have exceeded four editions. Now, joining their ranks is *Behavior Analysis and Learning* by David Pierce and Carl Cheney, which, with this printing, celebrates its fifth edition. The book was first published in 1994, and the fifth edition will now be published on the eve of its twentieth anniversary. The book's success is due in large part to a number of features that make it unique among its competitors.

First, as the title indicates and the authors make clear, the book covers not just learning and behavior, but behavior analysis as "a comprehensive, natural science approach to the study of the behavior of organisms." In so doing, Pierce and Cheney address not only the experimental foundations of the science, but its conceptual framework, philosophical implications, and applications to real-world behavioral problems. Concerning the latter, each chapter has a section—*On the Applied Side*—in which the authors illustrate how the basic concepts or principles presented in the chapter have been used to ameliorate some socially significant behavior.

Second, Pierce and Cheney present behavior analysis as a member of the family of biological sciences, which, as a selectionist science, emphasizes Skinner's concept of selection by consequences at three levels: genes (i.e., natural selection), the behavior of individual organisms (i.e., operant conditioning), and cultural practices (i.e., cultural selection). In fact, the authors acknowledge that the capacity for learning itself is an evolved trait, and that the behavior of scientists who study it is, in part, a function of cultural contingencies.

Third, a new feature of *Behavior Analysis and Learning*, and one that should increase the appeal of the book even more, especially beyond behavior-analytic circles, is the inclusion in almost every chapter of a *New Directions* section that relates the topic of the chapter to recent developments in behavioral neuroscience. The authors reiterate a point made by Skinner and later behavior analysts—that even though knowledge of neurological events and processes is not necessary for the prediction and control of behavior, such knowledge contributes to a more complete understanding of its proximate, or immediate, causes. Thus, *Behavior Analysis and Learning* places learning and the natural science that studies it—behavior analysis—in the broader context of the biological sciences, alongside evolutionary biology and neuroscience. Thereby, the book makes a strong case for a unified science of behavior that incorporates both proximate (i.e., immediate) and ultimate (i.e., remote) causes of behavior.

Fourth, Pierce and Cheney provide examples of how laboratory-derived principles of learning can be used to understand the results of studies carried out by nonbehavior-analytic psychologists. Many of these studies address interesting phenomena and observe and measure important behaviors, but all too often the explanations suffer from references to unobserved constructs. By interpreting the results of these studies according to behavior-analytic principles, Pierce and Cheney show that when it comes to experiments conducted by other psychologists, we need not throw out the baby with the bath water; we can take their behavioral data at face value and provide more parsimonious explanations. Such an exercise once again demonstrates the capacity of a behavior-analytic approach to offer a unified theory of behavior.

Finally, a related feature of *Behavior Analysis and Learning* that makes it stand out as a superior textbook is that, in addition to presenting the experimental foundations of behavior analysis and showing how they can be used to improve socially significant behaviors, Pierce and Cheney demonstrate how the basic principles of behavior detailed in the book can be used to interpret behavior that is either novel, too complex to be studied in the lab, or seemingly mentalistic or cognitive. Interpretation is fundamental to all of the experimental sciences, and behavior analysis is no different. By demonstrating how laboratory-derived principles of behavior can be used to understand complex behaviors that go by such names as language, memory, consciousness, and perception, Pierce and Cheney broaden the reach of behavior-analytic theory.

The fifth edition of *Behavior Analysis and Learning* improves on the fourth and previous editions, not by adding fluff, but by incorporating cutting-edge basic and applied research in the context of a unifying set of theoretical concepts and principles.

Beginning with the first edition, *Behavior Analysis and Learning* has been dedicated to B. F. Skinner, and I can think of no better tribute to him than a book which not only details the basic principles of the science that he helped to establish, but which does so in the context of the selectionist principles that he championed, and which demonstrates how, to paraphrase Skinner, we can use those principles to act to save the world.

Henry D. Schlinger, Jr.
California State University, Los Angeles
16 September 2012

Preface

W. Frank Epling, Ph.D. was coauthor of the first two editions of *Behavior Analysis and Learning*. He was a great personal friend of ours, an excellent teacher, and a productive colleague. We hope that this fifth edition is as good as Frank would accept, and we dedicate it to his memory.

The goal of this textbook is to present and describe the philosophy, methods, findings, principles, and applications of the natural science of behavior analysis. This fifth edition presents the history, current status, and projections for the future of humans investigating what accounts for their behavior.

We have received a great deal of welcome positive feedback from readers of earlier editions, which we greatly appreciate. This fifth edition retains much of the major organization, information, and unique features of the previous editions, yet, as with any revision, we have made several alterations in topics, presentation, and resources. We responded to user and reviewer comments and to the availability of much new information from the literature. Reviewers reported that, although this is a basic experimental analysis text, they enjoyed the applied human and nonhuman examples, and so we have expanded and continued this feature. A single college textbook cannot do justice to both basic and applied behavior analysis, and our focus has remained primarily basic so as to provide the fundamentals, where they came from, and how they may apply in diverse situations. It is our belief that, given a solid understanding of the behavior principles presented in this text, the reader will be equipped to analyze, design research or treatment, carry out an effective behavioral assessment, and be successful with the behavior management of most species.

Many readers indicated an appreciation of the use of Francis Mechner's notation system as a clear depiction of the experimental contingencies and the independent variables that control behavior. Dr. Mechner remains active and thoughtful in producing creative and challenging research in behavior analysis (see Chapter 1 on thinking), and we have used his system since graduate school.

Users and reviewers also encouraged us to include more biobehavioral findings, which we were pleased to do. For example, the reports of "mirror" neurons and their possible involvement in imitation and empathetic behavior have been expanded. We have also noted important research relating activity in the brain area called the nucleus accumbens to choice behavior, and the involvement of the amygdala in conditioned reinforcement. An elaboration of the evolution of the human vocal apparatus and verbal behavior contributes, we feel, to the synthesis of biology and behavior. Although we remain dedicated to behavior analysis as a discipline of its own, we appreciate the movement toward a synthesis of a science of behavior with neuroscience. Ultimately the brain is responsible for nearly all behavior (headless cockroach data being one exception), and eventually our knowledge of brain mechanisms together with understanding of the environmental features that contribute to behavioral contingencies will provide a means of prediction and control beyond what we may have thought possible.

The pedagogical features in the fifth edition have proven successful and include the *Focus On* inserts, *Advanced Sections*, and *On The Applied Side* presentations. The placement of *Advanced Sections* at the end of chapters allows instructors to address basic material without the intrusion of more complicated issues. We now include sections on *New Directions* in behavior and neuroscience in most chapters to highlight the links between behavior analysis and direct observation of neural systems and processes. As in the past, we continue to provide *Chapter Summaries*, which we expect will improve students' mastery of the material.

In this edition we have updated nearly all areas, topics, and coverage with new findings (there are more than 300 new citations), and we have incorporated several different study features. For readers/users all study questions, PowerPoint presentations, video vignettes illustrating specific points, and other material considered helpful, are available on a dedicated website at www.psypress. com/cw/Pierce. Using this system, the authors (and instructor) can add, delete, or alter material as considered appropriate. Many additional websites are indicated which can guide the reader to current material of interest. Websites are a major resource, and we encourage the instructor to incorporate web assignments whenever appropriate. A thorough reading of the text is sufficient to acquire the basic principles; however, most students nowadays are fluent with the web, and actually expect to access information via this medium.

The fifth edition continues to be primarily about the way the world works with respect to operant behavior and operant conditioning. We continue, however, to provide an extensive, updated, and detailed chapter on respondent (classical) conditioning, although the *Advanced Section* is abbreviated and less demanding than in previous editions. As in the past, we address respondent conditioning with regard to the habitual use of drugs and the concepts of tolerance, craving, and withdrawal.

The sections on behavior analysis applied in education settings, autism, and health (e.g., breast self-examination, obesity, and anorexia) have been extensively expanded, as has the emphasis on principles of selection and the biological context of conditioning. New findings in the area of epigenetics have contributed to our highlighting of the contribution of the early and developing environment to behavior. Behavior analysts, of course, recognize the essential nature of biological contributions and constraints while simultaneously emphasizing what can be done with arbitrary selective procedures (contingency management) to alter socially important (in fact all) behavior.

The organization of the book has not changed, because we consider it now to be a systematic and reasonable progression of behavior science, as a book format requires. We recommend assigning and treating the material in the order in which it is presented; of course, individual adjustments and adaptations are possible for personal considerations best left to the instructor. Chapters 1 and 2 set the boundaries of behavior science and introduce many of the critical historical features and individuals relevant to placing behavior analysis in a context familiar to the reader. At this point, the basic behavior paradigm and the three-term operant contingencies of positive reinforcement and extinction are described in detail. Chapter 4 on reinforcement and extinction is followed by schedules of reinforcement, which is the major independent variable of behavior analysis. The section on reinforcement schedules promotes the fact that all operant behavior varies in rate and form with the existing contingencies, both in the laboratory and in the everyday world of organisms. Next, we introduce the topic of the use of aversive procedures, and the by-products of aversive control are detailed and emphasized. Many contingencies in the world are based on aversive consequences, so although we do not recommend their use, we believe that the reader needs be aware of what behavior science has to offer with regard to this issue. This particular order of the chapters allows us to more fully address the contingencies of positive and negative punishment, and negative reinforcement (escape and avoidance). By this point in the book all of the basic contingencies have been introduced and shown to be operative in both research and observations of everyday life.

After presenting the basic principles, the text moves to the interrelationship of operant and respondent contingencies and the biological context of behavior—showing that operant and respondent processes often (if not always) work together, sometimes in opposition, in complex interacting relations. At this point, we consider issues of antecedent stimulus control and the regulation of higher-order behavioral processes such as conditional discrimination, remembering, and concept formation. Choice and preference analysis based on concurrent schedules of reinforcement are the next logical step; here we present a thorough treatment of the matching law for concurrent and single operant situations. Under choice, we now address research on optimal foraging and extensively describe the research, concepts, and applications of behavioral economics, attempting to clarify the breadth and application of these areas of investigation. As the natural science of behavior continues to mature—this is about the 50th anniversary of "Behaviorism at Fifty", published by Skinner in 1963 (*Science, 140*, 951–958)—we believe that there will be an even greater expansion of these areas of analysis to more complex behavior involving multifaceted contingencies. One example of this is conditioned reinforcement and the regulation of behavior by concurrent-chain schedules of reinforcement. In this edition, we have expanded the coverage of concurrent-chain procedures and how these contingencies are used to evaluate delay discounting and other accounts of conditioned reinforcement.

Imitation and rule-governed behavior are important issues in the analysis of human behavior that are inadequately treated in most basic behavior-science textbooks. We have substantially updated Chapter 11, which is devoted to these topics, adding a neuroscience dimension to imitation learning. The analysis of rule-governed behavior of the listener sets up Chapter 12 on verbal behavior and analysis of the behavior of the speaker. We have expanded the book's treatment of verbal behavior, adding new issues, research, and analyses (e.g., autoclitics and naming). The chapter now provides the basic rationale and fundamental components of Skinner's analysis, as well as more current analyses that link verbal behavior to human communication and social interaction. The issues of private events and equivalence relations are discussed, as are some current reports from the *Journal of Verbal Behavior*.

As mentioned, we have significantly updated the chapter on applied behavior analysis (Chapter 13) with more examples, new issues, and recent material. It is nearly impossible and unnecessary to separate basic from applied behavior analysis but, due to its social importance and interest to students, a separate applied chapter is warranted. Behavior principles are so compelling that students often invent new applications when they first encounter the concepts of reinforcement and extinction. Our discipline has become more recognized and appreciated from the visible effects on human behavior in applied situations than from the possibly more important, but clearly more esoteric, findings from the laboratory. Applied behavior analysis is part and parcel of the experimental analysis of behavior, and we include it wherever possible.

We end the book with a discussion of three levels of selection: natural selection, selection by reinforcement, and selection at the cultural level. Each of these sections is updated with new findings and new issues. For example, we now provide a discussion of evolution, behavioral dynamics, and modern neuroscience. The three levels of selection are described and repeatedly mentioned in our classes and lectures. It seems to require some repetition and time for many students to grasp the breadth and significance of what exactly the point is here. The utilization of virtually the same process (selection by consequences) to generate functional relations and explanations at vastly different levels of resolution should be impressive. Selection by consequences is the way the world works, with few hard-wired actions, but an ability to benefit (i.e., change behavior), depending upon the consequences of any action. The consequences of behaving—whether these are a response of the salivary gland, a child's babbling, or the protests of a political group—are what influence the likelihood of repetition of those actions.

Behavior analysis has always been an exciting scientific field, and we hope that we have communicated our own enthusiasm for the discipline described in this book. By its very nature, the study of why we do the things we do appeals to nearly everyone very quickly. The formal aspects of behavior analysis and learning are having an impact on education, industry, therapy, animal management, medicine, clinical psychology, and environmental protection, to name only a few areas of successful application. There is an explicit technology available to those who master the principles of behavior, and readers can use these principles to change their own and others' behavior.

However, our major focus has been to present the fundamental principles and procedures that form the foundation of a science of behavior.

We thank the many people who have directly and indirectly contributed to this text, and we appreciate them all. Our personal worldview began to take shape during our upbringing, and was formed and promoted by family, friends, personal experience, and our teachers, colleagues, and students. We thank them all for what we are and for what we have produced.

W. David Pierce
Carl D. Cheney

A Science of Behavior: Perspective, History, and Assumptions

1

1. Find out about *learning*, a science of behavior and behavior analysis.
2. Discover how *selection by consequences* extends from evolution to the behavior of organisms.
3. Focus on behavior analysis and neuroscience.
4. Delve into the early beginnings of behavior analysis and learning.
5. Learn how to analyze feeling and thinking as behavior.

Learning refers to the acquisition, maintenance, and change of an organism's *behavior* as a result of lifetime events. The **behavior** of an organism is everything it does, including private and covert actions like thinking and feeling (see section on assumptions in this chapter). An important aspect of human learning concerns the experiences arranged by other people. From earliest history, people have acted to influence the behavior of other individuals. Rational argument, rewards, bribes, threats, and force are used in attempts to promote learning or change the behavior of people. In civilized societies, people are required to learn socially appropriate behaviors. As long as a person conforms, no one pays much attention. As soon as conduct substantially departs from cultural norms, people get upset and socially reject the non-conformist—ensuring that most of us comply (Williams & Nida, 2011). All societies have codes of conduct and laws that their people have to learn; people who break moral codes or civil laws face penalties ranging from minor fines to capital punishment. Clearly, all cultures are concerned with human learning and the regulation of human conduct. Without regulation, anarchy and confusion eventually destroy the civil order of society.

Theories of learning and behavior have ranged from philosophy to natural science. When Socrates was told that new discoveries in anatomy proved that bodily movement was caused by the arrangement of muscles, bones, and joints, he replied, "That hardly explains why I am sitting here in a curved position talking to you" (Millenson, 1967, p. 3). About 2300 years later, in 1934, the great philosopher Alfred North Whitehead and the famous behaviorist B. F. Skinner were seated together at dinner involved in a discussion about the behaviorist approach to psychology. After listening to Skinner's interpretations of human behavior based on principles discovered in the laboratory, Whitehead challenged the behaviorist to account for the generative nature of human language. He said, "Let me see you account for my behavior as I sit here saying, 'No black scorpion is falling upon this table'" (Skinner, 1957, p. 457). Whitehead's point was that no theoretical or empirical system existed to account for the spontaneous and generative nature of human language.

Although there was no satisfactory behavioral account of complex human behavior and language in the 1930s, the science of behavior is currently addressing such puzzling questions.

Human behavior has been attributed to a great variety of causes. The causes of behavior have been located both within and outside of people. Internal causes have ranged from metaphysical entities like the soul to hypothetical structures of the nervous system. Suggested external causes of behavior have included the effect of the moon and tides, the arrangement of stars, and the whims of gods. Unfortunately, some of these bizarre, prescientific attempts to explain human behavior remain popular today. For example, the use of astrological forecasts is even found in modern corporations, as demonstrated in the following passage taken from *The Economist*.

> Is astrology the ultimate key to competitive advantage? That is what Divinitel, a French company specializing in celestial consulting, claims. For FFr350 ($70) a session, the firm's astrologers offer advice on anything from the timing of takeovers to exorcisms. For the busy executive, Divinitel's galaxy of services can be reached via Minitel, France's teletext system. The firm is even planning a flotation on France's over-the-counter stock market in March 1991.
>
> So who is daft enough to pay for such mystical mumbo-jumbo? About 10% of French businesses are, according to a study by HEC, a French business school. A typical client is the boss of a small or medium-sized company who wants a second, astrological opinion on job applicants. The boss of one plastics company even uses Divinitel's advice on star signs to team up salesmen.
>
> ("Twinkle, twinkle," *The Economist*, 22 December 1990, p. 95)

The use of metaphysical phenomena to account for human behavior has even permeated the social sciences. In the respected *Journal of Personality and Social Psychology*, Daryl Bem, a prominent social psychologist, reported a series of nine experiments on "feeling the future" (Bem, 2011). The idea is that people show conscious awareness (precognition) and affective apprehension (premonition) of future events, knowing what will happen before it does. These claims for time reversal and precognition hinge on the reliability and validity of the methods and statistics used in these studies. However, critics of these psi experiments question the soundness of the experiments and the statistical assumptions used for data analysis, concluding that there is little or no evidence to support such paranormal effects (Shermer, 2011; Wagenmakers, Wetzels, Borsboom, & van der Maas, 2011).

The trouble with precognition, astrology, and other primitive and metaphysical accounts of behavior is that they are not scientific. That is, these theories do not hold up to testing and scrutinizing by scientists who follow the scientific method. Over the last century, a scientific model of learning and behavior has developed. Behavior theory states that all behavior is due to a complex interaction between genetic influence and environmental experience. The theory is based on observation and controlled experimentation, and it provides a natural-science account of the learning and behavior of organisms, including humans. This book is concerned with such an account.

SCIENCE AND BEHAVIOR

The **experimental analysis of behavior** is a natural-science approach to understanding behavior regulation. Experimental analysis is concerned with controlling and changing the factors that affect the behavior of humans and other animals. For example, a behavioral researcher in a classroom may use a computer to arrange corrective feedback for a student's mathematical performance. The relevant condition that is manipulated or changed by the experimenter may involve presenting corrective feedback on some days and withholding it on others. In this case, the researcher would probably observe more accurate mathematical performance on days when feedback was presented.

This simple experiment illustrates one of the most basic principles of behavior—the principle of **reinforcement**.

The principle of reinforcement (and other behavior principles) provides a scientific account of how people and animals learn complex actions. When a researcher identifies a basic principle that governs behavior, this is called an analysis of behavior. Thus, the experimental analysis of behavior involves specifying the basic processes and principles that regulate the behavior of organisms. Experiments are then used to test the adequacy of the analysis.

Experimental analysis occurs when, for example, a researcher notices that more seagulls fly around a shoreline when people are on the beach than when the beach is deserted. After checking that changes in climate, temperature, time of day, and other conditions do not affect the behavior of the seagulls, the researcher offers the following analysis: People feed the birds and this reinforces flocking to the beach. When the beach is abandoned, the seagulls are no longer fed for congregating on the shoreline. This is a reasonable guess, but it can only be tested by an experiment. Pretend that the behavior analyst owns the beach and has complete control over it. The experiment involves changing the usual relationship between the presence of people and food. Simply stated, people are not allowed to feed the birds, and food is placed on the beach when people are not around. Over time, the behavior analyst notes that there are fewer and fewer seagulls on the beach when people are present, and more and more gulls when the shoreline is deserted. The behaviorist concludes that people regulated coming to the beach because the birds were fed, or reinforced, for this behavior only when people were present. This is one example of an experimental analysis of behavior.

Behavior Analysis: A Science of Behavior

Experimental analysis is the fundamental method for a **science of behavior**. Contemporary researchers no longer refer to their science as behavioral psychology, recognizing that psychology is focused on mental or cognitive events rather than on the behavior of organisms. Today, a science of behavior is called *behavior analysis*. This term implies a more general scientific approach that includes assumptions about how to study behavior, techniques for carrying out the analysis, a systematic body of knowledge, and practical implications for society and culture (Ishaq, 1991).

Behavior analysis is a comprehensive, natural-science approach to the study of the behavior of organisms. Primary objectives are the discovery of principles and laws that govern behavior, the extension of these principles across species, and the development of an applied technology for the management of behavior. In the seagull example, the underlying principle is called *discrimination*. The principle of discrimination states that an organism will respond differently to two situations (e.g., presence or absence of people) if its behavior has been reinforced in one setting but not in the other (*differential reinforcement*). Two assumptions should be noted here. First, behavior is a product of the organism's past and current interaction with the environment, as well as its biological or evolutionary history (primarily coded by the genes). Secondly, the principles (e.g., discrimination) discovered by an experimental analysis have wide generality, applying to all animal life.

The principle of discrimination may be extended to human behavior and social reinforcement. You may discuss dating with Carmen, but not Tracey, because Carmen is interested in such conversation while Tracey is not. In a classroom, the principle of discrimination can be used to improve teaching and learning. The use of behavior principles to solve practical problems is called **applied behavior analysis**, and is discussed at some length in Chapter 13.

As you can see, behavior analysis has a strong focus on environment–behavior relationships. The focus is on how organisms alter their behavior to meet the ever-changing demands of the environment. When an organism learns new ways of behaving in reaction to the changes that occur in its environment, this is called *conditioning*. The two basic kinds of conditioning are called respondent and operant.

Two Types of Conditioning

A **reflex** involves **respondent** behavior that is *elicited* by a biologically relevant stimulus. When a stimulus (S) automatically elicits (→) a stereotypical response (R) or *respondent*, the S → R *relationship* is called a reflex. The reflex is inherited in the sense that those animals that quickly and reliably responded to particular stimuli were more likely than other organisms to survive and reproduce. For instance, animals that startle and run in response to a sudden noise may escape a predator, and the startle reflex may provide an adaptive advantage over organisms that do not run, or that run less quickly in response to the noise. Thus, reflexes are selected across the history of the species. Of course, different species of organisms exhibit different sets of reflexes.

Respondent Conditioning

Respondent conditioning occurs when a neutral or otherwise meaningless stimulus is paired with an *unconditioned stimulus*. For example, respondent conditioning is shown when the buzz of a bee (neutral stimulus) is *paired* with the pain of a sting (unconditioned stimulus). After this conditioning, a buzzing bee usually causes people to escape it (respondent). The Russian physiologist *Ivan Petrovich Pavlov* made explicit this form of conditioning at the turn of the 20th century. He observed that dogs salivated when food was placed in their mouths. This relation between the food stimulus and salivation is an unconditioned reflex, and it occurs because of the animals' biological history. However, when Pavlov rang a bell just before feeding the dogs, they began to salivate at the sound of the bell. In this way, a new feature (the sound of the bell) came to control the respondent behavior of salivation. As shown in Figure 1.1, the respondent is now elicited by the new *conditioned stimulus*.

Respondent conditioning is one way in which organisms meet the challenge of change in their environments. A grazing animal that conditions to the sound of rustling grass and runs away is less likely to become a meal than one that waits to see the predator. All species that have been tested, including humans, show this kind of conditioning. In terms of human behavior, many of what we call our likes and dislikes are based on respondent conditioning. When good or bad things happen to us, we usually have an emotional reaction. These emotional responses can be conditioned to other people who are present when the positive or negative events occur (Byrne, 1971). Thus, respondent conditioning plays an important role in our social relationships—determining, to a great extent, how we feel about our friends as well as our enemies. Respondent conditioning is covered in more detail in Chapter 3.

FIG. 1.1 Simple respondent conditioning. In a reflex for a dog, food in the mouth produces salivation as respondent behavior. Next, a bell rings (new stimulus) just before feeding the dog; after several pairings of bell and food the dog begins to salivate at the sound of the bell.

Operant Conditioning

Operant conditioning involves the *regulation of behavior by its consequences*. B. F. Skinner called this kind of behavior regulation **operant conditioning** because, in a given situation or setting (S^D), behavior (R) operates on the environment to produce effects or consequences (S^r). An **operant** is any behavior that operates on the environment to produce an effect. The effect or consequence in turn changes the likelihood that the operant will occur again in a similar situation. During operant conditioning, an organism emits operant behavior based upon its genetic endowment; the operant produces an effect that increases (or decreases) the frequency of the response in a given situation (Skinner, 1938, p. 20). In the laboratory, a hungry rat in a chamber may receive food if it presses a lever when a light is on. If lever pressing increases in the presence of the light, then operant conditioning has occurred, and food functions as *reinforcement* (S^r) for the operant response (Figure 1.2).

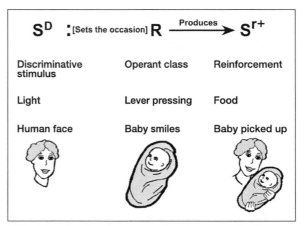

FIG. 1.2 Simple operant conditioning. In an operant chamber, lever pressing produces food for a hungry rat. The consequences of lever pressing (presentation of food) increase its frequency in that setting. In another example, a baby smiles to a human face and is picked up. The consequence of smiling (social attention) increases the frequency of this behavior in the presence of human faces.

In this example, the light (S^D) eventually *sets the occasion for* lever pressing in the sense that *the operant is likely to occur* when the light is on, and is unlikely to occur when it is off. That is, the frequency of lever pressing increases in the presence of the light (S^D). Turning the light on, however, does not force or elicit lever pressing as with a conditioned stimulus; it simply increases the probability of the lever-pressing response when the light is on. The control by the light stimulus is based on the past history of reinforcement for lever pressing in the presence of the light and no reinforcement when it is off.

Most of what we commonly call voluntary, willful, or purposive action is analyzed as operant behavior. *Operant conditioning* occurs when a baby smiles to a human face and is picked up. If smiling to faces increases in frequency because of social attention, then smiling is an operant and the effect is a result of conditioning. The presentation of a human face (S^D) *sets the occasion for* infant smiling only after a history of operant conditioning. When a face appears, the frequency of smiling increases; also, smiling has a low frequency of occurrence when no one is around. In a more complex example of video games, the presence of targets on the screen (S^D) *sets the occasion for* pressing a sequence of buttons (operant) that result in hitting a target (S^r), and increasing the probability of the response sequence. Other examples of operant behavior include driving a car to work, talking on the phone for fun, taking lecture notes to pass a test, walking to the store to buy groceries, reading a book for pleasure, writing a term paper for grades, and conducting an experiment to resolve a scientific question. In each case, the operant is said to be *selected by its consequences*.

The Consequences of Human Behavior

The consequences that follow human behavior are often arranged by other people, and are usually referred to as rewards. If the person is instructed to do something to get the reward, we call the reward an incentive. Both rewards and incentives are some of the social consequences of human behavior. A student who studies hard throughout the term may receive the grade of A+ as her reward. Another student may be instructed to study hard throughout the term to get a high grade. In both cases, the reward or incentive may or may not act as a reinforcing consequence for studying. Only when a high grade increases (or maintains) your subsequent studying is the grade acting as reinforcement. Thus, rewards and incentives are not equal to reinforcers.

One person may work hard for grades, while another does not make any effort to get them. Both have received the reward (A+), but one is now more likely to study while the other is not.

What makes a reward act as reinforcement for one person and not for another? The answer is a bit complicated at this point, but behavior analysts emphasize each person's *past history of reinforcement*. In one family, receiving high grades has resulted in many other reinforcing effects, such as praise and approval, which ultimately are related to basic reinforcers involving shelter and sustenance. Under these conditions, high grades (or the A+) have become a *conditioned reinforcer* for academic performance (see Chapter 10 for details). In another family, high grades have not led to other reinforcing effects, and grades do not act as reinforcement for academic behavior. One rat will work to turn a light on if the light has signaled food in the past; another rat without this experience will not work to activate the light. The reinforcing effects of the light for the rat and the grade for the student both depend on a prior history of reinforcement. The distinction between rewards and reinforcers is raised again in Chapter 4 in the section on rewards and intrinsic motivation.

Selection as a Causal Process

B. F. Skinner (1938) viewed psychology as the study of the behavior of organisms. From this point of view, psychology is a subfield of biology. The main organizing principle of contemporary biology is evolution through natural selection (Dawkins, 1996). Skinner generalized this concept to a broader principle of **selection by consequences**. Selection by consequences applies at three levels: (1) the selection over generations for genes related to survival and reproduction (natural or Darwinian selection); (2) the selection for behavior within the lifetime of an individual organism (selection by operant conditioning); and (3) the selection for behavior patterns (practices, traditions, rituals) of groups of human beings that endure beyond the lifetime of a single individual (cultural selection). In all three cases, it is the consequences arranged by the environment that select for (or against) the frequency of genetic, behavioral, and cultural forms (see Chapter 14).

Selection by consequences is a form of causal explanation. In science we talk about two kinds of causation: immediate and remote. **Immediate causation** is the kind of mechanism studied by physics and chemistry—the "billiard ball" sort of process where we try to isolate a chain of events that directly result in some effect. For example, chemical reactions are explained by describing molecular interactions. In the study of behavior, an immediate causal explanation might refer to the physiology and biochemistry of the organism. For example, the bar pressing of a rat for food or a gambler playing roulette could each involve the release of endogenous opiates and dopamine in the hypothalamus (Shizgal & Arvanitogiannis, 2003).

In contrast, **remote causation** is typical of sciences like evolutionary biology, geology, and astronomy. In this case, we explain some phenomenon by pointing to remote events that made it likely. Thus, the causal explanation of a species characteristic (e.g., size, coloration, exceptional vision, etc.) involves the working of natural selection on the gene pool of the parent population. An evolutionary account of species coloration, for example, would involve showing how this characteristic improved the reproductive success of organisms in a given ecological environment. That is, natural selection for coloration explains the current frequency of the characteristic in the population.

On the behavioral level, the principle of selection by consequences is a form of explanation by remote causation called *functional analysis*. When a rat learns to press a lever for food, we explain the rat's behavior by pointing to its past consequences (the function of behavior). Thus, the current frequency of bar pressing is explained by the **contingency** between bar pressing and food in the past. The rat's behavior has been *selected by its history of reinforcement*.

Both immediate and remote causal explanations are acceptable in science. Behavior analysts have emphasized functional analysis and selection by consequences (remote causation), but are also interested in direct analysis of physiological and neurochemical processes (immediate causation). Ultimately, both types of causal explanation will provide a more complete account of learning and behavior.

NEW DIRECTIONS: Behavior Analysis and Neuroscience

Behavior analysis is becoming more involved with the scientific analysis of the brain and nervous system (neuroscience). That is, researchers who primarily study the behavior of organisms are often interested in the brain processes that participate in the regulation of behavior (see special issue on Relation of Behavior and Neuroscience (2005) in *Journal of the Experimental Analysis of Behavior, 84,* 305–667). The word *participate* is used because the brain shows **neuroplasticity**, or changes in the interconnections of neurons (nerve cells; Kandel, 2006) and glia (non-neuronal cells; Fields, 2009), as the organism interacts with the world in which it lives. That is, the brain is not a static structure that determines behavior, but a malleable organ that constantly adjusts to the behavioral requirements of everyday life or the laboratory (Draganski, Gaser, Busch, Schuierer, Bogdahn, & May, 2004; Kempermann, Gast, & Gage, 2002; for the role of learning experiences in modification of brain structure that in turn affects behavior, see Schlinger, 2004). For example, brain mechanisms (neurons or groups of neurons) obviously participate in the regulation of behavior (bar pressing) by its consequences (food). Describing how neurons assemble, code for, and respond to reinforcement is an important and exciting addition to a behavior analysis—telling us more about what happens when behavior is shaped by its effects or consequences (Fiorillo, Tobler, & Schultz, 2003).

At the practical level, knowing the reinforcement contingencies (arrangements of the environment) for lever pressing is sufficient by itself to allow us to predict and control the rat's behavior. That is, we can get the rat to increase or decrease its lever pressing by providing or denying food reinforcement for this behavior—there is no need to look at neural systems. However, we gain a more complete account of how a rat's behavior increases when the action of neurons (and neural systems) is combined with the analysis of behavior. For example, in some cases it may be possible to "sensitize" or "de-sensitize" a rat to the behavioral contingencies by drugs that activate or block the action of specialized neurons (e.g., Bratcher, Farmer-Dougan, Dougan, Heidenreich, & Garris, 2005). Research at the neural level could, in this way, add to the practical control or regulation of behavior by its consequences (Hollerman & Schultz, 1998).

Neural processes also may participate as immediate consequences (local contingencies) for behavior that had long-range benefits for organisms (remote contingencies, as in evolution and natural selection) (Tobler, Fiorillo, & Schultz, 2005). The so-called *neural basis of reward* involves the interrelationship of the endogenous opiate and dopamine systems (as well as other neural processes) (Fiorillo, Tobler, & Schultz, 2003). For example, rats that are food restricted and allowed to run in wheels increase running over days—up to 20,000 wheel turns. Wheel running leads to the release of neural opiates that reinforce this behavior (Pierce, 2001). If wheel running is viewed as food-related travel, one function of neural reinforcement is to promote locomotion under conditions of food scarcity. The long-range or remote contingency (travel produces food: travel → food) is supported proximally by the release of endogenous opiates (physical activity → release of endogenous opiates) that "keep the rat going" under conditions of food scarcity (e.g., famine, drought, etc.). In later chapters we shall see that this process also plays a key role in human anorexia.

The integration of the science of behavior with neuroscience (**behavioral neuroscience**) is a growing field of inquiry. Areas of interest include the effects of drugs on behavior (behavioral pharmacology), neural imaging and complex stimulus relations, choice and neural activity, and the brain circuitry of learning and addiction. We shall examine some of this research in subsequent chapters in sections that focus on behavior analysis and neuroscience (FOCUS ON sections) or in sections that emphasize applications (ON THE APPLIED SIDE sections).

The Evolution of Learning

When organisms were faced with unpredictable and changing environments in their evolutionary past, natural selection favored those individuals whose behavior could be conditioned. Organisms who condition are more flexible, in the sense that they can learn new requirements and relationships in the environment (see section on "Behavioral Flexibility" in Chapter 14 for recent evidence by Mery and Kawecki (2002) on the link between learning ability and improved fitness in the fruit fly, *Drosophila melanogaster*). Such behavioral flexibility must reflect an underlying structural change of the organism. Genes code for the anatomical and physiological characteristics of the individual. Such structural physical changes allow for different degrees of functional behavioral flexibility. Thus, differences in the structure of organisms based on genetic variation give rise to differences in the regulation of behavior. Processes of learning, like operant and respondent conditioning, lead to greater (or lesser) reproductive success. Presumably, those organisms that changed their behavior as a result of experience during their lives survived and had offspring, while those that were less flexible did not. Simply stated, this means that *the capacity for learning is inherited.*

The evolution of learning processes had an important consequence. Behavior that was closely tied to survival and reproduction could be influenced by experience. Specific physiological processes typically regulate behavior related to survival and reproduction. However, for behaviorally flexible organisms, this control by physiology may be modified by experiences during the lifetime of the individual. The extent of such modification depends on the amount and scope of behavioral flexibility (Baum, 1983). For example, sexual behavior is closely tied to reproductive success and is regulated by distinct physiological processes. For many species, sexual behavior is rigidly controlled by genetically driven mechanisms. In humans, however, sexual behavior is also influenced by socially mediated experiences. It is these experiences, not genes, that come to dictate when sexual intercourse will occur, how it is performed, and who can be a sexual partner. Powerful religious or social controls can make people abstain from sex. This example demonstrates that even the biologically relevant behavior of humans is partly determined by life experience.

The Biological Context of Behavior

Behavior analysts recognize and promote the importance of biology and evolution, but focus more on the interplay of the organism and its environment, which is behavior. To maintain this focus, the evolutionary history and biological status of an organism are examined as part of the *context of behavior* (see Morris, 1988, 1992). This contextualist view is seen in B. F. Skinner's analysis of imprinting in a duckling:

> Operant conditioning and natural selection are combined in the so-called imprinting of a newly hatched duckling. In its natural environment the young duckling moves towards its mother and follows her as she moves about. The behavior has obvious survival value. When no duck is present, the duckling

behaves in much the same way with respect to other objects. Recently it has been shown that a young duckling will come to approach and follow any moving object, particularly if it is the same size as a duck—for example, a shoebox. Evidently survival is sufficiently well served even if the behavior is not under the control of the specific visual features of a duck. Merely approaching and following is enough.

Even so, that is not a correct statement of what happens. What the duckling inherits is the *capacity to be reinforced by maintaining or reducing the distance between itself and a moving object* [italics added]. In the natural environment, and in the laboratory in which imprinting is studied, approaching and following have these consequences, but the contingencies can be changed. A mechanical system can be constructed in which movement *toward* an object causes the object to move rapidly away, while movement *away from* the object causes it to come closer. Under these conditions, the duckling will move away from the object rather than approach or follow it. A duckling will learn to peck a spot on the wall if pecking brings the object closer. Only by knowing what and how the duckling learns during its lifetime can we be sure of what it is equipped to do at birth.

(Skinner, 1974, pp. 40–41)

The duckling's biological history, in terms of providing the capacity for reinforcement by proximity to a duck-sized object, is the context for the regulation of its behavior. Of course, the anatomy and physiology of the duck allow for this capacity. However, the way the environment is arranged determines the behavior of the individual organism. Laboratory experiments in behavior analysis identify the general principles that govern the behavior of organisms, the specific events that regulate the behavior of different species, and the arrangement of these events during the lifetime of an individual.

The Selection of Operant Behavior

Early behaviorists like John Watson (1903) used the terminology of stimulus–response (S–R) psychology. From this perspective, stimuli force responses much like meat in a dog's mouth elicits (or forces) salivation. In fact, Watson based his stimulus–response theory of behavior on Pavlov's conditioning experiments. Stimulus–response theories are mechanistic in the sense that an organism is compelled to respond when a stimulus is presented. This is similar to a physical account of the motion of billiard balls. The impact of the cue ball (stimulus) determines the motion and trajectory (response) of the target ball. Although stimulus–response conceptions are useful for analyzing reflexive behavior and other rigid response patterns (i.e., Newtonion mechanics), the push–pull model is not as useful when applied to voluntary actions or operants. To be fair, Watson talked about "habits" in a way that sounds like operant behavior, but he lacked the experimental evidence and vocabulary to distinguish between respondent and operant conditioning.

It was B. F. Skinner (1935, 1937) who made the distinction between two types of conditioned reflex, corresponding to the difference between operant and respondent behavior. In 1938, he introduced the term "operant" in his classic book, *The Behavior of Organisms*. Eventually, Skinner rejected the mechanistic (S–R) model of Watson and based operant conditioning on Darwin's principle of selection. The basic idea is that an individual *emits* behavior that produces effects, consequences, or outcomes. Based on these consequences, those performances that are appropriate increase, becoming more frequent in the population or class of responses for the situation; at the same time, inappropriate forms of response decline or become extinct. Julie Vargas is the daughter of B. F. Skinner and was a professor of behavior analysis at West Virginia University. She has commented on her father's model of causation:

Skinner's paradigm is a *selectionist* paradigm not unlike Darwin's selectionist theory of the evolution of species. Where Darwin found an explanation for the evolution of species, Skinner looked for variables functionally related to changes in behavior over the lifetime of an individual. Both explanations assumed variation; Darwin in inherited characteristics, Skinner in individual acts. Skinner, in other words, does not concern himself with why behavior varies, only with how patterns of behavior are drawn out from the variations that already exist. In looking at the functional relationships between acts and their effects on the world, Skinner broke with the S–R, input–output transformation model.

(Vargas, 1990, p. 9)

Skinner recognized that operants are selected by their consequences. He also noted that operant behavior naturally varies in form and frequency. Even something as simple as opening the door to your house is not done exactly the same way each time. Pressure on the doorknob, strength of pull, and the hand that is used change from one occasion to the next. If the door sticks and becomes difficult to open, a forceful response will eventually occur. This response may succeed in opening the door and become the most likely performance for the situation. Other forms of response will occur at different frequencies depending on how often they succeed in opening the door. Thus, *operants are selected by their consequences*.

Similarly, it is well known that babies produce a variety of sounds called "babbling." These natural variations in sound production are important for language learning. When sounds occur, parents usually react to them. When the infant produces a familiar sound, parents often repeat it more precisely. Unfamiliar sounds are usually ignored. Eventually, the baby begins to produce sounds (we say talk) like other people in their culture or verbal community. Selection of verbal behavior by its social consequences is an important process underlying human communication and language (Skinner, 1957).

Culture and Behavior Analysis

Although much of the basic research in the experimental analysis of behavior is based on laboratory animals, contemporary behavior analysts are increasingly concerned with human behavior. The behavior of people occurs in a social environment. Society and culture refer to aspects of the social environment, the context, that regulate human conduct. One of the primary tasks of behavior analysis is to show how individual behavior is acquired, maintained, and changed through interaction with others. An additional task is to account for the practices of the group, community, or society that affect an individual's behavior (Lamal, 1997).

Culture is usually defined in terms of the ideas and values of a society. However, behavior analysts define **culture** as all the conditions, events, and stimuli arranged by other people that regulate human action (Glenn, 1988; Skinner, 1953). The principles and laws of behavior analysis provide an account of how culture regulates an individual's behavior. A person in an English-speaking culture learns to speak in accord with the verbal practices of that community. People in the community provide reinforcement for a certain way of speaking. In this manner, a person comes to talk like and share the language of other members of the public and, in doing so, contributes to the perpetuation of the culture. The customs or practices of a culture are therefore maintained through the social conditioning of individual behavior.

Another objective is to account for the evolution of cultural practices. Behavior analysts suggest that the principle of selection (by consequences) also occurs at the cultural level. Cultural practices therefore increase (or decrease) based on consequences produced in the past. A cultural practice of making containers to hold water is an advantage to the group because it allows for the transportation and storage of water. This practice may include using shells or hollow leaves, or making fired-clay containers. The cultural form that is selected (e.g., clay jars) is the one that proves most efficient. In other words, the community values those containers that last the longest, hold the most, and are easily stored. Thus, people manufacture clay pots, and the manufacture of less efficient containers declines.

Behavior analysts are interested in cultural evolution because cultural changes alter the social conditioning of individual behavior. Analysis of cultural evolution suggests how the social environment is arranged and rearranged to support specific forms of human behavior. On a more practical level, behavior analysts suggest that the solution to many social problems requires a technology of cultural design. B. F. Skinner addressed this possibility in his utopian book, *Walden Two* (Skinner, 1948). Although this idealistic novel was written some five decades ago, contemporary behavior analysts are conducting small-scale social experiments based on Skinner's ideas (Komar, 1983). For example, behavioral technology has been used to manage environmental pollution, encourage energy conservation, and regulate overpopulation (Glenwick & Jason, 1980).

FOCUS ON: Burrhus Frederic Skinner

B. F. Skinner (1904–1990) was the intellectual force behind behavior analysis. He was born and named Burrhus Frederic Skinner on March 20, 1904 in Susquehanna, Pennsylvania. When he was a boy, Skinner spent much of his time exploring the countryside with his younger brother. He had a passion for English literature and mechanical inventions. His hobbies included writing stories and designing perpetual-motion machines. He wanted to be a novelist, and went to Hamilton College in Clinton, New York, where he graduated with a degree in English. After graduating from college in 1926, Skinner reported that he was not a great writer because he had nothing to say. He began reading about behaviorism, a new intellectual movement, and as a result went to Harvard in 1928 to learn more about a science of behavior. He earned his master's degree in 1930 and his PhD the following year.

Skinner (Figure 1.3) began writing about the behavior of organisms in the 1930s, when the discipline was in its infancy, and he continued to publish papers until his death in 1990. During his long career, he wrote about and researched topics ranging from utopian societies to the philosophy of science, teaching machines, pigeons that controlled the direction of missiles, air cribs for infants, and techniques for improving education. Some people considered him a genius, while others were upset by his theories.

Skinner was always a controversial figure. He proposed a natural-science approach to human behavior. According to Skinner, the behavior of organisms, including humans, was determined. Although common sense suggests that we do things because of our feelings, thoughts, and intentions, Skinner stated that behavior resulted from genes and environment. This position bothered many people who believed that humans have some degree of self-determination. Even though he was constantly confronted with arguments against his position, Skinner maintained that the scientific facts required the rejection of feelings, thoughts, and intentions as causes of behavior. He said that these internal events were not explanations of behavior; rather these events were additional activities of people that needed to be explained:

FIG. 1.3 B. F. Skinner. Reprinted with permission from the B. F. Skinner Foundation, Cambridge, MA.

> The practice of looking inside the organism for an explanation of behavior has tended to obscure the variables which are immediately available for a scientific analysis. These variables lie outside the organism in its immediate environment and in its environmental history. They have a physical status to which the usual techniques of science are adapted, and they make it possible to explain behavior as other subjects are explained in science. These independent variables [causes] are of many sorts and their relations to behavior are often subtle and complex, but we cannot hope to give an adequate account of behavior without analyzing them.
>
> (Skinner, 1953, p. 31)

One of Skinner's most important achievements was his theory of operant behavior. The implications of behavior theory were outlined in his book, *Science and Human Behavior* (Skinner, 1953). In this book, Skinner discussed basic operant principles and their application to human behavior. Topics included self-control, thinking, the self, social behavior, government, religion, and culture. Skinner advocated the principle of positive reinforcement and argued against the use of punishment. He noted how governments and other social agencies often resort to punishment for behavior control. Although punishment works in the short run, he noted that it has many negative side effects. Positive reinforcement, Skinner believed, is a more effective means of behavior change—people act well and are happy when behavior is maintained by positive reinforcement.

People have misunderstood many of the things that Skinner has said and done (Catania & Harnard, 1988; Wheeler, 1973). One popular misconception is that he raised his children in an experimental chamber—the so-called "baby in a box." People claimed that Skinner used his daughter as an experimental subject to test his theories. A popular myth is that this experience drove his child crazy. His daughter, Julie, was confronted with this myth and recalls the following:

> I took a class called "Theories of Learning" taught by a nice elderly gentleman. He started with Hull and Spence, and then reached Skinner. At that time I had read little of Skinner, and I could not judge the accuracy of what was being said about Skinner's theories. But when a student asked whether Skinner had any children, the professor thought Skinner had children. "Did he condition his children?" asked another student. "I heard that one of the children was crazy." "What happened to his children?" The questions came thick and fast.
>
> What was I to do? I had a friend in the class, and she looked over at me, clearly expecting action. I did not want to demolish the professor's confidence by telling who I was, but I couldn't just sit there. Finally, I raised my hand and stood up. "Dr. Skinner has two daughters and I believe they turned out relatively normal," I said, and sat down.
>
> (Vargas, 1990, pp. 8–9)

In truth, the "box" that Skinner designed for his children had nothing to do with an experiment. The air crib is an enclosed bed that allows air temperature to be controlled. Because of this feature no blankets are needed, so the baby is free to move and there is no danger of suffocating. The air crib was designed to keep the child warm, dry, and safe. Most importantly, the infant spent no more time in the air crib than other children do in ordinary beds (Skinner, 1945).

Although Skinner did not experiment with his children, he was always interested in the application of conditioning principles to human issues. His many books and papers on applied behavioral technology led to the field of applied behavior analysis. Applied behavior analysis is concerned with the extension of behavior principles to socially important problems. In the first issue of the *Journal of Applied Behavior Analysis*, Baer, Wolf, and Risley outlined a program of research based on Skinner's views:

> The statement [of behavior principles] establishes the possibility of their application to problem behavior. A society willing to consider a technology of its own behavior apparently is likely to support that application when it deals with socially important behaviors, such as retardation, crime, mental illness, or education. Better applications, it is hoped, will lead to a better state of society, to whatever extent the behavior of its members can contribute to the goodness of a society. The differences between applied and basic research are not differences between that which "discovers" and that which merely "applies" what is already known. Both endeavors ask what controls the behavior under study. . . . [Basic] research is likely to look at any behavior, and at any variable which may conceivably relate to it. Applied research is constrained to look at variables which can be effective in improving the behavior under study.
>
> (Baer, Wolf, & Risley, 1968, p. 91)

One area of application that Skinner wrote about extensively was teaching and learning. Although Skinner recognized the importance of behavior principles for teaching people with learning disabilities, he claimed that the same technology could be used to improve our general educational system. In his book, *The Technology of Teaching*, Skinner (1968) offered a personalized system of positive reinforcement for the academic performance of students. In this system, teaching involves arranging materials, designing the classroom, and programming lessons to shape and maintain the performance of students. Learning is defined objectively in terms of answering questions, solving problems, using grammatically correct forms of the language, and writing about the subject matter.

An aspect of Skinner's history that is not generally known is his humor and rejection of formal titles. He preferred to be called "Fred" rather than Burrhus, and the only person who called him Burrhus was his close friend and colleague Fred Keller, who felt that he had prior claim on the name Fred (he was a few years older than Skinner). One of Skinner's earliest collaborators, C. B. Ferster, tells about a time early in his acquaintance when Skinner tried to get Ferster to call him "Fred." The story goes (Ferster, personal communication to Paul Brandon) that one day Ferster walked into the living room of Skinner's house to see Skinner seated on the sofa with a large sign around his neck saying "FRED."

In the later part of his life, Skinner worked with Margaret Vaughan (Skinner & Vaughan, 1983) on positive approaches to the problems of old age. Their book, *Enjoy Old Age: A Program of Self-Management*, is written for the elderly reader and provides practical advice on how to deal with daily life. For example, the names of people are easy to forget, and even more so in old age. Skinner and Vaughan suggest that you can improve your chances of recalling a name by reading a list of people you are likely to meet before going to an important occasion. If all else fails "you can always appeal to your age. You can please the friend whose name you have forgotten by saying that the names you forget are always the names you most want to remember" (Skinner & Vaughan, 1983, p. 52).

Skinner, who held the Edgar Pierce Chair in Psychology, officially retired from Harvard University in 1974. Following his retirement, he continued an active program of research and writing. Each day he walked 2 miles to William James Hall, where he lectured, supervised graduate students, and conducted experiments. Eight days before his death on August 18, 1990, B. F. Skinner received the first (and only) Citation for Outstanding Lifetime Contribution to Psychology from the American Psychological Association (Schlinger, 2011). The citation for the award, published in the *American Psychologist*, read "Few individuals have had such a dynamic and far-reaching impact on the discipline"

(1990, p. 1205). In a study of renowned psychologists by Haggbloom (2002), Skinner ranked as the most eminent psychologist of the 20th century. Skinner's contributions to psychology and a science of behavior are documented in the film *B. F. Skinner: A Fresh Appraisal* (1999). Murray Sidman, a distinguished researcher in the experimental analysis of behavior, narrated the film (available from the bookstore of the Cambridge Center for Behavioral Studies, www.behavior.org).

A BRIEF HISTORY OF BEHAVIOR ANALYSIS

Contemporary behavior analysis is based on ideas and research that became prominent at the turn of the 20th century. The Russian scientist Ivan Petrovich Pavlov discovered the conditional reflex (a reflex that only occurs under a particular set of conditions, such as the pairing of stimuli), and this was a significant step towards a scientific understanding of behavior.

Ivan Petrovich Pavlov (1849–1936)

Pavlov (Figure 1.4) was born the son of a village priest in 1849. He attended seminary school in order to follow his father into the priesthood. However, after studying physiology he decided on a career in the biological sciences. Although his family protested, Pavlov entered the University of St. Petersburg, where he graduated in 1875 with a degree in physiology. After completing his studies in physiology, Pavlov was accepted as an advanced student of medicine. He distinguished himself and obtained a scholarship to continue his studies of physiology in Germany. In 1890, Pavlov was appointed to two prominent research positions in Russia. He was Professor of Pharmacology at the St. Petersburg Medical Academy and Director of the Physiology Department. For the next 20 years, Pavlov studied the physiology of digestion, and in 1904 he won the Nobel Prize for this work, the year that B. F. Skinner was born.

FIG. 1.4   Ivan Petrovich Pavlov. Reprinted with permission from the Archives of the History of American Psychology, Center for the History of Psychology, The University of Akron.

Ivan Pavlov worked on the salivary reflex and its role in digestion. Pavlov had dogs surgically prepared to expose the salivary glands in the dogs' mouths. The animals were brought into the laboratory and put in restraining harnesses. As shown in Figure 1.5, food was then placed in the dogs' mouths and the action of the salivary glands was observed.

The analysis of the salivary reflex was based on prevailing notions of animal behavior. At this time, many people thought that animals, with the exception of humans, were complex biological machines. The idea was that a specific stimulus elicited a particular response in much the same way that turning a key starts an engine. In other words, animals reacted to the environment in a simple cause–effect manner. Humans, on the other hand, were seen as different from other animals in that their actions were purposive. Humans were said to anticipate future events. Pavlov noticed that his dogs began to salivate at the sight of an experimenter's lab coat *before* food was placed in the animal's mouth. This suggested that the dogs anticipated food. Pavlov recognized that such a result challenged conventional wisdom.

Pavlov made an important observation in terms of the study of behavior. He reasoned that anticipatory reflexes were learned or conditioned. Further, Pavlov concluded that these conditioned reflexes were an essential part of the behavior of organisms. Although some behaviors were described as innate reflexes, other

FIG. 1.5   A dog in the experimental apparatus used by Pavlov.

actions were based on conditioning that occurred during the animal's life. These **conditioned reflexes** (termed conditional reflexes in Pavlov, 1960) were present to some degree in all animals, but were most prominent in humans.

The question was how to study conditioned reflexes systematically. Pavlov's answer to this question represents a major advance in the experimental analysis of behavior. If dogs reliably salivate at the sight of a lab coat, Pavlov reasoned, then any arbitrary stimulus that preceded food might also be conditioned and evoke salivation. Pavlov replaced the experimenter's lab coat with a stimulus that he could systematically manipulate and reliably control. In some experiments, a metronome (a device used to keep the beat while playing the piano) was presented to a dog just before it was fed. This procedure resulted in the dog eventually salivating to the sound of the metronome. If a particular beat preceded feeding while other rhythms did not, the dog salivated most to the sound associated with food.

Although Pavlov was a physiologist and believed in mental associations, his research was directed at observable responses and stimuli. He discovered many principles of the conditioned reflex. These principles included spontaneous recovery, discrimination, generalization, and extinction. The later part of his career involved an experimental analysis of neurosis in animals. He continued these investigations until his death in 1936.

John Broadus Watson (1878–1958)

Pavlov's research became prominent in North America, and the conditioned reflex was incorporated into a more general theory of behavior by the famous behaviorist John B. Watson (Figure 1.6). Watson acknowledged Pavlov's influence:

> I had worked the thing out [conditioning] in terms of *Habit* formation. It was only later, when I began to dig into the vague word *Habit*, that I saw the enormous contribution Pavlov had made, and how easily the conditioned response could be looked upon as the unit of what we had been calling *Habit*. I certainly, from that point on, gave the master his due credit.
>
> (Watson, personal communication to Hilgard & Marquis, 1961, p. 24)

FIG. 1.6   John Watson. Reprinted with permission from the Archives of the History of American Psychology, Center for the History of Psychology, The University of Akron.

Watson went on to argue that there was no need to make up unobservable mental associations to account for human and animal behavior. He proposed that psychology should be a science based on observable behavior. Thoughts, feelings, and intentions had no place in a scientific account, and researchers should direct their attention to muscle movements and neural activity. Although this was an extreme position, Watson succeeded in directing the attention of psychologists to behavior–environment relationships.

Watson was a rebellious young man who failed his last year at Furman University because he handed in a final-exam paper "backwards."[1] He graduated in 1899, when he was 21 years old. After spending a year as a public-school teacher, Watson decided to further his education and was admitted to graduate studies at the University of Chicago. There he studied philosophy with John Dewey, the famous educator. He never really appreciated Dewey's ideas, and later in his life commented "I never knew what he was talking about then, and, unfortunately for me, I still don't know" (Watson, 1936, p. 274). While a graduate student at the University of Chicago, he also studied psychology with James Angell and biology and physiology with Henry Donaldson and Jacques Loeb (Pauley, 1987). In 1903, he obtained his doctorate for research with laboratory rats. The experiments concerned learning and correlated changes in the brains of these animals.

Watson (1903) published a book called *Animal Education: An Experimental Study on the Psychical Development of the White Rat, Correlated with the Growth of Its Nervous System*, which was based on his doctoral research. The book demonstrated that Watson was a capable scientist who could clearly present his ideas. Ten years later, he published his most influential work in *Psychological Review*, "Psychology as the Behaviorist Views It" (Watson, 1913). This paper outlined Watson's views on **behaviorism** and argued that objectivity was the only way to build a science of psychology:

> I feel that *behaviorism* is the only consistent logical functionalism. In it one avoids [the problem of mind–body dualism]. These time-honored relics of philosophical speculation need trouble the student of behavior as little as they trouble the student of physics. The consideration of the mind-body problem affects neither the type of problem selected nor the formulation of the solution of that problem. I can state my position here no better than by saying that I should like to bring my students up in ignorance of such hypotheses as one finds among other branches of science.
>
> (Watson, 1913, p. 166)

In this paper, Watson also rejected as scientific data what people said about their thoughts and feelings. Further, he pointed to the unreliability of psychological inferences about another person's mind. He also noted that the psychology of mind had little practical value for behavior control and public affairs. Modern behavior analysts, informed by the writings of Watson and B. F Skinner, study what people say as verbal behavior regulated by the social environment (behavior of other people), not reports on the mind or mental states. Behavior analysts study thinking and remembering as private behavior often related to challenges or problems faced by the person. That is, a person may "think about the house key" and check her coat pocket just before leaving for work, especially if she has been locked out in the past. Notice that thinking about the key is not treated as a cause of behavior (as in cognitive psychology), but as more behavior to be explained by its interaction with the environment (history of being locked out of the house).

In addition to his influence on modern behaviorism, Watson is best known for his early studies of conditioning. Perhaps Watson's most famous experiment was the study of fear conditioning with Little Albert (Watson & Rayner, 1920). Little Albert was a normal, healthy infant who attended a day-care center. Watson and his assistant used classical-conditioning procedures to condition fear of

---

1 This description of John Watson is partially based on a paper by James Todd and Edward Morris (1986) on "The Early Research of John B. Watson: Before the Behavioral Revolution."

a white rat. At first Little Albert looked at the rat and tried to touch it. The unconditioned stimulus was the sound of a hammer hitting an iron rail. This sound made Little Albert jump, cry, and fall over. After only six presentations of the noise and rat, the furry animal alone also produced the fear responses. The next phase of the experiment involved a series of tests to see if the child's fear reaction transferred or *generalized* to similar stimuli. Albert was also afraid when presented with a white rabbit, a dog, and a fur coat.

At this point, Watson and Rayner discussed a number of techniques that could be used to eliminate the child's fear. Unfortunately, Little Albert was removed from the day-care center before counter-conditioning could be carried out. In his characteristic manner, Watson later used the disappearance of Little Albert to poke fun at Freud's method of psychoanalysis. He suggested that as Albert got older, he might go to an analyst because of his strange fears. The analyst would probably convince Albert that his problem was the result of an unresolved Oedipal complex. But, Watson remarked, we would know that Albert's fears were actually caused by conditioning—so much for Freudian analysis.

Watson had many interests, and he investigated and wrote about ethology, comparative animal behavior, neural function, physiology, and philosophy of science. Based on his controversial views and charisma, he was elected president of the American Psychological Association in 1915 when he was only 37 years old. After leaving Johns Hopkins University, he became successful in industry by applying conditioning principles to advertising and public relations (Buckley, 1989). Watson implemented the use of subliminal suggestion and the pairing of hidden symbols in advertising— techniques that are still used today.

Edward Lee Thorndike (1874–1949)

Watson's behaviorism emphasized the conditioned reflex. This analysis focuses on the events that precede action and is usually called a stimulus–response approach. Another American psychologist, Edward Lee Thorndike (Figure 1.7), was more concerned with how success and failure affect the behavior of organisms. His research emphasized the events and consequences that follow behavior. In other words, Thorndike was the first scientist to systematically study operant behavior, although he called the changes that occurred **trial-and-error learning** (Thorndike, 1898).

Edward L. Thorndike was born in 1874 in Williamsburg, Massachusetts. He was the son of a Methodist minister and had no knowledge of psychology until he attended Wesleyan University. There he read William James's book, *Principles of Psychology* (James, 1890), which had a major impact on him. After reading the book, Thorndike was accepted as a student at Harvard, where he studied with William James. It is important to note that James's psychology focused on the mind and used the method of introspection (people's reports of feelings and thoughts). Thus, in contrast to John Watson, Thorndike was concerned with states of mind. In terms of contemporary behavior analysis, Thorndike's contribution was his systematic study of the behavior of organisms rather than his mental interpretations of animal and human behavior.

FIG. 1.7 Edward Thorndike. Reprinted with permission from the Archives of the History of American Psychology, Center for the History of Psychology, The University of Akron.

Thorndike was always intrigued by animal behavior. While he was at Harvard, his landlady became upset because he was raising chickens in his bedroom. By this time, James and Thorndike were good friends, and Thorndike moved his experiments to the basement of James's house when he could not get laboratory space at Harvard. He continued his research and supported himself by tutoring students for 2 years at Harvard. Then Thorndike moved to Columbia University, where he studied with James McKeen Cattell, the famous expert on intelligence testing. Thorndike took two of his "smartest" chickens with him to Columbia, but soon switched to investigating the behavior of cats.

At Columbia University, Thorndike began his famous experiments on trial-and-error learning in cats. Animals were placed in what Thorndike called a "puzzle box" and food was placed outside the box (Chance, 1999). A cat that struggled to get out of the box would accidentally step on a treadle, pull a string, and lift a latch. These responses resulted in opening the puzzle-box door. Thorndike found that most cats took less and less time to solve the problem after they were repeatedly returned to the box (i.e., repeated trials). From these and additional observations, Thorndike developed the first formulation of the **law of effect**:

> The cat that is clawing all over the box in her impulsive struggle will probably claw the string or loop or button so as to open the door. And gradually all the other *non-successful impulses will be stamped out and the particular impulse leading to the successful act will be stamped in by the resulting pleasure* [italics added], until after many trials, the cat will, when put in the box, immediately claw the button or loop in a definite way.
>
> (Thorndike, 1911, p. 40)

Today, Thorndike's law of effect is restated as the principle of reinforcement. This principle states that all operants may be followed by consequences that increase or decrease the probability of response in the same situation. Notice that references to "stamping in" and "pleasure" are not necessary and that nothing is lost by this modern restatement of the law of effect.

Thorndike was appointed to the Teachers College, Columbia University as a professor in 1899, and he spent his entire career there. He studied and wrote about education, language, intelligence testing, comparison of animal species, the nature–nurture problem, transfer of training, sociology of the quality of life, and most importantly, animal and human learning. Thorndike published more than 500 books and journal articles. His son (Robert Ladd Thorndike, 1911–1990) became a well-known educational psychologist in his own right, and in 1937 joined the same department of psychology as his father. Edward Lee Thorndike died in 1949.

B. F. Skinner and the Rise of Behavior Analysis

The works of Pavlov, Watson, Thorndike, and many others have influenced contemporary behavior analysis. Although the ideas of many scientists and philosophers have had an impact, B. F. Skinner (1904–1990) is largely responsible for the development of modern behavior analysis. In the "Focus on: Burrhus Frederic Skinner" section above, we described some details of his life and some of his accomplishments. An excellent biography is available (Bjork, 1993), and Skinner himself wrote a three-volume autobiography (Skinner, 1976, 1979, 1983). Here we will outline his contribution to contemporary behavior analysis.

Skinner was studying at Harvard during a time of intellectual change. He wanted to extend the work of Pavlov to more complicated instances of the conditioned reflex. Rudolph Magnus was a contemporary of Ivan Pavlov, and he had been working on the conditioning of physical movement. Skinner had read his book *Korperstellung* in the original German and was impressed by it, saying "I began to think of reflexes as behavior rather than with Pavlov as 'the activity of the cerebral cortex' or, with Sherrington, as 'the integrative action of the nervous system'" (Skinner, 1979, p. 46).

The idea that reflexes could be studied as behavior (rather than as a reflection of the nervous system or the mind) was fully developed in Skinner's book, *The Behavior of Organisms* (Skinner, 1938). In this text, he distinguishes between Pavlov's reflexive conditioning and the kind of learning reported by Thorndike. Skinner proposed that respondent and operant conditioning regulated behavior. These terms were carefully selected to emphasize the study of behavior for its own sake. Pavlov interpreted reflexive conditioning as the study of the central nervous system, and Skinner's respondent conditioning directed attention to environmental events and responses. Thorndike's trial-and-error learning was based on unobservable states of mind, and Skinner's operant conditioning focused on the functional relations between behavior and its consequences. Both operant and respondent conditioning required the study of observable **correlations** among objective events and behavior.

Skinner soon talked about a "science of behavior" rather than one of physiology or mental life. Once stated, the study of behavior for its own sake seems obvious, but consider that most of us say that we do something because we have made up our mind to do it or, in more scientific terms, because of a neural connection in our brain. Most people accept explanations of behavior that rely on descriptions of brain, mind, intelligence, cognitive function, neural activity, thinking, or personality. Because these factors are taken as the cause(s) of behavior, they become the focus of investigation. Skinner, however, suggested that remembering, thinking, feeling, the action of neurons, etc., are more behavior of the organism that requires explanation. He further proposed that the action of organisms could be investigated by focusing on behavior and the environmental events that precede and follow it.

Skinner's behavioral focus was partially maintained and influenced by his lifelong friend, Fred Simmons Keller. Skinner and Keller attended Harvard graduate school together, and Keller encouraged Skinner to pursue a behavioral view of psychology. By 1946, Skinner had formed a small group of behaviorists at Indiana University. At the same time, Fred Keller and his friend Nat Schoenfeld organized another group at Columbia University (Keller, 1977, Chapters 2 and 6).

Although the number of **behavior analysts** was growing, there were no sessions on behavioral issues at the American Psychological Association annual meetings. Because of this, Skinner, Keller, Schoenfeld, and others organized their own conference at Indiana University. This was the first conference on the experimental analysis of behavior (see Figure 1.8). These new-style behaviorists rejected the extreme views of John B. Watson and offered an alternative formulation. Unlike Watson, they did not reject genetic influences on behavior; they extended the analysis of behavior to operant conditioning, and they studied behavior for its own sake.

These new behavior analysts found it difficult to get their research published in the major journals of psychology. This was because they used a small number of subjects in their experiments, they did not use statistical analysis, and their graphs of response rate were not appreciated. By 1958, the group was large enough to start its own journal, and the first volume of the

FIG. 1.8 Photograph taken at the first conference on the experimental analysis of behavior, held in 1946 at Indiana University. From left to right in front row: Dinsmoor, Musgrave, Skinner, Keller, Schoenfeld, Lloyd. Middle row: Ellson, Daniel, Klein, Jenkins, Wyckoff, Hefferline, Wolin. Back row: Estes, Frick, Anderson, Verplanck, Beire, Hill, Craig. From the *Journal of the Experimental Analysis of Behavior, 5,* 456. © 1958 by the Society for the Experimental Analysis of Behavior, Inc. Reprinted with permission.

Journal of the Experimental Analysis of Behavior (JEAB) was published. As research accumulated, the practical implications of behavior principles became more and more evident, and applications to mental illness, retardation, rehabilitation, and education increased. In 1968, the *Journal of Applied Behavior Analysis (JABA)* was published for the first time.

By 1964, the number of behavior analysts had grown so much that the American Psychological Association established a special division. Division 25 is called The Experimental Analysis of Behavior and has several thousand members. Subsequently, the Association for Behavior Analysis (ABA) was founded in the late 1970s, and it is now called the Association for Behavior Analysis International (ABAI). This association holds an annual international conference that is attended by behavior analysts from many countries. The association publishes a journal of general issues called *The Behavior Analyst*.

In addition to ABA, Robert Epstein, one of B. F. Skinner's last students, and past editor of the well-known magazine, *Psychology Today*, founded the Cambridge Center for Behavioral Studies in 1981. The Cambridge Center is devoted to helping people find effective solutions to behavior problems (e.g., in education, business, and other applied settings). As part of this mission, the Center maintains an information website (www.behavior.org) for the public, publishes books and journals, and sponsors seminars and conferences on effective behavior management in applied settings (e.g., the annual conference *Behavioral Safety Now* in the field of industrial safety).

A continuing issue in the field of behavior analysis is the separation between applied behavior analysis and basic research. During the 1950s and 1960s, no clear distinction existed between applied and basic investigations. This was because applied behavior analysts were trained as basic researchers. That is, the first applications of behavior principles came from the same people who were conducting laboratory experiments. [As an aside, Skinner's second book, after his basic text called *The Behavior of Organisms* (Skinner, 1938), was a novel describing the application of behavior principles in a Utopian community, *Walden Two* (Skinner, 1948)]. The applications of behavior principles were highly successful, and this led to a greater demand for people trained in applied behavior analysis. Soon applied researchers were no longer working in the laboratory or reading the basic journals.

This separation between basic and applied research was first described by Sam Deitz (1978), who noted the changing emphasis from science to technology among applied behavior analysts (see also Hayes, Rincover, & Solnick, 1980; Michael, 1980; Pierce & Epling, 1980). Donald Baer (1981) acknowledged the technical drift of applied behavior analysis, but suggested that this was a natural progression of the field that may have positive effects. One positive effect has been the substantial rise in membership and impact of the international organization (ABAI) due to the large influx of behavioral technicians in areas such as the treatment of autism, behavioral safety, and behavioral medicine. However, behavioral technicians are concerned with procedures to improve or help those with severe disorders, and are less connected to the basic science of behavior. One possibility is that those with a help-oriented focus will establish a new organization to represent their legitimate interests, while researchers who remain in the ABAI may continue to emphasize analysis and basic principles.

Applied researchers with a basic focus usually report their findings in the *Journal of Applied Behavior Analysis*. In addition to application research, this journal publishes applied articles based on modern behavior principles (e.g., Ducharme & Worling, 1994), as well as reviews of basic research areas (e.g., Mace, 1996). Currently, there is a call for more translational research that ties basic principles to socially important problems, especially when there are limited funding opportunities for basic research with animals (see Critchfield, 2011). We have written this book assuming that an acquaintance with basic research is important, even for those who are primarily concerned with behavioral applications and translational studies. Students can study this text for a basic grounding in behavioral science, or for a solid foundation in human behavior and application.

SCIENCE AND BEHAVIOR: SOME ASSUMPTIONS

All scientists make assumptions about their subject matter. These assumptions are based on prevailing views in the discipline and guide scientific research. In terms of behavior analysis, researchers assume that the behavior of organisms is lawful. This means that it is possible to study the interactions between an organism and its environment in an objective manner. To carry out the analysis, it is necessary to isolate behavior–environment relationships. The scientist must identify events that reliably precede the onset of some action and the specific consequences that follow behavior. If behavior systematically changes with variation in the environmental conditions, then behavior analysts assume that they have explained the action of the organism. There are other assumptions that behavior analysts make about their science.

The Private World

Contemporary behavior analysts include internal events as part of an organism's environment. This point is often misunderstood; internal functioning like an upset stomach, full bladder, and low blood sugar, is part of a person's environment. Internal physical events have the same status as external stimuli such as light, noise, odor, and heat. Both external and internal events regulate behavior. Although this is so, behavior analysts usually emphasize the external environment. This is because external events are the only stimuli available for behavior change. The objective procedures of psychological experiments are giving instructions and observing how the person acts. From a behavioral view, the instructions are external stimuli that regulate both verbal and nonverbal behavior. Even when a drug is given to a person and the chemical alters internal biochemistry, the direct injection of the drug is an external event that subsequently regulates behavior. To make this clear, without the drug injection neither the biochemistry nor the behavior of the person would change.

Many psychological studies involve giving information to a person in order to change or activate cognitive processes. Thus, cognitive psychologists ". . . invent internal surrogates which become the subject matter of their science" (Skinner, 1978, p. 97), and cognitive psychology has been defined as ". . . an approach to scientific psychology—that encourages psychologists to infer unobservable constructs on the basis of observable phenomena" (Baars, 1986, p. ix). In the cognitive view, thoughts are used to *explain* behavior. The problem is that the existence of thoughts (or feelings) is often inferred from the behavior to be explained, leading to circular reasoning. For example, a child who peers out of the window at around the time her mother usually comes home from work is said to do this because of an "expectation." The expectation of the child is said to explain why the child peers out of the window. In fact, there is no explanation because the cognition (expectation) is inferred from the behavior it is said to explain. Cognitions could explain behavior if the existence of thought processes were based on some evidence other than behavior. In most cases, however, there is no independent evidence that cognitions caused behavior, and the explanation is not scientifically valid. One way out of this problem of logic is not to use thinking and feeling as causes of behavior. That is, thinking and feeling are treated as more behavior to be explained.

Feelings and Behavior

Most people assume that their feelings and thoughts explain why they act as they do. Contemporary behavior analysts agree that people feel and think, but they do not consider these events as causes of behavior. They note that these terms are more correctly used as verbs rather than nouns. Instead of talking about thoughts, behavior analysts point to the action word "thinking." And instead of analyzing feelings as things we possess, the behavioral scientist focuses on the action of feeling or sensing. In other words, thinking and feeling are activities of the organism that require explanation.

Feelings: Real But Not Causes

Because feelings occur at the same time as we act, they are often taken as causes of behavior. Although feelings and behavior necessarily go together, it is the environment that determines how we act, and at the same time how we feel. Feelings are real, but they are the result of the environmental events that regulate behavior. Thus, a behavioral approach requires that the researcher trace feelings back to the interaction between behavior and environment.

Pretend that you are in an elevator between the 15th and 16th floors when the elevator suddenly stops, and the lights go out. You hear a sound that appears to be the snapping of elevator cables. Suddenly, the elevator lurches and then drops 2 feet. You call out, but nobody comes to your rescue. After about an hour, the elevator starts up again, and you get off on the 16th floor. Six months later, a good friend invites you to dinner. You meet downtown, and you discover that your friend has made reservations at a restaurant called The Room at the Top, which is located on the 20th floor of a skyscraper. Standing in front of the elevator, a sudden feeling of panic overwhelms you. You make a socially appropriate excuse like, "I don't feel well," and you leave. What is the reason for your behavior and the accompanying feeling?

There is no question that you feel anxious, but this feeling is not why you decide to go home. Both the anxious feeling and your decision to leave are easily traced to the negative experience in the elevator that occurred 6 months ago. It is this prior conditioning that behavior analysts emphasize. Notice that the behavioral position does not deny your feelings. These are real events. However, it is your previous interaction with the broken elevator that changed both how you feel and how you act.

Reports of Feelings

You may still wonder why behavior analysts study overt behavior instead of feelings—given that both are changed by experience. The answer concerns the accessibility of feelings and overt behavior. Much of the behavior of organisms is directly accessible to the observer or scientist. This public behavior provides a relatively straightforward subject matter for scientific analysis. In contrast, feelings are largely inaccessible to the scientific community. Of course, the person who feels has access to this private information, but the problem is that reports of feelings are highly unreliable.

This unreliability occurs because we learn to talk about our feelings (and other internal events) as others have trained us to do. During socialization, people teach us how to describe ourselves, but when they do this they have no way of accurately knowing what is going on inside us. Parents and teachers rely on public cues to train self-descriptions. They do this by commenting on and correcting verbal reports when behavior or events suggest a feeling. A preschooler is taught to say "I feel happy" when the parents guess that the child is happy. The parents may base their judgment on smiling, excitement, and affectionate responses from the child. Another way in which this training occurs is that the child may be asked "Are you happy?" in a circumstance where the parents expect the child to feel this way (e.g., on Christmas morning). When the child appears to be sad, or circumstances suggest this should be so, saying "I am happy" is not reinforced by the parents. Eventually, the child says "I am happy" in some situations and not in others.

Perhaps you have already noticed why reports of feelings are not good scientific evidence. Reports are only as good as the training of correspondence between public conditions and private events. In addition to inadequate training, there are other problems with accurate descriptions of feelings. Many of our internal functions are poorly correlated (or uncorrelated) with public conditions, and this means that we cannot be taught to describe such events accurately. Although a doctor may ask for the general location of a pain (e.g., the abdomen), he or she is unlikely to ask whether the hurt is in the liver or the spleen. This report is simply inaccessible to the patient because there is no way to teach the correspondence between exact location of damage and public conditions. Generally, we are able to report in a limited way on private events, but the unreliability of such reports makes them questionable as scientific observations. Based on this realization, behavior analysts focus on the study of behavior rather than feelings.

Thinking as Behavior

Behavior analysts have also considered thinking and its role in a science of behavior. In contrast to views that claim a special inner world of thought, behavior analysts suggest that human thought is human behavior. Skinner stated that:

> The history of human thought is what people have said and done. Symbols are the products of written and spoken verbal behavior, and the concepts and relationships of which they are symbols are in the environment. Thinking has the dimensions of behavior, not a fancied inner process which finds expression in behavior.
>
> (Skinner, 1974, pp. 117–118)

A number of behavioral processes, such as generalization, discrimination, matching to sample, and stimulus equivalence (see later chapters), give rise to behavior that, in a particular situation, may be attributed to higher mental functions. From this perspective, thinking is treated as private behavior (see Moore, 2003, and Tourinho, 2006 on private events).

Thinking as Private Behavior

One of the more interesting examples of thinking involves **private behavior** or behavior that is only accessible to the person doing it. Thinking as private behavior is observed in a game of chess (Figure 1.9). We may ask another person "What is the player thinking about?" A response like "She is probably thinking of moving the castle" refers to thinking that precedes the move itself. Sometimes this prior behavior (Skinner called it *precurrent behavior*) is observable—the player may place a hand on the castle in anticipation of the move, showing a high probability of moving the castle given the layout of the chessboard. At other times, such behavior is private and cannot be observed by others. An experienced chess player may think about the game, evaluating the consequences of moving the castle to different locations. Of course, evaluating the consequences of chess moves itself depends on the actual consequences of such moves in the past (*history of reinforcement*). How often did the move result in a capture or checkmate?

Presumably, the private behavior of playing chess is overt when a person learns to play the game. For example, first the basic rules of the game are explained and a novice player is shown how the pieces move and capture. In moving the pieces from place to place, the player is asked to describe the relationships between the opposing chess pieces. This establishes the behavior of viewing and describing the layout of the board and possible moves. As the player receives additional corrective feedback and reinforcement, viewing the layout becomes more skillful. The novice

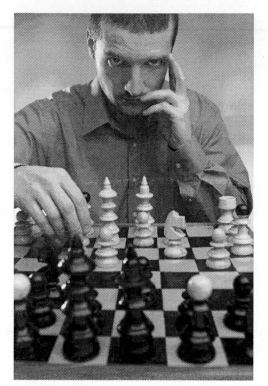

FIG. 1.9 Photograph showing a man playing chess, illustrating that thinking is operant behavior. The photo depicts visualizing the layout of the board as precurrent behavior preceding the move. © Shutterstock.

begins to see relationships and moves that were not previously apparent. During the first few games, new players are often given instructions like "Don't move your knight there, or you'll lose it." Additionally, the player may be told "A better move would have been . . .," and a demonstration of the superior move is usually given. After playing a number of games, the student is asked to explain why a particular move was made, and the explanation is discussed and evaluated. Eventually, the teacher stops prompting the player and encourages the person to play chess in silence. At this point, viewing the layout of the board (e.g., white controls the center of the board) and describing the possible consequences of moves (e.g., moving the knight to this square will split the two rooks) becomes covert and private.

As skill at chess further improves, the player no longer relies on viewing the board and its layout, but increasingly relies on thinking about the game. Blindfolded chess masters report that their thinking does not use mental images as surrogates for viewing the board, but rather *abstractions with minimal or no physical features*. Mechner (2010) suggests that "visualizing the board" involves private verbalizing rather than mental imaging—something like verbal chess notation. In chess notation, a letter and the coordinate of the destination square indicate each move of a piece. For example, a sequence of moves might be as follows: move a bishop to position e5 (**Bxe5**), move a knight to f3 (**Nf3**), and move a pawn to c5 (**c5** with no initial).

Verbal concepts drawn from a player's pre-existing behavior repertoire are used for conceptualizing moves (a form of personal notation), not mental representations of the external world as suggested by cognitive psychology. To illustrate this, verbal concepts linked to vision might include the vocabulary of color (black or white), movement in space (coordinates), and distance to and between objects (knight to bishop on e5). Chess masters appear to use their full range of verbal concepts to "conceptualize certain of [the chess position] relational and dynamic attributes" (Mechner, 2010, p. 376). The term "conceptualize" is used by Mechner to refer to verbal "discrimination between [stimulus] classes and generalization within classes," not some mental entity.

The function of thinking, as *private behavior*, is to increase the effectiveness of practical action. People conceptualize the game privately without committing themselves publicly. An advantage is that thinking about a sequence of moves (high probability response) is not revealed to your opponent; also thinking may be revoked if the judged consequences are not reinforcing based on your recent *history of reinforcement*. Once a conceptualization is implemented, the player faces the objective consequences. If conceptualizing guides actions resulting in checkmate, then this kind of thinking is strengthened. On the other hand, conceptualizing moves that result in loss of the game weakens this sort of thinking in the future. Overall, thinking is operant behavior (mostly verbal) controlled by its consequences. Thinking about a move that guides effective action is likely to occur again, while thinking that prompts ineffective performance declines (see Moore, 2000; Wilson & Hayes, 2000 for more details about thinking and feeling as behavior; also see Schlinger, 2008, 2009 on listening as behaving verbally at the sub-vocal, private level and mediated by speech production and motor regions of the brain).

In this section, we have discussed thinking as covert and private behavior. There are many other ways in which the term "thinking" is used. When a person remembers, we sometimes talk about thinking in the sense of searching and recalling. Solving problems often involves private behavior that furthers a solution. In making a decision, people are said to think about the alternatives before a choice is made. The creative artist is said to think of novel ideas. In each of these instances, it is possible to analyze thinking as private behavior that is regulated by specific features of the environment. The remainder of this book discusses the behavioral processes that underlie all behavior, including thinking.

CHAPTER SUMMARY

This chapter has introduced the idea that behavior often is acquired during one's lifetime as a result of experience. At birth we emit behavior with very little organized activity. However, as our behaviors cause consequences, some responses are strengthened while others are weakened. The consequences of behavior function to select and establish a behavior repertoire. Several prominent persons were introduced to illustrate the history of the science of behavior analysis. In particular, B. F. Skinner was described as the major force behind the experimental and applied analysis of behavior, which is the topic of this book. This approach is related to biology in that behavior is considered to be a product of genes interacting with the organism's environment. Behavior analysis can be extended to the understanding of feelings and to complex behavior involving problem solving and thinking.

KEY WORDS

Applied behavior analysis

Behavior

Behavior analysis

Behavior analyst

Behavioral neuroscience

Behaviorism

Conditioned reflexes

Contingency

Correlation

Culture

Experimental analysis of behavior

Immediate causation

Law of effect

Learning

Operant

Operant conditioning

Private behavior

Reflex

Reinforcement

Remote causation

Respondent

Respondent conditioning

Science of behavior

Selection by consequences

Trial-and-error learning

ON THE WEB

www.bfskinner.org The B. F. Skinner Foundation was established in 1987 to educate the public about B. F. Skinner's work, and to promote an understanding of the role of contingencies in human behavior.

www.behavior.org The website for the Cambridge Center for Behavioral Studies is useful for learning more about behavior analysis, behaviorism, and applied behavior analysis. The Center publishes several journals, is host to the Virtual Behavioral Community, and offers recent publications through an online bookstore.

http://web.utk.edu/~wverplan William S. Verplanck, a major contributor to the experimental analysis of behavior and behaviorism, died in September 2002. This award-winning site provides information on his past activities, publications, and addresses, plus interesting issues in psychology and the study of behavior.

www.abainternational.org Go to the web page for the Association for Behavior Analysis International to find out about the annual convention, the official journals (*The Behavior Analyst* and *Verbal Behavior*), and membership of the Association.

http://psych.athabascau.ca/html/aupr/ba.shtml Find the resource website for the behavior analysis and learning program at Athabasca University in Canada. Many useful links are given for students who want to explore a range of issues in the field. Many of these sites can be accessed to supplement your learning from each chapter in the textbook.

BRIEF QUIZ

1. _____ is the alteration (or maintenance) of an organism's behavior due to _____.
   (a) behavior; causes
   (b) learning; lifetime events
   (c) culture; social norms
   (d) evolution; genes

2. The experimental analysis of behavior is:
   (a) a natural-science approach to understanding behavior regulation
   (b) concerned with controlling and changing factors that affect behavior
   (c) concerned with the principle of reinforcement
   (d) all of the above

3. A _____ is behavior that is elicited by a biologically relevant stimulus, while a _____ is behavior that is controlled by its consequences.
   (a) reflex; respondent
   (b) respondent; voluntary
   (c) reflex; operant
   (d) operant; respondent

4. Selection by consequences occurs at three levels. What are these?
   (a) natural selection, behavior selection, and cultural selection
   (b) artificial selection, culture, and linguistic selection

(c) natural selection, artificial selection, and cultural selection

(d) artificial selection, natural selection, and linguistic selection

5. What does a duckling inherit in terms of imprinting?

    (a) the behavior of following its mother

    (b) the behavior of following a "duck-sized object"

    (c) the capacity to be reinforced by reducing the distance between itself and a moving object

    (d) the capacity to follow its mother as she obtains food in an ecological area

6. Skinner stated that behavior (including human behavior) resulted from _____.

    (a) genes

    (b) environment

    (c) self-determination

    (d) both (a) and (b)

7. According to Baer, Wolf and Risley (1968), what is the difference between basic and applied behavior analysis?

    (a) basic research is likely to look at any behavior and any variable

    (b) applied research looks at variables that could improve behavior

    (c) both (a) and (b)

    (d) none of the above

8. Which of the following statements is true of Pavlov and his contributions?

    (a) he won the Nobel Prize

    (b) he investigated the salivary reflex

    (c) he discovered the conditioned (or conditional) reflex

    (d) all of the above

9. Which of the following statements are true of the new-style behaviorists (behavior analysts) and their views?

    (a) they adopted the behaviorism of John B. Watson

    (b) they studied behavior for its own sake

    (c) they rejected genetic influences

    (d) all of the above

10. How are thinking and feeling treated from a behavioral perspective?

    (a) more behavior to be explained

    (b) the causes of overt behavior

    (c) the relationship between the mental and the physical

    (d) the mind and its regulation of behavior

Answers to Brief Quiz: 1, b (p. 1); 2, d (p. 2); 3, c (p. 4); 4, a (pp. 9–10); 5, c (p. 9); 6, d (p. 11); 7, c (p. 13); 8, d (pp. 14–15); 9, b (p. 19); 10, a (p. 21).

The Experimental Analysis of Behavior

1. Learn about a *functional* analysis of behavior.
2. Discover how perception is analyzed with behavior principles.
3. Inquire about the method of experimental analysis of behavior.
4. Focus on drugs and behavioral baselines.
5. Learn how to design and assess behavioral experiments.

The experimental analysis of behavior (EAB) refers to a method of analyzing behavior–environment relationships. This method is called functional analysis. **Functional analysis** involves *classifying behavior* according to its response functions and analyzing the *environment* in terms of stimulus functions. The term *function* refers to the *characteristic effect produced* by either a behavioral or an environmental event. Once a reliable classification has been established, the researcher uses experimental methods to show a causal relationship between the environmental event and a specified response. Because of this objective method, behavior analysts need not restrict their findings to one or a few species. The principles of behavior–environment relationships hold for all animals. Based on this assumption, and for convenience, researchers often use nonhuman subjects (e.g., rats and pigeons) as their "tools" for discovering principles of behavior, in the same way that geneticists use the fruit fly (*Drosophila melanogaster*) to establish laws of genetics.

FUNCTIONAL ANALYSIS OF BEHAVIOR

There are two ways to classify the behavior of organisms: structurally and functionally. In the **structural approach**, behavior is categorized by age to infer stages of development. For example, many developmental psychologists are interested in the intellectual growth of children. These researchers often use what a person does at a given point in the life cycle to test theories of intellectual development. Children may be said to show "object permanence" when they look for a familiar object that has just been hidden. The structure of the response or what the child does (e.g., looking for and finding the hidden object) is used to make an inference about cognitive development. The form or structure of behavior is emphasized because it is said to reveal the underlying "stage" of intellectual growth—knowing that objects exist even when they are out of sight. That is, the *structural approach* studies behavior to draw inferences about hypothetical cognitive abilities such as object permanence. These cognitive abilities in turn are used to explain the child's behavior in finding hidden objects. That is, the child can find hidden objects *because she has developed object permanence*. One problem with using structure to explain behavior is circular reasoning—the behavior of finding the hidden object is used to infer cognitive abilities (object permanence), and these abilities are then

FIG. 2.1 A child finding an object hidden in a handbag. The conditioning of finding hidden objects (object permanence) begins at birth when a child pulls at her mother's clothing to uncover the breast for feeding, is further refined by finding things under her blanket in the crib or play pen, and is directly trained as gift opening on birthdays or holidays and hunting for chocolate eggs at Easter.
© Shutterstock.

used to explain the behavior. Notice that nothing about the child's behavior is actually explained with the structural approach.

In the previous chapter, we noted that behavior analysts study behavior *for its own sake* and at its own level. To keep attention focused on behavior, structure and function are interrelated. A particular form of response by a child, such as opening and looking inside a handbag for a hidden object, is traced to its characteristic effects, outcomes, or consequences (Figure 2.1). The form, structure, or **topography** of response occurs because that way of doing it has been highly efficient, relative to other ways of opening the bag. Thus, the current topography (structure) of a response is determined by the function (effects or consequences) of this behavior.

In the example of a child who finds a hidden object, a *functional analysis* suggests that this behavior has resulted in specific consequences— the child usually has discovered the hidden toy or object. Rather than infer the existence of some intellectual stage of development or cognitive ability (object permanence), the behavior analyst suggests that a particular **history of reinforcement** is responsible for the child's capability. Presumably, from a behavioral perspective, a child who demonstrates object permanence (searching for objects when they are not in sight) has had numerous opportunities to search for and find missing or hidden objects. One advantage of this functional account is that it is testable.

A mother who breastfeeds her newborn often removes some of her clothing just before feeding the baby. After some experience, the baby may tug at the mother's blouse when she is hungry. This is one potential instance of the early conditioning of searching for hidden objects. A few months later, the infant may inadvertently cover up a favorite rattle. In this situation, getting the toy reinforces pulling back the cover when things are hidden. As children get older, they are directly taught to find hidden objects. This occurs when children are given presents to open at birthdays and when they hunt for Easter eggs. A functional analysis of object permanence accounts for the behavior by pointing to its usual effects or consequences. That is, object permanence occurs because searching for out-of-sight objects has usually resulted in finding them. Also, children who do not have these or similar experiences (playing peek-a-boo) will perform poorly on a test of object permanence, but should be able to learn this behavior by systematic instruction of the component skills (Bruce & Muhammad, 2009).

Response Functions

Behavior is not always composed of discrete responses. In fact, it is better to consider behavior as a *performance* that follows a specific stimulus and at some point results in a particular consequence. (One memorable three-term notation system used to denote this arrangement is A → B → C, which stands for antecedent stimulus (A), behavior (B), and consequence (C), as detailed in Chapter 13.) Although we shall use the term *response* throughout this book, this term does not always refer to a discrete movement like a muscle twitch or a lever press. *A response is an integrated set of movements, or a behavioral performance*, that is functionally related to environmental events or happenings in the world. In fact, some writers have referred to a behavioral stream into which antecedent and consequence events are inserted.

Functional response classes		
Response class	**Function**	**Controlling event**
Respondent	Elicited	Stimulus preceding the response
Operant	Emitted	Stimulus following the response

FIG. 2.2 Summary of the concepts used for a functional classification of behavior. The response classes are either respondent or operant. Respondent behavior is elicited by a stimulus preceding the response, either an unconditioned or conditioned stimulus; operant behavior is emitted and increased (or decreased) by a stimulus that has followed the response in the past.

Functionally, we speak of two basic types or classes of behavior: respondent and operant (Figure 2.2). These behavioral classes were briefly discussed in Chapter 1 and will be discussed further throughout the book, but here we shall emphasize the functional classification of behavior. The term **respondent** is used to refer to behavior that increases or decreases by the presentation of a stimulus (or event) that *precedes* the response. We say that the *presentation of the stimulus regulates or controls the response*. Respondent behavior is **elicited**, in the sense that it reliably occurs when the unconditioned stimulus is presented. The notation system used with elicited behavior is S → R (see section on contiguity in Chapter 3 for stimulus to stimulus or S–S conditioning, not base on response elicitation). The stimulus S causes (arrow) the response R. The constriction (and dilation) of the eye pupil is respondent behavior. It occurs when a bright light is directed into (away from) the eye. Salivation is another respondent, which is elicited by food in the mouth. The stimulus S (light or food) elicits the response R (constriction of the pupil or salivation). For the moment you may consider respondents to be the activity of smooth muscles or glands.

There is another large class of behavior that does not depend on an eliciting stimulus. This behavior is **emitted** at some frequency on the basis of genetic endowment. For example, human infants emit a random pattern of vocal sounds, usually referred to as "babbling." These sounds contain the basic elements of all human languages. English-speaking parents attend to and repeat back babbling that sounds like English, and the baby soon begins to emit more English sounds, especially when the parents are present. When emitted behavior is strengthened or weakened by the events that follow the response, it is called **operant** behavior. Thus, operants are emitted responses that occur more or less often depending on the consequences they produce in a given situation. To make clear the subtle distinction between emitted behavior and operants, consider the action word *walking* versus the phrase *walking to the store*. Walking is emitted behavior, but it has no specified function. In contrast, walking to the store is an operant that is defined by getting food at the store. Pecking a disk is emitted behavior by a pigeon, but it is an operant when pecking the disk has resulted in food. Generally, operants are emitted responses based on an organism's genetic endowment, occurring without an eliciting stimulus; effects or consequences of behavior control these responses.

Operant and respondent behaviors often occur at the same time when dealing with a single organism. When you step out of a movie theater in the middle of a bright afternoon you may show both types of responses. The change from dark to bright light will elicit pupil contraction (reflex). This smooth muscle activity is *respondent* behavior that decreases the amount of light entering the eye. At the same time, you may shade your eyes with a hand or put on a pair of sunglasses. This latter behavior is *operant* because it is strengthened by the removal of the brightness—the aversive stimulus. In another example, you find that you have failed an important exam. The bad news may elicit a number of conditioned emotional responses (respondents), such as heart palpitations, changes in blood pressure, and perspiration. You probably interpret these physiological responses as dread or anxiety. The person standing next to you as you read the results of the exam asks "How did you do on the test?" You say, "Oh, not too bad" and walk down the hall with your head down. Your reply and posture is *operant* behavior that avoids the embarrassment of discussing your poor performance. Although operant and respondent behaviors often occur at the same moment, we will usually analyze them separately to simplify and clarify the environmental conditions that regulate such behavior.

Response Classes

When a person emits a relatively simple operant such as putting on a coat, the performance changes from one occasion to the next. The coat may be put on using either the left or right hand; it may be grasped at the collar or held up by a sleeve. Sometimes one arm is inserted first, while in other circumstances both arms may be used. Careful observation of this everyday action will reveal an almost infinite variety of responses. The important point is that each variation of response has the common effect of staying warm by putting on a coat. To simplify the analysis, it is useful to introduce the concept of a class of responses. A **response class** refers to all the topographic forms of the performance that have a similar function (e.g., putting on a coat to keep warm). In some cases, the responses in a class have close physical resemblance, but this is not always the case. A response class for "convincing an opponent" may include dramatic gestures, giving sound reasons, and paying attention to points of agreement. To get service from a restaurant server, you may call out as he or she passes, wave your hand in the air, or ask the bus-person to send the server to your table.

FUNCTIONAL ANALYSIS OF THE ENVIRONMENT

In Chapter 1, we noted that behavior analysts use the term **environment** to refer to events and stimuli that change behavior. These events may be external to the organism or may arise from internal physiology. The sound of a jet aircraft passing close overhead or an upset stomach may both be classified as aversive by their common effects on behavior. That is, both events strengthen any behavior that removes them. In the case of a passing jet, people may cover their ears; a stomach pain may be removed by taking antacid medication.

The location of the source of stimulation, internal versus external, is not a critical distinction for a functional analysis. There are, however, methodological problems with stomach pains that are not raised by external events like loud sounds. Internal sources of stimulation must be indirectly observed with the aid of instruments or inferred from observable behavior–environment interactions. Evidence for stomach pain, beyond the verbal report, may include the kinds of foods recently eaten, the health of the person when the food was ingested, and current external signs of discomfort.

Stimulus Functions

All events and stimuli, whether internal or external, may *acquire* the capacity to affect behavior. When the occurrence of an event changes the behavior of an organism, we may say that the event has a **stimulus function**. Both respondent and operant conditioning are ways to create stimulus functions (see Figure 2.3). During respondent conditioning, an arbitrary event such as a tone, when paired with food, an *unconditioned stimulus* based on the animal's evolutionary history, comes to elicit a particular response, like salivation. Initially, food in the animal's mouth elicits salivation. After repeated pairings of the food and tone, the sound on its own elicits salivation. The tone is presented and salivation follows. Once the tone is effective, it is said to have a **conditioned-stimulus function** for salivation. In the absence of a conditioning history, the tone may have no specified function and does not affect behavior.

Functional stimulus classes			
Type of conditioning	**Stimulus function**	**Temporal location**	**Effect on behavior**
Respondent	Unconditioned	Before	Elicits response
	Conditioned	Before	Elicits response
Operant	Discriminative	Before	Occasions response
	Reinforcement	After	Increases response

FIG. 2.3   Summary of the concepts used for a functional classification of the environment. The type of conditioning or arrangement of behavior–environment relationships is either respondent or operant. For respondent conditioning, the stimulus that comes before behavior (temporal location) can be either an unconditioned or a conditioned stimulus. An unconditioned stimulus elicits a response based on the genetic endowment of the animal (food elicits salivation). A conditioned stimulus elicits a response based on a history of pairings with the unconditioned stimulus (tone elicits salivation). For operant conditioning, a stimulus that comes after a response (key pecking produces food) subsequently increases the rate of response (key pecking for food increases). A discriminative stimulus (key light) precedes reinforcement of the response (operant) and eventually *sets the occasion for* the response, making the response more likely when the stimulus is presented (key light increases pecking for food).

Similarly, operant conditioning generally results in establishing or changing the functions of stimuli. Any stimulus (or event) that follows a response and increases its frequency is said to have a **reinforcement function** (see Chapter 1). An event or stimulus that has this function is called a reinforcing stimulus or reinforcer (S^r). When an organism's behavior is reinforced, those events that reliably precede responses come to have a **discriminative function**. Events with a discriminative function *set the occasion for* behavior in the sense that an operant is more likely when the event occurs (see Chapter 1). Events, settings, and situations that precede operant behavior and increase its probability are called **discriminative stimuli**. Discriminative stimuli (S^D) acquire this function because they predict (have been followed by) reinforcement of operant behavior. In the laboratory, a pigeon's key pecks may be followed by food when the key is illuminated red, but not reinforced when the key is blue. After some time, the red key color is said to *set the occasion for* the response. In everyday language, the red key "tells" the bird when pecking will be reinforced. More technically, the red key is a discriminative stimulus, since the probability of reinforcement for pecking is higher when the key is red than when it is blue. That is, the bird discriminates or makes a *differential response* to red and blue.

The concept of stimulus function is an important development in the analysis of behavior. Humans and other animals have evolved in such a way that they can sense those aspects of the environment that have been important for survival. Of all the stimuli that can be physically measured and sensed by an organism, at any one moment, only some affect behavior (have a stimulus function). Imagine you are sitting on a park bench with a friend on a nice sunny day. The physical stimuli include heat, wind current, sounds and smells from traffic, birds, insects, rustling leaves, tactile pressure from sitting, and the sight of kids playing ball, people walking in the park, and the color of flowers, grass, and trees. Although all of these (and many more) stimuli are present, only some will affect your behavior—in the sense that you will turn your face to the sun, comment on the beauty of the flowers, wrinkle your nose to the odor of exhaust, and look in the direction of a passing fire truck. The remaining stimuli, at this moment in time, either have no function or serve as the context for those events that do.

Stimulus Classes

In a preceding section, we noted that responses that produce similar effects might be many and varied. To encompass response variation in form, behavior analysts use the term *response class*. Stimuli that regulate operant and respondent behavior also vary from one time to the next. When stimuli vary across physical dimension but have a common effect on behavior, they are said to be part of the same **stimulus class**. Bijou and Baer have used the concept of stimulus class in an analysis of child development and have made the point that:

> A mother's face has a fair consistency to it, we may think, in that we know our mother's face from anyone else's face. But careful observations show that it is sometimes shiny, sometimes dusty, some-times wet; occasionally creased into its facial lines, but sometimes smooth; the eyes range between fully open and fully closed, and assume a wide range of angles of regard; sometimes hairs fall in front of the face, sometimes not. Then let us remember that whenever we speak of a stimulus, we will almost surely mean a class of stimuli.
>
> (Bijou & Baer, 1978, p. 25)

It is important to note that a stimulus class is defined entirely by its common effect on behavior. That is, a stimulus class cannot be defined by the apparent similarity of the stimuli. Consider the words *boring* and *uninteresting*. In common English, we say that they have the same meaning. In behavior analysis, since these words have a similar effect on the person who reads or hears them, they belong to the same stimulus class even though they have completely different physical dimen-sions. Other stimuli may appear physically similar but belong to different stimulus classes. For example, mushrooms and toadstools look somewhat similar, but for an experienced woods person these stimuli have different functions—you pick and eat mushrooms but avoid toadstools.

Classes of Reinforcing Stimuli

The concept of stimulus class may also be used to categorize the consequences of behavior. When behavior operates on the environment to produce effects, it is an operant; the effects that increase the frequency of response are a class of reinforcing stimuli. Some consequences strengthen behavior when they are presented, such as money for a job well done, and others strengthen it when they are removed, such as scratching an itch. In this case, we can divide the general class of reinforcing stimuli into two subsets. Those events that increase behavior when presented are called **positive reinforcers**, and those that increase behavior when removed are **negative reinforcers**. For example, a smile and a pat on the back may increase the probability that a child will complete his or her home-work; thus, the smile and pat are positive reinforcers. The same child may stop dawdling and start working on a school project when a parent scolds the child for wasting time and the nagging stops when he gets going. In this case, reinforcement for working is based on the removal of scolding, and the reprimand is a negative reinforcer.

Motivation of Behavior

The relations between stimulus and response classes depend on the broader **context of behavior**. That is, environment–behavior relationships are always conditional—depending on other circum-stances. One of the most common ways to change environment–behavior relationships is to have the person (or other organism) experience a period of deprivation or satiation. For example, a pigeon will peck a key for food only if it is deprived of food for some period of time. More specifically, the peck-for-food contingency depends on level of food deprivation.

Michael (1982a) made an important distinction between the discriminative and motivational functions of stimuli. In that paper, he introduced the term **establishing operation (EO)** to refer to any environmental change that had two major effects: first, the change increased the momentary effectiveness of reinforcement supporting operant behavior, and second, the change increased momentarily the responses that had in the past produced such reinforcement (see also Michael, 1993, 2000). For example, the most common establishing operation is deprivation for primary reinforcement. The procedure involves withholding reinforcement for some period of time or, in the case of food, until the organism reaches 80% of its free-feeding body weight (see Chapter 5). This establishing operation of deprivation has two effects. First, food becomes an effective reinforcer for any operant that produces it. That is, the deprivation procedure *establishes* the reinforcement function of food. Second, behavior that has previously resulted in getting food becomes more likely—in the wild, a bird may start to forage in places where it has previously found food. Formally, an establishing operation is defined as "any change in the environment which alters the effectiveness of some object or event as reinforcement and simultaneously alters the momentary frequency of the behavior that has been followed by that reinforcement" (Michael, 1982a, pp. 150–151).

Establishing operations regularly occur in everyday life and depend on a person's conditioning history. For example, television commercials are said to influence a person's attitude toward a product. One way to understand the effects of TV commercials is to analyze them as establishing operations (technically, *conditioned establishing operations* or CEOs). In this case, an effective commercial alters the reinforcement value of the product and increases the likelihood of purchasing the item or using it if available. For example, dairy farmers advertise the goodness of ice-cold milk. Those who are influenced by the commercial are likely to go to the fridge and have a glass of milk. Of course, this immediate effect of the commercial depletes the amount of milk you have on hand, and eventually you buy more milk.

In contrast to the establishing operation, an **abolishing operation (AO)** decreases the effectiveness of behavioral consequences, and momentarily reduces behavior that has resulted in those consequences in the past (Michael, 1982a). Thus, providing frequent social attention for a period (*noncontingent* attention) functions as an abolishing operation. That is, a period of noncontingent attention subsequently decreases the effectiveness of attention as a social reinforcer, and reduces self-injurious behavior maintained by adult attention (Fischer, Iwata, & Worsdell, 1997). Furthermore, problem behavior maintained by attention may increase and decrease in the same child when noncontingent attention is withheld or provided (McGinnis, Houchins-Juarez, McDaniel, & Kennedy, 2010).

To capture both the establishing and abolishing effects of events that precede reinforced behavior (or punishment), it is useful to introduce a more inclusive concept. The **motivating operation (MO)** refers to any event that alters the reinforcement effectiveness of behavioral consequences and changes the frequency of behavior maintained by those consequences (see Laraway, Snycerski, Michael, & Poling, 2003). Figure 2.4 shows that the motivational operation (MO) comes before the three-term contingency of reinforcement [SD: R → Sr] increasing or decreasing the effectiveness of the contingency. In the operant laboratory, a period of food

$$\text{MO } [\text{S}^{\text{D}} : \text{R} \rightarrow \text{S}^{\text{r}}]$$

| Deprive of food | Key Light ON | Press lever | Food pellets |
| Provide noncontingent attention | Teacher explaining lesson | Talk out loud to other students | Teacher attention |

FIG. 2.4 The motivating operation (MO) that functions to alter the effectiveness of the contingency of reinforcement (S^D: R → S^r). In the laboratory, food deprivation (MO) increases the effectiveness of food reinforcement and also increases the probability of food-related behavior, responses previously reinforced by food in this situation (bar pressing for a rat). In a classroom, prior non-contingent attention (MO) reduces the reinforcement value of teacher attention and decreases the probability that the student will talk out loud for the period of instruction.

deprivation (MO) increases the effectiveness of lever pressing for food when the light comes on. In the classroom, a period of noncontingent attention (MO) reduces the effectiveness of talking out loud for teaching attention when the teacher is explaining the lesson. Motivating operations can have many diverse effects on behavior. In one study, events such as delaying planned activities or sleep deprivation had multiple motivating effects on problem behavior of boys with developmental disabilities (Horner, Day, & Day, 1997). For one boy, sleep deprivation reduced the effectiveness of staff praise as reinforcement for problem behavior (AO effect) and increased the effectiveness of food items as reinforcers (EO effect).

A recent study of alcohol and social bonding indicates that consumption of alcohol has motivational effects (MO) on human social interaction in addition to the reinforcing effects of alcohol itself (Sayette, Creswell, Dimoff, Fairbairn, Cohn, Heckman et al., 2012). In this study, researchers created groups of three strangers who drank cranberry juice (control drink), tonic water mixed with cranberry juice (placebo drink), or vodka mixed with cranberry juice (alcohol drink) in a social setting. Social interactions in these groups were video recorded, and facial expressions as well as speech behaviors were systematically coded. Alcohol consumption had behavior-enhancing effects (MO) compared with control and placebo groups. Alcohol use increased interpersonal smiling, speaking to others, participants' ratings of social bonding, and ratings of the reinforcing effects of the group. The motivational effects of alcohol on social contingencies of reinforcement (social reinforcement from interaction with others) may explain its continued use across diverse cultures.

TACTICS OF BEHAVIORAL RESEARCH

To discover elementary relationships between functional stimuli, responses, and consequences, behavior analysts have relied on experimental methods developed in biology, medicine, and behavior analysis (Bernard, 1927; Bushell & Burgess, 1969; Johnston & Pennypacker, 1993; Sidman, 1960). In 1865, the French physician Claude Bernard outlined the central objectives for experimental analysis. He stated that:

> We can reach knowledge of definite elementary conditions of phenomena only by one road, viz., by *experimental analysis*. Analysis dissociates all the complex phenomena successively into more simple phenomena, until they are reduced, if possible, to just two elementary conditions. Experimental science, in fact, considers in a phenomenon only the definite conditions necessary to produce it.
>
> (Bernard, 1927, p. 72)

In his book, *An Introduction to the Study of Experimental Medicine*, Bernard provided a classic example of experimental analysis:

> One day, rabbits from the market were brought into my laboratory. They were put on the table where they urinated, and I happened to observe that their urine was clear and acid. This fact struck me, because rabbits, which are herbivora, generally have turbid and alkaline urine; while on the other hand carnivora, as we know, have clear and acid urine. This observation of acidity in the rabbits' urine gave me an idea that these animals must be in the nutritional condition of carnivora. I assumed that they had probably not eaten for a long time, and that they had been transformed by fasting, into veritable carnivorous animals, living on their own blood. Nothing was easier than to verify this preconceived idea or hypothesis by experiment. I gave the rabbits grass to eat; and a few hours later, their urine became turbid and alkaline. I then subjected them to fasting and after twenty-four hours, or thirty-six hours at most, their urine again became clear and strongly acid; then after eating grass

their urine became alkaline again, etc. I repeated this very simple experiment a great many times, and always with the same result. I then repeated it on a horse, an herbivorous animal that also has turbid and alkaline urine. I found that fasting, as in rabbits, produced prompt acidity of the urine, with such an increase in urea that it spontaneously crystallizes at times in the cooled urine. As a result of my experiments, I thus reached the general proposition which then was still unknown, to wit, that all fasting animals feed on meat, so that herbivora then have urine like that of carnivora.

But to prove that my fasting rabbits were really carnivorous, a counter proof was required. A carnivorous rabbit had to be experimentally produced by feeding it with meat, so as to see if its urine would then be clear, as it was during fasting. So I had rabbits fed on cold boiled beef (which they eat very nicely when they are given nothing else). My expectation was again verified, and as long as the animal diet was continued, the rabbits kept their clear and acid urine.

(Bernard, 1927, pp. 152–153)

Bushell and Burgess (1969) provided an outline of the basic tactics of experimental analysis used by Bernard in the rabbit experiment. The following account is loosely based on their outline. Notice that Bernard made an observation that, as a physiologist, seemed unusual and puzzling—namely, that the rabbits from the market had urine that was characteristic of that of carnivores. Only a trained physiologist familiar with carnivores and herbivores would notice the anomaly of the urine. Most of us would run and get a cloth to wipe it up. The point is that a researcher must have a thorough familiarity with the subject matter to find a significant problem.

Once Bernard had identified the *problem*, he stated it in terms of a conjecture. The problem statement related type of diet to the chemistry of the urine. That is, fasting results in the animal living off its own body stores, and this produces acidity of the urine. On the other hand, when herbivores eat their usual diet of grass, their urine is alkaline. Thus, there is a clear relationship between type of diet and the nature of the animal's urine.

Experimentally, Bernard's statement suggests that we change, manipulate, or control the type of diet and measure the chemistry of the urine. The condition that is changed by the experimenter (i.e., type of diet) is called the **independent variable** (variable X), because it is free to vary at the discretion of the researcher. Bernard changed the animal's diet and measured the effect on the urine. The measured effect in an experiment is called the **dependent variable** (variable Y), because a change in it depends on a change in the independent variable. Whether the urine was acid or alkaline (dependent variable) depended on the nature of the diet (independent variable). Figure 2.5 explains the terms used in this section.

The purpose of any experiment is to establish a cause-and-effect relationship between the independent (X) and dependent (Y) variables. To establish such a relationship, the researcher must show that changes in the independent variable are functionally related to changes in the dependent variable. This is called showing covariation of the X and Y variables. In addition, the experimenter must show that the changes in the independent variable preceded changes in the dependent variable. Both of these conditions are seen in Bernard's experiment.

In Figure 2.6, you can see that changes between fasting and grass diet reliably alter the chemistry of the rabbits' urine. Thus, changes in the type of diet (the X

Independent variable	Dependent variable
• What is changed in an experiment	• What is measured in an experiment
• X variable	• Y variable
• Commonly called a *cause*	• Commonly called an *effect*
• In Bernard's experiment, type of diet	• In Bernard's experiment, chemistry of urine
• In behavioral experiments, environmental change	• In behavioral experiments, behavior of the organism

FIG. 2.5 Scientific terms used to discuss cause-and-effect relationships.

FIG. 2.6 The results of Bernard's experiment. Notice that the change in diet (independent variable) reliably changes the chemistry of the urine (dependent variable). Each time the diet is changed, the urine changes from acid to alkaline, or vice versa. Based on results reported by D. Bushell, Jr. and R. L. Burgess, *Behavioral Sociology*, 1969, p. 133. Reprinted with permission of Robert Burgess.

variable) may be said to covary with degree of acidity of the urine (the Y variable of Figure 2.6). Recall that Bernard changed the type of diet and then measured its effects on the urine. This procedure of manipulating the independent variable ensures that a change in X (type of diet) precedes the change in Y (chemistry of urine). At this point, Bernard has shown two of the three important conditions for causation—first, covariation of X and Y, and second, the independent variable precedes a change in the dependent variable.

The central question in all experiments is whether the changes in the dependent variable are uniquely *caused* by changes in the independent variable. The problem is that many other factors may produce changes in the dependent variable, and the researcher must rule out this possibility. In the Bernard experiment, the initial change from fasting to grass diet may have been accompanied by an illness caused by contaminated grass. Suppose that the illness changed the chemistry of the animals' urine. In this case, changes from fasting to grass, or from grass to fasting, will change the chemistry of the urine, but the changes are caused by the unknown illness rather than the type of diet. That is, the unknown illness *confounds* the effects of type of diet on the acidity of the urine. At this point, stop reading and look again at Bernard's description of his experiment and at Figure 2.6. Try to determine how Bernard eliminated this rival hypothesis.

One procedure for eliminating rival explanations is the systematic introduction and elimination of the grass diet. Notice that Bernard withholds and gives the grass diet and then repeats this sequence. Each time he introduces and removes the grass, a rapid change occurs from alkaline to acid (and vice versa). This rapid and systematic change makes it unlikely that illness accounts for the results. How can an animal recover from and contract an illness so quickly? Another procedure would be to use different batches of grass, because it is unlikely that they would all be contaminated. However, the most convincing feature of Bernard's experiment, in terms of eliminating rival explanations, is his final procedure of introducing a meat diet. The meat diet is totally consistent with Bernard's claim that the animals were living off their body stores, and counteracts the rival explanation that the animals were ill. More generally, the reversal of conditions and the addition of the meat diet help to eliminate most other explanations.

The Reversal Design and Behavior Analysis

Bernard's experimental design for physiology is commonly used to study behavior–environment relationships. The design is called an **A–B–A–B reversal**, and is a powerful tool used to show causal relationships among stimuli, responses, and consequences. The reversal design is ideally suited to show that specific features of the environment control the behavior of a single organism. This kind of research is often called a *single-subject experiment* and involves several distinct phases. The A-phase, or **baseline**, measures behavior before the researcher introduces an environmental change. During baseline, the experimenter takes repeated measures of the behavior under study, and this establishes a criterion against which any changes (caused by the independent variable) may be assessed. Following the baseline phase, an environmental condition is changed (B-phase) and behavior is repeatedly measured. If the independent variable or environmental condition has an effect, then the behavioral measure (dependent variable) will change (increase or decrease).

At the same time, as we have indicated, the researcher must rule out rival explanations for the change in behavior, such as simple coincidence. To do this, the baseline phase is reintroduced (A) and behavior is repeatedly measured. When the treatment is removed, behavior should return to pretreatment or baseline levels. Finally, the independent variable is changed again and the behavior is carefully measured (B). According to the logic of the design, behavior should return to a level observed in the initial B-phase of the experiment. This second application of the independent variable helps to ensure that the behavioral effect is caused by the manipulated condition.

An Application of the Reversal Design

An example of the reversal design, as used in behavior analysis, is seen in an experiment conducted in an elementary school classroom (Hasazi & Hasazi, 1972). The teacher reported a problem with an 8-year-old boy named Bob who had difficulty in adding numbers that yielded two-digit sums. Given the problem 5 + 7, Bob would write 21, reversing the digits. Today we call this kind of behavior "dyslexia" and say that the child has a learning disability. Behavior analysis suggests another possibility: dyslexia in reading or mathematics is often operant behavior inadvertently maintained by academic reinforcement, especially the extra help or attention provided by the child's teacher (the experimental problem). To test this possibility, the researchers designed an experiment to manipulate the contingency between Bob's digit-reversal responses and teacher attention (reinforcement). Basically, digit-reversal responses were expected to occur at high frequency when followed by "extra help" (attention) from the teacher, but should decrease when no longer supported by teacher-arranged consequences.

For each day of the study, at the same time in the morning, the teacher gave Bob 20 arithmetic problems with two-digit sums. Thus, the maximum number of digit reversals for a day was 20 responses. For the initial baseline (Baseline 1), the teacher used her usual method for checking problems. After Bob had completed the 20 additions, he raised his hand and the teacher came to his desk to check the worksheet. The teacher marked correct answers with "C" and digit reversals with an "X" for incorrect, explaining "This one is incorrect. You see (pointing), you reversed the numbers in the answer." Next, the teacher gave Bob "extra help" on incorrect answers by taking him through the adding process and providing verbal and physical prompts to obtain the correct answer.

For the first experimental phase (Experimental 1), the researchers changed the contingency between digit-reversal responses and teacher attention. All digit reversals were now marked with a "C", assuming that incorrect responses (and the mark "X") had acquired a conditioned reinforcement function. Also, the teacher no longer made comments about digit reversals, no longer supplied "extra help" for reversals, and Bob's statements about reversal errors were ignored. As in the past, correct sums were marked with a "C" and followed by the usual teacher consequences of a smile, a pat on the back, and the comment "This one is *very* good." As you can see, the experimental procedures no longer reinforced Bob's digit reversals with teacher attention. Technically, digit-reversal behavior was placed on *extinction* (no longer reinforced) while correct sums continued to be reinforced (*differential reinforcement* for correct sums).

The Baseline 2 phase reinstated the teacher's usual method of checking problems as in the initial baseline—assuming that digit reversals would increase once more. The Experimental 2 phase replicated the procedures used in the first experimental phase; the teacher again used *differential reinforcement* of correct sums—no longer giving attention to Bob's digit reversals, and supplying attention only for correct sums. Digit-reversal responses were expected to decrease when placed on *extinction* once again. The results of this experiment are shown in Figure 2.7.

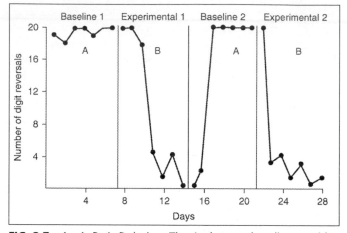

FIG. 2.7 An A–B–A–B design. The A phase or baseline provides a measure of digit-reversal responses when the teacher used her usual method of "extra help" for digit reversals. Next, the reinforcement contingency for digital reversals (B) is changed, placing these responses on extinction while maintaining reinforcement of correct sums. For the third phase (A reinstated), the teacher again follows digit reversals with "extra help." Finally, the experimental contingencies are once more in effect (B reinstated)—extinction for digit reversals and reinforcement of correct sums. Adapted from "Effects of teacher attention on digit-reversal behavior in an elementary school child" by J. E. Hasazi & S. E. Hasazi, 1972, *Journal of Applied Behavior Analysis, 5*, 157–162. © 1972 Society for Advancement of Behavior Analysis. Published with permission.

The experimental design is an A–B–A–B reversal. The A phase provides a measure of digit-reversal responses when the teacher used her usual method of "extra help" for digit reversals. Next, the researchers manipulated the reinforcement contingency for digital reversals (B), placing these responses on extinction while maintaining reinforcement of correct sums. During the third phase (A reinstated), the usual contingency arranged by the teacher was again in effect—supporting digital reversals with "extra help." Finally, the experimental contingencies were once more in effect (B reinstated)—extinction for digit reversals, and reinforcement of correct sums. The independent variable for this experiment is the contingency of reinforcement—reinforcement versus extinction for digit reversals. The dependent variable is the number of digit-reversal responses that Bob produced during each phase of the experiment (maximum of 20). As you can see in Figure 2.7, the dependent variable reliably changes in the expected direction with changes in the contingency of reinforcement (i.e., teacher attention for digit reversals). Clearly, in this experiment, digit reversals are operant responses that are inadvertently maintained by teacher-arranged reinforcement, and not some kind of learning disability residing inside the student.

Limitations to Use of the Reversal Design

The A–B–A–B reversal design is the most fundamental research design used in the experimental analysis of behavior. There are, however, difficulties that may make this design inappropriate for a given research question. One major problem is that behavior, once changed, may not return to baseline levels. Consider what might happen if you used a reinforcement technique to teach an illiterate adult to read. You could measure reading level, introduce your teaching technique, and after some time withdraw reinforcement for reading. It is very unlikely that the student will again become illiterate. In behavioral terms, the student's reading is maintained by other sources of reinforcement, such as getting information that enables the student to behave effectively (e.g., reading a menu, traffic signs, and books).

Another difficulty is that it is sometimes unethical to reverse the effects of a behavioral procedure. Suppose that a behavioral program to eliminate the use of crack cocaine works, but the doctors who run the program are not absolutely certain that the decline in drug use is caused by reinforcement procedures. It would be highly unethical to remove and reinsert the reinforcement therapy to be certain about causation. This is because removing the reinforcement procedure could lead to an increase in drug use. Nonetheless, when this and other difficulties are not encountered, the A–B–A–B reversal design is a preferable mode of analysis.

Throughout this book, we address research that uses the reversal design, modified-reversal designs (e.g., adding other control conditions), and other forms of designs for experimental analysis. We have concentrated on the reversal design in this chapter because it demonstrates the basic logic of behavioral experimentation. The task of all behavioral experiments is to establish with high certainty the cause-and-effect relationships that govern the behavior of organisms. Based on these causal relationships, behavior analysts search for general principles that organize experimental findings (e.g., principle of reinforcement).

NEW DIRECTIONS: Operant Baselines and Behavioral Neuroscience

In a given setting, behavior that is reinforced in a particular way (e.g., every 10 responses produce food) becomes very stable (low variability) over repeated experimental sessions. An animal might show a run of responses followed by a break (or time without responding) and then another run. This pattern might be repeated over and over again after long exposure to the reinforcement procedure (called **steady-state performance**). Stable performance under a contingency of reinforcement can be used as a baseline for the effects of other independent variables. That is, when behavior is very stable under a given arrangement of the environment, it is possible to investigate other conditions that disrupt, increase, or decrease the steady-state performance of animals (Sidman, 1960). Recognizing this advantage, behavioral neuroscientists often use steady-state operant behavior as baselines (control conditions) to investigate the effects of drugs on the brain and behavior.

Regarding drugs and baselines, the more stable the baseline the easier it is to detect the effects of small doses of the drug. If an animal's average number of responses for 20 experimental sessions is 10 per minute, with a range of ± 1 responses per minute (more stable baseline), a smaller dose of a drug would show an effect than if the baseline had the same average with a range of ± 5 responses per minute (less stable baseline). Notice that the same drug dose that produces a detectable effect for the stable baseline is claimed to be ineffective when inserted on the less stable baseline. The point is that we can detect small effects of drugs (and other variables) if the operant baseline is very stable during steady-state performance.

Operant baselines are said to show sensitivity to drugs. **Baseline sensitivity** means that a low dose of a drug such as amphetamine (a dopamine agonist) can cause substantial changes in baseline behavior. In contrast, the same operant baseline may not show sensitivity to doses of morphine (a opioid agonist). One implication of this kind of finding is that the effectiveness of the reinforcement contingency on behavior may involve the dopamine system more than the endogenous opiates. Based on this inference, the behavioral neuroscientist can further explore how the dopamine system participates in the control of the behavior and what neural structures are involved. Subsequent research could involve anatomical and physiological studies as well as further experiments using behavioral baselines.

Behavioral neuroscientists have used operant baselines to investigate the role of drugs in punished behavior (for reviews, see Sepinwall & Cook, 1978; Morgan, Carter,

DuPree, Yezierski, & Vierck, 2008). In a series of classic experiments, rats in an operant chamber were trained to respond for presentations of sweetened condensed milk (Geller & Seifter, 1960; Geller, Kulak, & Seifter, 1962). Next, when a clicker sounded, each lever press resulted in the milk and also an electric shock to the floor grid. Data (cumulative records, see Chapter 4) on typical performance by the rats showed that responding was greatly reduced during periods of punishment. A series of sedative or tranquilizing drugs were then administered, and the most interesting findings were that the tranquilizers did not affect overall responding for milk, but they increased responding during the clicker/shock periods. The clicker period is when there is a conflict between responding for milk (positive reinforcement) and receiving the electric shock (punishment). Apparently, the class of drugs called tranquilizers prevented the usual effects of punishment, while the other classes of drugs used by the researchers did not have this effect.

SINGLE-SUBJECT RESEARCH

Generalizing from **single-subject research** is a well-founded scientific strategy. A single individual (rat, pigeon, or human) is exposed to the values of the independent variable, and the experiment may be conducted with several subjects. Each subject replicates the experiment; if there are four subjects, the investigation is repeated four separate times. Thus, every additional individual in a single-subject experiment constitutes a **direct replication** of the research and adds to the **generality** of the research findings. Direct replication involves manipulating the independent variable in the same way for each subject in the experiment.

Another way to increase the generality of a finding is by **systematic replication** of the experiment. Systematic replication uses procedures that are different but are logically related to the original research question (see Sidman, 1960, for a detailed discussion of direct and systematic replication). For example, in Bernard's research with the rabbits, changing the diet from fasting to grass altered the chemistry of the urine and may be considered an experiment in its own right. Feeding the animals meat may be viewed as a second experiment—systematically replicating the initial research using a grass diet. Given Bernard's hypothesis that all fasting animals become carnivores, it logically follows that meat should change the chemistry of the urine from alkaline to acid.

In a behavioral experiment, such as the teacher attention and digit-reversal study (Hasazi & Hasazi, 1972), the researchers could have established generality by using a different teacher and a different kind of reinforcement (e.g., tactile contact such as hugging). Here the central idea is that the **contingency of reinforcement** is the critical factor that maintained the dyslexic behavior of the child. That is, the observed change in digit reversals did not depend on the specific teacher or the nature of the reinforcer (positive attention). In fact, many behavioral experiments have shown that contingencies of reinforcement generalize across species, type of reinforcement, diverse settings, and different operants.

Generality and Single-Subject Research

A common misunderstanding about single-subject experiments is that generalizations are not possible because the scores of a few individuals do not represent the larger population. Some social scientists believe that experiments must include a large group of individuals to make general statements (called the *statistical groups design*). This position is valid if the social scientist is interested in descriptions of what the average individual does. For example, single-subject research is inappropriate for questions like "What sort of advertising campaign is most effective for getting people in Los Angeles to recycle garbage?" In this case, the independent variable might be type of advertising and the dependent variable the number of citizens in Los Angeles who recycle their waste. The central question is concerned with how many people recycle, and a group experiment is the appropriate way to approach the problem.

Behavior analysts are less interested in aggregate or group effects. Instead the analysis focuses on the behavior of the individual. These researchers are concerned with predicting, controlling, and interpreting the behavior of single organisms. The generality of the effect in a behavioral experiment is established by **replication**. A similar strategy is sometimes used in chemistry. The process of electrolysis can be observed in an unrepresentative sample of water from Logan, Utah. A researcher who follows the procedures for electrolysis will observe the same result in all samples of water, whether they are from Logan or from the Ganges. Importantly, the researcher may claim—on the basis of a single experiment—that electrolysis occurs in all water, at all times, and in all places. Of course, only replication of the experiment will increase confidence in this empirical generalization.

Assessment of Experimental Control and Behavior Change

Single-subject experiments require a pre-intervention baseline period of measurement. This baseline serves as a comparison or reference for any subsequent change in behavior produced by the independent variable. The baseline is essential to know if your independent variable has any effect. To construct an appropriate baseline, it is necessary to define the *response class* objectively and clearly.

Definition and Measurement of the Response

In the animal laboratory, the response class of pressing a lever is most often defined by the closure of an electrical switch. There is no dispute about the state of the switch; it is either on or off. An animal may press the lever in many different ways. The left or right paw may be used as well as the hind foot, nose, or mouth. The point is that no matter how the response is made, all actions that result in a switch closure define the operant class. Once the response class is defined, the number of times the response occurs can be counted and a baseline constructed.

Outside of the laboratory, response classes are usually more difficult to define. Imagine that you are asked to help manage the behavior of a troublesome child in a classroom setting. The teacher complains that the child is disruptive and interferes with her teaching. On the surface, measuring the disruptive behavior of the child seems easy. Further reflection, however, suggests that it is not easy to define the operant class. What exactly does the teacher mean when she says "the child is disruptive"? After talking to the teacher and observing the child in the classroom, several "disruptive" responses may be identified. The child is often *out of her seat* without permission and at times when a lesson is being taught. Another behavior that occurs is *talking loudly* to other children during study periods. Both of these responses are more clearly defined than the label "disruptive," but objective measurement may still be difficult. Notice that each response is partially defined by prior events (permission) and the current situation (study periods). In addition, terms like *loud* and *out of seat* are somewhat subjective. How loud is loud, and is sitting on the edge of the desk out of seat? The answer is to keep refining the response definition until it is highly objective. When two observers can agree most of the time on whether a response has occurred, a baseline can be established.

In addition to defining the response class, assessment of experimental control and behavior change requires *measurement of the response*. During the baseline, repeated measures of the target

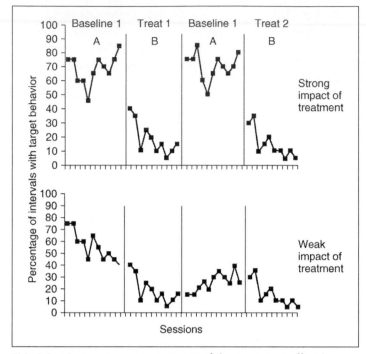

FIG. 2.8   Compare your assessment of the treatment effect in the strong-impact (top) and weak-impact (bottom) graphs. What visual properties of the two graphs lead you to assess the treatment (environmental manipulation) as effective in the top graph but not in the bottom one?

behavior are taken and plotted to assess *response variability*. Figure 2.8 portrays an idealized experiment to modify the out-of-seat behavior of the child in the foregoing classroom example. Pretend that the teacher is requested to pay attention and give tokens to the child only when she is sitting quietly in her seat during instruction sessions. At the end of the school day, the tokens may be exchanged for small prizes. For each 5-minute interval of an instruction session, the teacher records whether an out-of-seat or target response has occurred (see Chapter 13 on interval recording), and the percentage of intervals with target responses is calculated. Does this procedure alter the child's behavior?

Assessment of Experimental Control of the Response

The upper and lower panels of Figure 2.8 show two possible results of an A–B–A–B reversal study of this classroom intervention or treatment (attention and tokens for sitting quietly). Compare your assessment of the treatment effect in the two panels. You probably judge that the reinforcement procedure was effective in the top panel (strong impact) but possibly not in the lower one (weak impact). What do you suppose led to your conclusion?

A standardized visual assessment of treatment effectiveness uses several features of the graphed data (Kratochwill, Hitchcock, Horner, Levin, Odom, Rindskopf et al., 2010). These features are displayed in Figure 2.9, which shows four graphic displays of the classroom intervention for the child's out-of-seat behavior. The display labeled "Level" shows the **change in level** or average for the baseline and treatment (reinforcement) phases, with 10 instruction sessions per phase. Compared with the baseline phases, the teacher's reinforcement for sitting quietly (treatment) is expected to decrease the level of out-of-seat responses. Also, when the teacher removes the reinforcement contingency for sitting quietly (Baseline 2), it is expected that target responses will return to the initial baseline level (Baseline 1). These shifts in level in the appropriate direction are large and convincing for the high-impact graph but not for the low-impact plot.

Changes in level produced by the treatment must also be assessed in terms of the **range of variability** of the dependent variable (percentage of intervals with out-of-seat responses). The range of variability is the difference between the highest and lowest values (percentages), and is shown in Figure 2.9 for each phase of the study in the display labeled "Variability." In terms of the high-impact results (top), you can see that the scores for both baselines lie outside the range of scores in

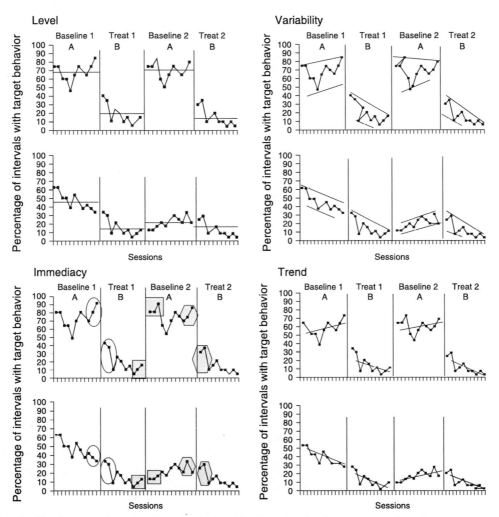

FIG. 2.9 The four panels portray the standardized features for visual assessment of treatment (environmental manipulation) effectiveness. The first panel (Level) shows the change in level or average for the strong-impact (top) and weak-impact (bottom) graphs from Figure 2.8. A second property is the range of variability of the scores for each phase of the experiment, as portrayed in the second panel (Variability). Immediacy of the change in the dependent variable is also used to assess the effectiveness of treatment, and is portrayed in the third panel (Immediacy). Note that both change in level and immediacy of change are assessed relative to the range in variability. Finally, the fourth panel (Trend) depicts the changes in trend or drift in the scores for the strong- and weak-impact graphs. Drift from baseline to treatment, in the direction of treatment (downward), is a distinct problem for the A–B–A–B reversal design. Stable baselines without trend are required to attribute causation to the treatment or independent variable.

the treatment phases. Inspection of the *range of variability* for the low-impact data shows that the baseline phases overlap the score variation in the treatments. This overlap of the percentage scores from phase to phase makes the results less convincing, in the sense of attributing any change in level to the effects of the treatment (reinforcement for sitting quietly in your seat). One reasonable strategy would be to increase the power of the intervention. In this case, the attempt is to produce a larger shift in behavior, relative to the baseline. For example, the small prizes earned at the end of the school day may be changed to more valuable items. Notice that this tactic leads to refinement of the procedures used in the experiment. This increases the experimenter's control over the subject matter—a primary objective of the experimental analysis of behavior.

You also may have taken into account the **immediacy of change** from baseline to treatment and from treatment to return to baseline (Baseline 2). You are using an assumption that the cause of a change in behavior must immediately precede the change. In behavior analysis, immediacy is assessed using the last three data points of the baselines and the first three data points for the treatment phases (ovals and hexagons of the "Immediacy" chart in Figure 2.9). You also probably assessed the immediacy of change from treatment 1 to the return to baseline (Baseline 2), encompassed by the squares. Notice that, for the high-impact results (top display of chart), the change in the dependent variable is almost immediate with the changes in the independent variable (from baseline to treatment or treatment to baseline). Now inspect the low-impact display and you are less convinced that the changes in the behavioral measures are caused by the teacher's reinforcement of sitting quietly in your seat.

A fourth visual feature used for assessment involves **trend**—a systematic rise or decline in the values of the scores. The trend is assessed by visually depicting a "best-fitting" straight line moving through the data points for each phase of the experiment. These lines are shown in Figure 2.9 in the chart labeled "Trend." For the high-impact findings (top display) there is an upward trend for the baseline phases, indicating that the out-of-seat responses are increasing. There is, however, a downward trend for each treatment phase, suggesting that the teacher's reinforcement of sitting quietly decreases the out-of-seat target behavior.

Now inspect the low-impact display for trend. Notice that the downward trend in the initial baseline (Baseline 1) is carried into the first treatment phase (Treatment 1). A drift in baseline measures can be problematic when the treatment is expected to produce a change in the same direction as the trend. In this case, the child is decreasing out-of-seat behavior before the intervention and continuing to decline in the treatment phase. Perhaps the child's parents are receiving more complaints from the school, and as the complaints mount they put more pressure on the child to "sit quietly in class." You can try to think up other reasonable hypotheses for the downward drift. The trends for the return to baseline (Baseline 2) and Treatment 2 are seemingly in the appropriate directions for the teacher's intervention, but could also reflect some kind of cyclical variation in the response measure. In summary, the trend data for the low-impact results do not suggest effective control by the teacher's reinforcement contingency. Generally, single-subject research requires a large shift in the level or direction of behavior relative to baseline. This shift must be clearly observed when the independent variable is introduced and withdrawn.

ADVANCED SECTION: Perceiving as Behavior

Most of us believe that we accurately perceive the world around us and are able to report on this with some reliability. In everyday language and in psychology, perception is an inferred, underlying cognitive process that determines behavior. In contrast, behavior analysis suggests that *perceiving is behavior* that must be accounted for by environment–behavior relationships.

In the traditional account of perception, the person is said to transform the sensations from the sense organs (eyes, ears, and nose) by mentally organizing the input into a meaningful representation of the situation. From a behavioral perspective, the difficulty with this view of perception is that the mental organization and representation of sensory input are not directly observable. That is, there is no objective way of obtaining information about such hypothetical events except by observing the behavior of the organism. Such **hypothetical** constructs are not always undesirable in science, but when used to account for behavior, these terms usually lack explanatory power because they are grounded in the very behavior that they are used to explain. This problem of explanatory power is seen in the traditional perception account of the well-known Stroop effect (Stroop, 1935).

Perception and the Stroop Effect

Figure 2.10 gives an example of the Stroop effect that you can try for yourself. First, look at the dots about the line at the top of the figure. Now, as fast as you can, say out loud whether each dot is positioned above or below the line—go! How many errors did you make and about how long did it take? OK, now look at the words ABOVE or BELOW about the line at the bottom of the figure. As fast as you can, say whether each word is positioned above or below the line—go! How many errors did you make this time and how long did it take? Most people do pretty well when the problem involves dots (top), but poorly when they have to say the position of the words (bottom). Why do you think it is harder to do the problem with the words? Read on to find out.

One account involves perception and cognition, as in the following: ". . . the highly practiced and almost automatic perception of word meaning [ABOVE or BELOW] facilitates reading. However, this same perception automatically makes it difficult to ignore meaning and pay attention only to [the position of the word] stimulus. Thus, the Stroop effect is a failure of selective perception" (Darley, Glucksberg, & Kinchla, 1991, p. 112).

Behavior Analysis of the Stroop Effect

From a behavior analysis perspective, the foregoing account restates the fact that your performance is better with the dots than with the words. The meanings and attention referred to in the passage are inferences from behavior with no independent evidence for their occurrence. Without evidence, the selective-perception explanation is not satisfying to the behavior analyst. The question is: How do environment–behavior relationships regulate performance on this task?

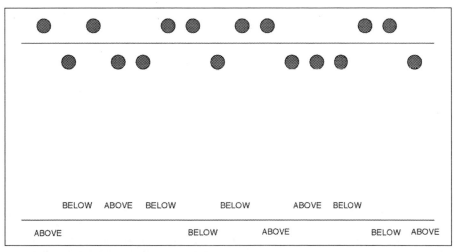

FIG. 2.10 The Stroop effect using dots above and below a line (top) and words for position (bottom). The bottom problem is more difficult in the sense that the position and the word (ABOVE vs. BELOW) compete for the response, "saying the position of the word."

The first thing to notice is that all of us have extensive experience of identifying the position of objects as above or below some reference point (the line in Figure 2.10). That is, the position of the object comes to set the occasion for the response of saying "above" or "below." We also have a long history of reinforcement for reading the words ABOVE and BELOW; in books these words correspond to the position of objects in pictures, as in "the airplane is above the ground" or "the sun is below the horizon." Because of this learning, the physical position (location of object X) and written words for position ("above/below") come to control the response class ("object X is above [or below) the reference point"). When written words for location are presented in positions that do not correspond to the word (word = ABOVE; position = below), the two properties of the complex stimulus (word/position) compete for the respective responses. Based on the simultaneous control of behavior by two aspects of the blended stimulus, the time to complete the task increases and errors occur. Consider what you might do if you were driving and came to an intersection with a red-hexagon sign that had the word PROCEED painted on it. You would probably wonder what to do and show "brake and go" responses. Instead of using an account based on selective perception, the behavior analysts would point to *response competition and reinforcement history* as reasons for your hesitation.

The Effect of the World on What We See

There are other interesting implications of a functional analysis of perceiving. For example, you walk into a room and look around, believing that you are taking in reality. But what do you see? Seeing itself is something an organism is prepared to do based on its genetic endowment, but seeing a particular object on a given occasion may be analyzed as respondent or operant behavior. That is, seeing an object or event is behavior that is either elicited by the event, has a high probability due to past consequences, or becomes likely due to motivating conditions (e.g., hunger, thirst, or aversive stimulation).

Imagine that you have gone camping with several friends. After supper you decide to entertain your friends by telling a horror story about an axe murder that took place in the same area a few years ago. One of your companions is finishing supper, and the fried egg on her plate begins to look like a giant dead eye that is about to explode with yellow "glop." As the night gets darker, another camper hears ominous sounds and begins to see figures moving in the brush. In everyday words, your friends are imagining these events. Behaviorally, the frightening story may be analyzed as a motivating condition that momentarily increases the probability of seeing things that appear to be threatening.

B. F. Skinner has described other conditions that affect seeing as a conditioned response. He stated that:

> Conditioned seeing explains why one tends to see the world according to one's previous history. Certain properties of the world are responded to so commonly that "laws of perception" have been drawn up to describe the behavior thus conditioned. For example, we generally see completed circles, squares, and other figures. An incomplete figure presented under deficient or ambiguous circumstances may evoke seeing a completed figure as a conditioned response. For example, a ring with a small segment missing when very briefly exposed may be seen as a completed ring. Seeing a completed ring would presumably not be inevitable in an individual whose daily life was concerned with handling incomplete rings.
>
> (Skinner, 1953, pp. 267–268)

Skinner later points out that operant conditioning can also affect what is seen:

> Suppose we strongly reinforce a person when he finds a four-leaf clover. The increased strength of "seeing a four-leaf clover" will be evident in many ways. The person will be more inclined to look at four-leaf clovers than before. He will look in places where he has found four-leaf clovers. Stimuli that resemble four-leaf clovers will evoke an immediate response. Under slightly ambiguous circumstances he will mistakenly reach for a three-leaf clover. If our reinforcement is effective enough, he may even see four-leaf clovers in ambiguous patterns in textiles, wallpaper, and so on. He may also "see four-leaf clovers" when there is no similar visual stimulation—for example, when his eyes are closed or when he is in a dark room. If he has acquired an adequate vocabulary for self-description, he may report this by saying four-leaf clovers "flash into his mind" or he "is thinking about" four-leaf clovers.
>
> (Skinner, 1953, p. 271)

You should realize that no one knows what a person "sees." What we know is what the perceiver says she sees. The person tells us she sees (or does not see) something and this statement is itself an operant; as an operant the verbal statement of seeing "X" is regulated by its past history of consequences, including the social consequences provided by other people. Let us apply this kind of analysis to a recent cognitive study of so-called "mindfulness" and visual perception.

Social Regulation of Visual Acuity

Most of us would say that 20/20 vision, evaluated by an eye-chart test, is an accurate measure of our eyes' ability to detect reality. But is visual acuity a straightforward fact or does it depend on a history of conditioning? An ingenious study by Langer, Djikic, Pirson, Madenci, and Donohue (2010) helps to answer this question. In the Langer study, students with at least 20/20 vision at the Massachusetts Institute of Technology (MIT) in the Reserve Officers Training Corp (ROTC), none of whom were pilots, volunteered to participate. All of the participants ranked vision as one of the three most important characteristics for being a pilot. Participants assigned to the pilot (experimental) group were asked to be Air Force pilots and were taken to a jet aircraft flight simulator and positioned in the pilot's seat. With the aid of the experimenter in the co-pilot seat, each participant performed simple flight maneuvers while looking at a flight simulator screen. As part of the simulation, the ROTC students were asked to hold the jet on a stable and level course while they identified markings on the wings of approaching aircraft. These wing insignias were actually taken from lines of a standardized eye chart and, unknowingly, students were taking a test for vision accuracy. Other ROTC students assigned to the nonpilot (control) group were treated in the same fashion as the pilot group, except that they were told the flight simulator was "broken"; nonpilot students could play the role of a pilot by holding on to the steering wheel, pretending to fly the jet fighter. As in the pilot condition, nonpilot ROTC students were asked to identify markings on the wings of approaching aircraft—the visual acuity test.

The pilot and nonpilot ROTC students did not differ on an eye-chart test before the study, but 40% of the pilots improved their eye-test scores on the equivalent vision test taken in the flight simulator (i.e., markings on aircraft wings). None of the nonpilot participants improved their eye-test scores, and one nonpilot showed a decline in visual acuity; none of the pilots showed a decrease in their scores on the vision tests. These findings were replicated in a second flight simulator study that included other control conditions.

A Behavior Analysis of Visual Acuity

Langer et al. (2010) have provided a cognitive interpretation of improved visual performance based on the pilots' "mind-sets" and beliefs. This explanation is regrettable, as it does not say much beyond the fact that the pilots increased their eye-test scores. The question is how we can explain the improvement in visual acuity for the participants who flew the jet fighter in the simulator.

A behavior analysis points to the ROTC students' history of conditioning and the current conditions arranged by flying in a simulator. In terms of *conditioning history*, notice that ROTC students have been trained in military discipline and the requirements to carry out the mission to the best of their ability. For example, at rifle practice, ROTC students would have been punished for inaccurate shots (off target) by low scores in marksmanship and reprimands from the training officer. Also, many of the ROTC students who volunteered for the pilot study "aspired to be fighter pilots" and "strongly associated good vision with pilots" (Langer et al., 2010, p. 662). That is, these students discriminated the operating contingencies for recruitment and selection of fighter pilots. To gain admission to military flight school, cadets must show strong performance on visual tasks; low performance leads to rejection by the Air Force.

Next, let us analyze the *current conditions* faced by the students. The flight simulator approximates the actual conditions of a military flight mission—that is, discriminating fine details, such as military insignias on another aircraft. In this context, going off course and losing control of the aircraft would punish instrument and guidance errors, while precision flying would avoid these consequences. It is behavior that military pilots have to get right. Flying in a simulator probably also functions as a *motivating operation* for those who aspire to be jet fighter pilots, increasing the momentary effectiveness of social punishment (evaluation by the training officer or experimenter), and reducing the probability of guidance errors, including those of vision (higher scores on the wing-marking test). Generally, the Langer study shows that *motivational conditions, together with contingencies of discrimination and punishment,* often regulate how well we see objects in the world.

Psychologists have called conditioned seeing effects "perceptual set," "search image," and "mind-set." In fact, many psychologists do not consider seeing as operant or respondent behavior. These researchers prefer to study perception as a cognitive process that underlies behavior. Although the issue is not resolved here, Skinner makes it clear that analyzing seeing as behavior is one way to understand such processes. That is, perceiving may be treated like *signal detection* rather than mental states and processes (Green & Swets, 1966; Wickens, 2002). The behavior analysis of seeing (or, more generally, perceiving) also applies to other sensory dimensions such as hearing, feeling, and smelling. Notice that such an analysis accounts for perceiving without reference to mental events.

CHAPTER SUMMARY

In summary, this chapter introduces the science of behavior analysis. In particular, it is the assessment of the antecedents and consequences of behavior as aspects of the environment that can be manipulated and affect the behavior in question. Innumerable formal and informal studies have determined that the events that follow a specific response will influence whether that response is likely occur again. If a response has a destructive, obnoxious, painful or otherwise unpleasant outcome, an animal will not repeat it. It will either be killed (as by eating toxic plants) or injured (as by touching a leaf with sharp spines), and the behavior is gone. The point is that behaviors have functions in the sense that something happens as a result. We are built by natural evolutionary processes to behave, to walk, to pick up things, to vocalize, etc. We look around and we see different sights; our head turning has a function—it moves our eyes so that we see in different directions. Behavior analysts work to discover the functions of behavior and also to provide functions that end up creating novel behaviors.

A functional analysis is conducted in several uniform and proven effective sets of procedures. A major tactic is the A–B–A–B reversal process whereby the researcher determines if a certain functional outcome (an applied consequence) does indeed control the appearance of a behavior. If a rat gets a pellet for lever pressing, the rat presses the lever and when pellets stop coming he stops pressing. The behavior of organisms can be studied objectively and scientifically, and that is why several issues are described concerning replication, validity, generalization and assessment. The experimental analysis of behavior is a systematic set of tactics for the exploration of the controlling variables of behavior.

KEY WORDS

A–B–A–B reversal design

Abolishing operation

Baseline

Baseline sensitivity

Change in level (baseline to treatment)

Conditioned-stimulus function

Context of behavior

Contingency of reinforcement

Dependent variable

Direct replication

Discriminative function

Discriminative stimuli

Elicited (behavior)

Emitted (behavior)

Environment

Establishing operation

Functional analysis

Generality

History of reinforcement

Hypothetical construct

Immediacy of change (baseline to treatment)

Independent variable

Motivating operation

Negative reinforcer

Operant

Positive reinforcer

Range of variability (in assessment)

Reinforcement function

Replication (of results)

Respondent

Response class

Single-subject research

Steady-state performance

Stimulus class

Stimulus function

Structural approach to classifying behavior

Systematic replication

Topography

Trend (as in baseline)

ON THE WEB

http://seab.envmed.rochester.edu/jeab/articles_selected/index.html The homepage for the *Journal of the Experimental Analysis of Behavior (JEAB)*—a journal that illustrates the experimental method discussed in Chapter 2. Early issues of the journal are helpful in terms of basic design (A–B–A–B reversal).

http://seab.envmed.rochester.edu/jaba The web page for the *Journal of Applied Behavior Analysis (JABA)*—a journal that is devoted to the application of behavior principles. The articles often illustrate the basic designs used in behavior analysis, especially in earlier issues of the journal.

www.michaelbach.de/ot Visit the website of Michael Bach and enjoy the 92 visual illusions he has assembled. Most of these illusions are used to reveal how humans perceive the world. A behavior analysis turns perception on its head, asking how the world controls what we see. Try to explain the illusions by referring to your previous history of reinforcement and the current contingencies set up by the illusion. Discuss the illusions with your classmates and instructor.

www.dharma-haven.org/science/myth-of-scientific-method.htm A site maintained by Terry Halwes, who argues that scientists deviate in important ways from the logical hypothesis-testing view taught in most scientific methods books. He states that "the procedure that gets taught as 'The Scientific Method' is entirely misleading. Studying what scientists actually do is far more interesting."

⬛ BRIEF QUIZ

1. In terms of finding an object that is missing or hidden:

    (a) a structural account points to stages of development and object permanence
    (b) a behavioral account points to a particular history of reinforcement
    (c) the form or structure of behavior is used by behavior analysts to infer mental stages
    (d) both (a) and (b) are true

2. The term _____ refers to behavior that is elicited, and the term _____ refers to behavior that is emitted.

    (a) operant; respondent
    (b) respondent; operant
    (c) reflexive; flexible
    (d) flexible; reflexive

3. Any stimulus (or event) that follows a response and increases its frequency is said to have:

    (a) a reinforcement function
    (b) a discriminative function
    (c) a conditioned-stimulus function
    (d) a consequence function

4. In functional analysis, positive and negative reinforcers are examples of:

    (a) response classes
    (b) stimulus classes

(c) conditioned stimuli

(d) unconditioned stimuli

5. In terms of behavior–environment relations, establishing operations:

(a) are used to construct the foundations of behavior

(b) increase the momentary effectiveness of reinforcement

(c) increase momentarily responses that produce reinforcement

(d) both (b) and (c)

6. The variable manipulated by the experimenter is the _____, and the measured effect is the _____.

(a) dependent; independent

(b) extraneous; dependent

(c) independent; dependent

(d) independent; extraneous

7. In terms of the reversal design and behavioral experiments:

(a) the A-phase is called the baseline

(b) the B-phase is the experimental manipulation

(c) the design is used in single-subject experiments

(d) all of the above are true

8. Baseline sensitivity means that:

(a) behavior is sensitive to a low dose of drug

(b) behavior is sensitive to a high dose of drug

(c) behavior is sensitive to both high and low doses of drug

(d) behavior is sensitive to stimuli that accompany the drug dose

9. The presence of trend in baseline measures:

(a) refers to a systematic rise or decline in the baseline values

(b) is problematic when the treatment is expected to produce a change in the direction of the trend

(c) can be helpful when inferring that an independent variable has produce and effect

(d) is characterized by both (a) and (b)

10. **ADVANCED SECTION:** In terms of the Stroop effect, behavior analysts point to _____ and _____ as reasons for hesitation.

(a) response competition; learning

(b) learning; reinforcement

(c) response competition; history of reinforcement

(d) history of reinforcement; memory

Answers to Brief Quiz: 1, d (pp. 29–30); 2, b (p. 31); 3, a (p. 33); 4, b (p. 34); 5, d (p. 35); 6, c (p. 37); 7, d (pp. 38–39); 8, a (p. 41); 9, d (p. 46); 10, c (p. 48).

Reflexive Behavior and Respondent Conditioning

1. Learn about *fixed action patterns (FAPs), modal action patterns (MAPs),* and reaction chains.
2. Investigate the primary laws of the reflex and the process of habituation.
3. Study *Pavlov's* experiments on respondent conditioning of salivation.
4. Learn about the complexities of second-order and compound conditioning.
5. Discover the basis of drug tolerance and how context affects drug overdose.

A biological imperative, faced by all creatures, is to survive long enough to reproduce. Because of this, behavior related to survival and reproduction often appears to be built into the organism. That is, organisms are born with a range of behavior that aids survival and reproduction. Creatures that fly to avoid predators are likely to be born with the ability to fly. Thus, flying does not need to be learned; it results from the organism's species history. The complex array of motor movement and coordination involved in flying could be learned, but it is much more dependable when this behavior is based on genetic endowment.

For most animals, survival at birth depends on being able to breathe, digest food, and move about. When a worm is dangled over a young robin's head, this stimulus elicits opening of the mouth and chirping. The behavior of the chick is the result of biological mechanisms and is elicited by the sight of the dangling worm. The relationship between the dangling worm (stimulus) and the open mouth (response) is called a reflex. Presumably, in the evolutionary history of robins, chicks that presented a gaping mouth and chirped were fed and those that did not may have been ignored. That does not mean that there are no learned modifications of such initial behaviors (Walker, 1987, p. 21–26). For example, Tinbergen and Kuenen (1957) observed that if feeding did not follow gaping to a realistic, artificial stimulus, thrush chicks stopped responding. In humans, reflexive crying to discomfort or hunger by an infant ensures more effective care from the child's parents. Parents engage in a variety of caretaking behaviors in attempts to stop crying. Usually, parental responses such as changing a soiled diaper, feeding, or burping the infant will stop the fussing.

PHYLOGENETIC BEHAVIOR

Behavior relations that are based on the genetic endowment of an organism are described as **phylogenetic**, and are present on the basis of species history. Behavior that aids survival or procreation is often (but not always) unlearned. This is because past generations of organisms that engaged in such behavior survived and reproduced. These animals passed to the next generation the characteristics, by means of genes, that allowed similar behavior. Thus, species history provides the organism with a basic repertoire of responses that are elicited by environmental conditions. Darwin said that these characteristics were naturally selected since they occurred through no action or intervention by man.

Sequences of Behavior

Fixed action patterns or FAPs are sequences of behavior (a series of connected movements) that are phylogenetic in origin. All members of a particular species (often all males or all females) engage in the FAP when the appropriate releasing stimuli are presented. Fixed action patterns have been observed and documented in a wide range of animals and over a large number of behaviors related to survival and reproduction. To illustrate this, Tinbergen (1951) noted that the male stickleback fish responds with a stereotyped sequence of aggressive displays and movements when other male sticklebacks intrude on its territory during the mating season. The female spider *Cupiennius salei* constructs a cocoon and deposits her eggs in it by engaging in a fixed sequence of responses (Eibl-Eibesfeldt, 1975). A greylag goose presented with an egg outside its nest will automatically roll the egg into the nest by reaching over the egg (with its bill) and pulling it carefully toward the nest. If the egg is removed, the bird continues with the fixed sequence of egg-retrieval actions. That is, the bird continues behaving as though the egg is present even though it has been removed. The following passage describes the fixed action pattern that the squirrel *Sciurus vulgaris* L. engages in while putting nuts away for the winter:

> The squirrel . . . buries nuts in the ground each fall, employing a quite stereotyped sequence of movement. It picks a nut, climbs down to the ground, and searches for a place at the bottom of a tree trunk or a large boulder. At the base of such a conspicuous landmark it will scratch a hole by means of alternating movements of the forelimbs and place the nut in it. Then the nut is rammed into place with rapid thrusts of the snout, covered with dirt with sweeping motions and tamped down with the forepaws.
>
> (Eibl-Eibesfeldt, 1975, p. 23)

Ethologists refer to such predictable and stereotypic behaviors as fixed action patterns to imply that these behaviors are built in and immutable. They are looking for heritable genetic factors with which to account for behavior. On the other hand, the behavior science model prefers to consider all behaviors as flexible and adaptable, at least to some degree. So, given the adaptive ability of most animals, Barlow (1968) refers to this behavior as a modal action pattern (MAP). Although the topographic features of these reflex sequences may appear similar across most individuals and situations (mode), the concept of MAP denotes the numerous idiosyncratic differences in behavior—implying flexibility rather than rigid genetic control. For example, all robins (*Turdus americanus*) build nests that appear very similar in construction. However, it is clear that they do not all build in the same location, or use the same materials. There is great individual variation in all phases of nest construction, suggesting modification by the environment (ontogeny).

Reaction chains are similar to FAPs, but with one major difference—each set of responses in a reaction chain requires an appropriate stimulus to set it off. Recall that once a fixed action pattern (or MAP) begins, the animal will continue the sequence even when the stimuli that set off the behavior are removed. In the previous squirrel example, if the nut is taken away from the squirrel, the animal will continue to dig a hole and bury a nonexistent nut. In contrast, a reaction chain requires the presence of a specific stimulus to elicit each link in a patterned sequence of behavior. An organism's performance produces stimuli that set off the next set of responses in the chain; these behaviors produce the next set of stimuli followed by another set of responses. Presenting stimuli that elicit responses ordinarily occurring in the middle part of the sequence will start the chain at that point rather than at the beginning. Also, unlike fixed action patterns, if the stimuli that elicit behavior are removed, the sequence is disrupted.

The courtship ritual of the male and female stickleback fish (*Gasterosteus aculeatus*) is a reaction chain and is presented in Figure 3.1. Reaction chains often show behavioral flexibility similar

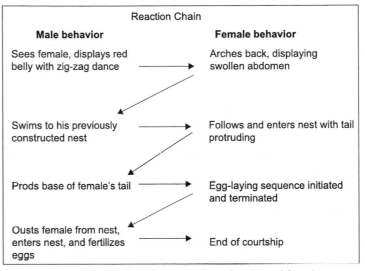

FIG. 3.1   The reaction chain for courtship of male and female sticklebacks. This sequence of reflexive responses is initiated in the breeding season when the male stickleback spies a female and begins his zigzag dance, displaying his red belly. The female responds by arching her back, revealing her swollen abdomen full of eggs. Upon seeing the swollen abdomen, the male stickleback swims to the nest that he has already prepared. The female follows the male into the nest with her tail protruding, allowing the male to nibble and prod at her tail. This prodding of the tail sets off egg laying in the female, and when this is completed the male ousts her from the nest and fertilizes the eggs, thereby completing the courtship chain.

to the MAP, but here we describe an idealized behavioral sequence. During the mating season, the chain is initiated when a male stickleback sees a female and begins a zigzag dance, displaying his red underbelly. For a receptive female with eggs, the male's display functions as a stimulus that causes the female to arch her back and reveal her swollen abdomen. This initiates swimming by the male to a previously constructed nest. The female follows and enters the nest with her tail protruding, causing the male to nibble at the base of her tail and initiate the egg-laying sequence. Once the female has deposited her eggs, the male ousts her from the nest, enters the nest and fertilizes the eggs, thereby completing the reaction chain.

This courtship chain may be terminated at any point if the behavioral displays by either fish are inadequate or inappropriate to function as a stimulus for the next link in the chain. Thus, red-bellied males that skillfully perform the zigzag dance are more likely to attract females to their nests and fertilize eggs than males that execute the dance less skillfully. **Sexual selection,** by providing more chances to mate, ensures that genes related to skillful execution of the dance are more represented in the next generation and that the offspring have a high probability of successful courtship and reproduction.

Reflexive Behavior

The principles that describe the reflex (and its conditioning) are similar for many different kinds of reflexes. For example, the laws that govern pupil contraction when a light is shone in the eye or the principles that describe the relationship between a sudden loud noise and a startle response also hold for the salivation produced when you eat a meal. Early work by Sherrington (1906) focused on the reflex, and the relationships that he discovered, over a century ago, generalize to a remarkable variety of stimulus–response relationships. When food is placed in a dog's (or human's) mouth, the salivary glands produce saliva. This relationship between food in the mouth and salivation is a reflex that is based on the genetic endowment of the organism and is not learned. Many reflexes serve defensive, protective, or survival functions. Frequently such reflexes are not learned because they have to function before adequate experience is provided.

All organisms are born with a built-in set of reflexes, but many of these are particular to a species. Thus, humans are born with an array of responses elicited by specific stimuli. For example, tactile stimulation of the human infant's cheek evokes the rooting response—turning toward the stimulation with the mouth open, which then receives the nipple. Also, as we have noted, in young robins the so-called "begging" reflex (open mouth and chirping) serves a similar function—getting fed. Because these relationships are relatively invariant and biologically based, we refer to the eliciting event as the **unconditioned stimulus (US)**. The related behavior following the stimulus is called the **unconditioned response (UR)**. The term *unconditioned* is used because the reflex does not depend on an organism's experience or conditioning during its lifetime (i.e., learning).

When an unconditioned stimulus elicits an unconditioned response (US → UR), the relationship is called a **reflex**. Reflexive behavior is automatic in the sense that a physically healthy organism will always produce the unconditioned response when presented with an unconditioned stimulus. You do not choose to salivate or not when you have food in your mouth; the US (which is "food in the mouth") draws out or **elicits** the UR of salivation. This is the way the animal (i.e., you) is built. However, there are times and conditions described below where the US does not elicit the UR. When repeated presentations of the US lead to a reduction of the UR we call that process *habituation*.

Laws of the Reflex

Around 350 BC, Aristotle developed principles of association that were rediscovered by psychologists, and by Pavlov (a physiologist), in the 1900s (Hothersall, 1990, p. 22). Sherrington (1906) studied many different types of reflexes, and formulated the laws of reflex action. Because reflexive behavior occurs across most or all animal species, from protozoa and sponges (Wawrzyncyck, 1937; Meech, 2008) to humans (Watson & Rayner, 1920; Knikou, Angeli, Ferreira, & Harkema, 2009), and because associative or respondent conditioning builds on reflexive behavior, it is important to describe the laws of the reflex. These laws are general in that they hold for all eliciting or unconditioned stimuli (e.g., food in the mouth, a touch of a hot surface, a sharp blow just below the knee, a light shining in the eye) and the corresponding unconditioned responses (salivation, quick finger withdrawal, an outward kick of the leg, pupil contraction).

The unconditioned stimuli that elicit unconditioned responses may vary in intensity. For example, light that is shining in the eye may be bright enough to hurt or so faint that it is difficult to detect. A tap below the knee, causing a kick, may vary from a modest to a heavy blow. The intensity of the eliciting US has direct effects on the elicited reflex. Three **primary laws of the reflex** describe these effects.

1. The **law of the threshold** is based on the observation that at very weak intensities a stimulus will not elicit a response, but as the intensity of the eliciting stimulus increases, there is a point at which the response is elicited. That is, *there is a point below which no response is elicited*

and above which a response always occurs. The uncertainty region, where roughly 50% of the stimuli that are presented produce a response, is called the threshold.

2. The **law of intensity–magnitude** describes the relationship between the intensity of the eliciting stimulus and the size or magnitude of the elicited response. *As the intensity of the US increases, so does the magnitude of the elicited UR*. A light tap on the patella tendon (just below the kneecap) will evoke a slight jerk of the lower leg; a stronger tap will produce a more vigorous kick of the leg (the patellar reflex). Of course, there are upper limits to the magnitude of the tap. If a hammer is used to smash into the knee, the result is a broken kneecap and no movement for a long time.

3. The **law of latency** concerns the time between the onset of the eliciting stimulus and the appearance of the reflexive response. Latency is a measure of the amount of time that passes between these two events. *As the intensity of the US increases, the latency to the appearance of the elicited UR decreases*. Thus, a strong puff of air will elicit a quick blink of the eye. A weaker puff will also elicit an eye blink, but the onset of the response will be delayed.

These three laws of the reflex are basic properties of all reflexes. They are called primary laws because, taken together, they define the relationship between the intensity of the eliciting stimulus (US) and the unconditioned response (UR). Reflexes, however, have other characteristics and one of these, habituation, has been shown in animals as simple as protozoa and as complex as humans.

Habituation

One of the more documented secondary properties of the reflex is called **habituation**. Habituation is observed to occur when an unconditioned stimulus repeatedly elicits an unconditioned response and the response gradually declines in magnitude. When the UR is repeatedly elicited it may eventually fail to occur at all. For example, Wawrzyncyck (1937) repeatedly dropped a 4 g weight onto a slide that the protozoa *Spirostomum ambiguum* were mounted on. The weight drop initially elicited a contraction or startle response that steadily declined to near zero with repeated stimulation.

An interesting report of human habituation, in a dangerous setting, appeared in the July 1997 issue of *National Geographic* (Figure 3.2). The small island of Montserrat has been home to settlers since 1632. Unfortunately, the relatively silent volcano on the island reawakened in July 1995. Suddenly the quiet existence that had characterized living on Montserrat was rudely interrupted. Before the major eruption of the volcano, a large group of inhabitants refused to evacuate the island, and these people suffered through several small volcanic explosions:

> . . . Gerard Dyer and his wife, Judith, [have] been staying with friends in St. John's, about as far north of the volcano as you can get. . . . People could get passes to visit the unsafe zone, which is how Gerard came to be working on the flanks of Soufriere Hills that bright morning.
>
> "If you have animals and crops, you can't just leave them" said Gerard as we walked back to his truck. "You have to come look after them and hope nothing happen." As he spoke, the volcano made a crackling sound like distant thunder—blocks of solid lava rolling down the side of the dome. Gerard didn't even look up.
>
> Montserratians have become so used to the volcano's huffing and puffing that the initial terror has gone. As one woman said, "At first when there was an ashfall, everybody run. Now when the ash falls, everybody look."
>
> (Williams, 1997, p. 66)

In this example, Gerard has been repeatedly exposed to the sound (US) of minor volcanic explosions. At first, this sound elicited a startle/panic response, accompanied by running, but these

FIG. 3.2 A volcano repeatedly threatening to erupt, without a major eruption, results in habituation of people's startle/panic responses, including running away. © Shutterstock.

URs habituated to near zero with repeated eruptions of the volcano. A similar process is observed when people live under an airport flight path; initially the sound of a jet taking off or landing is bothersome, but after some time the sound is barely noticed.

There are a number of general properties that characterize habituation (Thompson & Spencer, 1966; Rankin, Abrams, Barry, Bhatnagar, Clayton, et al., 2009). Some of the more important principles of habituation are as follows. First, the decrease in the habituated response is large initially, but this decrement gets progressively smaller as habituation is continued. Second, if the unconditioned stimulus is withheld for some time, the habituated response recovers. Third, when habituation is repeatedly produced, each series of stimulus presentations generates progressively more rapid habituation. In other words, habituation occurs more quickly on a second series of unconditioned stimulus presentations than on the first, and then even faster on a third set. This may represent the simplest form of learning and also a rudimentary form of memory (Tighe & Leaton, 1976).

Habituation is a behavioral process that has come about because of phylogenetic history. Those animals that habituated were more likely to survive and produce offspring. A herbivore that runs away each time the grass rustles gets less to eat than one that stands its ground. A rustling grass sound may indicate the presence of a predator, or simply the wind blowing. Repeated activation of respondent mechanisms, when unnecessary, stresses the animal as well, which is not good in terms of health and physiology.

ONTOGENETIC BEHAVIOR

In addition to phylogenetic history, the behavior of an organism is affected by environmental experience. Each organism has a unique **ontogenetic** history or lifetime of conditioning. Changes in behavior, as a result of such experience, are called *learning* and consist of organism–environment interactions. Events in the physical and social world impact the behavior of organisms. Learning builds on species or *phylogenetic* history to determine when, where, and what kind of behavior will occur at a given moment.

For example, salivation is involved in the digestion of food. People do not learn to salivate to the taste of food; this is a phylogenetic characteristic of the species. After some experience where you learn that McDonald's goes with food, you may salivate to the sight of the golden arches of McDonald's, especially if you are hungry and like hamburgers. Salivating at the sight of McDonald's arches occurs because of respondent conditioning—you were not born that way. It is, however, important to note that respondent conditioning and other learning processes themselves evolved because they provided some sort of reproductive advantage. Those organisms whose behavior came under the control of arbitrary (but important) environmental events presumably gained an advantage over those whose behavior did not. Through Darwinian evolution and selection, respondent conditioning became a means of behavioral adaptation. In other words, *organisms with a capacity for respondent learning were more likely to survive and reproduce*— increasing their genes in the population.

Respondent Conditioning

Respondent conditioning involves the transfer of the control of behavior from one stimulus to another by S–S pairing. In Chapter 1, we saw that the sound of a bell could come to elicit salivation after the bell had been associated with food. This kind of conditioning occurs in all species, including humans, and is common in everyday life. Imagine that you are out for an early-morning walk and pass a bakery where you smell fresh doughnuts. When this happens, your mouth begins to water and your stomach starts to growl. These conditioned responses occur because, in the past, the smell has been associated (paired) with food in the mouth (doughnuts).

Figure 3.3 shows the classical conditioning of salivation described by Pavlov (1960). The upper panel indicates that an arbitrary stimulus such as a light (CS) is presented just before food (US) is placed in a dog's mouth. After several pairings of the light with the food, the light is presented alone. If the light now elicits salivation (test phase), it is called a **conditioned stimulus (CS)**, and salivation to the light is called the **conditioned response (CR)**.

Notice that a new feature of the environment (a light) has come to regulate the behavior (salivation) of the organism. Thus, classical (Pavlovian or respondent) conditioning involves the transfer of behavior control to new and often arbitrary aspects of the environment. To experience this sort of conditioning, try the following: Read the word *lemon* and consider the last time you ate a slice of lemon. Many people salivate at this CS because the word has been contiguously (near in time) paired with the sour taste of the fruit. This shift in controlling stimulus from food to word is possible because of the anatomy involving the critical synapse onto the final common neural pathway. In this case, input to the visual system ends up activating the neuron that innervates the salivary gland.

Because the CR is a response elicited by the CS, it is often called a **respondent**. The terms *conditioned response* and *respondent* are interchangeable throughout this text. The process of presenting stimuli together in time (pairing or associating stimuli) so that a CS comes to regulate the occurrence of the conditioned response is called **respondent conditioning**. Technically, respondent conditioning involves establishing a conditional probability between the CS and US (the occurrence of the US is conditional on the presence of the CS).

Note that the association is between the CS and US (i.e., the word *lemon* and the real fruit in the mouth) because they have been paired together at some time in the past—not because of some cognitive (internal mental) association of events. This is an important point: The word "association" is sometimes taken to mean an internal mental process that a person or other animal performs. We hear people say "The

FIG. 3.3 Simple respondent conditioning. An arbitrary stimulus such as a light (CS) is presented just before food is placed in a dog's mouth (US). After several pairings of light and food, the light is presented alone. If the light now elicits salivation, it is called a conditioned stimulus (CS), and salivation to the light is a conditioned response (CR).

dog salivates when the bell is sounded because it has associated the sound with the food." In contrast, a behavior analyst points to the physical association of stimuli (CS and US) that occurred in the past. In other words, the association is between events—it does not refer to mental associations. The word *lemon* (CS) elicits salivation (CR) because the word has occurred at a time and place when the chemistry of a lemon (US) produced salivation (UR).

The usual *measures* of behavior for respondent conditioning are magnitude (amount of saliva-tion) and latency (time to salivation) of response following presentation of the US or CS. Magnitude and latency make sense as behavioral measures because respondent conditioning often involves the actions of smooth muscles and glands or responses such as eye-blinks and skin resistance (the UR or CR) that vary on these two dimensions.

Relative Nature of Stimuli

The conditioned stimulus (CS) is defined as an event that initially does not elicit the target response, while the US does (US → UR). A sweet-flavored liquid may function as a CS in taste-aversion conditioning, and drug-induced sickness (lithium chloride) may serve as the US. After repeated pairings of the flavor with the drug, the animal shows avoidance of the sweet-flavored solution, an effect known as **conditioned taste aversion (CTA)**.

Now consider a different procedure, where the CS is a particular place or location and the sweet-flavored solution is the US. In this case, we give the animal the solution in one distinct chamber (with stripes) but not in another (white), and the animal shows a preference by a choice test for the location paired with the solution, an effect known as **conditioned place preference (CPP)**. Notice that the tasty solution functioned as a CS for CTA conditioning, but as a US for CPP learning. That is, the same stimulus or event may function as either a CS or a US, depending on its relation to other stimuli in the situation.

Contiguity of Stimuli

When stimuli or events occur near in time they become similar in function. That is, a neutral stim-ulus paired with (occurring close in time with) an effective unconditioned stimulus takes on the eliciting features of the US, often referred to as stimulus to stimulus (S–S) conditioning (Rescorla & Wagner, 1972). To be most effective, the conditioning procedure should arrange that the neutral stimulus predicts (comes just before) the unconditioned stimulus. The importance of **contiguity** or pairing of stimuli in time cannot be overestimated, as it occurs everywhere from moment to moment. Although many non-human studies of respondent conditioning are cited in this textbook, these prin-ciples account for an enormous amount of human behavior.

In humans, conditioning by contiguity happens all the time. However, if it happens repeatedly on several occasions, the previously neutral stimulus acquires a conditioned stimulus (CS) function similar to the US. When the features of a person are paired with sexual gratification, these features take on the positive aspects of sexual stimulation. Many social relationships are enhanced by the pairing of pleasant events and other positive stimuli with the presence of particular persons. Mother–infant bonding is a product of good USs from the mother (such as mother's milk) being paired with mom's facial features, her odor, her stroking, the sound of her voice, and perhaps her heartbeat, many aspects that can become very potent signals for the mother (see Blass, Ganchrow, & Steiner, 1984 for conditioning in infants 2–48 hours of age; see Sullivan and Hall, 1988 for odor (CS) conditioning by presentations of milk and stroking of fur (US) in 6-day-old rat pups). Similar conditioning occurs between lovers, and can result in exclusive commitment to that person. Advertising often involves enhancing product appeal by pairing it with something that is already attractive. Thus, Bierley, McSweeney and Vannieuwkerk (1985) showed that human preference ratings were greater for neutral stimuli (colored geometric figures) that predicted pleasant music (music from *Star Wars*) than for stimuli that predicted the absence of music. These preferences also transferred to other stimuli resembling those used during conditioning.

The attractiveness of the human face has been an important component in human dating and mating, and a prominent feature in the reproductive success of humans (Rhodes, 2006). Research indicates that attractive faces function as reinforcers or unconditioned stimuli (US), suggesting that attractive human faces are capable of conditioning other objects or events (CS) paired with them (close temporal contiguity). Additional research, using brain imaging technology, has revealed neural activity to presentations of attractive faces in the reward structures of the brain. In the advertising industry, many television commercials and magazine advertisements involve arranging contiguity between products (e.g., cars, clothing, and beer) and attractive people, implying that the US value of attractive human faces can transfer to commercial products by conditioning procedures.

Given that attractive human faces appear to have US value, Bray and O'Doherty (2007) asked whether human participants would show conditioning when arbitrary stimuli (fractal or self-similar shapes) were paired with attractive and unattractive faces. The study also used functional magnetic resonance imaging (fMRI) of the participants' brains to reveal neural reward areas active during conditioning. The results showed increases from pre-conditioning to post-conditioning in partici- pants' positive ratings or evaluations of the fractal shapes (CS) paired with and predicting attractive female faces (US). Also, the fMRI imaging showed increased activity in the ventral striatum on attractive-face presentations (compared with unattractive-face presentations) that diminished over conditioning trials in accord with the S–S model of conditioning proposed by Rescorla and Wagner (1972) (see also the Advanced Section of this chapter). These findings indicate that an arbitrary stimulus acquires CS value when paired with pleasant social stimuli (attractive female faces), and this conditioning works on the reward centers in the brain related to the dopamine neurons in the ventral striatum. The results also suggest how commercial advertments linking products with attractive social stimuli act on the brain's reward system to influence consumer preference and the purchasing of goods and services.

Respondent Acquisition

When a conditioned stimulus (CS) is repeatedly paired with an unconditioned stimulus (US), the CS comes to produce the conditioned response (CR). The increase in the CR to the presentation of the CS is called **respondent acquisition**. In one experiment, Anrep (1920) demonstrated the condi- tioning of the salivary reflex to a tone stimulus. The acquisition procedure involved turning on the tone for a brief period, and then placing food in a dog's mouth. Anrep measured the conditioned response as the number of drops of saliva during 30-s intervals wherein the tone occurred without food. Figure 3.4A (acquisition) shows that the amount of salivation to the tone increases rapidly during the first 25 trials and then levels off, or reaches its maximum, called the asymptote. In other words, with repeated pairings of the CS and US, the magnitude of the conditioned response increases. Once the conditioned reflex reaches asymptote, however, further CS–US pairings have no addi- tional effects.

It is important to note that the asymptote for the conditioned response depends on the intensity of the unconditioned stimulus. As the intensity of the US increases, the magnitude of the UR also increases up to a point. The magnitude of the UR limits the maximum strength of the CR. Thus, the more food a dog is given the greater the amount of salivation. If a dog is given 60 g of meat, there will be more salivation than if it is presented with 30 g. A tone that is associated with 60 g of food will elicit salivation as a CR at a higher level (at asymptote) than a tone associated with 30 g of food. It is clear that these relationships are limited by an organism's physiology. If a dog is given 450 g of steak, it will probably salivate at maximum strength, and a change to 900 g will have no further

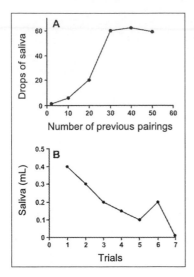

FIG. 3.4 The acquisition and extinction of salivation. The acquisition curve (A) is taken from an experiment by Anrep (1920), who paired a tone (CS) with food placed in a dog's mouth (US). The extinction curve (B) is from Pavlov (1960, p. 53), who presented the CS (sight of food) in the absence of the US (food in the mouth). The results are portrayed as a single experiment.

effect. Similar limits are observed for reflexes such as variation in pupil size in response to light, magnitude of the knee jerk in response to a tap, and the degree of startle in response to noise.

Conditioned and Unconditioned Responses

Notice that the conditioned response of salivation appears to be identical to the unconditioned response. That is, when conditioning to the tone has occurred, turning it on will elicit salivation. This response to the tone seems to be the same as the salivation produced by food in the dog's mouth. In fact, early theories of learning held that the tone substituted for the food stimulus. This implies that the CS–CR relationship is the same as the US–UR relation. If the CS–CR and the US–UR relationships are the same, then both should follow similar laws and principles. And the *laws of the reflex* govern the US–UR relationship, as you have seen.

If the CS–CR and US–UR relationships are the same, then the law of intensity magnitude should hold for conditioned stimuli and responses. That is, a rise in the intensity of the CS should increase the magnitude of the CR. In addition, the CS–CR relation should follow the law of latency. An increase in the intensity of the CS should decrease the latency between the CS onset and the conditioned response. Research has shown that these, and other laws of the reflex, typically do *not* hold for the CS–CR relationship (Millenson, 1967). Generally, a change in the intensity of the conditioned stimulus decreases the strength of the conditioned response. In the experiment by Anrep (1920), the tone occurred at a particular intensity, and after conditioning it elicited a given magnitude and latency of salivation. If Anrep had increased the sound, there would have been less salivation and it would have taken longer to occur. Thus, the CS–CR relation is specific to the original conditioning and does not follow the laws of the reflex. One reason for this is that the CS–CR relationship involves processes such as respondent discrimination (see below).

Respondent Extinction

Pavlov (1960) reported a very simple experimental procedure that he called **respondent extinction**. The procedure involves repeatedly presenting the CS and not presenting the US. Figure 3.4B (extinction) shows the decline in salivation when Pavlov's assistant, Dr. Babkin, repeatedly presented the CS but no longer fed the dog. As you can see, the amount of salivation declines and reaches a minimal value by the seventh trial. This minimum level of the CR is often similar to the value obtained during the first trial of acquisition, and probably reflects the **respondent level** of this behavior. Respondent level, or baseline, refers to the strength of the target response (e.g., salivation) before any known conditioning has occurred. Extinction can be valuable as a therapeutic procedure for reducing or removing unwanted emotional responses such as claustrophobia or arachnophobia. Simply present the CS (the small space or the spider) but do not present the fearful or frightening US component. The phobic CR will then gradually decrease with repeated trials.

A distinction should be made between extinction as a procedure and extinction as a behavioral process. The procedure involves presenting the CS but not the US after conditioning has occurred. As a behavioral process, extinction refers to the decline in the strength of the conditioned response when an extinction procedure is in effect. In both instances, the term *extinction* is used correctly. Extinction is the procedure of breaking the CS–US association, resulting in the decline of the CR.

The decline in the strength of the CR is often rapid. This statement is true for the conditioning of salivation, but other types of conditioned responses may vary in resistance to extinction. Even with salivation, Pavlov noted that as the time between trials increased, the CR declined more slowly. A test trial is any instance in which the CS is given in the absence of the unconditioned stimulus. Of course, repeated test trials are the same as extinction. The slower extinction of salivation with longer intervals between test trials may reflect what is called spontaneous recovery.

Spontaneous Recovery

Spontaneous recovery is the observation of an increase in the conditioned response after respondent extinction has occurred. Recall that after repeated presentations of the CS without the US, the conditioned response declines to respondent level. Following extinction of the response to respondent level, after some time has passed, the CS will again elicit the CR, and the more time that elapses between the first and second extinction sessions the more the spontaneous recovery (Brooks & Bouton, 1993).

The typical effect is seen in Figure 3.5, which shows the course of extinction and spontaneous recovery from another experiment by Pavlov (1960). In this experiment, the CS was the sight of meat powder, and the US was food in the dog's mouth. As you would expect, the sight of meat powder eventually elicited a conditioned response of salivation. When extinction began, the dog responded with 1 mL of salivation at the sight of the CS. By the fifth extinction trial, the animal showed almost no salivation to the sight of food powder, but after 20 minutes of rest without stimulus presentations, the CS again elicited a conditioned response. Note, however, that the amount of salivation on the spontaneous-recovery trial is much less than the amount elicited on the first extinction trial.

Pavlov (1960) argued that spontaneous recovery shows little weakening of the CS–CR relationship during extinction. He went on to suggest that "internal inhibition" came to block the connection between stimuli and responses. Pavlov viewed conditioning phenomena as an index of brain processes, and in this regard saw behavior as a reflection of central nervous system functioning. In this sense, spontaneous recovery reflected underlying physiological processes, and one of these was an active but temporary "dampening" of associative connections between the CS and the conditioned response. Pavlov called this apparent physiological blocking of the CS–CR relationship "internal inhibition."

In contrast to Pavlov's hypothetical physiological account (he did not actually observe any neural activity), a behavioral analysis of spontaneous recovery suggests that the CS–CR relation is weakened by extinction, but the context or features of the situation in general maintain some level of control over the conditioned response. During respondent conditioning, many stimuli not specified by the researcher as the CS, but present in the experimental situation, come to regulate behavior. For example, background odors, general

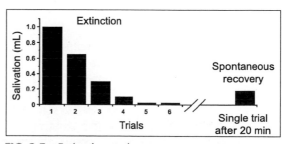

FIG. 3.5 Extinction and spontaneous recovery of salivation elicited by the sight of meat powder (Pavlov, 1960), with data replotted from Bower & Hilgard (1981, p. 51).

illumination of the room, the presence of particular researchers, the passage of time, and all the events that signal the start of a conditioning series come to exert some control over the conditioned response. Each time a recovery test is made, some part of the situation that has not yet been extinguished evokes the CR. This gradual decline in **contextual stimulus** control through repeated extinction also accounts for progressively less recovery of the conditioned response. The role of extinction in spontaneous recovery is currently being confirmed by investigations in behavioral neuroscience (Zelinski, Hong, Tyndall, Halsall, & McDonald, 2010).

NEW DIRECTIONS: Neuroscience and Learning in Honey Bees

A report published in 2007 by Giurfa describes the integrated use of overt behavior with neurophysiological techniques to provide a more complete account of associative learning in an organism not often considered to be a model for humans—the common honey bee. Actually bees are excellent models for this type of research for several reasons (Giurfa, 2007). They have rich behavioral repertoires, they have a social lifestyle, their motor and sensory systems are well developed and sensitive, they travel relatively large distances for food, water, and information, they see color, and they are able to learn, remember, and communicate. Honey bees are easy to train individually and to observe communally. They exhibit both operant and respondent conditioning and, because these forms of learning rely on the association of specific stimuli, it is possible to study where and how such stimuli activate brain areas and neural pathways. That is, the location and interactions of the neural pathways involved and how they are modified by experience are available for examination in the everyday honey bee. Such research is also worthwhile in terms of learning about honey bees themselves, since they are currently experiencing a nationwide increase in death rate from some unknown disease (Johnson, 2010).

In the appetitive learning situation (positive US or reinforcer), one specific odor CS is paired with a sucrose US, which elicits a proboscis extension UR, and ultimately a CR to the CS (Bitterman, Menzel, Fietz, & Schafer, 1983). In the aversive method the same (or a different) CS is followed by an electric foot-shock US that elicits a stinger extension defense response (UR or CR). One goal of this work is to identify the dopaminergic neuronal circuit involved and whether that circuit differs in the appetitive and aversive learning procedures (Vergoz, Roussel, Sandoz, & Giurfa, 2007). Another objective is to identify the role of dopamine and octopamine, the latter being a major biogenic amine neurotransmitter in the honey bee which is especially involved in appetitive learning of behavior (e.g., flying) related to energy regulation (Hammer & Menzel, 1998). Virtually all abused drugs increase dopamine levels in specific parts of the brain, and these areas appear to be part of a general neural reward system. It is the presence of this common neurotransmitter in man and other animals, including insects, which allows research findings with lower organisms such as the honey bee to be extended to humans in the search for the neural underpinnings of associative learning, and eventually the treatment of compulsions and addictions based on respondent and operant learning (Volkow, Fowler, & Wang, 2003).

To research the neuroscience of honey-bee behavior, individual bees are tethered (with a really tiny harness) and receive implanted electrodes in the nervous system, using extension of the proboscis or stinger extension as the response. There are many different protocols that use bees, but most of them involve the use of sucrose as the reinforcer (or US), and flying to a visually cue-signaled food source. (A variant of this procedure is being used to train bees to locate hidden mines in a field, or hidden drugs in airport luggage; Shaw, Seldomridge, Dunkle, Nugent, Spangler, Bromenshenk et al., 2005.) Honey bees in particular, and insects in general, make convenient subjects for neuroscience research, just as the common fruit fly (*Drosophila melanogaster*) is an excellent model for genetic research. Eric Kandel received a Nobel Prize primarily for his work on the neuronal basis of memory using the marine snail *Aplysia*, illustrating how fundamental behavioral neuroscience often extends to a more complete understanding of human behavior.

Respondent Generalization and Discrimination

Generalization

Pavlov conducted a large number of conditioning experiments and discovered many principles that remain useful today. One of his important findings concerned the principle of **respondent generalization**. *Respondent generalization* occurs when an organism shows a conditioned response to values of the CS that were not trained during acquisition. For example, respondent acquisition will occur when a specific stimulus, such as a 60-dB tone at a known frequency (e.g., 375 Hz), is associated with a US (e.g., food). After several pairings, the CS elicits a conditioned response, in this case salivation. If a 60-dB tone of 375 Hz is now presented without the US (a test trial), the animal will salivate at maximum level. To show generalization, the researcher varies some property of the conditioned stimulus. For example, a 60-dB tone of 75, 150, 225, 300, 375, 450, 525, 600, and 675 Hz is presented on test trials, and the magnitude of the conditioned response is measured. Figure 3.6 shows possible results of such an experiment. As you can see, the amount of salivation declines as the test stimulus departs in both directions from the value used in training. This graph, which plots stimulus value against magnitude of response, is called a **generalization gradient**.

Interestingly, a similar generalization gradient may not occur if the intensity rather than the tonal quality of the CS is varied. That is, if decibels rather than cycles per second (Hertz) are varied in the generalization test, a different result might occur. A few studies have shown that as the intensity of the CS increases, so does the magnitude of the conditioned response (Heinemann & Chase, 1970; Razran, 1949). Heinemann and Chase (1970) found that proportionally more conditioned responses were elicited as the sound intensity of the CS increased. Based on this finding, Heinemann and Chase suggest that there may be consistent increases in the strength of the CR as the intensity of the CS increases, although not all research has supported this finding (Ernst, Engberg, & Thomas, 1971). A conservative conclusion is that as the CS

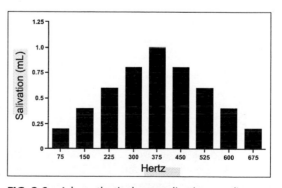

FIG. 3.6   A hypothetical generalization gradient for the salivary response. In this idealized experiment, training would occur at 375 Hz and then CSs ranging from 75 to 675 Hz would be presented.

greatly departs from the value that was originally established, the conditioned response becomes weaker (Thomas & Setzer, 1972; see Rescorla, 2006 for an account of differences in breadth of generalization gradients for excitatory and inhibitory conditioning).

Generalization is an adaptive process that allows the organism to respond similarly even when conditions do not remain exactly the same from trial to trial. Consider a situation in which a predator's approach (US) is associated with the sound of snapping twigs, rustling grass, and waving shrubs (CS). An organism that runs away (CR) only in the presence of these exact stimulus conditions would probably not last long. This is because the events that occurred during conditioning are never precisely repeated—each approach of a predator produces variations in sounds, sights, and smells. Even in the laboratory, where many features of the environment are controlled, there is some variation in stimuli from one trial to the next. When a bell is paired with food, the dog may change its orientation to the bell and thereby alter the sound; room humidity and other factors may also produce slight variations in tonal quality. Because of generalization, a CS–CR relationship can be strengthened even though the stimulus conditions are never exactly the same from trial to trial. Thus, generalization was likely to have been an adaptive process, allowing organisms to respond to the vagaries of life.

Discrimination

Another conditioning principle that Pavlov discovered is called differentiation or discrimination. **Respondent discrimination** occurs when an organism shows a conditioned response to one stimulus but not to other similar events. This is a process at the other end of the continuum from generalization. A discrimination-training procedure involves presenting both positive and negative conditioning trials. For example, a positive trial occurs when a CS^+ such as a 60-dB tone is associated with an unconditioned stimulus like food. On negative trials, a 40-dB tone is presented (CS^-) but never paired with food. Because of stimulus generalization, the dog may salivate to both the 60-dB (CS^+) and 40-dB (CS^-) tones on the early trials. However, if the procedure is continued, the animal will no longer salivate to the CS^- (40-dB tone), but will show a response to the CS^+ (60-dB tone). Once such a differential response occurs, we may say that the dog discriminates between the tones.

Respondent discrimination is another adaptive process. It would be a chaotic world if an animal spent its day running away from most sounds, sights, and smells, generalizing to everything. Such an animal would not survive and reproduce because there would be no time for other essential activities, such as eating, drinking, and procreating. Discrimination allows an organism to budget its time and responses in accord with the requirements of the environment. In the predator example, noises that are reliably associated with an animal that considers you a main course should become CS^+ for flight or fight. Similar noises made by the wind or harmless animals are CS^- for such behavior. Notice, however, that there is a fine line between discrimination and generalization in terms of survival.

Pre-Exposure to Stimuli

Recall that people who are first exposed to the rumblings of a volcano startle and run away, but after repeated exposure to volcano sounds without a major eruption their responses show habituation. This suggests that familiar events or stimuli do not elicit as intense a reaction as novel ones. The same is true for respondent conditioning, where novelty of the CS or US increases its effectiveness. Repeated exposure to or familiarity of the CS or US, however, reduces the effectiveness of the CS or US and retards respondent acquisition.

Considerable research indicates that pre-exposure to the CS weakens subsequent conditioning with the US—an outcome termed the **CS-pre-exposure effect** or **latent inhibition** (Lubow & Moore, 1959). The term latent inhibition is used to denote that the animal's learning of the CS–US relation is reduced or inhibited by pre-exposure of the CS, revealed by an acquisition test following the conditioning phase.

As we have seen, conditioned taste aversion (CTA) occurs when we present a distinctive flavor or taste that is followed by drug-induced illness. Compared with animals without pre-exposure to the taste (novel taste), those that experience pre-exposure to the flavor (familiar taste) show weaker CTA on a test for acquisition. You may have had similar experiences. For example, you eat a juicy steak with your meal, adding sauce béarnaise to the steak for the first time. Later, you become extremely sick (perhaps with a flu virus) and subsequently avoid the béarnaise sauce, eating your steak instead with good old familiar ketchup. Now consider what would happen if you had eaten sauce béarnaise repeatedly with your meals without any ill effects, but now had the steak dinner with the sauce and became extremely sick. Given the repeated pre-exposure to the sauce béarnaise without illness, it is unlikely that you will condition to the taste of the sauce. That is, you will not show avoidance of the sauce for your next steak dinner. Latent inhibition and CTA have been studied extensively, and the neurophysiological underpinnings are now a central focus of research in associative or respondent conditioning (Lubow, 2009).

Other research has focused on the novelty of the US by giving pre-exposure to the US before using it in subsequent conditioning. That is, animals are first given repeated exposures to the US by itself and then a series of CS → US pairings (conditioning). Compared with animals given pairings with a novel US, those familiar with the US (pre-exposed) show weaker and slower conditioning on the acquisition test—a result called the **US-pre-exposure effect**.

When a sweet saccharin CS is followed by injections of lithium chloride (US), animals become sick and avoid the sweet taste, reducing their consumption of the flavored solution on an acquisition test. When the drug (US) is injected repeatedly by itself (pre-exposure) before being used in conditioning (CS → US), animals show less avoidance of the sweet taste than other animals without a history of pre-exposure to the drug (Hall, 2009). The weaker conditioning following pre-exposure to the drug is not due to simple habituation of the unconditioned stimulus. Research has shown that the context in which the drug US is injected can function as a CS. That is, even when the drug is injected alone, aspects of the context or background acquire CS functions. When the sweet saccharin CS is subsequently conditioned in the same context, the contextual cues that signal the upcoming injection block conditioning to the sweet saccharin CS, resulting in weak or no avoidance of the sweet solution on the acquisition test (De Brugada, Hall, & Symonds, 2004).

TEMPORAL RELATIONS AND CONDITIONING

Delayed Conditioning

There are several ways of arranging the temporal relationship between the presentation of a CS and the unconditioned stimulus (US). So far we have described a procedure in which the CS is presented a few seconds before the US occurs. This procedure is called **delayed conditioning** (the presentation of the US is slightly delayed relative to the CS) and is shown in Figure 3.7A.

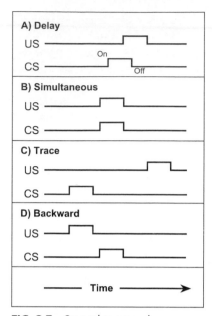

FIG. 3.7 Several temporal arrangements between CS and US commonly used for simple respondent conditioning. Time is shown in the bottom panel of the figure and moves from left to right. The other panels depict the temporal arrangement between US and CS for four basic respondent conditioning arrangements. For example, delayed conditioning is shown in panel A, where the CS is turned on and, a few seconds later, the US is presented.

Delayed conditioning is considered the most effective way to condition simple autonomic reflexes such as salivation. In the diagram, the CS is turned on, and 3 s later the US is presented. The interval between the onset of the CS and the onset of the US (called the CS–US interval) determines the effectiveness of conditioning. For autonomic responses, such as salivation, blood pressure, skin temperature, hormone levels, and sweat secretion, a CS–US interval of between 5 and 30 s appears to be most effective. A brief CS–US interval of about 0.5 s seems to be optimal for the conditioning of quick skeletal responses, such as a knee jerk, eye blinks, and retraction of a limb from a hot surface. In human eye-blink conditioning, a delay of 0.4 s between the CS and the US produces the fastest conditioning in young adults, but a longer delay of about 1 s is more effective with older people (Solomon, Blanchard, Levine, Velazquez, & Groccia-Ellison, 1991).

Simultaneous Conditioning

Another temporal arrangement is called **simultaneous conditioning**, where the CS and US are presented at the same time. This procedure is shown in Figure 3.7B, where the CS and US are presented at the same moment. For example, at the same time that the bell rings (CS), food is placed in the dog's mouth (US). Compared with delayed conditioning, where the CS precedes the US briefly, simultaneous conditioning produces a weaker conditioned response (Smith & Gormezano, 1965; White & Schlosberg, 1952). One way to understand this weaker effect is to note that the CS does not signal the impending occurrence of the US in simultaneous conditioning. Based on this observation, many researchers have emphasized the predictiveness of the CS as a central feature of classical conditioning (see Rescorla, 1966). That is, the CS works because it provides information that "tells" the organism a US will follow. In simultaneous conditioning, however, there can be no predictive information given by the CS, and yet some conditioning occurs. This suggests that predictiveness may facilitate conditioning, but is not *necessary* for it (Papini & Bitterman, 1990).

Trace Conditioning

The procedure for trace conditioning is shown in Figure 3.7C. The CS is presented for a brief period, on and off, and after some time the US occurs. For example, a light is flashed for 2 s, and 20 s later food is placed in a dog's mouth. The term **trace conditioning** comes from the idea of a "memory trace," and refers to the fact that the organism must remember the presentation of the CS. Generally, as the time between the CS and US increases, the conditioned response becomes weaker (Ellison, 1964; Lucas, Deich, & Wasserman, 1981). For eye-blink conditioning (a puff of air in the eye US → an eye blink UR), the response to the CS does not occur when the CS and US are separated by as little as 2 s (Schneiderman, 1966). When compared with delay conditioning with the same interval, between the onset of the CS followed by the US, trace conditioning is not as effective—producing a weaker conditioned response. Contemporary research has extended trace conditioning to taste aversion learning (see Chapter 7) and to neural changes in the cerebellum that help to bridge stimulus associations over the trace interval (Misanin, Goodhart, Anderson, & Hinderliter, 2002; Cheng, Disterhoft, Power, Ellis, & Desmond, 2008).

Backward Conditioning

As shown in Figure 3.7D, **backward conditioning** stipulates that the US comes on and goes off before the CS comes on. The general consensus has been that backward conditioning is unreliable, and many researchers question whether it occurs at all (but see Barnet & Miller, 1996, and Heth, 1976, for supportive views). It is true that backward conditioning usually does not produce a conditioned response. That is, if you place food in a dog's mouth and then ring a bell, the bell will not elicit the response of salivation when presented later. Most conditioning experiments have used arbitrary stimuli, such as lights, tones, and shapes, as the conditioned stimulus. However, Keith-Lucas and Guttman (1975) found backward conditioning when they used a biologically significant CS.

These researchers reasoned that following an unsuccessful attack by a predator, the sights, sounds, and smells of the attacker would be associated with pain from the attack. Consider a situation in which a grazing animal is unaware of the approach of a lion. The attack (US) comes swiftly and without warning (no CS), as depicted in Figure 3.8. The prey animal survives the onslaught and manages to run away. In this case, the pain inflicted by the attack is a US for flight that precedes the sight of the predator (CS). For such a situation, backward conditioning would have adaptive value, since the prey animal would learn to avoid lions.

Keith-Lucas and Guttman (1975) designed an experiment to test this adaptive-value hypothesis. Rats were placed in an experimental chamber and fed a sugar pellet in a particular location. While eating the pellet, the rats were given a one-trial presentation of electric shock (US). After the shock, the chamber was made completely dark for 1, 5, 10, or 40 s. When the light in the chamber came back on, a toy hedgehog (CS) was presented to the rat. To make this experiment clear, eating sugar pellets was viewed as the laboratory equivalent of grazing, the shock represented an attack, and the appearance of the toy hedgehog substituted for the predator. Two control groups were run under

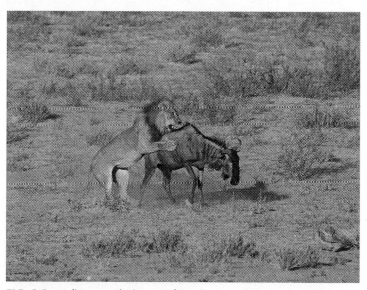

FIG. 3.8   A lion attacks its prey fron the rear. If the prey escapes the attack, backward conditioning (US → CS) would result in the avoidance of lions. © Shutterstock.

identical conditions, except that one group saw the hedgehog but did not get shocked and the other group received the shock but did not see a hedgehog.

On the next day, each animal was returned to the situation and a number of responses were measured. Compared with the control groups, backward conditioning was found after a delay of 1, 5, and 10 s but not after 40 s. Relative to control animals, experimental subjects showed greater avoidance (fear) of the hedgehog, spent less time in the presence of the hedgehog, and ate less food. Presumably, the shock (US) elicited a fear–flight reaction (UR), and backward conditioning transferred this reaction to the toy hedgehog (CS). The fear induced by the hedgehog (CR) interfered with eating and produced avoidance of the toy animal. This experiment shows that with a biologically relevant CS, backward conditioning is possible. Despite this outcome, most researchers suggest that the backward arrangement of US and then CS does not result in reliable conditioning (but see Cole & Miller, 1999; Siegel & Domjan, 1971; Tait & Saladin, 1986 for backward inhibitory conditioning; see also Arcediano & Miller, 2002 for timing and backward conditioning).

SECOND-ORDER RESPONDENT CONDITIONING

So far we have considered only first-order conditioning. To briefly review, in **first-order conditioning** an apparently neutral stimulus is paired with an unconditioned stimulus. After several such pairings, the control of the response to the US is transferred to the neutral stimulus, which is now called a conditioned stimulus (CS). Second-order conditioning extends this transfer of control to events that have not been directly associated with the unconditioned stimulus. These events gain control over the response because of their pairing with an established conditioned stimulus. Thus, **second-order conditioning** involves pairing a second CS_2 with an already functional CS_1, rather than pairing a CS and US (Rizley & Rescorla, 1972). Such higher-order conditioning is important because it extends the range of behavioral effects produced by respondent conditioning, especially with regard to learning word meanings (Staats, 1975) and evaluative conditioning in humans (for a review, see De Houwer, Thomas, & Baeyens, 2001).

Some phobic reactions (i.e., an intense and seemingly irrational fear) that people have may be caused by higher-order conditioning. Consider a person who refuses to sit with friends in the backyard on a nice summer day. The sight of flowers greatly upsets her and she says that "with so many flowers there are probably bees." A possible interpretation is that the person has been stung (US) by a bee (CS_1), and she has noticed that bees hover around flowers (CS_2). The "phobic" fear of flowers occurs because of the pairing of bees (CS_1) with flowers (CS_2). Thus, phobic reactions and other emotional responses may sometimes involve higher-order respondent conditioning (see Martin & Pear, 2006, on systematic desensitization and the fear hierachy).

ON THE APPLIED SIDE: Drug Use, Abuse, and Respondent Conditioning

Basic research on simple and complex (i.e., including contextual effects) respondent conditioning has major applied importance. One example of this involves factors that affect drug use and abuse. Several experiments have shown that conditioned stimuli can produce drug-like effects in both humans and other animals. In addition, stimuli that have been paired with drugs sometimes produce internal conditioned responses that are opposite to the unconditioned effects of the drug. For example, when animals are injected with insulin (US), the unconditioned response is a reduction in blood sugar levels (UR). The response to a stimulus (CS) that has been paired with insulin is exactly the opposite—blood sugar levels increase (Siegel, 1972, 1975).

Similar counteractive effects have been found with drugs other than insulin. For example, amphetamine reduces appetite, but a CS that has been paired with it increases food intake (Poulos, Wilkinson, & Cappell, 1981). Pentobarbital is a sedative, but the response to a conditioned stimulus associated with pentobarbital counteracts the drowsiness ordinarily associated with the drug (Hinson, Poulos, & Cappell, 1982).

Effects such as these suggest that respondent conditioning plays a major role in drug tolerance. Here is how it works. With repeated pairings of a drug (US) and a CS (e.g., injection process), the conditioned response (CR) gains in strength and increasingly opposes the unconditioned (UR) effects of the drug. This means that larger and larger amounts of the US will be needed for the user to experience the same degree of effect. In everyday life, conditioned stimuli arise from the time of day that a drug is taken, the way it is administered (e.g., using a needle), the location (e.g., in a tavern or at home), and social events (e.g., a party or dance). Notice that tolerance, which is a reduction in the effect of the drug (UR), is not due to habituation, but rather it is the result of the counteractive effects (CR) to the injection process and setting (CS). When more of a drug (US) is needed to obtain the same drug effects (UR), we talk about drug **tolerance** *(Baker & Tiffany, 1985). Thus, the counteractive effects of CSs are major components of drug tolerance.*

NOTE ON: Physiology and the Control of Preparatory Responses by Conditioned Stimuli (CS)

The concept of homeostasis helps to clarify the control by the CS over conditioned responses opposite to those induced by the US. **Homeostasis** is the tendency for a system to remain stable and to resist change. In terms of a biological system, homeostasis refers to the regulation of the system by negative feedback loops. For example, the body maintains a temperature within a very fine tolerance. If the environment warms up or cools down, physiological mechanisms (sweating or shivering) involving the sympathetic and parasympathetic nervous systems are activated to reduce the drift from normal body temperature. In terms of drug exposure, when a drug (US) is administered it upsets the stability of the system—that is, it may increase heart rate or reduce respiration (UR). If some aspect of the environment is consistently present when the drug is delivered (e.g., drug paraphernalia, a person, or the room), that stimulus becomes a conditioned stimulus

(CS) capable of eliciting a conditioned response that is often preparatory and compensatory (CR). If the US drug causes the heart rate to increase, the conditioned compensatory (homeostatic) response (CR) will be a decrease in heart rate—that is, the learned component ($CS_{needle} \rightarrow CR_{heart\ rate\ decrease}$) counteracts the unlearned response to the drug ($US_{drug} \rightarrow UR_{heart\ rate\ increase}$). This counteracting homeostatic effect may be so great that it nullifies the responses to the drug, and the user no longer experiences the typical high—a process called *tolerance*. The onset of tolerance can be dangerous for the drug user. If a larger dose of the drug is taken to overcome tolerance and the compensatory counteracting response is not produced, an overdose can occur. Further, if the preparatory stimuli (CSs) elicit their responses and the drug (US) is not delivered, a condition that we call *craving* or *withdrawal* occurs.

Heroin Overdose and Context

To consider drug tolerance as a result of a conditioned response helps to explain instances of drug overdose. Heroin addicts are known to survive a drug dose that would kill a person who did not regularly use the drug. Despite this high level of tolerance, approximately 1% of heroin addicts die from drug overdose each year. These victims typically die from drug-induced respiratory depression. Surprisingly, many of these addicts die from a dose that is similar to the amount of heroin they usually took each day. Siegel, Hinson, Krank, and McCully (1982) proposed that these deaths resulted from "a failure of tolerance. That is, the opiate addict, who can usually tolerate extraordinarily high doses, is not tolerant on the occasion of the overdose" (p. 436). They suggested that when a drug is administered in the usual context (CS^+), the CRs that counteract the drug allow for a large dose. When the situation in which the drug is taken is changed, the CSs are not present, the opposing conditioned response does not occur, and the drug is sufficient to kill the user. Siegel and associates designed an animal experiment to test these ideas.

In one study, rats were injected with heroin every other day for 30 days. The amount of heroin was gradually increased to a dose level that would produce tolerance to the drug. On non-heroin days, these rats were injected with dextrose solution (i.e., sugar and water). Both heroin and dextrose injections were given in one of two distinctive contexts—the ordinary colony room that the rats lived in, or a different room with constant white noise. A control group of rats was injected only with the dextrose solution in the two situations. The researchers predicted that experimental animals would develop a tolerance to the drug; this tolerance would occur if aspects of the room in which heroin injections were given became CSs that elicited opposing responses (CRs) to the drug.

To test this assumption, Siegel and colleagues (1982) on the test day doubled the amount of heroin given to experimental animals. The same high dose of heroin was given to the control group, who had no history of tolerance. Half of the experimental animals received this larger dose in the room where the drug was usually administered. The other addicted rats were injected with the higher dose in the room where they usually received a dextrose injection.

Figure 3.9 shows the results of this experiment. As you can see, the large dose of heroin killed almost all of the animals in the control group. For the two groups of animals with a history of heroin exposure, one group (same room) received the higher dose in the room where they were usually injected with heroin. Only 32% of the rats died in this condition, presumably because the CSs set off the opposing conditioned responses. This inference is supported by the mortality rate of rats in the different room group. These rats were injected with the double dose of heroin in a room that had never been associated with heroin administration. Twice as many animals in this condition died from the larger dose (64%) when compared with the same room group. It seems that the effects of context during this kind of respondent conditioning can be a matter of life or death—tolerance to heroin (and perhaps other drugs) is relative to the situation in which the conditioning has occurred, and in humans involves conditioning of both external and internal events (Siegel, 2001, 2005).

What happens when the drug-related CS is presented without the drug US, as in the classical extinction procedure? In this case the elicited respondents are often called "cravings", and the process is known as **conditioned withdrawal**. The CS elicits reactions that are ordinarily countered by the US. However, when the US is not delivered and if those CR reactions occur, the subject experiences what is called withdrawal. A heroin addict can have their withdrawal symptoms immediately terminated by a heroin injection. If you are accustomed to having a cigarette after a meal, the craving you experience can be alleviated with a smoke.

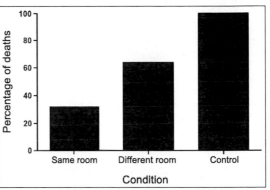

FIG. 3.9 Results of the experiment by Siegel, Hinson, Krank, and McCully (1982). The same room group of rats received the higher dose in the room where they usually were injected with heroin, and only 32% died. Twice as many animals in the different room condition died from the larger dose, presumably because they were injected in a room where heroin had not been given. Heroin killed almost all of the animals in the control group. Adapted from "Heroin 'Overdose' Death: The Contribution of Drug-Associated Environmental Cues," S. Siegel, R. E. Hinson, M. D. Krank and J. McCully, 1982, *Science, 216*, 436–437. © American Association for the Advancement of Science. Published with permission.

Conditioned Immunosuppression

Conditioned immunosuppression is another example of environmental influences altering what are generally considered to be internal and autonomously controlled processes. In this procedure, a CS (e.g., a novel flavor) is paired with a US drug that suppresses immune system function, such as the production of antibodies. (Note that drugs like cyclophosphamide are commonly administered to suppress rejection of a transplanted organ.) After several pairings, the CS is presented alone and the immune system reaction is measured. Ader and Cohen (1981, 1985, 1993) were the first to systematically investigate and describe this phenomenon. Clearly the next question is whether the immune system can also be conditioned to increase immune reaction. It appears that it can. In a human study, Buske-Kirschbaum, Kirschbaum, Stierle, Jabaij, and Hellhammer (1994), after pairing a flavor CS and an adrenaline injection US, subsequently raised natural killer (NK) cell production.

The issue of conditioned enhancement of the immune system also speaks to the findings of **placebo effects**. How can a neutral substance, a placebo, have any effect on a person's physiological well-being? Many studies have shown that groups which receive a sugar pill do as well as those in the legitimate treatment group (Brody, 2000). How can this be possible when the placebo, by definition, cannot directly cause any change? The obvious conclusion is that respondent conditioning is occurring. A CS, say the patient's "belief" (resulting from experience with doctors and medication) that they are receiving treatment, is presented, and this verbal stimulus acts as a placebo to elicit the CR mechanisms of improvement. Even sham (fake) arthroscopic surgery for arthritis is as functional as actual surgery, and of course with fewer side effects and less cost (Moseley, O'Malley, Petersen, Menke, Brody, Kuykendall et al., 2002). One thing that these types of studies indicate is that there is much greater two-way interaction between the environment and physiological mechanisms than had been suspected. Organisms are adaptive and they learn. It appears that organs (e.g., salivary glands) and organ systems (e.g., the immune system) can also alter their functions as a result of experience. Obviously we need more research to expand and validate these topics.

ADVANCED SECTION: Complex Conditioning

ASPECTS OF COMPLEX CONDITIONING

Conditioning and Compound Stimuli

We have so far examined CS and US relationships in isolation, ignoring for the most part the context or background in which these events occur. To investigate the effects of context on respondent behavior, researchers have arranged situations involving **compound stimuli**. In these cases, and to keep things somewhat simple, two conditioned stimuli (e.g., tone and light) are presented together before (delayed) or during (simultaneous) a US. This arrangement of two controllable stimuli (compound CSs) presented together can be shown to acquire the capacity to elicit a single conditioned response.

In an everyday example, the odor of food at a bakery or restaurant probably becomes a CS for salivation, having been paired with donuts or burgers and fries (US). However, other related stimuli such as the name, the order clerk, the location of the store, and the outdoor signs are also paired with eating. These additional features of the fast food experience become conditioned stimuli that function as the context (compound CS) which evokes salivation. Differences in conditioning procedures related to compound stimuli result in the behavioral processes called blocking and overshadowing.

Overshadowing

Pavlov (1960) first described **overshadowing**. A compound stimulus consisting of two or more simple stimuli are presented at the same time. For example, a faint light and loud tone (compound CS) may be turned on at the same time and paired with an unconditioned stimulus such as food. Pavlov found that the most salient element of the compound stimulus came to regulate exclusively the conditioned response. In this case the loud tone and not the faint light will become a CS and elicit salivation. The tone is said to overshadow conditioning to the light. This happens even though the weak light could function as a CS if it was originally presented by itself and was paired with a US.

Blocking

Kamin (1969) reported an effect related to overshadowing that also involved compound stimuli. This effect is called **blocking**, and describes a situation in which one CS paired with a US blocks a subsequent CS–US association. In blocking, a CS is paired with a US until the conditioned response reaches maximum strength. Following this conditioning, a second stimulus is presented at the same time as the original CS, and both are paired with the unconditioned stimulus. On test trials, the original CS evokes the CR but the second stimulus does not. For example, a tone (CS) may be associated with food (US) until the tone reliably evokes salivation. Next, the tone plus a light are presented together as a compound CS and both are associated with food (US). On test trials, the tone will elicit salivation but the light will not. The previously conditioned tone blocks conditioning of the light stimulus.

Kamin (1969) used a procedure called **conditioned suppression** (see Estes & Skinner, 1941). In conditioned suppression, a previously neutral stimulus (e.g., tone, light, etc.) is paired with an aversive US such as an electric shock. After several pairings, the originally neutral stimulus becomes a conditioned aversive stimulus (CS^{ave}). The CS^{ave} is said to elicit a conditioned emotional response (CER) that is commonly called anxiety or fear. Once the CS^{ave} has been conditioned, its effects may be observed by changes in an organism's operant behavior. For example, a rat may be trained to press a lever for food. After a stable rate of response is established, the CS^{ave} is introduced. When this occurs, the animal's lever pressing is disrupted, presumably because of the CER elicited by the CS^{ave}. Basically, we could say that the CS^{ave} frightens the animal and it stops pressing the bar. Conditioned suppression is a widely used procedure in respondent conditioning, and as you will see later it is important in the study of human emotions.

Using a conditioned-suppression procedure, Kamin (1969) discovered the phenomenon of blocking. Two groups of rats were used: a blocking group and a control group. In the blocking group, rats were presented with a tone (CS^{ave}) that was associated with electric shocks for 16 trials. Following this, the rats received 8 trials during which the compound stimulus tone and light were followed by shock. The control group did not receive the 16 light-shock conditioning trials but did have the 8 trials of tone and light paired with shock. Both groups were tested for conditioned suppression of lever pressing in the presence of the light. That is, the light was presented alone and suppression of bar pressing for food indicated the occurrence of the conditioned emotional response (CER). Kamin found that the light suppressed bar pressing in the control group but did not affect lever pressing in the blocking group. In other words, prior conditioning with the tone blocked or prevented conditioning to the light. Functionally, the light was a CS^{ave} in the control group but not in the blocking group.

Blocking and overshadowing may also be interpreted as cases of redundant stimuli. If two or more stimuli have been paired with the same US then only one CS element of the compound is required for eliciting the CR. We intentionally generate compound stimuli (actually we can hardly avoid doing so) so that some aspect or the other of the environment will gain eliciting properties. All stimulus manipulations are conducted in some place, be it the lab or elsewhere, and elements of that environment will be paired with the stimuli of interest. It is the repeated, consistent, and predictable nature of the specific CS–US pairing that tends to restrict the connection to only some stimuli.

THE RESCORLA–WAGNER MODEL OF CONDITIONING

The occurrence of overshadowing and blocking has led many researchers to the conclusion that cognitive processes underlie conditioning. This is because these effects (and others) seem to imply that an animal learns to expect certain events on the basis of predictive cues. That is, the sight of a predator becomes a predictive cue because the animal expects an attack. The CS is said to provide information about the occurrence of the US, and redundant information, as in blocking, is not processed by the organism.

Although this may be an intuitively satisfying account, inferring cognitive processes is not necessary to describe most of the research in respondent conditioning. Bolles has commented as follows:

> Are we now in a position to conclude that conditioning is really a cognitive process, that it involves the expectancy of a . . . [US], and that the expectancies reflect predictive relationships the animal perceives between cues and consequences? Some psychologists have come to this conclusion. But others have shown restraint. Indeed, it turns out to be possible to account . . . [for many conditioning effects], all without recourse to any cognitive concepts. It can all be done with the clever application of [temporal pairing of stimuli] and other S–R principles. This remarkable development is the work of Wagner, and surprisingly, Rescorla himself. They have produced what is widely known as the Rescorla–Wagner model.
>
> (Bolles, 1979, p. 158)

As Bolles (1979) notes, the **Rescorla–Wagner model** (Rescorla & Wagner, 1972; Wagner & Rescorla, 1972) is an S–R pairing theory of respondent conditioning. That is, the Rescorla–Wagner model is a behavioral theory that does not make inferences about underlying cognitive/informational processing.

The basic idea of the Rescorla–Wagner model is that a conditioned stimulus acquires a limited amount of **associative strength** on any trial. We use the term "associative strength" to describe the relation between the CS and the magnitude of the conditioned response (CR). In general, associative strength increases over conditioning trials and reaches some maximum level. It is apparent that a given CS can acquire only so much control over a conditioned response. This is the **maximum associative strength** for the CS. Thus, a tone (CS) that is paired with 1 g of food will have maximum associative strength when salivation (CR) to the tone is about the same as salivation (UR) to the 1 g of food (US). That is, an unconditioned stimulus elicits a given magnitude of the unconditioned response. This magnitude sets the upper limit for the conditioned response. The CS cannot elicit a greater response than the one produced by the unconditioned stimulus.

A conditioned stimulus gains a certain amount of associative strength on any one trial. The amount of gain or increment depends on several factors. One obvious factor is the maximum associative strength that may accrue to the conditioned stimulus. As noted, this maximum is set by the magnitude of the US–UR relationship. An intense US will set a higher maximum value than a weaker one.

Another factor that affects the increment in associative strength on any trial is the **change in associative strength** or the difference between the present strength of the CS and its maximum possible value. As conditioning trials proceed, the CS gains associative strength, and this means that the difference between present and maximum strength decreases; there is less and less to gain on each trial. For example, assume a 10-trial experiment in which 1 g of meat evokes 2 mL of saliva and the meat is paired with a tone. In terms of change in associative strength, the most gain will occur on the first trial, there will be less gain by the fifth trial, and there will be almost no gain in associative strength by the tenth trial.

The change in associative strength of a conditioned stimulus (CS_1) is also affected by the strength of other conditioned stimuli (CS_2, CS_3, etc.) that elicit the conditioned response in that situation. Because there is a maximum associative strength set by the US, it follows that the associative strength of each CS will add together and reduce the difference between the present associative strength and the maximum possible value. Thus, if a tone has been frequently paired with meat, it will evoke almost maximum salivation. If a light is now introduced and presented along with the tone, it will show little control over salivation, since most of the possible associative strength has accrued to the tone (blocking).

The Rescorla–Wagner model of respondent conditioning describes a large number of findings and has stimulated a great deal of research. The model makes counterintuitive predictions that have been confirmed in a variety of experimental settings. Since the early 1970s, scores of experiments have been conducted to test some of the implications of the model.

FOCUS ON: The Rescorla–Wagner Equation

The three limiting conditions of maximum associative strength, difference between the current strength and the maximum strength, and the number of additional CSs in the situation are represented by an equation suggested by Rescorla and Wagner (1972; see also Wagner & Rescorla, 1972), but simplified here for presentation:

$$\Delta V = S (V_{MAX} - V - V_{SUM})$$ (Equation 3.1)

The symbol ΔV stands for the amount of *change in associative strength* (or change in value of the stimulus, V) of any CS that occurs on any one trial. The symbol S is a constant that varies between 0 and 1, and may be interpreted as the **salience** (e.g., dim light versus bright light) of the CS based on the sensory capacities of the organism. The constant S (salience) is estimated after conditioning, and determines how quickly the associative strength of the CS rises to maximum. That is, a larger salience coefficient makes the associative strength of the CS rise more quickly to its maximum. The value V_{MAX} represents the maximum associative strength as measured by the magnitude of the unconditioned response (UR). The symbol V represents the associative strength already accrued to the CS_1, and V_{SUM} is any associative strength gained by any other stimuli in the situation ($V_{SUM} = CS_2 + CS_3 + \ldots CS_N$).

Acquisition

Figure 3.10 is a table of values for an idealized experiment on the acquisition of a conditioned response based on Equation 3.1. Figure 3.11 is the graph of the associative strength V based on the data in the table. In this hypothetical experiment, a tone CS is repeatedly paired with an unconditioned stimulus such as food. In the figure, S is set at 0.25 and the asymptote (or maximum possible strength) is 10 arbitrary units of the conditioned response (e.g., salivation). The value of V_{SUM} is assumed to be zero, so that all associative strength accrues to the CS. The value of ΔV is given by the equation when we substitute $S = 0.25$,

Trial	ΔV	V	
1	2.5	2.5	V = associate strength
2	1.9	4.4	or value
3	1.4	5.8	$S - 0.25$
4	1.1	6.9	$V_{MAX} = 10$
5	0.8	7.7	$V_{SUM} = 0$
6	0.6	8.3	
7	0.4	8.7	
8	0.3	9.0	
9	0.25	9.3	
10	0.18	9.4	

FIG. 3.10 A table of values for a 10-trial acquisition experiment based on solving the Rescorla–Wagner equation (our Equation 3.1). The symbols V and ΔV refer to associative strength and change in associative strength for a given trial. The values of V_{MAX}, V_{SUM} and S are also given in the table. See text for details.

$V_{MAX} = 10$, and the value of V is zero ($V = 0$) before conditioning begins. Based on Equation 3.1, the increase in associative strength from no conditioning to the first trial is:

$$\Delta V = 0.25 (10 - 0) = 2.50.$$

Notice that the value of V has changed from 0 to 2.50 (check this with the tabled values of Figure 3.10).

On each subsequent trial, the associative strength of the CS is 0.25 (salience) of the remaining distance to the asymptote or maximum. Thus for trial 2 we substitute the value 2.50 for V and obtain an increase of 1.88 for ΔV:

$$\Delta V = 0.25 (10 - 2.50) = 1.88.$$

The associative strength of the CS (V), after the second trial, is 2.50 + 1.88, or 4.38. This means that roughly one-half of the maximum associative strength ($V_{MAX} = 10$) of the CS has been acquired by trial 2.

The change in associative strength for trial 3 uses $V = 4.38$ from the second trial and obtains the value:

$$\Delta V = 0.25 (10 - 4.38) = 1.40.$$

And the new estimate of V is 4.38 + 1.40, or 5.78 (used to obtain ΔV on the fourth trial). Estimates of ΔV and V for all 10 trials of the experiment are obtained in the same way, using Equation 3.1.

As you can see in Figure 3.11, the equation yields a negatively accelerating curve for the associative strength, V, which approaches but never quite reaches maximum associative strength. You can see from the horizontal and perpendicular lines that the largest increase in associative strength is on the first trial, and this change corresponds to the difference in associative strength between trial 0 and trial 1 (2.5-unit increase). The change in associative strength (ΔV) becomes smaller and smaller over trials (check this out in the table of Figure 3.10). Notice how the values of ΔV and V depend on the salience, S, of the CS (tone). If the salience of the tone were different, say $S = 0.50$ rather than $S = 0.25$, a new set of estimates would be given by Equation 3.1 for ΔV and V.

FIG. 3.11 The acquisition curve predicted by the Rescorla–Wagner equation (our Equation 3.1). Gain in associative strength, from trial to trial, declines as the CR comes closer to the asymptote. The asymptote or flat upper portion of the curve is set in the equation by the value V_{MAX}. The curve is based on the data in Figure 3.10.

Extinction

Equation 3.1 can also be used to account for respondent extinction. In this case, the decline in associative strength (ΔV is determined by the values of S, V_{MAX}, V, and V_{SUM}. As before, assume that a tone is paired with food until the tone (CS) elicits a conditioned response that is close to maximum; there are no other relevant stimuli so $V_{SUM} = 0$ and cancels out of the equation. Since the procedure is respondent extinction, the curve must decline toward no associative strength, which means that V_{MAX} must be zero. If $S = 0.25$ and $V_{MAX} = 0$, the decline in associative strength on the first extinction trial is:

$$\Delta V = 0.25\,(0 - 10) = -2.50.$$

Thus, the value of the tone (CS) after the first extinction trial is 10.00 − 2.50, or 7.50 ($V = 7.50$). Other values of the CS during extinction are determined in a similar fashion (compare with respondent acquisition). Figure 3.12 shows that the predicted extinction curve is the *exact opposite of the acquisition curve* of

FIG. 3.12 The extinction curve predicted by the Rescorla–Wagner model. Notice that V_{MAX}, or the asymptote, is zero because extinction is in effect.

Figure 3.11. It is important to note that the actual associative strength of the tone before extinction is never exactly equal to the V_{MAX}, but for simplicity we have assumed that it is in Figure 3.12.

As you can see, the Rescorla–Wagner equation describes many of the basic aspects of respondent conditioning (acquisition, extinction, and blocking), as well as others not discussed here (e.g., latent inhibition). The equation is usually said to describe processes of associative learning but, as Pear (2001, p. 427) notes, it is also possible to derive equations for operant choice (see Chapter 9) from the Rescorla–Wagner model, and vice versa. Thus, both respondent and operant behavior could be related at the most fundamental levels. Advances in neuroscience may help to show how this is possible in terms of the circuitry of the brain (e.g., Zink, Pagnoni, Martin-Skurski, Chappelow, & Berns, 2004; Fiston, 2010).

CHAPTER SUMMARY

This chapter has introduced reflexive behavior, which is based on species history or phylogeny. It has explored reflexive sequences or patterns set off by a releasing stimulus and reaction chains where each response requires an appropriate stimulus to keep the sequence going. Reflexive behavior obeys the three laws of the reflex (threshold, magnitude, and latency) and secondary principles such as reflex habituation. Next, the discussion turned to the ontogeny of behavior and respondent conditioning, which involved pairing a CS (tone) with a US (food in mouth). Respondent behavior is elicited by the US, and conditioning establishes this function for the CS. The functions of the US and the CS are relative to the temporal arrangement of stimuli. A sweet flavor stimulus may be a CS for conditioned taste aversion and a US for conditioned taste preference. Both respondent acquisition and extinction were described, and research examples were provided. Spontaneous recovery that occurs during respondent behavior was also discussed.

Organisms show generalization of respondent behavior over a stimulus gradient, but also show discrimination (a differential response) when the US is presented with one stimulus and withheld to other values of the stimulus array. In addition to simple conditioning effects, temporal relationships between the CS and US are important, as in delayed, simultaneous, trace, and backward conditioning—and the phenomenon known as second-order conditioning. The implications of respondent conditioning were extended to an analysis of drug use and abuse, with some attention to context and drug tolerance. Finally, more advanced issues of complex conditioning and compound stimulus effects such as overshadowing and blocking were introduced. The Rescorla–Wagner model of conditioning was described, and how the model could be expressed as an equation. This equation predicts the increase in the respondent over time (acquisition) and the decrease during extinction.

KEY WORDS

Associative strength

Backward conditioning

Blocking

Change in associative strength

Compound stimuli

Conditioned place preference

Conditioned response

Conditioned stimulus

Conditioned suppression

Conditioned taste aversion

Conditioned withdrawal

Contextual stimuli

CS-pre-exposure effect

Delayed conditioning

Elicited (behaviour)

First-order conditioning

Fixed action pattern

Generalization gradient

Habituation

Homeostasis

Latent inhibition

Law of intensity–magnitude

Law of latency

Law of the threshold

Maximum associative strength

Modal action pattern

Ontogenetic

Overshadowing

Phylogenetic

Placebo effect

Primary laws of the reflex

Reaction chain

Reflex

Rescorla–Wagner model

Respondent

Respondent acquisition

Respondent conditioning

Respondent discrimination

Respondent extinction

Respondent generalization

Respondent level

Salience

Second-order conditioning

Sexual selection

Simultaneous conditioning

Spontaneous recovery

Temporal pairing

Tolerance

Trace conditioning

Unconditioned response

Unconditioned stimulus

US-pre-exposure effect

ON THE WEB

www.flyfishingdevon.co.uk/salmon/year3/psy337DrugTolerance/drugtolerance.htm – Introduction Learn more about drug use, abuse, and tolerance from the website of Paul Kenyon. Some neat data on conditioning and tolerance are provided and discussed.

www.simplypsychology.org/classical-conditioning.html This webpage tells you about John Watson and has a video presentation of his fear conditioning experiment with the infant known as Little Albert.

www.youtube.com/watch?v=LcojyGx8q9U One application of respondent conditioning is called systematic desensitization—an effective treatment for anxiety and phobia. This video clip outlines the basic procedure of graded exposure to the fear stimulus, a snake.

BRIEF QUIZ

1. Behavior relations based on the genetic endowment of the organism are described as:
   (a) operants
   (b) reflexes
   (c) ontogenetic
   (d) phylogenetic

2. Complex sequences of released behaviors are called:
   (a) traits
   (b) reaction chains
   (c) fixed action patterns
   (d) second-order conditioned reflexes

3. Reflexive behavior is said to be _____ and _____.
   (a) built in; flexible
   (b) involuntary; elicited
   (c) respondent; emitted
   (d) voluntary; inflexible

4. Primary laws of the reflex do not include:
   (a) the law of latency
   (b) the law of threshold
   (c) the law of habituation
   (d) the law of magnitude

5. A diminution in the UR due to repeated presentation of the US is called:
   (a) habituation
   (b) extinction
   (c) forgetting
   (d) sensitization

6. Respondent conditioning might also be called:

   (a) S–R conditioning
   (b) S–S pairing
   (c) CS–CR association
   (d) R–S learning

7. To do away with an unwanted CR, one should:

   (a) present the CS without the CR
   (b) present the CR without the US
   (c) present the US without the CS
   (d) present the CS without the US

8. Drug tolerance has been shown to be a result of:

   (a) generalization
   (b) metabolization
   (c) elicited CRs
   (d) US habituation

9. Which of the following is not a traditional way of relating the CS and a US?

   (a) trace
   (b) simultaneous
   (c) delayed
   (d) overshadowing

10. The Rescorla–Wagner theory suggests that a CS becomes effective:

   (a) gradually
   (b) through backward conditioning
   (c) by conditioned inhibition
   (d) following tolerance

Answers to Brief Quiz: 1, d (p. 55); 2, c (p. 56); 3, b (p. 58); 4, c (pp. 58–59); 5, a (p. 59); 6, b (p. 62); 7, d (pp. 64–65); 8, c (p. 73); 9, d (pp. 70–71); 10, a (p. 78)

Reinforcement and Extinction of Operant Behavior

1. Learn about operant behavior and the basic contingencies of reinforcement.
2. Discover whether reinforcement undermines intrinsic motivation.
3. Learn how to carry out experiments on operant conditioning.
4. Delve into reinforcement of variability, problem solving, and creativity.
5. Investigate operant extinction and resistance to extinction.

A hungry lion returns to the waterhole where it has successfully ambushed antelope and other prey. A person who plays a slot machine and wins a large jackpot is more likely to play again than a person who does not win. Students who ask questions and are told "That is an interesting point worth discussing" are prone to ask more questions. When a professor ignores questions or gives fuzzy answers, students eventually stop asking questions. In these cases (and many others), the consequences that follow behavior determine whether it will be repeated in the future.

Recall that operant behavior is said to be emitted (Chapter 2). When operant behavior is followed by reinforcing consequences it is selected, in the sense that it increases in frequency. Behavior that is not followed by reinforcing consequences decreases in frequency. This process, called **operant conditioning** is a major way that the behavior of organisms is changed on the basis of *ontogeny* or life experience (i.e., learning). It is important, however, to recognize that operant conditioning, as a process, has evolved over species history and is based on genetic endowment. That is, operant (and respondent) conditioning as a *general behavior-change process* is based on phylogeny or species history. In other words, those organisms whose behavior changed on the basis of consequences were more likely to survive and reproduce than animals that did not.

OPERANT BEHAVIOR

Operant behavior is commonly described as intentional, free, voluntary, or willful. Examples of operant behavior include conversations with others, driving a car, taking notes, reading a book, and painting a picture. From a scientific perspective, operant behavior is lawful and may be analyzed in terms of its relationship to environmental events. Formally, responses that produce a change in the environment and increase in frequency due to that change are called operants. The term **operant** comes from the verb *to operate* and refers to behavior that operates on the environment to produce consequences that in turn strengthen the behavior. The consequences of operant behavior are many and varied and occur across all sensory dimensions. When you turn on a light, dial a telephone

85

number, drive a car, or open a door, these operants result in visual clarity, conversation, reaching a destination, or entering a room. A **positive reinforcer** is defined as any consequence that increases the probability of the operant that produced it. For example, suppose that your car will not start, but when you jiggle the ignition key it fires right up. Based on past reinforcement, the operant—jiggling the key—is likely to be repeated the next time the car will not start.

Operants are defined by the consequences they produce. Opening the door to reach the other side is the operant, not the physical movement of manipulating the door. Operants are a class of responses that may vary in **topography**. Topography refers to the physical form or characteristics of the response. Consider the number of different ways you could open a door—you may turn the handle, push it with your foot, or (if your arms are full of books) ask someone to open it for you. All of these responses vary in form or topography and result in reaching the other side of the door. Because these responses result in the same consequence, they are members of the same **operant class**. Thus, the term *operant* refers to a class of related responses that may vary in topography but produce a common environmental consequence (Catania, 1973).

Discriminative Stimuli

Operant behavior is **emitted** in the sense that it often occurs without an observable stimulus preceding it. This is in contrast to reflexive responses, which are **elicited** by a preceding stimulus. Reflexes are tied to the physiology of an organism and, under appropriate conditions, always occur when the eliciting stimulus is presented. For example, Pavlov showed that dogs automatically salivated when food was placed in their mouths. Dogs do not learn the relationship between food and salivation; this reflex is a characteristic of the species. Stimuli may also precede operant behavior. However, these events do not force the occurrence of the response that follows them. A stimulus that precedes an operant, and *sets the occasion for behavior*, is called a **discriminative stimulus**, or S^D (pronounced esse-dee).

Discriminative stimuli change the probability that an operant will be emitted based on a history of differential reinforcement. **Differential reinforcement** involves reinforcing an operant in one situation (S^D) but not in another (S^{Δ}). The probability of emitting an operant in the presence of an S^D may be very high, but these stimuli do not have a one-to-one relationship with the response that follows them. For example, a telephone ring increases the chances that you will emit the operant, answering the telephone, but it does not force you to do so. Similarly, a nudge under the table may *set the occasion for* changing the conversation or just shutting up. The events that occasion operant behavior may be private as well as public. Thus, a private event such as a headache may set the occasion for taking an aspirin.

Discriminative stimuli are defined *by setting the occasion for* specific behavior. The probability of raising your hand in class is much greater when the instructor is present than when she is absent. Thus, the presence of an instructor is an S^D for asking questions in class. The teacher functions as an S^D only when her presence changes the student's behavior. The student who is having difficulty with a math problem may ask questions when the teacher enters the room. However, a student who is easily mastering the material is unlikely to do this. Based on the contingencies, the teacher functions as an S^D (for asking questions) for the first student but not the second. This discussion should make it clear that a stimulus is defined as an S^D only when it changes the probability of operant behavior. You may typically stop when you pull up to a traffic sign that reads STOP; the sign is a discriminative stimulus. If, however, you are driving a badly injured friend to the hospital, the same sign may not function as an S^D. Thus, discriminative stimuli are not defined by physical measures (e.g., color, size, tone); rather, they are defined as stimuli that precede and alter the probability of operant responses.

The consequences that follow operant behavior establish the control exerted by discriminative stimuli. When an S^D is followed by an operant that produces positive reinforcement, the operant is more likely to occur the next time the stimulus is present. For example, a student may ask a particular teaching assistant questions because in the past that teaching assistant has provided clear and concise answers. In this example, the assistant is an S^D and asking questions is the operant that increases in his or her presence. When an operant does not produce reinforcement, the stimulus that precedes the response is called an **S-delta**, or S^Δ (pronounced esse-delta). In the presence of an S^Δ, the probability of emitting an operant declines. For example, if a second teaching assistant answers questions in a confused and muddled fashion, the student will be less likely to ask that person questions. In this case the second teaching assistant becomes an S^Δ and the probability of asking questions declines in his or her presence.

Contingencies of Reinforcement

A **contingency of reinforcement** defines the relationship between the events that set the occasion for behavior, the operant class, and the consequences that follow this behavior. In a dark room (S^D), when you flip on a light switch (R), the light usually comes on (S^r). This behavior does not guarantee that the room will light up—the bulb may be burned out, or the switch broken. It is likely that the light will come on, but it is not certain. In behavioral terms, the probability of reinforcement is high, but it is not absolute. This probability may vary between 0 and 100%. A high probability of reinforcement for turning the switch to the "on" position will establish and maintain a high likelihood of this behavior.

Discriminative stimuli that precede behavior have an important role in the regulation of operant responses (Skinner, 1969). Signs that read OPEN, RESUME SPEED, or RESTAURANT, green traffic lights, and a smile from across the room are examples of simple discriminative stimuli that may set the occasion for specific operants. These events regulate behavior because of a *history of reinforcement* in their presence. A smile from across a room may set the occasion for approaching and talking to the person who smiled. This is because, in the past, people who smiled reinforced social interaction.

Each of these events—the occasion, the operant, and the consequences of behavior—makes up the *contingency of reinforcement*. Consider the example of this three-part contingency shown in Figure 4.1. The telephone ring is a discriminative stimulus that sets the occasion for the operant class of answering the phone. This behavior occurs because, in the past, talking to the other party reinforced the operant. The probability of response is very high in the presence of the ring, but it is not inevitable. Perhaps you are in the process of leaving for an important meeting, or you are in the bathtub.

Discriminative stimuli regulate behavior, but they do not stand alone. The consequences that follow behavior determine the probability of response in the presence of the discriminative stimulus. For example, most people show a high probability of answering the telephone when it rings. However, if the phone is faulty so that it rings but you cannot hear

FIG. 4.1   The three-term contingency of reinforcement. A discriminative stimulus (S^D) sets the occasion for operant behavior (R) that is followed by a reinforcing consequence (S^r).

the other party when you answer it, the probability of answering the phone decreases as a function of no reinforcement. In other words, you stop answering a phone that does not work.

Four Basic Contingencies

There are four basic contingencies of reinforcement. Events that follow behavior may be either presented or removed (environmental operation). These events can increase or decrease behavior (effect on behavior). The cells of the matrix in Figure 4.2 define the basic contingencies of reinforcement.

Positive Reinforcement

Positive reinforcement is one of the four basic contingencies of operant behavior. **Positive reinforcement** is portrayed in Figure 4.2 (cell 1), where a stimulus follows behavior and, as a result, the rate of that behavior increases. For example, a child is praised for sharing a toy (operant behavior), and the child begins to share toys more regularly (increase in response strength). Positive reinforcers usually include consequences such as food, praise, and money. *These events, however, cannot be called positive reinforcers until they have been shown to increase behavior.*

Negative Reinforcement

When an operant results in the removal of an event, and this procedure increases the rate of response, the contingency is called **negative reinforcement**. This contingency is shown in cell 3 of the matrix in Figure 4.2. Negative reinforcement is commonly misunderstood as punishment. However, the matrix makes it clear that negative reinforcement involves completely different procedures and effects to positive or negative punishment.

Negative reinforcement plays a major role in the regulation of everyday human behavior. For example, you put on sunglasses because in the past this behavior *removed* the glare of the sun. You open your umbrella when it is raining because doing so has prevented you from getting wet. You leave the room when someone is rude or critical because this behavior has ended other similar conversations. Suppose that you live in a place with a very sensitive smoke detector. Each time you are cooking, the smoke detector goes off. You might remove the sound by tripping the breaker or fuse that controls the alarm. In fact, you will probably learn to do this each time before cooking. As a final example, a mother may pick up and rock her crying baby because, in the past, comforting the child has stopped the crying. In each of these instances, removing an aversive event strengthens an operant.

Stimulus following behavior	Effect on behavior	
	Increase	Decrease
On/presented	1 Positive reinforcement	2 Positive punishment
Off/removed	3 Negative reinforcement	4 Negative punishment

FIG. 4.2 The four basic contingencies of reinforcement. The stimulus following a response (consequence) can be either presented (turned on) or removed (turned off). The effect of these procedures is to increase or decrease the rate of response. The cells of the matrix in this figure define the contingencies of reinforcement. A particular contingency of reinforcement depends on whether the stimulus following behavior is presented or removed and whether behavior increases or decreases in frequency.

Positive Punishment

Cell 2 of the matrix in Figure 4.2 depicts a situation in which an operant produces an event and the rate of operant behavior decreases. This contingency is called **positive punishment**. For example, spanking a child for running onto a busy road is positive punishment if the child now stops (or turns) before reaching the road. In everyday life, people often talk about punishment (and reinforcement) without reference to behavior. For example, a mother scolds her child for playing with matches. The child continues to play with matches, and the parents may comment "punishment doesn't work with Nathan." In behavior analysis, positive punishment is defined functionally (i.e., by its effects). When behavior is not changed by apparently aversive events, punishment has not occurred. In other words, the parents are arranging an ineffective contingency. The parents could identify an aversive event that reliably decreases behavior; however, this strategy may backfire. For example, as you will see in Chapter 6, punishment may produce serious emotional and aggressive behavior. Because of this, punishment should be used only as a last resort for the modification of severe behavior problems.

Negative Punishment

Punishment can also be arranged by removing stimuli contingent on behavior (cell 4 in Figure 4.2). This contingency is called **negative punishment**. In this case, the removal of an event or stimulus decreases operant behavior. For example, two children are watching a favorite television program and begin to fight with one another. The parent says, "That's enough fighting" and turns off the television. You tell a sexist joke and people stop talking to you. At school, a student who is passing notes is required to leave the room for a short period of time. In these examples, watching television, talking to others, and participating in classroom activities are assumed to be reinforcing events. When removal of these events contingent on fighting, telling sexist jokes, or passing notes decreases such behavior, negative punishment has occurred.

FOCUS ON: Rewards and Intrinsic Motivation

Over the past 30 years, many social psychologists and educators have been critical of the practice of using rewards in business, education, and behavior modification programs. The concern is that rewards (the terms "reward" and "reinforcement" are often used similarly in this literature) are experienced as controlling, thereby leading to a reduction in an individual's self-determination, intrinsic motivation, and creative performance (see, for example, Deci, Koestner, & Ryan, 1999). Thus, when a child who enjoys drawing is rewarded for drawing, with praise or with tangible rewards such as points or money, the child's motivation to draw is said to decrease. From this perspective, the child will come to draw less and enjoy it less once the reward is discontinued. In other words, the contention is that reinforcement undermines people's intrinsic motivation (see Figure 4.3). This view has been enormously influential and has led to a decline in the use of rewards and incentive systems in many applied settings.

In an article published in 1996 in *American Psychologist*, Robert Eisenberger and Judy Cameron provided an objective and comprehensive analysis of the literature concerned with the effects of reinforcement/reward on people's intrinsic motivation. Contrary to the belief of many psychologists, their findings indicated no inherent negative property of reward. Instead, their research demonstrates that reward has a much more favorable effect on interest in activities than is generally supposed (Eisenberger & Cameron, 1996).

Research Findings and Implications

Those who oppose the use of rewards support their position by citing experimental studies on reward and intrinsic motivation and claiming that rewards have pervasive negative effects (Deci, Koestner, & Ryan, 1999). One common-sense reason for doubting this claim is that we do not give rewards and awards to criminals for illegal behavior in the hope of undermining their intrinsic motivation to commit crime. Just think about rewarding theft by additional monetary

FIG. 4.3   A boy receiving a monetary reward, perhaps for bringing home good grades. This kind of reward is said to undermine the child's intrinsic motivation for academic subjects. Research suggests, however, that tangible rewards tied to high performance can be used to increase intrinsic motivation as well as perceived competence and self-determination. © Shutterstock.

payments or public recognition of doing a good job. When the rewards stop, the thief should lose interest in criminal activities and give up his life of crime. Intuitively, this scenario does not make sense.

To organize and interpret the diverse findings on rewards and intrinsic motivation, Cameron, Eisenberger, and Pierce (the author of this textbook) conducted several quantitative analyses of this literature (Cameron & Pierce, 1994, 2002; Cameron, Banko, & Pierce, 2001; Eisenberger & Cameron, 1996; Pierce & Cameron, 2002). Using a statistical procedure known as meta-analysis, Cameron et al. (2001) analyzed the results from 145 experiments on rewards and intrinsic motivation in order to answer the question "Do rewards have pervasive negative effects on intrinsic motivation?"

The findings indicated that rewards could be used effectively to enhance or maintain an individual's intrinsic interest in activities. Specifically, verbal rewards (praise, positive feedback) were found to increase people's performance and interest on tasks. In terms of tangible rewards such as money, the results showed that these consequences increased performance and interest for activities that were initially boring or uninteresting. Children who find little interest in reading or mathematics may gain intrinsic motivation from a well-designed reward program that ties rewards to increasing mastery of the material.

For activities that people find inherently interesting and challenging, the results from the meta-analysis point to the *reward contingency* as a major determinant of intrinsic motivation. Cameron et al. (2001) found that tangible rewards loosely tied to performance produce a slight decrease in intrinsic motivation. One interpretation is that people who are rewarded simply for showing up or for doing a job, even an interesting one, repetitively carry out the task, put in low effort, and lose interest (see also the discussion of stereotypy and variability in the section on "Reinforcement and Problem Solving" in this chapter).

When tangible rewards are offered for achieving high performance or exceeding the performance of others, intrinsic interest is maintained or enhanced. In the work world, employees who are offered rewards for high performance assign high ratings to their perceived competence and self-determination (Eisenberger & Shanock, 2003)—findings contrary to the claim that rewards are perceived as controlling and reduce personal autonomy. Furthermore, rewards that are tied to progressively increasing levels of achievement or mastery instill higher intrinsic interest than rewards for meeting a set, unchanging standard of performance (Cameron, Pierce, Banko, & Gear, 2005). Overall, rewards do not have pervasive negative effects on intrinsic motivation. Rewards tied to high performance, achievement, and progressive mastery increase intrinsic motivation, perceived competence, and self-determination.

Identifying a Reinforcing Stimulus

How do we know if a given event or stimulus will function as reinforcement? To identify a *positive reinforcer*, you devise a test. The test is to find out whether a particular consequence *increases* behavior. If it does, the consequence is defined as a positive reinforcer. Such tests are common in science. For example, a litmus test in chemistry tells us whether the solution is acid or base. One hundred dollars is defined as a positive reinforcer because it increases the frequency of betting 25 cents and pulling the handle on the slot machine. Notice that the test for a reinforcer is not the same as explaining the behavior. We explain behavior by pointing to the contingencies of reinforcement ($S^D: R \rightarrow S^r$) and basic principles, not by merely identifying a reinforcing stimulus. For example, we can explain a person's betting in a casino by pointing to the schedule of monetary reinforcement (involving large intermittent payoffs) that has strengthened and maintained this behavior.

The Premack Principle

Another way to identify a positive reinforcer is based on the **Premack principle**. This principle states that *a higher-frequency behavior will function as reinforcement for a lower-frequency behavior*. For example, for a person who spends little time practicing on the piano but lots of time playing basketball, the Premack principle means that playing basketball (high-frequency behavior) will reinforce practicing the piano. Generally, David Premack (1959) proposed that reinforcement involved a contingency between two sets of behaviors, operant behavior and reinforcing behavior (behavior$^{operant} \rightarrow$ behavior^{Sr}), rather than between an operant (behavior) and a stimulus ($R \rightarrow S^r$). That is, Premack suggests it is possible to describe reinforcing events as actions of the organism rather than as discrete stimuli. Thus, reinforcement involves eating rather than the presentation of food, drinking rather than provision of water, and reading rather than the effects of textual stimuli.

In his 1962 experiment, Premack deprived rats of water for 23 h and then measured their behavior in a setting in which they could run on an activity wheel or drink water. Of course, the animals spent more time drinking than running. Next, Premack arranged a contingency between running and drinking. The rats received a few seconds of access to drinking tubes when they ran on the wheels. Running on the wheel increased when it produced the opportunity to drink water— showing that drinking reinforced running. In other words, the rats ran on the wheel to get a drink of water. At this point in the experiment, Premack (1962) gave the rats free access to water. Now, when the rats were allowed to choose between drinking and running, they did little drinking and a lot more running. Premack reasoned that running would reinforce drinking because running occurred at a

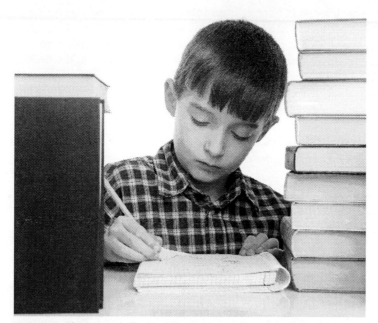

FIG. 4.4 Photograph illustrating the Premack principle. In this example, homework is a low-frequency behavior and watching television is a high-frequency response. The parents have set the contingency that the boy can watch television if he accurately completes his homework after coming home from school. © Shutterstock.

higher frequency than drinking. The running wheel was locked and the brake was removed if the rats licked the water tube for a few seconds. Based on this contingency, Premack showed that drinking water increased when it produced running. That is, the animals drank water for opportunities to run on the wheels. Overall, this experiment shows that drinking reinforces running when rats are motivated to drink. On the other hand, running reinforces drinking when running is the preferred activity. Thus, when behavior is measured in a situation that allows a choice among different activities, those responses that occur at a higher frequency may be used to reinforce those that occur at a lower frequency.

Premack's principle has obvious applied implications, and it provides another way to identify reinforcement in everyday settings. Behavior is measured in a situation where all relevant operants can occur without restriction; any behavior of relatively higher frequency will reinforce an operant of lower frequency. To illustrate, a child is observed in a situation where doing homework, watching television, playing with toys, and recreational reading may all freely occur. Once baseline measures of behavior have been taken, the Premack principle holds that any higher-frequency (or longer-duration) behavior may serve as reinforcement for any behavior of lower frequency. If television watching is longer in duration than doing homework, watching television may be made contingent on completing homework assignments (see Figure 4.4). This contingency will usually increase the number of homework assignments completed, as most parents know from experience.

Reinforcement and Response Deprivation

The Premack principle states that a higher-frequency behavior can reinforce a lower-frequency operant. In a free-choice setting, several behaviors will occur at different frequencies—yielding a **response hierarchy**. Any response in the hierarchy will reinforce any behavior below it; also, that response will be reinforced by any behavior above it.

An important observation is that depriving an animal of the opportunity to engage in a given behavior changes the response frequencies and hierarchy. Depriving a rat of water ensures that drinking occurs at a higher frequency than wheel running, and drinking will reinforce running (or behavior such as lever pressing); on the other hand, restriction of running increases its frequency relative to drinking, and running will now reinforce drinking. Thus, response deprivation leads to a reordering of the response hierarchy and determines which behaviors will function as reinforcement at a given moment.

Equilibrium analysis (Timberlake & Allison, 1974; Timberlake, 1993) makes a distinction between the instrumental and contingent responses. The **instrumental response** is the behavior that produces the opportunity to engage in some activity; the **contingent response** is the activity obtained by making the instrumental response. When a contingency is set between the instrumental and contingent responses, equilibrium is disturbed—the animal is deprived of the contingent response. One implication is that the animal will perform the instrumental response to get back to free choice or baseline levels of the contingent response. Generally, **response deprivation** occurs when access to the contingent behavior is restricted and falls below its baseline (or free-choice) level of occurrence.

Timberlake and Allison (1974) showed that the reason for a reinforcement effect is not the relative frequencies of behavior as stated in the Premack principle; rather, it is due to response deprivation and the disequilibrium imposed by the contingency (e.g., do homework before watching TV). In fact, it is possible to obtain a reinforcement effect with a low-frequency behavior if the person is deprived of the activity by setting a behavioral contingency. That is, equilibrium analysis and response deprivation have a wider range of application than the Premack principle.

OPERANT CONDITIONING

Operant conditioning refers to an increase or decrease in operant behavior as a function of a contingency of reinforcement. In a simple demonstration of operant conditioning, an experimenter may alter the consequences that follow operant behavior. The effects of environmental consequences on behavior were first described in 1911 by the American psychologist E. L. Thorndike, who reported results from a series of animal experiments that eventually formed the basis of operant conditioning. Cats, dogs, and chicks were placed in situations in which they could obtain food by performing complex sequences of behavior. For example, hungry cats were confined to an apparatus that Thorndike called a puzzle box, shown in Figure 4.5. Food was placed outside the box, and if the cat managed to pull out a bolt, step on a lever, or emit some other behavior, the door would open and the animal could eat the food.

FIG. 4.5 Thorndike's puzzle box for cats. Food was placed outside the box, and if the cat managed to pull out a bolt or step on a lever, the door would open and the animal could get out of the box and eat the food. When cats were given repeated trials in the box, they became faster and faster at getting out. Redrawn from *Animal Intelligence: Experimental Studies*, by E. L. Thorndike, 1911, p. 30, Macmillan Co., New York, with permission.

After some time in the box, the cat would accidentally pull the bolt or step on the lever and the door would open. Thorndike measured the time from closing the trap door until the cat managed to get it open. This measure, called **latency**, tended to decrease with repeated exposures to the box. In other words, the cats took less and less time to escape from the apparatus as they were given more trials. According to Thorndike, the puzzle-box experiment demonstrated learning by trial and error. That is, the cats repeatedly tried to get out of the box and made fewer and fewer errors. Thorndike made similar observations with dogs and chicks and, on the basis of these observations, formulated the **law of effect**. A modern paraphrase of this law is the principle of reinforcement, namely that operants may be followed by the presentation of contingent consequences that increase the rate (frequency of response divided by time) of this behavior. Skinner has commented on Thorndike's analysis of trial-and-error learning:

> Thorndike thought he solved his problem by saying that the successful cat used trial-and-error learning. The expression is unfortunate. "Try" [from trial] implies that a response has already been affected by relevant consequences. A cat is "trying to escape" if it engages in behavior which either has been selected in the evolution of the species because it has brought escape from comparable situations or has been reinforced by escape from aversive stimulation during the life of the cat. The term "error" does not describe behavior; it passes judgment on it. The curves for trial-and-error learning plotted by Thorndike and many others do not represent any useful property of behavior—certainly not a single process called problem solving. The changes which contribute to such a curve include the adaptation and extinction of emotional responses, the conditioning of reinforcers, and the extinction of unrelated responses. Any contribution made by an increase in the probability of the reinforced response is hopelessly obscured.
>
> (Skinner, 1988, p. 219)

In other words, Skinner suggests that simply measuring the time (or latency) taken to complete a task misses changes that occur across several operant classes. Responses that resulted in escape and food were selected while other behavior decreased in frequency. Eventually those operants that produced reinforcing consequences came to dominate the cat's behavior, allowing the animal to get out of the box in less and less time. Thus, latency was an indirect measure of a change in the animal's operant behavior. Today, **rate of response** or operant rate (the number of responses in a specified interval) is considered a better measure of operant behavior. Operant rate provides a direct measure of the selection of behavior by its consequences.

NEW DIRECTIONS: Behavioral Neuroscience and Operant Conditioning of the Neuron

> When the behavior of an organism acts upon the environment in which it lives, it changes that environment in ways that *often affect the organism itself* [emphasis added]. Some of these changes . . . are generally referred to technically as reinforcers: when they follow behavior in this way they increase the likelihood that the organism will behave in the same way again.
>
> (Ferster & Skinner, 1957, p. 1)

How does the environment "affect the organism itself" during the process of operant conditioning? One possibility is that reinforcement and operant conditioning occur at the level of brain units or elements. Skinner (1953, pp. 93–95) addressed brain units when he stated that ". . . the element rather than the response [is] the unit of behavior. It is a sort of behavioral atom, which may never appear by itself upon any single occasion but is the essential ingredient or component of all observed instances [of behavior]." At the time that Skinner made this claim he had no way of knowing the basic element or "behavioral atom" of operant conditioning. Today, the evidence is mounting that the basic units of reinforcement are not complex brain structures of whole responses but elements as small as the neuron itself.

It is possible to investigate the neuron and reinforcement by the method of *in-vitro* **reinforcement** or **IVR** (Stein, Xue, & Belluzzi, 1994). The idea is that calcium bursts or firings (L-type Ca^{2+}) of a neuron are reinforced by dopamine (a neurotransmitter) binding to specialized receptors. Furthermore, the process of neuronal conditioning can be investigated *"in vitro"* using brain-slice preparations and drug injections that stimulate the dopamine receptor (dopamine agonists).

In these IVR experiments, a small injector tube (micropipette) is aimed at cells of the brain slice (hippocampal cells from pyramidal cell layer of CA1). During operant conditioning, micropressure injections of a dopamine drug (agonist) are applied to the cell for 50 ms following bursts of activity (amplified action potentials). When the computer identifies a predefined burst of activity for the target neuron, the pressure-injection pump delivers a minute droplet of the drug to the cell. Drug-induced increases in bursting indicate operant conditioning if the *contingency* between neuron bursts and drug presentation is critical. To be sure that the drug is not just stimulating burst activity, the same drug is given independently of bursting on a *non-contingent* basis.

The results showed that the bursting responses of individual neurons increase in a dose-related manner by response-contingent injections of dopamine agonists. Also, non-contingent presentation of the same drug injections did not increase the bursting responses of the neurons. The findings indicate that reinforcement occurs at the level of individual neural units (Skinner's atoms of behavior), and suggest that subtypes of dopamine neurons (D1, D2, or D3 types) are involved in cellular and behavioral operant conditioning.

Additional IVR experiments indicate that bursting responses of CA1 pyramidal neurons also increase with injections of cannabinoid drugs, whereas the firings of CA3 neurons increase with drugs that stimulate the opiate receptors (Stein & Belluzzi, 1988; Xue, Belluzzi & Stein, 1993). When these drug injections are administered independent of cellular activity, bursting responses do not increase and often are suppressed. Furthermore, contingent and non-contingent glutamate injections to the CA1 neurons over a range of doses fail to increase bursting or decrease this response. Thus, drug agonists that target specific receptors implicated in reward and addiction (e.g., dopamine, cannabinoid, and opioid) act as reinforcement for neural bursting, whereas glutamate, an excitatory transmitter that is not associated with behavioral reinforcement, does not augment cellular activity or even suppresses it.

New research has revealed the conditioning of single neurons in the brains of live Japanese monkeys (*Macaca fuscata*) as the animals performed a visual fixation task (Kobayashi, Schultz, & Sakagami, 2010). Monkeys were mildly deprived of fluid and were seated in a primate chair with their head fixed, facing a computer monitor that presented images on each trial. The researchers isolated and monitored single neurons in the lateral prefrontal cortex (LPFC), an area of the brain associated with intentional, purposive action (operant behavior), and reinforced neuronal spikes that exceeded an established criterion. When the neuron emitted a spike in the established range, the monkeys received juice in the mouth as reinforcement. Control conditions involved all of the procedures of the experimental phase, including visual fixation and presentation of juice, but there was no contingency between neuron firing and reinforcement. Evidence indicated that individual neurons in the LPFC showed operant conditioning. Further experiments in the series indicated that LPFC neurons would respond in accord with the schedule of reinforcement. The researchers noted that alternative explanations such as simple reward prediction, attention, and arousal were unlikely to account for the findings. Also, the LPFC has few motor neurons, so it is unlikely that neuron activity in this region directly coincides with movement of the animal. One possibility is that LPFC neurons contribute to behavioral flexibility—a neural substrate for operant behavior. These neurons may "enhance the action signals [in other brain areas] to ensure the motor execution when operant control is required" (Kobayashi et al., 2010, p. 1854; see also Schafer & Moore, 2011).

Operant conditioning is a major adaptive mechanism for animals that change behavior on the basis of lifetime experiences (ontogeny). That is, operant conditioning allows for behavioral flexibility, survival, and reproduction. Evidence is accumulating that behavioral flexibility is based on **neuroplasticity**—that is, the alteration of neurons and neural interconnections during a lifetime by changes in environmental contingencies. *In-vitro* reinforcement experiments show that endogenous brain chemicals binding to particular types of receptors increase the likelihood of neuronal activity. These molecular neural processes presumably underlie the large-scale changes in operant behavior that occur as humans and other animals interact with the world in which they live, from moment to moment, over a life span.

Procedures in Operant Conditioning

Operant Rate and Probability of Response

Rate of response refers to the number of operant responses that occur in some defined unit of time. For example, if you ask 5 questions during a 2-h class, your rate is 2.5 questions per hour. An animal that presses a lever 1000 times in a 1-h session generates a rate of 1000 bar presses per hour (or 16.7 responses per minute). Skinner (1938) proposed that rate of response is the basic datum (or measure) for operant analysis. **Operant rate** is a measure of the probability of behavior (the **probability of response**). In other words, an operant that occurs at a high rate in one situation has a high probability of being emitted in a similar situation in the future. This increased probability of response is observed as a change in operant rate. Of course, probability of response may decrease, and in this case is seen as a decline in rate.

The Free Operant Method

In the **free operant method**, an animal may repeatedly respond over an extensive period of time (see Perone, 1991). The organism is free to emit many responses or none at all. That is, responses can be made without interference from the experimenter. For example, a laboratory rat may press a lever for food pellets. Lever pressing is under the control of the animal, which may press the bar rapidly, slowly, or quit pressing. Importantly, this method allows the researcher to observe changes in the rate of response. This is important because rate of response is used as a measure of response probability. Rate of response must be free to vary if it is used to index the future probability of operant behavior.

The analysis of operant rate and probability of response is not easily accomplished when an organism is given a series of trials (as in the Thorndike experiments). This is because the experimenter largely controls the animal's rate of behavior. For example, a rat that runs down a T-maze for food reward is picked up at the goal box and returned to the starting point. Because the experimenter sets the number of trials and response opportunities, changes in the rate of response cannot be directly observed and measured. Comparing the T-maze trial procedure with the free operant method, it is clear that the free operant method is more suitable for studying the probability of response in a given situation. The free operant method is clearly demonstrated by the procedures used in operant conditioning.

The Operant Chamber

To study operant conditioning in a laboratory, a device called an **operant chamber** is used (see Ator, 1991). Of course, operant conditioning is also investigated outside laboratories. Nonetheless, investigating the behavior of animals in operant chambers has resulted in the discovery of many principles of behavior. Figure 4.6 shows a student setup of an operant chamber designed to accommodate a laboratory rat (note that a research setup would involve much more experimental control, such as a sound-attenuating enclosure and "white noise" to mask sounds from outside). The chamber is a small enclosed box that contains a lever with a light above it, and a food magazine or cup connected to an external feeder. The feeder delivers a small food pellet (typically 45 mg) when electronically activated. In this situation, the food pellet serves as reinforcement for lever pressing. The operant chamber structures the situation so that the desired behavior will occur and incompatible behavior is reduced. Thus, lever pressing is highly likely, while behavior such as running away is minimized. A school classroom also attempts to structure the behavior of students with regard to learning. The classroom, unlike the operant chamber, often contains many distractions (e.g., looking out of the window) that interfere with on-task behavior and concentrating on the material being presented.

Establishing Motivation: Deprivation

Because the delivery of food is used as reinforcement, an animal must be motivated to obtain food. An objective and quantifiable measure of motivation for food is percentage of free-feeding body weight (note that another way of quantifying deprivation is a timed cycle that specifies the time since the rat last consumed the reinforcer). Prior to a typical experiment, an animal is brought from a commercial (or research) colony into a laboratory, placed in a cage, given free access to food, and weighed on a daily basis. The average weight is calculated, and this value is used as a baseline. Next,

FIG. 4.6 A student set-up of an operant chamber for a rat. The chamber is a small box that has a lever that the animal can press. There is a light above the lever that can be turned on or off. A food magazine or cup is connected to an electronically activated feeder. The feeder delivers a small, 45-mg food pellet to the cup. In this situation, the food pellet serves as reinforcement for lever pressing. Reprinted with permission of Gerbrands Corporation, Arlington, MA.

the daily food ration is reduced until the animal reaches 85% of its free-feeding weight. The procedure of restricting access to food (the potentially reinforcing stimulus) is called a **deprivation operation** (see section on motivational operations in Chapter 2). At this point, the experimenter assumes, but does not know, that food is a reinforcing stimulus. This is because food delivery must increase the frequency of an operant before it can be defined as a reinforcer.

The weight-loss or deprivation criterion is less severe than it first appears. Laboratory animals typically have food freely available 24 h a day, whereas animals in the wild must forage for their food. The result is that lab animals tend to be heavier than their free-ranging counterparts. Alan Poling and his colleagues (Poling, Nickel, & Alling, 1990) nicely demonstrated this point by showing that captured free-range pigeons gained an average 17% body weight when housed under laboratory conditions. Notice that weight gain, for these birds, is roughly equal to the weight loss typically imposed on laboratory animals.

Magazine Training

After food deprivation is established, **magazine training** starts. For example, a rat is placed in an operant chamber and a microcomputer periodically turns on the feeder. When the feeder is turned on, it makes a click and a small 45-mg food pellet falls into the food magazine. Because the click and the appearance of food are associated in time, you would, after training, observe a typical rat staying close to the food magazine; also, the animal would move quickly toward the magazine when the feeder operated and the click occurred. Because the click of the feeder reliably precedes the appearance of food, it becomes a conditioned positive reinforcer (see Chapter 11 for a more complete discussion of conditioned reinforcement). A **conditioned reinforcer** is an event or stimulus that acquires its reinforcing function over the lifetime of the organism (ontogeny). In this case, following the click of the feeder by the presentation of food establishes the sound of the feeder as a conditioned reinforcer for the rat.

The Operant Class

Staying close to the food cup and moving toward it are operants that have been selected by their reinforcing consequences. In other words, these responses have been reliably followed by food presentation, and as a result they increase in frequency. However, hovering around a food cup and moving toward it are operants that are difficult to measure objectively. In contrast, a lever press may be easily defined as a switch closure that makes an electrical connection. Any behavior emitted by the rat that results in a switch closure defines the **operant class**. A lever press with the left or right paw produces an identical electrical connection. Another advantage of lever pressing as an operant is that it may be emitted at high or low rates of response. This is an advantage because the primary focus of operant research is on the conditions that affect the rate (probability) of operant behavior.

Operant Level and Continuous Reinforcement

After magazine training, the food-deprived rat is again placed in the operant chamber. The researcher may first want to measure the rate of lever pressing before these responses produce food pellets. Rats emit many exploratory and manipulative responses, and as a result may press the lever at some low frequency, even when this behavior is not reinforced with food. This baseline rate of response is called the **operant level** or the rate of response before any known conditioning. Next, the environment is arranged so that each lever press results in the click of the feeder (conditioned reinforcement) and the delivery of a food pellet (primary reinforcement). When each response produces food, the schedule of reinforcement is called **continuous reinforcement (CRF)**. The food pellets are contingent on lever pressing. This contingency between the operant behavior and food reinforcement increases the frequency of lever pressing above operant level.

Shaping: the method of successive approximation

In the preceding example, we took advantage of a rat's behavioral repertoire. The animal's **repertoire** refers to the behavior it is capable of naturally emitting on the basis of species and environmental history. Suppose you want to train some response that the animal does not emit. For example, you may want the rat to activate the switch by an upward thrust of its nose. A baseline period of observation shows that the animal fails to emit this response (in other words, the *operant level is zero*). In this case, the researcher could use **shaping** or the method of **successive approximation** to establish the response (see Gleeson, 1991). This method involves reinforcing closer and closer approximations to the final performance (i.e., nosing the lever).

We begin to shape lever pressing for food (final performance) with a rat that has already been conditioned to eat from the pellet feeder. At first, the rat is reinforced for standing in the vicinity of the lever. It is important to note that the most immediate consequence is the sound of the pellet feeder, and it is this conditioned reinforcer that is used to shape the desired response.

Once the rat is reliably facing the lever, a movement of the head toward the lever is reinforced with a click of the feeder and presentation of food. Next, closer and closer approximations to depressing the lever with the right paw are reinforced, as shown in Figure 4.7. Each step of the procedure involves reinforcing closer approximations to the final performance and no reinforcement (extinction) of more distant responses. Eventually, the rat consistently emits responses with sufficient force to activate the electrical switch (final performance). Many novel forms of behavior may be established in animals and humans by the method of successive approximation or shaping (Pryor, 1999).

Shaping of key pecking in the pigeon uses the same principles as shaping of lever pressing in a rat. Skinner (1953) described how to train a bird to peck a spot in its cage using successive approximation to the final performance. Skinner emphasizes how the distribution of responses for the response class of "pecking a spot for food" is moved from an initial near zero probability toward a high and stable rate of response:

> We first give the bird food when it turns slightly in the direction of the spot from any part of the cage. This increases the frequency of such behavior. We then withhold reinforcement until a slight movement is made toward the spot. This again alters the general distribution of behavior without producing a new unit. We continue by reinforcing positions successively closer to the spot, then by reinforcing only when the head is moved slightly forward, and finally only when the beak actually makes contact with the spot. . . . The original probability of the response in its final form is very low; in some cases it may even be zero. In this way we can build complicated operants, which would never appear in the repertoire of the organism otherwise. By reinforcing a series of successive approximations, we bring a rare response to a very high probability in a short time. . . . The total act of turning toward the spot from any point in the box, walking toward it, raising the head, and striking the spot may seem to be a functionally coherent unit of behavior; but it is constructed by a continual process of differential reinforcement from undifferentiated behavior, just as the sculptor shapes his figure from a lump of clay.
>
> (Skinner, 1953, pp. 92–93)

Notice that shaping makes use of **behavioral variability**—the animal's tendency to emit variations in response form in a given situation. The range of behavioral variation is related to an animal's capabilities based on genetic endowment, degree of neuroplasticity, and previous interactions with

Steps in shaping lever pressing

- Standing near the lever reinforced
- Facing lever reinforced
- Moving head towards lever reinforced
- Touching lever with parts of body (nose) reinforced
- Touching lever with paws reinforced
- Touching lever with specified (right) paw reinforced
- Partially depressing lever with right paw reinforced
- Raising and depressing lever with right paw reinforced
- Raising and depressing lever completely with right paw reinforced

FIG. 4.7 The possible steps in shaping the rat towards the final performance of pressing the lever with sufficient force to activate the feeder and deliver the food pellet.

the environment. Behavioral variability allows for selection by reinforcing consequences, and is analogous to the role of genetic variability in natural selection (Neuringer, 2009, p. 319). Shaping by successive approximation uses undifferentiated operant behavior (a lump of clay) that is moved toward "a functionally coherent unit" (pecking a spot for food) by a process of **ontogenetic selection** (differential reinforcement).

Recording Operant Behavior

A commonly used laboratory instrument that records the frequency of operant behavior in time is called a **cumulative recorder**. Figure 4.8 illustrates this device, which was used in the early research on operant conditioning. Each time a lever press occurs, the pen steps up one increment. When reinforcement occurs, this same pen makes a downward deflection. Once the pen reaches the top of the paper, it resets to the bottom and starts to step up again. Since the paper is drawn across the roller at a constant speed, the *cumulative recorder depicts a real-time measure of the rate of operant behavior*. The faster the lever presses, the steeper the slope or rise of the **cumulative record**.

FIG. 4.8 A laboratory instrument used to record operant responses, called a cumulative recorder. This device was used in the early research on operant conditioning. The recorder gives a real-time measure of the rate of operant behavior. The faster the lever presses, the steeper the slope or rise of the cumulative record. This occurs because paper is drawn across the roller at a constant speed and the pen steps up a defined distance for each response. Modern laboratories show response records on computer screens, along with additional behavioral measures. Reprinted with permission of Gerbrands Corporation, Arlington, MA.

A cumulative record of key pecking by a pigeon is shown in Figure 4.9. In this illustration, a bird responded 50 times to produce one food delivery. Notice that periods of responding are followed by reinforcement (indicated by the deflection of the pen). After reinforcement, the rate of response is zero, as indicated by the plateaus or flat portions of the cumulative record.

In a modern operant laboratory, the cumulative record is portrayed on a computer screen to provide the experimenter with an immediate report of the animal's behavior. Researchers have discovered many basic principles of behavior by examining cumulative records (e.g., Ferster & Skinner, 1957). Today, microcomputers allow researchers to collect, display, and record measures of behavior (e.g., rate of response) that are later submitted to complex numerical analyses (see Gollub, 1991). In this book, we present examples of cumulative records and numerical analyses that have been important to the experimental analysis of behavior.

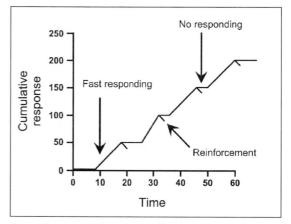

FIG. 4.9 A cumulative record of key pecking by a pigeon. In this illustration, a bird responded 50 times to produce one food delivery. Notice that 50 pecks are followed by reinforcement, and that this is indicated by a downward deflection of the pen. Following reinforcement, the rate of response is zero, as indicated by the plateaus or flat portions of the record.

A Model Experiment

In the previous discussion of operant behavior, some basic principles were illustrated using the laboratory rat. It is important to realize that these same principles can be extended to a variety of species (later chapters will focus more on human behavior). In the following demonstration of operant conditioning, pigeons are used as the experimental subjects. Pigeons are placed in an operant chamber and required to peck a small plastic disk or *key* that is illuminated by a white light. A peck at the key activates a microswitch and makes an electrical connection that controls a food hopper. Presentation of food functions as reinforcement for pecking. A food hopper filled with grain swings forward and remains available for a few seconds. The bird can eat the grain by sticking its head through an opening. Figure 4.10 shows an operant chamber designed for birds. Note that the chamber is very similar to the one used to study the operant behavior of rats.

Before an experiment, the bird is taken from its home colony and is placed alone in a cage. Each pigeon is given free access to food and water. The bird is weighed each day for about a week, and its baseline weight is calculated. Next, the daily food ration is reduced until the bird reaches approximately 80% of free-feeding or **ad libitum weight**. After the deprivation procedure, the pigeon is placed in the operant chamber for magazine training.

When the bird is placed in the chamber for the first time, it may show a variety of emotional responses, including wing flapping and defecating. This is because the chamber presents a number of novel features that initially function as aversive stimuli. For example, the operation of the feeder makes a loud sound that may startle the bird. Eventually, these emotional responses are extinguished by repeated exposure to the apparatus. As the emotional responses dissipate, the bird explores the environment and begins to eat from the food magazine. Since the sound of the hopper is paired with

FIG. 4.10   An operant chamber for birds. The chamber contains a small plastic disk illuminated by a light. A peck at the disk activates a microswitch and makes an electrical connection. When reinforcement is scheduled to occur, the food hopper swings forward and remains available for a few seconds. The bird can eat grain from the hopper by sticking its head through the opening in the chamber wall. In principle, the chamber is similar to the one used to study the operant behavior of rats. Adapted from Ferster, C. B. & Skinner, B. F. (1957). *Schedules of reinforcement*. New York: Appleton-Century-Crofts.

food, the sound becomes a conditioned positive reinforcer. At this point, the bird is said to be magazine trained.

The purpose of this demonstration is to train the pigeon to peck the key for food reinforcement. To show that the behavior occurs because of the contingency between pecking and food, an operant level or baseline of pecking the key must be measured. This is accomplished by placing the bird in the operant chamber and recording pecks on the key before a peck–food contingency is established. In other words, pecking the key does not produce food during this phase of the experiment. The operant level serves as a baseline or control period for assessing a change in behavior.

A bird's operant level of key pecking is typically very low, and it is convenient to train these responses by the method of successive approximation. Shaping key pecking in pigeons is similar to shaping lever pressing in rats; in both cases, shaping involves reinforcing closer and closer approximations to the final performance (i.e., pecking the key hard enough to operate the microswitch). As each approximation occurs, it is reinforced with the presentation of the food hopper. Earlier approximations are no longer reinforced and reduce in frequency. This process of reinforcing closer approximations, and withholding reinforcement for earlier approximations, eventually results in the pigeon pecking the key with sufficient force to operate the microswitch. The key peck that operates the microswitch to produce food is the *first definable response*. The switch closure and electrical connection define the operant class of pecking for food. At this point, a microcomputer is programmed so that each key peck results in the presentation of food for a few seconds. Because each response produces reinforcement, the schedule is called continuous reinforcement, or CRF.

Figure 4.11 shows the acquisition of key pecking on continuous reinforcement (the bird has presumably been shaped to peck the key for food). Notice that the rate of response is low when the pigeon is initially placed in the chamber. This period is called the warm-up, and probably occurs because of the abrupt change from home cage to the operant chamber. After the brief warm-up period, the rate of response is high and stable.

Finally, the record shows that rate of response declines, and the plateau indicates that the bird stops pecking the key. This latter effect is called **satiation**, and it occurs because the bird has eaten enough food. More technically, *rate of response declines because repeated presentations of the reinforcer weaken its effectiveness*. A satiation operation decreases the effectiveness of reinforcement. This effect is opposite to deprivation, in which withholding the reinforcer increases its effectiveness.

To be sure that an increase in the rate of response is caused by the contingency of reinforcement, it is necessary to withdraw that contingency. In other words, if food is no longer presented, the pigeon should give up pecking the key. If the peck–food contingency caused key pecking, then withdrawal of the contingency will result in a decline in key pecking toward the operant level.

Figure 4.12 presents cumulative records for periods in which pecking produces or does not produce food. The initial peck–food contingency produces a steady rate of response. When pecking no longer produces food, the rate of response declines and eventually key pecking stops. Thus, key pecking clearly depends upon the contingency of reinforcement.

FIG. 4.11   Typical acquisition of key pecking on CRF or continuous reinforcement. Because every response is reinforced, downward deflections indicating reinforcement are omitted. The rate of response is low when the animal is initially placed in the chamber. After this brief period, the rate of response is high and stable. Finally, the rate of response declines and then levels off. This latter effect is caused by satiation.

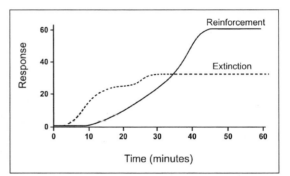

FIG. 4.12   Performance on CRF and extinction. Responses are maintained when they are reinforced. However, when responding is no longer reinforced, the rate of response declines and key pecking eventually stops.

⌕ FOCUS ON: Reinforcement and Problem Solving

Reinforcement and Response Stereotypy

Barry Schwartz (1980, 1982a) carried out a series of experiments with pigeons to show that reinforcement produced response stereotypy. In these experiments, reinforcement produced a set pattern of responding that occurred over and over again. Once he had established this result in pigeons, Schwartz (1982b) used similar procedures with college students to demonstrate the presumed negative effects of reinforcement for human problem solving.

College students were given points on a counter when they completed a complex sequence of responses. The responses were left and right key presses that moved a light on

FIG. 4.13 The matrix task used by Schwartz (1982b). A right key press moved the light one square to the right; a left key press moved the light down one square.

a checkerboard-like matrix of 25 illuminated squares. Figure 4.13 shows the matrix, with the light in the top left square. The task required that the subject press the keys to move the light from the top left corner to the bottom right square. A press on the right key moved the light one square to the right. When the left-hand key was pressed, the light moved one square down. Schwartz required exactly four left (L) and four right (R) presses in any order (e.g., LRLRLRLR, LLLLRRRR, etc.). There were 72 different orders of left and right key presses that would move the light to the bottom right corner. When the light reached the bottom right corner, a point registered on the counter. The points were later exchanged for money. If the subject pressed any key a fifth time (e.g., RRRRR), all of the matrix lights were turned off and the trial ended without reinforcement.

In a series of experiments, Schwartz found that students developed a stereotyped pattern of responding. The point is that as soon as a student hit on a correct sequence, he or she repeated it and rarely tried another pattern. In other experiments (Schwartz, 1982b), participants were explicitly reinforced for varying their response pattern. When this was done, the students developed higher-order stereotypes. From these experiments, Schwartz concluded that reinforcement interfered with problem solving, because it produced stereotyped response patterns.

FIG. 4.14 Dr. Allen Neuringer. Photograph by Vera Jagendorf, Portland, OR. Published with permission.

Reinforcement and Response Variability

Allen Neuringer (Figure 4.14) is a behavior analyst who investigates variability, randomness, and behavior. He suggested that the contingencies of the Schwartz experiments produced response stereotypy and that this was not an inevitable outcome of reinforcement. In the Schwartz experiments, the response patterns were constrained by the requirement to emit exactly four pecks on each key in any order. This constraint means that of the 256 possible sequences of pecks, only 72 patterns resulted in reinforcement; also, a fifth peck to either left or right keys resulted in a time out from reinforcement (negative punishment). This time-out contingency punished many instances of response variability, reducing its occurrence.

A classic study by Page and Neuringer (1985) eliminated these constraints imposed by Schwartz and tested the assumption that variability could actually increase with reinforcement. The experiment involved pigeons pecking left and right keys on the light matrix task. Each session consisted of numerous trials with the bird emitting 8 pecks to the two keys on each trial—ending with food for 8 pecks that met the criterion for variability and a short time out for other sequences. The contingency for the variability phase (VAR) involved lags in which the current sequence of 8 pecks had to differ from the pattern of pecks emitted on some previous trials. The number of previous trials defined the LAG value. For example, using a Lag 3 contingency, the current sequence of 8 pecks to left and right keys had to diverge from each of the patterns for the previous three trials for the current trial to end in food reinforcement; other "incorrect" sequences of pecks resulted in a time out. Birds met the schedule requirements for variability even at Lag 50 by responding almost randomly (like coin flipping) on the left and right keys, not by "remembering" what they did over the past 50 trials.

At this point in the experiment, the researcher introduced a critical comparison phase where the birds were reinforced at the end of some of the 8-peck trials, but the presentation of food did not depend on the bird's variability. Reinforcements were now tied or *yoked* to the earlier pattern of reinforcements delivered in the VAR phase. If a bird had been reinforced on a given trial of the VAR session, then the equivalent trial in the yoked phase also ended with reinforcement—regardless of whether the lag contingency had been met. By yoking each bird's reinforcements in the two phases, the researchers ensured that the allocation of reinforcements was identical for a given bird, and that the only difference was that variable sequences of some Lag were *required* for reinforcement in the VAR phase, but not in the yoked phase, where variability was simply *permitted*. Would response variability be higher when variability produced reinforcement than when reinforcement occurred independently of variability? The answer was a clear yes. Birds were highly variable when reinforced for varying (VAR), but tended to repeat pecks to one of the keys when reinforcement did not require response variability (yoked). One conclusion is that variability is an operant dimension of behavior (much like force of response or speed of response) regulated by the contingency of reinforcement.

Assessment of Reinforcement and Problem Solving

The current evidence indicates that *variability is an operant* that increases with reinforcement of behavioral variation (Neuringer, 2002, 2009; Lee, Sturmey, & Fields, 2007). To date, the reinforcement of variability has been shown in a number of species, including pigeons, dolphins, rats, and human adults and children (Goetz & Baer, 1973; Machado, 1997; Neuringer, 1986; Pryor, Haag, & O'Reilly, 1969; Stokes, Mechner, & Balsam, 1999; van Hest, van Haaren, & van de Poll, 1989). In addition, different experimental procedures have been used to produce variability with a number of different response forms (Blough, 1966; Eisenberger & Shanock, 2003; Goetz & Baer, 1973; Machado, 1989; Morgan & Neuringer, 1990; Odum, Ward, Barnes, & Burke, 2006; Pryor et al., 1969). Variability, constraints by task and contingencies, and artistic creativity have also been of interest (Stokes, 2001).

In summary, Barry Schwartz argues that reinforcement produces behavioral inflexibility and rigidity. In contrast, the research of Allen Neuringer and other researchers suggests that response stereotypy is not an inevitable outcome of reinforcement. If the contingencies of reinforcement support stereotyped behavior, then this will occur. On the other hand, contingencies may generate novel, even creative, sequences of behavior if these patterns result in reinforcement (Neuringer, 2004; Machado, 1989, 1992, 1997). Generally, a close analysis of the contingencies is required in problem-solving situations because "what you reinforce is what you get" (stereotypy or variability).

EXTINCTION

The procedure of *withholding reinforcement for a previously reinforced response* is called **extinction**. Skinner (1938) conducted the first extensive study of extinction and its related principles. To produce extinction, you would disconnect the food hopper after the bird had been reinforced for key pecking. It is important to note that the procedure of extinction is a contingency of reinforcement. The contingency is defined as zero probability of reinforcement for the operant response. Extinction is also a behavioral process and, in this case, refers to a *decline in rate of response caused by withdrawal of reinforcement*. For example, you may raise your hand to ask a question and find that a certain professor ignores you. Asking questions may decline because the professor no longer reinforces this behavior.

Behavioral Effects of Extinction

Extinction produces several behavioral effects in addition to a decline in the rate of response. In the section that follows, we consider the range of effects generated by the cessation of reinforcement. Many of the responses of organisms to the cessation of reinforcement make sense from an evolutionary perspective. Presumably, when things no longer worked (extinction), natural selection favored organisms that repeated behavior that had "worked" in the past, made a greater range of responses in the situation (behavioral variability), emitted more forceful responses to the circumstances, and attacked other members of the species associated with the cessation of reinforcement.

Extinction Burst

When extinction is started, operant behavior tends to increase in frequency. That is, organisms repeat behavior that has been reinforced. A pigeon will initially increase the rate of key pecking, and you may raise your hand more often than you did in the past. You may explain your increased tendency to raise your hand by telling a friend "The instructor doesn't see me; I have an important point to make." If the bird could talk it might also "explain" why it was pecking at an increased rate. The point is that an initial increase in the rate of response, or **extinction burst**, occurs when reinforcement is first withdrawn.

Operant Variability

In addition to extinction bursts, operant behavior becomes increasingly variable as extinction proceeds (**operant variability**). Behavioral variation increases the chances that the organisms will reinstate reinforcement or contact other sources of reinforcement. You may wave your hand about in an attempt to catch the professor's eye; the bird may strike the key in different locations and with different amounts of force. A classic experiment by Antonitis (1951) demonstrated this effect. Rats were taught to poke their noses through a 50-cm-long slot for food reinforcement. When this occurred, a photocell was triggered and a photograph of the animal was taken. The position of the rat and the angle of its body were recorded at the moment of reinforcement. After the rat reliably poked its nose through the slot, it was placed on extinction. Following this, reinforcement was reinstated, then extinguished, and in a final phase the operant was again reinforced.

Antonitis reported that reinforcement produced a stereotyped pattern of response. The rat repeatedly poked its nose through the slot at approximately the same location, and the position of its body was held at a particular angle. When extinction occurred, the nose poking and position of the body varied. During extinction, the animal poked its nose over the entire length of the slot. Reinforcing the operant after extinction produced even more stereotyped behavior than the original conditioning.

Pear (1985) found a similar effect with pigeons. When birds were reinforced for pecking a key after an average of only 15 s, they stayed close to the key and emitted routine patterns of head and body movements. When these animals were reinforced on a similar schedule, but one that required an average wait of 5 min, they strayed further from the key. Both of these patterns developed during extinction, but as extinction continued their behavior became much more variable.

Force of Response

Reinforcement may be made contingent on the **force of response** (or other properties) resulting in **response differentiation**. Notterman (1959) measured the force that rats used to press a lever during periods of reinforcement and extinction. During reinforcement sessions, animals came to press the lever with a force that varied within a relatively narrow range. When extinction occurred, the force of lever pressing became more variable. Interestingly, some responses were more forceful than any emitted during reinforcement or during operant level. This increase in response force may be due to emotional behavior generated by extinction procedures.

For example, imagine that you have pushed a button for an elevator but the elevator does not arrive, and you have an important appointment on the 28th floor. At first you increase the frequency of pressing the elevator button; you also change the way you hit the button. You probably feel angry and frustrated, and you may smash the button. These responses and accompanying feelings occur because of the change from reinforcement to extinction.

Emotional Responses

Consider what happens when someone puts money in a vending machine and is not reinforced with an item (e.g., a beverage). The person who is placed on extinction may hit the machine, curse, and engage in other emotional behavior. Soda machines once killed several US soldiers. Young soldiers at the peak of physical fitness are capable of emitting forceful operants. When some of the soldiers put money in soda machines that failed to operate, extinction-induced emotional behavior became so powerful that the men pulled over the 2-ton machines. Thus, their deaths were an indirect outcome of emotional behavior produced by extinction.

A variety of **emotional responses** occur under conditions of extinction. Birds flap their wings, rats bite the response lever, and humans may swear and kick at a vending machine. One important kind of emotional behavior that occurs during extinction is aggression. Azrin, Hutchinson, and Hake (1966) trained pigeons to peck a key for food. After training, a second immobilized pigeon was placed in the operant chamber. The "target" bird was restrained and placed on an apparatus that caused a switch to close whenever the bird was attacked. Attacks to the target reliably occurred when the contingencies of reinforcement were changed from CRF to extinction. Many of the attacks were vicious and unrelenting, lasting up to 10 min.

In children with severe behavior disorders, the modification of self-injurious behavior (SIB) maintained by social attention often uses extinction procedures. Two commonly observed side effects with the onset of extinction are the extinction burst (a sudden increase in the SIB) and extinction-induced aggression. Lerman, Iwata, and Wallace (1999) analyzed 41 sets of data on individuals who received extinction treatment for SIB, and found that bursts and aggression occurred in nearly 50% of the cases. When extinction was accompanied by other procedures, such as differential reinforcement of alternative behavior (DRA), bursting and aggression were substantially reduced.

The recommendation is to use other reinforcement and stimulus control procedures with extinction to lessen the side effects of bursting and aggression.

Discriminated Extinction

Suppose that a pigeon was reinforced for pecking a key in the presence of a green light. However, when a red light came on, pecking was not reinforced. During the course of training, the animal would emit emotional responses and extinction bursts when the red light was turned on. Following training, the bird would not emit this behavior and it would simply stop responding when the light changed from green to red. The red light became a *discriminative stimulus (S^D) that signaled a period of extinction.* This effect is called **discriminated extinction**, and is commonly observed in human behavior. A sign on a vending machine that reads OUT OF ORDER is an S$^\Delta$ that signals extinction for putting money in the machine.

The respondent procedures for rapid extinction (see Chapter 3) seem close to the operant procedure of discriminated extinction. Comparing the procedures, we assume that the conditioned response to the light is similar to the emission of an operant on a given occasion. Discriminative extinction involves signaling extinction periods with an exteroceptive stimulus, such as a change in key color from green to red. This change from green to red in the operant procedure is like adding the tone during respondent extinction. When the key is green, a pigeon is trained to peck it for food. Every once in a while the key color changes to red, and reinforcement for pecking no longer occurs. During these extinction periods, rate of response should decline. This decline would occur more rapidly when extinction is signaled by a change in color than when the key color remains the same. Finally, since the red key is consistently associated with extinction, it acquires a discriminative function (S$^\Delta$), suppressing responding when it is presented.

Resistance to Extinction

As extinction proceeds, emotional behavior subsides and the rate of response declines. When extinction has been in effect long enough, behavior may return to operant level. In practice, however, a return to operant level is rarely accomplished. This is because many extinction sessions are usually required before operant level is attained. Extinction is typically measured as the number of responses emitted in some amount of time. For example, a bird may be reinforced on CRF for ten consecutive daily sessions; following this, extinction is initiated. The pigeon's responses are recorded over three extinction sessions. The number of responses emitted by the bird or the rate of response during the last session may be used to index **resistance to extinction**. Operants are rapidly extinguished after a few reinforced responses, but when operants are reinforced many times, resistance to extinction increases. Experiments have shown that resistance to extinction reaches a maximum after 50 to 80 reinforced responses (Hearst, 1961; Perin, 1942).

Partial Reinforcement effect (PRE)

Resistance to extinction is substantially increased when a partial or **intermittent schedule of reinforcement** has been used to maintain behavior. On an intermittent reinforcement schedule, only some responses are reinforced. For example, instead of reinforcing each response (CRF), the experimenter may program reinforcement after 100 key pecks have been emitted. In this situation, the bird must emit 100 pecks before food is presented. This intermittent schedule will generate many more responses during extinction than continuous reinforcement. When people are described as having a persistent or tenacious personality, their behavior may reflect the effects of intermittent reinforcement.

Nevin (1988) indicates that the **partial reinforcement effect (PRE)** is the result of two basic processes: reinforcement and discrimination. According to Nevin's analysis, reinforcement has the single effect of increasing resistance to change. That is, *the higher the rate of reinforcement for an operant, the greater the resistance to change.* The implication is that behavior maintained by a CRF schedule is more resistant to change than behavior controlled by an intermittent schedule of reinforcement.

However, extinction occurs more rapidly on CRF compared with intermittent reinforcement. One reason for the discrepancy is that *discrimination* between reinforcement and extinction is more rapid on CRF rather than intermittent reinforcement. That is, an organism discriminates the difference between a high and steady rate of reinforcement (CRF) and no reinforcement (extinction) more easily than the difference between a low and intermittent rate of reinforcement and no reinforcement. In tests for resistance to extinction, the discrimination factor overrides the rate of reinforcement variable, and animals show greater resistance on intermittent than CRF schedules. If the effects of discrimination (between reinforcement and extinction) are controlled, behavior maintained by CRF is in fact more resistant to extinction than on intermittent schedules of reinforcement.

An additional reason for increased resistance to extinction following intermittent reinforcement involves *contact with the contingencies.* A rat that is reinforced for every 100 responses must emit 100 responses before contacting the change from reinforcement to extinction. In contrast, an animal that is reinforced for each response contacts the extinction contingency immediately. Since each response is a non-reinforced occurrence, the animal repeatedly encounters the change to extinction. If an animal on CRF emits 50 responses during extinction, it has contacted the extinction contingency 50 times. A rat on intermittent reinforcement may have to emit 5000 responses to have equal experience with the change in contingencies.

Discriminative Stimuli and Extinction

Intermittent reinforcement is not the only factor that determines the return to operant level during extinction. Resistance to extinction is also affected by discriminative stimuli that are conditioned during sessions of reinforcement. Skinner showed that "maximal responding during extinction is obtained only when the conditions under which the response was reinforced are precisely reproduced" (Skinner, 1950, p. 204).

Pigeons were trained to peck a yellow triangle on an intermittent schedule of food reinforcement. After training, a red triangle was substituted for the yellow one and extinction was started. During 15 min of extinction in the presence of the red triangle, the rate of response substantially declined. At this point, the yellow triangle replaced the red one but extinction was continued. The effect of introducing the yellow triangle was that rapid responding began immediately, and the usual extinction curve followed. This effect is portrayed in Figure 4.15, in which responding in the presence of the yellow triangle is at a high rate during the first 30 min of intermittent reinforcement. When the red triangle and extinction were introduced, the rate of response declined. Finally, extinction was continued and the yellow triangle was reinstated. Notice that the rate of response immediately recovers and then declines toward extinction.

Spontaneous Recovery

An interesting phenomenon that occurs during extinction is **spontaneous recovery**. After a session of extinction, the rate of response may be close to operant level. At this point, the animal is taken out of the operant chamber and returned to a holding cage. The next day, the organism is again placed in the operant chamber and extinction is continued. Surprisingly, the animal begins to respond

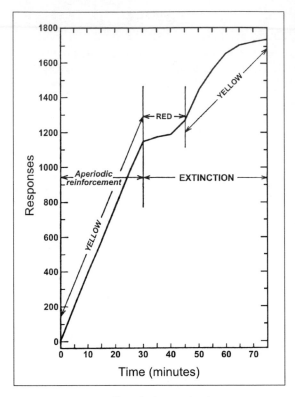

FIG. 4.15 Responding during extinction as a function of discrimination. Responding in the presence of the yellow triangle is high during the first 30 min of intermittent reinforcement. When the red triangle and extinction are introduced, the rate of response declines. Extinction is continued and the yellow triangle is reinstated. When the yellow triangle is presented, the rate of response recovers and then declines toward extinction. From "Are theories of learning necessary?" by B. F. Skinner, 1950, *Psychological Review, 57,* 193–216. Reprinted with permission of the American Psychological Association.

above operant level, and this defines spontaneous recovery. Over repeated sessions of extinction, the amount of recovery decreases. If many sessions of extinction are provided, the rate of response will no longer recover.

Spontaneous recovery is really not spontaneous. Stimuli that have accompanied reinforced responding are usually presented at the beginning of extinction sessions (habituation may also be involved; see Pear, 2001, p. 63). Skinner (1950) has noted that handling procedures and the stimulation arising from being placed in an operant chamber set the occasion for responding at the beginning of each extinction session. Skinner states:

> No matter how carefully an animal is handled, the stimulation coincident with the beginning of an experiment must be extensive and unlike anything occurring in the latter part of an experimental period. Responses have been reinforced in the presence of, or shortly following, this stimulation. In extinction it is present for only a few moments. When the organism is again placed in the experimental situation the stimulation is restored; further responses are emitted as in the case of the yellow triangle [see aforementioned experiment]. The only way to achieve full extinction in the presence of the stimulation of starting an experiment is to start the experiment repeatedly.
>
> (Skinner, 1950, pp. 199–200)

Human behavior also shows spontaneous recovery. Imagine that you are stranded in a secluded mountain cabin during a week-long snowstorm. The telephone rings, you answer, but all you get is the dial tone. You shout at the dial tone and bang the disconnect button repeatedly. Next, you try to contact the telephone company and discover that you are not able to dial out. Over the course of the first day the phone rings many times, you answer it, but it does not work. By the end of the day, you may not be inclined to answer the telephone—you just let it keep on ringing. The next morning you are having breakfast and the phone rings. What do you do? The best guess is that you will again answer the phone. You may say to yourself "Perhaps they have fixed the line." On this second day of extinction, you answer the phone but give up more quickly. On day 3, the phone rings at 10:00 a.m. and even though you doubt that it will work, you answer it "just to check it out." By day 4, you have had it with the "damn phone and the stupid telephone company," and extinction is complete.

Reinstatement of Responding

Another kind of response recovery, called **reinstatement**, involves the recovery of behavior when the reinforcer is presented alone after a period of extinction (Bouton, 2004; Bouton & Swartzentruber, 1991). In an operant model of reinstatement, Baker, Steinwald, and Bouton (1991) established responding for food reinforcement and then extinguished the lever-pressing response by withholding food. After extinction, reinstatement involved response-independent delivery of food without the response levers (using retractable levers), followed by tests with the response levers available. On these tests, animals that were given response-independent food deliveries showed more reinstatement of lever pressing than control animals. The findings from three experiments ruled out superstitious reinforcement and discriminative after-effects of food as the basis of reinstatement. Instead, the results indicated that response-independent reinforcement activates contextual S^Ds from the original learning situation that set the occasion for previously reinforced behavior (lever pressing).

At the practical level, reinstatement is often observed in the treatment of drug addiction. After becoming a drug addict (acquisition), the addict may seek help for his addiction, and treatment may involve drug withdrawal (extinction) in a therapeutic setting. When the client is returned to his former neighborhood and drug culture (original setting), drugs may be available on a response-independent basis, handed out on street corners to get him hooked or freely available from his friends. Free hits of drugs would activate the original setting events that have set the occasion for obtaining and using drugs in the past, reinstating drug use.

A similar analysis can be applied to the problem of obesity. In this case, the operant is selection and consumption of palatable high-calorie foods (acquisition). Dieting and choice of low-calorie alternatives may be analyzed as an extinction procedure for eating high-calorie foods (extinction). Response reinstatement occurs when palatable snacks and foods are freely available in the cupboard or refrigerator, following the dieting. Or perhaps you have your friends over and prepare rich desserts that are freely available after the guests have gone home. Response-independent presentation of palatable foods would re-establish control by setting events (S^Ds) that have regulated selection and eating of high-calorie foods. The obese person may have to throw out all the high-fat/sugar foods and avoid getting together with friends. Even these drastic measures may not work.

Unfortunately, it is impossible to eliminate all of the setting events that control eating of high-calorie foods. The best solution is to learn new ways of acting in the original setting—for example, when offered a piece of pie, ask for blueberries. Requests for calorie-wise food must be maintained initially by social reinforcement ("good choice" from friends and family) until the long-term consequences of weight loss and health can have an effect.

Extinction and Forgetting

During extinction, operant behavior decreases over time. People often talk about the weakening of behavior as loss of memory or forgetting. An important question concerns the procedural differences between forgetting and extinction. Extinction is a procedure in which a previously reinforced response no longer produces reinforcement. The opportunity to emit the operant remains available during extinction. Thus, the pigeon may still peck the illuminated key, or the rat may continue to press the response lever. In contrast, forgetting is said to occur after the mere passage of time. An organism that has learned a response is tested for retention after some amount of time has passed. In this case, there is no apparent opportunity to emit the behavior.

Skinner (1938) designed an experiment to assess the behavioral loss that occurs after the passage of time. In this experiment, four rats were trained to press a lever, and each animal received

FIG. 4.16 Average extinction curves of four rats, 1 day after training and 45 days after training. Curves are taken from B. F. Skinner, 1938, *The Behavior of Organisms*, Appleton-Century-Crofts, New York.

100 reinforced responses. After 45 days of rest, each animal was placed in the operant chamber and responding was extinguished. The number of responses emitted during extinction was compared with the performance of four other rats selected from an earlier experiment. These animals were similar in age, training, and number of reinforced responses to the experimental subjects. The comparison animals had received extinction 1 day after reinforced bar pressing.

Figure 4.16 shows the results of Skinner's experiment. The results are presented as the cumulative-average number of responses emitted by each group of animals. The group that received extinction 1 day after response strengthening emitted an average of 86 responses in 1 h. The group that was extinguished after 45 days made an average of 69 responses in 1 h. Notice that both groups of animals show a similar number of responses during the first few minutes of extinction. In other words, the animals in both groups immediately began to press the lever when placed in the operant chamber. This shows that the rats that received extinction after 45 days had not forgotten what to do to get food (Skinner, 1938).

Following the first few minutes of extinction, there is a difference in the cumulative-average number of responses for the two groups. Resistance to extinction is apparently reduced by the passage of time. Rats that were required to wait 45 days before extinction generated fewer responses per hour than those that were given extinction 1 day after reinforcement. Although the curves rise at different rates, animals in both groups appear to stop responding after approximately 90 non-reinforced lever presses. Overall, the results suggest that the passage of time affects resistance to extinction, but a well-established performance is not forgotten (for an account of remembering in elephants, see Markowitz, Schmidt, Nadal, & Squier, 1975; see also Dale, 2008).

ON THE APPLIED SIDE: Extinction of Temper Tantrums

Williams (1959) has shown how extinction effects play an important role in the modification of human behavior. In this study, a 20-month-old child was making life miserable for his parents by having temper tantrums when put to bed. If the parents stayed up with the child, he did not scream and cry, and he eventually went to sleep. A well-known source of reinforcement for children is parental attention, and Williams reasoned that this was probably maintaining the bedtime behavior. That is, when the parents left the bedroom, the child began screaming and crying. These tantrums were reinforced by the return of the parents to the bedroom. The parental behavior stopped the tantrum, and withdrawal of screaming by the child reinforced the parental behavior of returning to the bedroom. Based on these contingencies, the parents were spending a good part of each evening in the child's room waiting for him to go to sleep. At this point, the parents were advised to implement extinction by leaving the room and closing the door after the child was put to bed. Figure 4.17 demonstrates the rapid decline in duration of crying when this was done (first extinction).

When extinction was first attempted, the child screamed and cried for 45 min. However, on the next night he did not cry at all. On the third night, the child emitted tantrums for 10 min.

By the end of 10 days, the boy was smiling at his parents when they left the room. Unfortunately, his aunt, who reinforced crying by staying in the room with him, put the boy to bed and his temper tantrums reoccurred. A second extinction procedure was then implemented. The duration of crying was longer for the second than for the first period of extinction. The higher probability of response during the second extinction phase is presumably caused by the intermittent reinforcement of tantrums. Recall that intermittent reinforcement increases resistance to extinction. Fortunately, the boy was not reinforced again, and his tantrums eventually declined to a zero rate. At a 2-year follow-up, the parents reported that his bedtime tantrums had been completely eliminated.

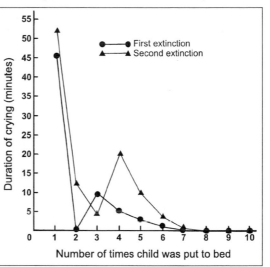

FIG. 4.17 First and second extinction procedures for a child's temper tantrums. Adapted from "The elimination of tantrum behavior by extinction procedures," by C. D. Williams, 1959, *Journal of Abnormal and Social Psychology, 59*, p. 269.

CHAPTER SUMMARY

In this important chapter, we have addressed the concept that behavior is a function of its consequences. Operants are responses that operate on the environment to produce changes and as a result have an increased (or decreased) probability of occurrence. The measure of the probability of response is most often the rate of operant behavior. If the rate of the particular behavior (or class of behaviors) increases as a result of some specific consequence, then that consequence is defined as a positive reinforcer. The exact definition of a positive reinforcer as a stimulus or event that increases or maintains the rate of the response upon which it is contingent is fundamental to the science of behavior. The reinforcer is contingent (dependent) upon (i.e., delivered after) the response, and no matter what the stimulus, it increases the frequency of operant behavior.

Other situations exist that require formal definitions. For example, when you encounter a disturbing event you may turn away or cover your ears; these behaviors are strengthened by the removal or reduction in occurrence of the event. This is a type of response strengthening called negative (subtracts the event) reinforcement (increases the escape response). Other consequences reduce the rate of the response that produces them and are called punishers. The procedure of making a punisher contingent on a response and the response decreases is called punishment.

If some behavior has a low probability of occurrence, the response can be shaped by reinforcement of successive approximations. In this way new behavior is generated from the variability existing in the response repertoire. When reinforcement is no longer delivered, the rate of the response declines back to baseline. This is the process of extinction. For example, if a rat presses a lever and food pellets are delivered, it will continue to press the lever as long as some responses are followed by food. When no pellets are delivered, however, the rate of lever pressing eventually declines to zero. This simple demonstration of reinforcement followed by extinction illustrates the central point of the chapter—behavior is a function of its consequences.

Behavior analysis is a formal discipline based on manipulating consequences and thereby shaping, directing, and altering the behavior of organisms. Precise procedures and apparatus have been invented in order to systematize this analysis.

KEY WORDS

Ad libitum weight

Behavioral variability

Conditioned reinforcer

Contingency of reinforcement

Contingent response

Continuous reinforcement (CRF)

Cumulative record

Cumulative recorder

Deprivation operation

Differential reinforcement

Discriminated extinction

Discriminative stimulus (S^D)

Elicited (behavior)

Emitted (behavior)

Emotional response

Extinction

Extinction burst

Force of response

Free operant method

Instrumental response

Intermittent schedule of reinforcement

In-vitro reinforcement

Latency

Law of effect

Magazine training

Negative punishment

Negative reinforcement

Neuroplasticity

Ontogenetic selection

Operant

Operant chamber

Operant class

Operant conditioning

Operant level

Operant rate

Operant variability

Partial reinforcement effect (PRE)

Positive punishment

Positive reinforcement

Positive reinforcer

Premack principle

Probability of response

Rate of response

Reinstatement (of behavior)

Repertoire (of behavior)

Resistance to extinction

Response deprivation

Response differentiation

Response hierarchy

Satiation

S-delta (S^Δ)

Shaping

Spontaneous recovery

Successive approximation

Topography

ON THE WEB

http://psych.athabascau.ca Click on the sidebar on Positive Reinforcement. The purpose of this site is to teach the concept of positive reinforcement and also to provide an idea of the kind of self-instructional exercises that are used at Athabasca University.

www.wagntrain.com/OC A website for all those seeking to use positive reinforcement in animal training. If you have a dog or cat, you can use the "clicker training" method of positive reinforcement to teach your animal new behavioral sequences and skills.

www.karawynn.net/mishacat This website is about the toilet training of Mischa the cat. The trainer does not provide the general principles that lead a cat from the litter box to the toilet, but many of the principles are outlined in Chapter 4. See if you can figure out how to train any cat to do what Mischa did.

BRIEF QUIZ

1. The term operant comes from the verb _____ and refers to behavior that _____.

   (a) opponent; opposes its consequences in a given environment
   (b) opendum; opens the door to its effects on a given occasion
   (c) operates; operates on the environment to produce effects
   (d) opara; presents the opportunity to respond on a given occasion

2. What defines a contingency of reinforcement?

   (a) discriminative stimulus
   (b) operant
   (c) reinforcement
   (d) all of the above

3. Which of the following is *not* one of the four basic contingencies?

   (a) positive reinforcement
   (b) positive extinction
   (c) negative punishment
   (d) negative reinforcement

4. In terms of rewards and intrinsic motivation, Cameron et al. (2001) conducted a statistical procedure called _____, and one of the findings indicated that verbal rewards _____ performance and interest on tasks.

   (a) multivariate analysis; decreased
   (b) meta-analysis; decreased
   (c) meta-analysis; increased
   (d) multivariate analysis; increased

5. The Premack principle states that a higher-frequency behavior will:

   (a) function as reinforcement for a lower-frequency behavior
   (b) function as punishment for a high-frequency behavior
   (c) function as intermittent reinforcement for a low-frequency behavior
   (d) none of the above

6. To experimentally study the probability of response, a researcher uses _____ as the basic measure and follows the _____ method.

   (a) latency; T-maze
   (b) latency; free operant
   (c) operant rate; T-maze
   (d) operant rate; free operant

7. Shaping of behavior involves:

   (a) the molding of a response class by the physical arrangement of the operant chamber
   (b) reinforcing closer and closer approximations to the final performance
   (c) withholding and giving food for correct performance of a specified level of response
   (d) none of the above

8. A classic experiment on the effects of extinction by Antonitis (1951) involved:

   (a) nose poking by rats for food reinforcement
   (b) photographs of the rats' position and body angle
   (c) increased variability of nose poking during extinction
   (d) all of the above

9. In terms of response stereotypes, variability, and reinforcement, the work by Barry Schwartz shows that reinforcement can produce _____ patterns of behavior, while the work of Neuringer and his colleagues indicates that reinforcement can produce _____.

   (a) stereotyped; response variability
   (b) response variability; stereotyped
   (c) stereotyped; response stability
   (d) response stability; response variability

10. Which of the following is involved in the partial reinforcement effect?

   (a) longer extinction on intermittent reinforcement compared with CRF
   (b) the higher the rate of reinforcement the greater the resistance to change
   (c) discrimination between reinforcement and extinction is more rapid on CRF
   (d) all of the above

Answers to Brief Quiz: 1, c (p. 85); 2, d (p. 87); 3, b (Fig. 4.2); 4, c (p. 90); 5, a (p. 91); 6, d (p. 95); 7, b (p. 99); 8, d (p. 106); 9, a (p. 105); 10, d (p. 109).

Schedules of Reinforcement

1. Learn about *schedules of reinforcement* and why they are important.
2. Investigate rates of reinforcement and how behavior is made resistant to change.
3. Inquire about behavior during transition between schedules of reinforcement.
4. Discover how schedules of reinforcement are involved in cigarette smoking.
5. Learn about the molecular and molar accounts of performance on schedules of reinforcement.

The stimuli that precede operants and the consequences that follow them may be arranged in many different ways. A **schedule of reinforcement** describes this arrangement. In other words, a schedule of reinforcement is a prescription that states how and when discriminative stimuli and behavioral consequences will be presented (Morse, 1966). In the laboratory, sounding a buzzer in an operant chamber may be a signal (S^D) that sets the occasion for each lever press (operant) to produce food (consequence). A similar schedule operates when a dark room sets the occasion for a person to turn on a lamp that is followed by light in the room.

At first glance, a rat pressing a lever for food and a person turning on a light seem to have little in common. Humans are very complex organisms—they build cities, write books, go to college, go to war, conduct experiments, and do many other things that rats cannot do. In addition, pressing a bar for food appears to be very different from switching on a light. Nonetheless, performances controlled by schedules of reinforcement have been found to be remarkably similar for different organisms, many types of behavior, and a variety of reinforcers. When the schedule of reinforcement is the same, a child solving math problems for teacher approval may generate a pattern of behavior that is comparable to a bird pecking a key for water.

IMPORTANCE OF SCHEDULES OF REINFORCEMENT

Schedules of reinforcement have been investigated over the last six decades. They were first described by B. F. Skinner in the 1930s and were a major discovery. Charles Ferster and B.F. Skinner reported (Ferster & Skinner, 1957) the first and most comprehensive study of schedules ever conducted. Their work on this topic is unsurpassed and represents the most extensive study of this critical independent variable in behavior science. Today, few studies focus directly on simple schedules of reinforcement. However, the lawful relations that have emerged from the analysis of schedules remain an important part of the science of behavior, and are used in virtually every study reported in the *Journal of the Experimental Analysis of Behavior*.

FOCUS ON: C. B. Ferster and Schedules of Reinforcement

In 1957, Charles Bohris Ferster (Figure 5.1) together with B. F. Skinner published *Schedules of Reinforcement*, the most comprehensive description of the behavior (performance) generated by different contingencies of reinforcement. Charles was born in Feehold, New Jersey on 1 November 1922 in the Depression years and, even though life was difficult for the Ferster family, he completed high school and entered Rutgers University in 1940. After receiving his BS degree at Rutgers and doing military service from 1943 to 1946, Charles went on to Columbia University where he studied the reinforcing effects of stimuli (conditioned reinforcers) presented during intermittent reinforcement. He obtained his PhD in 1950 and took a Research Fellowship at Harvard in the behavioral laboratory of B. F. Skinner.

At the Harvard laboratory, Charlie (as he was called) impressed Skinner by vastly improving the design of the equipment used to study the performance of pigeons on a variety of schedules of reinforcement. For example, he made several improvements to the cumulative recorder that eventually resulted in the design by Ralph Gerbrands of the first modern-style instrument, as shown in Chapter 4. In the laboratory, Charlie worked night and day, and together with Skinner made Grand Rounds each morning, inspecting cumulative records of pigeons' rates of response and making changes to the programmed schedules. Often there were surprises as Ferster and Skinner tried to predict the performance of the birds under complex schedules; they would then add a new piece of control equipment such as a clock or timer to see what would happen—and again the researchers found the results surprising and dramatic. Charlie said that over a year he stopped predicting the outcomes of experiments, as the prediction was often incorrect and "the pigeon really did know best what it was he was likely to do and the conditions under which he would do it" (Ferster, 2000, p. 306).

Ferster and Skinner noted that the only contact that the pigeons had with the programming equipment was at the *moment of reinforcement* but that many stimuli could be involved at this moment, determining the current rate of response and changes in response rates. Stimuli arising from the passage of time and from the number of responses made on the schedule were obvious sources of stimulus control. Ferster and Skinner designed experiments to enhance these stimuli so as to observe the effects in the cumulative records. In recalling these experiments and interactions with Skinner, Ferster states:

FIG. 5.1   C. B. Ferster. © 1961 Society for the Experimental Analysis of Behavior, Inc. Published with permission.

> There were many personal and natural consequences of completing a successful experiment [other than the results from the actual behavior of the birds]. A successful experiment led to conversations about the data, the new devices we could build, the new experiments that had to be started, and the new ways we could organize our past experience from the laboratory.
>
> When we discovered a new degree of orderliness or an unexpected but rewarding result on morning rounds, there was always much excitement

and talk about where the experiment might go next and how to manage the equipment for the next experiment that was burning to be done because of the new result.

When new discoveries accumulated too fast . . . there were planning sessions which were always great fun and very exciting. . . . I learned the value of large sheets of paper which we used to aid our thought and to chart our progress. . . . The theoretical structures [organized by the charts] and programmatic aspects of our work appeared as [headings . . .] to appear as chapter and subchapter titles in *Schedules of Reinforcement*. Each entry prompted rearrangements of the theoretical pattern and suggested new experiments and programs which in turn prompted further rearrangements of the data. The interactions between these theoretical exercises and changes in ongoing experiments in the laboratory were continuous and constituted an important reinforcer.

(Ferster, 2000, p. 307)

Looking back on his own experience of writing *Schedules of Reinforcement* and what he had learned, Charlie Ferster stated that:

a potential reinforcing environment exists for every individual, however, if he will only emit the required performances on the proper occasion. One has merely to paint the picture, write the symphony, produce the machine, tell the funny story, give affection artfully or manipulate the environment and observe the behavior of the animal, and the world will respond in kind with prestige, money, social response, love, and recognition for scientific achievement.

(Ferster, 2000, p. 311)

The knowledge that has accumulated about the effects of schedules is central to understanding behavior regulation. G. S. Reynolds underscored this point and wrote:

Schedules of reinforcement have regular, orderly, and profound effects on the organism's rate of responding. The importance of schedules of reinforcement cannot be overestimated. No description, account, or explanation of any operant behavior of any organism is complete unless the schedule of reinforcement is specified. Schedules are the mainsprings of behavioral control, and thus the study of schedules is central to the study of behavior. . . . Behavior that has been attributed to the supposed drives, needs, expectations, ruminations, or insights of the organism can often be related much more exactly to regularities produced by schedules of reinforcement.

(Reynolds, 1966b, p. 60)

Modern technology has made it possible to analyze performance on schedules of reinforcement in increasing detail. Nonetheless, early experiments on schedules remain important. The experimental analysis of behavior is a progressive science in which observations and experiments build on one another. In this chapter, we shall present early and later research on schedules of reinforcement. The analysis of schedule performance will range from a global consideration of cumulative records to a detailed consideration of the time between responses.

BEHAVIOR ANALYSIS: A PROGRESSIVE SCIENCE

The experimental analysis of behavior is a progressive enterprise. Research findings are accumulated and integrated to provide a general account of the behavior of organisms. Often, simple animals in highly controlled settings are studied. The strategy is to build a comprehensive theory of behavior that rests on direct observation and experimentation.

The field emphasizes a descriptive approach and discourages speculations that go beyond the data. Such speculations include reference to the organism's memory, thought processes, expectations, and undocumented accounts based on presumed physiological states. For example, a behavioral account of schedules of reinforcement provides a detailed description of how behavior is altered by contingencies of reinforcement. One such account is based on evidence that a particular schedule sets up differential reinforcement of the time between responses (interresponse times, or IRT; see later in this chapter). An alternative account is that behavior is integrated into larger units of performance according to the molar or macro contingencies of reinforcement (overall rate of reinforcement). Both of these analyses provide an understanding of an organism's behavior in terms of specific environment–behavior relationships.

Recall that behavior analysts study the behavior of organisms, including people, for its own sake. Behavior is not studied to make inferences about hypothetical mental states or real physiological processes. Although most behaviorists emphasize the importance of biology and physiological processes, they focus on the interplay of behavior with the environment.

Contemporary behavior analysis continues to build on previous research. The extension of behavior principles to more complex processes and especially to human behavior is of primary importance. The analysis remains focused on the environmental conditions that control the behavior of organisms. Schedules of reinforcement concern the arrangement of environmental events that support behavior. The analysis of schedule effects is currently viewed within a biological context. In this analysis, biological factors play several roles. One way in which biology affects behavior is through specific physiological events that function as reinforcement and discriminative stimuli (see Chapter 1). Biological variables may also constrain or enhance environment–behavior relationships, as we have noted. As behavior analysis and the other biological sciences progress, an understanding of biological factors becomes increasingly important for a comprehensive theory of behavior.

Schedules and Patterns of Response

Patterns of response develop as a result of the organism interacting with a schedule of reinforcement (Ferster & Skinner, 1957). These patterns come about after an animal has experience with the *contingency of reinforcement* ($S^D : R \rightarrow S^r$ arrangement) defined by a particular schedule. Subjects are exposed to a schedule of reinforcement and, following an acquisition period, behavior typically settles into a consistent or **steady-state performance** (Sidman, 1960). It may take many experimental sessions before a particular pattern emerges, but once it does, the orderliness of behavior is remarkable.

The first description of schedule performance was provided by B. F. Skinner in his book, *The Behavior of Organisms* (Skinner, 1938). In the preface to the seventh printing of that book, Skinner writes that "the cumulative records . . . purporting to show orderly changes in the behavior of individual organisms, occasioned some surprise and possibly, in some quarters, suspicion" (p. xii). Any suspicion was put to rest when Skinner's observations were replicated in many other experiments (see Morse, 1966, for a review of early work on schedules of reinforcement).

The steady-state behavior generated when a fixed number of responses are reinforced illustrates one of these patterns. For example, a hungry rat might be required to press a lever 10 times to get a food pellet. Following reinforcement, the animal has to make another 10 responses to produce the next bit of food, then 10 more responses. In industry this requirement is referred to as piece rate.

When organisms (rats, pigeons, or humans) are reinforced after a fixed number of responses, a pause-and-run pattern of behavior develops. Responses required by the schedule are made rapidly and result in reinforcement. Following each reinforcement there is a pause in responding, then another quick burst of responses (see the section on fixed ratio later in this chapter for more detail). This pattern repeats over and over again and occurs even when the size of the schedule is changed. A pause-and-run pattern has been found for many species, including horses (Myers & Mesker, 1960), chickens (Lane, 1961), a vulture (Witoslawski, Anderson, & Hanson, 1963), and children (Orlando & Bijou, 1960).

COMMENT ON: Inner Causes, Schedules, and Response Patterns

We sometimes speak of people being "highly motivated" when we observe them investing energy or time in some project. Motivation seems to explain why people behave as they do. Schoolchildren are said to be unmotivated when they put off or fail to do assignments; in contrast, children are highly motivated when they study hard and overachieve. From a behavioral perspective, there is no need to infer a hypothetical internal process of motivation to understand this kind of behavior. Schedules of reinforcement generate unique and predictable patterns of behavior that are often taken as signs of high motivation; other schedules produce pausing and low rates of response used as indicators of low motivation. In both cases, behavior is due to environmental contingencies rather than the inferred inner cause of motivation.

Similarly, habits or personality traits are said to be "response dispositions that are activated automatically by context cues that co-occurred with responses during past performance" (Neal, Wood & Quinn, 2006). Here reference is made to internal dispositions that account for regular and frequent actions. Instead of inferring dispositions as internal causes, one might say that habits or traits are patterns of steady-state responding; these regularities of behavior are maintained by the consistency of the schedule of reinforcement. That is, a consistent or reliable schedule of reinforcement generates stable rates and patterns of responding. It is these characteristics of behavior that are often used to infer dispositional causes. A behavior analysis indicates that the real causes are the behavioral contingencies rather than dispositional states within us.

Schedules and Natural Contingencies

In the everyday environment, behavior is often reinforced on an intermittent basis. That is, operants are reinforced occasionally rather than each time they are emitted. Every time a child cries, she is not reinforced with attention. Each time a predator hunts, it is not successful. When you dial the number for airport information, sometimes you get through, but often the exchange is busy. Buses do not immediately arrive when you go to a bus stop. It is clear that persistence is often essential for survival, and therefore being able to account for such behavior on the basis of the schedule that maintains it is a major discovery. In concluding his review of schedule research, Dr. Michael Zeiler states:

> It is impossible to study behavior either in or outside the laboratory without encountering a schedule of reinforcement: whenever behavior is maintained by a reinforcing stimulus, some schedule is in

effect and is exerting its characteristic influences. Only when there is a clear understanding of how schedules operate will it be possible to understand the effects of reinforcing stimuli on behavior.

(Zeiler, 1977, p. 229)

Consider a bird foraging for food. The bird turns over sticks or leaves and once in a while finds a seed or insect. These bits of food occur only every now and then, and the distribution of reinforcement is the schedule that maintains the animal's foraging behavior. If you were watching this bird hunt for food, you would probably see the animal's head bobbing up and down. You might also see the bird pause and look around, change direction, and move to a new spot. This sort of activity is often attributed to the animal's instinctive behavior patterns. However, labeling the behavior as instinctive does not explain it. Although biology certainly plays a role in this episode, perhaps as importantly, so does the schedule of food reinforcement.

Carl Cheney (one of the authors of this textbook) and his colleagues created a laboratory analog of foraging that allowed pigeons to choose between two food patches by pecking keys (Cheney, Bonem, & Bonem, 1985). The density of food available from pecking either key was based on two concurrent progressive ratio schedules of reinforcement that increased or decreased the ratio requirement with the amount of foraging. As reinforcers were removed from one patch they became more scarce and required more responses to produce them; this was a progressively increasing ratio schedule (or depleting patch of food). Concurrently, the number of responses for each reinforcement decreased in the other patch (or a repleting patch of food)—a progressively decreasing ratio schedule. As would be expected, this change in reinforcement density up and down generated switching back and forth between the two patches. However, to change patches the center key had to be pecked, which simulated travel time and effort between patches (the side keys). Cheney and his colleagues found that the cost of hunting (the schedule of reinforcement for pecking) in a patch, the effort (number of responses) required to change patches, and the rate of food replacement in the alternative patch all contributed to the likelihood that an animal would change patches. This research is an interesting example of an animal model of foraging that uses schedules of reinforcement to simulate natural contingencies in the wild.

Ongoing Behavior and Schedule Effects

Zeiler's point that schedules of reinforcement typically affect operant behavior (Zeiler, 1977) is well taken. Experimenters risk misinterpreting results when they ignore possible schedule effects. This is because schedules of reinforcement may interact with a variety of other independent variables and produce characteristic effects. For example, Azrin (1959) found that when every response on a fixed-ratio schedule of reinforcement (reinforcement occurs after a fixed number of responses) was shocked, the pause length after reinforcement increased. However, once the animal emitted the first response, the operant rate to finish the run was unaffected. In other words, the pause increased but otherwise behavior on the schedule remained the same. A possible conclusion is that punishment (shock) reduces the tendency to begin responding; however, once started, behavior is not suppressed by contingent aversive stimulation.

This conclusion is not completely correct, because further experiments have shown that punishment has other effects when behavior is maintained on a different schedule of reinforcement (Azrin, 1958; Azrin & Holz, 1961). When behavior is reinforced after a fixed amount of time (rather than responses), an entirely different result occurs. On this kind of schedule, when each operant is punished, the pattern of behavior remains the same and the rate of response declines. It is obvious that conclusions concerning the effects of punishment on pattern and rate of response cannot be drawn without considering the schedule of reinforcement maintaining the behavior.

In summary, schedules of reinforcement produce reliable patterns of response, and these patterns are consistent for different reinforcers, organisms, and a variety of different operants. In our everyday environment, schedules of reinforcement are so common that we take such effects for granted. We wait for a taxi to arrive, line up at a bank to negotiate a transaction, or solve 10 math problems for homework. All of these behavior–environment interactions illustrate schedules of reinforcement in our everyday lives.

FOCUS ON: A System of Notation

We have found that using a notation system greatly improves the understanding of contingencies between antecedents, behavior, and consequences. This notation system is based on Mechner's description of reinforcement contingencies (Mechner, 1959). We have simplified the notation and relabeled some of the symbols. The system of notation only describes independent variables, and is similar to a flow chart sometimes used in computer programming. That is, **Mechner notation** describes what the experimenter (instrumentation or computer) does, not the behavior of organisms. In other words, Mechner notation represents the way (sequence of events, the requirements, etc.) that schedules of reinforcement are arranged. Cumulative records or other data collected by computers describe what a subject does (i.e., the dependent variable) on those schedules.

Symbol	Event
S	Stimulus or event
S^r	Reinforcer
S^{r+}	Positive reinforcer
S^{r-}	Negative reinforcer (aversive stimulus)
S^D	Discriminative stimulus (event signaling reinforcement)
S^Δ	S-delta (a discriminative stimulus that signals extinction)
S^{ave}	Conditioned aversive stimulus (an event that has signaled punishment)
R	Response (operant class)
R_a	Response of type a (i.e., a response on lever a)

Time and Number Symbols

F	Fixed
V	Variable
T	Time
N	Number

Relationships

The horizontal arrow connecting two events (i.e., A → B) indicates that one event follows another. When the arrow leads to a consequence, as in R → S^r, the arrow is read as *produces*. In this case, a response (R) *produces* a consequence (S^r). If the arrow leads to a response, as in R_a → R_b, it is read as *produces a condition where*. In other words, response R_a "sets up" or allows response R_b to produce an effect. For example, a press on lever "a" creates a situation where a press on lever "b" results in food.

Brackets

All conditions listed vertically inside a bracket go into effect simultaneously (Figure 5.2). For example, A and B are conditions that occur at the same time, and the occurrence of B leads to event C.

When a vertical arrow cuts across a horizontal arrow (Figure 5.3), it means that the diagrammed event is prevented. In the following example, A and B occur at the same time. Event A leads to condition C, but event B blocks the A → C relationship. In other words, A leads to C but not if A and B occur together.

When events repeat (Figure 5.4), this may be shown by a horizontal arrow that starts at the end of a sequence and goes back to the beginning. In the presence of A, the event B produces C, and after C occurs, the sequence repeats.

Mechner notation is especially helpful when complex contingencies are involved and the experimenter has to program a computer or other instrumentation for contingencies arranged in an operant chamber. Using this notation system also aids students in specifying exactly what the events, requirements, and their interactions are in an experiment. Finally, the notation makes explicit the programmed contingencies that control the behavior of organisms.

FIG. 5.2   Relations within brackets in Mechner notation. A and B occur and B produces event C.

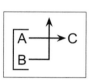

FIG. 5.3   Relations within brackets in Mechner notation. A and B occur; A produces event C, but not if B occurs.

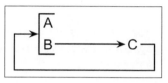

FIG. 5.4   Relations within brackets in Mechner notation. A and B occur, and B produces event C. After C occurs the sequence repeats.

SCHEDULES OF POSITIVE REINFORCEMENT

Continuous Reinforcement

Continuous reinforcement, or **CRF**, is probably the simplest schedule of reinforcement. On this schedule, every operant required by the contingency is reinforced. For example, every time a hungry pigeon pecks a key, food is presented. When every operant is followed by a reinforcer, responses are emitted relatively quickly depending upon the consummatory time for the reinforcer. The organism continues to respond until it is satiated. Simply put, when the bird is hungry (food deprived), it rapidly pecks the key and eats the food until it is full (satiated). If the animal is again deprived of the reinforcer and exposed to a CRF schedule, this pattern of responding followed by satiation occurs again. Figure 5.5 is a typical cumulative record of performance on continuous reinforcement. As mentioned previously in this chapter, the typical vending machine delivers products on a continuous (CRF) schedule.

CRF and Resistance to Extinction

Continuous reinforcement generates little resistance to extinction compared with intermittent reinforcement (Harper & McLean, 1992; Jenkins & Stanley, 1950). Recall from Chapter 4 that *resistance to extinction* is a measure of persistence when reinforcement is discontinued. This perseverance can be measured in several ways. The most obvious way to measure resistance to extinction is to count the number of responses and measure the length of time until *operant level* is reached. Again, remember from Chapter 4 that operant level refers to the rate of a response before behavior is reinforced. For example, a laboratory rat could be placed in an operant chamber with no explicit contingency of reinforcement in effect. The number of times the animal pressed the response bar during a 2-h exploration of the chamber is a measure of operant level, or in this case baseline. Once extinction is in effect, measuring the time taken and number of responses made until operant level is attained is the best gauge of resistance to extinction.

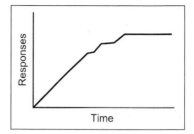

FIG. 5.5 Performance on a continuous reinforcement schedule. Hatch marks indicating reinforcement are omitted since each response is reinforced. The flat portion of the record occurs when the animal stops making the response because of satiation.

Although continuing extinction until operant level is obtained provides the best measure of behavioral persistence, this method requires considerable time and effort. Therefore, arbitrary measures that take less time are usually used. Resistance to extinction may be estimated by counting the number of responses emitted over a fixed number of sessions. For example, after exposure to CRF, reinforcement could be discontinued and the number of responses made in three daily 1-h sessions counted. Another index of resistance to extinction is based on how fast the rate of response declines during nonreinforced sessions. The point at which no response occurs for 5 min may be used to index resistance. The number of responses and time taken to that point are used as an estimate of behavioral persistence. These measures and others may be used to indicate resistance to extinction. The important criterion is that the method must be quantitatively related to extinction responding.

Hearst (1961) investigated the resistance to extinction produced by CRF and intermittent schedules. In this experiment, birds were trained on CRF and two intermittent schedules that provided reinforcement for pecking a key. The number of extinction responses that the animals made during three daily sessions of nonreinforcement was then counted. Basically, Hearst found that the birds made many more extinction responses after training on an intermittent schedule than after exposure to continuous reinforcement.

Response Stereotypy on CRF

On continuous reinforcement schedules, the form or topography of response becomes stereotypical. In a classic study, Antonitis (1951) found that, on CRF, operants were repeated with very little change or variability in topography. In this study, rats were required to poke their noses anywhere along a 50-cm horizontal slot to get a food pellet (see Figure 5.6). Although not required by the contingency, the animals frequently responded at the same position on the slot. Only when the rats were placed on extinction did their responses become more variable. These findings are not limited to laboratory rats, and may reflect a principle of behavior.

FIG. 5.6 The apparatus used by Antonitis (1951). Rats could poke their noses anywhere along the 50-cm horizontal slot to obtain reinforcement.

Further research with pigeons suggests that response variability may be inversely related to the rate of reinforcement. In other words, as more and more responses are reinforced, less and less variation occurs in the members of the operant class. Herrnstein (1961a) reinforced pigeons for pecking on an intermittent schedule. The birds pecked at a horizontal strip and were occasionally reinforced with food. When some responses were reinforced, most of the birds pecked at the center of the strip—although they were not required to do so. During extinction, the animals made fewer responses to the center and more to other positions on the strip. Eckerman and Lanson (1969) replicated this finding in a subsequent study, also with pigeons. They varied the rate of reinforcement and compared response variability under CRF, intermittent reinforcement, and extinction. Responses were stereotypical on CRF and became more variable when the birds were on extinction or on an intermittent schedule.

One interpretation of these findings is that organisms become more variable in their responding as reinforcement becomes less frequent or predictable. When a schedule of reinforcement is changed from CRF to intermittent reinforcement, the rate of reinforcement declines and response variability increases. A further change in the rate of reinforcement occurs when extinction is started. In this case, operants are no longer reinforced and response variation is maximal. The general principle appears to be "When things no longer work, try new ways of behaving." Or, as the saying goes, "If at first you don't succeed, try, try again."

When solving a problem, people usually employ a solution that has worked in the past. When the usual solution does not work, people try novel approaches to solving the problem. Suppose that you are a camper who is trying to start a fire. Most of the time, you gather leaves and sticks, place them in a heap, strike a match, and start the fire. This time the fire does not start. What do you do? If you are like most of us, you try different ways to get the fire going, many of which may have worked in the past. You may change the kindling, add newspaper, use lighter fluid, swear at the fire pit, or even build a shelter. Clearly, your behavior becomes more variable when reinforcement is withheld after a period of success. This increase in topographic variability during extinction after a period of reinforcement has been referred to as **resurgence** (Epstein, 1983, 1985), and can contribute to the development of creative or original behavior.

In summary, CRF is the simplest schedule of positive reinforcement. On this schedule, every response produces a reinforcer. Continuous reinforcement produces little resistance to extinction. This schedule also generates stereotypical response topographies. Both resistance to extinction and variation in form of response increase on intermittent schedules.

RATIO AND INTERVAL SCHEDULES OF REINFORCEMENT

On intermittent schedules of reinforcement, some rather than all responses are reinforced. **Ratio schedules** are response based—that is, these schedules are set to deliver reinforcement following a prescribed number of responses; the ratio specifies the number of responses for each reinforcer. **Interval schedules** pay off when one response is made after some amount of time has passed. Interval and ratio schedules may be fixed or variable. Fixed schedules set up reinforcement after a fixed number of responses have occurred, or after a constant amount of time has passed. On variable schedules, response and time requirements vary from one reinforcer to the next. Thus, there are four basic schedules—fixed ratio, variable ratio, fixed interval, and variable interval. In this section, we shall describe these four basic schedules of reinforcement (shown in Figure 5.7) and illustrate the typical patterns that they produce. We also present an analysis of some of the reasons for the effects produced by schedules.

Ratio Schedules

Fixed Ratio

A **fixed ratio (FR)** schedule is programmed to deliver reinforcement after a fixed number of responses have been made. Continuous reinforcement (CRF) is FR 1—that is, the ratio is one reinforcer for one response. Figure 5.8 presents a fixed-ratio schedule diagrammed in Mechner notation. The notation is read, "In the presence of a discriminative stimulus (S^D), a fixed number (N) of responses (R) produces an unconditioned reinforcer (S^{R+})." In a simple animal experiment, the S^D is sensory stimulation arising from the operant chamber, the response is a lever press, and food functions as reinforcement. On fixed-ratio 25 (FR 25), 25 lever presses must be made before food is presented. After reinforcement, the returning arrow indicates that another 25 responses will again produce the reinforcer.

The symbol N is used to indicate that fixed-ratio schedules can assume any value. Of course, it is unlikely that very high values (say, FR 100,000,000) would ever be completed. Nonetheless, this should remind you that Mechner notation describes independent variables, not what the organism does. Indeed, FR 100,000,000 could be easily programmed, but this schedule is essentially an extinction contingency because the animal will never complete the response requirement for reinforcement.

In 1957, Ferster and Skinner described the FR schedule and the characteristic effects, patterns, and rates, along with cumulative records of performance on about 15 other schedules of reinforcement (see section on C. B. Ferster in this chapter). Their observations remain valid after literally thousands of replications: *FR schedules produce a rapid run of responses, followed by reinforcement, and then a pause in responding* (Ferster & Skinner, 1957; Weissman & Crossman, 1966). An idealized cumulative record of behavior on fixed ratio is presented in Figure 5.9. The record looks somewhat like a set of stairs (except at very small FR values, as shown by Crossman, Trapp, Bonem, & Bonem, 1985). There is a steep period of responding (the *run of responses*), followed by reinforcement (oblique line), and finally a flat portion (the pause)—a pattern known as **break and run**.

		Reinforcement contingent on	
		Responses	Time*
Response/time requirement	Fixed	Fixed ratio (FR)	Fixed interval (FI)
	Variable	Variable ratio (VR)	Variable interval (VI)

*The first response after a given amount of time

FIG. 5.7 A table of the four basic schedules of positive reinforcement. Adapted from *Behavior Principles*, by C. B. Ferster, S. Culbertson, and M. C. P. Boren, 1975, Prentice-Hall, Englewood Cliffs, NJ.

FIG. 5.8 A fixed-ratio schedule of positive reinforcement diagrammed in Mechner notation. In the presence of an S^D, a fixed number of responses results in reinforcement (S^{r+}). As indicated by the returning arrow, the sequence repeats such that another fixed number of responses will again produce reinforcement.

FIG. 5.9 A cumulative record of well-developed performance on FR 100. The typical pause-and-run pattern is presented. Reinforcement is indicated by the hatch marks. This is an idealized record that is typical of performance on many fixed-ratio schedules.

During extinction, the break-and-run pattern shows increasing periods of pausing followed by high rates of response. In a cumulative record of a pigeon's performance for the transition from FR 60 (after 700 reinforcements) to extinction, the pausing after reinforcement comes to dominate the record. However, a high rate of response (approximately 5 pecks per second) is also notable when it does occur (Ferster & Skinner, 1957, Bird 31, p. 58).

The flat part of the cumulative record is often called the **postreinforcement pause (PRP)**, to indicate where it occurred. The pause in responding after reinforcement does not occur because the organism is consuming the food. Skinner (1938, p. 288) indicated that the length of the PRP depended on the preceding reinforcer, a postreinforcement pause. He noted that on FR schedules (and fixed interval schedules) one reinforcer never immediately follows another. Thus, the occurrence of a reinforcer became discriminative for non-reinforcement (S^Δ), and the animal paused. Subsequent research has shown that the moment of reinforcement contributes to the length of the PRP, but is not the only controlling variable (Schlinger, Derenne, & Baron, 2008).

Detailed investigations of PRP on FR schedules indicate that the *upcoming ratio requirement* is critical. As the ratio is increased, longer and longer pauses appear in the cumulative record. At extreme ratios there may be almost no responding. However, if responding occurs at all the animal responds at high rates, even though the number of responses per reinforcement is very high. Mixed FR schedules described later in this chapter also illustrate the influence of to-be-completed response requirements on FR pausing. The number of responses required and the size of the reinforcer have both been shown to influence PRP (Inman & Cheney, 1974). Calling this pause a "post"-reinforcement event accurately locates the pause, but the upcoming requirements exert predominant control over the PRP. Hence, researchers often refer to the PRP as a **preratio pause** (e.g., Derenne & Baron, 2002; Derenne, Richardson, & Baron, 2006; Schlinger et al., 2008).

Conditioned reinforcers such as money, praise, and successful completion of a task also produce a pause when they are scheduled on fixed ratio. Consider what you might do if you had five sets of 10 math problems to complete for a homework assignment. A good bet is that you would solve 10 problems, then take a break before starting on the next set. When constructing a sun deck, one of the authors bundled nails into lots of 50 each. This had an effect on the "nailing behavior" of friends who were helping to build the deck. The pattern that developed was to put in 50 nails, then stop, drink some beer, look over what had been accomplished, have a chat, and finally start nailing again. In other words, a break-and-run pattern typical of FR was generated by this simple scheduling of the nails.

These examples of FR pausing suggest that the analysis of FR schedules has relevance for human behavior. We often talk about procrastination and people who put off or postpone doing things. It is likely that some of this delay in responding is similar to the pausing induced by the ratio schedule. That is, a person who has a lot of upcoming work to complete (preratio size) may show a period of low or no productivity. Human procrastination may be modeled by animal performance on ratio schedules; however, translational research linking human productivity to animal performance has yet to be attempted (Schlinger et al., 2008).

Variable Ratio

Variable-ratio (VR) schedules are similar to FRs except that the number of responses required for reinforcement changes after each reinforcer is presented. A variable ratio schedule is literally a series of FRs with each FR of a different size. The average number of responses is used to define the schedule. A subject may press a lever for reinforcement 5 times, then 15, 7, 3, and 20 times. Adding these response requirements for a total of 50 and then dividing by the number of separate response runs (5) yields the schedule value, VR 10. The symbol V in Figure 5.10 indicates that the number of responses required for any one reinforcer is variable. Other than this change, the contingency is identical to fixed ratio (see Figure 5.8).

In general, ratio schedules produce a high rate of response. When VR and FR schedules are compared, responding is typically faster on VR. One reason for this is that pausing after reinforcement (PRP) is reduced or eliminated when the ratio contingency is changed from fixed to variable. This provides further evidence that the PRP does not occur because the animal is tired or is consuming the reinforcer (i.e., eating food). A rat or pigeon responding for food on VR does not pause as many times, or for as long after reinforcement. When VR schedules are not excessive, postreinforcement pauses do occur (Kintsch, 1965; Webbe, DeWeese, & Malagodi, 1978), although these pauses are typically smaller than those generated by FR schedules (Mazur, 1983). Figure 5.11 portrays a typical pattern of response on a VR schedule of positive reinforcement.

A VR schedule with a low mean ratio can contain some very small ratio requirements. For example, on a VR 10 schedule there cannot be many ratio requirements above 20 because, to offset those high ratios and average 10, there will have to be many very low ratios. It is the *occasional occurrence of a reinforcer right after another reinforcer (the short runs to reinforcement) that reduces the likelihood of pausing on a VR schedule of reinforcement.* Variable-ratio schedules with high mean ratios (e.g., VR 100) have fewer short ratios following one another and typically generate longer PRPs.

The change from VR reinforcement to extinction initially shows little or no change in rate of response. A pigeon on VR 110 shows a high steady rate of response (approximately 3 pecks per second). With the onset of extinction, the bird continues to respond at a similar high rate for about 3000 responses, followed by a shift to a somewhat lower rate of response for 600 responses. The last part of the record shows long pausing and short bursts of responses at a rate similar to the original VR 110 performance. The pauses become longer and longer and eventually all responding stops, as it does on FR schedules (Ferster & Skinner, 1957, pp. 411–412).

FIG. 5.10   A variable-ratio schedule of positive reinforcement. The symbol V indicates that the number of responses required for reinforcement is varied from one sequence to the next. The average number of responses required for reinforcement indexes the schedule. That is, a VR 10 requires an average of 10 responses before reinforcement is presented.

FIG. 5.11   A cumulative graph of typical responding on a variable-ratio schedule of reinforcement. Reinforcement is indicated by the hatch marks. Notice that PRPs are reduced or eliminated when compared with fixed-ratio performance.

An additional issue concerning VR schedules is that the number of responses for reinforcement is unpredictable, but it is not random. In fact, the sequence repeats after all the programmed ratios have been completed and, on some VR schedules, short ratios may occur more frequently than with a random sequence. A schedule with a pseudo-random pattern of response to reinforcement values is called a random ratio (RR) schedule of reinforcement. Research has shown that performance on RR schedules resembles that on a VR schedule, but these probabilistic schedules "lock you in" to high rates of response, as in gambling, by early runs of payoffs and by the pattern of unreinforced responses (Haw, 2008; Turner & Horbay, 2004).

In everyday life, variability and probability are routine. Thus, ratio schedules involving probabilistic payoffs (or RR schedules) are more common than strict VR or FR contingencies from the laboratory. You may have to hit one nail three times to drive it in, and the next nail may take six swings of the hammer. It may, on average, take 70 casts with a fly rod to catch a trout, but any one strike is probabilistic. In baseball, the batting average reflects the player's schedule of reinforcement. A batter with a .300 average gets 3 hits for 10 times at bat on average, but nothing guarantees a hit for any particular time at bat. The schedule depends on a complex interplay among conditions set by the pitcher and the skill of the batter.

Interval Schedules

Fixed Interval

On **fixed-interval (FI)** schedules, an operant is reinforced after a fixed amount of time has passed. For example, on a fixed-interval 90-s schedule (FI 90 s), one bar press after 90 s results in reinforcement. Following reinforcement, another 90-s period goes into effect, and after this time has passed another response will produce reinforcement. It is important to note that responses made before the time period has elapsed have no effect. Notice that in Figure 5.12, one response (R) produces reinforcement (S^{r+}) after the fixed time period (FT) has passed. (Note that there is a schedule called *fixed time (FT)* in which reinforcement is delivered without a response following a set, or fixed, length of time. This is also referred to as a *response-independent schedule*. Unless otherwise specified, one should always assume that a response is required on whatever schedule is in effect.)

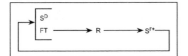

FIG. 5.12 A fixed-interval schedule. In the presence of an S^D, one response is reinforced after a fixed amount of time. Following reinforcement, the returning arrow states that the sequence starts again. This means that the fixed-time interval starts over and, after it has elapsed, one response will again be reinforced.

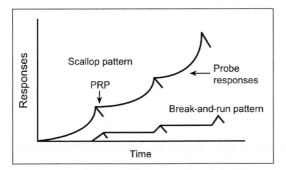

FIG. 5.13 Fixed-interval schedules usually produce a pattern that is called scalloping. There is a PRP following reinforcement, and then a gradual increase in the rate of response to the moment of reinforcement. Less common is the break-and-run pattern. Break and run occasionally develops after organisms have considerable experience on FI schedules. There is a long pause (break) after reinforcement, followed by a rapid burst (run) of responses.

When organisms are exposed to interval contingencies and they have no way of telling time, they typically produce many more responses than the schedule requires. Fixed-interval schedules produce a characteristic steady-state pattern of responding. There is a pause after reinforcement (PRP), then a few probe responses, followed by more and more rapid responding to a constant high rate as the interval times out. This pattern of response is called **scalloping**. Figure 5.13 is an idealized cumulative record of FI performance. Each interreinforcement interval can be divided into three distinct classes—the PRP, followed by a period of gradually increasing rate, and finally a high terminal rate of responding.

Suppose that you have volunteered to be in an operant experiment. You are brought into a small room, and on one wall there is a lever with a cup under it. Other than those objects, the room is empty. You are not allowed to keep your watch while in the room, and you are told "Do anything you want." After some time, you press the lever to see what it does. Ten dollars fall into the cup. A good prediction is that you will press the lever again. You are not told this, but the schedule is FI 5 min. You have 1 h per day to work on the schedule. If you collect all 12 (60 min ÷ 5 min = 12) of the scheduled reinforcers, you can make $120 a day.

Assume you have been in this experiment for 3 months. Immediately after collecting a $10 reinforcer, there is no chance that a response will pay off (discriminated extinction). However, as you are standing around, or doing anything else, the interval is timing out. You check out the contingency by making a probe response (you guess the time might be up). The next response occurs more quickly because even more time has gone by. As the interval continues to time out, the probability of reinforcement increases and your responses are made faster and faster. This pattern of responding is described by the scallop shown in Figure 5.13, and is typical of FI schedules (Dews, 1969; Ferster & Skinner, 1957).

Following considerable experience with FI 5 min, you may get very good at judging the time period. In this case, you would wait out the interval and then emit a burst of responses. Perhaps you begin to pace back and forth during the session, and you find out that after 250 steps the interval has almost elapsed. This kind of mediating behavior may develop after experience with FI schedules (Muller, Crow, & Cheney, 1979). Other animals behave in a similar way and occasionally produce a *break-and-run* pattern of responding, similar to FR schedules (Ferster & Skinner, 1957).

Humans use clocks and watches to keep track of time. Based on this observation, Ferster and Skinner (1957, pp. 266–278) asked about the effects of adding a visible clock to an FI schedule. The "clock" for pigeons was a light that grew in size as the FI interval ran out. The birds generated FI scallops which were much more uniform than without a clock, showing the control exerted by a timing stimulus. Another indication of the stimulus control occurred when the clock was reversed (i.e., the light grew smaller with the FI interval). Under these conditions, the scallop also reversed such that immediately following reinforcement a high response rate occurred, leading to a pause at the end of the interval. However, the FI contingencies quickly overrode the stimulus control by the reverse clock, shifting the pattern back to a typical curve. When a stimulus such as a clock results in behavior that is inefficient with respect to the schedule, behavior eventually conforms to the schedule rather than the controlling stimulus.

In everyday life, FI schedules are arranged when people set timetables for trains and buses. Next time you are at a bus stop, take a look at what people do while they are waiting for the next bus. If a bus has just departed, people stand around and perhaps talk to each other for a while. Then, the operant of "looking for the bus" begins at a low rate of response. As the interval times out, the rate of looking for the bus increases and most passengers are now looking for the arrival of the next bus. The passengers' behavior approximates the scalloping pattern we have described in this section. Schedules of reinforcement are a pervasive aspect of human behavior, but we seldom recognize the effects of these contingencies.

☉ FOCUS ON: Generality of Schedule Effects

The **assumption of generality** implies that the effects of contingencies of reinforcement extend over species, reinforcement, and behavior (Morse, 1966, p. 59; Skinner, 1969, p. 101). For example, a fixed-interval schedule is expected to produce the scalloping pattern for a pigeon pecking a key for food, as well as for a child solving math problems for teacher approval.

Lowe (1979) conducted numerous studies of fixed-interval performance with humans, who press a button to obtain points that are later exchanged for money.

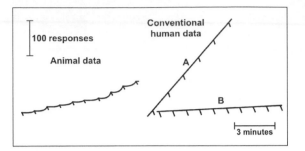

FIG. 5.14 Typical animal performances on FI schedules along with the high- and low-rate performance usually seen with adult humans. Adapted from Lowe (1979, p. 162). © John Wiley & Sons, Ltd. Reproduced with permission.

Figure 5.14 shows typical performances on fixed-interval schedules by a rat and two human subjects. Building on research by Harold Weiner (1969), Lowe argues that animals show the characteristic scalloping pattern, and humans generally do not. Humans often produce one of two patterns—an inefficient, high, steady rate of response, or an efficient, low-rate, break-and-run performance. Experiments by Lowe and his colleagues have focused on the conditions that produce the high- or low-rate patterns in humans.

The basic idea is that schedule performance in humans reflects the influence of language (see Chapter 12 on verbal behavior). In conditioning experiments, people generate some verbal rule and proceed to behave according to the rule rather than the experimentally arranged contingencies. Lowe, Beasty, and Bentall (1983) commented that:

> Verbal behavior can, and does, serve a discriminative function that alters the effects of other variables such as scheduled reinforcement. Unlike animals, most humans are capable of describing to themselves, whether accurately or inaccurately, environmental events and the ways in which those events impinge upon them; such descriptions may greatly affect the rest of their behavior.
>
> (p. 162)

FIG. 5.15 Infant John in study of FI schedules had to touch the metal cylinder to receive small snack items like pieces of fruit, bread, and candy. The FI values were 10, 20, 20, and 50 s. From C. F. Lowe, A. Beasty and R. P. Benthall, 1983, "The role of verbal behavior in human learning: Infant performance on fixed-interval schedules," *Journal of the Experimental Analysis of behavior, 39,* 157–164. © 1983 Society for the Experimental Analysis of Behavior. Reproduced with permission.

In most cases, people who follow self-generated rules satisfy the requirements of the schedule, obtain reinforcement, and continue to follow the rule. For example, one person may say "I should press the button fast" while another says "I should count to 50 and then press the button." Only when the contingencies are arranged so that self-generated rules conflict with programmed reinforcement do people reluctantly abandon the rule and behave in accord with the contingencies (Baron & Galizio, 1983). Humans also naturally find it easy to believe a statement or rule and effortful to reject one (Harris, Sheth, & Cohen, 2007).

One implication of Lowe's analysis is that humans without language skills will show characteristic effects of schedules. Lowe et al. (1983) designed an experiment to show typical FI performance by children less than 1 year old. Figure 5.15 shows an infant (John) seated in a high chair and able to touch a round metal cylinder. Touching the cylinder produced a small bit of food (pieces of fruit, bread, or candy) on fixed-interval schedules of reinforcement. A second infant, Ann, was given 4 s of music played from a variety of music boxes on the same schedules. Both infants produced response patterns similar to the rat's performance in Figure 5.14. Thus, infants who are not verbally skilled behave in accord with the FI contingencies. There is no doubt that humans become more verbal as they grow up. However, there are many other changes that occur from infancy to adulthood. An important consideration is the greater experience that adults have with ratio-type contingencies of reinforcement. Infants rely on the caregiving of other people. This means that most of the infant's reinforcement is delivered on the basis of time and behavior (interval schedules). A baby is fed when the mother has time to do so, although fussing may decrease the interval. As children get older, they begin to crawl and walk and reinforcement is delivered more and more on the basis of their behavior (ratio schedules). When this happens, many of the contingencies of reinforcement change from interval to ratio schedules. The amount of experience with ratio schedules of reinforcement may contribute to the differences between adult human and animal/infant performance on fixed-interval schedules.

Research by Wanchisen, Tatham, and Mooney (1989) has shown that rats perform like adult humans on FI schedules after a history of ratio reinforcement. The animals were exposed to variable-ratio reinforcement and were then given 120 sessions on a fixed-interval 30-s schedule (FI 30 s). Two patterns of response developed on the FI schedule—a high-rate pattern with little pausing and a low-rate pattern with some break-and-run performance. These patterns of performance are remarkably similar to the schedule performance of adult humans (see Figure 5.14). One implication is that human performance on schedules may be explained by a special history of ratio reinforcement rather than self-generated verbal rules. At this time, it is reasonable to conclude that both reinforcement history and verbal ability contribute to fixed-interval performance of adult humans.

Variable Interval

On a **variable-interval (VI)** schedule, responses are reinforced after a variable amount of time has passed (see Figure 5.16). For example, on a VI 30 s schedule, the time to each reinforcement changes but the average time is 30 s. The symbol V indicates that the time requirement varies from one reinforcer to the next. The average amount of time required for reinforcement is used to index the schedule.

Interval contingencies are common in the ordinary world of people and other animals. People line up, sit in traffic jams, wait for elevators, time a boiling egg, and are put on hold. In everyday life, variable time periods occur more frequently than fixed ones. Waiting in line to get to a bank teller may take 5 min one day and half an hour the next time you go to the bank. A wolf pack may run down prey following a long or short hunt. A baby may cry for 5 s, 2 min, or 15 min before a parent picks up the child. A cat waits varying amounts of time in ambush before a bird becomes a meal. Waiting for a bus is rarely reinforced on a fixed schedule, despite the efforts of transportation officials. The bus arrives around an average specified time and waits only a given time before leaving. A carpool is an example of a VI contingency with a limited hold. The car arrives more or less at a specified time but waits for a

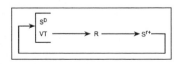

FIG. 5.16   A variable-interval schedule. The symbol V stands for variable and indicates that the schedule is indexed by the average time requirement for reinforcement.

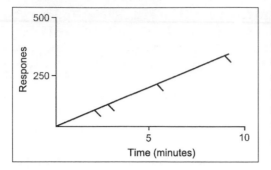

FIG. 5.17   Idealized cumulative pattern of response produced by a variable-interval schedule of reinforcement.

rider only a limited (and usually brief) time. In the laboratory, this **limited-hold** contingency—where the reinforcer is available for a set time after a variable interval—when added to a VI schedule increases the rate of responding by reinforcing short interresponse times (IRTs). In the case of the carpool, people on the VI schedule with limited hold are ready for pick-up and rush out of the door when the car arrives.

Figure 5.17 portrays the pattern of response generated on a VI schedule. On this schedule, rate of response is moderate and steady. The pause after reinforcement that occurs on FI does not usually appear in the variable-interval record. Notably, this steady rate of response is maintained during extinction. Ferster and Skinner (1957, pp. 348–349) described the cumulative record of a pigeon's performance for the transition from VI 7 min to extinction. The bird maintains a moderately stable rate (1.25 to 1.5 pecks per second) for approximately 8000 responses. After this, the rate of response continuously declines to the end of the record. Generally, VI response rates initially remain stable on extinction, showing an overall large and stable output of behavior. Because the rate of response is steady and moderate to high, VI performance is often used as a *baseline for evaluating other independent variables*. Rate of response on VI schedules may increase or decrease as a result of experimental manipulations. For example, tranquilizing drugs such as chlorpromazine decrease the rate of response on variable-interval schedules (Waller, 1961), while stimulants increase VI performance (Segal, 1962). Murray Sidman has commented on the usefulness of VI performance as a baseline:

> An ideal baseline would be one in which there is as little interference as possible from other variables. There should be a minimal number of factors tending to oppose any shift in behavior that might result from experimental manipulation. A variable-interval schedule, if skillfully programmed, comes close to meeting this requirement.
>
> (Sidman, 1960, p. 320)

In summary, VI contingencies are common in everyday life. These schedules generate a moderate steady rate of response. Because of this pattern, VI performance is frequently used as a baseline.

NOTE ON: VI Schedules, Reinforcement Rate, and Behavioral Momentum

Behavioral momentum refers to behavior that persists or continues in the presence of a stimulus for reinforcement despite disruptive factors (Nevin, 1992; Nevin & Grace, 2000; see PRE effect and behavioral momentum in Chapter 4). Thus, response rate declines more slowly (relative to its baseline level) in the presence of a stimulus for high-density reinforcement than a stimulus for low-density reinforcement (Shull, Gaynor, & Grimer, 2002). If you are working at the computer, and you keep working even though you are called to dinner, that is an example of behavioral momentum. Also, if you have a tendency to do some specific activity, despite alternative sources of reinforcement, that too shows behavioral momentum.

The analysis of behavioral momentum emerged when it was observed that behavior in a situation associated with a higher rate of reinforcement was less disrupted than behavior in a setting associated with a lower reinforcement rate, when challenged with some distraction. The procedure employed by Nevin (1974) involved a multiple schedule of reinforcement with two separate VI reinforcement conditions, each with a discriminative stimulus (S^D) and separated by a third dark component. Rates of responding were naturally higher in the richer VI component. Then, when free food was provided in the third component (disruption), responding decreased less in the VI condition with the higher rate of reinforcement. That is, behavior in the component with the richer VI schedule (higher rate of reinforcement) showed greater momentum. It continued to keep going despite the disruption by free food (see also Cohn, 1998; Lattal, Reilly, & Kohn, 1998).

A study by Nevin and associates compared the resistance to change (momentum) of behavior maintained on ratio and interval schedules of reinforcement (Nevin, Grace, Holland, & McLean, 2001). Pigeons pecked keys on a multiple schedule of random-ratio (RR) random-interval (RI) reinforcement to test relative resistance to change. On this multiple schedule, a distinctive stimulus (S^D) signaled each component schedule, either RR or RI, and the researchers ensured that the reinforcement rates for the RR component were equated with those of the RI segment. Disruptions by free feeding between components, extinction, and pre-feeding (before the session) were investigated. The findings indicated that, with similar obtained rates of reinforcement, *interval schedule performance was more resistant to change (higher momentum) than performance on ratio schedules.* Notice that resistance to change is exactly the opposite to the findings for rate of response on these schedules—ratio schedules maintain higher rates of response than interval schedules.

Many behavior analysts have investigated predictions and analyses based on momentum theory (e.g., Harper & McLean, 1992) and have made suggestions for applying the theory to everyday problems (Brandon & Houlihan, 1997). Currently, researchers are using behavioral momentum theory to evaluate the long-term effects of reinforcement programs on the persistence of targeted responses when challenged by disruptions (Wacker, Harding, Berg, Lee, Schieltz, Padilla et al., 2011). In one applied study, two individuals with severe mental retardation performed self-paced discriminations on a computer using a touch-sensitive screen and food reinforcement (Dube & McIlvane, 2001). Responses on two separate problems were differentially reinforced. The researchers found that on-task behavior with the higher reinforcement rate was more resistant to change due to pre-feeding, free snacks, or alternative activities. Thus, the disruptive factors reduced task performance depending on the prior rates of reinforcement. That is, when performance on a task received a high rate of reinforcement it was relatively impervious to distraction compared with performance maintained on a lower rate schedule.

Progressive Ratio Schedules and Reinforcement Efficacy

On a **progressive ratio (PR) schedule** of reinforcement the ratio requirements for reinforcement are increased systematically, typically after each reinforcer (Hodos, 1961). In an experiment, the first response requirement for reinforcement might be set at a small ratio value such as 5 responses.

Once the animal emits 5 responses resulting in reinforcement, the next ratio requirement might increase by 10 responses (the step size). Now reinforcement occurs only after the animal has pressed the lever 15 times, followed by ratio requirements of 25 responses, 35, 45, 55, and so on (adding 10 responses on each step). The increasing ratios (5, 15, 25, 35 . . .) are the progression and give the schedule its name. At some point in the progression of ratios, the animal fails to achieve the requirement. The highest ratio value completed on the PR schedule is designated the **breakpoint**.

The type of progression on a PR schedule may be arithmetic, as when the difference between any two ratio requirements is a constant value (e.g. 10). Another kind of progression is geometric, as when each ratio after the first is found by multiplying the previous one by a fixed number. A geometric progressive ratio might be 2, 6, 18 . . ., where 3 is the fixed value. The type of progression (arithmetic or geometric) is an important determinant of behavior on PR schedules. In a recent study of PR schedules, Killeen, Posadas-Sanchez, Johansen, and Thraikill (2009) found that response rates on arithmetic and geometric PR schedules increased as the ratio requirement progressed and then decreased. Response rates maintained on arithmetic PR schedules decreased in a linear manner—as the ratio size increased there was a linear decrease in response rates. However, responses rates on geometric PR schedules showed a negative deceleration toward a low and stable response rate—as ratio size increased geometrically response rates rapidly declined and then leveled off. Thus, the relationship between response rates and ratio requirements of the PR schedule depends on the type of progression—arithmetic or geometric. These relationships can be described by mathematical equations, and this is an ongoing area of research (Killeen et al., 2009).

PR Schedules, Behavioral Pharmacology, and Neuroscience

The PR schedule has also been used in applied research (Roane, 2008). Most of the applied research on PR schedules uses the giving-up or breakpoint as a way of measuring **reinforcement efficacy** or effectiveness, especially of drugs like cocaine. The breakpoint for a drug indicates how much operant behavior the drug will sustain at a given dose. For example, a rat might self-administer morphine on a PR schedule as the dose size is varied and breakpoints are determined for each dose size. It is also possible to determine the breakpoints for different drugs (e.g. stimulants or opioids), assessing the drugs' relative reinforcement effectiveness. In these tests, it is important to recognize that the time allotted to complete the ratio (e.g. 120 min) and the progression of the PR schedule (a particular progression of ratio sizes) have an impact on the breakpoints—potentially limiting conclusions about which drugs are more "addictive," and how the breakpoint varies with increases in drug dose (dose–response curve).

Progressive ratio schedules allow researchers to assess the reinforcing effects of drugs prescribed to control problem behavior. A drug prescribed to control hyperactivity might also be addictive—an effect recommending against its use. The drug Ritalin® (methylphenidate) is commonly used to treat attention deficit hyperactivity disorder (ADHD) and is chemically related to Dexedrine® (d-amphetamine). Amphetamine is a drug of abuse, as are other stimulants, such as cocaine. Thus, people who are given methylphenidate to modify ADHD might develop addictive behavior similar to behavior maintained by amphetamine. A study by Stoops, Glaser, Fillmore, and Rush (2004) used human drug-abusing volunteers to study the reinforcing efficacy of three doses of methylphenidate (16, 32, and 48 mg) and d-amphetamine (8, 16, and 24 mg), including a placebo. The reinforcing efficacy of the drug was assessed by a modified PR schedule (over days) where participants had to press a key on a computer (50, 100, 200, 400, 800, 1600, 3200, and 6400 times) to earn capsules of the drug; completion of the ratio requirement resulted in oral self-administration of the drug. Additional monetary contingencies were arranged to ensure continued participation in the study. As shown in Figure 5.18, the results indicated that the number of responses to the breakpoint increased at the intermediate dose of methylphenidate and d-amphetamine compared with the placebo control. Thus methylphenidate is similar in reinforcement effectiveness to d-amphetamine. One conclusion is that using Ritalin® to treat ADHD may be contraindicated due to its potential for abuse (see Stoops, 2008 for a review of the reinforcing effects of stimulants in humans on PR schedules).

Recently, PR schedules have been used to study the reinforcement efficacy of palatable food for over-eating and obesity. Leptin is a protein that is produced mostly in the adipocytes (fat cells) of the white adipose (fat) tissue. The basic function of leptin is to signal when to stop eating—counteracting neuropeptides that stimulate feeding. Based on a genetic mutation, the ob/ob (obese-prone) mouse is deficient in the production of leptin—overeating and gaining excessive body weight

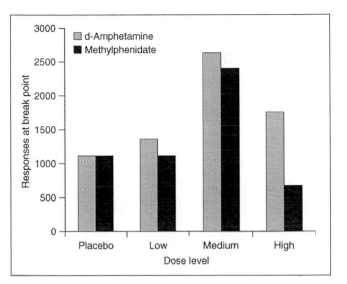

FIG. 5.18 Breakpoints produced by 10 drug-abusing volunteers who self-administered low, medium, and high doses of two stimulants (methylphenidate and d-amphetamine) as well as a placebo control. The medium doses of each drug differ from the placebo, but the two drugs do not reliably differ from each other. Based on data for average breakpoints in W. W. Stoops, P. E. A. Glaser, M. T. Fillmore, and C. R. Rush, 2004, "Reinforcing, subject-rated, performance and physiological effects of methylphenidate and d-amphetamine in stimulant-abusing humans," *Journal of Psychopharmacology, 18*, 538

compared with the lean-prone littermates of the same strain (see Figure 5.19). That is, overeating and obesity vary with genotype (obese-prone vs. lean-prone) of these rodents.

New research by Finger, Dinan, and Cryan (2010) investigated whether the reinforcing efficacy of palatable food varies by genotype of the ob/ob mouse. Obese-prone and lean-prone mice were trained to make nose-poke responses for flavored sucrose pellets (detected by photo beams in the

food magazine). Next, the mice were tested on a PR3 schedule, requiring an increase or step of 3 responses for each pellet, using a linear progression of ratio values (3, 6, 9, 12, 15 . . .) with 3 as the first ratio requirement. The highest ratio completed within a 15-min timing-out period was defined as the breakpoint. All mice received 16 daily sessions to attain stability on the PR3 schedule. After establishing the PR3 baselines, both obese-prone and lean-prone mice were administered low and high doses of an anorexic drug (fenfluramine) and given more sessions on the PR3 schedule. The results for breakpoints showed that the obese-prone genotype did not reliably differ from the lean-prone mice. The reinforcing efficacy of palatable food was

FIG. 5.19 The ob/ob obese-prone mouse and lean-prone littermate. The ob/ob genotype has a deficiency in leptin production that results in obesity when food is freely available.

similar for both genotypes. Also, the anorexic drug reduced PR3 breakpoints in a dose–response manner, but this effect did not differ by genotype (obese-prone vs. lean-prone). Apparently, the overeating and excessive weight gain of leptin-deficient (ob/ob) mice is not due to differences in the reinforcement efficacy of palatable food.

One problem with this conclusion is that animals were only given 15 min to complete the ratio requirement, and some animals did not achieve stable baselines on the PR3 schedule, even after 16 days. The safest conclusion is that further studies of ob/ob mice on PR schedules are necessary to determine the reinforcing efficacy of palatable food for these obese-prone rodents.

SCHEDULE PERFORMANCE IN TRANSITION

We have described typical performances generated by different schedules of reinforcement. The patterns of response on these schedules take a relatively long time to develop. Once behavior has stabilized, showing little change from day to day, the organism's behavior is said to have reached a *steady state*. The pause-and-run pattern that develops on FR schedules is a steady-state performance and is only observed after an animal has considerable exposure to the contingencies. Similarly, the steady-state performance generated on other intermittent schedules takes time to evolve. When an organism is initially placed on any schedule of reinforcement, typically behavior patterns are not consistent or regular. This early performance on a schedule is called a **transition state**. Transition states are the periods between initial steady-state performance and the next steady state (see Sidman, 1960, for steady-state and transition-state analysis).

Consider how you might get an animal to press a lever 100 times for each presentation of food (FR 100). First, you shape the animal to press the bar on continuous reinforcement (see Chapter 4). After some arbitrary steady-state performance is established on CRF, you are faced with the problem of how to program the steps from CRF to FR 100. Notice that in this transition there is a large shift or step in the ratio of reinforcement to bar pressing. This problem has been studied using a *progressive-ratio schedule*, as we described earlier in this chapter. The ratio of responses following each run to reinforcement is programmed to increase in steps. Stafford & Branch (1998) employed the PR schedule to investigate the behavioral effects of step size and criteria for stability. If you simply move from CRF to the large FR value, the animal will probably show **ratio strain** in the sense that it pauses longer and longer after reinforcement. One reason is that the time between successive reinforcements contributes to the postreinforcement pause. The pause gets longer as the **interreinforcement interval** (IRI, or time between reinforcement) increases. Because the PRP makes up part of the IRI and is controlled by it, the animal eventually stops responding. Thus, there is a negative-feedback loop between increasing PRP length and the time between reinforcements in the shift from CRF to the large FR schedule.

Transitions from one reinforcement schedule to another play an important role in human development. Developmental psychologists have described periods of life in which major changes in behavior typically occur. One of the most important life stages in Western society is the transition from childhood to adolescence. Although this phase involves many biological and behavioral processes, one of the most basic changes involves schedules of reinforcement.

When a youngster reaches puberty, parents, teachers, peers, and others require more behavior and more skillful performance than they did during childhood. A young child's reinforcement schedules are usually simple, regular, and immediate. In childhood, food is given when the child says "Mom, I'm hungry" after playing a game of tag, or is scheduled at regular times throughout the day. On the other hand, a teenager is told to fix his or her own food and clean up the mess. Notice that the schedule requirement for getting food has significantly increased. The teenager may search through the refrigerator, open packages and cans, sometimes cook, get out plates, eat the food, and clean up. Of course, any part of this sequence may or may not occur depending on the disciplinary practices of the parents. Although most adolescents adapt to this transition state, others may show signs of ratio strain and extinction. Poor eating habits among teenagers may reflect the change from regular to intermittent reinforcement.

Many other behavioral changes may occur during the transition from childhood to adolescence. Ferster, Culbertson, and Boren (1975) have noted the transition to intermittent reinforcement that occurs in adolescence:

> With adolescence, the picture may change quite drastically and sometimes even suddenly. Now money becomes a reinforcer on a fixed-ratio schedule instead of continuous reinforcement as before. The adolescent may have to take a job demanding a substantial amount of work for the money which heretofore he received as a free allowance. Furthermore, he now needs more money than when he was younger to interact with people he deals with. A car or a motorcycle takes the place of the bicycle. Even the price of services such as movies and buses is higher. Money, particularly for boys, frequently becomes a necessary condition for dealing with the opposite sex. The amount of work required in school increases. Instead of simple arithmetic problems, the adolescent may now have to write a long term paper, cover more subjects, or puzzle through a difficult algebra problem which will require much trial and error.
>
> (pp. 416–417)

There are other periods of life in which our culture demands large shifts in schedules of reinforcement. A current problem involves a rapidly aging population and the difficulties generated by forced retirement. In terms of schedules, retirement is a large and rapid change in the contingencies of reinforcement. Retired people face significant alterations in social, monetary, and work-related consequences. For example, a person who has enjoyed his or her academic career as a professor is no longer reinforced for research and teaching by the university community. Social consequences for these activities may have included approval by colleagues, academic advancement, the interest of students, and intellectual discussions. Upon retirement, these social reinforcers are reduced in frequency or completely eliminated. It is not surprising, therefore, that retirement is an unhappy time of life for many people. Although retirement is commonly viewed as a problem of old age, a behavior analysis points to the abrupt change in rates and sources of reinforcement (Skinner & Vaughan, 1983).

ON THE APPLIED SIDE: Schedules and Cigarettes

As we have seen, the use of drugs is operant behavior maintained in part by the reinforcing effects of the drug. One implication of this analysis is that reinforcement of an incompatible response (i.e., abstinence) can reduce the probability of taking drugs. The effectiveness of an abstinence contingency depends on the magnitude and schedule of reinforcement for nondrug use (e.g., Higgins, Bickel, & Hughes, 1994).

In applied behavior analysis, contingency management involves the systematic use of reinforcement to establish desired behavior and the withholding of reinforcement or punishment of undesired behavior (Higgins & Petry, 1999). An example of contingency management is seen in a study using reinforcement schedules to reduce cigarette smoking. Roll, Higgins, and Badger (1996) assessed the effectiveness of three different schedules of reinforcement for promoting and sustaining drug abstinence. These researchers conducted an experimental analysis of cigarette smoking because cigarettes can function as reinforcers, smoking can be reduced by reinforcement of alternative responses, and it is relatively more convenient to study cigarette smoking than illicit drugs. Furthermore, cigarette smokers usually relapse within several days following abstinence. This suggests that reinforcement factors regulating abstinence exert their effects shortly after the person stops smoking and it is possible to study these factors in a short-duration experiment.

Sixty adults, who smoked between 10 and 50 cigarettes a day, took part in the experiment. The smokers were not currently trying to give up cigarettes. Participants were randomly assigned to one of three groups: progressive reinforcement, fixed rate of reinforcement, and a control group. They were told to begin abstaining from cigarettes on Friday evening so that they could pass a carbon monoxide (CO) test for abstinence on Monday morning. Each person in the study went for at least 2 days without smoking before reinforcement for abstinence began. On Monday through Friday, participants agreed to take three daily CO tests. These tests could detect prior smoking.

Twenty participants were randomly assigned to the progressive reinforcement group. The progressive schedule involved increasing the magnitude of reinforcement for remaining drug free. Participants earned $3.00 for passing the first carbon monoxide test for abstinence. Each subsequent consecutive CO sample that indicated abstinence increased the amount of money participants received by $0.50. The third consecutive CO test passed earned a bonus of $10.00. That is, passing the first CO test yielded $3.00, passing the second test yielded $3.50, passing the third test yielded $14.00 ($4.00 and bonus of $10.00), and passing the fourth test yielded $4.50. In addition, a substantial response cost was added for failing a CO test. If the person failed the test, the payment for that test was withheld and the value of payment for the next test was reset to $3.00. Three consecutive CO tests indicating abstinence following a reset returned the payment schedule to the value at which the reset occurred (Roll et al., p. 497), supporting efforts to achieve abstinence.

Participants in the fixed reinforcement group (N = 20) were paid $9.80 for passing each CO test. There were no bonus points for consecutive abstinences and no resets. The total amount of money available for the progressive and fixed groups was the same. Smokers in both the progressive and fixed groups were informed in advance of the schedule of payment and the criterion for reinforcement. The schedule of payment for the control group was the same as the average payment obtained by the first 10 participants assigned to the progressive condition. For these people, the payment was given no matter what their carbon monoxide levels were. The control group was, however, asked to try to cut their cigarette consumption, reduce CO levels, and maintain abstinence.

Smokers in the progressive and fixed reinforcement groups passed more than 80% of the abstinence tests, while the control group only passed about 40% of the tests. The effects of the schedule of reinforcement are shown in Figure 5.20A. The figure indicates the percentage of participants who passed three consecutive tests for abstinence and then resumed smoking over the 5 days of the experiment. Only 22% of those on the progressive schedule resumed smoking, compared with 60% and 82% in the fixed and control groups, respectively. Thus, the progressive schedule of reinforcement was superior in terms of preventing the resumption of smoking (after a period of abstinence).

Figure 5.20B shows the percentage of smokers who gave up cigarettes throughout the experiment. Again, a strong effect of schedule of reinforcement is apparent. Around 50% of those on the progressive reinforcement schedule remained abstinent for the 5 days of the experiment, compared with 30% and 5% of the fixed and control participants, respectively.

In a subsequent experiment, Roll and Higgins (2000) found that a progressive reinforcement schedule with a response–cost contingency increased abstinence from cigarette use

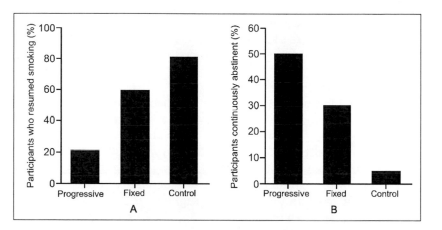

FIG. 5.20   Percentage of participants in each group who obtained three consecutive abstinences, but then resumed smoking (A). Also shown is the percentage of smokers in each group who were abstinent on all trials during the entire experiment (B). From "An experimental comparison of three different schedules of reinforcement of drug abstinence using cigarette smoking as an exemplar," by J. M. Roll, S. T. Higgins, and G. J. Badger, 1996, *Journal of Applied Behavior Analysis, 29*, 495–505. © 1996 Society for the Experimental Analysis of Behavior, Inc. Republished with permission.

compared with a progressive schedule without the response cost or a fixed incentive-value schedule. Overall, these results indicate that a progressive reinforcement schedule, combined with an escalating response cost, is an effective short-term intervention for abstinence from smoking. Further research is necessary to see whether a progressive schedule maintains abstinence after the schedule is withdrawn. Long-term follow-up studies of progressive and other schedules are necessary to assess the lasting effects of reinforcement schedules on abstinence. What is clear, at this point, is that schedules of reinforcement may be an important component of stop-smoking programs.

ADVANCED SECTION: Schedule Performance

Each of the basic schedules of reinforcement (FR, FI, VR, and VI) generates a unique pattern of responding. Ratio schedules produce a higher rate of response than interval schedules. A reliable pause after reinforcement (PRP) occurs on fixed-ratio and fixed-interval schedules, but not on variable-ratio or variable-interval schedules.

Rate of Response on Schedules

The issue of what produces rapid responding on ratio schedules and moderate rates on interval schedules has not been resolved. The two major views concern molecular versus molar conceptions of schedule control. **Molecular accounts of schedule performance** focus on small moment-to-moment relationships between behavior and its consequences. The molecular analysis is based on the fact that some behavior precedes the response (peck or lever press) that is reinforced. This is the behavior that occurs between successive responses, and it is measured as the interresponse time (IRT). **Molar accounts of schedule performance** are concerned with large-scale factors that occur over the length of an entire session, such as the overall rate of reinforcement, and the relation between response rate and reinforcement rate (called the feedback function).

Molecular Account of Rate of Response

The time between any two responses, or what is called the **interresponse time (IRT)**, may be treated as an operant. Technically, IRTs are units of time and cannot be reinforced. The behavior between any two responses is indirectly measured as IRT, and it is this behavior that produces reinforcement. Consider Figure 5.21, in which 30-s segments of performance on VR and VI schedules are presented. Responses are portrayed by the vertical marks, and the occurrence of reinforcement is denoted by the familiar symbol S^{r+}. As you can see, IRTs are much longer on VI than on VR. On the VR segment, 23 responses occur in 30 s, which gives an average time between responses of 1.3 s. The VI schedule generates longer IRTs, with a mean of 2.3 s.

Generally, ratio schedules produce shorter IRTs and consequently higher rates of response than interval schedules. Skinner (1938) suggested that this came about because ratio and interval schedules reinforce short and long interresponse times, respectively. To understand this, consider the definition of an operant class. It is a class of behavior that may increase or decrease in frequency on the basis of contingencies of reinforcement. In other words, if it could be shown that the time between responses changes as a function of selective reinforcement, then the IRT is by definition an operant in its own right. To demonstrate that the IRT is an operant, it is necessary to identify an IRT of specific length (e.g., 2 s between any two responses) and then reinforce that interresponse time, showing that it increases in frequency.

Computers and other electronic equipment have been used to measure the IRTs generated on various schedules of reinforcement. A response is made and the computer starts timing until the next response is emitted. Typically, these interresponse times are slotted into time bins. For example, all IRTs between 0 and 2 s are counted, followed by those that fall in the 2- to 4-s range, and then the number of 4- to 6-s IRTs. This method results in a distribution of interresponse times. Several experiments have shown that the distribution of IRTs may in fact be changed by selectively reinforcing interresponse times of a particular duration (for a review, see Morse, 1966). Figure 5.22 shows the results of a hypothetical experiment in which IRTs of different duration are reinforced on a VI schedule.

On the standard VI, most of the IRTs are 2–4 s long. When an additional contingency is added to the VI schedule that requires IRTs of 10–12 s, the IRTs increase in this category. Also, a new distribution of IRTs is generated. Whereas on a VR the next response may be reinforced regardless of the IRT, on VI the combination pause plus response is required for reinforcement.

Anger (1956) conducted a complex experiment demonstrating that IRTs are a conditionable property of behavior. In this experiment, the IRT was also considered to be a stimulus that set the occa-

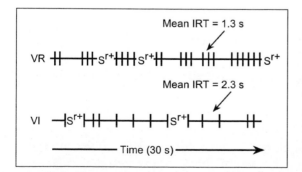

FIG. 5.21 Idealized distributions of response on VR and VI schedules of reinforcement. Responses are represented by the vertical marks, and S^{r+} denotes reinforcement.

FIG. 5.22 Hypothetical distributions of interresponse times (IRTs) for an animal responding on a standard VI schedule of reinforcement and on a VI that only reinforces IRTs that fall between 10 and 12 s.

sion for the next response (S^D). Reynolds (1966a) subsequently showed that the IRT controlled performance that followed it. In other words, IRTs seem to function as discriminative stimuli for behavior. The difficulty with this conception is that stimulus properties are inferred from performance. Zeiler has pointed out:

> If the IRT is treated as a differentiated response unit [an operant], unobservable stimuli need not be postulated as controlling observable performance. Given the one-to-one correspondence between response and inferred stimulus properties, however, the two treatments appear to be equivalent.
>
> (Zeiler, 1977, p. 223)

We treat the IRT as an operant rather than as a discriminative stimulus. As an operant, the IRT is considered to be a conditionable property of the response that ends the time interval between any two responses. For example, a rat may press a lever R_1, R_2, R_3, R_4, and R_5 times. The time between lever presses R_1 and R_2 is the interresponse time associated with R_2. In a similar fashion, the IRT for R_5 is the elapsed time between R_4 and R_5. This series can be said to constitute a homogeneous chain that is divisible into discrete three-term-contingency links.

As part of Anger's experiment, animals were placed on a VI 300-s schedule of reinforcement (Anger, 1956). On this schedule, the response that resulted in reinforcement had to occur 40 s or more after the previous response. If the animal made many fast responses with IRTs of less than 40 s, the schedule requirements would not be met. In other words, IRTs of more than 40 s were the operant that was reinforced. Anger found that this procedure shifted the distribution of IRTs toward 40 s. Thus, the IRT that is reinforced is more likely to be emitted than other interresponse times. Additional experiments have demonstrated a similar effect (Dews, 1963; Ferster & Skinner, 1957; Kelleher, Fry, & Cook, 1959; Platt, 1979; Shimp, 1969), and Morse (1966) provides a formal analysis supporting the conclusion that IRTs are a conditionable property of operant behavior. Lattal and his colleagues at West Virginia University have extended these findings. Their research on delay of reinforcement suggests that basic behavioral units, like IRTs, are conditioned even when the contingencies of reinforcement do not directly require it (Arbuckle & Lattal, 1988; Lattal, 1984; Lattal & Ziegler, 1982).

Ratio schedules generate rapid sequences of responses with short interresponse times (Gott & Weiss, 1972; Weiss & Gott, 1972). On a ratio schedule, consider what the probability of obtaining reinforcement is following a burst of very fast responses (short IRTs) or a series of responses with long IRTs. Recall that ratio schedules are based on the number of responses that are emitted. Bursts of responses with short IRTs rapidly count down the ratio requirement and are more likely to be reinforced than sets of long IRT responses (slow responding). Thus, ratio schedules, because of the way they are constructed, differentially reinforce short IRTs. According to the molecular IRT view of schedule control, this is why the rate of response is high on ratio schedules.

When compared with ratio schedules, interval contingencies generate longer IRTs and consequently a lower rate of response. Interval schedules pay off after some amount of time has passed and a response is made. As the IRTs become longer, more and more of the time requirement on the schedule elapses and the probability of reinforcement increases. In other words, longer IRTs are differentially reinforced on interval schedules (Morse, 1966). In keeping with the molecular view, interval contingencies differentially reinforce long IRTs, and the rate of response is moderate on these schedules.

Molar Accounts of Rate Differences

There are several problems with the IRT account of rate differences on ratio and interval schedules. One problem is that experiments on selective reinforcement of IRTs do not prove that IRTs are controlled in this way on interval or ratio schedules. Also, there is evidence that when long IRTs are reinforced, organisms continue to emit short bursts of rapid responses. Animals typically produce these bursts even on schedules that never reinforce a fast series of responses (differential reinforcement of low rate, DRL). For these reasons, molar hypotheses have been advanced about the rate of response differences on reinforcement schedules.

Molar explanations of rate differences are concerned with the overall relationship between responses and reinforcement. In molar terms, the *correlation between responses and reinforcement or feedback function* produces the difference in rate on interval and ratio schedules. Generally, if a high rate of response is associated with a higher rate of reinforcement in the long run, animals will respond rapidly. When an increased rate of response does not affect the rate of reinforcement, organisms do not respond faster (Baum, 1993).

Consider a VR 100 schedule of reinforcement. On this schedule, a subject could respond 50 times per minute and in a 1-h session obtain 30 reinforcers. On the other hand, if the rate of response was 300 per minute (not outside the range of pigeons or humans), the number of reinforcers earned would increase to 180 an hour. According to supporters of the molar view, this correlation between increasing rate of response and increased frequency of reinforcement is responsible for rapid responding on ratio schedules.

A different correlation between rate of response and rate of reinforcement is set up on interval schedules. Recall that interval schedules program a reinforcer after time has passed and one response is made. Suppose you are responding on a VI 3-min schedule for $5 reinforcers. You have 1 h a day to work on the schedule. If you respond at a reasonable rate, say 30 lever presses per minute, you will get most or all of the 20 scheduled reinforcers. Now pretend that you increase your rate of response to 300 lever presses a minute. The only consequence is a sore wrist, and the rate of reinforcement remains at 20 per hour. In other words, after some moderate value, it does not pay to increase the rate of response on interval schedules—hence lower rates are maintained on interval schedules.

Molar and Molecular Control of Response Rates

A substantial number of studies have attempted to experimentally separate the molecular and molar determinants of response rates on schedules of reinforcement (Reed, 2007). One way to analyze the control exerted by the molar and molecular determinants of response rate is to use a blended schedule of reinforcement, having both VR and VI properties.

McDowell and Wixted (1986) designed a schedule with the molar properties of a VR schedule, higher rates of response correlating with higher rates of reinforcement (linear feedback), but with the molecular properties of a VI schedule—differential reinforcement of longer IRTs. The schedule is called the *variable interval plus linear feedback (VI+)*. In this study, humans pressed a lever for monetary reinforcement on VR and VI+ schedules. The results indicated that both schedules produced high response rates, a finding consistent with molar control by the feedback function (correlation between rates of response and rates of reinforcement) but inconsistent with molecular contingency of differential reinforcement of long IRTs (and low response rate).

Studies with rats generally have not found equivalent high rates of response on VR and VI+ schedules. Evidence from rodents indicates that VI+ generates response rates similar to conventional VI schedules when matched for the rate of reinforcement (Reed, Soh, Hildebrandt, DeJongh, & Shek, 2000). That is, the IRTs on the VI+ schedules were more similar to VI and considerably longer than on the VR schedule. Overall, rats show sensitivity to the molecular contingency of IRT reinforcement and minimal control by the molar feedback function arranged by the VI+ schedule.

As you can see, studies using a VI+ schedule to separate molar and molecular control of response rates reach different conclusions for rats and humans. Rats are sensitive to the reinforcement of IRTs arranged by the VI+ schedule, whereas humans show sensitivity to the feedback function (correlation between response rate and reinforcement rate) of the schedule. One difference between rats and humans (other than species) is that humans may have responded at higher rates than rats on the VI+. The higher response rates would allow differential conditioning of high rates. Also, variability in high rates would allow sampling of the correlation between response rate and reinforcement rate, resulting in sensitivity to the molar feedback function. One implication of this is that rats would be sensitive to the molar feedback function of the VI+ schedule if the animals responded at high rates.

In a series of experiments that compared VR, VI, and VI+ schedules, Reed (2007) demonstrated that at lower rates of response rats were controlled by the reinforcement of IRTs, showing higher response rates on VR than on VI or VI+ schedules. In contrast, when procedures were arranged to maintain high response rates, rats showed sensitivity to the molar feedback function, responding as fast on VI+ as on VR, and faster on both than on a yoked VI schedule (which obtained reinforcement the same as VI+). Variability in the response rate also resulted in more sensitivity to the molar characteristics of the schedule. Overall, sensitivity to molecular and molar determinants of schedules of reinforcement requires contact with the contingencies. Low rates of responding contact the molecular contingencies related to interresponse times (IRT). High response rates contact the molar contingencies that involve the correlation between rate of response and rate of reinforcement.

In terms of human behavior, Baum (2010) has argued that IRT regularities at molecular levels may be of little use. The contingencies that regulate children responding for teacher attention or employees working for pay seldom involve moment-to-moment contiguity between responses and reinforcement. Thus, employees would be more likely to contact the molar correlation between rates of productivity and wages, varying their work rates over time to match the rate of payoff. It is the molar contingencies that control human behavior from Baum's point of view.

Although human behavior may not show obvious control by molecular contingencies, there are industries, such as Lincoln Electric, which use incentive systems directly tied to IRTs (assembly piece rate) as well as molar profit sharing (Hodgetts, 1997). Notably, Lincoln Electric has been highly successful even in hard economic times, and has never used employee layoffs to cut costs. Planned incentive systems that arrange both molecular and molar contingencies may yield high performance and satisfaction for both workers and management (Daniels & Daniels, 2004).

Postreinforcement Pause on Fixed Schedules

Fixed-ratio and fixed-interval schedules generate a pause that follows reinforcement. Accounts of pausing on fixed schedules may also be classified as molecular or molar. Molecular accounts of pausing are concerned with the moment-to-moment relationships that immediately precede reinforcement. Such accounts are concerned with the relationship between the number of bar presses that produce reinforcement and the subsequent postreinforcement pause. In contrast, molar accounts of pausing focus on the overall rate of reinforcement for a session and the average pause length.

Research shows that the postreinforcement pause (PRP) is a function of the *interreinforcement interval (IRI)*. As the IRI becomes longer, the PRP increases. On fixed-interval schedules, in which the time between reinforcement is controlled by the experimenter, the PRP is approximately half of the IRI. For example, on an FI 300-s schedule (in which the time between reinforcements is 300 s), the average PRP will be 150 s. On fixed ratio, the evidence suggests similar control by the IRI (Powell, 1968)—as the ratio requirement increases, the PRP becomes longer.

There is, however, a difficulty with analyzing the PRP on FR schedules. On ratio schedules, the IRI is partly determined by what the animal does. That is, the animal's rate of pressing the lever affects the time between reinforcements. Another problem with ratio schedules, for an analysis of pausing, is that the rate of response goes up as the size of the ratio is increased (Boren, 1961). Unless the rate of response exactly coincides with changes in the size of the ratio, adjustments in ratio size alter the IRI. For example, on FR 10 a rate of five responses per minute produces an IRI of 2 min. This same rate of response produces an IRI of 4 min on an FR 20 schedule. Thus, changes in postreinforcement pause as the ratio size is increased may be caused by the ratio size, the IRI, or both.

Molar Interpretation of Pausing

We have noted that the average PRP is half of the interreinforcement interval. Another finding is that the PRPs are normally distributed (bell-shaped curve) over the time between reinforcements. In other words, on an FI 320-s schedule, pauses will range from 0 to 320 s, with an average pause of around 160 s. As shown in Figure 5.23, these results can be accounted for by considering what would happen if the normal curve moved upward so that the mean pause was 225 s. In this case, many of the pauses would exceed the FI interval and the animal would get fewer reinforcements for the session. An animal that was sensitive to *overall rate of reinforcement* or the long range payoffs (maximization; see Chapter 9) should come to emit pauses that are on average half of the FI interval, assuming a normal distribution. Thus, maximization of reinforcement provides a molar account of the postreinforcement pause (Baum, 2002).

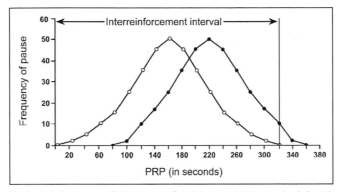

FIG. 5.23 Two possible distributions of PRPs on a fixed-interval 320-s schedule. The distribution given by the open circles has a mean of 160 s and does not exceed the interreinforcement interval (IRI) set on the FI schedule. The bell curve for the distribution with the dark circles has an average value of 225 s, and many pauses exceed the IRI.

Molecular Interpretations of Pausing

There are two molecular accounts of pausing on fixed schedules that have some degree of research support. One account is based on the observation that animals often emit other behavior during the PRP (Staddon & Simmelhag, 1971). For example, rats may engage in grooming, sniffing, scratching, and stretching after the presentation of a food pellet. Because this other behavior reliably follows reinforcement, it is said to be induced by the schedule. *Schedule-induced* behaviors (see Chapter 7) may be viewed as operants that automatically produce reinforcement. For example, stretching may relieve muscle tension, and scratching may eliminate an itch. One interpretation is that pausing occurs because the animal is maximizing local rates of reinforcement. That is, the rat gets food for bar pressing as well as the automatic reinforcement from the induced activities (see Shull, 1979). The average pause should therefore reflect the allocation of time to induced behavior and to the operant that produces scheduled reinforcement (food). At present, experiments have not ruled out or clearly demonstrated the induced-behavior interpretation of pausing (e.g., Derenne & Baron, 2002).

A second molecular account of pausing is based on the **run of responses** or amount of work that precedes reinforcement (Shull, 1979, pp. 217–218). This "work-time" interpretation holds that the previously experienced run of responses regulates the length of the postreinforcement pause. Work time affects the PRP by altering the value of the next scheduled reinforcement. In other words, the more effort or time that is expended for the previous reinforcer, the lower the value of the next reinforcer and the longer it takes for the animal to initiate responding (pause length). Interestingly, Skinner made a similar interpretation in 1938 when he stated that pausing on fixed-ratio schedules occurred because "the preceding run which occurs under reinforcement at a fixed ratio places the [reflex] reserve in a state of strain which acts with the temporal discrimination of reinforcement to produce a pause of some length" (p. 298). Skinner's use of the strained reserve seems to be equivalent to the more current emphasis on work time. Overall, this view suggests that the harder one works for reinforcement, the less valuable the next reinforcement is, and therefore the longer it takes to start working again.

Neither the induced behavior nor the work-time accounts of pausing are sufficient to handle all that is known about patterning on schedules of reinforcement. A schedule of reinforcement is a procedure for combining a large number of different conditions that regulate behavior. Some of the controlling factors arise from the animal's behavior, and others are set by the experimenter. This means that it is exceedingly difficult to unravel the exact processes that produce characteristic schedule performance. Nonetheless, the current interpretations of pausing point to some of the more relevant factors that play a role in the regulation of behavior on fixed schedules.

The Dynamics of Schedule Performance

There are reasons for detailed research on the PRP and interresponse time. The hope is to analyze schedule effects in terms of a few basic processes. This area of research is called **behavioral dynamics**, or the study of behavior allocation through time. Behavioral dynamics involve feedback processes that move the system (organism) from an unstable, transitional state toward steady-state equilibrium. If performance on schedules can be reduced to a small number of fundamental principles, either laws of dynamics or law of equilibrium, then reasonable interpretations may be made about any particular arrangement of the environment (schedule). Also, it should be possible to predict behavior more precisely from knowledge of the operating contingencies and the axioms that govern dynamic behavior systems. Evidence has accumulated that the basic principles may be molar, involving laws of equilibrium and the matching of time allocation among activities. Even at the smallest time scales of the key peck or the switch from one activity to another, a molar law describes the behavioral dynamics of the system (Baum, 2010; see Chapter 9 on choice).

Behavioral dynamics is currently at the leading edge of behavior analysis and, like most scientific research, it requires a high level of mathematical sophistication. Both linear and nonlinear calculus is used to model the behavioral impact of schedules of reinforcement. In the 1990s, an issue of the *Journal of the Experimental Analysis of Behavior* was devoted to this important subject, and included topics such as a chaos theory of performance on fixed-interval schedules, dynamics of behavioral structure, behavioral momentum, resistance to behavior change, and feedback functions for variable-interval schedules (see Baum, 1992; Killeen, 1992; Marr, 1992; Nevin, 1992; Rachlin, 1992; Shimp, 1992; Zeiler, 1992). In that same issue, Peter Killeen, a professor at Arizona State University, builds on his previous work and suggests that "behavior may be treated as basic physics" with responses viewed as movement through behavioral space (Killeen, 1992). Although these issues are beyond the scope of this book, the student of behavior analysis should be aware that the physics of schedule performance is an advanced area of the science of behavior.

CHAPTER SUMMARY

A schedule of reinforcement describes the arrangement of stimuli, operants, and consequences. Such contingencies were outlined by Ferster and Skinner (1957) and are central to the understanding of behavior regulation in humans and other animals. The research on schedules and performance patterns is a major component of the science of behavior, a science that progressively builds on previous experiments and theoretical analysis. Schedules of reinforcement generate consistent, steady-state performances involving runs of responses and pausing that are characteristic of the specific schedule (ratio or interval). In the laboratory, the arrangement of progressive ratio schedules can serve as an animal model of foraging in the wild, and intermittent reinforcement plays a role in most human behavior, especially social interaction.

To improve the description of schedules as contingencies of reinforcement, we have introduced the Mechner system of notation. This notation is useful for programming contingencies in the laboratory or analyzing complex environment–behavior relations. In this chapter, we have outlined continuous reinforcement (CRF) and resistance to extinction on this schedule. CRF also results in response stereotypy based on the high rate of reinforcement. Fixed-ratio (FR) and fixed-interval (FI) schedules were introduced, as well as the postreinforcement pausing (PRP) on these contingencies. Adult humans have not shown classic scalloping or break-and-run patterns on FI schedules, and the performance differences of humans relate to language or verbal behavior as well as histories of ratio reinforcement. Variable-ratio (VR) and variable-interval (VI) schedules produce less pausing and higher overall rates of response. Adding a limited hold to a VI schedule increases the response rate by reinforcing short interresponse times (IRT). When rates of reinforcement are varied on VI schedules, the higher the rate of reinforcement the greater the behavioral momentum.

The study of behavior during the transition between schedules of reinforcement has not been well researched, due to the boundary problem of steady-state behavior. Transition states, however, play an important role in human behavior—as in the shift in the reinforcement contingencies from childhood to adolescence or the change in schedules from employment to retirement. Reinforcement schedules also have applied importance, and research shows that cigarette smoking can be regulated by a progressive schedule combined with an escalating response–cost contingency. Finally, in the advanced section of this chapter, we addressed molecular and molar accounts of response rate and rate differences on schedules of reinforcement. We emphasized the analysis of IRTs for molecular accounts, and the correlation of overall rates of response and reinforcement for molar explanations.

KEY WORDS

Assumption of generality

Behavioral dynamics

Break and run

Breakpoint

Continuous reinforcement (CRF)

Fixed interval (FI)

Fixed ratio (FR)

Interreinforcement interval (IRI)

Interresponse time (IRT)

Interval schedules

Limited hold

Mechner notation

Molar account (of schedule performance)

Molecular account (of schedule performance)

Postreinforcement pause (PRP)

Preratio pause

Progressive ratio schedule

Ratio schedule

Ratio strain

Reinforcement efficacy

Resurgence

Run of responses

Scalloping

Schedule of reinforcement

Steady-state performance

Transition state

Variable interval (VI)

Variable ratio (VR)

ON THE WEB

www.youtube.com/watch?v=I_ctJqjlrHA This YouTube video discusses basic schedules of reinforcement, and B. F. Skinner comments on variable ratio schedules, gambling, and the belief in free will.

www.pigeon.psy.tufts.edu/eam/eam2.html This module demonstrates basic schedules of reinforcement as employed in a variety of operant and discrimination procedures involving animals and humans.

http://opensiuc.lib.siu.edu/cgi/viewcontent.cgi?article=1255&context=tpr&sei-redir=1–search="conjugate schedule reinforcement" A review of the impact of Ferster and Skinner's publication of *Schedules of Reinforcement* (Ferster and Skinner, 1957), from the study of basic schedules to the operant analysis of choice, behavioral pharmacology, and microeconomics of gambling. Contingency detection and causal reasoning by infants, children, and adults are addressed as areas influenced by schedules of reinforcement.

www.wadsworth.com/psychology_d/templates/student_resources/0534633609_sniffy2/sniffy/download.htm If you want to try out shaping and basic schedules with Sniffy the virtual rat, go to this site and use a free download for 2 weeks of fun. After this period, you will have to pay to continue your investigation of operant conditioning and schedules of reinforcement.

BRIEF QUIZ

1. Schedules of reinforcement were first described by:

   (a) Charles Ferster
   (b) Francis Mechner
   (c) B. F. Skinner
   (d) Fergus Lowe

2. Infrequent reinforcement generates responding that is persistent. What is this called?

   (a) postreinforcement pause
   (b) partial reinforcement effect
   (c) molar maximizing
   (d) intermittent resistance

3. Mechner notation describes:

   (a) stimulus effects
   (b) dependent variables
   (c) response contingencies
   (d) independent variables

4. Resurgence happens when:

   (a) behavior is put on extinction
   (b) reinforcement magnitude is doubled
   (c) high-probability behavior persists
   (d) response variability declines

5. Schedules that generate predictable stair-step patterns are:

(a) fixed interval
(b) fixed ratio
(c) variable ratio
(d) random ratio

6. Variable-ratio schedules generate:

(a) postreinforcement pauses
(b) locked rates
(c) break-and-run performance
(d) high rates of response

7. Schedules that combine time and responses are called:

(a) partial reinforcement schedules
(b) complex schedules
(c) interval schedules
(d) fixed-time schedules

8. The shape of the response pattern generated by an FI is called a:

(a) scallop
(b) ogive
(c) break and pause
(d) accelerating dynamic

9. Human performance on FI differs from animal data due to:

(a) intelligence differences
(b) self-instruction
(c) contingency effects
(d) alternative strategies

10. Behavior is said to be in transition when it is between:

(a) a rock and a hard place
(b) stable states
(c) one schedule and another
(d) a response run

Answers to Brief Quiz: 1, c (p. 117); 2, b (p. 135); 3, d (p. 123); 4, a (p. 126); 5, b (Fig. 5.9); 6, d (p. 127); 7, c (Fig. 5.7); 8. A (Fig. 5.13); 9, b (p. 132); 10, b (p. 138).

Aversive Control of Behavior

6

Aversive stimuli are those events that organisms evade, avoid, or escape from. Stings, attacks, foul odors, bright light, and very loud noises are events that organisms are prepared to evade on the basis of phylogeny. Escaping or avoiding these **primary aversive stimuli** was adaptive, presumably because those animals that emitted this behavior in the presence of these kinds of events survived and reproduced. In other words, organisms do not learn that these are aversive stimuli; they are biologically prepared to avoid or escape such events.

Other stimuli acquire aversive properties when associated with primary aversive events during an animal's lifetime. For people, **conditioned aversive stimuli** (S^{ave}) include threats, public criticism, a failing grade, a frown, and verbal disapproval. To affect behavior, these events usually depend on a history of punishment. A 1-week-old infant is not affected by a reprimand such as "Don't do that!" However, by the time the child is 2 years old, the command may stop the toddler from tearing pages out of your favorite book. Animals also learn responses to conditioned stimuli as aversive events. People commonly shout "No!" when pets misbehave, and this auditory stimulus eventually reduces the probability of the response it follows (e.g., chewing on your new chair).

AVERSIVE CONTROL IN EVERYDAY LIFE

Aversive Control, Elephants, and Bees

Elephants are said to run away from mice, but recent research indicates that they are more likely to escape from the sounds of African bees (King, Douglas-Hamilton, & Vollrath, 2011). The "buzz" of bees is conditioned as an aversive stimulus when followed by bee stings inside the elephant's trunk—an event that is apparently extremely painful, with swelling that lasts for several weeks. In Kenya, farmers and elephants are often in conflict over crops that elephants raid and destroy. Rumors among game wardens suggested that elephants avoid trees with beehives, leading King and her colleagues to

FIG. 6.1   A herd of African elephants. These herds often invade the crops of farmers, eating the crops and destroying the farmers' property. The sound of bees and the presence of beehives keep the elephants away, based on the elephants' conditioning history involving bee stings to the inside of their trunks. © Shutterstock.

test the behavioral effects of a 4-min recording of bee sounds with 17 herds of elephants in Kenya's Buffalo Springs and Samburo National Reserves. The "buzzing" worked as 16 of the 17 herds took off running, and one herd even ran across a river to get away (Figure 6.1). On average, the elephants moved 64 m away from the speakers when "buzzing" sounds were played, but only 20 m when the sounds of random white noise were played. The equipment for playing bee sounds is too expensive (think of the extension cords that would be needed) for farmers. However, beehives with real bees are a feasible alternative that also provides farmers with extra food and income. The scientists placed beehives every 10 m along a 1700-m "beehive fence" on farms in Northern Kenya, which were usually protected only by thorn-bush barriers. Over a period of 2 years, only one elephant broke through the beehive fence, compared with 31 invasions through the thorny barriers. The evidence suggests that bees and their "buzz" are a deterrent for elephants, presumably as a result of a conditioning history of bee stings and social learning.

Aversive Control of Human Behavior

Elephants' avoidance of bees shows that a large amount of animal behavior is regulated by naturally occurring aversive stimuli. Humans also extensively use and arrange aversive stimuli to control the behavior of others at the individual, societal, and institutional levels. Nathan Azrin and William Holz, pioneers in the analysis of punishment, considered the possibility of eliminating punishment from our world. They stated:

> At the institutional level, it would seem to be quite possible to eliminate the use of physical punishment. Conceivably, administrative regulations could be altered such that public punishment in the form of flogging, spankings, or other physical abuse would be excluded. At the level of individual behavior, it seems somewhat more difficult but still not impossible to eliminate the use of physical punishment. *One type of punishment, however, seems to be virtually impossible to eliminate, and that is the punishing contingencies that are arranged by the physical world.* Whenever we interact with the physical world, there are many punishing contingencies awaiting us. . . . Elimination of punishing contingencies by the physical world would appear to require elimination of all behavior that involves interaction with the physical world.
>
> (Azrin and Holz, 1966, p. 438, emphasis added)

At least in the physical world, punishment is a fact of life. With regard to the social world, Sidman (2001) has documented our excessive reliance on coercion to control human behavior. The excessive use and advocacy of punishment by some groups is illustrated by the beating of children as a form of Christian discipline. In 2010, CBS News reported the beating to death of 7-year-old Lydia Schatz by her adopted parents. The beatings of Lydia and her 11-year-old sister, who recovered from her injuries, ironically took place in Paradise, California. The report stated:

> **CHICO, Calif. (CBS/KOVR)** Three years ago, Kevin Schatz and his wife Elizabeth did something so noble, a local television station featured them; the pair decided to adopt three children from Liberia. Now, they're accused of killing one of the children because she mispronounced a word. . . . Prosecutors say that the California couple used quarter-inch plastic tubing to beat their seven-year-old adopted daughter to death. Apparently, they got the idea from a fundamentalist Christian group, which promotes this as a way of training children to be obedient. Butte County District Attorney Mike Ramsey says for several hours the 7-year-old was held down by Elizabeth and beaten dozens of times by Kevin on the back of her body, which caused massive tissue damage.
>
> (Martinez, 2010; CBS News)

Subsequently, the couple pleaded guilty and Kevin Schatz was sentenced to 22 years in prison for murder, torture, and misdemeanor cruelty to a child. Elizabeth Schatz received a sentence of 13 years and 4 months for voluntary manslaughter, infliction of unlawful corporal punishment, and misdemeanor cruelty to a child (full story on CNN video; Tuckman, 2011). In the USA, for the year 2009 there were more than 2 million investigations of child maltreatment (mostly neglect and physical abuse), of which about 25% were substantiated (U.S. Department of Health and Human Services, Administration for Children & Families, 2009). The use of punishment and aversive control in child rearing is a pervasive practice in American culture. Figure 6.2 shows the percentage of American parents using all forms of corporal punishment by age of child (see Straus, 2001 and Gershoff, 2002 on the use of corporal punishment in America; also Park, 2002 points to the difficulty of isolating the effects of parental punishment from a "package" of disciplinary tactics).

Given the acceptance of punishment in our society, it is notable that today there is little basic research on aversive control and how best to minimize its side effects and reduce its prevalence (Catania, 2008). Most studies of the basic principles of punishment (and negative reinforcement) were conducted in the 1960s and 1970s, at which point studies of punishment almost stopped. A major

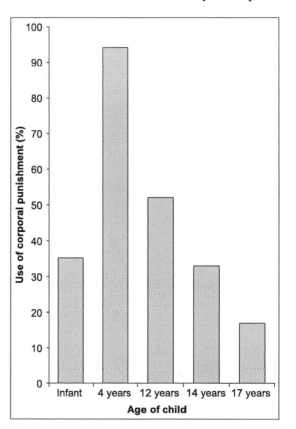

FIG. 6.2 The percentage of parents in the US using any form of corporal punishment by age of child. Use of corporal punishment begins in infancy and rises to a peak by 4 years of age, then declines as the child ages. Authors' illustration is based on data presented in Straus, M.A. & Stewart, J.H. (1999).

reason for this was that ethics committees at universities, influenced by changing cultural values and the animal activist movement, made it almost impossible to conduct experiments on punishment, believing it to be inhumane to subject animals to punishment. In this chapter, we present the accumulated findings on punishment and other forms of aversive control, assuming that knowledge about the effects and side effects of aversive control is a better strategy for improving the human condition than continued ignorance of the facts.

CONTINGENCIES OF PUNISHMENT

When a behavioral contingency results in a *decrease* in the rate of response, the contingency is called **punishment**. Any event or stimulus that decreases the rate of operant behavior is called a **punisher**. Figure 6.3 makes it clear that it is the relationship between the consequence and its effects on behavior that defines the contingency (see Sidman, 2006, p. 138 for an alternative definition of punishment by Skinner that does not include a decrease in behavior). At this point, we discuss contingencies of punishment; negative reinforcement is addressed later in this chapter.

Many operations other than a punishment contingency reduce the rate of response. These include satiation, extinction, behavioral contrast, restraint, precommitment, and richer alternative schedules of reinforcement. Each of these procedures is discussed throughout this textbook. Punishment is defined when an event is contingent on the occurrence of a specified response and the probability of that response is reduced. If shock is contingent on lever pressing, and lever pressing repeatedly has produced shocks, the rat is less likely to press the lever. The effect and the contingency are called positive punishment.

Positive Punishment

Positive punishment occurs when a stimulus is *presented* following an operant and the operant *decreases* in frequency. The contingency of positive punishment is shown in cell 2 of Figure 6.3.

Stimulus following behavior	Effect on behavior	
	Increase	Decrease
On/presented		2 Positive punishment
Off/removed	3 Negative reinforcement	4 Negative punishment

FIG. 6.3 Aversive contingencies of reinforcement and punishment (adapted from Figure 4.2 in Chapter 4). When a stimulus or event follows operant behavior, then the behavior increases or decreases in frequency. It is this relationship between behavior and consequence that defines the contingency.

When a parent spanks a child for running into the street and the child stops doing it, this is positive punishment. Of course, technically spanking is functioning as punishment only if it decreases the probability of running into the street. This is an important point because in usual language people talk about punishment without considering its effects on behavior. For example, you may shout and argue with another person when he or she expresses a particular political position. Your shouting is positive punishment only if the other individual stops (or decreases) talking about politics. In fact, the person may increase his or her rate of political conversation (as often happens in arguments). In this case, you have reinforced rather than punished arguing with you. Thus, positive punishment is defined as a decrease in operant behavior produced by the presentation of a stimulus that follows it. By this functional definition, punishment always works.

The Overcorrection Procedure

In applied behavior analysis, **overcorrection** is a positive punishment procedure that uses "restitution" to reduce or eliminate destructive or aggressive behavior. The person is required to "restore the disturbed situation to a greatly improved state" (Foxx & Azrin, 1972, p. 15). Thus, a patient in a mental institution who throws around the furniture in the lounge, scaring or annoying the other residents and ward staff, must overcorrect the environmental effects of his actions by rearranging the furniture of the entire room and apologizing to staff and residents. Overcorrection may also involve *positive practice*, requiring the violator to intensively practice an overly correct form of the action. Thus, Foxx and Azrin (1973) treated the self-stimulatory behavior of four autistic children using positive practice overcorrection. The children were required by commands or physical guidance to make a series of head and arm movements (approximations of self-stimulatory behavior) following bouts of self-stimulation. This procedure eliminated self-stimulatory behavior in each of the children.

Although Foxx and Azrin (1972) viewed overcorrection as an "educational" procedure, reviews of the literature make it clear that both restitution and positive practice involve behavioral effects similar to punishment imposed by electric shock (Mackenzie-Keating & McDonald, 1990; Milenberger & Fuqua, 1981). Note that overcorrection works to instill compliance with the rules and commands of an authority (parents, teacher, or staff). When the wrongdoer fails to comply, the authority adds other punishers such as physical restraint or removal from the situation. These back-up punishers make overcorrection an effective punishment contingency. Even so, overcorrection includes additional procedures such as differential reinforcement of alternative behavior or extinction, which contribute to the effectiveness of overcorrection as an intervention package. To date, detailed component analysis of the "package" has not been a primary focus of applied behavioral research.

Negative Punishment

Negative punishment is portrayed in cell 4 of Figure 6.3. When an ongoing stimulus is *removed* contingent on a response and this removal results in a *decrease* in the rate of behavior, the contingency is called **negative punishment** (or omission). In other words, if the organism responds, the stimulus is taken away and behavior decreases. A hungry bird is given continuous access to food, but if it pecks the key, food is removed. A child is watching TV, but if the child runs around, the television is turned off. A person has earned money and is fined for speeding. In these cases, positive reinforcement (i.e., provision of food, TV is turned on, or earned money) is removed contingent on behavior, and the behavior decreases.

Negative punishment is often confused with extinction. *Extinction occurs when a previously reinforced response no longer produces reinforcement.* In this case, a response has produced reinforcement; extinction for that response is in effect when the response → reinforcer contingency is discontinued. A pigeon may peck a key for food, but when extinction is programmed, pecking no longer produces the food reinforcer. Similarly, a child may be allowed to watch a favorite television show after completing homework assignments. When the TV is broken the contingency is no longer in effect and doing homework is on extinction.

In Figure 6.4, ongoing reinforcement could be eating a meal with the family, and responses $R_2 \ldots R_N$ may involve talking to a sister, passing food around the table, or turning on a compact

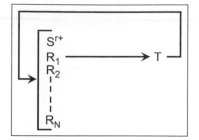

FIG. 6.4 Negative punishment occurs when operant responses R_2 through R_N do not affect ongoing reinforcement (S^{r+}). If the response R_1 is emitted, however, reinforcement is removed for some period of time (T). After that time period has elapsed, reinforcement is reinstated.

disk player. Licking your plate is represented by R_1 and results in father telling you to leave the table for a period of time (negative punishment). Forcing you to leave your supper reduces your tendency to engage in this nasty habit when you next have a meal with your family.

Timeout Procedures

In behavioral terms, "leaving the table" is timeout from positive reinforcement (Ferster & Appel, 1961), assuming that the procedure reduces "licking the plate." With **timeout** the wrongdoer loses access to positive reinforcement for a specified period of time for engaging in the undesirable behavior. In the classroom, timeout can involve either exclusion or non-exclusion (Cooper, Heron, & Heward, 2007). In timeout with non-exclusion the student is not physically removed from the situation. Timeout by non-exclusion occurs when the teacher uses planned ignoring of the behavior, withdrawal of a specific positive reinforcer, or handing the person a timeout ribbon that is later exchanged for a timeout period. Exclusion timeout, on the other hand, involves placing the person in a timeout room, using a partitioned space for timeout, or placing the violator in a school hallway.

For a timeout procedure to be effective, the teacher must ensure that the classroom activities are reinforcing for the student, define the responses that lead to timeout, and decide on the method to use (non-exclusion or exclusion). In addition, the duration of timeout (usually a brief period) must be specified, the exiting criteria should be established, and permission to use timeout must be obtained from the relevant parties, such as the school principal and parents. As in all behavioral interventions, the teacher should keep precise records to evaluate the effectiveness of the procedure.

Response–Cost Procedures

Response cost is another negative punishment procedure in which conditioned reinforcers (tokens) are removed contingent on behavior, and the behavior decreases. In humans, common response–cost contingencies involve the loss of money or privileges for disobedience, and this loss decreases rule breaking. In the laboratory, response cost is arranged by token reinforcers, which are subsequently subtracted or removed following a response. Thus, Weiner (1962) arranged for the responses of adult humans to result in detection of light signals on VI or FI schedules; each detection response resulted in 100 points (tokens) on a counter. In response–cost conditions, each response subtracted 1 point from the counter of accumulated points. This point-loss contingency resulted in suppression of response rates on the signal-detection schedules. Recent research with pigeons using light-emitting diodes (LEDs) as tokens exchanged for 2.5 s of access to food has confirmed the human findings. Birds show suppression of behavior by response–cost contingencies, and effects similar to traditional punishers such as electric shock (Pietras & Hackenberg, 2005).

Relativity of Punishment

In Chapter 4, we discussed the principle of reinforcement and the Premack principle (Premack, 1959, 1962). This principle states that the opportunity to engage in a higher-frequency behavior will reinforce a lower-frequency response. That is, *reinforcement is relative, not absolute*. Premack

(1971) extended this principle to the **relativity of punishment**. Consider a rat that can run in an activity wheel and drink water from a tube. The wheel apparatus is modified so that a brake can be activated, locking the wheel and preventing the rat from running. In addition, a motor is installed that permits the wheel to rotate at a set speed, forcing the rat to run. In this modified apparatus, withholding running while giving free access to water makes running the higher-frequency behavior. On the other hand, depriving the rat of water while giving it access to running makes drinking the more probable behavior.

At this point, forced running (motorized wheel) is made the consequence of drinking. That is, the rat's drinking is followed by bouts of forced running. What do you think happens? The answer is that it depends on the relative frequency of running and drinking. When running is more probable than drinking (deprivation for running), bouts of forced running reinforce drinking (drinking increases). In contrast, when running is less probable than drinking (deprivation for water), bouts of forced running punish drinking (drinking decreases). More generally, Premack's analysis indicates that, like reinforcement, *punishment is relative, not absolute.* Even electric shock, which is usually viewed as an aversive stimulus or punisher, can function as reinforcement under appropriate conditions—as when a fixed-interval schedule of shock is superimposed on a schedule of food reinforcement for lever pressing or on a schedule of brain stimulation reinforcement in humans and other animals (Heath, 1963; Sidman, Brady, Boren, Conrad, & Schulman, 1955).

How to Make Punishment Most Effective

Unlike reinforcement, contingencies of punishment do not teach or condition new behavior. Contingencies of punishment eliminate or, more often, temporarily suppress the rate of operant behavior. In this section, we describe some of the conditions that increase the effectiveness of punishment.

The study of punishment is complicated by the fact that punished responses are typically maintained on some schedule of positive reinforcement. In other words, a schedule of punishment is superimposed on a baseline of positive reinforcement. This means that we are really investigating the effects of punishment on behavior maintained by some schedule of positive reinforcement, and the results may reflect both of these contingencies.

Abrupt Introduction of Punishment

Azrin, Holz, and Hake (1963) found that birds would continue to respond even when intense levels of electric shock (130 V) were delivered for key pecks. This effect occurred when the punisher was introduced at 60 V or less and gradually increased. On the other hand, pigeons that suddenly received moderate-intensity shocks, at 80 V, completely quit responding (see also Azrin, 1959; Miller, 1960). Behavior that produced sudden shock of sufficient intensity was irreversibly suppressed.

Consider the following scenario. Mike has bought a new stereo system and his friend, Joe, and Joe's 2-year-old daughter drop in for a visit. The child is eating a glob of peanut butter and makes a beeline for the new equipment. Nervously, Mike looks at his friend, who says "Emily, don't touch— that's Mike's new disk player." The child continues to fondle the knobs on Mike's $900 music system, and Joe says "Please leave that alone!" Emily is still smearing peanut butter on Mike's investment, so Joe glowers at his child and loudly says "I said stop that!" Emily does not stop, and is now threatened with "If you don't stop, Dad will give you a spanking!" Emily still plays with the stereo. In desperation, Joe gives Emily a light tap on the bottom, which she ignores. In this circumstance, presumed punishers are introduced at low intensity and gradually increased. Laboratory research suggests that this is a formula for creating a masochist. Of course, the best solution for the stereo problem would be to wipe the child's hands, or place the equipment out of reach.

Intensity of Punishment

The preceding discussion should make it clear that if punishment is going to be used, it should be introduced at a moderate intensity on the first occasion. Generally, higher intensity of punishment results in greater response suppression. Low-intensity positive punishment may leave behavior relatively unaffected, while severe values of the punisher may permanently change behavior (Appel & Peterson, 1965; Azrin, 1960). Several experiments have shown that intense punishment can completely eliminate responding (Appel, 1961; Storms, Boroczi, & Broen, 1962). One interesting implication is that once complete suppression of responding occurs, behavior is unlikely to recover for some time even when the punishment contingency is withdrawn. This is because the organism stops responding and never contacts the changed environment.

If an animal does respond again when reinforcement is available after punishment has been withdrawn, behavior eventually recovers to pre-punishment levels. These observations led Skinner and others to suggest that punishment only produces a temporary suppression of behavior:

> Recently, the suspicion has . . . arisen that punishment does not in fact do what it is supposed to do. An immediate effect in reducing a tendency to behave is clear enough, but this may be misleading. The reduction in strength may not be permanent.
>
> (Skinner, 1953, p. 183)

This passage reflects Skinner's lifelong objection to the use of punishment for behavior regulation. That is, he argued against the use of punishment and for the use of positive reinforcement in human affairs. Remember, however, that both reinforcement and punishment are defined by a change in the behavior; if the rate of response does not change, neither reinforcement nor punishment can be said to have occurred.

Nonetheless, research shows that high-intensity positive punishment can permanently eliminate responding. This elimination of responses does not seem to be affected by time away from the experimental situation (Azrin, 1959, 1960). For example, Masserman (1946) placed cats in a situation in which they had been punished 20 months earlier. The animals did not emit the punished response, even though the punishment contingency was discontinued. Thus, high-intensity punishment can reduce the rate of response to absolute zero, and this appears to be an enduring effect. Have you ever touched a wire conducting 110 V of electricity more than once?

Immediacy of Punishment

Punishment is most effective at reducing responses when it closely follows behavior (Azrin, 1956; Cohen, 1968). This effect can be missed easily because punishment generates emotional behavior that may disrupt operant responses. In other words, when it is first introduced, *positive punishment elicits reflexive behavior that prevents the occurrence of operant behavior.* Watch a child (or adult) who has just been chastised severely for making rude noises. You will probably see the child sit quietly, possibly cry, or look away from others. In common language, we may say that the child is pouting, but in fact what is happening is that reflexive emotional behavior is disrupting all operant behavior. If punishment follows immediately for making rude noises (the target behavior), those noises (as well as many other operants) would decrease in frequency. Making noises, however, would be relatively unaffected if punishment did not closely follow the target response.

Estes (1944) punished some rats immediately after they made a response, while another group received *delayed* punishment. Both groups of animals showed a similar reduction in bar pressing. This finding was replicated 11 years later by Hunt and Brady (1955), and suggests that positive punishment reduces operant responses because it elicits competing respondent behavior. Later research by Azrin (1956) found that after the first hour of exposure to positive punishment, immediate versus delayed punishment makes a large difference. Responses that were punished after a time delay recovered substantially, but when the punisher was delivered immediately, responses were often completely eliminated. Thus, it appears that the introduction of punishment generates conditioned emotional responses that may at first disrupt operant behavior. However, the contingency is eventually contacted and, in the long run, makes a large difference. To make punishment most effective, it should be delivered immediately after the response.

Schedule of Punishment

In general, positive punishment is most effective when it is delivered after each response and continuously (Zimmerman & Ferster, 1963), rather than intermittently (Filby & Appel, 1966). Azrin, Holz, and Hake (1963) trained pigeons to peck a key on a VI 3-min schedule of food reinforcement. Once responding was stable, shocks were presented after 100, 200, 300, 500, or 1000 key pecks. Rate of response substantially declined even when punishment was delivered after 1000 responses. As the rate of punishment increased, the number of responses per hour declined. In other words, as more responses were punished, the operant rate decreased. Continuous punishment (FR 1) produced the greatest response suppression. The effect is similar to increasing the intensity of the punisher—to maximize suppression of responses, deliver the punisher as frequently as possible and at high intensity.

Rate of response patterns on various schedules of punishment (FR, FI, VI, and VR) are usually *opposite* to the patterns produced on similar schedules of positive reinforcement. For example, an FI schedule of punishment when superimposed on a VI schedule of reinforcement for key pecking by pigeons produces an *inverse scallop* (recall that FI reinforcement often yields a scalloping pattern). That is, the occurrence of each punisher is followed by an immediately high rate of pecking that gradually declines as the time to the next punishment approaches (Azrin, 1956).

In summary, to make punishment most effective one should abruptly deliver an intense aversive stimulus immediately following the response and do this every time the response occurs.

🔎 FOCUS ON: Use of Punishment in Treatment

There are behaviorally deficient and psychotic people who, for a variety of reasons, engage in self-destructive behavior. This behavior may escalate to the point at which the person is hitting, scratching, biting, or gouging himself most of the day. In some cases, self-injurious acts are so frequent and intense that the person is hospitalized. Occasionally physical injury is irreversible, as when a child bangs his or her head on a wall until brain damage occurs. Although positive-reinforcement programs have been used to alleviate severe behavior problems, these contingencies are not always successful. Because of this, behavior therapists have resorted to punishment as a way of reducing self-destructive behavior.

One seemingly benign type of punishment used to suppress self-injurious behavior is water misting (Osborne, 2002). The literature indicates that contingent misting in the face reduces self-injurious behavior by 30–90% depending upon alternative sources of reinforcement. However, water misting as an effective—if not completely effective—punishment procedure has not been formally used for several years.

Misting and other techniques of positive punishment such as electric shock have been controversial, resulting in a **punishment debate** (Feldman, 1990). Opponents of punishment argue that such procedures are morally wrong, and they advocate a total ban on their use (e.g., Guess, Helmstetter, Turnbull, & Knowlton, 1986; Sobsey, 1990). These researchers also suggest that punishment is not necessary because many positive methods are available to treat severe behavior problems. In fact, research shows that positive behavioral support is as effective as punishment for eliminating severe behavior problems in young autistic children (up to 90% reduction), especially when the treatment program is based on a behavioral assessment of the functions (e.g. social attention, automatic reinforcement, self-stimulation) of the self-injurious responses (Horner, Carr, Strain, Todd, & Reed, 2002). Thus, it is possible to use only positive behavior management with young children who show severe problem behavior.

On the other side of the issue are the therapists and parents of self-abusive children who do not show reductions in life-threatening or self-damaging behavior. These people advocate the individual's right to effective treatment (e.g., Matson & Taras, 1989; Van Houten, Axelrod, Bailey, Favell, Foxx, Iwata et al., 1988). The proponents of effective treatment claim that a combination of positive behavioral support and punishment is the best way to manage severely self-injurious behavior (see review by Minshawl, 2008). Notice, however, that the predominant strategy from all perspectives is positive behavior management, regardless of whether punishment is added to the overall program. No one in applied behavior analysis is advocating the sole or predominant use of punishment without an overall positive behavioral program.

One reason given for not using punishment in applied settings is that aversive techniques may generate emotional distress and aggression (LaVigna & Donnellan, 1986; Lohrman-O'Rourke & Zirkel, 1998; Meyer & Evans, 1989). In a treatment setting, these effects and several side effects of punishment imply that aversive therapy for self-injurious behavior may produce as many problems as it alleviates (Lerman & Vorndran, 2002; see also the section on "Side Effects of Aversive Procedures" later in this chapter). However, Salvy and her associates found that contingent electric shock plus a conditioned punisher eliminated severe head banging in a preschool child without any negative side effects (Salvy, Mulick, Butter, Bartlett, & Linscheid, 2004; see Vorndran & Lerman, 2006 for a less intrusive procedure using conditioned punishment). This finding is supported by research on the use of electric shock treatment for self-injurious and aggressive behavior in

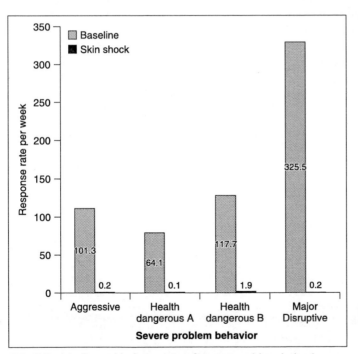

FIG. 6.5 Mean weekly frequency of severe problem behaviors (aggressive, health dangerous A, health dangerous B, and major disruptive behaviors) before and after contingent skin shock was added to the positive behavior program of a 14-year-old autistic boy at the Judge Rotenberg Center. Figure is based on the results reported in N. A. Blenkush, R. E. von Heyn, & M. L. Israel, 2007, "The effect of contingent skin shock on treated and untreated problem behaviors." Retrieved from www.judgerc.org/effectsofshock.html

pre-teens and teenagers with autism and conduct disorders (Oorsouw, Israel, von Heyn, & Duker, 2008).

In an early review of the research, Kushner (1970) supported the effective and justified use of electric shock in humans in a clinical context. This conclusion coincides with that of Blenkush, von Heyn, and Israel (2007), who found that dangerous and aggressive behaviors of a 14-year-old autistic boy were substantially reduced when contingent skin shocks were added to a positive comprehensive program of behavior management (Figure 6.5). Contingent shocks also had an indirect effect in decreasing other non-targeted problem behaviors, and completely eliminated the need for physical restraints. Subsequently, Israel, Blenkush, von Heyn, and Rivera (2008) replicated these findings with 60 autistic and conduct-disordered residents at a treatment facility, showing a 90% or greater reduction in aggressive behavior and a 98% decrease in injuries to treatment staff, presumably by reducing the need for physical restraint of the residents.

The Association for Behavior Analysis International (2010) reviewed the research on physical restraint and released a "Statement of Restraint and Seclusion" containing guiding principles for the use of restraint (punishment) procedures, as part of a positive behavior management program. If punishment is to be used in a behavioral program, contingent shocks actually might be preferable to repeated use of physical restraint and the potentially high rates of staff injuries. Unfortunately, the relative efficacy and generalizability of electric shocks, physical restraint, and other aversive procedures for treatment of self-injury have not been established convincingly (Prangnell, 2009). Inasmuch as punishment always works (by definition), only a very few presentations of the punishing stimulus should be delivered within the context of positive reinforcement. As anyone who has touched an electric wire knows, you do not usually touch it again. Repeated use of shock or physical restraint would indicate ineffective punishers or lack of effective reinforcement for alternative behavior. In either case, the program should be discontinued and a thorough behavioral assessment conducted. Continued use of aversive consequences without beneficial effects on behavior is unethical and not recommended by the authors or the Association for Behavior Analysis International.

NOTE ON: The Legal and Ethical Use of Electric Shock in a Residential Treatment Program

In the summer of 2012, a jury for a lawsuit in Dedham, Massachusetts saw a video of shock treatment recorded at the Judge Rotenberg Center (JCR) for developmentally disabled students. The video showed a teenager named Andre McCollins refusing to take off his coat, being restrained by staff, and being shocked repeatedly over time. The lawyer for the Center explained that the staff had followed the treatment plan for Andre and that these procedures were only administered after "prior parental, medical, psychiatric, human rights, peer review, and individual approval from a Massachusetts Probate Court" (Huffington Post, 2012).

On the other side of the issue, *Mother Jones* magazine argues that the Center is the only facility in the USA to use shocks to discipline students—"a form of punishment not inflicted on serial killers or child molesters or any of the 2.2 million inmates now incarcerated in U.S. jails and prisons" (Gonnerman, 2007). In defense of its treatment program, the Center insists that "JCR relies primarily on the use of positive programming and educational procedures to modify behaviors of its students. If, however, after giving these procedures a trial for an average of eleven months, they prove to be insufficiently effective, JCR then considers supplementing them with more intensive treatment procedures known as aversives" (Israel, undated).

Our answer to these legal and ethical issues relies on research evidence about aversive control of behavior. If shocks serve as punishers in a treatment procedure, these stimuli should immediately stop the self-injurious or aggressive behavior, allowing for positive reinforcement of alternative responses. To the extent that shocks, for whatever reason, do not immediately suppress the undesirable behavior, or positive reinforcements are unavailable to support alternative responses, the treatment program should be stopped and redesigned. The use of electric shocks without immediate suppressive effects on behavior is unwarranted and unethical from the evidence-based perspective of the authors of this textbook.

Reduce the Effectiveness of Positive Reinforcement

Punishment suppresses behavior more when positive reinforcement for the response is reduced in effectiveness (Dinsmoor, 1952). Azrin, Holz, and Hake (1963) trained pigeons to peck a key on a VI 3-min schedule of food reinforcement. After responding was stable, they introduced an intense 160-V shock for every 100th response. Birds were exposed to the schedule of reinforcement plus punishment at several levels of food deprivation. Recall that food deprivation is an *establishing operation* that should increase pecking of the key for food (and increase the reinforcement effectiveness of food). The animals were punished for responding at 60, 65, 70, 75, and 85% of free-feeding body weight. At 85% weight, punishment virtually stopped the birds' responding. However, at 60% weight the pigeons maintained a high, stable rate of response. As shown in Figure 6.6, rate of response was ordered by level of deprivation—the less the deprivation for food (satiation), the more effective punishment was.

Thus, behavior that is punished may be completely suppressed when the positive reinforcement contingency is made less effective through satiation. Interestingly, there is evidence that once complete suppression has occurred, the behavior does not recover even when the probability of responding for reinforcement is increased (Masserman, 1946; Storms et al., 1962). For example, a rat may be punished when it responds for food and its behavior completely eliminated. Next, the level of food deprivation is increased but responding remains at a zero rate.

These findings may have practical implications. Punishment is sometimes used to reduce the frequency of human behavior (see the preceding "Focus On: Use of Punishment in Treatment" section). And there are side effects of punitive regulation, suggesting that these techniques should be used with caution. Nonetheless, when

FIG. 6.6 Level of food deprivation and punished responding maintained by a VI food reinforcement schedule. Adapted from "Fixed-ratio punishment," by N. H. Azrin, W. C. Holz, and D. Hake, 1963, *Journal of the Experimental Analysis of Behavior, 6,* 141–148. © 1963 Society for the Experimental Analysis of Behavior, Inc. Published with permission.

people behave in ways that hurt themselves or others, punishment can be used to quickly suppress this behavior. Children who severely injure themselves by banging their heads, hitting themselves, or chewing on their flesh may benefit when positive punishment with electric shock is used to rapidly reduce self-injury (Lovaas and Simmons, 1969).

Temporary use of punishment can save a child from years of self-injury. Even so, animal research, as we have seen, suggests further ways to make punishment even more humane. Behavioral assessment shows that children who are treated with positive punishment often engage in self-injurious behavior due to social attention from adult caretakers. One way to refine the punishment procedure would involve satiation for caretaker attention. Adults would provide a high level of non-contingent attention to a child before using punishment of self-injury. This would be easy to implement; staff would hold, cuddle, and talk to the child for a few days before punishment was used. Once satiation for attention had occurred, even mild punishment might eliminate the self-injurious responses. Basic research, as we have seen, also suggests that when deprivation for attention increases again, self-destructive responding will not recover.

Response Alternatives

A straightforward way to make punishment more effective is to give a person another way to obtain reinforcement. When a reinforced response alternative is available, even moderate levels of punishment suppress behavior. To use a response alternative procedure, it is essential to identify the consequences that are maintaining the target behavior. Next, motivation may be reduced and the person given another way to obtain the same reinforcer. Herman and Azrin (1964) had people lever press on a VI schedule of reinforcement. Each lever press then produced an annoying buzzing sound, but the procedure only slightly reduced the rate of response. When people were given another response option that did not produce the buzzing sound, they quickly changed to that alternative and punished responses were eliminated (see also Azrin & Holz, 1966, p. 405).

Pretend that there is a convenience store in the middle of the block directly behind your house. You often walk to the store, but if you turn left to go around the block you pass a chained pit bulldog that lunges and growls at you. On the other hand, if you turn right you do not pass the dog. It is obvious that most people will choose the unpunished route to the store. If, however, turning right leads to a path that does not get you to the store, you may continue to walk past the dog. In reality, of course, you could walk on the other side of the street or drive to the store—these are also unpunished alternative responses.

PUNISHMENT: PERMANENCE AND PARADOX

Permanence of Punishment

One issue is whether punishment by itself, without additional procedures such as extinction or reinforcement of alternative behavior, can permanently eliminate undesirable behavior. In applied behavior analysis, the issue of permanence is cast as the maintenance of response suppression over extended periods. James O'Heare (2009; Weblog), a certified animal behavior consultant, has commented on the **permanence of punishment** and the maintenance of response suppression. He states:

> To suggest that punishment can eliminate a behavior is to conflate punishment with punishment plus other processes. If a behavior is exhibited then it has a reinforcement history; that contingency is in

place. When we impose a punishment contingency on that behavior, we merely add that contingency to the prevailing reinforcement contingency. If the reinforcer is stronger than the punisher then the behavior will continue to occur, although perhaps at a reduced rate or frequency. If the punishment is stronger than the reinforcer then the behavior will be suppressed to some extent, depending on just how much stronger it is. Indeed the behavior may be suppressed to a rate of zero. But as soon as the punishment contingency is discontinued, the existing reinforcement contingency prevails again and the behavior is expected to return to pre-punishment strength. . . . The main point here is to note that punishment alone does not eliminate the behavior; it merely suppresses it to some extent while that contingency is in effect. If the behavior is permanently eliminated, it is not because of the punishment contingency alone. What would have occurred is likely extinction simultaneously imposed, or more commonly the suppression allowed for the performance and reinforcement of other behaviors.

(from Weblog)

Although the permanence of punishment remains controversial, we have seen that highly intense electric shocks completely suppressed the behavior of cats even after 20 months (Masserman, 1946). However, the effects of early training and reinforcement history were not controlled; therefore these early studies and their findings must remain tentative. In applied settings, instances of punishment always involve other behavioral procedures as part of the "treatment package." On the other hand, Lerman and Vorndran (2002, p. 434) found that "common punishment procedures [used in treatment] . . . can be effective in the absence of extinction," a finding at odds with the claim that punishment effects are always confounded by other procedures. Overall, it is reasonable to conclude that punishment in combination with other positive procedures can have lasting suppressive effects on human behavior. Whether punishment (not including capital) by itself can permanently eliminate responding remains an unresolved question.

Paradoxical Effects of Punishment

If you touch a hot stove, you are less likely to do so again. That is just common sense. But what would you say if the response of touching the hot stove increased rather than decreased. That is, how could you understand responding to *produce* a painful event? Would you have to conclude that the child or person was a masochist and that hot stoves functioned as positive reinforcement for touching? It is exactly this kind of problem that behavior analysts confronted in research on the paradoxical effects of punishment.

Experiments have revealed that animals will sometimes work to produce punishers. In the laboratory, electric shock—an aversive event that can be precisely scheduled and varied in intensity—replaces the hot stove from our example. Morse and Kelleher (1977, pp. 193–198) described an experiment with a food-deprived squirrel monkey that was initially trained to press a lever for food on a variable-interval (VI) schedule of reinforcement. When responding for food was stable, the monkey was placed in a restraining chair with shock electrodes attached to its tail. The contingencies were arranged so that every 10 min the monkey's lever pressing produced a shock to its own tail (FI 10-min shock). At first, the FI 10-min shock was superimposed upon the VI schedule of food reinforcement. Thus, every 10 min a response for food resulted in the monkey shocking itself. At this point, the food schedule was eliminated and the monkey's lever pressing only resulted in shock on the FI schedule. Notice that now, if the monkey stops pressing the lever, it never receives an electric shock. However, the results showed that lever pressing for shock was maintained; this finding was also replicated with another monkey.

When the monkeys were given 11-min cycles of FI 10-min shock followed by 1 min where each response produced shock (FR 1-min shock), the animals showed accelerated responding on the

FI 10-min schedule (scalloping for shock) but suppressed responding in the last minute of the cycle. Thus, the same electric shocks maintained FI scalloping but suppressed lever pressing when each response produced a shock, indicating that the shocks are indeed punishers.

These **paradoxical effects of punishment** have been found across species (monkeys, cats, and rats) using both positive and negative reinforcement (lever pressing to postpone shock) to train and maintain initial responding (Pear, 2001, pp. 314–316). Generally, the findings indicate that while response-produced shock resembles some of the effects of positive reinforcement (FI scalloping), shocks do not actually function as positive reinforcement.

Jessica Long at West Virginia University proposed a resolution to the punishment paradox (Long, 2009). In four experiments with rats responding on a VI 40-s schedule of food reinforcement, she manipulated shock intensity and the time between consecutive responses (interresponse times, IRT) that produced shocks. Shocks contingent on long interresponse times reduced long IRTs leading to *increased* response rates (lever pressing rates). Shocks contingent on short interresponse times decreased short IRTs, resulting in decreased response rates. Furthermore, when long interresponse times produced shocks, low-intensity shocks reduced long IRTs and *increased* response rates. High-intensity shocks contingent on long IRTs suppressed a range of IRTs and decreased response rates. When short IRTs produced high-intensity shocks, the shocks punished short interresponse times, resulting in decreased response rates compared with shocks of low intensity. Overall, differential punishment of IRTs by the shock schedule and the intensity of the shocks explain why punishment procedures sometimes *increase* responding—an apparent reinforcement effect.

In humans, these findings suggest that victims of abuse would be more likely to instigate responding for physical punishers if the abuser (parent, teacher, or spouse) used weak to moderate punishers (spanking or slapping) contingent on long intervals between responses—the "Do it now, I said" effect. Harsh punishment (beatings), regardless of IRT contingency, should lead to decreases in the rate of targeted behavior, perhaps with other side effects.

FOCUS ON: Physical Punishment and Mental Disorders

In America, the use of physical punishment to discipline children in the absence of maltreatment or abuse is controversial. Physical punishment by parents includes the use of spanking, smacking, pushing, shoving, grabbing, slapping, or hitting when children are judged to misbehave. These methods of correction involve the intentional use of pain for the purpose of disciplining or reforming the wrongdoer. Thus, punishment is not functionally defined by its effects on behavior, but refers to painful procedures used to reform the disobedient child. One issue is whether the infliction of pain for disobedience is linked to mental disorders, even when there is an absence of more extreme maltreatment involving physical and sexual abuse, emotional abuse, physical and emotional neglect, and exposure to family violence.

A recent study used a nationally representative US sample to examine the long-term relationship between physical punishment and mental health (Afifi, Mota, Dasiewicz, MacMillan, & Sareen, 2012). The data were drawn from a 2004–2005 national survey using nearly 35,000 adult respondents, with abused and maltreated respondents excluded from further analyses. The results showed that frequent or harsh use of physical punishment in childhood occurred in about 6% of the national sample, with males reporting more harsh physical punishment than females. Also, respondents who indicated that they grew up in a dysfunctional family were more likely to report the use of harsh physical punishment by adult caretakers or parents. Using statistical techniques and controlling for socioeconomic variables, it was found that those who experienced physical punishment in childhood were more likely than non-punished respondents to indicate a diagnosis of major depression, mania and mood disorder, specific phobia, anxiety disorders, or alcohol or drug dependence.

Compared with studies using experimental designs and direct measurement of behavior, this national survey has several limitations, as has been noted by the researchers. One problem is that the data are based on retrospective reports of what happened in childhood, and these verbal responses may be influenced by many factors that distort recall, including the interview situation itself. Another limitation is that the survey design (which is cross-sectional) does not allow for any inference of causation between harsh physical punishment and mental disorders—the best one can say is that there may be a link or correlation. However, the experimental analysis of punishment in non-human animals suggests that a causal relationship is a possibility, especially when corporal punishment of children is arranged on the basis of whims and mistaken child-rearing beliefs of the care-takers (noncontingent punishment).

CONTINGENCIES OF NEGATIVE REINFORCEMENT

When an organism emits an alternative unpunished response, the behavior may be viewed as escape or avoidance. If the response is made while the punishing stimulus is occurring, it is an **escape** response. The vicious dog is growling at you, and you escape by crossing to the other side of the street. When the operant prevents the punishing stimulus, the behavior is **avoidance**. You turn right to go around the block and do not walk past the dog. In both cases, the removal or prevention of an event or stimulus *increases* operant behavior and the contingency is defined as **negative reinforcement** (cell 3 of Figure 6.3).

Any event or stimulus that increases operant rate by its removal (or prevention) is called a **negative reinforcer**. Notice that the same event—delivery of electric shock—is a punisher in a punishment procedure, and a negative reinforcer in a negative reinforcement procedure. When neither punishment nor negative reinforcement is well defined, we refer to the event as an *aversive stimulus*—a stimulus that the organism evades, escapes, or avoids.

In everyday life, the distinction between negative and positive reinforcement is occasionally uncertain (Michael, 1975), and continues to be a major topic of debate in behavior analysis (Baron & Galizio, 2005, 2006). For example, do you open a window on a hot day to get a cool breeze or to escape the heat? Putting on glasses clarifies vision but also removes a blurry view of the world. Hineline made this point when he stated:

> The addition of one event is the removal of another, and vice versa: Adding heat is removing cold; adding food is decreasing deprivation; adding a smile removes a frown. However, there is a funda-mental asymmetry, for if a stimulus or situation is to be reducible or removable by some response, that response must occur in its presence. In contrast, positively reinforced responses necessarily occur in the absence of the stimuli upon which reinforcement is based.
>
> (Hineline, 1984, pp. 496–497)

One issue is that physics tells us that there is no such thing as cold—there are only increases or decreases in heat. Thus, a person who places logs on a fire is adding heat and the behavior is controlled by positive reinforcement, not negative reinforcement (removing cold). On the other hand, there are many other instances where it may be difficult to tell the difference in everyday life. In the operant laboratory, however, the distinction between positive and negative reinforcement is reasonably easy to arrange, and experimental investigations of negative reinforcement are relatively clear-cut (Khalili, Daley, & Cheney, 1969). When a response results in the removal or postponement of a stimulus and the rate of response increases, negative reinforcement has occurred (see also Catania, 1973).

The distinction between escape and avoidance is somewhat artificial. Consider an experiment on escape, in which an animal makes a response that turns off a continuous electric shock. Hineline has suggested that in experiments like this:

> Electric shock continuously delivered may not be continuously received. For example, if it is grid shock the animal may produce intermittency by jumping up and down. Nevertheless the escape procedure is treated as a clear case of negative reinforcement by removal of shock. The experimenter may even arrange an escape procedure by explicitly presenting intermittent pulses of shock several times per second, rather than presenting it continuously. But if shock is presented several times per second, why not just twice per second, or once per second, or even less frequently? At some point we tend to stop labeling it continuous shock, and call it a stream of shocks. Responses are reinforced by interruption of (escape from) a stream of shocks. But as the pulses of shocks are spaced out still further, to one every five, ten, or twenty seconds, we tend to characterize suspension of this situation not as removal of shock . . . but as reduction in shock frequency [avoidance].
>
> (Hineline, 1977, p. 369)

To make this clear, when an animal presses a lever to turn off a stream of shocks that are occurring every 0.2 s, we call this escape. If, however, the same animal makes a response that interrupts shocks that are scheduled every 20 s, then shocks are postponed and the procedure is usually called avoidance.

The only difference between escape and avoidance, presented in Figure 6.7, is the time between shocks, or the **shock–shock interval (S–S)**. In both procedures, the time away from shock produced by responses is the same; the **response–shock interval (R–S)** is 10 s in both cases. Thus, *escape and avoidance represent endpoints on a continuum of negative reinforcement.*

In this chapter, however, we make the traditional distinction between escape and avoidance. In avoidance, an organism evades, prevents, or postpones some event; in escape, it removes the stimulus (or itself) from the situation. A person escapes a boring party by leaving it, or the party is avoided by never going to it. That is, a person who avoids going to the party presumably has a history of boring parties that are prevented by staying at home. Thus, the person who escapes the party and the one who avoids it are both showing the effects of negative reinforcement.

FIG. 6.7 In the escape contingency, shocks (indicated by the vertical lines) are scheduled once every second, and a response (R) delays the aversive stimulus for 10 s. The amount of time by which a response delays shock onset is called the response–shock interval. During avoidance, shocks occur once every 10 s, and a response produces a 10-s delay. Notice that the only difference between the two procedures is the time between shock deliveries, called the shock–shock interval.

Escape

In escape learning, an operant changes the situation from one in which a negative reinforcer is present to one in which it is absent, for some period of time. A pigeon is exposed

FIG. 6.8 (Left) An escape contingency. In the presence of a negative reinforcer (S^{r-}), an operant (R) produces a period of time (T) in which the aversive stimulus is absent. The increase in the operant is the process of negative reinforcement. (Right) A shuttle box that may be used to condition escape responses in dogs. The animal is placed in the left compartment at the start of a trial. Electric shock is turned on, and the dog can escape the aversive stimulus by jumping the hurdle and going to the safe area, on the right side of the box.

to continuous loud white noise, and when the bird pecks a key the noise is turned off. If pecking the key increases, then this defines the procedure as negative reinforcement. People reprimand others who are bothering them with statements such as "Stop that," or "Don't do that, it's not nice" and other forms of disapproval. Research shows that such reprimands are controlled by negative reinforcement in the form of escape from the aggravating behavior (Miller, Lerman, & Fritz, 2010). In a different situation, a dog jumps across a barrier to escape electric shock. Figure 6.8 is a diagram of a shuttle-box apparatus that is used to train escape in dogs. The figure also shows the notation for an escape contingency. Notice that there are many responses that may be emitted, but only R_1 removes the negative reinforcer.

In general, organisms acquire escape responses more readily than avoidance responses. This is easy to understand. In escape (but not avoidance), there is an *immediate change* from the presence to the absence of the negative reinforcer.

Another factor that affects how quickly an escape response occurs is its compatibility with reflexive behavior elicited by the negative reinforcer. Evolution has ensured that organisms respond to aversive stimuli. In the everyday world, animals may only get one chance to save their life in the presence of an aversive event. Running like crazy makes good sense (in many cases) when a predator appears. Those animals that "ponder over" the situation are likely to have contributed calories to the predator, but not genes to the next generation. Thus, natural selection has ensured that species-specific reflexes often are elicited by aversive stimuli that also function as negative reinforcers. When rats are presented with intense electric shock, they typically freeze—emitting a response that interferes with escape conditioning. That is, depressing and releasing a lever is incompatible with freezing, the species-typical response to shock. If the animal is simply required to press the lever and hold it down, the escape response is more readily acquired; this is because holding the lever down is compatible with freezing. Generally, *negative reinforcement frequently elicits reflexive behavior that interferes with the acquisition of operant behavior supported by the removal of the negative reinforcer.* Khalili and Cheney (1969), however, developed a program of shock-off titration that reduced interference by reflexive behavior. With this procedure, rats were trained to lever press for shock removal on fixed-ratio (FR) schedules as high as 80 responses.

Conditioning escape behavior is easier when the *operant is similar to reflexive behavior elicited by the aversive stimulus.* A rat can be readily trained to run on a wheel to escape electric shocks, but conditioning the animal to stand up is much more difficult (Bolles, 1970). Running is a species-typical response to electric shock, but standing is not. Although respondent and operant conditioning interact during escape training, behavior eventually comes under the control of the operant contingency. For example, rats that are trained to run on a wheel (or hold down a lever) to escape shock will stop running (or bar holding) if this response does not terminate the negative reinforcer. The species-specific response does not predominate over behavior required by the contingencies of reinforcement.

🔍 FOCUS ON: Escape and Infant Caregiving

Parents frequently are confronted with a crying baby. Crying is a normal response of infants that is usually interpreted as a way in which the baby communicates her wants and needs. Excessive and persistent crying, however, is a major factor linked to infant abuse (e.g., shaking the baby), and a leading cause of severe injury and death. One possibility is that infant crying arranges an aversive stimulus for the parents or caregivers that is usually removed by caretaking behavior (e.g., feeding, playing, and rocking). That is, the infant and caregiver are locked in a social interaction; this interaction involves escape contingencies where actions of the caregiver are negatively reinforced by the removal of crying by the baby. In this view, infant abuse is the result of inescapable crying where nothing the parent or caregiver does removes the aversive stimulus (Donovan, 1981; see also see section on "Learned Helplessness" later in this chapter).

To study experimentally the effects of infant crying on caretaking behavior it is necessary to manipulate the contingencies of reinforcement. Thus, infant crying must be controlled by the researcher and its removal made contingent on specified actions of adult caretakers. One method is an experimental simulation of infant caretaking where the removal of recorded infant cries requires specific responses by the adult caregivers. In a study by Thompson, Bruzek, and Cotnoir-Bichelman (2011), infant crying was recorded as the parents rocked their baby in a chair before naps. Next, undergraduate students with some experience in infant caretaking were recruited as participants. They were placed in an experimental setting that included a crib, baby doll, blanket, toys, bottle, and a tape recording of infant cries controlled from an adjacent observation room. Participants were told that the study simulated a caretaking situation and they should "do what comes naturally." Negative reinforcement involved the presentation of recorded infant crying until the participant performed the target response (horizontal rocking, vertical rocking, feeding, or playing). An extension of the reversal design (A–B–A) compared negative reinforcement to an extinction phase that arranged response-independent crying; in addition, the target behavior differed by participant and phase of the experiment.

The results in Figure 6.9 show the cumulative number of seconds engaged in the target and the alternative responses for three participants (P-7, P-8, and P-9). Notice the increase in time spent on the target response for each participant in the initial negative reinforcement (S^{r-}) phase. When the contingency is changed to another target response, cumulative time on this response increases while the previously reinforced response drops to near zero level or reaches a plateau. During extinction the target response decreased, but responses that were previously effective in removing crying increased, indicating resurgence of caretaking responses based on a history of negative reinforcement (see also Bruzek, Thompson, & Peters, 2009).

Overall, the results indicate that infant caretaking is under the control of crying emitted by an infant. Furthermore, the findings suggest that negative reinforcement by escape is part of the early parent–infant relationship. Clearly this need not be the case in practice. If the caretaker is attending to the child, signals from the infant will indicate child needs (hunger, wet diaper, etc.) prior to the crying. Caretakers, who "change a diaper" or "begin breastfeeding" based on infant signals, would reinforce signaling behavior as an early form of human communication.

FIG. 6.9 Cumulative duration of caregiving (in seconds) (*y*-axis) for participants P-7, P-8, and P-9. Data are depicted in 1-min bins on the *x*-axis, and breaks in the data paths indicate the start of a new session. Reprinted from R. H. Thompson, J. Bruzek, and N. Cotnoir-Bichelman, 2011, "The role of negative reinforcement in infant caregiving: An experimental simulation," *Journal of Applied Behavior Analysis, 44,* 295–304. © 2011 Society for the Experimental Analysis of Behavior. Published with permission.

Avoidance

When an operant prevents the occurrence of an aversive stimulus, the contingency is called avoidance. You typically walk the shortest distance to the university, but recently an acquaintance has joined you at the halfway mark, blabbing on and on about boring topics. Now you walk a longer distance than necessary to the university because that route does not take you past the boring person's house. During their annual migration, young wildebeests stop to drink at a river infested with large crocodiles. The crocodiles wait each year for this gourmet lunch and "pig out" on rare wildebeest. Survivors of the crocodile picnic choose a different watering spot the next year.

Discriminated Avoidance

Avoidance may involve responding when a warning signal precedes an aversive stimulus. Because the organism only responds when the warning signal occurs, the procedure is called **discriminated avoidance**. A parent may say to a child, "Nathan, keep the noise down or else you will have to go to bed." An antelope may smell a lion and change the direction in which it is traveling. In these cases, the child is told what not to do and the antelope detects what direction to avoid. Pretend that you are all set to go to a party but are told that Dr. Hannibal Sloat will be attending. Dr. Sloat is an unusually obnoxious professor, and you have just flunked his human sexuality class. In this case, the warning that he will be at the bash may result in you avoiding the party. Figure 6.10 is a diagram of discriminated avoidance in an experimental situation. In the presence of a warning stimulus (S^{ave}), a response postpones for some time, T, the onset of a negative reinforcer (S^{r-}). If the response does not occur, the negative reinforcer is presented and after some time the warning stimulus comes on again.

In the operant laboratory, discriminated avoidance is typically acquired only after many hours of training. Rats will quickly learn to lever press for food, but take a surprisingly long time to acquire lever pressing to avoid electric shock (Solomon & Brush, 1956). Pigeons are also slow at acquiring avoidance behavior when they are required to peck a key to avoid an aversive event. A major reason for this is that, in the discriminated avoidance procedure, the warning stimulus (S^{ave}) is also a CS that elicits respondent behavior (like freezing) that interferes with operant behavior (Meyer, Cho, & Wesemann, 1960). As stated in the section on escape conditioning, other responses such as running and jumping are elicited by shock and are acquired much more readily than lever pressing. For example, Macphail (1968) reported that pigeons required 120 trials of signaled avoidance to run down a straight alley to avoid shock. Notice that running to a warning stimulus for shock is not species-typical behavior for pigeons—birds usually fly away. Rats, on the other hand, required only two or three trials to learn to jump onto a platform when a warning stimulus occurred (Baum, 1965, 1969). For rats, jumping to safety is respondent behavior to the warning stimulus; this behavior was also compatible with the operant avoidance contingency.

In an interesting series of experiments, Modaresi (1990) found that lever pressing to avoid shock was acquired more readily if the lever was high on the wall, and if lever pressing not only avoided the shocks but also resulted in access to a platform to stand on. Additional experiments showed that these two aspects of the situation were in accord with the rats' species-specific behavior. That is, rats naturally stretch upward

FIG. 6.10 Discriminated avoidance occurs when a warning stimulus (S^{ave}) leads to a condition in which, after some time (T), a negative reinforcer (S^{r-}) is presented. If a response (R) is made, the negative reinforcer is delayed and further responses continue to prevent the onset of the aversive stimulus. Once the negative reinforcer is presented, some amount of time elapses and the warning stimulus again comes on.

and seek a safe area when faced with painful aversive stimuli from the floor. Thus, to produce rapid acquisition of avoidance responses, choose behavior that is naturally elicited by the negative reinforcer.

Nondiscriminated (Sidman) Avoidance

In the laboratory, a rat may press a lever to avoid the delivery of an electric shock. Shocks are scheduled every 60 s, and each lever press prevents the shock and starts another 1-min cycle (a postponement schedule of negative reinforcement). The shocks are simply programmed to occur on the basis of time, and there is *no warning signal* that they are about to be presented. When there is no warning stimulus, the contingency is called **nondiscriminated avoidance**. Some people compulsively wash their hands to get rid of unseen germs. In this case, hand washing is the operant, and reduction in the rate of anxiety negatively reinforces washing. As you will see in later chapters, negative reinforcement appears to underlie many so-called abnormal behavior patterns. Figure 6.11 illustrates simple nondiscriminated avoidance in which the aversive event is presented without a warning signal.

This book was written on a computer, and an unexpected power failure could result in many hours of lost work. To prevent this event, the authors regularly emitted the behavior of *hitting the save key*. This avoidance response saves the text to a disk or hard drive and is maintained because it has prevented computer crashes from costing the authors a day's work. Over time, however, pressing the save key is so effective that loss of work rarely occurs and the rate of response begins to decline—we say we forgot to save or were careless. At this point, a computer crash or equivalent "shock" happens and reinstates the avoidance behavior. Thus, avoidance is inherently cyclical. It is a paradox that the more effective the avoidance response the less shocks are received, but the fewer shocks that are received the weaker the avoidance behavior becomes. Like all operant behavior, avoidance responses must be negatively reinforced at least occasionally for the behavior to be maintained at high strength. In *Coercion and Its Fallout*, Murray Sidman pointed to the avoidance paradox when he compared contingencies of avoidance and positive reinforcement. He stated:

> The avoidance paradox reveals a critical difference between positive reinforcement and negative reinforcement by avoidance. With avoidance, success breeds failure; the behavior weakens and will stop unless another shock brings it back. With positive reinforcement, success breeds more of the same; the behavior continues. If the only reason a student studies is to keep from failing, an occasional failure or near-failure will be necessary to keep the studying going. A student who studies because of the options that new learning makes available will stop only if the products of learning become irrelevant. If citizens keep within the law only because that keeps them out of jail, they will eventually exceed the speed limit, cheat on their income taxes, give or accept bribes, or worse. Citizens who keep within the law because of the benefits from participating in an orderly community will not face cyclic temptations to break the law.
>
> (Sidman, 2001, p. 145)

FIG. 6.11 A Mechner diagram of nondiscriminated avoidance. A response (R) produces some time (T) in which negative reinforcers (S^{r-}) are not presented.

The use of check stops by police and audits by the tax department ensure that drivers and taxpayers encounter or are threatened with occasional negative reinforcers. Without these occasional "shocks" there would be far fewer honest people in our society. More generally, moral behavior that is learned as avoidance will weaken and stop if there is no socially arranged negative reinforcement backing it up.

Murray Sidman (1953) was the first to investigate nondiscriminated avoidance, and the procedure is often called **Sidman avoidance** or free operant avoidance. Periodic shocks were given to a rat unless the animal emitted an operant response. The time between shocks was (and still is) called the *shock–shock* (S–S) interval. When a response occurred, it delayed the onset of shock for some specified period of time called the *response–shock* (R–S) interval (see Figure 6.4 again). *Avoidance responding is learned more rapidly when the R–S interval is longer than the S–S interval* (Leaf, 1965; Sidman, 1962). In other words, when the operant delays the negative reinforcer (R–S) for a period greater than the time between shocks (S–S), conditioning is enhanced (see Baron, 1991, p. 191).

Most of the research on avoidance has used shock as the aversive stimulus. Recent research, however, has shown that *timeout from positive reinforcement* (delivery of food) has functional properties similar to shocks. Response rates to avoid timeout from reinforcement were a function of both magnitude (food quality) and rate of food-pellet delivery (Richardson and Baron, 2008).

DETERMINANTS AND ANALYSIS OF AVOIDANCE BEHAVIOR

Pretend that you live in a world in which evil professors have absolute authority over students. One day you walk into class and your professor says "Class, from today until the end of term you are subjects in a shocking experiment." You notice the straps attached to your desk and the two large electrodes embedded in your chair. Although you protest vigorously, the teaching assistant straps you to the chair and says "Press the button on your desk, if you want to." You look at the button and wish you had taken another course. A powerful (but your professor says harmless) electric shock is delivered every 20 s (S–S = 20 s). In desperation, you press your button and notice that the frequency of shocks declines (you get fewer shocks). Each press of the button delays the next shock for 30 s (R–S = 30 s), and after some experience you regularly press your button and avoid most or all of the shocks. Consider, however, what would happen if the S–S interval remained at 20 s but the R–S interval changed to 5 s. Pressing the button would increase the frequency of shocks unless you maintained a high rate of response. This occurs because a response brings the next shock closer than does not responding (5 s versus 20 s). Animal research suggests that under these conditions avoidance behavior is poorly maintained.

Shock Frequency and Avoidance Behavior

Avoidance behavior is poorly maintained when responses do not reduce the frequency of aversive stimulation (Sidman, 1962). In a classic experiment, Herrnstein and Hineline (1966) exposed 18 rats to a random sequence of electric shocks. The animals could press a lever to reduce the frequency of shocks, but some responses were still followed by the negative reinforcer. That is, bar pressing reduced the number of shocks per second but did not completely eliminate them. Seventeen of the 18 rats in this experiment showed avoidance responding—they reliably pressed the lever.

This finding has generated a debate over the critical factors that regulate avoidance behavior. Essentially, the issue concerns molar versus molecular control of behavior in avoidance. From a **molecular perspective**, the moment-to-moment time between shocks (S–S) and the time from response to shock (R–S) represent the essential variables regulating avoidance responses (Dinsmoor, 1977, 2001a, 2001b). Nonetheless, the bulk of the evidence supports a **molar perspective** (Baum,

2001), suggesting that the molar variable, *overall reduction in shock frequency* (or sensitivity to rates of shock), establishes and maintains operant avoidance (Gardner & Lewis, 1976; Hineline, 1970; Lewis, Gardner, & Hutton, 1976; Mellitz, Hineline, Whitehouse, & Laurence, 1983).

Consider what happens when your friend persistently nags you to stop watching television and start working on your term paper. You may say to the person "Leave me alone, I'll get to it after the movie is over." This will likely reduce the frequency of nagging but not eliminate it. In fact, your reply may sometimes be followed by "I can't understand how you can just sit there glued to the idiot box when you have so much to do." Assuming that the nagging is a negative reinforcer, how can your vocal operant ("Leave me alone . . .") be maintained? The answer, of course, is that it has reduced the overall number of nagging episodes while you are engrossed in *Return of the Killer Tomatoes*.

The basic question concerning avoidance is how the lack of a contingent consequence—the aversive stimulus is cancelled and does not occur—can maintain operant responding. How can "nothing" reinforce something? In discriminated avoidance the warning stimulus becomes aversive, and therefore a response that stops the discriminative stimulus also cancels the impending aversive stimulus. This can therefore be accounted for as an escape contingency, since the contingent consequence of the response is the termination of the CS. But when there is no change in the context as a result of a response it is difficult to account for the operant behavior. This remains a topic of concern and research in the experimental analysis of behavior.

Avoidance as Impending Doom

Hackenberg and Hineline (1987) used a conditioned-suppression paradigm to show the interrelations between avoidance and behavior maintained by positive reinforcement. *Conditioned suppression* is a procedure in which a conditioned aversive stimulus (a tone that has signaled shock) is presented when an animal is responding for food reinforcement. The tone usually suppresses the operant behavior regulated by food. Hackenberg and Hineline (1987) introduced an interesting twist to show that a similar effect could be obtained when a period of avoidance either preceded or followed entire sessions of food reinforcement.

In their experiment, eight rats were trained to press a lever for food on a fixed-interval 3-min schedule (FI 3 min). After response rates were stable on the FI schedule, animals were exposed to 100 min of unsignaled shock avoidance. During this period, shocks occurred every 5 s (S–S = 5 s) unless the rat pressed a lever that postponed the shocks for 20 s (R–S = 20 s). These avoidance periods were presented to four rats just before the food reinforcement sessions. The other four animals were given the avoidance period immediately after they responded for food. The question was whether the avoidance periods would suppress responding during food reinforcement sessions.

The results indicated that operant responding for positive reinforcement was disrupted when avoidance periods either preceded or followed the food sessions. This suppression occurred even though the response rates of the rats remained high enough to obtain most of the available food. The avoidance periods had an effect that did not depend on interference with behavior maintained by positive reinforcement. When avoidance periods came after food reinforcement sessions, there was more disruption of food-related behavior than when avoidance periods preceded fixed-interval responding for food. In addition, when avoidance was discontinued, operant responses for food took longer to recover if the avoidance periods came after the sessions of positive reinforcement.

In everyday language, the rats seemed worried about their appointment with doom (remember that the animals had experienced these appointments in the past). This is not unlike a student who has difficulty studying because she is scheduled to have a wisdom tooth extracted a few hours later. People, and apparently rats, respond to *long-term aversive consequences in their environment*. This disruption of responding is severe when long-term aversive consequences are impending. Immediately delivered aversive events can also suppress operant behavior but, all things being equal, do not appear to affect responses as strongly as long-term aversive consequences. By implication, a child who receives reprimands from a teacher for talking out of turn will show little disruption of play and school work. In contrast, a student who is regularly harassed by a bully after school is over may show *general disruption* of school activities throughout the day.

Timeout from Avoidance

We all value a holiday from the stress of school requirements or the duties and obligations of the work world. One way to analyze work and holidays is to recognize that much of our behavior as students and employees is maintained by schedules of avoidance. We get our reports and essays in on time to avoid the reprimands, low grades, or low performance evaluations that we received from our boss or teacher in the past. Avoidance contingencies are so prevalent that we spend much of our day engaged in avoiding the aversive stimuli arranged by others and the natural world.

Now consider how much we value holidays, leaves of absence, and other periods that temporarily suspend or remove the everyday "shocks" and behavioral requirements that pervade our lives. These periods of **timeout from avoidance** may be analyzed as negative reinforcement of behavior that terminates, prevents, or postpones the avoidance contingencies. For example, university professors are given sabbatical leave (suspension of teaching and administration duties) contingent on writing a sabbatical application outlining a program of research and academic inquiry. A strong record of publishing and obtaining research grants is part of the Faculty assessment for granting sabbaticals. Professors with high publication records and large research grants are judged worthy of sabbaticals as well as monetary merit awards. Obviously, sabbatical leave, as timeout from avoidance, is part of the reinforcement contingencies that maintain much of the academic behavior of university professors.

Timeout from avoidance has been studied experimentally in a procedure developed by Perone and Galizio (1987). Rats could press either of two levers. Responses on the right lever postponed electric foot shocks arranged on a Sidman avoidance schedule. Pressing the left lever intermittently produced 2 min of timeout from avoidance. Insertion or withdrawal of the response levers, illumination of the chamber, and auditory white noise signaled periods of time in and timeout of avoidance. In a number of experiments using the two-lever procedure, timeout from avoidance maintained behavior on a variety of interval and ratio schedules of reinforcement (Foreman, 2009). Thus, taking a holiday from avoidance has proved to be effective as negative reinforcement.

But what is it about a holiday that makes it function as negative reinforcement? The timeout period involves three distinct changes in the environment. A stimulus change from avoidance to timeout occurs, the frequency of shocks (stressors) is reduced, and the response requirements for avoidance and timeout are suspended, resulting in reduced response effort. Research shows that the stimulus change from avoidance to timeout does not maintain responding on the timeout lever (Perone & Galizio, 1987). Additional research indicates that reduction in shock frequency plays a relatively minor role in maintaining timeout behavior, while reduction in response effort is the key factor (Courtney and Perone, 1992; Foreman, 2009). That is, people may value holidays, leaves of absence, and sabbaticals because these are periods of reduced response effort during which many of the behavioral requirements of life are suspended.

SIDE EFFECTS OF AVERSIVE PROCEDURES

There are obvious ethical reasons for not using punishment contingencies to change behavior. In addition to ethical concerns, there are serious side effects that often arise when contingencies of punishment and negative reinforcement are employed. Skinner (1953, 1971) has consistently argued against the use of punishment techniques:

> The commonest technique of control in modern life is punishment. The pattern is familiar: if a man does not behave as you wish, knock him down; if a child misbehaves, spank him; if the people of a country misbehave, bomb them. Legal and police systems are based on such punishments as fines, flogging, incarceration, and hard labor. Religious control is exerted through penances, threats of excommunication, and consignment to hell-fire. Education has not wholly abandoned the birch rod. In everyday personal contact we control through censure, snubbing, disapproval, or banishment. In short, the degree to which we use punishment as a technique of control seems to be limited only by the degree to which we can gain the necessary power. All of this is done with the intention of reducing tendencies to behave in certain ways. Reinforcement builds up these tendencies; punishment is designed to tear them down.
>
> (Skinner, 1953, pp. 182–183)

The use of punishment for the social regulation of behavior maintained by positive reinforcement has serious side effects, to which we shall now turn.

Behavioral Persistence

As we have seen, punishment may under some circumstances produce a rapid decline in behavior. Thus, negative reinforcement by removal of problem behavior ensures that individuals who use punishment effectively are more likely to use it on future occasions (Miller et al., 2010). This is an important point—the "successful" use of punishment leads to further use of the technique, which produces the additional side effects of aversive control.

Operant–Respondent Interactions and Persistence

Consider a person who has received a painful wasp sting. The sight and buzzing of the insect precede the sting and (for some people) become powerful conditioned stimuli (CS) that elicit anxiety. The CS^- that is established is likely to generalize to similar sights and sounds (i.e., the sight of other flying insects, the buzzing of a harmless fly). The CS^- also has a dual function. In terms of Pavlovian conditioning, it elicits anxiety; in an operant sense, it functions as a conditioned aversive stimulus (S^{ave}) and will strengthen behavior that removes it (negative reinforcement). To extinguish the effects of the CS^-, it must be presented in the absence of the unconditioned stimulus (respondent extinction). Under ordinary circumstances the CS^- would rapidly extinguish, since buzzing sounds and flying insects (CS^-) are rarely accompanied by pain (US). However, people who are afraid of wasps and bees avoid places in which these insects may be found, and leave locations in which they encounter buzzing sounds and flying insects. That is, *avoidance behavior maintained by operant conditioning prevents respondent extinction.*

One way to place avoidance behavior on extinction is to expose the organism to aversive stimulation while preventing effective escape responses. A rat may be trained to press a lever to turn off electric shock, but during extinction bar presses have no effect. Extinction occurs most rapidly when it is clearly signaled—a buzzer could be turned on during extinction and turned off when responses prevented shock. However, in many everyday settings, escape and avoidance responses are resistant to extinction. This *persistence occurs when the difference between the acquisition and extinction setting is low* (extinction is not clearly signaled). When the difference between the extinction setting and conditions under which the contingency is in effect is slight, extinction is not discriminated, and avoidance responding continues. For example, in everyday life, a particular dentist's office smells and looks similar to one in which pain was experienced or flying insects and buzzing sounds were accompanied by a sting.

Learned Helplessness

A similar persistence effect occurs when animals are exposed to inescapable aversive stimulation and are then given an opportunity to escape. In the phenomenon called **learned helplessness**, an animal is first exposed to inescapable and severe aversive stimulation. Eventually the animal gives up and stops attempting to avoid or escape the situation. Next, an escape response, which under ordinary circumstances would be acquired easily, is made available, but the animal does not make the response. In an early experiment, Seligman and Maier (1967) exposed dogs to intense, inescapable electric shock. Following this, they attempted to teach the animals to avoid signaled shocks by jumping across a shuttle-box barrier (see Figure 6.5). The dogs failed to avoid the shocks, and even after the shocks came on (for 50 s) they would not escape by crossing the barrier to safety. The researchers suggested that the dogs had learned to give up and become helpless when presented with inescapable aversive stimulation. Of course, dogs that are not first exposed to inescapable shock learn quickly to escape and avoid shocks in a shuttle box.

Learned helplessness has been found in a large number of experiments, and has been documented in other animals (Baker, 1976; Glazer & Weiss, 1976a, 1976b; Maier, 1970; Maier, Albin, & Testa, 1973; Maier & Seligman, 1976; Maier, Seligman, & Solomon, 1969; Overmier & Seligman, 1967; Seligman & Maier, 1967). For example, Jackson, Alexander, and Maier (1980) found that rats in a maze had difficulty learning to escape electric shocks after exposure to inescapable aversive stimuli.

Similar results have been reported for humans. Hiroto and Seligman (1975) exposed college students to a series of inescapable loud noises. Following this procedure, the students had to solve a number of anagram problems. Students who were exposed to inescapable noise had more difficulty solving problems than students who were not exposed to the loud noise. Most control subjects solved all of the anagrams and reached solutions faster and faster. In contrast, students who were exposed to inescapable noise failed many problems and made slow improvements in performance.

The practical implication of these findings seems obvious. When people are exposed to inescapable "shocks," they may learn to give up and become helpless. A parent who spanks a child on the basis of his or her mood rather than for the child's misbehavior may create a socially withdrawn individual. The child has learned that "No matter what I do, I get a spanking." A husband who frequently "blows up" for no apparent reason might produce a similar set of responses in his partner.

Helplessness, Punishment, and Avoidance

Inescapable social "shocks" are not the only way to learn helplessness. Indiscriminant punishment and avoidance contingencies were brutally arranged by the Nazi guards of concentration camps to instill a kind of helplessness and docility in Jewish prisoners (Figure 6.12). Many people have

FIG. 6.12   A French postage stamp depicting Holocaust survivors after liberation by the Allies in 1945. The survivors showed the profound effects of indiscriminant use of punishment and avoidance contingencies by the Nazi guards. © Shutterstock.

questioned how so many people could have gone to their deaths without resisting the Nazi captors. The answer lies in the power of aversive control, which far exceeds what we can imagine.

The jailors often used unpredictable and arbitrary slaughter of prisoners to maintain control after using death by execution for any minor act of resistance. That is, the Jewish captives learned to avoid death by doing what they were expected to do. Once this helpless avoidance had been set up, the SS guards could keep it going by occasionally selecting a few prisoners to shoot or exterminate on an arbitrary whim. These executions were unrelated to anything that the victims did or did not do—they were unavoidable. Sidman explains that imposing indiscriminate death by execution on learned avoidance of death was the basis of the observed helplessness:

> If the shock had merely been painful [instead of death], the Jews might have resisted, welcoming death as the ultimate escape. With death itself as the shock, however, escape from death was the controlling contingency. That shock, delivered frequently with machinelike ruthlessness, was at first contingent on the prisoners' actions—when they resisted, for example, or failed to obey orders. Later, the shocks bore no relation to anything they actually did or failed to do. Because the original contingencies had generated required avoidance behavior—docility—the subsequent noncontingent shocks [arbitrary shooting of prisoners] kept that form of avoidance going. An outside observer, or a historian, could see that their quiet march to the ovens was futile. The change in the rules had come without notice, however, and those who were about to be murdered were simply doing what the original contingencies [of avoidance] had taught them was necessary for survival. Their deaths served to maintain the docility of those who remained.
>
> (Sidman, 2001, pp. 147–148)

It is important to recognize that helplessness had nothing to do with the Jewish people being unable to resist. Anyone exposed to similar kinds of coercive control would behave in a similar fashion, regardless of race, ethnicity, or religious orientation. Helplessness does not rest within the victims of violence, but with the powerful behavioral effects engendered by the aversive contingencies.

Helplessness and Depression

Seligman (1975) argued that the research on learned helplessness with animals provides a model for clinical depression. For example, there is evidence that helplessness is involved in the relationship between alcohol dependence and depression (Sitharthan, Hough, Sitharthan, & Kavanagh, 2001). More generally, thousands of people each year are diagnosed as depressive. These individuals show insomnia, report feeling tired, often say that life is not worth living, have difficulty performing routine tasks, and may be suicidal. Clinical depression is severe, long lasting, and not easily traced to a recent environmental experience.

Although animal experiments may shed light on human depression, there are differences (Abramson, Seligman, & Teasdale, 1978; Peterson & Seligman, 1984). For the most part, Seligman points to differences that occur because of human verbal behavior. That is, people talk about their problems and attribute them to either internal or external causes. When people attribute their difficulties to personal causes (e.g., "I am a failure"), these responses could function to occasion giving up (as in rule-governed behavior, discussed in Chapter 11). In terms of treatment, Seligman suggested that depressed individuals be placed in situations in which they cannot fail. In this manner, the person may eventually learn appropriate responses in the presence of aversive events.

Seligman has also suggested how to prevent learned helplessness and depression. A person who has already learned to escape from punitive control may be "immunized" against the effects of inescapable aversive events. Such an effect is suggested by experiments in which animals initially learn some response (e.g., wheel running) to escape electric shocks. That is, the animals first learn an effective escape response to negative reinforcement contingencies. Next, the animals are exposed to the typical learned-helplessness procedures of inescapable shocks. Finally, the subjects are tested in a situation where a new response produces escape from shocks (e.g., switching sides in a shuttle box). The typical effect of pre-exposure to escape is that this experience blocks the learned helplessness usually brought on by inescapable aversive stimulation (Maier & Seligman, 1976; Williams & Lierle, 1986; but see Dos Santos, Gehm, & Hunziker, 2010 for negative evidence).

Helplessness, Depression, and Neuroscience

In addition to behavioral approaches that immunize against learned helplessness, neuroscience research is currently analyzing the underlying brain mechanisms. The objective is to identify the brain structures, neuronal systems, and neurochemistry implicated in learned helplessness and depression, in the hope of discovering new medical treatments.

One promising brain structure relating inescapable shocks (or stressors) to behavioral depression is the medial prefrontal cortex, which is rich in 5-hydroxytryptamine (5-HT) receptors that are activated by the neurotransmitter serotonin (Amat, Baratta, Paul, Bland, Watkins, & Maier, 2005). The 5-HT receptors modulate the release of many neurotransmitters and hormones related to stress and "reward-negative" reactions, including the neurotransmitter dopamine. In this regard, a line of research links dopamine and several brain sites to behavioral depression induced by learned helplessness. Drugs that target the dopaminergic pathways may eventually offer a treatment for clinical depression (Bertaina-Anglade, La Rochelle, & Scheller, 2006; Besson, Privat, Eschalier, & Fialip, 1999; Kram, Kramer, Ronan, Steciuk, & Petty, 2002; Takamori, Yoshida, & Okuyama, 2001), especially when combined with behavioral interventions focused on overcoming and preventing learned helplessness.

At the cellular level, depressive behavior is poorly understood. Neurons in the lateral habenula (LHb) near the dorsal thalamus are implicated, as they allow communication between the forebrain and midbrain areas associated with learning about "reward-negative" events. Importantly, LHb neurons project to, and modulate, dopamine nerve cells in the ventral tegmental area (VTA) of the midbrain. Dopamine neurons in the VTA in turn participate in the control of depressive behavior induced by inescapable shock. A recent study in *Nature* showed that learned-helplessness procedures increased excitatory synaptic responses of LHb neurons projecting to the VTA (Li, Piriz, Mirrione, Chung, Proulx, Schulz et al., 2011). Furthermore, enhancement of LHb synaptic activation results from presynaptic release of a neurotransmitter, and correlates with an animal's depressive behavior. Repeated electrical stimulation of LHb afferent nerves depletes the release of the neurotransmitter, substantially decreases excitatory synaptic responses of LHb neurons in brain slices, and significantly reduces learned helplessness behavior in rats. Overall, the results indicate that transmitter release onto LHb neurons contributes to the rodent model of learned helplessness and depression. Also, the electrical stimulation method used to deplete transmitter release and reduce learned helplessness is a promising treatment for patients diagnosed with clinical depression.

NEW DIRECTIONS: Social Defeat and Behavioral Neuroscience

Psychiatric disorders that include depression, social phobia, and post-traumatic stress disorder (PTSD) have been linked to social withdrawal and to abnormalities of the dopaminergic system. To gain a better understanding of these links, Berton, McClung, DiLeone, Krishnan, Renthal, Russo et al. (2006) used a social defeat procedure that profoundly alters the social interactions of rodents.

In their study, mice were given daily episodes of social defeat, followed by a period of protected exposure to the larger aggressor—both animals were placed in a cage separated by a barrier to allow for sensory contact. The test mice were subjected to defeat by different aggressors over a period of 10 days, and measures of social behavior were obtained. The researchers measured social approach to an unfamiliar mouse enclosed in a wire cage, using a video-tracking system. Control animals (undefeated) spent most of the time in close proximity to the unfamiliar mouse. Defeated mice displayed intense aversion responses and spent less time near the unfamiliar mouse in the cage, but not when the wire cage was empty. Thus, the response was to the social target (unfamiliar mouse), not the novel wire cage. When tested again after 4 weeks, mice with a history of social defeat still displayed avoidance of the social target. These avoidance responses were greater to the aggressor, but also generalized to unfamiliar mice that were physically distinct from the aggressor.

Next, the researchers showed that antidepressant drugs used with humans improved the social interaction of defeated mice, but anxiety-related drugs did not have this effect. One possibility is that antidepressant drugs operate on the dopaminergic pathways of the brain.

To characterize the neurobiological mechanisms of social aversion induced by defeat, Berton et al. (2006) targeted the dopamine neurons of the mesolimbic brain in the ventral tegmental area (VTA), as well as the projections of these neurons to the nucleus accumbens (NAc). Previous research has shown that these pathways are associated with emotionally salient stimuli and avoidance behavior. The neurotrophic factor BDNF (brain-derived neurotrophic factor) is a major regulator of the mesolimbic dopamine pathway—modulating the release of dopamine. BDNF is also involved with dopamine release in the NAc via the TrkB receptor on the dopamine nerve terminals. The findings showed that BDNF levels in the NAc were increased by social defeat, and this effect occurred 24 h and 4 weeks after the episodes of social defeat.

The source of the BDNF protein in the NAc is thought to be the VTA, where the messenger RNA (mRNA) for BDNF is expressed. Berton et al. (2006) deleted the gene encoding for BDNF in the VTA of adult mice and found an *antidepressant-like effect*; the deletion of the gene for BDNF and dopamine release reduced the acquisition of social avoidance behavior in defeated mice. This finding and other control conditions indicated that *BDNF from the VTA neurons is required for a social target to become an aversive stimulus that regulates the avoidance behavior of defeated mice.*

One implication is that humans diagnosed with affective disorders may be showing avoidance responses acquired by a history of social punishment and defeat. These behavioral effects may involve BDNF and the dopaminergic pathways. Behavior therapy when combined with specialized antidepressant drugs could be especially effective at reducing social aversion and increasing socially appropriate behavior. In addition, innovative neurochemical research is linking learned helplessness and social defeat procedures to common brain mechanisms, with the objective of yielding a more complete account of major depressive disorder (Amat, Aleksejev, Paul, Watkins, & Maier, 2010; Hammack, Cooper, & Lezak, 2012).

Aggression

Reflexive Aggression

When two rats are placed in the same setting and painful shocks are delivered, the animals may attack one another (Ulrich & Azrin, 1962; Ulrich, Wolff, & Azrin, 1964). The fighting generated by these contingencies is called **reflexive aggression** (or pain-elicited aggression), because the attack follows the presentation of aversive events. Attack occurs even though neither animal is responsible for the occurrence of the shocks. Elicited aggression has been documented in several species, including humans (Azrin, Hutchinson, & Hake, 1963; Hutchinson, 1977), and has been found with painful stimuli other than electric shock (Azrin, Hake, & Hutchinson, 1965). Most people recognize that they are more prone to aggression when exposed to painful stimuli. When you are feeling good you may never shout at your partner, but you may do so if you have a severe toothache.

In these early experiments (O'Kelly and Steckle, 1939), rats were placed in a small enclosure and electric shock occurred periodically, no matter what the animals did (a procedure similar to learned helplessness, but with two rats). When the rats were periodically shocked, they began to fight. Twenty-three years later, Ulrich and Azrin (1962) systematically investigated the fighting behavior of rats to inescapable and intermittent shocks. These researchers began by testing whether two rats would fight when simply placed in a small operant chamber. They noted that the animals did not usually attack one another when placed in a confined space. However, when random shocks were delivered, the animals would immediately stand up and vigorously strike and bite one another (see Figure 6.13).

FIG. 6.13 Two rats in the attack position induced by electric shock. Reprinted from "Reflexive fighting in response to aversive stimulation" by R. E. Ulrich and N. H. Azrin, 1962, *Journal of the Experimental Analysis of Behavior, 5,* 511–520. © 1962 Society for the Experimental Analysis of Behavior, Inc. Republished with permission.

Shocks were delivered at increasing frequencies, and the number of attacks increased as more shocks were presented. In addition, Ulrich and Azrin (1962) found that the probability of attack for any single shock increased as the number of shocks increased. When the animals received one shock every 10 min, attack followed approximately 50% of the shocks. When the animals received 38 shocks a minute, fighting followed 85% of the shocks. The probability that a painful event will induce aggressive behavior is greater following high rates of inescapable aversive stimulation.

Painful stimulation also produces attack-like responses in humans and monkeys (Azrin & Holz, 1966; Azrin, Hutchinson, & Sallery, 1964; Hutchinson, 1977). In one experiment, squirrel monkeys were strapped into a small test chamber and electric shock was delivered to the animals' tails (Azrin et al., 1964). As with rats, attack was elicited by electric shocks. The animals attacked other monkeys, rats, mice, and inanimate objects, such as a stuffed doll, a round ball, and a rubber hose that they could bite. As shock intensity increased, so did the probability and duration of the attacks—a result that parallels the findings with rats.

In a review of the side effects of aversive control, Hutchinson (1977) described bite reactions by humans to aversive stimulation. Subjects were paid volunteers who were exposed to inescapable loud noise at regular intervals. Because the noise was delivered on a predictable basis, the subjects came to discriminate the onset of the aversive stimulus. Unobtrusive measures indicated that humans would show aggressive responses (or, more precisely, bite on a rubber hose) following the presentation of loud noise. The humans' response to noise parallels the elicited fighting found in monkeys and other animals. However, Hutchinson suggests that the human results should be interpreted with caution. The subjects were told that they would receive aversive stimulation, but the intensity would be tolerable. Also, he noted that subjects were paid to stay in the experiment, and most people would leave such a situation in everyday life.

Operant Aggression

When one person punishes another's behavior, the punished individual may retaliate. This is not difficult to understand; one way to escape from punishment is to eliminate or neutralize the person who is delivering it (Azrin & Holz, 1966). This strategy is called **operant aggression**, and it is shaped and maintained by negative reinforcement (i.e., removal of the punishment). When two people have a fistfight, the winner of the combat is reinforced by the absence or reduction of punches from the other person. Unfortunately, this analysis suggests that physical aggression will increase in frequency for people who successfully use counteraggression to stop the punishment arranged by others.

Consider a situation in which a husband and wife argue and the husband loses his temper and strikes his spouse—suppressing her yelling and screaming at him. Because men are typically larger and stronger than women, this probably ends the argument and the husband is negatively reinforced (by the wife's submission) for his physical abuse. Although this does not completely explain spouse abuse, it does suggest that negative reinforcement plays a large role in many cases.

Investigating Human Aggression

Although human aggression is easily recognized, it is difficult to study in the laboratory. This is because aggressive behavior is a dangerous form of human conduct. Realizing the danger, researchers have developed procedures that protect the victim from harm. In the laboratory situation, participants are led to believe that they have an opportunity to hurt another person when in reality they do not (e.g., Baron, Russell, & Arms, 1985; Gustafson, 1989; Vasquez, Denson, Pedersen, Stenstrom, & Miller, 2005; Zillmann, 1988). In a typical experiment, participants are told that they can deliver a punisher (e.g., loud noise, electric shock, or hand immersion in ice water) to another person by pressing a button on a response panel or indicating how long the hand must stay submerged in ice water. The other person is in fact an accomplice or confederate of the researcher, and acts the role of victim but does not receive the aversive stimulus.

There has been a debate about the reality or **external validity** of these procedures. However, evidence suggests that these methods constitute a reasonable analog of human aggression in everyday life. Participants in aggression experiments are convinced that their actions harmed the confederate (Berkowitz & Donnerstein, 1982). When the accomplice provokes the subjects (e.g., with insults), they deliver greater amounts of painful stimulation than when they are not provoked (Baron & Richardson, 1993). Finally, people who are known to be violent usually select and deliver stronger levels of aversive stimulation than those without such a history (Gully & Dengerink, 1983; Wolfe & Baron, 1971).

Aggression Breeds Aggression

Operant and respondent principles suggest that the presentation of an aversive stimulus may elicit or set the occasion for aggressive behavior. Provocation by others is a common form of aversive stimulation that occurs in a variety of social settings. Consider a situation in which you have worked extremely hard on a term paper and you feel it is the best paper you have ever written. Your professor calls you to his office and says "Your paper is rubbish. It lacks clarity, scholarship, and organization, and is riddled with grammatical mistakes. Only an idiot could write and submit such trash!" You probably protest the unfair treatment, but to no avail. You storm out of the office mumbling a few choice words, and once down the hall you kick the elevator door. Later in the term you are asked to fill out a teaching evaluation and, in retaliation, you score the professor as one of the worst teachers you have ever known. In this example, the professor's insulting remarks generated aggressive responses that ranged from kicking a door to counterattack by negative evaluation. Generally, aggression breeds aggression (Patterson, 1976).

Skinner described the cycle of aggression in his account of a game played by sailors during the 18th century:

> Sailors would amuse themselves by tying several boys or younger men in a ring to a mast by their left hands, their right hands remaining free. Each boy was given a stick or whip and told to strike the boy in front of him whenever he felt himself being struck by the boy behind. The game began by striking one boy lightly. This boy then struck the boy ahead of him, who in turn struck the boy next ahead, and so on. Even though it was clearly in the interest of the group that all blows be gentle, the inevitable result was a furious lashing. The unstable elements in this interlocking system are easy to identify. We cannot assume that each boy gave precisely the kind of blow he received because this is not an easy comparison to make. It is probable that he underestimated the strength of the blows he gave. The slightest tendency to give a little harder than he received would produce the ultimate effect. Moreover, repeated blows probably generate an emotional disposition in which one naturally strikes harder. A comparable instability is seen when two individuals engage in a casual conversation which leads to a vituperative quarrel. The aggressive effect of a remark is likely to be underestimated by the man who makes it, and repeated effects generate further aggression. The principle is particularly dangerous when the conversation consists of an exchange of notes between governments.
>
> (Skinner, 1953, p. 309)

Skinner's analysis is confirmed by controlled experiments showing that both physical and verbal provocation produce aggression. In terms of physical provocation, experiments show that people respond to attacks with escalating counterattacks (Borden, Bowen, & Taylor, 1971; O'Leary & Dengerink, 1973; Taylor & Pisano, 1971). In these experiments, participants tried to beat their opponents on a reaction-time game in which the loser received an electric shock. In fact, there were no actual opponents, but the participants received shocks that were programmed by the researchers. In this game, subjects were made to lose on a number of trials, and the shocks from the fictitious opponent increased in magnitude. Faced with increasing physical provocation, subjects retaliated by escalating the intensity of the shocks they gave when the "opponent" lost (see also Anderson, Buckley & Carnagey, 2008, for a discussion of a history of generalized aggression or trait aggression as an influence on aggression level in this situation).

A related study of physical aggression compared individuals and three-person groups from different ethnic backgrounds (Israeli, European Russian, Caucasian, and Georgian) who administered bogus shocks for "incorrect" answers to a learner (who was in fact a confederate). Although not required to do so, individuals escalated the level of shocks given for incorrect answers (punishers), and groups of three used higher levels of escalating shocks, presumably because individual responsibility is reduced in groups. These findings were replicated for all of the ethnic groups, suggesting that escalation of aggression to social punishment (incorrect responses) occurs for individuals and groups regardless of cultural background. Additional evidence indicated that social learning of aggression by ethnic background played a role in the levels of physical aggression (which were highest among Georgian immigrants) that participants chose to use in the study (Jaffe, Shapir, & Yinon, 1981).

Experiments on provocation and aggressive behavior further support and refine Skinner's analysis of aggression (Skinner, 1953). In one study, people matched their level of aggression to the level of provocation (Juujaevari, Kooistra, Kaartinen, & Pulkkinen, 2001). Also, people retaliated more when they were provoked and subsequently presented with a minor annoyance than when they were only provoked or received no provocation. The minor annoyance became a "trigger" for retaliation when it was preceded by provocation; by itself it had no effect on aggressive behavior (Pedersen, Gonzales, & Miller, 2000).

Verbal insults also evoke and set the occasion for strong counterattacks. Wilson and Rogers (1975) suggest that verbal provocation can lead to physical retaliation, and they noted incidents that began with verbal taunts escalating into violent fistfights. In a laboratory study of verbal insults, Geen (1968) found that subjects who were exposed to unprovoked, nasty comments from a confederate would retaliate with physical aggression. The subjects in this study were allowed to deliver shocks to the insulting confederate (in fact no shocks were actually given). Compared with personal frustration (a confederate preventing them from completing an assigned task) and task frustration (the task not having a solution), verbal insults produced the highest level of aggression toward the confederate.

A field study of 6th-grade children supports the findings from the laboratory. In this study, the context of the insults and reactions of other children increased perceived hostility of insults from classmates (level of punishment) and the amount of verbal escalation that followed. Insults related to permanent social attributes (e.g., ethnic identity) elicited humiliation and escalated the violence from verbal insults to physical aggression for both boys and girls (Geiger & Fischer, 2006).

Escalation of violence from insults to physical aggression occurs more often in males who come from a "culture of honor" (e.g., males from the southern USA) than in those who do not (e.g., males from the northern USA). For males who value honor, insults diminish the person's reputation, and retaliation involves behavior that previously restored status and respect (Cohen, Nisbett, Bowdle, & Schwarz, 1996; see McAndrew, 2009 for a discussion of challenges to status, testosterone levels, and aggression in the human male). Generally, aggression breeds more aggression, and aggressive episodes escalate toward harmful levels of physical violence, especially in cultures that propagate dignity and honor (see Skinner, 1971 on other problems of freedom and dignity).

The dictum that aggression breeds aggression can also be extended to problems of violence in American schools and other social situations. One common form of group behavior involves social exclusion of others based on their characteristics and behavior. For example, a student who shows a high level of accomplishment in academic subjects may be excluded from the "in group", whose members call him a "nerd." Can this kind of group behavior instigate aggression in those who receive it? A recent experiment investigated this question in the laboratory (Twenge, Baumeister, Tice, & Stucke, 2001). Human participants were exposed to social exclusion by telling them that other participants had rejected them as part of the group. Social exclusion caused participants to behave more aggressively in various contexts.

When insulted by another person (the target), excluded people retaliated by "blasting" the target with higher levels of aversive noise. In another experiment, the target received the same aggressive treatment even though he or she had not insulted the excluded people. This suggests that it is social exclusion itself that instigated the aggressive behavior. A further experiment showed that the effects of social exclusion on aggression could be mitigated if the target provided social praise to the excluded person. That is, provision of social rewards prevented the retaliation induced by exclusion from the group. The researcher indicated that these responses were specific to social exclusion as opposed to other kinds of misfortune. One implication is that schoolchildren who are excluded or rejected by their classmates may show aggressive behavior directed toward group members—another instance of aggression breeding aggression (see DeWall, Twenge, Gitter, & Baumeister, 2009, for an account of generalized effects of social exclusion on aggressive behavior—including judgments of ambiguous actions or words as aggressive).

Social Disruption

When punishment is used to decrease behavior, the attempt is usually made to stop a particular response. The hope is that other unpunished behavior will not be affected. Two factors work against this—the person who delivers punishment and the setting in which punishment occurs can both become conditioned aversive stimuli (S^{ave}). Because of this conditioning, individuals will attempt to escape from or avoid the punishing person or setting. Azrin and Holz have called this negative side effect of punishment **social disruption**:

> It is in the area of social disruption that punishment does appear to be capable of producing behavioral changes that are far-reaching in terms of producing an incapacity for an effective life. . . . For example, a teacher may punish a child for talking in class, in which case it is desired that the unauthorized vocalization of the child be eliminated but his other behaviors remain intact. We have seen previously, however, that one side effect of the punishment process was that it reinforced tendencies on the part of the individual to *escape from the punishment situation itself.* In terms of the example we are using, this means that punishment of the vocalization would not only be expected to decrease the vocalization, but also increase the likelihood of the child leaving the classroom situation. Behavior such as tardiness, truancy, and dropping out of school would be strengthened. The end result would be termination of the social relationship, which would make any further social control of the individual's behavior impossible. This side effect of punishment appears to be one of the most undesirable aspects of having punishment delivered by one individual against another individual, since the socialization process must necessarily depend upon continued interaction with other individuals.
>
> (Azrin and Holz, 1966, pp. 439–440, emphasis added)

It is also worth recalling the general suppressive effects of aversive stimuli. A teacher, parent, or employer (social agent) who frequently uses aversive techniques *becomes a conditioned punishing stimulus.* Once this occurs, the mere presence of the social agent can disrupt all ongoing operant behavior. This means that positive behavior falls to low levels when this person is present (see section on "New Directions: Social Defeat and Behavioral Neuroscience" in this chapter).

ON THE APPLIED SIDE: Coercion and its Fallout

In his book titled Coercion and its Fallout, Sidman (2001) provides a behavior analysis of coercion and its frequent use in North American society. **Coercion** *is defined as the "use of punishment and the threat of punishment to get others to act as we would like, and . . . our practice of rewarding people just by letting them escape from our punishments and threats" (p. 1). That is, coercion involves the basic contingencies of punishment and negative reinforcement. An interesting part of this book concerns escape and "dropping out" of the family, community, and society (Figure 6.14).*

Dropping out—one kind of escape contingency—is a major social problem of our time. People drop out of education, family, personal and community responsibility, citizenship, society, and even life. Sidman (2001, p. 101) points out that the common element in all of these forms of conduct is negative reinforcement. Once they are involved in an aversive system, people can get out by removing themselves from the coercive situation, and this strengthens the behavior of dropping out. Sidman notes that society is the loser when people cease to participate; dropping out is nonproductive since dropouts no longer contribute to their own or society's welfare.

An unfortunate, but common, example is the school dropout. Day after day, students are sent to schools where coercion is a predominant way of teaching. Students show increasingly severe forms of dropping out. Tardiness, feigned illness, "playing hooky," and never showing up for school are common responses to the escalation of coercion in schools. Sidman summarizes the problem as follows:

> *The current discipline and dropout crises are the inevitable outcome of a history of educational coercion. One may long for the days when pupils feared their teachers, spoke to them with respect, accepted extra work as punishment, submitted to being kept after school, and even resigned themselves to being beaten. But through the years, all these forms of coercive control were sowing the seeds of the system's destruction. Wherever and whenever coercion is practiced, the end result is loss of support of the system on the part of those who suffered from it. In every coercive environment, the coerced eventually find ways to turn upon the coercers. An adversarial relationship had developed between pupils and teachers, and the former victims, now parents, no longer support the system against their children.*
>
> *(Sidman, 2001, p. 107)*

FIG. 6.14 Teenagers hanging out rather than going to school illustrate the problem of school coercion and students dropping out of education.© Shutterstock.

Sidman goes on to note that not all teachers (or school systems) use coercion or negative reinforcement as a way to induce students to learn. Some teachers and educators are familiar with and use positive reinforcement effectively. A teacher who uses positive reinforcement looks to reward small steps of success rather than punish instances of failure. Schools that adopt positive reinforcement methods are likely to promote the enjoyment of learning as well as high levels of academic performance (Cameron and Pierce, 2002). Positive reinforcement turns dropping out into "tuning in." In this context, behavior analysts can offer new and constructive positive reinforcement techniques for teaching new behavior, and for establishing skillful academic repertoires (Sidman, 1993).

CHAPTER SUMMARY

This chapter highlighted the major contingencies of aversive control. The basic aversive contingencies were outlined in terms of positive and negative punishment and negative reinforcement. Positive punishment involves a decrease in operant behavior that produces or adds an event or stimulus. Negative punishment is a decrease in response that terminates or removes ongoing reinforcement. In both cases, punishment is defined by a reduced probability of response following a punishment procedure. We saw that punishment is relative and is made more effective by abrupt, intense, and immediate delivery of the punisher. The schedule of punishment (continuous is best), reduced effectiveness of positive reinforcement, and the availability of response alternatives also enhance the regulation of behavior by punishment contingencies.

Next, we turned to the control of behavior by negative reinforcement and the increase in operant behavior that removes or prevents the negative reinforcer. Two kinds of negative reinforcement were identified as escape and avoidance, with the only difference being the shock–shock intervals (see Figure 6.4). The section on avoidance introduced the molecular and molar perspectives in terms of analysis, the conditioned suppression paradigm, and the disruption of ongoing operant behavior by periods of scheduled avoidance.

We then turned to the side effects of aversive control, and noted that avoidance behavior is persistent because operant avoidance often prevents respondent extinction. A similar persistence effect was observed with exposure to inescapable punishers and learned helplessness. After a history of inescapable shocks, animals did not learn to escape the shocks; people and other animals fail to emit responses that could remove the punishing events (helplessness). The implications of learned helplessness for clinical depression and its neural basis in social defeat were addressed. Reflexive and operant aggression were analyzed as side effects of aversive control. Analysis showed that aggression breeds aggression, and the research on human aggression supported this observation. In fact, people who control behavior by punishment often become conditioned punishers themselves (social disruption).

Finally, we looked briefly at the analysis of coercion and its fallout by Sidman, emphasizing how coercive control may lead people to drop out of society and adolescents to drop out of the school system. The answer to this problem is to reduce coercive control in schools and increase the regulation of academic behavior by positive reinforcement.

KEY WORDS

Aversive stimulus

Avoidance

Coercion

Conditioned aversive stimulus (S^{ave})

Discriminated avoidance

Escape

External validity

Learned helplessness

Molar perspective

Molecular perspective

Negative punishment

Negative reinforcement

Negative reinforcer

Nondiscriminated avoidance

Operant aggression

Overcorrection

Paradoxical effects of punishment

Permanence of
    punishment

Positive punishment

Primary aversive stimulus

Punisher

Punishment

Punishment debate

Reflexive aggression

Relativity of punishment

Response cost

Response–shock interval

Shock–shock interval

Sidman avoidance

Social disruption

Timeout (from avoidance)

Timeout (from positive
    reinforcement)

ON THE WEB

http://morallowground.com/2011/08/16/kevin-elizabeth-schatz-christian-fundamentalists-spanked-7-year-old-daughter-to-death-because-god-wanted-them-to This is a link to the CNN story and video clip on Kevin and Elizabeth Schatz, the Christian fundamentalists who spanked their 7-year-old daughter to death. Discuss the pervasive use of corporal punishment in our society.

www.ppc.sas.upenn.edu/publications.htm Dr. Martin Seligman, who conducted the original research on learned helplessness, has turned to positive psychology, emphasizing the behaviors related to happiness and well-being. Take a look at his website at the Positive Psychology Center at the University of Pennsylvania.

www.teachervision.com/lesson-plans/lesson-10155.html This site is devoted to the Art of Teaching by the Council for Exceptional Children. The web page includes behavior management tips and advice for teachers, including classroom discipline, and behavior techniques, forms, and charts. Learn how to use positive behavior management rather than punishment to manage behavior.

BRIEF QUIZ

1. In terms of aversive stimuli, attacks and foul odors are _____, while threats and failing grades are _____.

    (a) potent; impotent
    (b) natural; secondary

(c) primary; conditioned

(d) primitive; cultured

2. If wheel running is a higher-frequency operant, then wheel running will_____ drinking; if wheel running is a lower-frequency operant, then wheel running will _____ drinking.

(a) decrease; increase

(b) reinforce; punish

(c) determine; undermine

(d) diminish; exacerbate

3. Research on the use of skin-shock punishment in the treatment of self-injurious behavior:

(a) shows many side effects of punishment

(b) indicates that skin shocks have no effect on non-targeted behavior

(c) found an increase in aggressive and destructive behavior with skin shocks

(d) indicates that skin-shock treatment eliminates the need for physical restraint

4. The time between shocks or the _____ interval and the time away from shocks produced by responses or the _____ interval are two aspects of escape and avoidance.

(a) temporal shock; response time

(b) shock–shock; response–shock

(c) shocking; responding

(d) aversive; postponement

5. The procedure of nondiscriminative avoidance is also called:

(a) signaled avoidance

(b) sensory aversion

(c) Sidman avoidance

(d) Stevens aversion

6. In terms of operant–respondent interactions, persistence, and avoidance:

(a) operant avoidance prevents respondent extinction

(b) operant avoidance interacts with respondent aggression

(c) operant avoidance competes with respondent avoidance

(d) operant avoidance sets the occasion for respondent aversion

7. For learned helplessness, pre-exposure to escape _____ the helplessness brought on by _____ aversive stimulation.

(a) enhances; noncontingent

(b) causes; excessive

(c) augments; expected

(d) blocks; inescapable

8. With regard to respondent aggression, Ulrich and Azrin (1962) found that the probability of attack for any single shock:

(a) decreased as the number of shocks increased

(b) remained constant as the number of shocks increased

(c) increased as the number of shocks went up

(d) increased and then decreased as the number of shocks went up

9. Skinner (1953) reported a game played by sailors in the 18th century. This game involved the following:

    (a) tying several boys in a ring
    (b) telling each boy to hit another boy when he himself was hit
    (c) a slight tap on one boy
    (d) all of the above

10. In terms of dropping out, Sidman (2001) indicates that one basic element is:

    (a) escape due to negative reinforcement
    (b) escape due to punishment
    (c) escape due to contingencies of avoidance
    (d) escape due to a history of inescapable shock

Answers to Brief Quiz: 1, c (p. 153); 2, b (p. 159); 3, d (p. 163); 4, b (p. 169); 5, c (p. 174); 6, a (p. 178); 7, d (p. 181); 8, c (p. 184); 9, d (p. 185); 10, a (p. 188)

Operant–Respondent Interrelationships: The Biological Context of Conditioning

7

1. Discover how operant and respondent contingencies interrelate.
2. Explore the processes of sign tracking, autoshaping, and negative automaintenance.
3. Investigate the role of operant contingencies for respondent behavior.
4. Learn about the biological context of conditioning and taste aversion learning.
5. Discover how eating and physical activity contribute to activity anorexia.

So far, we have considered operant and respondent behavior as separate domains. Respondent behavior is elicited by the events that precede it, and operants are strengthened (or weakened) by stimulus consequences that follow them. Assume that you are teaching a dog to sit and you are using food reinforcement. You might start by saying "Sit", push the animal into a sitting position, and follow this posture with food. After training, you present the dog with the discriminative stimulus "Sit," and it quickly sits. This sequence nicely fits the operant paradigm—the S^D "sit" sets the occasion for the response of sitting, and food reinforcement strengthens this behavior (Skinner, 1953).

In most circumstances, however, both operant and respondent conditioning occur at the same time. If you look closely at what the dog does, it is apparent that the "Sit" command also elicits respondent behavior. Specifically, the dog salivates just after you say "Sit." This occurs because the "Sit" command reliably preceded and was paired with the presentation of food, becoming a conditioned stimulus that elicits respondent salivation. For these reasons, the stimulus "Sit" is said to have a dual function. It is an S^D in the sense that it sets the occasion for operant responses, and it is a CS that elicits respondent behavior. Shapiro (1960) demonstrated that respondent salivation was positively correlated with operant lever pressing for fixed-interval food in dogs.

Similar effects are seen when a warning stimulus (a tone) is turned on that signals imminent shock if a rat does not press a lever. The signal is a discriminative stimulus that increases the probability of bar pressing, but it is also a CS that elicits changes in heart rate, hormone levels, and other physiological responses (all of which can be called fear). Suppose that you are out for a before-breakfast walk and you pass a doughnut and coffee shop. The aroma from the shop may be a CS that elicits salivation and also an S^D that sets the occasion for entering the store and ordering a doughnut. These examples should make it clear that in many settings respondent and operant conditioning are intertwined—probably sharing common neural pathways in the brain.

ANALYSIS OF OPERANT–RESPONDENT CONTINGENCIES

When biologically relevant stimuli such as food are contingent on an organism's operant behavior, species-characteristic, innate behavior is occasionally elicited at the same time. One class of species-characteristic responses that is elicited (when operant behavior is expected) is unconditioned reflexive behavior. This intrusion of reflexive behavior occurs because *respondent procedures are sometimes embedded in operant contingencies of reinforcement*. These respondent procedures cause species-characteristic responses that may interfere with the regulation of behavior by operant contingencies.

At one time, this intrusion of respondent behavior in operant situations was used to question the generality of operant principles and laws. The claim was that the biology of an organism overrode operant principles (Hinde & Stevenson-Hinde, 1973; Stevenson-Hinde, 1983; Schwartz & Lacey, 1982), and behavior was said to drift towards its biological roots.

Operant (and respondent) conditioning is, however, part of the biology of an organism. The neural capacity for operant conditioning arose on the basis of species history; organisms that changed their behavior as a result of life experience had an advantage over animals that did not do so. Behavioral flexibility and neuroplasticity (neural changes resulting from environmental contingencies) allowed for rapid adaptation to an altered environment. As a result, organisms that evolved behavioral flexibility by operant learning were more likely to survive and produce offspring.

Both evolution and learning involve selection by consequences. Darwinian evolution has produced both species-characteristic behavior (reflexes, modal-action patterns, and reaction chains) and basic mechanisms of learning (operant and respondent conditioning) through natural selection. Operant conditioning during an organism's lifetime selects response topographies, rates of response, and repertoires of behavior through the feedback from reinforcing consequences. One question is whether unconditioned responses (UR) in the basic reflex model (US → UR) are also selected by consequences. In this regard, it is interesting to observe that the salivary glands are activated when food is placed in the mouth; as a result, the food can be tasted, ingested (or rejected), and digested. That is, there are notable physiological effects following reflexive behavior. If the pupil of the eye constricts when a bright light is shown, the result is an escape from retinal pain, while at the same time avoiding retinal damage. It seems that reflexes have come to exist and operate because these responses do something; it is the effects of these responses that maintain the operation of the reflexive behavior. One might predict that if the effects of salivating for food or blinking at a puff of air to the eye did not result in improved performance (ease of ingestion or protection of the eye) then neither response would continue, as this behavior would not add to the fitness of the organism.

Respondent Contingencies Override Operant Regulation

The Breland and Breland Demonstration

Marion and Keller Breland worked with B. F. Skinner as students, and later established a successful animal training business. They conditioned a variety of animals for circus acts, arcade displays, advertising, and movies. In an important paper (Breland & Breland, 1961), they documented a number of instances in which species-specific behavior interfered with operant conditioning. For example, when training a raccoon to deposit coins in a box, they noted:

> The response concerned the manipulation of money by the raccoon (who has "hands" rather similar to those of primates). The contingency for reinforcement was picking up the coins and depositing them in a 5-inch metal box.
>
> Raccoons condition readily, have good appetites, and this one was quite tame and an eager subject. We anticipated no trouble. Conditioning him to pick up the first coin was simple. We started out by reinforcing him for picking up a single coin. Then the metal container was introduced, with the requirement that he drop the coin into the container. Here we ran into the first bit of difficulty: he seemed to have a great deal of trouble letting go of the coin. He would rub it up against the inside of the container, pull it back out, and clutch it firmly for several seconds. However, he would finally turn it loose and receive his food reinforcement. Then the final contingency: we put him on a ratio of 2, requiring that he pick up both coins and put them in the container.
>
> Now the raccoon really had problems (and so did we). Not only could he not let go of the coins, but he spent seconds, even minutes rubbing them together (in a most miserly fashion), and dipping them into the container. He carried on the behavior to such an extent that the practical demonstration we had in mind—a display featuring a raccoon putting money in a piggy bank—simply was not feasible. The rubbing behavior became worse and worse as time went on, in spite of non-reinforcement.
>
> (Breland & Breland, 1961, p. 682)

The Brelands documented similar instances of what they called instinctive drift in other species. **Instinctive drift** refers to species-characteristic behavior patterns that became progressively more invasive during training or conditioning (see Figure 7.1, which depicts a raccoon "shooting baskets" rather than depositing coins with the same hand-rubbing response). The raccoon is drifting toward the instinctive "hand rubbing" that evolved as a way of removing the exoskeleton of crayfish. The term *instinctive drift* is, however, problematic because the concept suggests a conflict between nature (biology) and nurture (environment). Behavior is said to drift toward its biological roots. However, there is no need to talk about behavior "drifting" toward some endpoint. Behavior is always appropriate to the operating environmental contingencies. Recall that *respondent procedures may be embedded in an operant contingency*, and this seems to be the case for the Brelands' raccoon. Let us examine why.

FIG. 7.1 Drawing of a raccoon performing "drop shots" into a basketball hoop, illustrating the animal tricks trained by the Brelands. The animals increasingly showed species-specific responses such as rubbing the ball rather than the reinforced operant of dropping it into the hoop—a process called instinctive drift. From Russell A. Dewey, *Instinctive Drift. Psychology: An Introduction.* Retrieved from www.intropsych. com/ch08_animals/instinctive_drift.html. Published with permission.

In the raccoon example, the coins were presented just before the animal was reinforced with food for depositing them in the box. For raccoons, as we have seen, food elicits rubbing and manipulating of food items. Since the coins preceded food delivery, they became a CS for the respondent behavior of rubbing and manipulating (coins). This interpretation is supported by the observation that the "rubbing" behavior increased as training progressed. As more and more reinforced trials occurred, there were necessarily more pairings of coins and food. Each pairing increased the associative strength of the $CS_{(coin)} \rightarrow CR_{(rubbing)}$ relationship, and the behavior became more and more prominent, interfering with the operant conditioning.

Respondent processes also occur as by-products of operant procedures with rats and children. Rats will hold on to marbles longer than you might expect when they receive food pellets for depositing a marble in a hole. Children will manipulate tokens or coins prior to banking or exchanging them. The point is that what the Brelands found is not that unusual or challenging to an operant account of behavior. Today, we talk about the interrelationship of operant and respondent contingencies rather than label these observations as a conflict between nature and nurture.

Sign Tracking

Suppose that you have trained a dog to sit quietly on a mat, and you have reinforced the animal's behavior with food. Once this conditioning is accomplished (the dog sits quietly on the mat), you start a second training phase. During this phase, you turn on a buzzer located on the dog's right side. A few seconds after the sound of the buzzer, a feeder delivers food to a dish that is placed 1.8 m in front of the dog. Figure 7.2 is a diagram of this sort of arrangement.

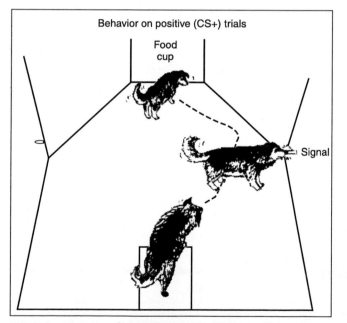

FIG. 7.2 Diagram of apparatus used in sign tracking with dogs. When the signal for food is given, the dog approaches the signal and makes "food-soliciting" responses rather than going directly to the food dish. Adapted from H. M. Jenkins, F. J. Barrera, C. Ireland, & B. Woodside, 1978, "Signal-centered action patterns of dogs in appetitive classical conditioning," *Learning and Motivation*, 9, 280.

When the buzzer goes off, the dog is free to engage in any behavior it is able to emit. From the perspective of operant conditioning it is clear what should happen. When the buzzer goes off, the dog should stand up, walk over to the dish, and eat. This is because the sound of the buzzer is an S^D that sets the occasion for the operant of going to the dish, and this response has been reinforced by food. In other words, the three-term contingency, SD: R $\rightarrow$ S^r, specifies this outcome and there is little reason to expect any other result. A careful examination of the contingency, however, suggests that the sign (sound) could be either an S^D (operant) that sets the occasion for approaching and eating the reinforcer (food), or a CS$^+$ (respondent) that is paired with the US (food). In this latter case, the CS $_{(food\ signal)}$ would be expected to elicit food-related conditioned responses.

Jenkins, Barrera, Ireland, and Woodside (1978) conducted an

experiment very similar to the one described here. Dogs were required to sit on a mat and a light/tone stimulus was presented either on the left or right side of the animal. When the stimulus was presented on one side, it signaled food, and when presented on the other side it signaled extinction. As expected, when the extinction stimulus came on, the dogs did not approach the food tray and for the most part ignored the signal. However, when the food signal was presented, the animals unexpectedly approached the signal (tone/light) and made what were judged by the researchers to be "food-soliciting responses" to the stimulus. Some of the dogs physically contacted the signal source, and others seemed to beg at the stimulus by barking and prancing. This behavior is called **sign tracking**, because it refers to approaching a sign (or stimulus) that has signaled a biologically relevant event (food).

The behavior of the dogs is not readily understood in terms of operant contingencies of reinforcement. As stated earlier, the animals should simply trot over to the food and eat it. Instead, the dogs' behavior appears to be elicited by the signal that precedes food delivery. Importantly, the ordering of stimulus → behavior resembles the CS → CR arrangement that characterizes classical conditioning. Of course, S^D: R follows the same time line, but in this case the response should be a direct approach to the food, not to the signal. In addition, behavior in the presence of the sign stimulus appears to be food directed. When the tone/light comes on, the dog approaches, barks, begs, prances, and licks the signal. Thus, the temporal arrangement of signal followed by response, and the topography of the responses, both suggest respondent conditioning. Apparently, in this situation the unconditioned stimulus (US) properties of the food are stronger (in the sense of regulating behavior) than the operant–reinforcement contingency. Because of this, the light/tone gains strength as a CS with each pairing of light/tone and food (US), ensuring that sign tracking predominates in the operant situation. A caution is that one cannot entirely dismiss the occurrence of operant conditioning in this experiment. If the dog engages in a chain of responses that is followed by food, you can expect the sequence to be maintained. The sequence of going to the signal and then to the food, however, is not required by the operant contingency, and actually delays getting the food reinforcer. Overall, respondent behavior seems to override operant control in sign-tracking situations.

Autoshaping

Shaping (differential reinforcement of successive approximations) is the usual way that a pigeon is taught to strike a response key (see Chapter 4). In the laboratory, a researcher operating the feeder with a hand-switch reinforces closer and closer approximations to the final performance (key pecking). Once the bird makes the first independent peck on the key, electronic programming equipment activates a food hopper and the response is reinforced. The contingency between behavior and reinforcement both during shaping and after the operant is established is clearly operant ($R → S^r$). This method of differential reinforcement of successive approximations requires considerable patience and a fair amount of skill on the part of the experimenter.

Brown and Jenkins (1968) reported a way to automatically teach pigeons to peck a response key. In one experiment, they first taught birds to approach and eat grain whenever a food hopper was presented. After the birds were magazine trained, automatic programming turned on a key light 8 s before the grain was delivered. Next, the key light went out and the grain hopper was presented. After 10–20 pairings of this key light followed by food procedure, the birds started to orient and move toward the lighted key. Eventually all 36 pigeons in the experiment began to strike the key even though pecking did not produce food. Figure 7.3 shows the arrangement between key light and food presentation. Notice that the light onset precedes the presentation of food and appears to elicit the key peck.

The researchers called this effect **autoshaping**, an automatic way to teach pigeons to key peck. Brown and Jenkins offered several explanations for their results. In their view, the most likely

FIG. 7.3 Autoshaping procedures are based on Brown and Jenkins (1968). Notice that the onset of the light precedes the presentation of food and appears to elicit the key peck.

explanation had to do with species-characteristic behavior of pigeons. They noted that pigeons have a tendency to peck at things they look at. The bird notices the onset of the light, orients toward it, and "the species-specific look–peck coupling eventually yields a peck to the [key]" (Brown & Jenkins, 1968, p. 7). In their experiment, after the bird made the response, food was presented, and this contiguity could have accidentally reinforced the first peck.

Another possibility was that key pecking resulted from respondent conditioning. The researchers suggested that the lighted key had become a CS that elicited key pecks. This could occur because pigeons make unconditioned pecks (UR) when grain (US) is presented to them. In their experiment, the key light preceded grain presentation and may have elicited a conditioned peck (CR) to the lighted key (CS). Brown and Jenkins comment on this explanation and suggest that although it is possible, it "seem[s] unlikely because the peck appears to grow out of and depend upon the development of other motor responses in the vicinity of the key that do not themselves resemble a peck at grain" (Brown & Jenkins, 1968, p. 7). In other words, the birds began to turn toward the key, stand close to it, and make thrusting movements with their heads, all of which led eventually to the key peck. It does not seem likely that all of these are reflexive responses. They seem more like operant approximations that form a chain culminating in pecking.

Notice that respondent behavior such as salivation, eye blinks, startle, knee jerks, pupil dilation, and other reflexes does not depend on the conditioning of additional behavior. When you touch a hot stove you rapidly and automatically pull your hand away. This response simply occurs when a hot object is contacted. A stove does not elicit approach to it, orientation toward it, movement of the hand and arm, and other responses. All of these additional responses seem to be clearly operant, forming a chain or sequence of behavior that includes avoiding contact with the hot stove.

Autoshaping extends to other species and other types of reinforcement and responses. Chicks have been shown to make autoshaped responses when heat was the reinforcer (Wasserman, 1973). When food delivery is signaled for rats by lighting a lever or by inserting it into the operant chamber, the animals lick and chew on the bar (Peterson, Ackil, Frommer, & Hearst, 1972; Stiers & Silberberg, 1974). These animals also direct social behavior toward another rat that signals the delivery of food (Timberlake & Grant, 1975). Rachlin (1969) showed autoshaped key pecking in pigeons using electric shock as negative reinforcement. The major question that these and other experiments raise is this: What is the nature of the behavior that is observed in autoshaping and sign-tracking experiments?

In general, research has shown that autoshaped behavior is at first respondent, but when the contingency is changed so that pecks are followed by food, the pecking becomes operant. Pigeons reflexively peck (UR) at the sight of grain (US). Because the key light reliably precedes grain presentation, it acquires a CS function that elicits the CR of pecking the key. However, when pecking is followed by grain, it comes under the control of contingencies of reinforcement and it is an operant. To make this clear, *autoshaping produces respondent behavior that can then be reinforced as operant behavior.* That is, once respondent behavior is elicited and reinforced, it is controlled by its consequences and is considered to be operant. A human example of respondents becoming operant might be crying. An injury may occur, causing reflexive tearing and vocalizing, and if a caretaker immediately provides comfort and a reduction in the pain, the actions of the caretaker reinforce the crying response. Subsequently, "crying" may occur simply for its consequences—comfort from caretakers.

Contingencies and Species-Specific Behavior

In discussing their 1968 experiments on autoshaping, Brown and Jenkins report that:

> Experiments in progress show that location of the key near the food tray is not a critical feature [of autoshaping], although it no doubt hastens the process. Several birds have acquired the peck to a key located on the wall opposite the tray opening or on a side wall.
>
> (Brown and Jenkins, 1968, p. 7)

This description of autoshaped pecking by pigeons sounds similar to sign tracking by dogs. Both autoshaping and sign tracking involve species-specific behavior that is elicited by food presentation. Instinctive drift also appears to be reflexive behavior that is elicited by food. Birds peck at grain and make similar responses to the key light. That is, birds sample or taste items in the environment by the only means available to them—beak or bill contact (see Figure 7.4). Dogs make food-soliciting responses to the signal that precedes food reinforcement. For example, this kind of behavior is clearly seen in pictures of wolf pups licking the mouth of an adult returning from a hunt. Raccoons rub and manipulate food items and make similar responses to coins that precede food delivery. And we have all seen humans rubbing dice together between their hands before throwing them. It is likely that autoshaping, sign tracking, and instinctive drift represent the same (or very similar) processes (see Hearst & Jenkins, 1974).

One proposed possibility is that all of these phenomena (instinctive drift, sign tracking, and autoshaping) are instances of **stimulus substitution**. That is, when a CS (light or tone) is paired with a US (food), the conditioned stimulus is said to substitute for, or generalizes from, the unconditioned stimulus. This means that responses elicited by the CS (rubbing, barking and prancing, pecking) are similar to the ones caused by the US. Although this is a parsimonious account, there is evidence that it is wrong.

Recall from Chapter 3 that the laws of the reflex (US → UR) do not hold for the CS → CR relationship, suggesting that there is no universal substitution of the CS for the US. Also, in many experiments, the behavior evoked by the US is opposite in direction to the responses elicited by the conditioned stimulus (see "On the Applied Side: Drug Use, Abuse, and Respondent Conditioning" in Chapter 3). In addition, there are experiments conducted within the autoshaping paradigm that directly refute the stimulus substitution hypothesis.

In an experiment by Wasserman (1973), chicks were placed in a very cool enclosure. In this situation, a key light was occasionally turned on and this was closely followed by the activation of a heat lamp. All of the chicks began to peck the key light in an unusual way. The birds moved toward the

FIG. 7.4 Pigeons in a park foraging for food illustrate that pecking for food is species-specific behavior under the control of the contingencies arranged in the natural setting or the laboratory. © Shutterstock.

key light and rubbed their beaks back and forth on it—behavior described as snuggling. These responses resemble the behavior that newborn chicks direct toward their mother when soliciting warmth. Chicks peck at their mother's feathers and rub their beaks from side to side—behavior that results in snuggling up to their mother.

At first glance, the "snuggling to the key light" seems to illustrate an instance of stimulus substitution. The chick behaves to the key light as it does toward its mother. The difficulty is that the chicks in Wasserman's experiment responded completely differently to the heat lamp compared with the way they responded to the key light. In response to heat from the lamp, a chick would extend its wings and stand motionless—behavior that it might direct toward intense sunlight (Wasserman, 1973). In this experiment, it is clear that the CS does not substitute for the US, because these stimuli elicit completely different responses (see also Timberlake & Grant, 1975).

Timberlake (1983, 1993) proposed an alternative to stimulus substitution. He suggested that each US (food, water, sexual stimuli, or a heat lamp) controls a distinct set of species-specific responses or a behavior system. That is, for each species there is a behavior system related to procurement of food, another related to obtaining water, and another still for securing warmth and comfort. For example, the presentation of food to a raccoon activates the **behavior system** that consists of procurement and ingestion of food. One of these behaviors, rubbing and manipulating the food item, may be activated, depending on the CS–US (key light paired with food) contingency. Other behaviors of the system, such as bringing the food to the mouth, chewing, and swallowing may not occur. Timberlake goes on to propose that the particular responses activated by the CS or signal depend, in part, on the physical properties or features of the stimulus for that species. Presumably, in the Wasserman experiment with chicks, properties of the key light (a visual stimulus raised above the floor) were more closely related to snuggling than to standing still and extending wings.

At the present time, it is not possible to predict which responses in a behavior system the CS will activate. That is, a researcher can predict that the CS will elicit one or more responses in the behavior system of food procurement, but cannot specify which responses will occur. One possibility is that the intensity of the reinforcer (food or heat) affects which responses are elicited by the CS–US contingency. For example, as the intensity of the heat source increases (approximating a hot summer day), the chick's response to the key light (sign) may change from snuggling to standing in the sun (i.e. with open wings and motionless). An analysis of an animal's ecology and evolutionary history is necessary to predict its behavior toward environmental contingencies that are encountered during its lifetime.

Operant Contingencies Override Respondent Regulation

We have seen that both operant and respondent conditioning can occur at the same time. Moreover, respondent contingencies sometimes regulate responses that are usually viewed as operant behavior (e.g., pecking a lighted key), and as such these responses are respondents. There are also occasions when behavior that appears to be respondent is regulated by its consequences and is therefore operant behavior. That is, operant contingencies can override respondent control of behavior.

Reinforcing Reflexive Behavior

In the 1960s, a number of researchers attempted to show that involuntary reflexive or autonomic responses could be conditioned by operant procedures (Kimmel & Kimmel, 1963; Miller & Carmona, 1967; Shearn, 1962). Miller and Carmona (1967) deprived dogs of water and monitored their respondent level of salivation. The dogs were separated into two groups. One group was reinforced with water for increasing salivation, and the other group was reinforced for a decrease. Both groups of animals showed the expected change in amount of salivation. That is, the dogs that were reinforced for increasing saliva flow showed an increase, and the dogs that were reinforced for less saliva flow showed a decrease.

At first glance, this result seems to demonstrate the operant conditioning of salivation. However, Miller and Carmona (1967) noticed an associated change in the dogs' behavior that could have produced the alteration in salivation. Dogs that increased their saliva flow appeared to be alert, and those that decreased it were described as drowsy. For this reason the results are suspect, as salivary conditioning may have been mediated by a change in the dogs' operant behavior. Perhaps drowsiness was operant behavior that resulted in decreased salivation, and being alert increased the reflex. In other words, the change in salivation could have been part of a larger, more general behavior pattern that was reinforced. Similar problems occurred with other experiments. For example, Shearn (1962) showed operant conditioning of heart rate, but this dependent variable can be affected by a change in the pattern of breathing.

The Miller Experiments

It is difficult to rule out operant conditioning of other behavior as a mediator of reinforced reflexes. However, Miller and DiCara (1967) conducted a classic experiment in which this explanation was not possible. The researchers reasoned that operant behavior could not mediate conditioning if the subject had its skeletal muscles immobilized. To immobilize their subjects, which were white rats, they used the drug curare. This drug paralyzes the skeletal musculature and interrupts breathing, and the rats were maintained by artificial respiration. When given curare, the rats could not swallow food or water. Miller and DiCara solved this problem by using electrical stimulation of the rats' pleasure center in the brain as reinforcement for visceral reflexes.

Before the experiment was started, the rats had electrodes permanently implanted in their hypothalamus. This was done in a way that allowed the experimenters to connect and disconnect the animals from the equipment that stimulated the neural-reward center. To ensure that the stimulation was reinforcing, the rats were trained to press a bar to turn on a brief microvolt pulse. This procedure demonstrated that the pulse was reinforcing, since the animals pressed a lever for the stimulation.

At this point, Miller and DiCara administered curare to the rats and reinforced half of them with electrical stimulation for decreasing their heart rate. The other animals were reinforced for an increase in heart rate. Figure 7.5 shows the results of this experiment. Both groups started out with heart rates in the range of 400–425 beats per minute. After 90 min of contingent reinforcement, the groups were widely divergent. The group that was reinforced for slow heart rate had rates of about 310 beats per minute, and the group reinforced for fast rate had heart rates of approximately 500 beats per minute.

Miller and Banuazizi (1968) extended this finding. They inserted a pressure-sensitive balloon into the large intestine of rats. This allowed them to monitor intestinal contractions. At the same

FIG. 7.5 Effects of curare immobilization of skeletal muscles and the operant conditioning of heart rate (Miller & DiCara, 1967). Half of the rats received electrical brain stimulation for increasing heart rate and the other half for decreasing heart rate.

time, the researchers measured the animals' heart rate. As in the previous experiment, the rats were administered curare and reinforced with electrical brain stimulation. In different conditions, reinforcement was made contingent on increased or decreased intestinal contractions. In addition, the rats were reinforced on some occasions for a decrease in heart rate, and at other times for an increase.

The researchers showed that reinforcing intestinal contractions or relaxation changed them in the appropriate direction. The animals also showed an increase or decrease in heart rate when brain stimulation was made contingent on this response. Finally, Miller and Banuazizi (1968) demonstrated that a change in intestinal contractions did not affect heart rate and, conversely, changes in heart rate did not affect contractions.

In these experiments the contingencies of reinforcement modified behavior that is usually considered to be reflexive or respondent, under conditions in which skeletal responses could not affect the outcome. Also, the effects were specific to the response that was reinforced, showing that brain stimulation was not generating general physiological changes that produced the outcomes of the experiment. It seems that responses that are usually elicited as URs can be conditioned using operant contingencies of reinforcement. Greene and Sutor (1971) extended this conclusion to humans, showing that a galvanic skin response or GSR could be regulated by negative reinforcement (for more on operant autonomic conditioning, see DiCara, 1970; Engle, 1993; Jonas, 1973; Kimmel, 1974; Miller, 1969).

Although this conclusion is probably justified, the operant conditioning of autonomic responses such as blood pressure, heart rate, and intestinal contractions has run into difficulties. Miller even had problems replicating the results of his own experiments (Miller & Dworkin, 1974), concluding "that the original visceral learning experiments are not replicable and that the existence of visceral learning remains unproven" (Dworkin & Miller, 1986). The weight of the evidence does suggest that reflexive responses are, at least in some circumstances, affected by the consequences that follow them. This behavior, however, is also subject to control by contiguity or pairing of stimuli. It is relatively easy to change heart rate by pairing a light (CS) with electric shock and then using the light to change heart rate (respondent contingency). It should be evident that controlling heart rate with an operant contingency is no easy task. Thus, autonomic behavior may not be exclusively tied to respondent conditioning, but respondent conditioning is particularly effective with these responses.

NOTE ON: Operants and Respondents

Clearly, the fundamental distinction between operant and respondent conditioning is operational. The distinction is operational because conditioning is defined by the operations that produce it. Operant conditioning involves a contingency between behavior and its consequences. Respondent conditioning entails the pairing of stimuli. Autonomic responses are usually respondents, and are best modified by respondent procedures. When these responses are changed by the consequences that follow them, they are operant responses (an operant class). Similarly, skeletal responses are usually operant and most readily changed by contingencies of reinforcement, but when modified by the pairing of stimuli they are respondents. The whole organism is impacted by contingencies (environmental arrangement of events), whether these are designed as operant or respondent procedures. That is, most contingencies of reinforcement activate respondent processes, while Pavlovian or respondent contingencies often involve the reinforcement of operant behavior.

THE BIOLOGICAL CONTEXT OF CONDITIONING

As we stated in Chapter 1, the evolutionary history, ontogenetic history, and current neurophysiological status of an organism are the **context for conditioning**. Context is a way of noting that the probability of behavior depends on certain conditions. Thus, the effective contingencies (stimuli, responses, and reinforcing events) may vary from species to species. A hungry dog can be reinforced with meat for jumping a hurdle, and a pigeon will fly to a particular location to get grain. These are obvious species differences, but there are more subtle effects of the **biological context**. The rate of acquisition and level of behavior, once established, may be influenced by an organism's neurophysiology, as determined by species history and lifetime interactions with the environment. Moreover, within species, discriminative stimuli, responses, and reinforcers depend on an animal's learning history and are specific to particular situations.

Although the effects of contingencies sometimes depend on the particular events and responses, principles of behavior such as extinction, discrimination, and spontaneous recovery show generality across species. The behaviors of schoolchildren working at math problems for teacher attention and of pigeons pecking keys for food are regulated by the principles of reinforcement even though the particular responses and reinforcers vary over species. As early as 1938, B. F. Skinner recognized that a comprehensive understanding of the behavior of organisms required the study of more than "arbitrary" stimuli, responses, and reinforcers (Skinner, 1938, pp. 10–11), and evolutionary history as well as neurophysiology had to be included. By using simple stimuli, responses that were easy to execute and record, and precise reinforcers, Skinner hoped to identify *general principles* of operant conditioning. By and large, this same strategy is used in the modern behavioral laboratory. Researchers today continue to search for general principles of learning, but remain sensitive to the interrelationships among conditioning, species history, and neurophysiology. These interrelationships are clearly present in the field of taste aversion learning.

Taste Aversion Learning

Taste aversion learning is illustrated by a study in which quail and rats were given a solution of blue salty water. After the animals drank the water, they were made sick. Following recovery, the animals were given a choice between water that was not colored but tasted salty, and plain water that was colored blue. The rats avoided the salty-flavored water, and the quail would not drink the colored solution. That is, the taste avoidance depends on the species. This finding is not difficult to understand—when feeding or drinking, birds rely on visual cues, whereas rats are sensitive to taste and smell. In the natural habitat of these animals, drinking liquids that produce illness should be avoided, and this has obvious survival value. Because quail typically select food based on its appearance, they avoided the colored water. In contrast, because rats usually select food by taste, they avoided the salty water associated with sickness (Wilcoxon, Dragoin, & Kral, 1971).

Notice that the taste and color of the water was a compound CS ($CS_1 + CS_2$) that was paired with the US of illness. Both species showed taste aversion learning. That is, the animals came to avoid one or the other of the CS elements based on species history. In other words, the biology of the organism dictated which feature became the CS, but the conditioning of the aversion by CS–US pairing (general behavior principle) was the same for both species. Of course, a bird that relied on taste for food selection would be expected to condition to the taste followed by illness

Type of aversive stimulus		Type of water	
		Bright-noisy	Flavored
	Shock	Bright-noisy drinking followed by shock	Flavored drinking followed by shock
	Poison	Bright-noisy drinking followed by poison	Flavored drinking followed by poison

FIG. 7.6 Conditions used to show taste aversion conditioning by rats in an experiment by Garcia and Koelling (1966). From description given in "Relation of cue to consequence in avoidance learning," by J. Garcia and R. A. Koelling, 1966, *Psychonomic Science, 4*, 123–124.

contingency. This phenomenon has been called **preparedness**—quail are biologically prepared to discriminate visual features that are associated with illness, and rats respond best to a flavor–illness association. Additional experiments have shown that animals of the same species are prepared to learn some particular CS–US associations and not others.

Garcia and his colleagues conducted many important experiments concerned with the conditions that produce taste aversions in rats.[1] Garcia and Koelling (1966) had thirsty rats drink tasty (saccharin-flavored) water or unflavored water accompanied by flashing lights and gurgling noises (bright-noisy water). After the rats drank the water, half of each group was immediately given an electric shock for drinking. The other animals were made ill by injecting them with lithium chloride or by irradiating them with X-rays. Lithium chloride and high levels of X-rays produce nausea roughly 20 min after administration. Figure 7.6 shows the four cue-to-consequence conditions of the experiment.

After aversion training and recovery, the rats were allowed to drink and their water intake was measured. The major results of this experiment are shown in Figure 7.7. Baseline measures of drinking were compared with fluid intake after shock or lithium or X-rays paired with a visual or flavor stimulus (CS). Both shock and illness induced by X-ray exposure suppressed drinking. Those rats that received shock after drinking the bright-noisy water and the ones that were made sick after ingesting the flavored water substantially reduced their fluid intake. Water intake in the other two groups was virtually unaffected. The animals that were made sick after drinking the bright-noisy water and those that were shocked after ingesting the flavored water did not show a conditioned aversion.

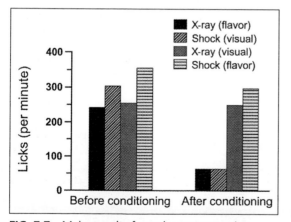

FIG. 7.7 Major results from the taste-aversion experiment by Garcia and Koelling (1966). Based on data from "Relation of cue to consequence in avoidance learning," by J. Garcia and R. A. Koelling, 1966, *Psychonomic Science, 4*, 123–124. © 1966 Psychonomic Society, Inc. Published with permission.

These results are unusual for several reasons. During traditional respondent conditioning, the CS and US typically overlap or are separated by only a few seconds. In the experiment by Garcia and Koelling (1966), the taste CS was followed much later by the US (drug or X-ray). Also, it is often assumed that the choice of CS and US is irrelevant for respondent conditioning. Pavlov claimed that the choice of CS was arbitrary—he said that anything would do. However, taste and gastrointestinal malaise produced aversion, but taste and

---

1 These rodents are ideal subjects for generalizing experimental results to humans. Like humans, rats are omnivorous, eating both meat and vegetables. Rats live wherever humans do, and are said to consume up to 20% of the world's human food supply.

shock did not. Therefore, it appears that for some stimuli the animal is *prepared* by nature to make a connection and for others it may even be *contraprepared* (Seligman, 1970). Generally, for other kinds of respondent conditioning many CS–US pairings are required, but aversion to taste is conditioned after a single, even delayed pairing of flavor with illness. In fact, the animal need not even be conscious for an aversion to occur (Provenza, Lynch, & Nolan, 1994). Finally, the animal must experience nausea for taste aversion to condition. Strychnine is a poison that inhibits spinal neurons but does not cause sickness. It also does not cause taste aversion (Cheney, van der Wall, & Poehlmann, 1987).

These results can be understood by considering how conditioning principles interact with the biology of the rat. These animals are omnivorous, eating a wide range of meat and vegetable foods. In their natural habitat, rats eat 10 to 16 small meals each day, and frequently ingest novel food items. They have evolved sensitivities to smell and taste but have relatively poor sight, and they cannot vomit. When contaminated, rotten, or naturally toxic food is eaten, it typically has a distinctive smell and taste. For this reason, taste and smell but not visual cues are associated with illness. Avoidance occurs after a long delay between CS and US because rats, sensitive to the delay between ingestion of a toxin and later nausea, survived and reproduced. It would be unusual for a rat to eat and for this to be quickly followed by an aversive stimulus such as electric shock (flavor–shock contingency); hence there is little conditioning. The fitness advantage of one-trial conditioning, or quickly avoiding food items that produce illness, is obvious—eat that food again and it may kill you!

NEW DIRECTIONS: Behavioral Neuroscience, Taste Aversion, and Urges for Addictive Behavior

Behavior is why the nervous system exists. Those organisms with a nervous system that allowed for behavioral adaptation and reproduction survived. To reveal the neural mechanisms that interrelate brain and behavior, neuroscientists often look for changes in behavior as a result of functional changes in the brain as the organism solves problems posed by its environment. This approach has been used to understand how organisms acquire aversions to food tastes and avoidance of foods with these tastes.

A recent study investigated the sites in the brain that are responsive to lithium chloride (LiCl), a chemical which is often used in conditioned taste aversion learning to induce nausea. The researchers used brain imaging to measure the presence of c-fos, a gene transcription factor and marker of neuronal activity, which is implicated in LiCl-induced illness (Andre, Albanos, & Reilly, 2007). The gustatory area of the thalamus showed elevated levels of c-fos following LiCl treatment, implicating this brain region as central to conditioned taste aversion. Additional research has implicated transcription factors such as c-fos as the biochemical substrate bridging the delay between the CS-taste and the onset of nausea (US) several hours later (Bernstein, Wilkins, & Barot, 2009). Other research by Yamamoto (2007) showed that two regions of the amygdala were also involved in taste aversion conditioning. One region is concerned with detecting the conditioned stimulus (e.g., distinctive taste) and the other is involved with the hedonic shift from positive to negative, as a result of taste aversion experience. Thus, brain research is showing that several brain areas and mechanisms are involved in linking the CS-taste to the delayed nausea from toxic chemicals (US), and the subsequent aversion to tastes predictive of such nausea.

Brain sites also contribute to our urges, cravings, and excessive behavior. The cortical brain structure called the insula helps to turn physical reactions into sensations of craving. A recent investigation reported in *Science* showed that smokers with strokes involving damage to the insula lost their craving for cigarettes (Naqvi, Rudrauf, Damasio, & Bechara, 2007). The insula area is also involved in behaviors whose bodily effects are experienced as pleasurable, such as cigarette smoking. Specific neural sites code for the physiological reactions to stimuli and "upgrade" the integrated neural responses into awareness, allowing the person to act on the urges of an acquired addiction. Since humans can learn to modulate their own brain activity to reduce the sensation of pain (deCharms, Maeda, Glover, Ludlow, Pauly, Soneji et al., 2005), they may also be able to learn to deactivate the insula and reduce cravings associated with excessive use of drugs.

Taste aversion learning has been replicated and extended in many different experiments (see Barker, Best, & Domjan, 1977; Reilly & Schachtman, 2009; Rozin & Kalat, 1971). Revusky and Garcia (1970) showed that the interval between a flavor CS and an illness-inducing US could be as much as 12 h. Other findings indicate that a novel taste is more easily conditioned than one with which an animal is familiar (Cheney & Eldred, 1980; Revusky & Bedarf, 1967). A novel setting (as well as taste) has also been shown to increase avoidance of food when a toxin is the unconditioned stimulus. For example, Mitchell, Kirschbaum, and Perry (1975) fed rats in the same container at a particular location for 25 days. Following this, the researchers changed the food cup and made the animals ill. After this experience, the rats avoided eating from the new container (see Parker, 2003, for an account of the difference between taste aversion and avoidance). Taste aversion learning also occurs in humans, of course (Arwas, Rolnick, & Lubow, 1989; Logue, 1979, 1985, 1988). Alexandra Logue at the State University of New York, Stony Brook, has concluded:

> Conditioned food aversion learning in humans appears very similar to that in other species. As in other species, aversions can be acquired with long CS–US delays, the aversion most often forms to the taste of food, the CS usually precedes the US, aversions [are] frequently generalized to foods that taste qualitatively similar, and aversions are more likely to be formed to less preferred, less familiar foods. Aversions are frequently strong. They can be acquired even though the subject is convinced that the food did not cause the subject's illness.
>
> (Logue, 1985, p. 327)

Imagine that on a special occasion you spend an evening at your favorite restaurant (Figure 7.8). Stimuli at the restaurant include your companion, waiters, candles on the table, china, art on the wall, and many more aspects of the setting. You order several courses, most of them familiar, and "just to try it out" you have *pasta primavera* for the first time (taste-CS). What you do not know is that a flu virus (US) has invaded your body and is percolating away while you eat. Early in the morning, you wake up with a clammy feeling, a rumbling stomach, and a hot acid taste in the back of your throat. You spew *primavera* sauce, wine, and several other ugly bits and pieces on the bathroom mirror and into the sink (UR).

The most salient stimulus at the restaurant was probably your date. Alas, is the relationship finished? Will you get sick at the next sight of your lost love? Is this what the experimental

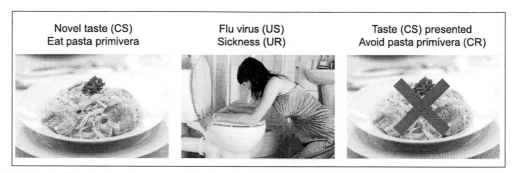

| Novel taste (CS) Eat pasta primavera | Flu virus (US) Sickness (UR) | Taste (CS) presented Avoid pasta primavera (CR) |

FIG. 7.8 An illustration of taste aversion learning in humans. Pasta primavera is a novel taste (CS) consumed at dinner. Later that night the flu virus (US) induces sickness (UR). Subsequently, the presentation of pasta primavera (CS) produces avoidance of the food (CR). © Shutterstock.

analysis of behavior has to do with romance novels? Of course, the answer to these questions is no. It is very likely that you will develop a strong aversion only to *pasta primavera* (taste-CS → CR-avoid). Interestingly, you may clearly be aware that your illness was caused by the flu, not the new food. You may even understand taste aversion learning but, as one of the authors (Cheney) of this book can testify, it makes no difference. The novel-taste CS, because of its single pairing (even though delayed by several hours) with nausea, is likely to be avoided in the future.

Taste Conditioning Induced by Physical Activity

Taste aversion learning is, as we have seen, a well-established conditioning process that generalizes over many species. Typically, a drug such as LiCl is used to condition taste aversion, but research on activity anorexia (Epling & Pierce, 1992; see the following section in this chapter, and also Chapter 13) has suggested that physical activity would condition an aversion to food tastes and flavors. To test this idea, Lett and Grant (1996) allowed hungry and thirsty rats 10 min in which to consume either a salt or sour solution, followed by 30 min of confinement in a running wheel. On separate unpaired trials (taste not paired with physical activity), these rats were allowed 10 min to consume the other solution and confined to 30 min in home cages (no physical activity). After three paired trials, rats avoided the solution paired with wheel running compared with the solution followed by placement in home cages. Lett and Grant (1996) concluded that rats show conditioned taste avoidance (CTA) when the flavored conditioned stimulus (CS) is repeatedly followed by the unconditioned stimulus (US) of wheel running, CS → US (see Boakes & Nakajima, 2009, for an account of CTA induced by swimming).

Recently, CTA induced by physical activity has been shown in humans (Havermans, Salvy, & Jansen, 2009). Participants either consumed or merely tasted a flavored solution prior to 30 min of running on a treadmill at 80% of maximum heart rate. In both the consumption and the tasting-only groups, flavors followed by a single bout of intense physical activity led to a negative shift in consuming the paired flavor by comparison with the evaluation of another flavor that was not explicitly paired with treadmill running, indicating a conditioned flavor aversion. The degree of exercise-related gastrointestinal distress did not predict evaluation ratings of the flavor paired with the physical activity, implying that such distress is not required to obtain CTA induced by running in humans.

Notice that CTA in both humans and rats involves a *forward conditioning* procedure in which the CS-taste is presented before the bouts of running (US). Salvy, Pierce, Heth, and Russell (2004) extended the running-wheel procedure to *backward conditioning*, in which the flavor CS follows the wheel-running US. Relative to unpaired controls, rats that were given backward pairings drank more of the CS flavor, showing a **conditioned taste preference** (CTP). The observed CTP suggests that the after-effects of wheel running act as positive reinforcement (Lett, Grant, Byrne, & Koh, 2000). If so, wheel running has bivalent properties (aversive *and* reinforcing) that produce different conditioning effects depending on the temporal placement of the CS-taste.

Subsequently, Hughes and Boakes (2008) tested the *bivalent effect of wheel running*. Rats were given access to one flavor before (CS_1) and a second flavor after (CS_2) 3 h of wheel running. Tests showed avoidance of the flavor given before running (CS_1), but preference for the flavor that followed running (CS_2). However, the bivalent effects were found only in those rats that were given eight pre-exposure sessions of wheel running, and not in rats without this experience. That is, the bivalent effects of wheel running seemed to depend on pre-exposure of the US-wheel.

Dobek, Heth, and Pierce (2012) hypothesized that the bivalent effect generalized to rats without pre-exposure to wheel running. In this study, palatable liquid food was used as a way to encourage rats to consume equally the flavor coming before (CS_1) and after (CS_2) wheel running. Also, the wheel-running sessions lasted for 40 min, rather than 3 h, to ensure that the bivalent effect was due to equalizing exposure to the CSs and not to higher intensity of the US-wheel. Rats were given six conditioning sessions, CS_1 (flavor) → US (wheel) → CS_2 (flavor), followed by flavor consumption tests. Figure 7.9 shows that relative to a third control flavor unpaired with wheel running, a taste coming before wheel running was consumed less (avoidance), and a taste that came after wheel running was consumed more (preference). That is, Dobek and colleagues obtained a bivalent effect (CTA and CTP) of wheel running that did not depend on pre-exposure to US-wheel.

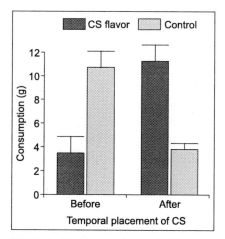

FIG. 7.9 Results are shown for the bivalent effects of wheel running. Compared with the control flavor, the flavor given before wheel running decreased on the consumption test, indicating conditioned taste aversion (CTA). The flavor given after wheel running, however, increased relative to the control flavor on the consumption test, indicating conditioned taste preference (CTP). The temporal location of the taste-CS with respect to the wheel-running US determines its effect—CTA or CTP. From "The bivalent effects of wheel running on taste conditioning" by C. Dobek, C. D. Heth, & W. D. Pierce, 2012, *Behavioural Processes, 89*, 36–38.

As a final point, it appears that the bivalent effects of wheel running do not depend on the nature of the CS (taste). Lett, Grant, Byrne, and Koh (2000) used rats to show that the after-effects of wheel running produced a *conditioned place preference (CPP)*. That is, a distinctive chamber paired with the after-effects of wheel running was preferred to an unpaired chamber. Also, Masaki and Nakajima (2008) obtained *conditioned place aversion (CPA)* induced by wheel running, using a forward conditioning procedure. To date, there have been no studies showing CPA to distinctive chamber preceding, and CPP to a chamber following, the same bouts of wheel running. However, the current evidence indicates that wheel running (and vigorous physical activity) has bivalent properties—both aversive and reinforcing—that result in aversion or preference, depending on the temporal location of the CS.

Adjunctive Behavior

On time-based and interval schedules, organisms may emit behavior patterns that are not required by the contingency of reinforcement (Staddon & Simmelhag, 1971). If you received $5 for pressing a lever once every 10 min you might start to pace, twiddle your thumbs, have a sip of soda, or scratch your head between payoffs. Staddon (1977) noted that during a fixed time between food reinforcers, animals engage in three distinct types of behavior. Immediately after food reinforcement, **interim behavior** such as drinking water may occur. Next, an organism may engage in **facultative behavior** that is independent of the schedule of reinforcement (e.g., rats may groom themselves). Finally, as the time for reinforcement gets close, animals engage in food-related activities called **terminal behavior,** such as orienting toward the lever or food cup. The first of these categories, called **interim** or adjunctive behavior,[2] is of most interest for the purposes of the present discussion, as it is behavior not required by the schedule but *induced by reinforcement.* Because the behavior is induced as a side effect of the reinforcement schedule, it is also referred to as **schedule-induced behavior**.

When a hungry animal is placed on an interval schedule of reinforcement, it will ingest an excessive amount of water if allowed to drink. Falk (1961, 1964, 1969) suggested that this **polydipsia** or excessive drinking is adjunctive behavior induced by the time-based delivery of food. A rat that is working for food pellets on an intermittent schedule may drink as much as half its body weight during a single session (Falk, 1961). This drinking occurs even though the animal is not water deprived. The rat may turn toward the lever, press for food, obtain and eat the food pellet, drink excessively, groom itself, and then repeat the sequence. Pressing the lever is required for reinforcement, and grooming may occur in the absence of food delivery, but polydipsia appears to be induced by the schedule.

In general, **adjunctive behavior** refers to any excessive and persistent behavior pattern that occurs as a side effect of reinforcement delivery. The schedule may require a response for reinforcement, or it may simply be time based, as when food pellets are given every 30 s no matter what the animal is doing. Additionally, the schedule may deliver reinforcement on a fixed-time basis (e.g., every 60 s) or it may be constructed so that the time between reinforcers varies (e.g., 20 s, then 75 s, 85 s, 60 s, and so on).

Schedules of food reinforcement have been shown to generate such adjunctive behavior as attack against other animals (Flory, 1969; Hutchinson, Azrin, & Hunt, 1968; Pitts & Malagodi, 1996), licking at an airstream (Mendelson & Chillag, 1970), drinking water (Falk, 1961), chewing on wood blocks (Villareal, 1967), and preference for oral cocaine administration (Falk & Lau, 1997; Falk, D'Mello, & Lau, 2001). Adjunctive behavior has been observed in pigeons, monkeys, rats, and humans; reinforcers have included water, food, shock avoidance, access to a running wheel, money, and for male pigeons the sight of a female (for reviews, see Falk, 1971, 1977; Staddon, 1977). Muller, Crow, and Cheney (1979) induced locomotor activity in college students and retarded adolescents with fixed-interval (FI) and fixed-time (FT) token delivery. Stereotypic and self-injurious behavior of humans with developmental disabilities has also been viewed as adjuctive to the schedule of reinforcement (Lerman, Iwata, Zarcone, & Ringdahl, 1994). Thus, adjunctive behavior occurs in different species, is generated by a variety of reinforcement procedures, and extends to a number of induced responses.

---

2 Induced behavior that immediately follows reinforcement has been described as "interim" (Staddon, 1977) and "adjunctive" (Falk, 1961, 1964, 1969). These terms are used interchangeably in this book.

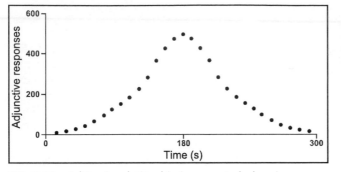

FIG. 7.10   A bitonic relationship is presented, showing time between food pellets and amount of adjunctive water drinking.

A variety of conditions affect adjunctive behavior, but the schedule of reinforcement delivery and the deprivation status of the organism appear to be the most important. As the time between reinforcement deliveries increases from 2 to 180 s, adjunctive behavior increases. After 180 s, adjunctive behavior drops off, and it reaches low levels at 300 s. For example, a rat may receive a food pellet every 10 s and drink only slightly more than a normal amount of water between pellet deliveries. When the schedule is changed to 100 s, drinking increases; polydipsia increases again if the schedule is stretched to 180 s. As the time between pellets is further increased to 200, 250, and then 300 s, water consumption goes down. This increase, peak, and then drop in schedule-induced behavior is illustrated in Figure 7.10, and is called a bitonic function. The function has been observed in species other than the rat, and occurs for other adjunctive behavior (see Keehn & Jozsvai, 1989, for contrary evidence).

In addition to the reinforcement schedule, adjunctive behavior becomes more and more exces-sive as the level of deprivation increases. A rat that is at 80% of its normal body weight and is given food pellets every 20 s will drink more water than an animal at 90% of its normal weight and on the same schedule. Experiments have shown that food-schedule-induced drinking (Falk, 1969), airstream licking (Chillag & Mendelson, 1971), and attack (Dove, 1976) increase as an animal's body weight goes down. Thus, a variety of induced activities escalate when deprivation for food is increased and when food is the scheduled reinforcer.

Falk has noted that "on the surface" adjunctive behavior does not seem to make sense:

> [Adjunctive activities] are excessive and persistent. A behavioral phenomenon which encompasses many kinds of activities and is widespread over species and high in predictability ordinarily can be presumed to be a basic mechanism contributing to adaptation and survival. The puzzle of adjunctive behavior is that, while fulfilling the above criteria, its adaptive significance has escaped analysis. Indeed, adjunctive activities have appeared not only curiously exaggerated and persistent, but also energetically quite costly.
>
> (Falk, 1977, p. 326)

Falk went on to note that adjunctive behavior is similar to **displacement behavior** of animals in the wild—actions that are seemingly irrelevant, incongruous, and out of context. For example, two skylarks might stop fighting and begin to peck the ground with feeding movements. One possibility is that both adjunctive and displacement behaviors occur in situations that are generally positive for the organism, but from which the animal is likely to escape, due to the delay arranged by the schedule of reinforcement. That is, the adaptive significance of adjunctive behavior is to maintain the animal on the schedule during a period (the delay) when it would be likely to leave or escape (Falk, 1977).

Adjunctive Behavior in Humans

Adjunctive behavior occurs in a variety of species, including humans. Excessive drug use by people may involve adjunctive behavior induced by the temporal arrangement of reinforcement. Thus, Doyle and Samson (1988) allowed human participants to drink beer while they played a gambling game that delivered monetary reinforcements. Participants on the FI 90-s payoff drank about twice as much as those assigned the FI 30-s schedule, which suggests that beer drinking was induced by the payoff schedule. In another study, Cherek (1982) allowed people to smoke while button pressing for monetary reinforcements. The average number of puffs an hour was a bitonic function of FI schedule values (30, 60, and 240 s). In both of these experiments, humans consumed higher levels of a drug (alcohol or nicotine) just after payoffs, which suggests that excessive drug taking and addiction may sometimes be schedule induced (Falk, 1998).

Another adjunctive behavior observed in humans is general restlessness, movement, and fidgeting. Lasiter (1979) monitored gross-movement activity of undergraduate students seated at a console and performing a signal-detection vigilance task. Relative to a control group (FT-control), both FT (detect only) and FI (observation-detect) schedules increased general activity, particularly in the period immediately following the delivery and detection of the signal. These increases in movements appeared to be schedule induced, showing high rate and temporal patterning. Subsequently, Porter, Brown, & Goldsmith (1982) asked female children to press a telegraph key that delivered M&M's® candies on FR 1, FI 30-, and FI 60-s schedules. Baselines (FR 1) were obtained before and after each FI value, and the schedules were equated for temporal lengths and the number of candies dispensed. Substantial increases in motor movements occurred after reinforcement for both FI schedules (post-reinforcement vocalization and drinking were also observed). One possibility is that fidgeting and general restlessness of children with attention deficit and hyperactivity disorder (ADHD) may be induced by the schedules of reinforcement arranged in the home and classroom.

Many developmentally delayed people show a variety of stereotyped behavior that may also be schedule induced. Hollis (1973) studied stereotyped wringing of hands and head-rolling movements in institutionalized females and developmentally delayed children. In the first experiment, delivery of M&M's® candies on FT 4-min and FT 30-s schedules induced the most stereotyped movements on the FT 30 s compared with baseline measures of stereotyped movements; baselines were taken when the children were fed and food-deprived, but without any delivery of candies. Increases in stereotyped movement occurred in bouts following each delivery of M&M's®. Notably, FT 30-s dispenser clicks (conditioned reinforcers) temporarily induced increased stereotyped movements, but FT 30-s doorbell rings did not. In another study of adjunctive stereotyped movements, three developmentally delayed, institutionalized adult males served as experimental participants (Wiesler, Hanson, Chamberlain, & Thompson, 1988). Responses on a motor task were reinforced by the delivery of 8 mL of a soft drink and praise. The baseline schedule was FR 1, and three FI schedules were programmed—FI 15 s, FI 90 s, and FI 180 s. The amount of stereotyped movement on the FI 15-s schedule was about twice as much as that for FR 1 for two of the participants; the increase was less dramatic for the third participant. Also, the amount of stereotyped movement increased with the FI value. The evidence suggests that excessive stereotyped movements in humans, often described as abnormal behavior, may be induced by schedules of reinforcement. Schedules involving activities and events on the ward may induce stereotyped and "bizarre" behavior as an unintentional by-product.

Overskeid (1992) rejected the research on adjunctive behavior in humans, pointing to the inadequate control or baseline conditions of most experiments. In contrast, Falk (1994) acknowledged that there were some problems with human experiments, but found that the totality of the evidence supported the hypothesis that schedules of reinforcement induce adjunctive behavior in humans. Our view is that convergent evidence from experiments with a number of species, including humans and other primates, indicates that interval- and time-based schedules induce excessive behavior following reinforcement. Many bizarre, displaced, and high-rate activities of humans may be induced inadvertently by schedules in the workplace, school, or home.

ON THE APPLIED SIDE: Activity Anorexia and Interrelations between Eating and Physical Activity

Eating and Physical Activity

In 1967, Carl Cheney (who was then at Eastern Washington State University) came across a paper (Routtenberg & Kuznesof, 1967) that reported self-starvation in laboratory rats. Cheney (one of the authors of this textbook) thought that this was an unusual effect, since most animals are reluctant to kill themselves for any reason. Because of this, he decided to repli-cate the experiment, and he recruited Frank Epling (former author of this textbook), who was an undergraduate student at the time, to help to run the research. The experiment was rela-tively simple. Cheney and Epling (1968) placed a few rats in running wheels and fed them for 1 h each day. The researchers recorded the daily number of wheel turns, the weight of the rat, and the amount of food eaten. Surprisingly, the rats increased wheel running to excessive levels, ate less and less, lost weight, and if allowed to continue in the experiment died of star-vation. Importantly, the rats were not required to run and they had plenty to eat, but they stopped eating and ran as much as 10–12 miles a day.

Twelve years later, Frank Epling, at the University of Alberta, Canada began to do collaborative research with David Pierce (author of this textbook), at the same university. They wondered if anorexic patients were hyperactive like the animals in the self-starvation experiments. If they were, it might be possible to develop an animal model of anorexia. Clin-ical reports indicated that many anorexic patients were indeed excessively active. For this reason, Epling and Pierce began to investigate the relationship between wheel running and food intake (Epling & Pierce, 1988, 1992; Pierce, 2001; Pierce & Epling, 1991). The basic finding was that physical activity decreases food intake, and that suppressed food intake through loss of body weight increases activity. Epling and Pierce call this feedback loop activity-based anorexia or just **activity anorexia***, and argue that a similar cycle occurs in anorexic patients (see Epling, Pierce, & Stefan, 1983; Epling & Pierce, 1992, 1996a; see also Davis, Kennedy, Ralevski, Dionne, Brewer, Neitzert et al., 1995).*

This analysis of eating and exercise suggests that these activities are interrelated. Depriving an animal of food should increase the reinforcing value of exercise. Rats that are required to press a lever to run on a wheel should work harder for wheel access when they are deprived of food. Additionally, engaging in exercise should reduce the reinforcing value of food. Rats that are required to press a lever for food pellets should not work as hard for food following a day of exercise. Pierce, Epling, and Boer (1986) designed two experiments to test these ideas, which are described below.

Reinforcement Effectiveness of Physical Activity

We asked whether food deprivation increased the reinforcing effectiveness of wheel running. If animals worked harder for an opportunity to exercise when deprived of food, this would show that running had increased in its capacity to support behavior. That is, depriving an animal of food should increase the reinforcing effectiveness of running. This is an interesting implication, because increased reinforcement effectiveness is usually achieved by withholding the reinforcing event. Thus, to increase the reinforcement effectiveness of water, a researcher typically withholds access to water, but (again) in this case food is withheld in order to increase the reinforcing effectiveness of wheel access.

Nine young rats of both sexes were used to test the reinforcing effectiveness of wheel running as food deprivation changed. The animals were trained to press a lever to obtain 60 s of wheel running. When the rat pressed the lever, a brake was removed and the running wheel was free to turn. After 60 s, the brake was again activated and the animal had to press the lever to obtain more wheel running. The apparatus that we constructed for this experiment is shown in Figure 7.11.

*Once lever pressing for wheel running was stable, each animal was tested when it was food deprived (75% of normal weight) and when it was at free-feeding weight. Recall that the animals were expected to work harder for exercise when they were food deprived. To measure the reinforcing effectiveness of wheel running, the animals were required to press the lever more and more for each opportunity to run—*a progressive ratio schedule *(see Chapter 5 for further information about this schedule). Specifically, the rats were required to press 5 times to obtain 60 s of wheel running, then 10, 15, 20, and 25 times, and so on. The point at which they gave up pressing for wheel running was used as an index of the reinforcing effectiveness of exercise.*

The results of this experiment are shown in Figure 7.12. All of the animals lever pressed for wheel running more when food deprived than when at normal weight. In other words, the animals worked harder for exercise when they were hungry. Further evidence indicated that the reinforcing effectiveness went up and down when an animal's weight was made to increase and decrease. For example, one rat pressed the bar 1567 times when food deprived, 881 times when at normal weight, and 1882 times when again food deprived. This indicated that the effect was reversible and was tied to the level of food deprivation (see Belke, Pierce, & Duncan, 2006, on substitutability of food and wheel running).

FIG. 7.11 Wheel-running apparatus used in the Pierce, Epling, and Boer (1986) experiment on the reinforcing effectiveness of physical activity as a function of food deprivation. From "Deprivation and satiation: The interrelations between food and wheel running," by W. D. Pierce, W. F. Epling, and D. P. Boer, 1986, *Journal of the Experimental Analysis of Behavior, 46,* 199–210. © 1986 Society for the Experimental Analysis of Behavior. Republished with permission.

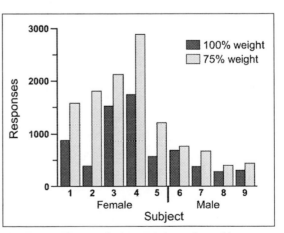

FIG. 7.12 The graph shows the number of bar presses for 60 s of wheel running as a function of food deprivation. From "Deprivation and satiation: The interrelations between food and wheel running," by W. D. Pierce, W. F. Epling, and D. P. Boer, 1986, *Journal of the Experimental Analysis of Behavior, 46,* 199–210. © 1986 Society for the Experimental Analysis of Behavior. Republished with permission.

Reinforcement Effectiveness of Food

In a second experiment, we investigated the effects of exercise on the reinforcing effectiveness of food. Four male rats were trained to press a lever for food pellets. When lever pressing occurred reliably, we tested the effects of exercise on each animal's willingness to work for food. In this case, we expected that a day of exercise would decrease the reinforcement effectiveness of food on the next day.

Test days were arranged to measure the reinforcing effects of food. One day before each test, animals were placed in their wheels without food. On some of the days before a test the wheel was free to turn, and on other days it was not. Three of the four rats ran moderately in their activity wheels on exercise days. One lazy rat did not run when given the opportunity. This animal was subsequently forced to exercise on a motor-driven wheel. All of the animals were well rested (3 to 4 h of rest) before each food test. This ensured that any effects were not caused by fatigue.

Counting the number of lever presses for food, as food became more and more difficult to obtain, allowed the reinforcement effectiveness of food to be assessed. For example, an animal had to press 5 times for the first food pellet, 10 times for the next, then 15, 20, and 25 times, and so on. As in the first experiment, the giving-up point was used to measure reinforcement effectiveness. Presumably, the more effective the reinforcer (i.e., food), the harder the animal would work for it.

Figure 7.13 shows that, when test days were preceded by a day of exercise, the reinforcing effectiveness of food decreased sharply. Animals pressed the lever more than 200 times when they were not allowed to run, but no more than 38 times when running preceded test sessions. Food no longer supported lever presses following a day of moderate wheel running, even though a lengthy rest period preceded the test. Although wheel running was moderate, it represented a large change in physical activity, since the animals were previously sedentary.

Prior to each test, the animals spent an entire day without food. Because of this, the reinforcing effectiveness of food should have increased. However, exercise seemed to override the effects of food deprivation, since responding for food decreased rather than increased. Other evidence from these experiments suggested that the effects of exercise were similar to those of feeding the animal. Although exercise reduces the reinforcement effectiveness of food, the effect is probably not because wheel running serves as an economic substitute for food consumption (Belke, Pierce, & Duncan, 2006).

The rat that was forced to run also showed a sharp decline in lever pressing for food (see Figure 7.13). Exercise was again moderate, but substantial relative to the animal's sedentary history. Because the reinforcement effectiveness of food decreased with forced exercise, we concluded that both forced and voluntary physical activity produce a decline in the value of food reinforcement. This finding suggests that people who increase their physical activity because of occupational requirements (e.g., ballet dancers), or just in order to get trim and fit, may value food less.

FIG. 7.13 The graph shows the number of bar presses for food when rats were allowed to run on a wheel as compared with no physical activity. From "Deprivation and satiation: The interrelations between food and wheel running," by W. D. Pierce, W. F. Epling, and D. P. Boer, 1986, *Journal of the Experimental Analysis of Behavior, 46*, 199–210. © 1986 Society for the Experimental Analysis of Behavior. Republished with permission.

The Biological Context of Eating and Activity

In our view, the motivational interrelations between eating and physical activity have a basis in natural selection. Natural selection favored those animals that increased their amount of travel in times of food scarcity. During a famine, organisms can either stay where they are and conserve energy, or become mobile and travel to another location. The particular strategy adopted by a species depends on natural selection. If travel led to reinstatement of food supply and staying where they were resulted in starvation, then those animals that traveled gained a reproductive advantage.

A major problem for an evolutionary analysis of activity anorexia is accounting for the decreased appetite of animals that travel to a new food patch. The fact that increasing energy expenditure is accompanied by decreasing caloric intake seems to violate common sense. From a homeostatic (i.e., energy-balance) perspective, food intake and energy expenditure should be positively related. In fact, this is the case if an animal has the time to adjust to a new level of activity and food supply is not greatly reduced (Dwyer & Boakes, 1997).

When depletion of food is severe, however, travel should not stop when food is infrequently contacted. This is because stopping to eat may be negatively balanced against reaching a more abundant food patch. Frequent contact with food would signal a replenished food supply, and this should reduce the tendency to travel. Recall that a decline in the reinforcing effectiveness of food means that animals will not work hard for nourishment. When food is scarce, considerable effort may be required to obtain it. For this reason, animals ignore food and continue to travel. However, as food becomes more plentiful and the effort to acquire it decreases, the organism begins to eat (see Dixon, Ackert, & Eckel, 2003, on recovery from activity anorexia). Food consumption lowers the reinforcement effectiveness of physical activity and travel stops (see also Belke, Pierce, & Duncan, 2006, on the partial substitution of food for physical activity). On this basis, animals that expend large amounts of energy on a migration or trek become anorexic.

Behavioral Neuroscience of Activity Anorexia: Role of NPY

Prominent features of activity anorexia are the suppression of food intake, escalating levels of physical activity, and a precipitous decline in body weight. These responses occur when animals face an environmental challenge of time-limited feeding (1 to 2 h a day) followed by the opportunity for food-related travel. As you can see, these behavioral observations do not suggest energy balance or homeostasis, which is the accepted model of biology.

In the homeostatic model, the hormone leptin is secreted by the fat cells in response to weight loss. High levels of leptin in turn activate neuropeptide Y (NPY), a brain peptide that stimulates eating and normalizes body weight. This energy-balance cycle is substantially altered in anorexic patients and rats in the activity anorexia challenge. Both activity-anorexic rats and anorexic humans show low body weight, low leptin levels, and high NPY levels (Diane, Pierce, Heth, Russell, Richard, & Proctor, 2011; Gendall, Kaye, Altemus, McConaha, & La Via, 1999)—a pattern that is clearly not homeostatic. Also, with high levels of NPY both activity-anorexic rats and anorexic humans should be eating, but they do not. Finally, activity-anorexic rats and anorexic humans are physically overactive, expending high levels of energy at a time when food is depleted (Epling & Pierce, 1992).

One possibility is that NPY acts differently when animals are challenged by severe food restriction and excessive weight loss. Under these extreme conditions, NPY may no longer act on the eating centers of the brain, but now acts to stimulate a search for food (travel) and inhibit food intake. To test this possibility, Nergardh and colleagues in Sweden gave brain infusions of NPY to rats that had access to running wheels, and varied the number of hours a day for which food was available (Nergardh, Ammar, Brodin, Bergstrom, Scheurink, & Sodersten, 2007). Rats in running wheels lost more weight than sedentary controls, and ran progressively more as the availability of food was reduced over experimental groups (24, 4, 2 and 1 h per day). When food was available for only 1 h per day, body weight plummeted and the rats in this group showed the typical activity-anorexic effect. These anorexic rats also showed high levels of NPY measured by assay. But were high levels of NPY working on the eating or food search centers of the brain? The critical test occurred in rats that were given food for 2 h each day. These animals increased wheel running and decreased food intake when given brain infusions of NPY. By contrast, NPY infusions increased eating, but not wheel running, in rats that had free access to food for 24 h. The results show that NPY, a brain peptide that usually stimulates eating, acts on brain receptors to activate travel and inhibit eating during periods of food shortage or famine.

ADVANCED SECTION: The Nature of Autoshaped Responses

Negative Automaintenance

When scientists are confronted with new and challenging data, they are typically hesitant about accepting the findings. This is because researchers have invested time, money, and effort in experiments that may depend on a particular view of the world. Consider a person who has made a career of investigating the free-operant behavior of pigeons, with rate of pecking a key as the major dependent variable. The suggestion that key pecking is actually respondent rather than operant behavior would not be well received by such a scientist. If key pecks are reflexive, then conclusions about operant behavior based on these responses are questionable. One possibility is to go to some effort to explain the data within the context of operant conditioning.

In fact, Brown and Jenkins (1968) suggested just this kind of explanation for their results. Recall that these experimenters pointed to the species-specific tendency of pigeons to peck at stimuli that they look at. When the light is illuminated, there is a high probability that the bird will look and peck at it. Some of these responses are followed by food, and pecking increases in frequency. Other investigators noted that when birds are magazine trained they stand in the general area of the feeder and the response key is typically at head height just above the food tray. Anyone who has watched a pigeon knows that they have a high frequency of bobbing their heads. Since they are close to the key and are making pecking (or bobbing) motions, it is possible that a strike at the key is inadvertently followed by food delivery. From this perspective, key pecks are superstitious in the sense that they are accidentally reinforced. The superstitious explanation has an advantage because it does not require postulation of a look–peck connection and it is entirely consistent with operant conditioning.

Although these explanations of pecking as an operant are plausible, the possibility remains that autoshaped pecking is respondent behavior. An ingenious experiment by Williams and Williams (1969) was designed to answer this question. In their experiment on **negative automaintenance**, pigeons were placed in an operant chamber and key illumination was repeatedly followed by food. This is, of course, the same procedure that Brown and Jenkins (1968) used to show autoshaping. The twist in the Williams and Williams procedure was that if the bird pecked the key when it was illuminated, food was not presented. This is called *omission training*, because if the pigeon pecks the key the reinforcer is omitted, or if the response is omitted the reinforcer is delivered.

The logic of this procedure is that if pecking is respondent, then it is elicited by the key light and the pigeon will reflexively strike the disk. If, on the other hand, pecking is operant, then striking the key prevents reinforcement and responses should not be maintained. Thus, the clear prediction is that pecking is respondent behavior if the bird continues to peck with the **omission procedure** in place. Using the omission procedure, Williams and Williams (1969) found that pigeons frequently pecked the key even though responses prevented reinforcement. This finding suggests that the sight of grain is an unconditioned stimulus for pigeons, eliciting an unconditioned response of pecking at the food. When a key light stimulus precedes grain presentation, it becomes a CS that

FIG. 7.14   For birds, the sight of grain (US) elicits pecking (UR) as species-specific behavior. Williams and Williams (1969) arranged omission procedures for pecking a lighted key that was usually followed by grain (autoshaping). When the key light-CS occurred, a peck at the key (CR) caused the key light to go out and no food was presented. If the bird did not peck the lighted key it received food. The birds pecked the key even though these responses prevented reinforcement.

elicits pecking at the key (CR). Figure 7.14 shows this arrangement between stimulus events and responses. It is also the case that by not presenting the food (US), the key light (CS) is no longer paired with the US, and the response (CR) undergoes extinction.

In discussing their results, Williams and Williams state that "the stimulus–reinforcer pairing overrode opposing effects of . . . reinforcement indicat[ing] that the effect was a powerful one, and demonstrat[ing] that a high level of responding does not imply the operation of . . . [operant] reinforcement" (1969, p. 520). The puzzling aspect of this finding is that in most cases pecking to a key is regulated by reinforcement and is clearly operant. Many experiments have shown that key pecks increase or decrease in frequency depending on the consequences that follow behavior.

The Nature of the Autoshaped Response

Because of this apparent contradiction, several experiments were designed to investigate the nature of autoshaped pecking. Schwartz and Williams (1972a) preceded grain reinforcement for pigeons by turning on a red or white light on two separate keys. The birds responded by pecking the illuminated disk (i.e., they were autoshaped). On some trials, the birds were presented with both the red and white keys. Pecks on the red key prevented reinforcement as in the omission procedure used by Williams and Williams (1969). Pecks on the white key, however, did not prevent reinforcement.

On these choice trials, the pigeons showed a definite preference for the white key that did not stop the delivery of grain. In other words, the birds more frequently pecked the key that was followed by the presentation of grain. Because this is a description of behavior regulated by an operant contingency (peck → food), autoshaped key pecks cannot be exclusively respondent behavior. In concluding their paper, Schwartz and Williams wrote:

A simple application of respondent principles cannot account for the phenomenon as originally described . . . and it cannot account for the rate and preference results of the present study. An indication of the way operant factors can modulate the performance of auto-maintained behavior has been given. . . . The analysis suggests that while automaintained behavior departs in important ways from the familiar patterns seen with arbitrary responses, the concepts and procedures developed from the operant framework are, nevertheless, influential in the automaintenance situation.

(Schwartz & Williams, 1972a, p. 356)

Schwartz and Williams (1972b) went on to investigate the nature of key pecking by pigeons in several other experiments. The researchers precisely measured the contact duration of each peck that birds made to a response key. When the omission procedure was in effect, pigeons produced short-duration pecks. If the birds were autoshaped, but key pecks did not prevent the delivery of grain, the duration of the pecks was long. These same long-duration pecks occurred when the pigeons responded for food on a schedule of reinforcement. Generally, it appears that there are two types of key pecks: short-duration pecks evoked (or perhaps elicited) by the presentation of grain, and long-duration pecks that occur when the bird's behavior is brought under operant control.

Other evidence also suggests that both operant and respondent conditioning is involved in autoshaping. For example, Bullock and Myers (2009) recently showed that autoshaped responding of the cynomolgus monkey (*Macaca fascicularis)* is sensitive to both negative (omission) and positive (response-dependent) contingencies, using banana pellets and stimulus-directed, touch-screen responses. It is likely, therefore, that autoshaped pecking by birds is initially respondent behavior elicited by light–food pairings. Once pecking produces food, however, it comes under operant control. Even when an omission procedure is in effect both operant and respondent, behavior is conditioned, suggesting that there is no uniform learning process underlying autoshaping (Papachristos & Gallistel, 2006). During omission training, a response to the key turns off the key light and food is not delivered. If the bird does not peck the key, the light is eventually turned off and food is presented. Notice that light offset (dark key) is always predictive of reinforcement and becomes a conditioned reinforcer in the omission procedure. In this analysis, pecking the key is maintained by immediate reinforcement from light offset. Hursh, Navarick, and Fantino (1974) provided evidence for this conditioned reinforcement view of negative automaintenance. They showed that birds quit responding during omission training if the key light did not immediately go out when a response was made.

CHAPTER SUMMARY

This chapter has considered several areas of research on respondent–operant interactions. Autoshaping showed that an operant response (key pecking for food) could actually be elicited by respondent procedures. Before this research, operants and respondents had been treated as separate systems subject to independent controlling procedures. The Brelands' animal training demonstrations provided a hint that the two systems were not distinct—with species-specific behavior being elicited by operant contingencies. Their work revealed the biological foundations of conditioning as well as the contributions made by biologically relevant factors. Animals are prepared by evolution to be responsive to specific events and differentially sensitive to various aspects of the environment.

Other experiments indicated that respondent behavior could be controlled by operant contingencies. The Miller studies used curare to immobilize rats, showing that heart rate—an autonomic response—could be reinforced by electrical stimulation of the brain. The implication again is that the neural systems regulating respondent and operant behavior are interrelated, allowing for operant conditioning of behavior (heart rate) that is often considered to be hard-wired.

Taste aversion is another example of biological factors underlying conditioning procedures. The findings of Garcia and Koelling indicate that interoceptive stimuli are paired with each other (flavor–sickness) better than crossing systems stimuli (flavor–shock), illustrating how organisms are prepared for conditioning based on evolution and natural selection. Work in this area contributes to the management of toxic plant ingestion by livestock, and to the prediction and control of diet selection. Finally, we discussed activity anorexia both as a real-world human problem and as an interesting research question. What neurophysiological–behavioral mechanisms could possibly interact to drive an organism to self-starvation? It turns out that a combination of restricted access to food and the opportunity to exercise are the conditions that lead to this deadly spiral.

KEY WORDS

Activity anorexia	Interim behavior
Adjunctive behavior	Negative automaintenance
Autoshaping	Omission procedure (training)
Behavior system	Polydipsia
Biological context	Preparedness
Conditioned taste preference	Schedule-induced behavior
Context for conditioning	Sign tracking
Displacement behavior	Stimulus substitution
Facultative behavior	Taste aversion learning
Instinctive drift	Terminal behavior

ON THE WEB

http://psych.rutgers.edu/program_areas/bbn/bbn_00.html Students who are interested in schedule-induced behavior or foraging models of behavior may be interested in this website for Biopsychology and Behavioral Neuroscience at Rutgers University. Click on the Faculty home pages for George Collier and John Falk.

www.jsu.edu/depart/psychology/sebac/fac-sch/spot-peck/spot-peck.html Go to this website to read an actual scientific article on "Stereotyped adjunctive pecking by caged pigeons", by Palya and Zacny (1980), from *Animal Learning and Behavior, 8*, 293–303.

www.ctalearning.com This website provides an annotated bibliography and overview of conditioned taste aversion by Anthony Riley of the Department of Psychology, Psychopharmacology Laboratory, American University, Washington, DC.

✎ BRIEF QUIZ

1. In terms of operant contingencies and the intrusion of reflexive behavior:

    (a) operant procedures elicit reflexive behavior directly by the contingencies of reinforcement
    (b) reflexive behavior is elicited by respondent procedures embedded in operant contingencies
    (c) respondent procedures cause species-characteristic responses
    (d) both (b) and (c) are true

2. What did Brown and Jenkins (1968) conclude about autoshaping in their pigeons?

    (a) the look–peck coupling is species-specific and results in pecks to the illuminated key
    (b) following illumination of the key with grain eventually caused the lighted key to elicit pecking
    (c) eventually an operant chain develops, culminating in pecking
    (d) all of the above

3. Phenomena such as instinctive drift, sign tracking, and autoshaping have been analyzed as:

    (a) stimulus substitution, where the CS substitutes for the US
    (b) behavior systems activated by the US and the physical properties of the CS
    (c) both (a) and (b)
    (d) none of the above

4. In terms of operant conditioning of reflexive behavior, the experiment by Miller and Carmona (1967):

    (a) showed conclusive results for operant conditioning of salivation
    (b) showed that salivation and heart rate were both susceptible to operant conditioning
    (c) showed that the increased flow of saliva was accompanied by the dogs being more alert
    (d) showed all of the above

5. What does the evidence suggest about the operant conditioning of reflexive behavior?

    (a) reflexes can be conditioned by operant procedures in some circumstances
    (b) reflexive behavior is hardly ever controlled by respondent procedures
    (c) reflexive behavior is generally controlled by operant procedures
    (d) only (b) and (c) are true

6. When a CS compound (color and taste) is associated with illness, different species show avoidance to the two parts of the compound. This phenomenon is called:

    (a) species readiness
    (b) species set
    (c) species preparedness
    (d) species activation

7. What did Lett and Grant (1996) suggest with regard to activity anorexia?

    (a) it could involve taste aversion induced by physical activity
    (b) it probably explains taste-aversion conditioning
    (c) it is the first stage in taste-aversion conditioning
    (d) both (b) and (c)

8. Excessive drinking is technically called:

    (a) polyhydration
    (b) polydipsia
    (c) polyfluidity
    (d) polydistation

9. According to Falk (1977), schedule-induced or adjunctive behavior occurs in situations that are generally positive for the organism but:

    (a) result in high levels of aggressive behavior
    (b) lead to impulses to retaliate
    (c) from which it is likely to escape
    (d) toward which it shows avoidance

10. What is the basic finding for activity anorexia?

    (a) decreased food intake increases physical activity
    (b) increased food intake increases physical activity
    (c) physical activity decreases food intake
    (d) both (a) and (c)

Answers to Brief Quiz: 1, d (pp. 195–196); 2, d (pp. 197–198); 3, c (pp. 199–200); 4, c (pp. 201); 5, a (p. 202); 6, c (pp. 203–204); 7, a (p. 207); 8, b (p. 209); 9, c (p. 210); 10, d (p. 212)

Stimulus Control

In the everyday world, human behavior is changed by signs, symbols, gestures, and spoken words. Sounds, smells, sights, and other sensory stimuli that do not depend on social conditioning also regulate behavior. When social or nonsocial events precede operant behavior and affect its occurrence, they are called controlling stimuli. A **controlling stimulus (S)** is said to alter the probability of an operant, in the sense that the response is more (or less) likely to occur when the stimulus is present.[1]

One kind of controlling stimulus that we discussed in Chapter 4 is the S^D or **discriminative stimulus**. An S^D is a controlling stimulus that sets the occasion for reinforcement of an operant. In a pigeon experiment, a red light may reliably signal the presentation of food for pecking a key. After some experience, the bird will immediately strike the key when it is illuminated with the red light. Thus, the discriminative stimulus sets the occasion for a high probability of response.

The discriminative stimuli that regulate human behavior may be as simple as that in the pigeon experiment, or far more complex. A green traffic light and the word WALK sets the occasion for pedestrians to cross a street. In a library, the call numbers posted above the stacks and on the books are discriminative stimuli for stopping, turning corners, and so on that result in finding a book. On the football field, a quarterback who is about to pass the ball must decide whether to pick the left or right receiver. Throwing the ball to a receiver is based on the degree of coverage (the number and proximity of defensive players). In this example, the degree of coverage is a complex S^D that controls the direction, speed, elevation, and probability of the quarterback's pass.

---

1 In this chapter, we present a classification scheme for stimuli that precede and set the occasion for reinforcement, extinction, or punishment of operant behavior. We introduce the generic term *controlling stimulus* (S) to stand for all events that exert stimulus control over operant behavior. There are three kinds of controlling stimuli: S^D, S^Δ, and S^{ave}. Notice that the controlling stimulus is modified to reflect its function based on the contingencies of reinforcement that have established it (i.e., reinforcement, extinction, or punishment). The notations S^+ and S^- are also commonly used to represent the S^D and S^Δ functions of stimuli.

Another kind of controlling stimulus is called an S^Δ **(S-delta)** or an **extinction stimulus**. An S^Δ is a stimulus that sets the occasion for nonreinforcement or extinction of an operant (see Chapter 4). For example, a rat may press a lever on a VI schedule of food reinforcement. Every now and then a tone comes on and a period of extinction is in effect. After some time, the rat will stop pressing the bar as soon as the tone is presented. Thus, the tone is defined as an S^Δ because lever pressing has a low probability of occurrence in its presence, due to extinction.

Extinction stimuli that regulate human behavior also range from simple to complex. When your car is almost out of gas, a service-station sign that says CLOSED is an S^Δ for turning into that station. A tennis opponent who usually wins the match may become an extinction stimulus for playing the game. In this case, you may play tennis with others, but not with the person who always wins. Sometimes breakdown of communication between married couples may be caused by stimuli that signal extinction for conversation. A wife may try to talk to her husband about a variety of issues, and he pretends to read the newspaper. The husband's behavior is an S^Δ for conversation if his wife reliably stops talking when he picks up the paper.

DIFFERENTIAL REINFORCEMENT AND DISCRIMINATION

Stimulus Control as a Three-Term Contingency

When an animal makes a response in one situation but not in another—that is, a differential response—we say that it discriminates between the situations. Alternatively, we may say that the situation exerts stimulus control over the animal's behavior. The simplest way to establish stimulus control and train a **differential response** or **discrimination** is to reinforce an operant in one situation and withhold reinforcement in the other. This procedure uses the basic three-term contingency involving a controlling stimulus (S^D), a response or performance (R), and reinforcement (S^r). For birds in a laboratory, the contingency takes the following form:

S^D (red key): R (peck) $\rightarrow$ S^r (food)
S^Δ (green key): R (peck) $\rightarrow$ extinction (no food)

In the presence of the red key, pecks produce food. When the key is green, pecks are on extinction (no food). Now this basic contingency can be used to establish stimulus control over the bird's behavior in the laboratory and extended to complex human behavior in everyday settings.

Figure 8.1 shows the development of a differential response to a single key that is alternately illuminated red and green for 5 min. The graph shows the cumulative number of responses over a 90-min session. Pecks to the red key by a pigeon are intermittently reinforced with food. Responses emitted in the presence of the green key are extinguished, never reinforced. The procedure of alternating between periods of reinforcement and extinction is termed *differential reinforcement*.

As you can see in this idealized experiment, the pigeon begins by emitting about the same number of responses to the red and green stimuli. After about 20 min, the cumulative response curves start to separate, indicating that the bird is pecking in the presence of red more than green. At about 60 min, the pigeon seldom responds when the key is green, as shown by the leveling off of the curve for this stimulus. Notice, however, that the cumulative curve for pecking the red key continues to rise. Because the bird pecks in the presence of a red stimulus, but does not respond when the key is green, we may say that the pigeon *discriminates* between these two colors. At this point, it is possible to label the red and green stimuli in terms of their stimulus functions. The red key is called a discriminative stimulus (S^D) and the green color is an extinction stimulus or S-delta (S^Δ).

FIG. 8.1   Development of a differential response in the presence of red and green stimuli. Cumulative number of responses over a 90-min session in which responses in the presence of red are reinforced and responses in the presence of green are on extinction.

Suppose the bird is returned to its home cage after 90 min of such *differential reinforcement*. On the next day, the pigeon is again placed in the operant chamber and the key is illuminated with the red light. During this test session, reinforcement is not given for pecking in the presence of either red or green stimuli. Because of its previous training, the bird has a high probability of pecking the red key. Over a 60-s period, the bird may emit many responses when the S^D is present. After 60 s, the key light is changed from red to green. When the green light comes on, the probability of response is low and the bird makes few pecks to the green key. By continuing to alternate between red and green, the researcher can show the stimulus control exerted by the respective colors.

Stimulus control refers to the change in behavior that occurs when either an S^D or an S^Δ is presented. When an S^D is presented, the probability of response increases; when an S^Δ is presented, the probability of response decreases. The stimuli that commonly control human behavior occur across all sensory dimensions. Stopping when you hear a police siren, coming to dinner when you smell food, expressing gratitude following a pat on the back, elaborating an answer because the student looks puzzled, and adding salt to your soup because it tastes bland are all instances of stimulus control in human behavior.

Stimulus Control of Behavior Sequences

Suppose that you have trained a bird to reliably peck for food on an intermittent schedule in the presence of a red key. How could you use the red key to establish a simple sequence of behavior? Let us require the bird to step on a foot treadle (a lever near the floor, operated by the foot) when the key is blue and then peck the key for food when the color changes to red. To establish this two-component sequence or **response chain** you will use the red key as reinforcement (S^r) for treadle pressing as well as the S^D to peck for food. That is, because the red key has set the occasion for food reinforcement of pecking, it has acquired two stimulus functions, both as an S^D and as an S^r.

You begin to establish the response chain by observing the bird in the chamber pecking for food on the red key. Next, you manually change the key light to blue and look for a foot response toward the treadle. Any movement of the foot in the direction of the treadle is immediately followed by presentation of the red key (conditioned reinforcement). Also, when the key changes to red the bird pecks the key and this response is reinforced with food. You again present the blue key, look for another approximation to a foot-treadle response, and reinforce (shape) it by changing the key color to red. The bird pecks the red key and is reinforced with food. You keep following this procedure until the first definable foot-treadle response occurs, at which point the entire sequence is carried out automatically by the programmed apparatus and the bird. Once the performance is established, a person unfamiliar with basic behavior principles would see a bird in the chamber standing near the key and food hopper. A blue key is illuminated and the bird steps on a treadle, followed by the key color changing to red; the bird then pecks the red key and the sequence is repeated. For your demonstration, you omit any food reinforcement at the end of the response chain. The bird's behavior looks mysterious, but can be entirely explained by the contingencies of reinforcement.

To make the performance even more impressive, you decide to add more components to the pigeon's response chain; these include ringing a bell, climbing a perch, and pulling a string. You establish each link in the chain using the same procedures, with separate S^Ds for each component. Thus, to establish pulling a string in the presence of an orange key as the next link, you use the blue key color as conditioned reinforcement. You continue to add new links once each performance is well established. Now you have a bird that rings a bell when the key is green, climbs a perch when the key changes to yellow, pulls a string when it shifts to orange, steps on a food treadle when it transitions to blue, and finally pecks the key when it turns to red. This is really impressive! These same steps can be used to train pigeons to "read" such English words as PECK or RING, by gradually fading in the letters over the colors and gradually fading out the colors (see section on Fading later in this chapter).

NEW DIRECTIONS: Stimulus Control, Neuroscience, and What Birds See

What do birds see and how do they see it? We actually do not know what humans "see," let alone birds. We do know a great deal about the structure and physiology of vision, but what is actually "seen" can only be speculation. Vision and other sensations are private experiences, even though the operation of the physiological system can be observed and analyzed.

The evolution of vision is an example of the natural selection of structures that enhance the organism's reproductive fitness (Dawkins, 1996). Many very primitive biological organisms have light-sensitive structures that contribute to that organism's survival even if it is only a matter of telling light from dark. Darker places are often safer than lighter places, and organisms that were sensitive to the difference produced more offspring. In terms of avian evolution it is apparent that both structure and function have interacted to produce the current forms of vision, making birds more viable (Goldsmith, 2006).

Vision occurs when light enters the eye and is transduced from one form of energy to another by processes in the retina—from light photons to neural impulses that travel from the eye via the optic nerve to the brain (see Donovan, 1978, on the structure and function of pigeon vision). Nothing is actually "seen" at any point. However, identifying the mechanisms in the retina and brain provides the basis for predicting how the organism might behave, as well as advancing our scientific knowledge of visual discrimination.

A direct demonstration of a bird's ability to see color, shape, and movement requires behavioral experiments wherein the subject has to discriminate aspects of these stimuli. D. S. Blough (1957) provided the first thorough behavioral assessment of color vision in pigeons, even though the anatomy of the bird eye had predicted such ability long before. Using a modified Blough procedure, Goldsmith and Butler (2005) trained parakeets to go to a yellow light for food. The researchers then presented a light composed of a mix of red and green as a comparison stimulus, and showed that with a certain mix (90% red and 10% green) the birds could not discriminate the mix from the yellow light.

These findings indicated to behavioral neuroscientists that separate retinal receptors (cones) are responsive to different hues and are used by birds to guide their behavior. Four types of cones were identified that contained different pigments and oil-droplet filters; one of these receptors is sensitive to ultraviolet (UV) wavelengths, allowing birds to discriminate colors that we cannot even imagine (see Carvalho, Knott, Berg, Bennet, & Hunt, 2010, for an account of UV vision in long-living parrots, macaws, and cockatoos; see Hogg, Neveu, Stokkan, Folkow, Cottrill, Douglas et al., 2011, for an account of the discovery of UV vision in Arctic reindeer). Subsequently, behavioral experiments using operant contingencies showed that birds could make the visual discriminations predicted from the analysis of retinal receptors. The evidence suggests that UV wavelengths are seen as separate colors by birds due to the presence of UV receptors. In the everyday world of birds, these receptors allow for differential mate selection (Griggio, Hoi, & Pilastro, 2010; Hausmann, Arnold, Marshall, & Owens, 2003), improved foraging (Hastad, Ernstdotter, & Odeen, 2005), and detection of rapidly moving prey (Rubene, Hastad, Tauson, Wall, & Odeen, 2010). Overall, visual sensitivity to the UV spectrum allows for operant discriminations of the world that improve the survival and reproductive success of birds.

Stimulus Control and Multiple Schedules

Behavior analysts often use multiple schedules of reinforcement to study stimulus control in the laboratory. On a **multiple schedule**, two or more simple schedules are presented one after the other and each schedule is accompanied by a distinctive controlling stimulus—in some cases two or more reinforcement schedules are presented, neither of which is extinction. The idealized experiment that we discussed near the beginning of this chapter is one example of a multiple schedule. Pecking was reinforced when a red light appeared on the key, and a schedule of extinction was in effect when the key color turned to green. The schedules and the associated stimuli alternated back and forth every 5 min. As indicated, these procedures result in a *differential response* to the colors.

In an actual experiment, presenting the component schedules for a fixed amount of time or on an FI schedule (e.g., 5 min) would confound the results. Without a test procedure, the researcher would not be sure that the bird discriminates on the basis of color rather than time. That is, time itself may have become a discriminative stimulus. For this reason, variable-interval (VI) schedules are often used for discrimination training (Guttman & Kalish, 1956; Harrison, 1991).

Figure 8.2 illustrates one example of a multiple variable-interval extinction schedule of reinforcement (MULT VI EXT). The Mechner notation shows that in the presence of the red S^D

FIG. 8.2 Mechner notation for a MULT VI 2-min, EXT 1-min schedule of reinforcement.

FIG. 8.3   Idealized results for a MULT VI 2-min, EXT 1-min schedule of reinforcement. Relative to the red VI component, pecking declines over sessions to almost zero responses per minute in the green extinction phase.

the first response after an average of 2 min produces reinforcement. Following reinforcement, the key light changes from red to the green S^{Δ}, and pecking the key no longer results in reinforcement. After an average of 2 min of extinction, the green light goes out and the red stimulus appears again. Pecking the key is now reinforced on the VI 2-min schedule, and the components continue to alternate in this fashion.

A likely result of this multiple schedule is shown in Figure 8.3. The graph portrays the total number of responses during the red and green components for 1-h daily sessions. Notice that the bird begins by pecking equally in the presence of the red and green stimuli. Over sessions, the number of pecks to the green extinction stimulus, or S^{Δ}, declines. By the last session, almost all of the responses occur in the presence of the red S^{D} and almost none when the green light is on. At this point, pecking the key can be controlled easily by presenting the red or green stimulus. When red is presented the bird will peck the key at a high rate, and if the color changes to green the pigeon will immediately stop pecking.

Multiple Schedules and the Discrimination Index

One way to measure the stimulus control exerted by the S^{D} and S^{Δ} at any moment is to use a **discrimination index (I_D)**. This index compares the rate of response in the S^{D} component with the sum of the rates in both S^{D} and S^{Δ} phases (Dinsmoor, 1951):

$$I_D = (S^D \text{ rate})/(S^D \text{ rate} + S^{\Delta} \text{ rate}).$$

Prior to discrimination training, the measure varies between 0.00 and 1.00. When the rates of response are the same in the S^{D} and S^{Δ} components, the value of I_D is 0.50, indicating no discrimination. When all of the responses occur during the S^{D} phase and no responses occur during the S^{Δ} component, the I_D is 1.00. Thus, a discrimination index of 1.00 indicates a perfect discrimination and maximum stimulus control of behavior. Intermediate values of the index signify more or less control by the discriminative stimulus.

A study by Pierrel, Sherman, Blue, and Hegge (1970) illustrates the use of the discrimination index. The experiment concerned the effects of sound intensity on acquisition of a differential response. The researchers were interested in sound-intensity relationships (measured in decibels) between the S^{D} and S^{Δ}. The basic idea was that the more noticeable the difference in sounds, the better the discrimination. For example, some people have doorbells for the front and back entrances to their houses. If the chimes are very similar in sound intensity, a ring will be confusing and you may go to the wrong door. One way to correct this problem is to change the intensity of sound for one of the chimes (of course, another is to replace one chime with a buzzer).

In one of many experimental conditions, 16 rats were trained to respond on a MULT VI 2-min, EXT schedule. The animals were separated into four equal groups, and for each group the auditory S^{D} for the VI component was varied while the S^{Δ} for the extinction phase was held constant. For each group, the S^Δ was a 60-dB tone but the S^D was different—a choice of 70, 80, 90, or 100 dB. Thus, the difference in decibels or sound intensity between the S^D and S^Δ increased over groups (70–60, 80–60, 90–60, and 100 versus 60 dB). The rats lived in operant chambers for 15 days. Two 8-h sessions of the multiple schedules were presented each day, with a 4-h break between sessions.

Figure 8.4 shows the average acquisition curves for each experimental group. A mean discrimination index based on the four animals in each group was computed for each 8-h session. As you can see, all of the groups begin with I_D values of approximately 0.50 or no difference in responding between the S^D and S^Δ components. As discrimination training continues, a differential response develops and I_D values rise toward 1.00 or perfect discrimination. The accuracy of the discrimination, as indicated by the maximum value of I_D, is determined by the difference in sound intensity between S^D and S^Δ. In general, more rapid acquisition and a more accurate discrimination occur when the difference between S^D and S^Δ is increased.

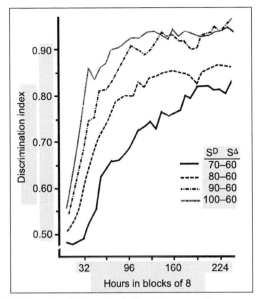

FIG. 8.4 Discrimination index (I_D) curves for different values of S^D and S . Each curve is a plot of the average I_D values based on a group of four animals that were repeatedly exposed to 8-h sessions of discrimination training. From Figure 1B, p. 22 in "Auditory discrimination: A three-variable analysis of intensity effects," by R. Pierrel, G. J. Sherman, S. Blue, and F. W. Hegge, 1970, *Journal of the Experimental Analysis of Behavior, 13,* 17–35. © 1970 Society for the Experimental Analysis of Behavior, Inc. The labels for the *x*- and *y*-axes have been simplified to promote clarity.

FOCUS ON: Discrimination and the "Bird-Brained" Pigeon

Pretend that you are doing a class assignment that involves training a pigeon to discriminate between red and green components of a multiple schedule. The assignment counts for 30% of the course grade, and you must show the final performance of the bird to your instructor. Students are given a pigeon, an operant chamber, and a microcomputer that allows them to control key color and the delivery of food from a hopper. Sessions are scheduled for 1 h a day over a 2-week period that ends with the professor's evaluation of your project. The pigeon has been food deprived, magazine trained, and taught to peck at a white-illuminated key on a VI 60-s schedule.

You and the other students follow the Mechner notation for a MULT VI 60-s EXT 60-s schedule in which you signal the VI component with a red-key light and 1 min of extinction by turning the key green. To create the VI schedule and the variable 60 s of extinction you use operant-conditioning software to program your computer. The software program is set up to record the number of key pecks in each component of the multiple schedule. Your program starts a session with the key illuminated red, and the first response after an average of 60s is reinforced with food (VI 60s). After food is presented, the key color changes to green and extinction is in effect for an average of 60s.

Day after day, your bird pecks at a similar rate in both the red and green components. You become more and more concerned because other students have trained their birds to peck when the key is red and stop when it is green. By the 11th session, you are in a panic because everyone else is finished, but your bird has not made much progress. You complain to your instructor that you were given a dumb or color-blind bird, and it is not fair for her to give you a low mark because you tried your best. Your professor is a strict behavior analyst who replies, "The fault is with the program, not with the pigeon; go study your computer program in terms of Mechner notation." You spend the night pondering the program and then, somewhat like Kohler's apes (Kohler, 1927), you "have an insight." Pecking in the extinction green-key component has been reinforced with the presentation of the red-key light!

You realize that the red color is always associated with food reinforcement and this suggests that the red stimulus has more than one function. It is obviously an S^D that sets the occasion for reinforced pecking. However, in addition, the stimulus itself is a conditioned reinforcer because of its association with food. Presumably, during the extinction component the bird sometimes pecked the green key, and on the basis of the computer program the color changed to red. This change in color accidentally or adventitiously reinforced pecking in the extinction component. From the bird's point of view, pecking the key during extinction turns on the red light that then allows food reinforcement. In fact, the pigeon's behavior is **superstitious**, because pecking in the green component does not affect the presentation of the red color.

Figure 8.5 shows how to solve the adventitious reinforcement problem in Mechner notation. The first part of the diagram presents the notation for a simple MULT VI 60-s EXT 60-s schedule. Enclosed within the dotted lines is an additional, critical contingency. This contingency prevents the onset of the red stimulus if responding is occurring at the moment when the extinction phase ends (or is supposed to do so). That is, if the extinction period ends with the bird pecking the key, the onset of the red stimulus is delayed. The added contingency is called **differential reinforcement of other behavior**, or **DRO**. Notice that when extinction ends, the DRO contingency requires an additional 2-s response-free period before the red stimulus is presented. During this DRO period, each response or peck resets the 2-s interval. If the bird does anything other than strike the key for 2s, the red stimulus occurs. (One might say that the green stimulus sets the occasion for behavior other than key pecking, which is reinforced by the appearance of the red key.)

With this insight, you rush to the laboratory and add DRO to your computer program. At the first opportunity, you place your "dumb or color-blind" pigeon in the operant chamber

FIG. 8.5 Mechner diagram for solving the adventitious reinforcement problem on a multiple schedule of reinforcement. The first part of the diagram presents the notation for a simple MULT VI 60-s EXT 60-s schedule. Notice that when extinction terminates, the DRO contingency requires an additional 2-s period before the red stimulus is presented. During this DRO time, each response or peck resets the 2-s interval. If the bird does anything other than strike the key for 2 s, the red stimulus occurs.

and initiate the program. As you watch the bird's performance on the cumulative recorder, the rate of response during the S^D and S^Δ components begins to separate. After two more sessions, the discrimination index (I_D) is almost 0.90, indicating good discrimination between reinforcement and extinction components. The instructor is impressed with your analytical skills, and you get the highest mark possible for the assignment (A+).

This analysis has implications for teaching and learning. When most people learn from instruction but a few do not, educators, psychologists, and parents often blame the poor student, confused client, or stubborn child. They see the failure to learn as a deficiency of the person rather than a problem of contingencies of reinforcement (called "blaming the victim"; Shaver, 1985). The individuals who fail to learn are said to be learning disabled, low in intelligence, or cognitively impaired. Of course, some people and animals may have neurological and/or sensory impairment (e.g., color blindness, deafness, organic brain damage) that contributes to their poor performance. Nonetheless, defective contingencies of reinforcement may also contribute to, or exclusively produce, problems of discrimination and learning. In the case of the apparently dumb pigeon, the fault was caused entirely by *adventitious reinforcement* of responding during extinction. A small change in the contingencies of reinforcement (adding DRO) made a "bird-brained" pigeon smart.

BEHAVIORAL CONTRAST

Consider an experiment by Guttman (1977) in which rats were exposed to a two-component multiple schedule with a variable-interval 30-s reinforcement schedule in both components (MULT VI 30 s VI 30 s). A sound (white noise) signaled one component and a light signaled the other. The sound and light alternated every 3 min, and the rats made about the same number of responses in each of the components. Next, in the presence of the sound stimulus the contingencies were changed from VI to extinction (MULT VI EXT). As you might expect, the rate of response declined in the extinction component. Surprisingly, the rate of response increased on the VI component signaled by the light. This increase in rate occurred even though the reinforcement contingencies for the VI component remained the same. Thus, changing the contingencies of reinforcement on one schedule affected reinforced behavior on another schedule.

This effect is called **behavioral contrast** (Reynolds, 1961a, 1961b, 1963). Contrast refers to a negative correlation between the response rates in the two components of a multiple schedule—as one goes up, the other goes down. There are two forms of behavioral contrast, positive and negative. **Positive contrast** occurs when the rate of response in an unchanged setting *increases* with a decline in behavior in another situation. **Negative contrast** occurs when the rate of response *decreases* in the unchanged component with increases in behavior in the other.

There are several alternative accounts of behavioral contrast. For example, when reinforcement is reduced in one component of a two-component multiple schedule, habituation to the reinforcer is less, resulting in more effective reinforcement in the unchanged component (McSweeney & Weatherly, 1998; see also McSweeney, Murphy, & Kowal, 2003, for the role of dishabituation). Other accounts of behavioral contrast include increased autoshaped key pecks in the unchanged component, fatigue or rest attributed to the amount of responding on the changed schedule, and compensating for response rate changes on the altered component (de Villiers, 1977; McSweeney, Ettinger, & Norman, 1981; Schwartz & Gamzu, 1977).

Behavioral Contrast and Relative Rates of Reinforcement

Although there is some dispute, one prominent account suggests that behavioral contrast results from changes in *relative rates of reinforcement*. On a two-component multiple schedule, relative rate of reinforcement for the unchanged component increases when the number of reinforcers goes down on the other schedule. Of course, relative rate of reinforcement for the unchanged component goes down when the number of reinforcers is increased on the changed schedule.

For example, on a MULT VI VI schedule, if an animal obtains 30 reinforcers each hour on the unchanged component and gets another 30 reinforcers on the other schedule, then 50% of the reinforcement occurs on both components. If the schedule is changed to MULT VI EXT, then 100% of the reinforcements occur on the unaltered component. As the *relative rate of reinforcement goes up on the unchanged component, so does the rate of response.* Similarly, response rate on the unaltered schedule would go down if the relative rate of reinforcement declines because of an increase in reinforcement on the changed component. Relative rates of reinforcement provide an account of performance on multiple schedules that is consistent with a behavioral analysis of choice and preference, using concurrent schedules of reinforcement (see Chapter 9). Thus, behavior principles of choice and preference, based on relative rates of reinforcement, can be extended to the findings on multiple schedules—extending the generality of these principles.

Experiments with food and alcohol reinforcement, however, indicate that the substitutability of the reinforcers on a multiple schedule limits the impact of relative rates of reinforcement on behavioral contrast (Ettinger & McSweeney, 1981; McSweeney, Melville, & Higa, 1988). Changes in relative rates of reinforcement produced positive contrast (i.e., the rate of response increased on the unchanged schedule) when food reinforcement was continued in one component and extinction for alcohol was introduced in the other. However, behavioral contrast *did not occur* when alcohol reinforcement was continued and responding for food was placed on extinction. One possibility is that *alcohol is an economic substitute for food* (as rice is for potatoes), but food is not a substitute for alcohol (I'll drink to that!). That is, alcohol and food are partial substitutes. Anderson, Ferland, and Williams (1992) also reported a dramatic negative contrast wherein rats stopped responding for food and switched exclusively to responding for electrical stimulation of the brain (ESB). Relative rates of reinforcement may produce contrast only when reinforcers are economic substitutes, based on reinforcement history or biology.

Behavioral Contrast in a Three-Component Multiple Schedule

Ben Williams investigated behavioral contrast using a sequencing of schedules and stimuli. That is, Williams (1981, 1990, 1992) investigated how contrast depends on the contingencies that precede or follow a schedule or component. For example, in the three-component multiple schedule, A → B → C, the schedule for the component B is changed and response rates for components A and C are monitored.

Generally, Williams (1981) found that the preceding B schedule produced a weak, variable, and transitory contrast effect on the C component. This transitory effect is shown in Figure 8.6 (panel A), where the rate of response is high following reinforcement and then drops off to pre-contrast levels. However, when the B schedule followed the A component, strong contrast occurred that increased as training progressed (see Figure 8.6, panel B). Williams called this strong contrast effect **anticipatory contrast**, to distinguish it from the weak elicited responding induced by the preceding schedule (respondent contingencies).

Suppose we arrange a three-component (A, B, and C) multiple schedule with a VI 3-min schedule in each component. Now let us change the schedule in the B component to VI 6 min. Of course, the first effect is that responding in the B component decreases. Responding in both the A and C components will increase, but the increase in component A will be more than that in component C. Also, the increase in component A will persist over the session, but the increase in the C component will be transitory. Thus, changing the rate of reinforcement on the B component has a greater effect on the component that it follows (the A component) than on the component that it precedes (the C component). Although this following-schedule effect is now well established (Williams, 2002), further experimental analysis is necessary to clarify why it works (Pear, 2001, pp. 154–158).

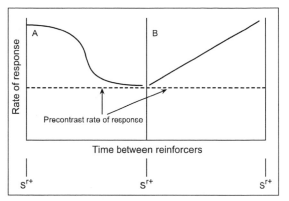

FIG. 8.6 Two patterns of behavioral contrast. The drop-off pattern presented in panel A is often elicited by contingencies that precede the target schedule. The linear pattern presented in panel B is called anticipatory contrast and is a function of the contingencies that follow the target schedule.

After hundreds of studies of behavioral contrast, it is clear that contrast effects may occur in pigeons, rats, and even humans (Simon, Ayllon, & Milan, 1982). In addition, contrast has been shown with various schedules of reinforcement (both ratio and interval), different kinds of responses (e.g., lever pressing, key pecking, and treadle pressing), and different types of reinforcement (e.g., food, water, and alcohol) in the component schedules. This suggests that behavioral contrast is an important process. An animal that forages successively in two patches would be expected to increase searching for food in one patch if the other patch became depleted (i.e., positive contrast). Similarly, negative contrast would occur when food in one of the patches became more abundant than that in the other. In this case, the animal would decrease foraging in the less plentiful location (Cheney, DeWulf, & Bonem, 1993; see also Bergvall, Rautio, Luotola, & Leimar, 2007 and Bergvall & Balogh, 2008, for negative contrast in the foraging behavior of fallow deer). Overall, behavioral contrast in the laboratory may relate to adaptive foraging strategies of animals in the wild.

GENERALIZATION

An organism that responds in one setting but not in another is said to discriminate between the settings. An organism that behaves similarly in different situations is said to generalize across circumstances. **Generalization** is a common observation in everyday life. A child may call all adult males "daddy," label all small furry animals as dogs, and drink anything that looks like juice (one reason for putting child-proof caps on containers of dangerous liquids). Some students call all university teachers "profs" even though professors are only the senior academics. Most of us have seen an old friend at a distance only to find out that the person was not who we expected. A rude person is one who tells vulgar jokes no matter who is listening. In these and many more examples, it appears that common properties of the different stimuli set the occasion for operant behavior.

The problem is that an observer cannot be sure of the stimulus properties that regulate a common response. That is, it is difficult to specify the geometry of dad's face, the physical characteristics that differentiate dogs from other animals, the common aspects of different audiences for the joke teller, and so on. In the operant laboratory, however, it is usually possible to specify the exact physical dimensions of stimuli in terms of wavelength, amplitude, size, mass, and other physical properties. On the basis of experiments that use well-defined stimuli, it is possible to account for everyday examples of generalization and discrimination.

Aspects of Stimulus Generalization

Formally, **stimulus generalization** occurs when an operant that has been reinforced in the presence of a specific discriminative stimulus (S^D) is also emitted in the presence of other stimuli. The process is called stimulus generalization because the operant is emitted to new stimuli that presumably share common properties with the discriminative stimulus. Generalization and discrimination refer to differences in the *precision of stimulus control*. Discrimination refers to the precise control of an operant by a stimulus, and generalization involves less precise regulation of operant behavior.

Generalization Gradients

Guttman and Kalish (1956) conducted a classic study of stimulus generalization. Pigeons were trained to peck a key on a VI 1-min schedule of reinforcement. The key was illuminated with a green light of wavelength 550 nanometers (nm)—a wavelength of light that is approximately in the middle of the color spectrum.[2] Once the rate of key pecking for food had stabilized in the presence of the green light, the researchers tested for stimulus generalization. To do this, they exposed the pigeons to 10 additional values of wavelength (variations in color) as well as the original green light. All 11 colors were presented in a random order, and each wavelength was shown for 30 s. During these test trials, pecking the key was not reinforced (extinction). After the 11 wavelengths had been presented (one block of trials), a new random series of the same colors was initiated. A total of 12 blocks of trials were given to the birds. Of course, as the test for generalization continued, key pecking decreased because of extinction, but the decline was equal over the range of stimuli, because different wavelengths were presented randomly.

FIG. 8.7 Stimulus generalization gradients of wavelength obtained from four groups of pigeons trained at different wavelengths. Adapted from "Discriminability and stimulus generalization," by N. Guttman and H. I. Kalish, 1956, Journal of Experimental Psychology, 51, 79–88.

As is shown in Figure 8.7, generalization gradients resulted from the experiment. A **generalization gradient** shows the relationship between probability of response and stimulus value. In the experiment by Guttman and Kalish (1956),

2 The visible color spectrum is seen when white light is projected through a prism. The spectrum ranges from violet (400 nm) at one end to red (700 nm) at the other.

probability of response is measured as the percentage of responses emitted by the pigeons, and stimulus value is the wavelength of light. As you can see, a symmetrical curve with a peak at 550 nm (yellow-green training stimulus) describes stimulus generalization for pigeons trained at this wavelength. The more the new stimulus differed from the wavelength used in training, the lower the percentage of responses. Importantly, these results were typical of the curves for individual birds. In addition, similar generalization gradients were found for three other groups of pigeons using 530, 580, and 600 nm as the training stimuli. Generally, probability of response is highest for a stimulus that has signaled reinforcement (S^D), less for stimuli that are close but not identical to the S^D, and low for stimuli that substantially depart from the discriminative stimulus.

Peak Shift

Multiple schedules may be used to study generalization gradients. Hanson (1959) reported an experiment with pigeons that was similar to the study by Guttman and Kalish (1956) just discussed. The procedural difference was that four groups of birds were exposed randomly to periods of VI reinforcement and extinction. For the experimental groups, the S^Δ period was 555, 560, 570, or 590 nm and the S^D phase was always 550 nm. A control group only received training on the VI schedule, with 550 nm of light on the response key. Notice that the S^D for all groups was a key light of 550 nm, replicating one of the stimulus values used by Guttman and Kalish.

Figure 8.8 shows the major results of the experiment by Hanson (1959). The control group that received only VI training produced a generalization gradient that replicates the findings of Guttman and Kalish. The peak of the distribution is at 550 nm, and is symmetrical around this value (check this out). In contrast, the experimental groups uniformly showed a shift in the peak of the distribution from 550 nm to 540 nm, moving away from the stimulus value of the S^Δ that was always greater

than 550 nm. For this reason, **peak shift** refers to the change in the peak of a generalization gradient to the side of the S^D away from the stimulus (S^Δ) that signals extinction. Peak shift effects have been observed in the "chick-a-dee" call notes of black-capped chickadees (Guillette, Farrell, Hoeschele, Nickerson, Dawson, & Sturdy, 2010) and in responses to a variety of signals in the natural ecology of animals (Cate & Rowe, 2007). In humans, peak shifts occur for spatial generalization and recognition of faces (see Cheng & Spetch, 2002; Spetch, Cheng, & Clifford, 2004), and peak shift gradients to complex sounds have been reported (Wisniewski, Church, & Mercado, 2009). A final point is that the number of responses made at the peak of each distribution is greater for the experimental groups than for the control condition (compare the peaks in Figure 8.8). This latter finding reflects *positive behavioral contrast* that occurs on multiple schedules with S^D and S^Δ components (see the previous section on "Behavioral contrast").

FIG. 8.8 Peak shift of a generalization gradient. The control shows a peak of the distribution at 550 nm that is symmetrical around this value (check this out). In contrast, the experimental groups uniformly show a shift in the peak of the distribution from 550 nm to 540 nm, moving away from the stimulus value of the S^Δ, which is always greater than 550 nm. Adapted from "Effects of discrimination training on stimulus generalization," by H. M. Hanson, 1959, *Journal of Experimental Psychology*, 58, 321–334.

ON THE APPLIED SIDE: Peak Shift in Anorexia Nervosa

A well-known aspect of anorexia nervosa is the so-called distortion of body image (Garner, Garfinkel, Stancer, & Moldofsky, 1976). In one version of the test for body image, the anorexic patient is given a photograph of herself and two alternative distorted photographs (Figure 8.9). One alternative is manipulated to look thinner and the other is altered to look heavier than the actual photograph. The person is asked to look at the three photographs and identify the one that is the most attractive or preferred. A general finding is that female anorexics typically choose the thinner photograph of themselves as the preferred image (body image distortion).

A behavioral interpretation of the body image test would view the photographs as stimuli on a gradient of generalization.[3] That is, we can think of body size as a stimulus dimension that varies from extremely thin and emaciated to morbidly fat and obese. You have probably heard about the body mass index or BMI—the ratio of weight (kg) to height squared (m^2)—as a way of characterizing your body size. An extremely thin body has a BMI of less than 18.5 kg/m^2, a body that is neither thin nor fat would have a BMI of around 20–24kg/m^2, and a severely obese body would have a BMI of around 40kg/m^2. When viewed as a stimulus dimension, the photograph of one's own body size can be analyzed as the S^D, and the distorted heavier photograph as the S^Δ, on a gradient of generalization. Selection of the thinner photograph as more attractive or preferred would then be analyzed as an instance of peak shift. The strongest response ("I prefer the thinner photograph") occurs to the stimulus shifted furthest from the S^Δ or heavier image on the other side of the S^D (photograph of self). From the perspective of behavior analysis, females who are anorexic do not have a problem of distorted cognitions of self, but are showing the behavioral effects of social conditioning and discrimination training as women living in a cultural of thinness and fitness (Epling and Pierce, 1992).

S^D $\qquad$ S^Δ

FIG. 8.9 The figure shows three photographs. The S^D is the photograph of the actual woman and the S^Δ is the altered photograph of the heavier woman. The other comparison photograph is the manipulated image of a thinner woman. The anorectic woman usually prefers the thinner photograph of herself showing peak shift on a gradient of generalization of body size. Illustration of peak shift in anorexia is adapted from a photograph taken by Dr. David Garner and published in Garner, D.M., Garfinkel, P.E., Stancer, H.C. and Moldofsky, H., 1976, "Body image disturbances in anorexia nervosa and obesity," Psychosomatic Medicine, 38, 327–336. Published with permission of Dr. David Garner, River Center Clinic.

---

3 The analysis of body image distortion as peak shift is based on a review of the textbook by Brady Phelps in the Department of Psychology at South Dakota State University. Brady indicates that he got the idea from Adam Derenne in the Department of Psychology at the University of North Dakota. We thank both for an interesting behavior analysis of cognitive disturbance in anorexia nervosa.

Absolute and Relative Stimulus Control

Peak shift is an unusual effect from the point of view of absolute control by a stimulus. **Absolute stimulus control** means that the probability of response is highest in the presence of the stimulus value used in training. In fact, this occurs when reinforcement is the only procedure used to establish stimulus control (no extinction training). This is clearly seen in the results of the study by Guttman and Kalish (1956) and in the control group of the experiment by Hanson (1959). In both studies, the peak of the generalization gradient is at the exact (or absolute) value of the stimulus presented during training (550 nm). When both S^D and S^Δ procedures are arranged (reinforcement and extinction), the peak of the distribution shifts away from the absolute value of the training stimulus—often analyzed as the interrelationship of excitatory and inhibitory stimulus gradients (Pear, 2001, pp. 158–162).

The shift in the peak of the generalization gradient may involve relative rather than absolute stimulus control. **Relative stimulus control** means that an organism responds to *differences* among the values of two or more stimuli. For example, a pigeon may be trained to peck the "larger" of two triangles projected on a response key, rather than respond to the absolute size of the discriminative stimulus. Similarly, the birds in the peak-shift experiments may have come under the control of the relative value of the wavelengths. That is, the S^D was "greener" than the yellow-green S^Δ used in discrimination training. Because of this, the birds pecked most at stimuli that were relatively "greener," shifting the peak to 540 nm.

Research indicates that pigeons can readily acquire visual discriminations based on both absolute and relational features. These findings are not surprising, as pigeons have excellent color vision on the basis of their biology. How would pigeons do when asked to respond along an auditory dimension to absolute and relational sequences of sounds? Murphy and Cook (2008) used sequences of sounds as experimental stimuli. Responses to *sequences of different sounds* using one set of pitches were reinforced, while responses to other different sound sequences made from another set of pitches, and to sequences of sounds of the same pitch repeatedly presented, were on extinction. In different experiments, the birds were asked to respond to absolute and relative features of the sound sequences, and the findings indicated that the absolute, fundamental pitch of the notes primarily controlled pigeons' behavior. Relational control occurred when the researchers increased the difficulty of the absolute discrimination, forcing the birds to rely on the relational aspects of the sounds. Birds naturally rely more on absolute pitch of sounds, but come under the control of relational features when this is required by the contingencies of reinforcement.

There are other ways of showing *relational control* by stimuli. To study generalization gradients and peak shift, researchers usually arrange the presentation of S^D and S^Δ so that one follows the other. This is called **successive discrimination**. An alternative procedure is labeled **simultaneous discrimination**—the S^D and S^Δ are presented at the same time, and the organism responds to one or the other. For example, a pigeon may be presented with two keys, both illuminated with white lights, but one light is brighter than the other. The bird may be reinforced for pecking the "dimmer" of the two keys. Pecks to the other key are on extinction. After training, the pigeon mostly pecks the darker of the two keys. To test that the bird's performance is caused by the difference between the two stimuli, it is necessary to present new values of luminosity and observe whether the pigeon pecks the dimmer of two keys.

Simultaneous discrimination tasks are often used in education. The television program *Sesame Street* teaches youngsters the relations of "same" and "different" by presenting several objects or pictures at the same time. The jingle "one of these things is just like the others" sets the occasion for the child to identify one of several items. After the child has made a covert response, something like "It's the blue ball," the matching item is shown. In this case, getting the correct answer is reinforcement for the discriminative response (see Wasserman & Young, 2010, for a discussion of same–different discriminations as the foundation for thought and reasoning).

ERRORLESS DISCRIMINATION AND FADING

When the S^D and S^Δ are presented alternately, as in successive discrimination, the organism initially makes many errors. That is, the animal or person continues to respond in the presence of the S^Δ on the basis of generalization. As extinction and reinforcement continue, a differential response gradually occurs to the S^D and S^Δ. A pigeon is taught to peck a green key for food. Once this behavior is well established, the color on the key is changed to blue and pecking is not reinforced. The blue and green colors are alternately presented (without a DRO), and the corresponding schedules of extinction or reinforcement are in effect. During the early sessions, the onset of extinction will often generate emotional behavior that interferes with ongoing operant behavior.

Extinction is an aversive procedure. Pigeons flap their wings in an aggressive manner and will even work for an opportunity to attack another bird during the presentation of the S^Δ on a multiple schedule. Birds will peck a different key if such pecking turns off the extinction stimulus, implying that the stimulus is aversive. There are other problems with successive discrimination procedures. Because emotional behavior is generated, discriminative responding takes a long time to develop. In addition, spontaneous recovery of S^Δ responding from session to session interferes with the acquisition of discrimination. Finally, even after extensive training, birds and other organisms continue to make errors by responding in the presence of the signal for extinction.

Errorless Discrimination

These problems can be eliminated with a discrimination procedure described by Terrace (1963, 1972). The method is called **errorless discrimination** because the trainer or teacher does not allow the animal or person to make mistakes by responding to the extinction stimulus. As described in his 1963 paper, Terrace used early progressive training to reduce errors of discrimination. This training began when pigeons were conditioned to peck a red key for food reinforcement. The birds were started on continuous reinforcement and moved gradually to a variable-interval 1-min schedule. Early in this training, the key light was occasionally turned off for 5 s and extinction was in effect. Thus, a brief dark key was the S^Δ in this early phase. It is important to note that pigeons do not usually peck at a dark key, and Terrace made use of this fact.

As discrimination training continued, the dark key was gradually illuminated with a green light. The light became progressively greener and brighter and remained on for longer and longer intervals, until it stayed on for the same amount of time as the red key light. At this point, the duration of the S^D (red) was abruptly increased to 3 min while the S^Δ (green) was gradually increased to 3 min.

Now the birds were responding on a MULT VI 1-min EXT 3-min schedule. On this schedule, the red key was presented for 3 min and the pigeons pecked for food on a VI 1-min schedule during this period. After 3 min in the reinforcement component, the key color was changed from red to green, and extinction was in effect for 3 min. With these new contingencies in effect, the pigeons had sufficient time in the S^Δ component to make numerous errors, but they did not respond in the presence of the green (S^Δ) key light.

When this early progressive training was compared with standard successive discrimination procedures, there were found to be far fewer mistakes with the errorless technique. Figure 8.10 shows that the three pigeons which were trained with errorless discrimination procedures made about 25 pecks each to the extinction stimulus (errors). Another three birds had the S^Δ introduced

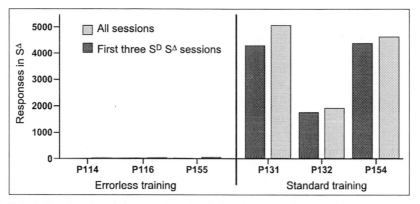

FIG. 8.10 Results of the errorless discrimination procedure used by Terrace. Adapted from Fig. 1 of "Discrimination leaning with and without 'errors'," by H. S. Terrace, 1963, *Journal of the Experimental Analysis of Behavior, 6,* 1–27.

later in the experiment, at full intensity and for 3 min (standard method); these pigeons made between 2000 and 5000 pecks to the S^Δ. Compared with the errorless group, most of the pecks to the S^Δ in the standard condition occurred during the first three sessions. Overall, errorless discrimination procedures result in faster acquisition of a discrimination and substantially less incorrect responding (see Arantes & Machado, 2011, for an account of the superiority of errorless learning of a conditional temporal discrimination in pigeons). In dolphins, errorless training methods were used to establish discriminations on auditory and visual tasks (see Roth, 2002). Errorless methods have also been used with developmentally challenged children and adults to teach a variety of visual, auditory, and temporal discrimination skills (Mueller, Palkovic, & Maynard, 2007), and with visually impaired children to teach tactile discriminations of the Braille alphabet (Toussaint, 2011). Additional research indicates that errorless learning methods can even be extended to complex human behavior involving flight simulation and the use of landing flares (Benbassat & Abramson, 2002).

Once discrimination has been established with errorless training, it may be difficult to reverse the roles of the S^D and S^Δ. Marsh and Johnson (1968) trained two groups of birds to discriminate between red (S^D) and green (S^Δ) stimuli. One group received errorless training and the other group received the standard discrimination procedure. After performance had stabilized, the S^D and S^Δ were reversed so that the green stimulus now signaled reinforcement and the red stimulus indicated extinction. The birds trained by the errorless method continued responding in terms of their initial training—they would not respond to the S^Δ (the new S^D from the point of view of the researcher) even when explicitly reinforced for such behavior. Birds given standard discrimination training were not as persistent, and quickly discriminated the change in contingencies.

These findings suggest that errorless procedures may be most useful in education when there is little chance of a change in the contingencies of reinforcement. For example, students may learn and retain better their multiplication tables, standard word spellings, rules for extracting a square root, and other types of rote learning with the errorless method. Students also enjoy learning more, learn very rapidly, and make few errors with errorless teaching procedures (Powers, Cheney, & Agostino, 1970; see Luciano, 1986, for an account of training verbal discriminations in language-delayed children). In problem-solving situations where there are many alternative solutions requiring error elimination, or where the contingencies of reinforcement change, the standard method of trial-and-error learning may produce more flexibility in responding and allow better remembering and recall, as when university students are preparing for exams (Anderson & Craik, 2006).

Fading

Errorless discrimination involves two basic procedures: early introduction of the S^{Δ} and gradual transfer of stimulus control. Educators and clinicians have emphasized the latter procedure, which is called **fading**. Fading involves transferring stimulus control from one value of a stimulus to another. This is done by gradually changing a controlling stimulus from an initial value to some designated criterion. When Terrace (1963) gradually changed the dark key toward the green color, this was fading in the S^{Δ}. Cheney and Tam (1972) used fading to transfer initial control by a color discrimination to subsequent control by line angle tilt in pigeons; the procedure involved gradually increasing the intensity of the line segments projected on the key while decreasing the intensity of the colors. Control transferred from color to mirror-image line angles with some, but very few, errors.

Sherman (1965) gave a practical example of fading when he used the procedure to get a mute psychotic to say his first words. He described the patient as:

> . . . a 63-year-old man, diagnosed, in 1916, as dementia praecox, hebephrenic type. He had been in the hospital continuously for 47 years, with a history of mutism for 45 of those years. At the time of this study he was not receiving any medication or participating in psychotherapy. Periodically, when seen on the ward, . . . [he] could be observed walking around mumbling softly to himself. However, all of this mumbling appeared to be nonsensical vocal behavior. In his 45-year history of mutism [he] had not exhibited any recorded instance of appropriate verbal behavior.
>
> (Sherman, 1965, p. 157)

After many sessions of reinforcement and imitation training, Sherman succeeded in getting the patient to say "food"—his first distinct utterance in 45 years. At this point, Sherman used fading to bring this response under appropriate stimulus control—responding "food" to the question "What is this?" The training was as follows:

> To obtain the word "food" from the subject when the experimenter asked "What is this?" a fading procedure was used. With the fading procedure, the experimenter continued to hold up a bite of food each time and to deliver instructions to the subject. The behavior of the subject—that is, saying "food"—was maintained with reinforcement while the instructions to the subject were gradually changed in the following steps: (a) "Say food"; (b) "Say foo_"; (c) "Say f___"; (d) "What is this? Say f___"; (e) "What is this? Say ____"; (f) "What is this?"
>
> (Sherman, 1965, p. 158)

This example shows that the patient initially replied "food" after the experimenter said "Say food." The original verbal stimulus for the response "food" was gradually faded out and replaced with a new stimulus of "What is this?"

Fading procedures have been regularly used with autistic children, as when the youngsters show resistance to drinking liquids such as milk. Both for health and nutritional benefits it is sometimes necessary for children to drink (or eat) things they usually reject. In one study (Luiselli, Ricciardi, & Gilligan, 2005), the researchers treated milk avoidance by a 4-year-old autistic girl by fading out a beverage she consumed 100% of the time and fading in the milk. That is, the amount of beverage was reduced and the amount of milk was increased over training sessions. Fading allowed rapid acquisition of milk consumption without interruptions to the fading sequence by the child's usual refusal and fussing.

In another example, three autistic youths were taught by fading procedures to engage in conversations during shopping trips to the community store—an essential skill for living independently. The youths initially had near zero verbal interactions with store staff, but were taught to use scripts in conversations during simulated shopping trips. The scripts were systematically faded, from last word to first word, as the rates of unscripted conversations increased. Subsequently, unscripted conversations showed generalization, occurring in the presence of new store staff on actual trips to local retail stores (Brown, Krantz, McClannahan, & Poulson, 2008; see also Dotto-Fojut, Reeve, Townsend, & Progar, 2011).

In everyday life, fading is an important aspect of complex human behavior, which often goes unrecognized because of its gradual nature. Children learn to identify many objects in the world by the step-by-step transfer of stimulus control. A parent may present a glass of apple juice to a 2-year-old child and state "Say juice." Eventually, the child says "juice" when a glass of juice is given. Once the response "juice" has been established, stimulus control may be gradually transferred from "Say juice" to questions such as "What is this?" by fading. In another example, a parent may initially stay at a day-care center in order to make the child comfortable in the new setting. Once the child starts to participate in activities, the parent sneaks out (fades) and stimulus control for a variety of behavior is transferred to the new situation and the teacher.

COMPLEX STIMULUS CONTROL

Up to this point, we have discussed the control of behavior by relatively simple configurations of stimuli, as when a red color signals reinforcement and green signals no reinforcement. There are other procedures that allow for the investigation of performance regulated by more complex stimulus arrays.

Matching to Sample

Discrimination of Identity

One procedure that is often used to investigate identity discriminations is called **matching to sample**. In a simple identity procedure, a pigeon may be presented with three keys, as illustrated in

Figure 8.11. Panel A shows a triangle projected onto the center key. The triangle is the *sample* stimulus in the sense that it is an instance of a larger set of geometric forms. To ensure that the bird attends to the sample, it is required to peck the sample key. When this *observing response* occurs, two side keys are illuminated with a triangle on one and a square on the other, which are called the *comparison* stimuli (the sample key goes off). If the bird then pecks the comparison stimulus that corresponds to the sample (a match), this behavior is reinforced and leads to the presentation of a new sample. Panel B shows a nonreinforced sequence in which pecks to the noncorresponding stimulus

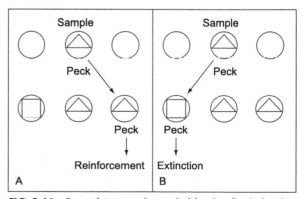

FIG. 8.11 Procedures used to train identity discrimination by a pigeon. Panel A shows that a peck to the sample key (triangle) results in two shapes on the side keys. A peck to the side key that matches the sample is reinforced. Panel B shows a sequence that is not reinforced.

FIG. 8.12 Photograph of Rio, a California sea lion, matching to sample (center key). Both Rio and another sea lion named Rocky eventually passed tests for generalized identity matching. © Dr. Colleen Reichmuth of the Institute of Marine Sciences, University of California Santa Cruz. Published with permission.

result in extinction and the next trial. Over a number of trials, the comparison stimuli appear on the left or right keys with equal probability. After some training, pigeons accurately match to sample even with new (never reinforced) samples and comparison stimuli (Blough, 1959, 1982). These generalization or transfer tests show that training resulted in a higher-order response class (generalized identity) controlled by the property of similarity or sameness of the stimulus items, a generalized stimulus class. That is, matching to sample across numerous exemplars (stimulus sets) leads to the formation of concepts (sameness) by pigeons.

Other animals (monkeys, chimpanzees, and dolphins) have passed transfer tests on matching-to-sample problems, indicating that the same–different relationship of stimulus items controlled their behavior. In one study, California sea lions (*Zalophus californianus)* were assessed in terms of their ability to generalize an identity concept (Kastak & Schusterman, 1994). After training two animals, Rocky and Rio, on 15 two-stimulus (visual configurations) matching-to-sample problems, the sea lions were tested for transfer of performance to 15 novel problems (Figure 8.12). The criteria for passing the transfer test included performance on the initial trial (pass/fail test item), performance on test trials compared with baseline, and performance on four-trial problem blocks. Both Rocky and Rio passed the transfer tests. Also, when given identity pairings (ring–ring; bat–bat) of stimuli previously learned as an arbitrary relation (ring–bat), both animals passed the identity generalization tests, with Rio passing on test 1 and Rocky passing on test 2. Rocky just needed a few more examples than Rio. The researchers concluded that the study conclusively demonstrates that California sea lions can learn and use a generalized identity-matching rule.

Delayed Matching to Sample and Remembering

A twist on the standard matching-to-sample task is called **delayed matching to sample (DMTS)**. This procedure was first described by Blough (1959), and involves adding a delay between the offset of the sample stimulus and the onset of the two comparison stimuli. For example, in Figure 8.13 a pigeon is presented with a center key (sample) that is illuminated with a red light. When the observing response occurs, the red sample turns off and a few seconds (e.g., 10 s) later, red and green comparison stimuli are presented on the side keys. A response to the stimulus that matches the sample is reinforced, and responses to the other stimulus are not. The basic finding is that the percentage of correct responses decreases as the delay increases (Blough, 1959; Grant, 1975).

Delayed matching to sample has been used to investigate behavior that is said to reflect cognition and memory. For example, the time between the offset of the sample stimulus and the onset of the comparison stimuli is usually called the **retention interval**. The idea is that during this interval the organism is covertly doing something that helps to retain the information about the sample. Thus, Grant (1981) found that pigeons would "forget" the sample if they were given a sign (a vertical line on the key) that indicated that the comparison stimuli would not appear on that trial. In terms of

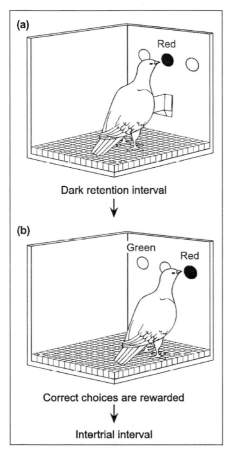

(a)

Red

Dark retention interval

↓

(b)

Green

Red

Correct choices are rewarded

↓

Intertrial interval

FIG. 8.13 Delayed matching to sample in a pigeon. The sequence begins with the pigeon pecking a red or green sample on the center response key. The chamber is darkened following the pigeon's response to the sample during a retention interval. Next, the pigeon chooses between red and green side keys; choices that match to the sample are reinforced with food and after a time interval another trial begins. Adapted from "Psychophysics of remembering: the discrimination hypothesis," by K. G. White, 2002, Current Directions in Psychological Science, 11, 141–145.

remembering the sample, Grant reported that the pigeons performed poorly if the forget cue was presented soon after the sample went off (see also Maki & Hegvik, 1980; Stonebraker, Rilling, & Kendrick, 1981). Performance was not as disrupted if the signal was given later in the interval. One interpretation is that the cue to forget interferes with covert rehearsal of the sample stimulus (Grant, 1981; Stonebraker & Rilling, 1981).

The cognitive metaphor of memory processes (encoding, storage, retrieval, rehearsal, etc.) is popular in psychology. Tulving (1983) explained that remembering an event involves mental encoding of the event and subsequent retrieval of the information from memory due to reactivation of the encoding operations. He proposed that encoding results in a memory trace or representation of the past event. The memory trace becomes manifest when combined with retrieval processes. Thus, cognitive memory research has emphasized how encoding produces mental representations that in turn aid retrieval.

Geoffrey White in the Department of Psychology at the University of Otago (Dunedin, New Zealand) has developed a behavioral approach to explaining memory using basic operant principles. White (2002) indicates that a behavior analysis of memory points to actions or choices (e.g., choosing between the comparison stimuli) based on current contingencies and how those choices are in part regulated by the reinforcement history for similar choices in the past. In this regard, he explains:

> **Remembering** is not so much a matter of looking back into the past or forward into the future as it is of *making choices at the time of remembering*. The [behavioral] approach treats remembering as a process of discriminating the relevant events from alternative possibilities. By analogy with the discrimination of objects at a physical distance, objects or events can be discriminated at a temporal distance. . . . That is, the discrimination is not made at the time of encoding, or learning, but at the time of remembering.
>
> (White, 2002, pp. 141–142, emphasis added)

One aspect of White's behavioral approach to memory is that it challenges the well-known finding that remembering gets worse as the retention interval increases. If the discrimination of a past event is made at the time of remembering, White suggests that it is possible to train pigeons to be accurate at a specific delay. In this case, the remembering of a stimulus would be more accurate at a specific delay than with less delay or no delay. That is, remembering would not decline in accord with the retention interval.

Using the delayed matching-to-sample procedure shown in Figure 8.13, Sargisson and White (2001) compared the performance of pigeons trained with a 0-s delay and those trained with one

FIG. 8.14 Selected data from the experiment by Sargisson and White (2001), showing the accuracy of matching to sample in different groups of pigeons trained with either a 0-s retention interval or a 4-s retention interval; pigeons were tested with retention intervals that varied from 0 to 10 s. The discriminability measure is the log of the ratio of correct to incorrect responses, and is not influenced by response bias. From "Psychophysics of remembering: the discrimination hypothesis," by K. G. White, 2002, *Current Directions in Psychological Science, 11,* 141–145. Reprinted with the permission of the American Psychological Society. © 2002 Blackwell Publishing Ltd.

specific delay at the outset. Typically, birds are trained to match to sample with a 0-s delay, and subsequently the delay or retention interval is gradually lengthened. In the new procedure, pigeons were trained in matching to sample at one specific delay (e.g., 4 s) and then asked to remember the sample at different retention intervals.

Figure 8.14 shows the discriminability of the sample for birds trained with a 0-s delay (circles). Notice that the accuracy of the discrimination decreases with the retention interval, as would be predicted by cognitive theories of memory. For pigeons trained with a 4-s delay, however, their accuracy does not systematically decrease over the retention interval (triangles). Instead, these birds were most accurate at the training delay of 4 s, a finding that argues against the mental representation of the sample with a declining memory trace. Notice also that the birds were not trained to perform with less accuracy at brief delays. That is, the discrimination of the "to be remembered color" should have been easier at short delays (e.g., 0 s) because the sample color was observed very recently. The data show, however, that the pigeons were less accurate at delays of less than 4 s, again disconfirming a cognitive representational account. Overall, the results of the experiment support a behavioral view that remembering involves discriminative operant behavior specific to the time interval of retrieval (see White & Wixted, 1999, for a discrimination model of remembering; see White, Parkinson, Brown, & Wixted, 2004, for an account of proactive interference and the role of reinforcement).

Reverse Forgetting: Withdrawal of Retroactive Interference

The research on improved remembering at long intervals suggests that it is possible to reverse the usual forgetting which occurs with the passage of time. In a DMTS task, forgetting involves the loss of accuracy in identifying the sample stimulus over the retention interval. In the cognitive view of memory, the memory trace of the sample color weakens with time, implying that accuracy in identifying the original color should be lower with longer delays. One way to challenge the memory trace account is to use a procedure that separates accuracy in remembering the sample from the passage of time. White and Brown (2011) reviewed research showing that memory traces are strengthened by memory rehearsal procedures and retarded by procedures that interfere with rehearsal—so-called retroactive interference. The aim of their study was to reverse the forgetting of pigeons during the retention interval on a DMTS task by inserting and later removing retroactive interference.

Pigeons usually perform DMTS in a dark chamber. Thus, interference with remembering the sample color can be arranged by activating the houselight at the beginning of the retention interval. The houselight can be turned on throughout short retention intervals or illuminated for only a few seconds and then turned off for long retention intervals. According to memory trace and retroactive interference theories, the insertion of the houselight would be expected to increase forgetting early in the retention interval, but accuracy in remembering the sample should not improve with the removal of the interference event. After removal of the interference, the memory trace would be expected to dissipate and accuracy would continue to decline.

White and Brown designed two DMTS experiments, but we shall only describe Experiment 2, which involved long retention intervals. Pigeons were trained in a dark chamber to peck a red or green sample (observing response) to initiate a retention interval that varied from 0.2 to 24 s. The retention interval ended with the red and green comparison stimuli presented on side keys. A correct choice of the comparison color resulted in food reinforcement followed by a dark period before the next trial. Incorrect choices were followed only by the dark period. The same pigeons were tested at all retention intervals with the chamber dark, with the houselight on for the first 3 s, or with the houselight on throughout the delay.

Figure 8.15 shows the results for the three experimental conditions. Notice that without any interference by the houselight (dark delay), accuracy (the proportion of correct choices) in identifying the original sample (red or green) declines over the retention interval, consistent with memory trace theory. Also, when the houselight remained on throughout the retention interval (HL throughout delay), the presumed retroactive interference (preventing rehearsal of the memorized sample) substantially reduced accuracy, as expected by a cognitive account. The critical condition involves turning on the houselight for the first 3 s of the retention interval but then turning it off, reinstating the dark chamber and removing the interference. Now accuracy drops for the 3-s delay, but recovers

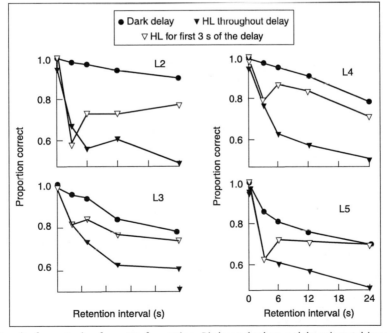

FIG. 8.15 Results from study of reverse forgetting. Birds worked on a delayed matching to sample task involving red and green samples and retention intervals that varied from 0.2 to 24 s. The same birds made choices after the different delays under three chamber-illumination conditions: the chamber was dark throughout the retention interval (dark delay), the chamber house light was illuminated for the entire retention interval (HL throughout delay), or the chamber was illuminated by the house light for the first 3 s of the retention interval and then the light was turned off for the rest of the delay (HL for the first 3 s of delay). The figure is a graph of the results (Experiment 2) taken from a study titled "Reversing the course of forgetting," by K. G. White and G. S. Brown, 2011, Journal of the Experimental Analysis of Behavior, 96, 177–189. © Society for the Experimental Analysis of Behavior. Published with permission.

at the 6-s delay and then tapers off as the delay increases. This finding of a reversal in forgetting at a longer delay (greater accuracy at 6 s than at 3 s) is contrary to a cognitive theory involving memory traces and retroactive interference.

Although further research is required, Brown and Davidson argue that the reversal of forgetting is in accord with a discriminative operant analysis of remembering at long intervals (Sargisson and White, 2001, as discussed previously). In the behavioral view, discriminations at short and long intervals are independent of one another and depend on the contingencies. In the case of withdrawing retroactive interference, turning on the houselight allows for extraneous sources of reinforcement of off-task behavior that compete with food reinforcement for correct choices of the comparison color. When the houselight is turned off, reinforcement of off-task behavior is withdrawn and on-task correct choices improve (greater accuracy at 6 s than at 3 s). A behavioral account in terms of extraneous sources of reinforcement fits the results without an appeal to inferred cognitive processes, and is consistent with the principles of choice discussed in Chapter 9 of this textbook.

 # FOCUS ON: Concept Formation by Pigeons

Principles of stimulus control are involved in many instances of concept formation and abstract reasoning. People usually assume that conceptual thinking is a defining feature of humans that separates them from other animals. Although this kind of behavior is common in humans, it occurs in a more limited way in other organisms. Herrnstein and Loveland (1964) designed an experiment to teach pigeons to distinguish humans from other objects (i.e., to learn the concept "human").

Consider what it means to know that this is a human being and other objects are not. Humans come in a variety of sizes, shapes, colors, postures, and so on. Characteristics of the stimulus "human" are abstract and involve multiple stimulus dimensions, rather than a single property such as wavelength of light. For example, human faces differ in terms of presence or absence of hair, geometric form, and several other factors. Defining characteristics of faces include bilateral symmetry, two eyes, a nose, a mouth, and many additional features common to all people.

Although a precise physical description of humans is elusive, Herrnstein and Loveland (1964) asked whether pigeons could respond to the presence or absence of human beings in photographs. If a bird can do this, its behavior may be said to be controlled by the abstract property of "humanness." There is no concrete set of attributes that visually equals a human being, but there are relations among such attributes that define the stimulus class. The bird's task is to respond correctly to instances of the stimulus class, and by doing so to demonstrate concept formation. Herrnstein and Loveland described the experiment as follows:

> It is well known that animals can use one or a few distinguishing features to discriminate stimuli such as simple visual arrays differing in size, shape, or color. In the experiment described here, however, pigeons were trained to detect human beings in photographs, a class of visual stimuli so diverse that it precludes simple characterization.
>
> [After pigeons were trained to peck at a translucent plate] . . . the plate was illuminated throughout each session with projections of 35-mm color slides from a projector that housed 81 slides. . . . Over 1200 unselected slides obtained from private and commercial sources were available. Before each session, the projector was loaded with 80 or 81 different photographs of natural settings, including countryside, cities, expanses of water, lawn,

meadow, and so on. For any one session, approximately half the photographs contained at least one human being; the remainder contained no human beings—in the experimenter's best judgment. In no other systematic way did the slides appear to differ. Many slides contained human beings partly obscured by intervening objects: trees, automobiles, window frames, and so on. The people were distributed throughout the pictures: in the center or to one side or the other, near the top or the bottom, close up or distant. Some slides contained a single person; others contained groups of various sizes. The people themselves varied in appearance: they were clothed, semi-nude, or nude; adults or children; men or women; sitting, standing, or lying; black, white, or yellow. Lighting and coloration varied: some slides were dark, others light; some had either reddish or bluish tints, and so on.

...Pictures containing people ... meant an opportunity to feed ... and pictures without people meant no such opportunity. ... Each day the slides themselves, and also the random sequence of positive (S^D) slides (that is, containing a person) and negative (S) slides (without people), were changed for each pigeon. Many slides were used again in later sessions, but never in the order with other slides in which they had appeared earlier. The pigeons had no opportunity, therefore, to learn groups of particular slides or sequences of positives and negatives in general.

(Herrnstein and Loveland, 1964, pp. 549–550)

The results showed that the pigeons could learn to discriminate between slides with people and slides without them. Within 10 sessions of this training, every bird was responding at a higher rate to slides with humans in them. Over several months, the performance of the birds steadily improved. After extensive training, the birds were given 80 (or 81) slides that they had never seen before. Pigeons pecked at a high rate to new slides with people and at lower rates to slides without them. Generally, this experiment shows that pigeons can differentially respond to the abstract stimulus class of human being.

Additional experiments on concept formation have been conducted with other stimulus classes and different organisms. Pigeons have discriminated trees (Herrnstein, 1979), geometric forms (Towe, 1954), letters of the alphabet (Blough, 1982), fish (Herrnstein & de Villiers, 1980), one person from another (Herrnstein, Loveland, & Cable, 1976), and aerial photographs of human-made objects (Lubow, 1974). Concept formation has also been reported for monkeys (Schrier & Brady, 1987), an African gray parrot (Pepperberg, 1981), and mynah birds (Turney, 1982). And pigeons trained to differentially respond to real objects show these responses to corresponding pictures of the objects—even when the pictures only contain novel views of the stimuli (Spetch & Friedman, 2006). Ravens have been shown to learn the concept "thief" after experience of caching food and having it removed by some human caretakers (Heinrich & Bugnyar, 2007).

Overall, this research suggests that animals can learn to differentially respond to abstract properties of stimulus classes. These stimulus classes are commonly called categories when humans make similar discriminations. When people describe different categories, they are said to "understand the concept." People can easily identify a computer disk and an automobile as human-made objects. When other animals show similar performances, we are reluctant to attribute the discriminative behavior to the creature's understanding of the concept.

Rather than attribute understanding to complex performances by humans or other animals, it is possible to provide an account based on evolution and the current demands of the environment. Natural selection shapes sensory capacities of organisms that allow for discrimination along abstract dimensions. Birds obtain food, navigate, care for their young, and find mates largely on the basis of visual stimuli (see the section on "Stimulus

Control, Neuroscience, and What Birds See" earlier in this chapter). Many of these activities require subtle adjustments to a complex and changing visual world. It is not surprising, therefore, that these creatures are readily able to discriminate abstract properties of visual objects, especially when reinforcement contingencies favor such discrimination.

Conditional Discrimination

In everyday life, stimuli that regulate behavior (S^D and S^Δ) often depend on the context. Consider a matching-to-sample experiment in which a bird has been trained to match to triangles or to squares based on the sample stimulus. To turn this experiment into a conditional-discrimination task, a red or green light illuminates the sample stimulus. The bird is required to match to the sample only when the background light is green, and to choose the noncorresponding stimulus only when the light is red. That is, when a green triangle is the sample, the bird must peck the comparison triangle, but when a red triangle is presented, pecks to the non-matching circle are reinforced. Of course, if a green circle is the sample, pecks to the circle are reinforced, and when the sample turns to a red circle, pecking the triangle is the correct response. Conditional matching to sample involves simultaneous discrimination of three elements in a display. The animal must respond to geometric form depending on the background color of the sample. It must also respond to the correspondence or noncorrespondence of the comparison stimuli.

Conditional discrimination is a common aspect of human behavior. A person who is hurrying to an appointment on the 15th floor of an office building will ordinarily enter the first available elevator. This same person may wait for the next lift if the elevator is full. Thus, getting on the elevator (operant) when the doors open (S^D) is conditional on the number of people in the car. In another example, you will say "8" when shown 3 + 5 and "15" if the relation is 3 × 5. Your response to the 3 and 5 is conditional on the + and × symbols. In the chapter on verbal behavior (Chapter 12), we shall see that conditional discrimination is also important for the emergence of symbolic behavior and communication. When people say and show that the spoken word "cat," the written word "cat," and a picture of a cat are equivalent, their behavior is a result of such complex discrimination training (for further information on conditional discrimination and stimulus equivalence, see Chapter 12).

 ## ON THE APPLIED SIDE: Quality Control and Detection of Signals by Animals

In industrial settings, workers are often hired as quality-control inspectors. Quality control is usually a monotonous job that involves checking samples of a product to identify any defects. The most important skills or attributes needed for such jobs are good visual acuity and color vision. Based on these visual requirements, Thom Verhave (1966) suggested to the management of a drug company that the laboratory pigeon (Columba livia domestica) would be a cheap and efficient quality-control inspector. Although skeptical, the director of research for the company gave Verhave the go-ahead to train pigeons as inspectors.

The procedures were similar to a matching-to-sample (identity-matching) task. Pigeons were trained to inspect a line of drug capsules, accepting those that met a fixed standard and rejecting defective ones. In this procedure (Figure 8.16), a bird compared a drug capsule with a standard sample (a perfect one) and pecked Key 1 if it matched or Key 2 if there was a defect (a skag).

The standard capsule was fixed in position behind an inspection window. A line of capsules passed by the same window one at a time; some were perfect and others were defective. In order to initiate an inspection, the pigeon pecked at the inspection window, activating a beam of light that illuminated the sample and the comparison capsules. During training, all of the capsules on the inspection line were pre-coded by an electrical switch as either perfect or skags. If a capsule on the line was precoded as perfect, then the pigeon's response to Key 1 (matching response) resulted in food, turned off the

FIG. 8.16 Drawing depicts the discrimination procedures of Verhave (1966) as described in the text. Pigeons were trained to inspect a line of drug capsules, accepting those that met a fixed standard and rejecting defective ones. From Behavior Principles. 2nd edition, p. 558, by C. B. Ferster, S. Culbertson and M. C. P. Boren, 1975, Englewood Cliffs, NJ: Prentice-Hall. Republished with permission. © 1975 Pearson Education, Inc.

beam of light behind the inspection window, and moved a new capsule into place. If a capsule was precoded as a skag, then a response to Key 2 (nonmatching response) turned off the illumination, moved a new capsule into the inspection window, and resulted in presentation of the food hopper. All other responses were false alarms or misses that were not reinforced and resulted in a 30-s blackout. With these contingencies in effect, the birds became about 99% accurate in identifying perfect capsules and skags.

One practical problem that Verhave faced concerned the persistence of a pigeon's performance on a real-life inspection line. In everyday life, there is no experimenter to designate perfect capsules, skags, misses, and false alarms. Without this monitoring, differential reinforcement for "hits versus misses" cannot be maintained, and a bird's performance will deteriorate over time to chance levels. A solution to this problem was to introduce capsules "known to be perfect or defective" occasionally onto the inspection line. Reinforcement or punishment was only in effect for "known" instances of matching (or nonmatching) to sample. With this procedure, sufficient differential reinforcement occurred to maintain stimulus control by the sample and comparison capsules.

In addition to the study by Verhave (1966), other researchers have attempted to use pigeons for navigation of missiles (Skinner, 1960) or to run assembly lines (Cumming, 1966). More recently, Azar (2002) reported that the US navy in the 1970s and 1980s used pigeons to find people stranded at sea. Navy scientist Jim Simmons, PhD, trained pigeons by operant conditioning for search-and-rescue missions. The pigeons were trained to recognize objects floating in the water from an aircraft and were 93% accurate, compared with only 38% accuracy for human flight crews. When combined with human searchers, the pigeons' detection rate rose to almost 100%.

Pigeons are excellent at detecting visual signals. Other animals are highly sensitive to olfactory (smell) stimuli, making them suitable for detection of chemical odors. Animals are often "clicker trained," using a portable hand-held device that makes a "clicking" sound (Pryor, 1999; see also Chapter 10 in this book). In preliminary training, the sound of the clicker is paired with food reinforcement. Once established, the sound of the clicker marks the response that matches the odor sample, and acts as conditioned reinforcement for the correct response. Withholding of clicks also acts as nonreinforcement for incorrect responses to comparison odors. The clicker allows the trainer to provide immediate reinforcement of the target behavior in a field setting where it is impossible to instantly provide food reinforcement. Clicker training with operant procedures (especially shaping and differential reinforcement) has allowed animals to perform odor-detection tasks that improve the everyday lives of people.

Landmines inflict injuries on people in more than 70 countries of the world, and more than half a million people have sustained life-changing injuries as a result of mine explosions. Dr. Allen Poling at Western Michigan University and his colleagues used African giant pouched rats (Cricetomys gambianus), trained by operant-conditioning procedures (clicker training), to detect the smell of the explosive chemical 2,4,6-trinitrotoluene (TNT) (Poling, Weetjens, Cox, Beyene, Bach, & Sully, 2011). After extensive training for accuracy in odor detection, the rats searched $93,400\,m^2$ of land in Gaza Province of Mozambique, finding 41 mines and 54 other explosive devices. Humans with metal detectors found no additional mines in this area. On average, the rats made 0.33 false alarms for every $100\,m^2$ searched, which is below the standards for accrediting mine-detection animals. These findings indicate that trained pouched rats make excellent mine-detection animals, allowing human populations to reclaim their land and live free of landmine disasters.

Dogs are also highly sensitive to olfactory stimuli, and are often used for detection of illegal drugs, chemical contaminants, and explosives (Browne, Stafford, & Fordham, 2006). A recent application of operant conditioning in medicine involves odor detection by dogs of chemical markers in the urine of cancer patients. The basic idea is that urine contains volatile organic compounds (VOCs) that mark the presence of prostate cancer (PC). These VOCs are absent from the urine of people who test negative for the disease. In a recent study of prostate cancer detection, a Belgian Malinois dog was clicker trained over a period of 24 months to detect the scent of urine samples from men known to have prostate cancer (Cornu, Cancel-Tassin, Ondet, Girardet, & Cussenot, 2011). After training, the dog's ability to discriminate PC samples from control urine was tested in a double-blind procedure. Samples of urine were obtained from 66 patients who had been referred to a urologist for elevated prostate-specific antigen or irregular digital rectal examination. All patients were given a prostate biopsy and divided into a group of 33 patients with cancer and a group of 33 controls with negative biopsies. For each detection test, the dog was required to identify the one cancer urine sample among six comparison samples (one sample from a person with cancer and five randomly selected control samples). The results showed that the dog correctly identified 30 of the 33 cancer cases, corresponding to an accuracy rate of 91%. Of the three incorrect identifications, one patient was given a second biopsy and found to have prostate cancer. Thus the corrected accuracy rate for the dog was 93%. Overall, a review of the evidence suggests that dogs can discriminate VOCs in the urine and exhaled breath of cancer patients, allowing for detection of several types of cancer (Moser & McCulloch, 2010). Behavioral applications using dogs and other animals are proving to be of benefit to human health and wellness.

CHAPTER SUMMARY

This chapter has presented research on and discussion of the stimulus conditions that set the occasion for operant behavior—changing its probability of occurrence. Control of the probability of responding is a matter of differential reinforcement in the presence or absence of a stimulus. Such control can be produced in the absence of "errors" by the judicious use of stimulus fading. Generalization across stimuli means that there is a lack of discrimination, and responding occurs in the presence of many different stimuli. The process of remembering (memory) is treated as a response probability issue in that the question is what the stimulus conditions are that enhance the likelihood of a specific response at a specific moment in time. The idea of a "concept" not as something inside the organism but as overt behavior under the control of precise stimuli was also presented. Birds were shown to learn the concept "human" when the contingencies supported responding to (identifying) pictures of humans and rejecting pictures without humans. Procedures such as matching to sample and training with only the S^D were discussed, and outcomes such as peak shift and behavioral contrast were highlighted. Several examples of training animals to make stimulus discriminations in everyday settings were given as evidence that operant procedures can be applied to important human problems.

KEY WORDS

Absolute stimulus control

Anticipatory contrast

Behavioral contrast

Conditional discrimination

Controlling stimulus (S)

Delayed matching to sample

Differential reinforcement

Differential reinforcement of other behavior (DRO)

Differential response

Discrimination

Discrimination index (I_D)

Discriminative stimulus (S^D)

Errorless discrimination

Extinction stimulus (S^Δ)

Fading

Generalization

Generalization gradient

Matching to sample

Multiple schedule

Negative contrast

Peak shift

Positive contrast

Relative stimulus control

Remembering

Response chain

Retention interval

Simultaneous discrimination

Stimulus control

Stimulus generalization

Successive discrimination

Superstitious behavior

ON THE WEB

www.youtube.com/watch?v=_eAGtAYW6mA This YouTube video of the HeroRAT shows rats detecting landmines in Africa. Listen for the sound of the clicker for correct identifications and the subsequent delivery of food reinforcement by the trainers.

www.youtube.com/watch?v=h5_zJIm1B_k See if you can analyze errorless learning in this YouTube video of the teaching of autistic children. In applied behavior analysis, the prompt is used to ensure correct responses to the S^D in early training, and high rates of reinforcement. The prompt is subsequently faded as the child comes under the control of the S^D, making few or no errors.

www.youtube.com/watch?v=yG12rqPaIdc Take a look at this YouTube video on teaching a visual matching-to-sample task to a dog. See if you can identify some of the basic operant procedures used by the trainer.

www2.vet.upenn.edu/labs/equinebehavior/cognition.htm The study of concept formation in the horse is the topic of this website. It is interesting that the researchers interpret the discriminative responses of the horses as evidence for animal cognition and mental representation. We suggest that mentalistic explanations of the horses' behavior are not necessary; an account in terms of the contingencies of reinforcement would be more appropriate.

BRIEF QUIZ

1. An S^Δ sets the occasion upon which a response is _____ reinforced.

    (a) sometimes
    (b) always
    (c) never
    (d) maybe

2. An S^D does not cause or elicit the appearance of a response the way a _____ does.

    (a) UR
    (b) US
    (c) CS
    (d) CR

3. In operant conditioning, what is the antecedent stimulus paired with reinforcement called?

    (a) S^Δ
    (b) S–R–S
    (c) S^D
    (d) CS

4. A two-component schedule in which both components have separate stimuli is called a:

    (a) MIX
    (b) CONC
    (c) TAND
    (d) MULT

5. To keep the onset of S^D from reinforcing responses in S^Δ one needs to add a _____ contingency.

    (a) EXT
    (b) IRT
    (c) DRO
    (d) PRP

6. If reinforcers on one schedule are depleted and responding in another schedule increases, we call this:

    (a) negative contrast
    (b) positive contrast
    (c) substitutability
    (d) anticipatory contrast

7. A change in maximal generalization responding, away from S^Δ to the other side of S^D, is called:

    (a) gradient shift
    (b) relative control
    (c) stimulus control
    (d) peak shift

8. A shaping procedure that gradually changes stimulus control from one element to another is called:

    (a) approximations
    (b) fading
    (c) transfer
    (d) conditional discrimination

9. If you trained a pigeon to turn in a circle when a TURN sign was presented, you could say that the bird was:

    (a) discriminating
    (b) conceptually oriented
    (c) reading
    (d) superstitious

10. With careful shaping and fading one might develop discrimination without:

    (a) reinforcement
    (b) extinction
    (c) contrast
    (d) errors

Answers to Brief Quiz: 1, c (p. 224); 2, b (p. 223); 3, c (p. 225); 4, d (p. 227); 5, c (Fig 8.5); 6, b (p. 231); 7, d (p. 235); 8, b (p. 240); 9, c (p. 226); 10, d (p. 238).

Choice and Preference

9

1. Find out about how to study choice and preference in the laboratory.
2. Learn about the matching law as a basic principle of behavioral choice.
3. Inquire about optimal foraging, behavioral economics, and self-control.
4. Investigate matching on a single schedule of reinforcement.
5. Discover mathematics and the behavior analysis of choice and preference.
6. Focus on behavioral neuroscience and concurrent schedules of reinforcement.

Over the course of a day, an individual makes many decisions that range from ones of great importance to ones of small consequence. A person is said to make a decision when buying a new car, when choosing to spend an evening with one friend rather than another, or when deciding what to eat for supper. Animals also make a variety of decisions; they may choose mates with particular characteristics, select one type of food over another, or decide to leave a territory.

From a behavioral view, the analysis of **choice** is concerned with the distribution of operant behavior among alternative sources of reinforcement (options). When several options are available, one alternative may be selected more frequently than others. When this occurs, it is called a **preference** for that particular option. For example, a person may choose between two food markets (a large supermarket and the corner store) on the basis of price, location, and variety. Each time the individual goes to one store rather than the other, she is said to have made a choice. Eventually, the person may shop more frequently at the supermarket than the local grocery, and when this occurs the person is showing preference for the supermarket alternative.

Many people describe choosing to do something, or a preference for one activity over another, as a subjective experience. For example, you may simply like one person better than others, and based on this you feel good about spending a day with that person. From a behavioral perspective, your likes and feelings are real but they do not provide an objective scientific account of why you decide to do what you do. To provide that account, it is necessary to identify the conditions that affected your attraction to (or preference for) the other person or friend.

EXPERIMENTAL ANALYSIS OF CHOICE AND PREFERENCE

For behavior analysts, the study of choice is based on principles of operant behavior. In previous chapters, operant behavior was analyzed in situations in which one response class was reinforced on a single schedule of reinforcement. For example, a child is reinforced with contingent attention from a teacher for correctly completing a page of arithmetic problems. The teacher provides one source of reinforcement (attention) when the child emits the target operant (math solutions). The single-operant analysis is important for the discovery of basic principles and applications. However, this same situation may be analyzed as a choice among behavioral options. The child may choose to do math problems or emit other behavior (e.g., look out of the window or talk to another child). This analysis of choice extends the operant paradigm or model to more complex environments in which several response and reinforcement alternatives are available.

In the everyday environment, there are many alternatives that schedule reinforcement for operant behavior. A child may distribute time and behavior among parents, peer group, and sport activities. Each alternative may require specific behavior and provide reinforcement at a particular rate and amount. To understand, predict, and change the child's behavior, all of these response–consequence relationships must be taken into account. Thus, the operant analysis of choice and preference begins to contact the complexity of everyday life, offering new principles for application. Even the issue of drug addiction is viewed today as matter of voluntary (operant) choice instead of an unfortunate disease. In fact, Gene Heyman (2009) makes a compelling case for attributing addiction to the dynamics of choice, and most effective treatments are based on an analysis of response alternatives.

The Choice Paradigm

The Two-Key Procedure

In the laboratory, choice and preference are investigated by arranging **concurrent schedules of reinforcement** (Catania, 1966). Figure 9.1 shows a concurrent operant setting for a pigeon. In the laboratory, two or more simple schedules (i.e., FR, VR, FI, or VI) are simultaneously available on different response keys (Ferster & Skinner, 1957). Each key is programmed with a separate schedule of reinforcement, and the organism is free to distribute behavior between the alternative schedules. The distribution of time and behavior among the response options is the behavioral measure of choice and preference. For example, a food-deprived bird may be exposed to a situation in which the left response key is programmed to deliver 20 presentations of the food hopper each hour, while the right key delivers 60 reinforcers an hour. To obtain reinforcement from either key, the pigeon must respond according to the schedule on that key. If the bird responds exclusively to the right key (and never to the left) and meets the schedule requirement, then 60 reinforcers will be delivered each hour. Because the bird could have responded to either side, we may say that it "prefers" to spend its time on the right alternative.

Concurrent schedules of reinforcement have received considerable research attention because they may be used as an analytical tool for understanding choice and preference. This selection of an experimental paradigm or model is based on the reasonable assumption that contingencies of reinforcement contribute substantially to choice behavior. Simply stated, all other factors being equal, the more reinforcement (higher rate) that is provided by

FIG. 9.1   A two-key operant chamber for birds. Schedules of food reinforcement are arranged simultaneously on each key.

an alternative, the more time and energy are spent on that alternative. For example, in choosing between spending an evening with either of two friends, the one who has provided the most social reinforcement will probably be the one selected. Reinforcement may be social approval, affection, interesting conversation, or other aspects of the friend's behavior. The experience of deciding to spend the evening with one friend rather than the other may be something like "I just feel like spending the evening with Fred." Of course, in everyday life choosing is seldom as uncomplicated as this, and a more common decision might be to spend the evening with both friends. However, to understand how reinforcement processes are working, it is necessary to control the other factors so that the independent effects of reinforcement on choice may be observed.

Concurrent Ratio Schedules

Figure 9.2 shows a two-key concurrent-operant setting for humans. (It is irresistible to point out the similarities of the following lab situation and the casino slot-machine case.) Consider that you are asked to participate in an experiment in which you may earn up to $50 an hour. As an experimental participant, you are taken to a room that has two response keys separated by a distance of 2.4 m. Halfway between the two keys is a small opening just big enough for your hand to fit. The room is empty, except for the unusual-looking apparatus. You are told to do anything you want. What do you do? You probably walk about and inspect your surroundings and, feeling somewhat foolish, eventually press one of the response keys. Immediately following this action, $1 is dispensed by a coin machine and is held on a plate inside the small opening. The dollar remains available for about 5 s, and then the plate falls away and the dollar disappears. Assuming that you have retrieved the dollar, will you press one of the keys again? In reality, this depends on several factors: perhaps you are wealthy and the dollar is irrelevant; perhaps you decide to "get the best of the experimenter" and show that you are not a rat; maybe you do not want to appear greedy, and so on. However, assume for the moment that you are a typical poor student and you press the key again. After some time pressing both keys and counting the number of key presses, you discover what seems to be a rule. The left key pays a dollar for each 100 responses, while the right side pays a dollar for 250 responses. Does it make sense to spend your effort on the right key when you can make money faster on the other alternative? Of course it does not, and you decide to spend all of your effort on the key that pays the most. This same result has been found with other organisms. When two ratio schedules (in this case FR 100 and FR 250) are programmed as concurrent schedules, the alternative that produces more rapid reinforcement is chosen exclusively (Herrnstein & Loveland, 1975).

Because ratio schedules result in exclusive responding to the alternative with the highest rate of payoff, these schedules are seldom used to study choice. We have discovered something about choice: Ratio schedules produce exclusive preference (see McDonald, 1988, on how to program concurrent ratio schedules to produce response distributions similar to those that occur on interval schedules). Although this result is interesting, it suggests that other schedules should be used to investigate choice and preference.

FIG. 9.2 A two-key operant chamber for humans. Pressing the keys results in money being issued from a coin dispenser (middle), depending on the schedules of reinforcement.

Once exclusive responding occurs, it is not possible to study how responses are distributed between the alternatives, which is the major objective of an experimental analysis of choice.

Concurrent Interval Schedules

Consider, however, what you might do if interval schedules were programmed on the two response keys. Remember that on an interval schedule a single response must occur after a defined or variable amount of time. If you spend all of your time pressing the same key, you will miss reinforcement that is programmed on the other alternative. For example, if the left key is scheduled to pay a dollar on average every 2 min and the right key on average every 6 min, then a reasonable tactic is to spend most of your time responding on the left key but every once in a while to check out the other alternative. This behavior will result in obtaining most of the money set up by both schedules. In fact, when exposed to concurrent interval schedules, most animals distribute their time and behavior between the two alternatives in such a manner (de Villiers, 1977). Thus, the first prerequisite of the choice paradigm is that *interval schedules* must be used to study the distribution of behavior.

Interval schedules are said to be independent of one another when they are presented concurrently. This is because responding on one alternative does not affect the rate of reinforcement programmed for the other schedule. For example, a fixed-interval 6-min schedule (FI 6 min) is programmed to deliver reinforcement every 6 min. Of course, a response must be made after the fixed interval has elapsed. Assume that you are faced with a situation in which the left key pays a dollar every 2 min (FI 2 min). The right key delivers a dollar when you make a response after 6 min (FI 6 min). You have 1 h a day in the experiment. If you just respond to the FI 2-min schedule, you would earn approximately $30. On the other hand, you could increase the number of payoffs an hour by occasionally pressing the FI 6-min key. This occurs because the left key pays a total of $30 each hour and the right key pays an additional $10. After many hours of choosing between the alternatives, you may develop a stable pattern of responding. This *steady-state performance* is predictable. You should respond for approximately 6 min on the FI 2-min alternative and obtain three reinforcers ($3). After the third reinforcer, you may feel like switching to the FI 6-min key, on which a reinforcer is immediately available. You obtain the money on this key and immediately return to the richer schedule (left key). This steady-state pattern of alternate responding may be repeated over and over with little variation.

Concurrent Variable-Interval Schedules

Recall that there are two major types of interval schedules. On variable-interval (VI) schedules, the time between each programmed reinforcer changes and the average time to reinforcement defines the specific schedule (VI 60 s). Because the organism is unable to discriminate the time to reinforcement on VI schedules, the regular switching pattern that characterizes concurrent FI FI performance does not occur. This is an advantage for the analysis of choice, because the organism must respond on both alternatives as switching does not always result in reinforcement. Thus, operant behavior maintained by concurrent VI VI schedules is sensitive to the rate of reinforcement on each alternative. For this reason, VI schedules are typically used to study choice.

Alternation: The Changeover Response

At this point, the choice paradigm is almost complete. Again, however, consider what you would do in the following situation. The two keys are separated and you cannot press both at the same time. The left key now pays a dollar on a VI 2-min schedule, while responses to the right key are reinforced on VI 6 min. The left key pays $30 each hour, and the right key delivers $10 if you respond perfectly. Assuming that you obtain all programmed reinforcers on both schedules, you earn $40 for each experimental session. What can you do to earn the most per hour? If you stay on the VI 2-min side, you end up missing the 10 reinforcers on the other alternative. However, if you frequently change over from key to key, most of the reinforcers on both schedules will be obtained. This is in fact what most animals do when faced with these contingencies (de Villiers, 1977).

Simple alternation between response alternatives prevents an analysis of choice because the distribution of behavior remains the same (approximately 50/50) no matter what the programmed rates of reinforcement. Frequent switching between alternatives may occur because of the correlation between rate of switching and overall rate of reinforcement (number of dollars per session). In other words, as the rate of switching increases, so does the hourly payoff. Another way of looking at this alternation is that organisms are accidentally reinforced for the **changeover response**. This alternation is called concurrent superstition (Catania, 1966), and it occurs because as time is spent on one alternative the other schedule is timing out. As the organism spends more time on the left key, the probability of a reinforcer being set up on the right key increases. This means that a changeover to the right key will be reinforced even though the contingencies do not require the changeover response. Thus, switching to the other response key is an operant that is inadvertently strengthened.

The Changeover Delay

The control procedure that is used to stop rapid switching between alternatives is called a **change-over delay**, or **COD** (Shull & Pliskoff, 1967). The COD contingency stipulates that responses will not have an effect immediately following a change from one schedule to another. After switching to a new alternative, a brief time interval is required before a response can be reinforced (e.g., a 3-s delay). For example, if an organism has just changed to an alternative that is ready to deliver reinforcement, there is a 3-s delay before a response is effective. As soon as the 3-s delay has elapsed, a response is reinforced. Of course, if the schedule has not timed out, the COD is irrelevant because reinforcement is not yet available. The COD contingency operates in both directions whenever a change is made from one alternative to another. The COD prevents frequent switching between alternatives. To obtain reinforcement, an organism must spend a minimal amount of time on an alternative before switching to another schedule. For example, with a 3-s COD, changing over every 2 s will never result in reinforcement. The COD is therefore an important and necessary feature of the operant-choice procedure.

Experimental Procedures for Studying Choice

The basic paradigm for investigating choice and preference is now complete. In summary, a researcher who is interested in behavioral choice should:

1. arrange two or more concurrently available schedules of reinforcement
2. program interval schedules on each alternative
3. use variable- rather than fixed-interval schedules
4. require a COD in order to stop frequent alternation between or among the schedules.

The Findley Procedure

Findley (1958) described an interesting variation on the basic choice procedure. The **Findley procedure** involves a single response key that changes color. Each color is a stimulus that signals a

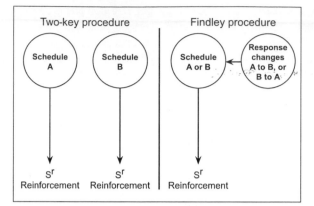

FIG. 9.3 Comparison of the two-key and Findley procedures. Notice that the Findley method highlights the changeover response.

particular schedule of reinforcement. The color and the programmed schedule may be changed by a response to a second key. This key is called the *changeover key*. For example, a pigeon may respond on a VI 30-s schedule that is signaled by red illumination of the response key. When the bird pecks a second changeover key, the color on the response key changes from red to blue and a new schedule is operative. In the presence of the blue light, the pigeon may respond on a VI 90-s schedule of reinforcement. Another response on the changeover key reinstates the red light and the VI 30-s schedule. The advantage of the Findley procedure is that *the response of changing from one alternative to another is explicitly defined and measured.* Figure 9.3 compares the two-key and Findley procedures, showing that the Findley method allows for the measurement and control of the changeover response.

Current evidence suggests that the same principles of choice account for behavior in both the two-key and changeover procedures. For this reason, researchers have not made a theoretical distinction between them. However, such a distinction may be important for the analysis of human behavior. Sunahara and Pierce (1982) suggested that the **two-key procedure** provides a model for social interaction. For example, in a group discussion a person may distribute talk and attention to several group members. These members may be viewed as alternative sources of social reinforcement for the person. On the other hand, the changeover-key procedure may model role taking, in which an individual responds differentially to the role of another person. In this case, the individual may change over between the reinforcement schedules provided by the other person as a friend or as a boss. For example, while at work the changeover may be made by saying "Could I discuss a personal problem with you?" In other words, a person who is both your friend and your supervisor at work may sometimes deliver social reinforcement as a friend and at other times as your boss. Your behavior changes when the other person provides differential reinforcement in these two different roles.

THE MATCHING LAW

In 1961, Richard Herrnstein (Figure 9.4) published an influential paper that described the distribution of behavior on concurrent schedules of positive reinforcement (a collection of related papers by Herrnstein, 1997, on the matching law was edited by Rachlin & Laibson). He found that pigeons matched relative rates of behavior to relative rates of reinforcement. For example, when 90% of the total reinforcement was provided by schedule A (and 10% by schedule B), approximately 90% of the bird's key pecks were on the A schedule. This equality or matching between relative rate of reinforcement and relative rate of response is known as the **matching law**. To understand this law, we turn to Herrnstein's (1961b) experiment.

Proportional Matching

Herrnstein's Experiment

In this study, Herrnstein investigated the behavior of pigeons on a two-key concurrent schedule. Concurrent VI VI schedules of food reinforcement were programmed with a 1.5-s COD. The birds were exposed to different pairs of concurrent VI schedules for several days. Each pair of concurrent schedules was maintained until response rates stabilized— that is, behavior on each schedule did not significantly change from session to session. After several days of stable responding, a new pair of schedule values was presented. Overall rate of reinforcement was held constant at 40 reinforcers per hour for all pairs of schedules. Thus, if the schedule on the left key was programmed to deliver 20 reinforcers an hour (VI 3 min), then the right key also provided 20 reinforcers. If the left key supplied 10 reinforcers, then the right key supplied 30 reinforcers. The schedule values that Herrnstein used are presented in Figure 9.5.

FIG. 9.4   Richard Herrnstein. Reprinted with permission.

The data in Figure 9.5 show the schedules operating on the two keys, A and B. As previously stated, the total number of scheduled reinforcers is held constant for each pair of VI schedules. This is indicated in the third column, in which the sum of the reinforcements per hour (Rft/h) is equal to 40 for each set of schedules. Because the overall rate of reinforcement remains constant, changes in the distribution of behavior cannot be attributed to this factor. Note that when key A is programmed to deliver 20 reinforcers an hour, so is key B. When this occurs, the responses per hour (Rsp/h) are the same on each key. However, the responses per hour (or absolute rate) are not the critical measure of preference. Recall that choice and preference are measured as the distribution of time or behavior between alternatives. To express the idea of distribution, it is important to direct attention to *relative* measures. Because of this, Herrnstein focused on the relative rates of response. In Figure 9.5, the relative rate of response is expressed as a proportion. That is, the rate of response on key A is the numerator and the sum of the response rates on both keys is the denominator. The proportional rate of response on key A is shown in the final column, labeled "Relative responses."

Calculation of Proportions

To calculate the proportional rate of responses to key A for the pair of schedules VI 4.5 min VI 2.25 min, the following simple formula is used:

$$B_a/(B_a + B_b).$$

The term B_a is behavior measured as the rate of response on key A, or 1750 pecks per hour. The rate of response on key B is

Key	Schedule	Rft/h	Rsp/h	Relative reinforcement	Relative responses
A	VI 3-min	20.00	2000	0.50	0.50
B	VI 3-min	20.00	2000	0.50	0.50
A	VI 9-min	6.7	250	0.17	0.08
B	VI 1.8-min	33.30	3000	0.83	0.92
A	VI 1.5-min	40.00	4800	1.00	1.00
B	Extinction	0.00	0	0.00	0.00
A	VI 4.5-min	13.30	1750	0.33	0.31
B	VI 2.25-min	26.70	3900	0.66	0.69

FIG. 9.5   A table of schedule values and data. Reinforcement per hour (Rft/h), responses per hour (Rsp/h), relative reinforcement (proportions), and relative responses (proportions) are shown. Adapted from Fig. 1 (bird 231) and text of "Relative and absolute strength of responses as a function of frequency of reinforcement," by R. J. Herrnstein, 1961b, *Journal of the Experimental Analysis of Behavior, 4,* 267–272.

3900 pecks per hour and is represented by the B_b term. Thus, the proportional rate of response on key A is:

$$1750/(1750 + 3900) = 0.31.$$

In a similar fashion, the proportion of reinforcement on key A may be calculated as:

$$R_a/(R_a + R_b).$$

The term R_a refers to the scheduled rate of reinforcement on key A, or 13.3 reinforcers per hour. The rate of reinforcement on key B is designated by the symbol R_b and is 26.7 reinforcers per hour. The proportional rate of reinforcement on key A is calculated as:

$$13.3/(13.3 + 26.7) = 0.33.$$

These calculations show that the relative rate of response (0.31) is very close to the relative rate of reinforcement (0.33). If you compare these values for the other pairs of schedules, you will see that the proportional rate of response approximates the proportional rate of reinforcement.

Importance of Relative Rates

Herrnstein showed that the major dependent variable in choice experiments was **relative rate of response**. He also found that relative rate of reinforcement was the primary independent variable. Thus, in an operant-choice experiment, the researcher manipulates the **relative rates of reinforcement** on each key and observes the relative rate of response to the respective alternatives.

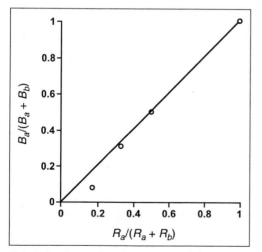

Figure 9.5 shows that Herrnstein manipulated the independent variable, relative rate of reinforcement on key A, over a range of values. Because there are several values of the independent variable and a corresponding set of values for the dependent variable, it is possible to plot the relationship. Figure 9.6 shows the relationship between proportional rate of reinforcement, $R_a/(R_a + R_b)$, and proportional rate of response, $B_a/(B_a + B_b)$, for pigeon 231 based on the values in Figure 9.5.

FIG. 9.6 Proportional matching of the response and reinforcement rates for bird 231. Figure is based on results from "Relative and absolute strength of responses as a function of frequency of reinforcement," by R. J. Herrnstein, 1961b, *Journal of the Experimental Analysis of Behavior, 4*, 267–272. © 1961 Society for the Experimental Analysis of Behavior, Inc.

The Matching Equation

As the relative rate of reinforcement increases so does the relative rate of response. Furthermore, for each increase in relative reinforcement there is about the same increase in relative rate of response. This equality of relative rate of reinforcement and relative rate of response is expressed as a proportion in Equation 9.1:

$$B_a/(B_a + B_b) = R_a/(R_a + R_b). \tag{9.1}$$

Notice that we have simply taken the $B_a/(B_a + B_b)$ and the $R_a/(R_a + R_b)$ expressions, which give the proportion of responses and reinforcers on key A, and mathematically stated that they are equal. In verbal form, we are stating that *relative rate of response matches (or equals) relative rate of reinforcement*. This statement, whether expressed verbally or mathematically, is known as the *matching law*.

In Figure 9.6, matching is shown as the solid black line. Notice that this line results when the proportional rate of reinforcement exactly matches the proportional rate of response. The matching law is an ideal representation of choice behavior. The actual data from pigeon 231 approximate the matching relationship. Herrnstein (1961b) also reported the results for two other pigeons that were well described by the matching equation.

EXTENSIONS OF THE MATCHING LAW

The Generality of Matching

The equality of rates of response and reinforcement is called a law of behavior because it describes how a variety of organisms choose among alternatives (de Villiers, 1977). Animals such as pigeons (Davison & Ferguson, 1978), wagtails (Houston, 1986), cows (Matthews & Temple, 1979), and rats (Poling, 1978) have demonstrated matching in choice situations. Interestingly, this same law applies to humans in a number of different settings (Bradshaw & Szabadi, 1988; Pierce & Epling, 1983). Reinforcers have ranged from food (Herrnstein, 1961b) to points that are subsequently exchanged for money (Bradshaw, Ruddle, & Szabadi, 1981). Behavior has been as diverse as lever pressing by rats (Norman & McSweeney, 1978) and conversation in humans (Conger & Killeen, 1974; Pierce, Epling, & Greer, 1981). Environments in which matching has been observed have included T-mazes, operant chambers, and open spaces with free-ranging flocks of birds (Baum, 1974a), as well as discrete-trial and free operant choice by human groups (Madden, Peden, & Yamaguchi, 2002). Also, special education students have been found to spend time on math problems proportional to the relative rate of reinforcement (e.g., Mace, Neef, Shade, & Mauro, 1994). Thus, the matching law describes the distribution of individual (and group) behavior across species, types of response, different reinforcers, and a variety of settings.

Matching and Human Communication

An interesting test of the matching law was reported by Conger and Killeen (1974). These researchers assessed human performance in a group discussion situation. A group was composed of three experimenters and one experimental participant. The participant was not aware that the other group members were confederates in the experiment, and was asked to discuss attitudes toward drug abuse. One of the confederates prompted the participant to talk. The other two confederates were assigned the role of an audience. Each listener reinforced the subject's talk with brief positive words or phrases when a hidden cue light came on. The cue lights were scheduled so that the listeners gave different rates of reinforcement to the speaker. When the results for several participants were combined, relative time spent talking to the listener matched relative rate of agreement from the listener. These results suggest that the matching law operates in everyday social interaction.

In a recent applied study by McDowell and Caron (2010), the matching law was used to describe the verbal behavior of boys at risk for delinquency, as they interacted with their friends. The boys' verbal responses were coded as either "rule-break talk" or "normative talk", and positive social responses from peers were recorded as the presumed reinforcers for the two verbal response classes. The matching law provided an excellent description of the boys' allocation of verbal behavior, with some undermatching and bias toward normative talk (as would be expected). Importantly, the undermatching became extreme and the bias toward normative talk lessened as the deviance of the child increased. The researchers suggested that extreme undermatching reflects the low reinforcement value of positive social responses for the deviant child, while bias away from normative talk is indicative of different histories of reinforcement and punishment during the upbringing of these delinquent boys (see Advanced Section of this chapter for a discussion of undermatching, bias, and the matching law).

Matching Time on an Alternative

Behavioral choice can also be measured as time spent on an alternative (Baum & Rachlin, 1969; Brownstein & Pliskoff, 1968). Time spent is a useful measure of behavior when the response is continuous, as in talking to another person. In the laboratory, rather than measuring the number of responses, the time spent on an alternative may be used to describe the distribution of behavior. The matching law can also be expressed in terms of relative time spent on an alternative. Equation 9.2 is similar to Equation 9.1, but states the matching relationship in terms of time:

$$T_a/(T_a + T_b) = R_a/(R_a + R_b). \tag{9.2}$$

In this equation, the time spent on alternative A is represented by T_a and the time spent on alternative B is denoted by T_b. Again, R_a and R_b represent the respective rates of reinforcement for these alternatives. The equation states that the relative time spent on an alternative equals the relative rate of reinforcement from that alternative. This extension of the matching law to continuous responses, such as standing in one place or looking at objects, is important. Most behavior outside of the laboratory does not occur as discrete responses. In this case, Equation 9.2 may be used to describe choice and preference.

Matching on More Than Two Alternatives

A consideration of either Equation 9.1 or Equation 9.2 makes it evident that in order to change behavior, the rate of reinforcement for the target response may be adjusted; alternatively, the rate of reinforcement for other concurrent operants may be altered. Both of these procedures manipulate the relative rate of reinforcement for the specified behavior. Equation 9.3 represents the relative rate of response as a function of several alternative sources of reinforcement:

$$B_a/(B_a + B_b + \ldots B_n) = R_a/(R_a + R_b + \ldots R_n). \tag{9.3}$$

In the laboratory, most experiments are conducted with only two concurrent schedules of reinforcement. However, the matching law also describes situations in which an organism may choose among several sources of reinforcement (Davison & Hunter, 1976; Elsmore & McBride, 1994; Miller & Loveland, 1974; Pliskoff & Brown, 1976). In Equation 9.3, behavior allocated to alternative A (B_a) is expressed relative to the sum of all behavior directed to the known alternatives ($B_a + B_b + \ldots B_n$). Reinforcement provided by alternative A (R_a) is stated relative to all known sources of reinforcement ($R_a + R_b + \ldots R_n$). Again, notice that an equality of proportions (matching) is stated.

Practical Implications of the Matching Law

The matching law has practical implications. A few researchers have shown that the matching equations are useful in applied settings (Borrero & Vollmer, 2002; Epling & Pierce, 1983; McDowell, 1981, 1982, 1988; Myerson & Hale, 1984; Plaud, 1992). One applied setting where the matching law has practical importance is the classroom, where students' behavior is often maintained on concurrent schedules of social reinforcement.

Matching, Modification, and Reinforcement Schedules

In a classroom, appropriate behavior for students includes working on assignments, following instructions, and attending to the teacher. In contrast, yelling and screaming, talking out of turn, and throwing paper airplanes are usually viewed as undesirable. All of these activities, appropriate or inappropriate, are presumably maintained by teacher attention, peer approval, sensory stimulation, and other sources of reinforcement. However, the schedules of reinforcement that maintain behavior in complex settings such as a classroom are not usually known. When the objective is to increase a specific operant and the concurrent schedules are unknown, Myerson and Hale (1984) recommend the use of VI schedules to reinforce target behavior.

Recall that on concurrent ratio schedules, exclusive preference develops for the alternative with the higher rate of reinforcement (Herrnstein & Loveland, 1975). Ratio schedules are in effect when a teacher implements a grading system based on the number of correct solutions for assignments. The teacher's intervention will increase the students' on-task behavior only if the rate of reinforcement by the teacher is higher than another ratio schedule controlling inappropriate behavior. Basically, an intervention is either completely successful or a total failure when ratio schedules are used to modify behavior. In contrast, interval schedules of reinforcement will always redirect behavior to the desired alternative, although such a schedule may not completely eliminate inappropriate responding.

When behavior is maintained by interval contingencies, interval schedules remain the most desirable method for behavior change. Myerson and Hale used the matching equations to show that behavior-change techniques based on interval schedules are more effective than ratio interventions. They stated that "if the behavior analyst offers a VI schedule of reinforcement for competing responses two times as rich as the VI schedule for inappropriate behavior, the result will be the same as would be obtained with a VR schedule three times as rich as the schedule for inappropriate behavior" (Myerson and Hale, 1984, pp. 373–374). Generally, behavior change will be more predictable and successful if interval schedules are used to reinforce appropriate behavior.

MATCHING ON SINGLE OPERANT SCHEDULES

The matching law suggests that operant behavior is determined by rate of reinforcement for one alternative relative to all other known sources of reinforcement. Even in situations in which a contingency exists between a single response and a reinforcement schedule, organisms usually have several reinforced alternatives that are unknown to the researcher. Also, many of the activities that produce reinforcement are beyond experimental control. A rat that is lever pressing for food may gain additional reinforcement from exploring the operant chamber, scratching itself, or grooming.

In a similar fashion, rather than working for teacher attention, a pupil may look out of the window, talk to a friend, or even daydream. Thus, even in a single-operant setting, multiple sources of reinforcement are operating. Richard Herrnstein argued this point and suggested that all operant behavior must be understood as behavior emitted in the context of other alternative sources of reinforcement (Herrnstein, 1970, 1974).

Based on these ideas, Herrnstein proposed a matching equation that describes the absolute rate of response on a single schedule of reinforcement. This mathematical formulation is called the **quantitative law of effect**. The law states that the *absolute rate of response on a schedule of reinforcement is a hyperbolic function of rate of reinforcement on the schedule relative to the total rate of reinforcement*, both scheduled and extraneous reinforcement. That is, as the rate of reinforcement on the schedule increases, the rate of response rapidly rises, but eventually further increases in the rate of reinforcement produce less and less of an increase in the rate of response (a hyperbolic curve, see Figure 9.7 for examples).

The rapid rise in rate of response with higher rates of reinforcement is modified by extraneous sources of reinforcement. **Extraneous sources of reinforcement** include any unknown contingencies that support the behavior of the organism. For example, a rat that is pressing a lever for food on a particular schedule of reinforcement could receive extraneous reinforcement for scratching, sniffing, and numerous other behaviors. The rate of response for food will be a function of the programmed schedule as well as the extraneous schedules controlling other behavior. In humans, a student's mathematical performance will be a function of the schedule of correct solutions as well as extraneous reinforcement for other behavior from classmates or teachers, internal neurochemical processes, and changes to the physical/chemical environment (e.g., the smell of food drifting from the cafeteria).

Extraneous reinforcement slows down the rise in rate of response with higher rates of reinforcement. One implication is that control of behavior by a schedule of reinforcement is reduced as the sources of extraneous reinforcement increase. A student who does math problems for a given rate of teacher attention will do less if extraneous reinforcement is available by looking out of the classroom window. Alternatively, the teacher will have to use higher rates of attention for problem solving when "distractions" are available than when there are few additional sources of reinforcement.

Experimental Evidence for the Quantitative Law of Effect

The quantitative law of effect has been investigated in laboratory experiments. In an early investigation, Catania and Reynolds (1968) conducted an exhaustive study of six pigeons that pecked a key for food on different variable-interval (VI) schedules. The rate of reinforcement ranged from 8 to 300 food presentations per hour. Herrnstein (1970) replotted the data on X and Y coordinates. Figure 9.7 shows the plots for the six birds, with reinforcements per hour on the x-axis and responses per minute on the y-axis.

Herrnstein used a statistical procedure to fit his hyperbolic equation to the data for each pigeon. Figure 9.7 presents the curves that best fit these results. Notice that all of the birds produce rates of response that are described as a hyperbolic function of rate of reinforcement. Some of the curves fit the data almost perfectly, while others are less satisfactory. Overall, Herrnstein's quantitative law of effect is well supported by these findings.

The quantitative law of effect has been extended to magnitude of food reinforcement, brain stimulation, quality of reinforcement, delay of positive reinforcement, rate of negative reinforcement, magnitude or intensity of negative reinforcement, and delay of negative reinforcement

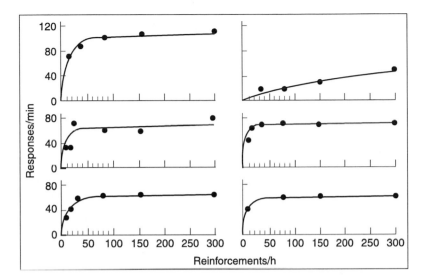

FIG. 9.7   Rate of response as a function of rate of food reinforcement for six pigeons on single VI schedules. Taken from "On the law of effect," by R. J. Herrnstein, 1970, *Journal of the Experimental Analysis of Behavior, 13,* 243–266. © 1970 Society for the Experimental Analysis of Behavior, Inc. Republished with permission.

(see de Villiers, 1977, for a thorough review). In a summary of the evidence, Peter de Villiers stated:

> The remarkable generality of Herrnstein's equation is apparent from this survey. The behavior of rats, pigeons, monkeys and ... people is equally well accounted for, whether the behavior is lever pressing, key pecking, running speed, or response latency in a variety of experimental settings. The reinforcers can be as different as food, sugar water, escape from shock or loud noise or cold water, electrical stimulation of a variety of brain loci, or turning a comedy record back on. Out of 53 tests of Equation [9.6] on group data, the least-squares fit of the equation accounts for over 90% of the variance in 42 cases and for over 80% in another six cases. Out of 45 tests on individual data, the equation accounts for over 90% of the variance in 32 cases and for over 80% in another seven cases. The literature appears to contain no evidence for a substantially different equation.... This equation therefore provides a powerful but simple framework for the quantification of the relation between response strength and both positive and negative reinforcement.
>
> (de Villiers, 1977, p. 262)

ON THE APPLIED SIDE: Application of the Quantitative Law of Effect

Dr. Jack McDowell from Emory University (Figure 9.8) was the first researcher to use Herrnstein's matching equation for a single schedule of reinforcement to describe human behavior in a natural setting. McDowell's expertise in mathematics and behavior modification spurred him to apply Herrnstein's matching equation for a single operant to a clinically relevant problem.

FIG. 9.8   Jack McDowell. Reprinted with permission.

Mathematics and Behavior Modification

Carr and McDowell (1980) were involved in the treatment of a 10-year-old boy who repeatedly and severely scratched himself. Before treatment the boy had a large number of open sores on his scalp, face, back, arms, and legs. In addition, the boy's body was covered with scabs, scars, and skin discoloration, where new wounds could be produced. In their 1980 paper, Carr and McDowell demonstrated that the boy's scratching was operant behavior. Careful observation showed that the scratching occurred predominantly when he and other family members were in the living room watching television. This suggested that the self-injurious behavior was under stimulus control. In other words, the family and setting made scratching more likely to occur.

Next, Carr and McDowell looked for potential reinforcing consequences maintaining the boy's self-injurious behavior. The researchers suspected that the consequences were social, because scratching appeared to be under the stimulus control of family members. In any family interaction there are many social exchanges, and the task was to identify those consequences that reliably followed the boy's scratching. Observation showed that family members reliably reprimanded the boy when he engaged in self-injury. Reprimands are seemingly negative events, but the literature makes it clear that both approval and disapproval may serve as reinforcement.

Although social reinforcement by reprimands was a good guess, it was still necessary to show that these consequences in fact functioned as reinforcement. The first step was to take baseline measures of the rate of scratching and the rate of reprimands. Following this, the family members were required to ignore the boy's behavior. That is, the presumed reinforcer was withdrawn (i.e., extinction), and the researchers continued to monitor the rate of scratching. Next, the potential reinforcer was reinstated; the family members again reprimanded the boy for his misconduct. Relative to baseline, the scratching decreased when reprimands were withdrawn and increased when they were reinstated. This test identified the reprimands as positive reinforcement for scratching. Once the reinforcement for scratching had been identified, behavior modification was used to eliminate the self-injurious behavior.

FIG. 9.9   Rate of social reinforcement and self-injurious scratching of a young boy. The data were fitted by Herrnstein's single-operant equation. Adapted from J. J. McDowell, 1981, in *Quantification of Steady-State Operant Behavior*, pp. 311–324, Elsevier/North-Holland, Amsterdam. Republished with permission of Jack McDowell.

In a subsequent report, McDowell (1981) analyzed the boy's baseline data in terms of the quantitative law of effect. He plotted the number of reprimands per hour on the x-axis and the number of scratches per hour on the y-axis. He then fitted the matching equation for a single schedule of reinforcement to the points on the graph. Figure 9.9 shows the plot and the curve of best fit. The matching equation provides an excellent description of the boy's behavior. You will notice that most of the points are on, or very close to, the hyperbolic curve. In fact, more than 99% of the variation in rate of scratching is accounted for by the rate of reprimands. McDowell has indicated the significance of this demonstration. He states:

> *The single-alternative hyperbola accounted for nearly all the variance in the data. This is especially noteworthy because the behavior occurred in an uncontrolled environment where other factors that might have influenced the behavior had ample opportunity to do so. It may be worth emphasizing that the rates of reprimanding . . . occurred naturally; that is, they were not experimentally arranged. . . . Thus, the data . . . demonstrate the relevance of matching theory to the natural ecology of human behavior.*
>
> *(McDowell, 1988, pp. 103–104)*

Overall, the quantitative law of effect or Herrnstein's hyperbolic equation has been an important contribution to the understanding of human behavior and to the modification of human behavior in applied settings (see Fisher & Mazur, 1997; Martens, Lochner, & Kelly, 1992).

CHOICE, FORAGING, AND BEHAVIORAL ECONOMICS

Optimal Foraging, Matching, and Melioration

One of the fundamental problems of evolutionary biology and behavioral ecology concerns the concept of "optimal foraging" of animals (Krebs & Davies, 1978). Foraging involves prey selection, where prey can be either animal or vegetable. Thus, a cow taking an occasional mouthful of grass in a field, or a redshank wading in the mud and probing with its beak for an occasional worm, are examples of foraging behavior. Because the function of foraging is to find food, foraging can be viewed as operant behavior regulated by food reinforcement. The natural contingencies of foraging present animals with alternative sources of food called *patches*. Food patches provide items at various rates (patch density), and in this sense are similar to concurrent schedules of reinforcement arranged in the laboratory.

Optimal foraging is said to occur when animals obtain the highest overall rate of reinforcement from their foraging. That is, over time organisms are expected to select between patches so as to optimize (obtain the maximum possible value from) their food resources. In this view, animals are like organic computers comparing their behavioral distributions with overall outcomes and stabilizing on a response distribution that **maximizes** the overall rate of reinforcement.

In contrast to the optimal foraging hypothesis, Herrnstein (1982) proposed a process of **melioration** (doing the best at the moment). Organisms, he argued, are sensitive to fluctuations in the momentary rates of reinforcement rather than to long-term changes in overall rates of reinforcement. That is, an organism remains on one schedule until the local rates of reinforcement decline relative to that offered by a second schedule. Herrnstein (1997, pp. 74–99) showed that the steady-state outcome of the process of melioration is the matching law where relative rate of response matches relative rate of reinforcement. Thus, in a foraging situation involving two patches, Herrnstein's melioration analysis predicts matching of the distributions of behavior and reinforcement (e.g., Herrnstein & Prelec, 1997). Optimal foraging theory, on the other hand, predicts maximization of the overall rate of reinforcement (Charnov, 1976; Nonacs, 2001).

It is not possible to examine all the evidence for melioration, matching, and maximizing in this chapter, but Herrnstein (1982) has argued that melioration and matching are the basic processes of choice. That is, when melioration and matching are tested in choice situations that distinguish matching from maximizing, matching theory has usually predicted the actual distributions of the behavior.

One example of the application of matching theory to animal foraging has been reported by Baum (1974a; see also Baum, 1983, on foraging) for a flock of free-ranging wild pigeons. The subjects were 20 pigeons that lived in a wooden-frame house in Cambridge, Massachusetts. An opening allowed them to freely enter and leave the attic of the house. An operant apparatus with a platform was placed in the living space opposite to the opening to the outside. The front panel of the apparatus contained three translucent response keys and, when available, an opening allowed access to a hopper of mixed grain. The pigeons were autoshaped to peck to the center key and, following this training, a perch replaced the platform so that only one pigeon at a time could operate the keys and obtain food. Pigeons were now shaped to peck the center key on a VI 30-s schedule of food reinforcement. When a stable performance occurred, the center key was no longer illuminated or operative, and the two side keys became active. Responses to the illuminated side keys were reinforced on two concurrent VI VI schedules. Relative rates of reinforcement on the two keys were varied and the relative rate of response was measured.

Although only one bird at a time could respond on the concurrent schedules of reinforcement, Baum (1974b) treated the aggregate pecks of the group as the dependent measure. When the group of 20 pigeons chose between the two side keys, each of which occasionally produced food, the ratio of pecks to these keys was approximately equal to the ratio of grain presentations obtained from them. That is, the aggregate behavior of the flock of 20 pigeons was in accord with the generalized matching equation, a form of matching equation based on ratios rather than proportions (see Advanced Section at the end of this chapter). This research suggests that the matching law applies to the behavior of wild pigeons in natural environments. Generally, principles of choice based on laboratory experiments can predict the foraging behavior of animals in the wild.

Preference for Choice

Animals foraging in the wild must select food items and search for food in different locations. Thus, making choices is part of the natural ecology of animals. For humans, it is notable that American society is uniquely founded on choice, and most Americans value freedom of choice as a fundamental right. Throughout the day, we make repeated choices by expressing our opinion on diverse social and political issues, selecting among an enormous variety of goods and services (see Figure 9.10), and choosing to form close relationships with others in our social network and community. Generally, we believe in choice.

The value of choice has been investigated in the operant laboratory by asking animals to select between choice and no-choice options. Catania (1975, 1980a) arranged for pigeons to peck an initial key to allow them to choose between two keys (choice condition) or to peck another initial key to allow them to respond on a single key (no-choice condition). The reinforcers (food) and the rates of reinforcement were identical for the choice and no-choice conditions, but the birds preferred the alternative with two keys, showing a **preference for choice** (see also Catania & Sagvolden, 1980; Voss & Homzie, 1970). That is, even without differential outcomes, making choices is preferred.

Preference for choice has been investigated with preschool children (Tiger, Hanley, & Hernandez, 2006). Six children were presented with three colored academic worksheets that allowed access to "choice," "no-choice," and "control" arrangements. Selection of the "choice" worksheet, followed by a correct academic response, resulted in praise and presentation of a plate of five identical candies from which the child could choose one. For selection of the "no-choice" worksheet, and a correct academic response, the child received praise and presentation of a plate with one candy on it. Selection of the "control" worksheet followed by a correct academic response resulted only in praise. Modeling and prompting by the experimenter ensured that the children always made the correct academic response. The findings showed that three children consistently selected the worksheet that led to a choice of candy, and two

FIG. 9.10   The photograph shows a busy shopping mall, illustrating the enormous variety of choice in America. Shoppers can choose to enter different stores within the mall and select from among the goods offered within each store. Americans, perhaps more than any other people, value freedom of choice. © Shutterstock.

other children showed an initial preference for choosing which was not maintained into later sessions. One child always selected the worksheet that led to the "no-choice" plate with one candy. Thus, five of the six children preferred choice, a finding that has been replicated in a subsequent study that equated the number of edible items presented on the choice and no-choice options (Schmidt, Hanley, & Layer, 2009).

Preference for choice has also been found with university students (Leotti & Delgado, 2011). On each trial, participants pressed a black key that resulted in a choice between striped and dotted keys for monetary rewards (choice condition), or pressed a white key that led to a single key, either striped or dotted, for monetary payoffs (no-choice condition). The levels and probability of monetary reward were the same for both the choice and no-choice arrangements. In this experiment, participants selected the black key leading to choice 64% of the time, which is reliably greater than would be expected by chance (50%). In another part of the study, a stimulus (circle, triangle) preceded choosing between blue and yellow keys for monetary rewards, and a second stimulus signaled pressing the key, either blue or yellow, as selected by the computer. All monetary outcomes were equated over the two signaling procedures. Participants were asked to rate the choice or no-choice cues on a scale of liking; the results showed that the stimulus associated with choice was rated higher than the one signaling no choice. The researchers also obtained brain scans showing activity in the ventral striatum, an area related to motivation and affect, when the cue signaled upcoming choice. The researchers claimed that choice is inherently rewarding.

Although preference for choice may be innately rewarding, a recent study indicates that a history of differential reinforcement is also involved (Karsina, Thompson, & Rodriguez, 2011). After initial training about the options, participants sat facing a computer screen and used a computer mouse to make responses (Figure 9.11). On choice trials, the computer screen initially displayed two grey boxes, one containing the words "You select" and the other containing the words "Numbers generated." A click on the "You select" box (free-choice option) deactivated the "Numbers generated" box and changed the screen image to an array of eight numbered squares. Clicks by the participant on any three of the eight squares transferred the chosen numbers to a game box and allowed for a possible win. Alternatively, a click on the "Numbers generated" box (restricted-choice

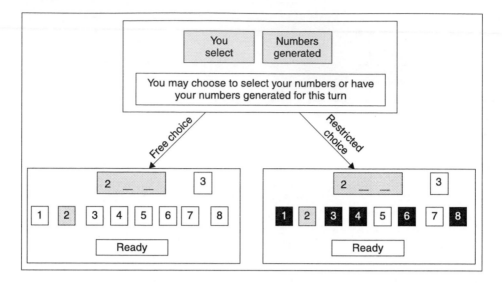

FIG. 9.11 The experimental arrangement for the study of reinforcement history and preference for choice. Participants selected either the "You select" or the "Numbers generated" box (top panel). Once a box had been selected, the other option became dark and inoperative, and a second computer screen appeared. For example, clicking on "You select" resulted in a screen with eight numbered keys, and the participant then picks any three numbers, transferring them to the game box (bottom left panel). In this example, the participant has chosen the number 2 and has two more numbers to select before clicking on "Ready." The participant is told that her numbers are checked for matches and if she wins, a point is added to her total (shown as 3 points). In contrast, selection of the "Numbers generated" box deactivates the free choice option and leads to eight keys, with only three keys operative. The participant clicks on the three numbers generated for her (restricted-choice option); in this case she has already transferred the number 2 to the game box and must select 5 and 7 before clicking "Ready" and finding out if she wins and gets a point for the trial. Points are actually allocated by random-ratio (RR) schedules of reinforcement (see text for further information). Taken from Karsina, A., Thompson, R. H., and Rodriguez, N. M, 2011, "Effects of a history of differential reinforcement on preference for choice," *Journal of the Experimental Analysis of Behavior, 95,* 189–202. © 2011 Society for the Experimental Analysis of Behavior. Republished with permission.

option) of the initial screen deactivated the "You select" option and changed the screen to the array of eight numbers, but only three, chosen by the computer, were available to transfer to the game box for a possible win. Participants were told that any number in the game box that matched three randomly drawn numbers resulted in a win, and a point registered on the screen. In fact, points for free-choice and restricted-choice arrangements were based on random-ratio (RR) schedules of reinforcement, allowing the probability of points for free-choice and restricted-choice options to be equated or varied as necessary.

Seven participants with no consistent preference, or a consistent preference for the restricted-choice option, were given differential reinforcement for selecting the free-choice option. That is, the probability of points was increased for free-choice selection and decreased for selection of the restricted-choice option. Differential reinforcement established a preference for choice in six of seven participants, a preference that lasted even when the probability of points was again equated for the free-choice and restricted-choice options. An overall conclusion is that preference for choice is a reliable finding and a history of reinforcement may establish and maintain this preference. Choice involves a history of selection between good versus better, or sooner versus later, but rarely between exactly equal alternatives. The simple option to "choose" suggests an opportunity to improve your situation, and is usually preferable.

Preference for choice has implications for a matching law analysis of behavior. The distribution of behavior on concurrent VI VI schedules of reinforcement should be biased toward a free-choice alternative, even when the rates of reinforcement on each schedule are equated. Bias toward freedom of choice may help to explain opposition to government regulation of the free-market system even when government control is required. It may also relate to the continual escalation of variety and choice in all aspects of our lives. Today, we may be overwhelmed by choice, as for example is seen when a restaurant offers so many items that we have great difficulty choosing. As noted by Schwartz (2004), Americans more than any other people have made a fetish out of choice, perhaps at the expense of our long-term happiness.

BEHAVIORAL ECONOMICS, CHOICE, AND ADDICTION

Choice and concurrent schedules of reinforcement have been analyzed from a microeconomic point of view (Rachlin, Green, Kagel, & Battalio, 1976). **Behavioral economics** involves the use of basic economic concepts and principles to predict, control, and analyze behavior in choice situations.

In economic terms, as the price of a commodity becomes more expensive, we consume less of it—our demand for it decreases. Behaviorally, price is varied by a ratio schedule of reinforcement. For example, an FR10 schedule requires 10 responses for each unit of food reinforcement (price). We could vary the price of food by changing the FR requirement. Thus, FR20 doubles the price while FR100 is 10 times the original price. By varying the price, it is possible to obtain a **demand curve** showing that as price increases consumption decreases (Figure 9.12). When consumption of a commodity (reinforcer) changes with price, the commodity is said to be elastic. Luxury items (e.g., a European vacation) are highly elastic, being sensitive to price. Consumption of necessities (groceries) does not change much with price, and these are said to be inelastic.

The elasticity of a commodity also depends on one's income. If the cost of going to the movies increases from $10 to $20 and you live on a fixed income of $500 a week, you would probably decrease the frequency with which you go to the movies (movies are a luxury and elastic). However, suppose that your income increases from $500 to $1000. You would now go to the movies as often as you did before (movies are inelastic). All this is to say that the shape of the demand curve for a given commodity (reinforcer) depends on one's income. In operant research with animals, "money" is operant responses and income is the number of responses available. In most operant experiments on choice, income is not restrained and the animal is free to vary the number of responses. If the price of a reinforcer increases (based on the schedule), the animal can adjust to the change by increasing its rate of response. If we place a rat on a budget and it only has 400 responses to allocate for a session, it is likely that the rat will be

FIG. 9.12 Two demand curves relating price (x-axis) to consumption (y-axis). For the inelastic demand curve, consumption does not show much decline with increases in price. In contrast, for the elastic demand curve, consumption shows an increasing decline with price.

sensitive to the price. How we set up a choice situation (free response vs. budget) makes a big difference to the outcome of our experiments.

Let us now turn to the classic economic problem of **substitutability**. How might a change in price of one reinforcer alter the consumption of a second reinforcer, if income is held constant? For some commodities, consumption decreases with price, but consumption of a second commodity increases. The two commodities are said to be *substitutes*. Butter and margarine are substitutes if a shift in the price of butter results in more consumption of margarine. Beverages such as Coke and Pepsi are another example of substitutes. Other commodities are *independents*. As the price of one commodity increases and its consumption decreases, the consumption of a second commodity does not change. Thus, your consumption of gasoline is independent of the price of theatre tickets. A third way in which commodities are related is as *complements*. As the price of one commodity increases and its consumption decreases, consumption of the other commodity also decreases. When the price of hot dogs increases and you eat less of them, your consumption of hot-dog buns also decreases, as does your consumption of relish, mustard, and ketchup. This analysis of substitutability makes it clear that different reinforcers are not necessarily equivalent. To predict the effects of one reinforcer we often need to know its substitutability with other (alternative) reinforcers.

Substitutability, Demand, and Addictive Behavior

Economic principles of demand and substitutability have been extended to laboratory experiments with animals working for addictive drugs such as alcohol, heroin, and cocaine. For example, Nader and Woolverton (1992) showed that a monkey's choice of cocaine over food was a function of drug dose, but that choosing cocaine decreased with the price (number of responses per infusion). That is, the reinforcing effects of the drug increased with dose, but these effects were modified by price, an economic factor. In another experiment, Carroll, Lac, & Nygaard (1989) examined the effects of a substitute commodity on the use of cocaine. Rats nearly doubled their administration of cocaine when water was the other option, compared with when a sweet solution was the other option. These effects were not found in a control group that self-administered an inert saline solution, which suggests that cocaine infusion functioned as reinforcement for self-administration, and the sweet solution substituted for cocaine. In this study, the presence of a substitute (sweet solution) altered the reinforcement value of the drug (see Carroll, 1993, for an account of similar effects with monkeys and the drug PCP). One possibility is that cocaine and the sweet solutions both operate on the neural reward centers, especially the dopamine pathway, establishing both as substitute commodities (Alsiö, Nordenankar, Arvidsson, Birgner, Mahmoudi, Halbout et al., 2011).

In a 2005 review of behavioral economics and drug abuse, Steven Hursh, a professor of behavioral biology at Johns Hopkins University, and his colleagues showed that a mathematical analysis of demand curves is a way of describing the reinforcing value of different drugs (Hursh, Galuska, Winger, & Woods, 2005). Demand curves for drugs yield quantitative measures of "motivation" to procure and consume drugs, and allow for comparison of the demand for similar types of drugs and between drugs that are quite different (e.g., cocaine vs. heroin). Behavioral economics also provides a way to conceptualize drug interventions, and offers new treatment strategies. For example, the analysis of substitute commodities (reinforcers) may be useful for understanding the treatment of heroin addicts with methadone, a less addictive opioid alternative. From an economic perspective, methadone is a partial substitute for heroin because it provides only some of the reinforcing effects of the actual drug. Also, methadone is administered in a clinical setting that is less reinforcing than the social context in which heroin is often used (Hursh, 1991). Based on this analysis, it is unlikely that availability of methadone treatment will, by itself, eliminate the use of heroin.

Addictive substances cause the release of dopamine in the nucleus accumbens, which is what makes a drug addictive. However, the dopamine system does not distinguish between addictive drugs and nonaddictive but rewarding substances. Drugs are used to excess because the benefits are immediate and certain and their costs are uncertain and delayed. Therefore, given a choice between immediate and delayed hedonic substances, the selection is nearly always impulsively in favor of now rather than later (Heyman, 2009).

FOCUS ON: Activity Anorexia and Substitutability of Food and Wheel Running

Activity anorexia occurs when rats are placed on food restriction and provided with the opportunity to run. The initial effect is that food intake is reduced, body weight declines, and wheel running increases. As running escalates, food intake drops off and body weight plummets downward, further augmenting wheel running and suppressing food intake. The result of this cycle is emaciation and, if allowed to continue, the eventual death of the animal (Epling & Pierce, 1992, 1996b; Epling, Pierce, & Stefan, 1983; Routtenberg & Kuznesof, 1967).

A behavioral economic model can describe the allocation of behavior between commodities such as food and wheel running. For example, the imposed food restriction that initiates activity anorexia can be conceptualized as a substantial increase in the price of food, resulting in reduced food consumption. Low food consumption in turn increases consumption of physical activity, which suggests that food and physical activity may be economic substitutes (see Green & Freed, 1993, for a review of behavioral economic concepts).

In two experiments, Belke, Pierce, and Duncan (2006) investigated how animals choose between sucrose (food) and wheel-running reinforcement. Rats were exposed to concurrent VI 30-s VI 30-s schedules of wheel running and sucrose reinforcement. Sucrose solutions varied in concentration (2.5, 7.5, and 12.5%). As the concentration increased, more behavior was allocated to sucrose and more reinforcements were obtained from that alternative. Allocation of behavior to wheel running decreased somewhat, but the obtained wheel-running reinforcement did not change. The results suggested that food-deprived rats were sensitive to changes in food supply (sucrose concentration) while continuing to engage in physical activity (wheel running). In the second study, rats were exposed to concurrent variable ratio (VR VR) schedules of sucrose and wheel running, wheel running and wheel running, and sucrose and sucrose reinforcement. For each pair of reinforcers, the researchers assessed substitutability by changing the prices for consumption of the commodities. The results showed that sucrose substituted for sucrose and wheel running substituted for wheel running, as would be expected. However, wheel running did not substitute for sucrose—the commodities were independent—but sucrose partially substituted for wheel running.

The partial substitutability of sucrose for wheel running in the experiments by Belke et al. (2006) reflects two energy-balance processes: the initiation and maintenance of travel induced by loss of body weight and energy stores (wheel running does not substitute for food), and the termination of locomotion as food supply increases (food does substitute for wheel running). In terms of activity anorexia, the fact that travel does not substitute for food ensures that animals with low energy stores keep going on a food-related trek, even if they eat small amounts along the way. As animals contact stable food supplies, the partial substitutability of food for wheel running means that travel would subside as food intake and body stores return to equilibrium. Behavioral economics therefore provides one way to understand the activity anorexia cycle (see also Belke & Pierce, 2009, who showed that demand for food (sucrose) became less elastic and wheel running became more elastic at low body weight).

Delay Discounting of Reinforcement Value

Demand curve analysis of reinforcement value makes an important contribution to basic research and applications. Another problem addressed by behavioral economics involves devaluation or discounting of reinforcement value. **Delay discounting** involves choosing between small–immediate and large–delayed rewards. If you are watching your weight, you often must choose between the immediate reinforcement from a piece of chocolate cake or the long-term reinforcement of body weight loss and improved health. If you are like most of us, you find yourself eating the cake and forgoing the weight loss. These kinds of decision traps are clarified when they are expressed in terms of immediate or delayed amounts of money.

Suppose that you have just received notification of a substantial inheritance from your grandfather, who has willed you $100,000 to be held in trust until your next birthday, 10 months from today (this example is based on Madden & Johnson, 2010). A discounting company has heard of your good fortune through another relative, and phones you offering $70,000 right now for the money being held in trust. If you accept the offer, you will have discounted your inheritance by more than 30%. That is, your inheritance has lost more than 30% of its value due to the 10-month delay. Now suppose that you only discount your inheritance by 20% or $80,000, and receive the offer of $70,000. Clearly, you will reject the offer, as $70,000 is less than $80,000. And if you discounted the offer by exactly 30% you would be hard pressed to make a decision, as the offer of $70,000 now is equivalent in value to the $100,000 in the future. Suppose that you accept the offer of $70,000, so that we know you have discounted your inheritance by more than 30%. We can use a procedure of gradually reducing the amount offered to find the point where you are indifferent to the choice between taking up the offer and waiting for your inheritance. If you are indifferent at $60,000, then your future inheritance is worth 60% of its full value, called its *present value*.

We can repeat this procedure to find the indifference points when $100,000 is delayed for different amounts of time (e.g., 0 to 40 months). Usually, we obtain 7 or 8 indifference points over the range of the delays. At each delay, the indifference point is plotted on a graph and a mathematical curve, called the **discounting curve**, is fitted to the points. Figure 9.13 shows the hypothetical discounting curve for your inheritance with delay in months on the x-axis and the discounted value on the y-axis. Your indifference point or present value for $100,000 at 10 months'

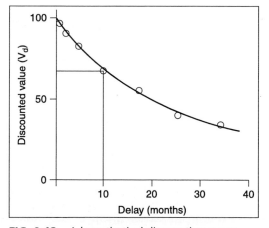

FIG. 9.13 A hypothetical discounting curve based on the inheritance of money problem described in the text. The x-axis shows delays in months and the y-axis is the discounted value (in thousands of dollars). The intersecting point on the curve is the indifference point or discounted value of $100,000 delayed 10 months and is $70,000. In a typical experiment, a number of indifference points are obtained for $100,000 at different delays (months), and a mathematical curve is fitted to the points.

delay is shown as $70,000. Six other indifference points (small circles) are also plotted. Notice that the present value drops quickly at first and then declines more slowly—the shape of the curve is *hyperbolic*.

Hyperbolic Discounting Equation

Considerable research in both human and nonhuman choice has supported a **hyperbolic discounting equation**, described by Mazur (1987).

$$V_d = \frac{A}{1 + kd} \qquad\qquad (9.4)$$

In Equation 9.4, we are predicting discounted values, V_d, of the reinforcer. The amount of the reinforcer, A, is $100,000 in our example, and the value d is the delay—the variable on the x-axis. The value k is called the *discounting rate*, which must be estimated to fit a curve to the indifference points (data) obtained from the experiment. The best-fitting curve is fitted to the data by a statistical technique called nonlinear regression (available from standard statistical programs such as Microsoft Excel).

To obtain the indifference points for pigeons, Mazur (1987) used an *adjusting delay procedure*. The pigeon chooses (pecks) between left and right colored (red and green) keys that provide a small food reward delivered after a fixed delay, or a larger food reward delivered after an adjusting delay. The experiment involves forced-choice and free-choice trials. On two forced-choice trials, the bird is forced to obtain the small reward with fixed delay on one trial and the large reward with adjusting delay on the other trial. The forced-choice trials are followed by two free-choice trials in which the bird is free to choose between the left and right colored keys. If the small reward of fixed delay is selected on both choice trials, the indifference point has not been obtained and the delay (in 1-s steps) to the larger reward is reduced on the next block of forced- and free-choice trials. On the other hand, if the bird chooses the larger, adjusting-delay reward on free-choice trials, the delay is increased in the next block of trials. Using this adjusting-delay procedure, it is possible to find the stable indifference point. The mean over several sessions of stability is used as the indifference point that is plotted on a graph. To obtain other indifference points, new fixed-delay values are set for the small reward, and the delay to the large food reward is again adjusted over trial blocks (see Madden & Johnson, 2010, for additional procedures to establish indifference points with nonhumans).

To establish delay discounting with humans, participants are often asked to choose between hypothetical amounts of money at given delays. In the original study by Howard Rachlin and his colleagues, participants were asked to choose between a hypothetical $1000 right now and $1000 after delays of 1 month to 50 years (Rachlin, Raineri, & Cross, 1991). At each delay value, the researchers used an *adjusting-amount procedure*, whereby the amount of money received immediately was adjusted relative to a fixed $1000 at a set delay ($990 now vs. $1000 in 1 month's time, adjusted in steps toward $1 now and $1000 in 1 month's time). At each delay, for half of the participants the amount of immediate reward was adjusted downward and then repeated with an ascending progression of values. The other participants received the ascending amounts first and then the descending progression. The indifference point was calculated as the average amount of the immediate reward, based on the value at which the participant switched to the immediate reward (downward progression) and no longer preferred the delayed reward (upward progression). Seven indifference points were calculated for the $1000 delayed for 1 month, 6 months, 1 year, 5 years, 10 years, 25 years, and 50 years. The hyperbolic equation (Equation 9.4) was calculated, and the indifference points were fitted as described previously (additional procedures with real rewards have confirmed the findings with hypothetical outcomes; see Madden & Johnson, 2010).

The equation provided a good fit to the data, and a better fit than an alternative equation suggested by economic theory (exponential discounting). That is, Mazur's hyperbolic equation provides a good description of how humans and other animals discount reinforcement value and the mechanisms involved. In contrast, evolutionary models (which are beyond the scope of this textbook) account for why organisms are short-sighted, often acting impulsively in the laboratory. Evolutionary models show that apparently irrational behavior (delay discounting) is a special case of decision rules that increased fitness in everyday ecological settings (see Fawcett, McNamara, & Houston, 2012).

Delay Discounting, Drug Abuse, and Gambling

Hyperbolic discounting has been extended to problems of impulsive behavior, especially behavior labeled as addictive (Madden & Bickel, 2010). The assumption is that people who abuse cigarettes, alcohol, and drugs are more impulsive than others and show steeper discounting of future outcomes, which in turn contributes to their addiction.

Using an adjusting-amount procedure, cigarette smokers (users of nicotine) were found to have higher discounting rates (k-values) for a hypothetical delayed reward ($1000) than non-smokers (Bickel, Odum, & Madden, 1999). This result also holds for people who abuse alcohol. Compared with light, social-drinking controls, both heavy drinkers and problem drinkers show higher discounting of the future rewards (Vuchinich & Simpson, 1999). The difference in discounting between light-drinking controls and problem drinkers was greater than that between controls and heavy drinkers, suggesting that both alcohol consumption and the consequences related to this consumption affect delay discounting.

Additional studies have investigated delay discounting in substance abusers. Heroin users discounted future money more than nondependent controls matched for age and gender (Madden, Petry, Badger, & Bickel, 1997). Heroin users also discounted future money ($1000) more than they did $1000 worth of heroin in the future. One possibility is that future money does not buy you heroin now, but future heroin ensures continued access to the drug (having a stash on hand). Cocaine users also show steeper discounting of delay rewards than appropriate controls, but no differences in discounting rate were observed between active cocaine users and those abstaining from cocaine use for at least a month (Heil, Johnson, Higgins, & Bickel, 2006). A history of cocaine use seems to be more related to impulsive behavior and discounting of reinforcement value than current use of the drug.

Research has also documented high delay discounting in compulsive gamblers, even in the absence of substance abuse. On a daily basis, compulsive gamblers face the choice between the maladaptive behavior (gambling) and the delayed benefits (financial and interpersonal) of alternative behavior. As with substance abusers, pathological gamblers discount the value of future rewards more steeply than matched controls. Also, moderately high discounting rates are linked to developing problem behavior with either drugs or gambling. Even higher discounting rates predict multiple problems involving both drugs and gambling (Petry & Madden, 2010).

One conclusion might be that substance abusers and gamblers share a general personality trait for impulsiveness. However, the relationship is inconsistent between measures of impulsivity and delay discounting (Odum & Baumann, 2010), although Odum (2011a, 2011b) has recently presented evidence for the influence of personality traits and genetic factors on discounting. A recent study of adolescent males with attention deficit hyperactivity disorder (ADHD) supported a link between impulsivity and discounting of hypothetical, but not real, rewards (Paloyelis, Asherson, Mehta, Faraone, & Kunts, 2010). However, other research on delayed and probabilistic rewards with gamblers argues against a general trait that includes an inability to delay gratification and a propensity for taking risks (Holt, Green, & Myerson, 2003). Evolutionary and neural factors do seem to play a role in delay-discounting situations, but further research is required to clarify this link (Stevens & Stephens, 2010; Winstanley, 2010). At the present time, the evidence suggests that impulsive behavior depends on the contingencies arranged at the moment of choice, as well as one's history of learning about immediate and delayed reinforcement.

Self-Control, Preference Reversal, and Commitment

Contingencies of immediate and delayed reinforcement are frequently involved in common problems of self-control. Students often face the choice of going out to party or staying at home and "hitting the books." Often, when given these options, students pick the immediate reward of partying with friends over the delayed benefits of studying, learning the subject matter, and achieving high grades. When a person (or other animal) selects the smaller, immediate payoff over the larger, delayed benefits, we may say that he or she shows **impulsive behavior**. On the other hand, a person who chooses the larger, delayed reward while rejecting the smaller, immediate payoff is said to show **self-control behavior**. In terms of a student's choice of whether to party or to study, choosing to party with friends is impulsive behavior, while choosing to stay at home and study is self-control behavior.

One of the interesting things about self-control situations is that our preferences change over time. That is, we may value studying over partying a week before the party, but value partying when the night of the party arrives. Based on a consideration of hyperbolic discounting, Howard Rachlin (1970, 1974) and George Ainslie (1975) independently suggested that such preference reversals could be analyzed as changes in reinforcement value with increasing delay. The **Ainslie–Rachlin principle** states that *reinforcement value decreases hyperbolically as the delay between making a choice and obtaining the reinforcer increases.*

As shown in Figure 9.14, the value of studying on the Friday night of the party (choice point) is lower than the value of having fun with friends (partying), because the payoffs for studying (learning and good grades) are delayed. At the end of the term, the value of studying is high, but it declines hyperbolically, ensuring that the value of studying is less than the value of partying on the Friday night (the choice point). Delayed discounting requires that, at the choice point, we usually behave impulsively, selecting the immediate, short-term payoff.

However, if we move back in time from the choice point to a week before the party, the value of studying relative to partying reverses. That is, adding delay to each reinforcement option before a choice is made reverses the value of the alternative reinforcers. More generally, at some time removed from making a choice, the value of the smaller, immediate reinforcer will be less than the value of the larger, delayed reward, indicating a **preference reversal**. When preference

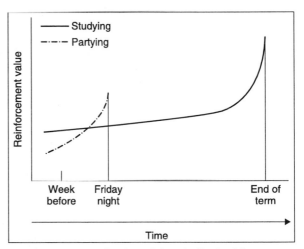

FIG. 9.14 An application of the Ainslie–Rachlin principle. The reinforcement value of studying (solid black curve) declines rapidly and then more gradually the further back in time the student is from the end of term. Notice that the value of studying is lower than the value of going to the party (dashed curve) on the night of the party. However, the value of going to the party declines below the value of studying a week before the party. That is, the student's preference reverses—she prefers to study.

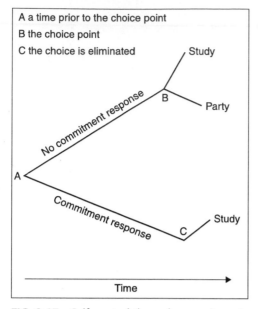

A a time prior to the choice point
B the choice point
C the choice is eliminated

FIG. 9.15 Self-control through commitment based on preference reversal, as required by the Ainslie–Rachlin principle (as in Figure 9.14). The student will make a commitment to study at point A (a week before the party) because the value of studying is higher than that of partying, but not at the choice point B (the night of the party). The commitment response removes going to the party as an option on the night of the party (C).

reversal occurs, people (and other animals) will make a commitment response to forgo the smaller, immediate reward and lock themselves into the larger, delayed payoff. Figure 9.15 shows the commitment procedure for eliminating the choice between studying and partying a week before the party. The **commitment response** is some behavior emitted at a time prior to the choice point that eliminates or reduces the probability of impulsive behavior. A student who has invited a classmate over to study on the Friday night of the party (commitment response) ensures that she will "hit the books" and give up the option of partying when the choice arrives.

Preference reversal and commitment occur over extended periods in humans, and involve many complexities (e.g. Green, Fry, and Myerson, 1994; Logue, Pena-Correal, Rodriguez, & Kabela, 1986). In animals, delays of reinforcement by a few seconds can change the value of the options, instill commitment, and ensure self-control over impulsiveness. As an example of preference reversal, consider an experiment by Green, Fisher, Perlow, and Sherman (1981) in which pigeons responded on two schedules of reinforcement, using a trials procedure. The birds were given numerous trials each day. On each trial a bird made its choice by pecking one of two keys. A single peck at the red key resulted in 2 s of access to grain, while a peck at the green key delivered 6 s of access to food. The intriguing aspect of the experiment involved adding a brief delay between a peck and the delivery of food. In one condition, there was a 2-s delay for the 2-s reinforcer (red key) and a 6-s delay for 6 s of access to food (green key). The data indicated that birds were impulsive, choosing the 2-s reinforcer on nearly every trial and losing about two-thirds of their potential access to food.

In another procedure, 18 additional seconds were added to the delays for each key, so that the delays were now 20 s for the 2-s reinforcer and 24 s for the 6 s of access to food. When the birds were required to choose this far in advance, they pecked the green key that delivered 6 s of access to food on more than 80% of the trials. In other words, the pigeons showed preference reversal and self-control when both reinforcers were further away.

Other research by Ainslie (1974) and Rachlin and Green (1972) shows that pigeons can learn to make a commitment response, thereby reducing the probability of impulsive behavior. Generally, animal research supports the Ainslie–Rachlin principle and its predictions. One implication is that changes in reinforcement value over extended periods also regulate self-control and impulsiveness in humans (see Ainslie, 2005; Rachlin, 2000; Rachlin & Laibson, 1997). In this way, behavior principles may help to explain the impulsive use of credit cards in our society, the fact that most people have trouble saving their money (self-control), and the world financial crisis of 2008 that involved short-term financial gains and the discounting of the long-term economic costs (Lewis, 2010).

ADVANCED SECTION: Quantification of Choice and Generalized Matching

The proportion equations (Equations 9.1, 9.2, and 9.3) describe the distribution of behavior when alternatives differ only in rate of reinforcement. However, in complex environments, other factors also contribute to choice and preference (see Poling, Edwards, Weeden, & Foster, 2011, for an account of different matching equations, empirical support, and a brief summary of applications).

Sources of Error in Matching Experiments

Suppose that a pigeon has been trained to peck a yellow key for food on a single VI schedule. This experience establishes the yellow key as a discriminative stimulus that controls pecking. In a subsequent experiment, the animal is presented with concurrent VI VI schedules of reinforcement. The left key is illuminated with a blue light and the right key with a yellow one. Both of the variable-interval schedules are programmed to deliver 30 reinforcers per hour. Although the programmed rates of reinforcement are the same, the bird is likely to distribute more of its behavior to the yellow key. In this case, stimulus control exerted by yellow is an additional variable that affects choice.

In this example, the yellow key is a known source of experimental **bias** that came from the bird's history of reinforcement. However, many unknown variables also affect choice in a concurrent-operant setting. These factors arise from the biology and environmental history of the organism. For example, sources of error may include different amounts of effort for the responses, qualitative differences in reinforcement (e.g., food versus water), a history of punishment, a tendency to respond to the right alternative rather than the left, and sensory capacities.

Matching of Ratios

To include these and other conditions within the matching law, it is useful to express the law in terms of ratios rather than proportions. A simple algebraic transformation of Equation 9.1 gives the matching law in terms of ratios:

1. Proportion equation: $B_a/(B_a + B_b) = R_a/(R_a + R_b)$.
2. Cross-multiplying: $B_a/(R_a + R_b) = R_a/(B_a + B_b)$.
3. Then: $(B_a \times R_a) + (B_a \times R_b) = (R_a \times B_a) + (R_a \times B_b)$.
4. Canceling: $B_a \times R_b = R_a \times B_b$.
5. Ratio equation: $B_a/B_b = R_a/R_b$.

In the ratio equation, B_a and B_b represent the rate of response or time spent on the A and B alternatives. The terms R_a and R_b express the rates of reinforcement. When relative rate of response matches relative rate of reinforcement, the ratio equation is simply a restatement of the proportional form of the matching law.

The Power Law

A generalized form of the ratio equation may, however, be used to handle the situation in which unknown factors influence the distribution of behavior. These factors produce systematic departures from ideal matching but may be represented as two constants (parameters) in the generalized matching equation, as suggested by Baum (1974b):

$$B_a/B_b = k(R_a/R_b)^a. \tag{9.5}$$

In this form, the matching equation is represented as a **power law** in which the coefficient k and the exponent a are values that represent two sources of error for a given experiment. When these parameters are equal to 1, Equation 9.5 is the simple ratio form of the matching law.

Bias

Baum suggested that variation in the value of k from 1 reflects preference caused by some factor that has not been identified. For example, consider a pigeon placed in a chamber in which two response keys are available. One of the keys has a small dark speck that is not known to the experimenter. Recall that pigeons have excellent visual acuity and a tendency to peck at stimuli that approximate a piece of grain. Given a choice between the two keys, a pigeon could show a systematic response *bias* for the key with a spot on it. In the generalized matching equation, the presence of such bias is indicated by a value of k different from 1. Generally, bias is some unknown asymmetry between the alternatives that affects preference over and above the relative rates of reinforcement.

Sensitivity

When the exponent a takes on a value other than 1, another source of error is present. A value of a greater than 1 indicates that changes in the response ratio (B_a/B_b) are larger than changes in the ratio of reinforcement (R_a/R_b). Baum (1974b) called this outcome **over-matching** because relative behavior increased faster than predicted from the relative rate of reinforcement. Although overmatching has been observed, it is not the most common result in behavioral-choice experiments. The typical outcome is that the exponent a takes on a value of less than 1 (Baum, 1979; Davison & McCarthy, 1988; Myers & Myers, 1977; Wearden & Burgess, 1982). This result is described as **undermatching**. Undermatching refers to a situation in which changes in the response ratio are less than changes in the reinforcement ratio.

One interpretation of undermatching is that changes in relative rates of reinforcement are not well discriminated by the organism (Baum, 1974b). Sensitivity to the operating schedules is adequate when the value of the a coefficient is close to 1. An organism may not detect subtle changes in the schedules, and its distribution of behavior lags behind the current distribution of reinforcement. This slower change in the distribution of behavior is reflected by a value of a less than 1. For example, if a pigeon is exposed to concurrent VI VI schedules without a COD procedure, then the likely outcome is that the bird will rapidly and repeatedly switch between alternatives. This rapid alternation usually results in the pigeon being less sensitive to changes in the reinforcement ratio, and under-matching is the outcome. However, a COD may be used to prevent the superstitious switching and increase sensitivity to the rates of reinforcement on the alternatives. The COD is therefore a procedure that reduces undermatching, and this is reflected by values of a close to 1.

Although problems of discrimination or sensitivity may account for deviations of a away from 1, some researchers believe that undermatching is so common that it should be regarded as an accurate description of choice and preference (Davison, 1981). If this position is correct, then matching is not the lawful process underlying choice. Most behavior analysts have not adopted this position, and view matching as a fundamental process. None-theless, the origin of undermatching remains a focus of debate and is not resolved at this time (Allen, 1981; Baum, 1979; Davison & Jenkins, 1985; Prelec, 1984; Wearden, 1983).

Estimating Bias and Sensitivity

Dr. William Baum (1974b) (Figure 9.16) formulated the **generalized matching law**, as shown in Equation 9.5. In the same article, he suggested that Equation 9.5 could be represented as a straight line when expressed in logarithmic form. In this form, it is relatively easy to portray and interpret deviations from matching (i.e., bias and sensitivity) on a line graph. Baum suggested that in linear form, the value of the slope of the line measured sensitivity to the reinforcement schedules, while the intercept reflected the amount of bias.

FIG. 9.16 William Baum. Reprinted with permission.

Algebra for a Straight Line

The algebraic equation for a straight line is:

$$Y = m + n(X)$$

In this equation, n is the slope and m is the intercept. The value of X (horizontal axis) is varied, and this changes the value of Y (vertical axis). Assume that X takes on values of 1 through 10, $m = 0$, and $n = 2$. When X is 1, the simple algebraic equation is $Y = 0 + 2 (1)$ or $Y = 2$. The equation can be solved for the other nine values of X and the (X, Y) pairs plotted on a graph. Figure 9.17 is a plot of the (X, Y) pairs over the range of the X values. The rate at which the line rises, or the slope of the line, is equal to the value of n and has a value of 2 in this example. The intercept m is zero in this case, and is the point at which the line crosses the Y-coordinate.

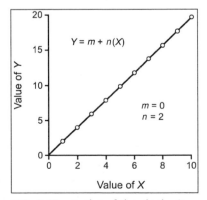

FIG. 9.17 A plot of the algebraic equation for a straight line. Slope is set at 2.0, and intercept at zero.

A Log-Linear Matching Equation

To write the matching law as a straight line, Baum suggested that Equation 9.5 be expressed in the logarithmic form of Equation 9.6:

$$\log(B_a/B_b) = \log k + [a \times \log(R_a/R_b)]. \qquad (9.6)$$

Notice that in this form, $\log(B_a/B_b)$ is the same as the Y value in the algebraic equation for a straight line. Similarly, $\log(R_a/R_b)$ is the same as the X value. The term a is the same as n and is the slope of the line. Finally, $\log k$ is the intercept, as is the term m in the algebraic equation.

The Case of Matching

Figure 9.18 shows the application of Equation 9.6 to idealized experimental data. The first and second columns give the number of reinforcers per hour delivered on the A and B alternatives. Notice that the rate of reinforcement on alternative B is held constant at 5 per hour, while the rate of reinforcement for alternative A is varied from 5 to 600 reinforcers per hour. The relative rate of reinforcement is shown in column 3, expressed as a ratio (i.e., R_a/R_b). For example, the first ratio for the data labeled "matching" is 5/5 = 1, and the other ratios may be obtained in a similar manner.

The fourth column is the logarithm of the ratio values. Logarithms are obtained from a calculator and are defined as the exponent of base 10 that yields the original number. For example, the number 2 is the logarithm of 100, since 10 raised to the second power is 100. Similarly, in Figure 9.18 the logarithm of the ratio 120 is 2.08, because 10 to the power of 2.08 equals the original 120 value.

Notice that logarithms are simply a transformation of scale of the original numbers. Such a transformation is suggested because logarithms of ratios plot as a straight line on X,Y coordinates, while the original ratios may not be linear. Actual experiments involve both positive and negative logarithms, since ratios may be less than 1. For simplicity, the constructed examples in Figure 9.18 only use values that yield positive logarithms.

Rft/h A	Rft/h B	(R_a/R_b)	X value log (R_a/R_b)	Slope (a)	Intercept (log k)	Y value log (Ba/Bb)
			MATCHING			
5	5	1	0.00	1.00	0.00	0.00
30	5	6	0.78	1.00	0.00	0.78
100	5	20	1.30	1.00	0.00	1.30
600	5	120	2.08	1.00	0.00	2.08
			UNDERMATCHING			
5	5	1	0.00	0.50	0.00	0.00
30	5	6	0.78	0.50	0.00	0.39
100	5	20	1.30	0.50	0.00	0.65
600	5	120	2.08	0.50	0.00	0.14
			BIAS			
5	5	1	0.00	1.00	1.50	1.50
30	5	6	0.78	1.00	1.50	2.28
100	5	20	1.30	1.00	1.50	2.80
600	5	120	2.08	1.00	1.50	3.58

FIG. 9.18   Application of log-linear matching equation (Equation 9.6) to idealized experimental data. Reinforcements per hour (Rft/h) for alternatives A and B, the ratio of the reinforcement rates (R_a/R_b), and the log ratio of the reinforcement rates (X values) are shown. The log ratios of the response rates (Y values) were obtained by setting the slope and intercept to values that produce matching, undermatching, or bias.

Columns 5 and 6 provide values for the slope and intercept for the log-ratio equation. When the relative rate of response is assumed to match (or equal) the relative rate of reinforcement, the slope (a) assumes a value of 1.00 and the value of the intercept ($\log k$) is zero. With slope and intercept so defined, the values of Y or $\log(B_a/B_b)$ may be obtained from the values of X or $\log(R_a/R_b)$, by solving Equation 9.5. For example, the first Y value of 0.00 for the final column is obtained by substituting the appropriate values into the log-ratio equation, $\log(B_a/B_b) = 0.00 + [1.00 \times (0.00)]$. The second value of Y is 0.78, or $\log(B_a/B_b) = 0.00 + [1.00 \times (0.78)]$, and so on.

Figure 9.19 (upper left) plots the "matching" data. The values of X or $\log(R_a/R_b)$ were set for this idealized experiment, and Y or $\log(B_a/B_b)$ values were obtained by solving Equation 9.5 when $a = 1$ and $\log k = 0$. Notice that the plot is a straight line that rises at 45°. The rate of rise in the line is equal to the value of the slope (i.e., $a = 1$). This value means that a unit change in X (i.e., from 0 to 1) results in an equivalent change in the value of Y. With the intercept ($\log k$) set at 0, the line passes through the origin ($X = 0$, $Y = 0$). The result is a matching line in which log ratio of responses equals log ratio of reinforcement.

Undermatching or Sensitivity

The data in Figure 9.18 labeled "undermatching" represent the same idealized experiment. The value of the intercept remains the same ($\log k = 0$). However, the slope now takes on a value less than 1 ($a = 0.5$). Based on Equation 9.6, this change in slope results in

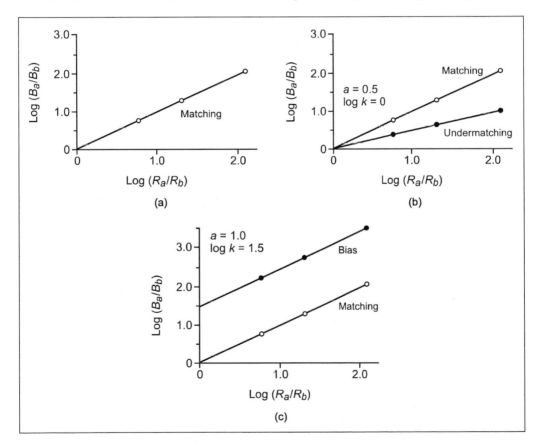

FIG. 9.19 (a) An X–Y plot of the data for "Matching" from Figure 9.18. The value of the slope is set at 1 ($a = 1$), and the intercept is set at zero ($\log k = 0$). The matching line means that a unit increase in relative rate of reinforcement [$\log(R_a/R_b)$] produces a unit increase in relative rate of response [$\log(B_a/B_b)$]. (b) An X–Y plot of the data for "Undermatching" from Figure 9.18. The value of the slope is set at less than 1 ($a = 0.5$), and the intercept is set at zero ($\log k = 0$). Undermatching with a slope of 0.5 means that a unit increase in relative rate of reinforcement [$\log(R_a/R_b)$] produces a half-unit increase in relative rate of response [$\log(B_a/B_b)$]. (c) An X–Y plot of the data for "Bias" from Figure 9.18. The value of the slope is set at 1 ($a = 1$), and the intercept is more than zero ($\log k = 1.5$). A bias of this amount indicates that the new plotted data on X–Y coordinates are deflected 1.5 units from the matching line.

new values of Y or $\log(B_a/B_b)$. Figure 9.19 (upper right) is a graph of the line resulting from the change in slope. When compared with the matching line ($a = 1$), the new line rises at a slower rate ($a = 0.5$). This situation is known as undermatching, and implies that the subject gives less relative behavior to alternative A [$\log(B_a/B_b)$] than expected on the basis of relative rate of reinforcement [$\log(R_a/R_b)$]. For example, if log-ratio reinforcement changes from 0 to 1, the log ratio of behavior will change only from 0 to 0.5. This suggests poor discrimination by the subject of the operating schedules of reinforcement (low sensitivity).

Response Bias

It is also possible to have a systematic bias for one of the alternatives. For example, a right-handed person may prefer to press a key on the right side more than to the left. This tendency to respond to the right side may occur even though both keys schedule equal rates of reinforcement. Recall that response bias refers to any systematic preference for one alternative that is not explained by the relative rates of reinforcement. In terms of the idealized experiment, the data labeled "bias" in Figure 9.18 show that the slope of the line is 1 (matching), but the intercept ($\log k$) now assumes a value of 1.5 rather than zero. A plot of the X or $\log(R_a/R_b)$ and Y or $\log(B_a/B_b)$ values in Figure 9.19 (lower panel) reveals a line that is systematically deflected 1.5 units from the matching line.

Experiments and Log-Linear Estimates

Setting the Values of the Independent Variable

In actual experiments on choice and preference, the values of the slope and intercept are not known until the experiment is conducted. The experimenter sets the values of the independent variable, $\log(R_a/R_b)$, by programming different schedules of reinforcement on the alternatives. For example, one alternative may be VI 30 s and the other VI 60 s. The VI 30-s schedule is set to pay off at 120 reinforcers per hour, and the VI 60-s schedule is set to pay off at 60 reinforcers per hour. The relative rate of reinforcement is expressed as the ratio 120/60 = 2. To describe the results in terms of Equation 9.6, the reinforcement ratio, 2, is transformed to a logarithm, using a calculator with logarithmic functions. Experiments are designed to span a reasonable range of log-ratio reinforcement values. The minimum number of log-ratio reinforcement values is 3, but most experiments program more than three values of the independent variable.

Each experimental subject is exposed to different pairs of concurrent schedules of reinforcement. The subject is maintained on these schedules until rates of response are stable, according to preset criteria. At this point, relative rates of response are calculated (B_a/B_b) and transformed to logarithms. For example, a subject on a concurrent VI 30-s VI 60-s schedule may generate 1000 responses per hour on the VI 30-s alternative and 500 responses per hour on the VI 60-s schedule. Thus, the response ratio is 1000/500 = 2, or 2 to 1. The response ratio, 2, is transformed to a logarithm. For each value of $\log(R_a/R_b)$, the observed value of the dependent variable $\log(B_a/B_b)$ is plotted on X, Y coordinates.

To illustrate the application of Equation 9.6, consider an experiment by White and Davison (1973). In this experiment, several pigeons were exposed to 12 sets of concurrent schedules. Each pair of schedules programmed a different reinforcement ratio. The pigeons were maintained on the schedules until key pecking was stable from day to day. The data for pigeon 22 are plotted in Figure 9.20 A on logarithmic coordinates. Plotting the reinforcement and response ratios on logarithmic coordinates is the same as plotting the log ratios on ordinary graph paper. Notice that actual results are not as orderly as the data of the idealized experiment. This is because errors in measurement, inconsistencies of procedure, and random events operate to affect response ratios in actual experiments. The results appear to move upward to the right in a linear manner, but it is not possible to draw a simple line through the plot.

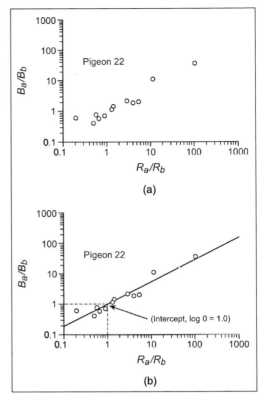

Estimates of Slope and Intercept

To find the line that best fits the results, a statistical technique (i.e., least-squares regression) is used to estimate values for the slope and intercept of Equation 9.6. The idea is to select slope and intercept values that minimize the errors in prediction. For a given value of the reinforcement ratio (x-axis), an error is the difference between the response-ratio value on the line (called the predicted value) and the actual or observed response ratio.

The mathematics that underlie this statistical technique are complicated and beyond the scope of this book. However, most personal computers have programs that will do the calculations for you. For example, you can use a program like Microsoft Excel with a PC to obtain the best-fitting line, using linear regression analysis. The estimate of slope was $a = 0.77$, indicating that pigeon 22 undermatched to the reinforcement ratios. The estimate of the intercept was zero (log $k = 0$), indicating that there was no response bias. With these estimates of slope and intercept,

FIG. 9.20 (a) Reinforcement and response ratios for pigeon 22 plotted on logarithmic coordinates. (b) The line of best fit for the data for pigeon 22. Taken from "Performance in concurrent fixed-interval schedules," by A. J. White and M. C. Davison, 1973, *Journal of the Experimental Analysis of Behavior, 19*, 147–153. © 1973 Society for the Experimental Analysis of Behavior, Inc. Republished with permission.

Equation 9.6 may be used to draw the best-fitting line.

In Figure 9.20B, the line of best fit has been drawn. You can obtain the line of best fit by substituting values for log(R_a/R_b) and finding the predicted log(B_a/B_b) values. You only need to find two points on the X, Y coordinates to draw the line. Notice that the data and best-fit line are plotted on a graph with logarithmic coordinates. Because there was no bias (log $k = 0$), the line must pass through the point $X = 1$, $Y = 1$ when R_a/R_b and B_a/B_b values are plotted on logarithmic paper.

As a final point, you may be interested in how well the matching equation fits the results of pigeon 22. One measure of accuracy is called explained variance. This measure varies between 0 and 1 in value. When the explained variance is 0, it is not possible to predict the response ratios from the reinforcement ratios. When the explained variance is 1, there is perfect prediction from the reinforcement ratios to the response ratios. In this instance, the explained variance is 0.92, indicating 92% accuracy. The **log-linear matching equation** is a good description of the pigeon's behavior on concurrent schedules of reinforcement.

NEW DIRECTIONS: Behavioral Neuroscience, Matching, and Sensitivity

The generalized matching law can be used to study neural events and processes using pharmacological interventions. A recent study by Bratcher, Farmer-Dougan, Dougan, Heidenreich, and Garris (2005) applied the generalized matching equation (Equation 9.5) to investigate how the brain is involved in the regulation of behavior by relative rates of reinforcement. The point was to detect the effects of specific drugs on choice behavior using the estimates of the slope *a* value (sensitivity) of the matching equation.

Dopamine, which is a neurotransmitter in the brain, is known to be a behavioral activator, and different dopamine receptors, D1-like or D2-like, appear to be involved in the regulation of different aspects of behavior. Thus, drug activation of D2 receptors was predicted to induce focused search for food, increased behavior directed at lever pressing, and overmatching (or matching) to relative reinforcement with estimates of slope *a* taking a value greater than 1. In contrast, drug activation of D1 receptors was predicted to elicit non-specific food-related behavior, increased behavior away from lever pressing, and subsequent undermatching to relative reinforcement with estimates of *a* taking a value of less than 1.

In this study, rats were trained to press levers for food on concurrent VI VI schedules, and drug or control treatments (saline) were administered 20 min before sessions. When behavior had stabilized, response and reinforcement ratios were determined and the generalized matching law was fitted, providing estimates of *a* or sensitivity to relative reinforcement. The results showed that the sensitivity value was slightly higher than baseline with quinpirole (the D2-like agonist) and was substantially lower than baseline with SKF38393 (the D1-like agonist). That is, as predicted, SKF38393 produced considerable undermatching (poor control by relative rate of reinforcement).

Analysis of video recordings of the rats' behavior indicated that quinpirole (the D2-like agonist) increased chewing and sniffing of the lever and food cup—behaviors compatible with lever pressing. The D1-like agonist (SKF38393) increased grooming and sniffing at some distance away from the lever—behavior that was incompatible with lever pressing and the reinforcement contingencies. Bratcher and colleagues suggested that "sensitivity to reward may have been due to changes in the value of the scheduled and/or any unscheduled reinforcers. That is, other behaviors elicited by D1 or D2 drug exposure ... may have taken on greater reinforcement value than operant responding" (Bratcher et al., 2005, pp. 389–390). These alternative behaviors were either compatible or incompatible with lever pressing for food, leading to the observed differences in the estimates of the slope *a* value. The researchers concluded that further study of the dopamine receptors in the regulation of operant behavior is warranted, and the matching law provides a powerful analytical basis for research on brain and behavior relationships.

CHAPTER SUMMARY

Why do people and other animals choose to do the things that they do? Are they compelled by impulses or is their behavior random? Behavior analysts have proposed a model based on the assumption that consequences influence behavior choices. Richard Herrnstein and William Baum have worked out many of the details of a law that states that relative rates of response to alternatives or options will match the relative rate of reinforcement. The matching law is the outcome of an experimental analysis of concurrent choice performance. This chapter describes the methods by which researchers have investigated this process. It has been determined that we are always confronted with at least two alternatives (take it or leave it), and that the alternative we choose is determined by the probability of reinforcement provided by that choice. This law can be stated in the form of a mathematical equation, and manipulations based on that equation have provided valuable insights into many components of choice behavior. Use of the matching law has been shown to work best in the laboratory with concurrent variable-interval schedules of reinforcement, but it also applies with free-ranging wild pigeons and in human social situations. Other applications of the matching law have proved useful in areas such as behavioral economics, substance addiction, self-control, and preference reversal. The generality of the matching equation is remarkable, and it will continue to improve the quantification of the relationship between rates of response and rates of reinforcement.

KEY WORDS

Ainslie–Rachlin principle

Behavioral economics

Bias

Changeover delay (COD)

Changeover response

Choice

Commitment response

Concurrent schedules of reinforcement

Delay discounting

Demand curve

Discounting curve

Extraneous sources of reinforcement

Findley procedure

Generalized matching law

Hyperbolic discounting equation

Impulsive behavior

Log-linear matching equation

Matching law

Maximization

Melioration

Overmatching

Power law for matching

Preference

Preference for choice

Preference reversal

Quantitative law of effect

Relative rate of reinforcement

Relative rate of response

Self-control behavior

Substitutability

Two-key procedure

Undermatching

ON THE WEB

www.pigeon.psy.tufts.edu/eam/eam7.htm This module is designed to illustrate the patch problems of optimal foraging. Students can control the rate of reinforcement within a patch, and its depletion rate.

www.youtube.com/watch?v=VO6XEQIsCoM Take a look at the lecture by Barry Schwartz on freedom and choice, called the Paradox of Choice. Schwartz states that freedom is necessary to maximize personal welfare, and that the way to freedom is to expand individual choice. However, in pursuing freedom of choice we often find that the more choice we have the less we gain, in terms of happiness and satisfaction with life.

www.youtube.com/watch?v=xLEVTfFL7ls Warren Bickel, a leading researcher in behavioral economics, distinguishes between the impulsive and executive areas of the brain. Subsequently, he relates these areas to decisions about the future in drug addicts. The talk provides a description of behavioral treatments for addiction that help to reduce the impulsiveness of drug users, or that enhance their consideration of future outcomes.

BRIEF QUIZ

1. In terms of behavior, choice is concerned with:

    (a) the distribution of behavior among alternative sources of reinforcement
    (b) the decision-making capabilities of the organism
    (c) the information processing during decision making
    (d) the differential reinforcement of alternative behavior

2. Which of the following is used to investigate choice in the laboratory?

    (a) a Skinner box with a single manipulandum
    (b) two cumulative recorders that are running successively
    (c) concurrent schedules of reinforcement
    (d) both (a) and (b)

3. In order to prevent switching on concurrent schedules:

    (a) program an intermittent schedule of reinforcement
    (b) program a changeover delay
    (c) program a multiple schedule
    (d) program a DRO contingency

4. To investigate switching on concurrent schedules:

    (a) use a Findley procedure
    (b) use a single-response key that changes color with the schedule
    (c) use a changeover key
    (d) use all of the above

5. The experiment by Herrnstein (1961b) using a two-key concurrent VI VI schedule is described by:

    (a) the matching law for a single alternative
    (b) the quantitative law of effect

    (c) the proportional matching equation

    (d) the non-matching function for multiple alternatives

6.   The matching law has described the choice behavior of:

    (a) pigeons

    (b) wagtails

    (c) rats

    (d) all of the above

7.   When the response is continuous rather than discrete, use a matching equation for:

    (a) time spent on each alternative

    (b) rate of response on each alternative

    (c) several concurrent schedules of reinforcement

    (d) the single operant

8.   The equation for matching of ratios of rates of response to rates of reinforcement:

    (a) is stated in terms of a power law

    (b) includes a value for bias

    (c) includes a value for sensitivity

    (d) is characterized by all of the above

9.   In contrast to optimal foraging, Herrnstein (1982) proposed a process of:

    (a) maximization

    (b) melioration

    (c) multiple schedule inference

    (d) monotonic matching

10. Behavioral economics involves the use of:

    (a) economic principles to describe and analyze behavioral choice

    (b) economic factors to predict animal behavior in the marketplace

    (c) economic indicators when pigeons are trading goods and services

    (d) economic satisfaction due to reinforcement

Answers to Brief Quiz: 1, a (p. 255); 2, c (p. 256); 3, b (p. 259); 4, d (p. 260); 5, c (p. 261); 6, d (p. 263); 7, a (p. 264); 8, d (p. 282); 9, b (p. 269); 10, a (p. 273).

Conditioned Reinforcement

10

---

1. Learn about conditioned reinforcement and chain schedules of reinforcement.
2. Investigate backward chaining and how it may be used to improve your golf game.
3. Find out why we prefer to observe events linked to good news rather than those linked to bad news.
4. Learn about generalized conditioned reinforcement and the token economy.
5. Investigate the delay-reduction model of conditioned reinforcement.

Human behavior is often regulated by consequences whose effects depend on a history of conditioning. Praise, criticism, good grades, and money are often consequences that may strengthen or weaken behavior. Such events acquire these effects because of the different experiences that people have had throughout their lives. Some people have learned the value of what others say about their actions—others are indifferent to it. Henry Ford marketed and sold cars because of monetary reinforcement, status, and power, but Mother Teresa took care of the poor for other reasons. In these examples, the effectiveness of a behavioral consequence depends on a personal history of conditioning. A positive reinforcer may be defined as a stimulus or event, the delivery of which will increase or maintain the rate of the response upon which it is contingent. The critical component is the influence on response rate, not what exactly the stimulus or event is.

Conditioned reinforcement occurs when behavior is strengthened by events that have an effect because of a conditioning history. The important aspect of the history involves a correspondence between an arbitrary event and a currently effective reinforcer. Once the arbitrary event becomes able to increase the frequency of an operant, it is called a **conditioned reinforcer**. (It may also be called a secondary reinforcer, but conditioned reinforcer is the best term.) For example, the sound of the pellet feeder operating becomes a conditioned reinforcer for a rat that presses a lever because the sound has preceded the presentation of food. The immediate effect of lever pressing or key pecking is the sound of the feeder, not the consumption of food. Food is a biological or **unconditioned reinforcer** that accompanies the sound of the feeder. "Magazine training" is the procedure of deliberately and contiguously pairing the sound of food delivery with immediate access to the food. The point in this case is to be able to deliver an auditory reinforcer, the feeder sound, wherever the subject is or whenever you wish. One way to demonstrate the conditioned reinforcement effectiveness of the feeder sound is to arrange a contingency between a new response (e.g., pressing a spot on the wall) and the presentation of the sound, the new response method. If the operant rate increases, the process is conditioned reinforcement and the sound is a conditioned reinforcer.

In his book, *The Behavior of Organisms*, Skinner (1938) described a procedure that resulted in conditioned reinforcement. Rats were exposed to a clicking sound and were given food. Later the animals were not fed, but the click was used to train lever pressing. Lever pressing increased, although it only produced the clicking sound. Because the click was no longer accompanied by food, each occurrence of the sound was also an extinction trial. For this reason, the sound declined in reinforcing effectiveness, and lever pressing for clicks decreased at the same time.

It should occur to you that establishing a conditioned reinforcer (click → food) is similar to the development of a CS in respondent conditioning. A previously neutral stimulus is contiguously presented with a functioning reinforcer, and this stimulus becomes capable of maintaining behavior upon which it is contingent. Of course, as in respondent conditioning, presenting the CS without the occasional US leads to the absence of the CR as the CS loses its associative strength.

NOTE ON: Clicker Training

There is a major industry built around the use of conditioned reinforcement in training animals. Karen Pryor (1999; www.clickertraining.com) has exploited the fact that a click from a little hand-held clicker followed (usually) by a food treat can be used to strengthen behavior. Clicker training is like the old game of "hot and cold" where a person is searching for something and the only help given is in the form of telling the searcher whether she is "hot" (meaning close) or "cold" (meaning further away). Clicks are used as indications of "hot" and no clicks mean "cold" for such behavior shaping (Peterson, 2004). Clicker training has been adopted by many zoo animal keepers (e.g., Lukas, Marr, & Maple, 1998; Wilkes, 1994), and is highly effective in training companion animals of all species (e.g., dogs and horses).

Animals typically engage in long and complex sequences of behavior that are often far removed from unconditioned reinforcement. This is particularly true for humans. People get up in the morning, take buses to work, carry out their jobs, talk to other workers, and so on. These operants occur day after day and are maintained by conditioned reinforcement. Thus, conditioned reinforcement is a durable process, but the new-response method does not always reveal how this occurs. Because of this, behavioral researchers have turned to additional procedures that seek to clarify the long-lasting effects of conditioned reinforcement.

CHAIN SCHEDULES AND CONDITIONED REINFORCEMENT

One way to investigate conditioned reinforcement is to construct sequences of behavior in the laboratory. A **chain schedule of reinforcement** involves two or more simple **schedules** (CRF, FI, VI, FR, or VR), each of which is presented sequentially and is signaled by an arbitrary stimulus. Only the final or terminal link of the chain results in unconditioned reinforcement. Figure 10.1 shows the Mechner notation for a three-component chain schedule of reinforcement. The schedule is a chain VI FR FI, and each link (or component) of the chain is signaled by a red, blue, or green light. For example, in the presence of the red light, a pigeon must emit a key peck after an average of 1 min has elapsed (VI 60 s). When the peck occurs, the light changes from red to blue and the bird must then peck the key 50 times (FR 50) to produce the green light. In the presence of the green light, a single peck after 2 min (FI 120 s) produces food and the light changes back to red (i.e., the chain starts over).

When the pigeon pecks in the red component, the only consequence is that the light changes to blue. Once the blue condition is in effect, 50 responses turn on the green light. If the bird pecks for the blue and green lights, the change in color is reinforcement. Recall that any stimulus that strengthens behavior is by definition a reinforcing stimulus. Thus, these lights have multiple functions. They are S^Ds that set the occasion for pecking the key in each link and also conditioned reinforcement, S^r(cond), for behavior that produces them. The notation in Figure 10.1 indicates that the red light is only a discriminative stimulus. You might suspect that it is a conditioned reinforcer, and it may have this function. However, the chain procedure as outlined does not require a separate response to produce the red light (the last response in the chain produces food, and afterwards the red light automatically comes on), and for this reason a conditioned reinforcing function is not demonstrated.

FIG. 10.1   Mechner notation for a three-component chain schedule of reinforcement, VI 60 s FR 50 FI 120 s. Notice that the red light only has a discriminative stimulus function, while the blue and green lights have multiple functions, including S^D and $S^{r(cond)}$.

Multiple-Stimulus Functions

Consider a sequence of two schedules, FR 50 FI 120-s, in which the components are not signaled. Formally, this is called a **tandem schedule**. A tandem is a schedule of reinforcement in which unconditioned reinforcement is programmed after completing two or more schedules, presented sequentially *without discriminative stimuli*. In other words, a tandem schedule as shown in Figure 10.2 is the same as an unsignaled chain.

FIG. 10.2   A tandem schedule of reinforcement is the same as an unsignaled chain.

Gollub (1958) compared the behavior of pigeons on similar tandem and chain schedules of reinforcement. On a tandem FI 60-s FI 60-s schedule, performance resembled the pattern observed on a simple FI 120-s schedule. The birds produced the typical scallop pattern observed on fixed-interval schedules—pausing after the presentation of food, and accelerating in response rate to the moment of reinforcement. When the tandem schedule was changed to a chain FI 60-s FI 60-s schedule by adding distinctive stimuli to the links, the effect of conditioned reinforcement was apparent. After some experience on the chain schedule, the birds responded faster in the initial link than they had on the tandem. In effect, the birds produced two FI scallops rather than one during the 120 s. This change in behavior may be attributed to the discriminative stimulus in the final link that also reinforced responses in the first component. In other words, the discriminative stimulus signaling the terminal link is also a conditioned reinforcer for responses in the first component of the chain (see also Ferster & Skinner, 1957).

Homogeneous and Heterogeneous Chains

Operant chains are classified as **homogeneous chains** when the topography or form of response is similar in each component. For example, in the chain schedule discussed earlier, the bird pecks the same key in each link. Because a similar response occurs in each component, this is a homogeneous chain. In contrast, a **heterogeneous chain** requires different responses for each link. Dog trainers make use of heterogeneous chains when they teach complex behavioral sequences to their animals. When going for a walk, a seeing-eye dog stops at intersections, moves forward when the traffic is clear, pauses at a curb, avoids potholes, and finds the way home. Each of these different responses is occasioned by specific stimuli and results in conditioned reinforcement. Although heterogeneous chains are common in everyday life and are created easily in the laboratory, they are usually too complex for experimental analysis. For this reason, conditioned reinforcement is typically investigated with homogeneous chains.

Chain schedules show how sequences of behavior are maintained by conditioned reinforcement in everyday life. Conditioned reinforcers in chains remain effective because the terminal link continues to schedule unconditioned reinforcement. Viewed as a heterogeneous chain schedule, going to a restaurant may involve the following links. A person calls and makes a reservation, gets dressed for the occasion, drives to the restaurant, parks their car, enters and is seated, orders dinner, and eats the meal. In this example, the S^Ds are the completion of the response requirements for each link. That is, being dressed for dinner (S^D) sets the occasion for going to the car and driving to the restaurant. Conditioned reinforcement involves the opportunity to engage in the next activity—bringing you closer to unconditioned reinforcement.

Of course, each of these components may be subdivided into finer and finer links in the chained performance. For example, dressing for dinner is comprised of many different responses with identifiable discriminative stimuli (e.g., putting on shoes sets the occasion for tying laces). Even tying shoelaces may be separated into finer and finer links of a heterogeneous chain. The degree of detail in describing a chain performance depends on the analytical problem. An analysis of going out for dinner does not require details about how a person ties their shoes. On the other hand, a behavior analyst teaching a retarded child to dress may focus on fine details of the chained performance.

 # FOCUS ON: Backward Chaining

Imagine that you have just been hired as a behavioral technician at a group home for retarded children. One of your first assignments is to use the principle of conditioned reinforcement to teach a child to make his bed. The child is profoundly retarded and cannot easily follow instructions or examples. He does have good motor coordination and is reinforced by potato chips. You and the child are in one of the bedrooms, with sheets, blankets, and pillowcases stacked on the bed. You have decided to use potato chips as a reinforcer for bed making.

Many people would start at the beginning of the sequence by unfolding a sheet, shaking it out, and placing it over the mattress. This tactic works for students (or children) who are easily able to follow instructions. However, this is not the case for this child, and the initial links of the chain are far removed from unconditioned reinforcement. Also, there are no conditioned reinforcers established along the way for completing the components.

The alternative way of teaching the child is to use a technique called **backward chaining**. The idea is to begin training at the end of the sequence. That is, you first teach the behavior in the final link of the chain. The child is reinforced with chips when he places the top of the bedspread over the pillow. Once this behavior is well established, the bedspread is pulled down further. Unconditioned reinforcement now occurs when the child pulls the covers up to the pillow and then finishes making the bed. In this manner, responses that are more and more remote from the final performance are maintained by conditioned reinforcement (engaging in the next sequence). Of course, you eventually pair chips with social approval (i.e., "Your bed looks great!") and maintain the behavior without direct unconditioned reinforcement.

In everyday life, backward chaining has been used to train athletic skills. O'Brien and Simek (1983) taught golf using principles of backward chaining (see Figure 10.3). In their article they state:

The teaching of sports has been largely unaffected by the advances in learning other operants. Golf, for example, is still routinely taught by handing the novice a driver and instructing him verbally how to get his body, arms and head to combine to hit a 250 yard drive. The usual result of such instruction is a series of swings that end in wiffs, tops and divots. This is followed by more verbal explanations, some highly complex modeling, and loosely administered feedback. Endless repetitions of this chain then follow.

A behavioral analysis of golf would suggest that the reinforcer for this exercise is putting the ball in the hole. The trip from tee to green represents a complex response chain in which the swing of the club up over the head and back to hit the ball is shortened as one gets closer to the hole. The final shot may be a putt of six inches or less leading to the reinforcement of seeing the ball disappear into the ground. This putt requires a backswing of only a few inches but involves the same basic stroke as the long backswinged shot from the tee. Since the short putt seems to be the simplest response and the one closest to reinforcement, it would seem appropriate to teach the golf chain by starting with the putt and working back to the drive.

(pp. 175–176)

The superiority of the backward-chaining method in athletics or other areas of learning results from the principle of conditioned reinforcement. Behavior that is closest to unconditioned reinforcement is taught first. By doing this, the instructor ensures that operants in the sequence are maintained by effective consequences. With the backward-chaining method, each step in the chain may be added as the previous link is mastered.

Step 1: Putt from lip of cup

Step 2: Move back from lip of cup to putt

Step 3: Increase distance from cup to putt

FIG. 10.3   Backward chaining in golf, beginning with putting into the cup (final performance). The first step is to simply tap the ball at the lip of the cup into the hole. Once this occurs consistently, the ball is moved back from the lip and the golfer putts (making a small swing of the club) the ball into the cup. After this performance is well established, more distance is added and the golfer must putt to the cup with more force. Once beyond the putting green, the golfer changes to other clubs appropriate to the distance, and the amplitude of the swing is systematically increased. The "tee shot" begins the chain and uses a club called a driver to provide the most distance and loft toward the putting green and cup.

CONDITIONED REINFORCEMENT: DETERMINANTS AND ANALYSIS

Operant chains show how complex sequences of behavior can be maintained by events that have acquired a reinforcement function based on the past experience of an organism. The task for experimental analysis is to identify the critical conditions that contribute to the strength of conditioned reinforcement. It is also important to specify the factors that determine the reinforcing effectiveness of conditioned stimuli.

Strength of Conditioned Reinforcement

Frequency of Unconditioned Reinforcement

The effectiveness of a conditioned reinforcer depends on the frequency of unconditioned reinforcement correlated with it. Autor (1960) found that preference for a conditioned reinforcer increased with the frequency of unconditioned reinforcement in its presence. The power or effectiveness of a conditioned reinforcer increases with more and more presentations of unconditioned reinforcement, but eventually levels off. As the frequency of unconditioned reinforcement goes up, the strength of a conditioned reinforcer reaches a maximum value. This relationship is strikingly similar to the increase in associative strength of a CS as described by the Rescorla–Wagner model of classical conditioning (see Chapter 3).

Variability of Unconditioned Reinforcement

Variability of unconditioned reinforcement also affects the strength of a conditioned reinforcer. Fantino (1967) showed that birds preferred a conditioned reinforcer that was correlated with an alternating schedule (FR 1 half of the time and FR 99 for the other half of the trials) to one that was associated with a fixed schedule with the same rate of payoff (FR 50). Thus, variability of unconditioned reinforcement increases the value of a conditioned reinforcer (see also Davison, 1969, 1972; Fantino, 1965; Herrnstein, 1964a). Variable schedules increase the effectiveness of conditioned reinforcement because these schedules occasionally program short intervals to unconditioned reinforcement. Compared with fixed schedules, these short intervals enhance responding and the value of stimuli correlated with this behavior (Herrnstein, 1964b).

Establishing Operations

The effectiveness of a conditioned reinforcer is enhanced by events that establish unconditioned reinforcement. A bird will respond for a light correlated with food more when it is hungry than when it is well fed. People attend to signs for washrooms, restaurants, or hospitals when their bladders are full, when they have not eaten for some time, or when they are sick. Generally, conditioned reinforcement depends on stimuli that establish unconditioned reinforcement (Michael, 1982a, see Chapter 2 on motivational operations).

Delay to Unconditioned Reinforcement

On a chain schedule, the longer the delay between a discriminative stimulus and unconditioned reinforcement, the less effective it is as a conditioned reinforcer. Gollub (1958) compared the performance of pigeons on three different schedules—FI 5 min, chain FI 1 FI 1 FI 1 FI 1 FI 1 min, and tandem FI 1 FI 1 FI 1 FI 1 FI 1 min. On the simple FI 5-min schedule a blue key light was on throughout the interval. On the chain, a different key color was associated with each of the five links. The components of the tandem schedule were not signaled by separate colored lights, but a blue key light was on throughout the links. Birds responded to the tandem as they did to the simple FI—producing the typical FI scallop. On the extended-chain schedule, responding was disrupted in the early components, and some of the birds stopped responding after prolonged exposure to the schedule (see also Fantino, 1969b). Disruption of responding occurs because the S^Ds in the early links (furthest from unconditioned reinforcement) signal a long time to unconditioned reinforcement and are therefore weak conditioned reinforcers. A similar effect occurs when people give up when faced with a long and complex task. Students who drop out of school may do so because the signs of progress are weak conditioned reinforcers—far removed from a diploma or degree.

Experimental Analysis of Conditioned Reinforcement

Many experiments have used extinction procedures to investigate conditioned reinforcement. A conspicuous stimulus such as the sound of a feeder is presented just before the delivery of food. To demonstrate conditioned reinforcement, the feeder sound is subsequently used to condition a new response (e.g., pressing a spot on the wall) while food is withheld—the **new-response method**. If the operant rate increases, the process is conditioned reinforcement and the sound is a conditioned reinforcer. The new-response method often results in short-lived effects. Because of respondent extinction (the sound without the food), the conditioned reinforcer quickly loses its effectiveness, maintaining few responses (see Kelleher & Gollub, 1962; Miller, 1951; Myers, 1958; Wike, 1966). On the other hand, Skinner (1938, p. 82 and his Figure 13) reported that "considerable conditioning can be effected before a state of more or less complete extinction is reached." This conclusion is in accord with Alferink, Crossman, and Cheney (1973), who found that trained pigeons continued to peck on an FR 300 schedule of hopper light presentation even with the hopper propped up so that food was always available.

Another extinction technique is called the **established-response method**. An operant that produces unconditioned reinforcement is accompanied by a distinctive stimulus, just prior to reinforcement. When responding is well established, extinction is implemented but half of the subjects continue to receive the stimulus that accompanied unconditioned reinforcement. The other subjects undergo extinction without the distinctive stimulus. Generally, subjects with the stimulus present respond more than the subjects who do not receive the stimulus associated with unconditioned reinforcement. This result is interpreted as evidence for the effects of conditioned reinforcement.

Both extinction methods for analyzing conditioned reinforcement involve the presentation of a stimulus closely followed by unconditioned reinforcement. This procedure is similar to the CS–US pairings used in respondent conditioning. One interpretation, therefore, is that conditioned reinforcement is based on classical conditioning. This interpretation is called the stimulus–stimulus or **S–S account of conditioned reinforcement**. That is, all CSs are also conditioned reinforcers. To provide a test of the S–S account, behavior analysts devised new ways to show sustained responding on schedules of reinforcement for brief stimulus presentations where the brief stimulus is intermittently paired with food.

A Brief Stimulus Procedure Using Second-Order Schedules

We have seen that a brief stimulus such as the clicking sound of a feeder, or the presentation of a hopper light, eventually comes to support operant behavior (pecking), indicating a conditioned reinforcement function. However, the extinction methods (new-response and established-response) do not show sustained responding for a brief stimulus only occasionally followed by food (unconditioned reinforcer). To remedy this problem, behavior analysts designed second-order schedules of brief stimulus presentations that ensured infrequent pairing of the brief stimulus with food, or unconditioned reinforcement. A **second-order schedule** involves two (or more) schedules of reinforcement in which completion of the requirements of one schedule is reinforced according to the requirements of a second schedule (see Wing & Shoaib, 2010, for an account of the use of this schedule in behavioral neuroscience).

Kelleher (1966) arranged a second-order schedule of brief stimulus presentations and infrequent delivery of food reinforcement and compared it with an identical second-order schedule (tandem) in which food never accompanied the brief stimulus. In the central experiment, pigeons responded on a second-order FR 15(FI4-min:W) schedule where a peck after 4 min produced a flash (0.7 s) of white light (W) on the response key for each FI 4-min component, and the birds had to complete 15 components for food reinforcement (FR15). On the 15th repetition of the FI component, the first response after 4 min produced the flash of light (W) followed immediately by presentation of the food hopper. The second-order schedule tested whether the flash of light (W) would sustain FI-component responding even though the minimum time between pairings of light with food was 1 h (S-paired condition). Comparison conditions scheduled brief (0.7 s) dark (D) key, or red key light (R) stimulus changes following each of 14 FI 4-min components; on the 15th repetition, the first response after 4 min produced food reinforcement without any presentation of the brief stimulus (S-unpaired conditions). In the S-paired condition, birds showed positively accelerated responding for the flash of white light (W) on the FI 4-min components, similar to scalloping on conventional FI schedules of food reinforcement. Omitting the white light (W) eliminated the scalloping pattern in the FI 4-min components (see Figure 10.4). Response rates increase over the fixed interval for the brief stimulus (W) paired with food, but not for the brief stimulus (D) unpaired with food. This finding indicates that the brief stimulus paired intermittently with food maintained operant behavior, functioning as a conditioned reinforcer. A complication of the findings is that response rates increased over the interval for the red light stimulus (R) that also was unpaired with food. Kelleher explained this observation by noting that the birds had extensive histories on various schedules of reinforcement that involved colored keys as discriminative stimuli. Thus, a brief stimulus paired with food functioned as conditioned reinforcement for response patterning on a schedule of reinforcement, but so did a brief stimulus with a previously established S^D function. The latter finding offers support for the **discriminative-stimulus account of conditioned reinforcement**, which states that an S^D also acquires value as a conditioned reinforcer and does not depend on being a CS associated with food.

There have been many experiments that have attempted to distinguish between the S^D and S–S accounts of

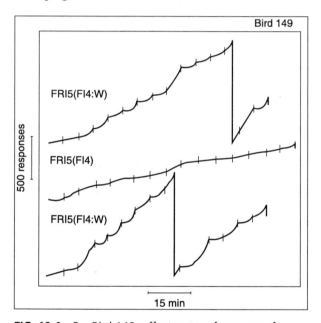

FIG. 10.4   For Bird 149, effects on performance of presenting the white light (W) on the FR15(FI4:W) second-order schedule, removing the white light on the FR15(FI4) tandem schedule, and reinstating it once again, FR15(FI4:W). Notice the elimination of scalloping in each FI4 component and the reduction of response rate when the light is removed, indicating the conditioned reinforcement efficacy of the white light. The short strokes for the FR15(FI4:W) schedule indicate 0.7-s presentations of white light. For the FR15(FI4) schedule there was no stimulus change and the short strokes indicate the end of each FI4 component. From R. T. Kelleher, 1966, "Conditioned reinforcement in second-order schedules," *Journal of the Experimental Analysis of Behavior, 9,* 475–485. © 1966 Society for the Experimental Analysis of Behavior. Republished with permission.

conditioned reinforcement (Fantino, 1977, 2008; Gollub, 1977; Hendry, 1969). For example, Schoenfeld, Antonitis, and Bersh (1950) presented a light for 1 s as an animal ate food. This procedure paired food and light, but the light could not be a discriminative stimulus, as it did not precede the food delivery. Following this training, the animals were placed on extinction and there was no effect of conditioned reinforcement. Given this finding, it seems reasonable to conclude that a stimulus must be discriminative to become a conditioned reinforcer. However, current research shows that *simultaneous pairing* of CS and US results in weak conditioning (see Chapter 3). For this and other reasons, it has not yet been possible to definitively test the S^D and S–S accounts of conditioned reinforcement.

On a practical level, distinguishing between these accounts of conditioned reinforcement makes little difference. In most situations, procedures that establish a stimulus as an S^D also result in that stimulus becoming a conditioned reinforcer. Similarly, when a stimulus is conditioned as a CS it almost always has an operant reinforcement function. In both cases, contemporary research (Fantino, 1977, 2008) suggests that the critical factor for conditioned reinforcement value is the temporal delay between the onset of the stimulus and the later presentation of unconditioned reinforcement.

NEW DIRECTIONS: Neuroscience and Conditioned Reinforcement

One major issue of behavioral neuroscience has been locating where in the nervous system response consequences are "evaluated" or assigned a hedonic value. That is, how does an event or stimulus such as money take on value and become a strong reinforcer? We know that conditioned reinforcers maintain behavior over long periods of time, and often in the absence of unconditioned reinforcers. These conditioned consequences also play a central role in complex social behavior.

Several brain areas (pain/pleasure centers) are known to code for hedonic value of stimuli (Olds & Milner, 1954), and continuing research has refined the brain circuits involved. Thus, for example, Parkinson, Crofts, McGuigan, Tomic, Everitt, and Roberts (2001) reported that the amygdala is critical for the conditioned reinforcement process in primates. They made lesions to the amygdala of marmosets and subsequently observed behavioral insensitivity to the absence of conditioned reinforcement for pressing a touch-screen panel. In contrast, responding for unconditioned reinforcement was not disrupted. Control subjects with an intact amygdala nearly ceased responding when conditioned reinforcement stopped, showing sensitivity to the contingencies. An intact and functioning amygdala seems to be necessary for the control of behavior by conditioned reinforcement.

The neurons of the basolateral (BL) amygdala are particularly important for encoding the value of a conditioned reinforcer (Baxter & Murray, 2002). Using second-order schedules, marmoset monkeys learned to respond on a computer screen for a tone and access to a banana milkshake (Roberts, Reekie, & Braesicke, 2007). Monkeys showed impairment of performance when given lesions to the BL amygdala. As the response requirements for access to the milkshake increased, and the frequency of the pairings between the tone (conditioned reinforcer) and the milkshake (unconditioned reinforcer) decreased, the lesioned monkeys became progressively more unable to maintain responding for contingent presentations of the tone. However, control monkeys without lesions continued to respond for presentations of the tone as pairings decreased. When the tone was omitted, lesioned monkeys showed insensitivity to the reinforcer efficacy—maintaining performance in the absence of the tone. Control monkeys, without impairment to the BL amygdala, were sensitive to the omission procedure and showed a marked decline in performance. The general finding is that an intact BL amygdala is required for sensitivity to contingencies of conditioned reinforcement (see also Ciano, 2008, for an account of drug seeking on second-order schedules, showing the role of the dopamine D_3 receptors in the BL amygdala).

Other recent evidence suggests that both aversive and rewarding stimuli, conditioned or unconditioned, affect similar brain areas. These areas include the orbitofrontal cortex, the prefrontal cortex, and the nucleus accumbens (Roberts et al., 2007; Ventura, Morrone, & Puglisi-Allegra, 2007). The nucleus accumbens septi (which is near the medial extension of the head of the caudate nucleus) is known to release dopamine in response to salient conditioned stimuli regardless of their hedonic valence (positive or aversive). Nucleus accumbens dopamine depletion slows the rate of operant responding and speeds the rate of acquisition by reducing the effectiveness of the reinforcer, not by impairing motor behavior (Salamone, Correa, Mingote, & Weber, 2003). And in-vivo microdialysis procedures have shown that high levels of dopamine from the nucleus accumbens are present in rats that learn response–outcome relationships, but not in rats that fail to learn these relationships (Cheng & Feenstra, 2006). Clearly, the nucleus accumbens and dopamine are involved in establishing and maintaining control of behavior by contingencies of reinforcement.

Behavioral neuroscience is providing a circuitry map for what goes on inside the brain when overt conditioning and learning are taking place. The interesting issue is how conditioning with arbitrary stimuli is supported by neural activity. Objects or events that were originally neutral can quickly become very attractive and valuable when specific brain activity occurs during conditioning. What is going on in the brain when this happens? Researchers are making progress in synthesizing how the brain and the environment work together—providing a more complete understanding of behavior and its regulation.

INFORMATION AND CONDITIONED REINFORCEMENT

Stimuli that provide information about unconditioned reinforcement may also become effective conditioned reinforcers. Egger and Miller (1962) used the extinction method to test for conditioned reinforcement. They conditioned rats by pairing two different stimuli (S_1 and S_2) with food. Figure 10.5 describes the procedures and major results. In their experiment (panel A), S_1 came on and S_2 was presented 0.5 s later. Both stimuli were turned off when the animals were given food. Both S_1 and S_2 were paired with food, but only S_1 became an effective conditioned reinforcer. In another condition (panel B), S_1 and S_2 were presented as before, but S_1 was occasionally presented alone. Food was never given when S_1 occurred by itself. Under these conditions, S_2 became a conditioned reinforcer.

To understand this experiment, consider the informativeness of S_2 in each situation. When S_1 and S_2 are equally correlated with food, but S_2 always follows S_1, then S_2 is *redundant*, providing no additional information about the occurrence of food. Because it is redundant, S_2 gains little conditioned reinforcement value. In the second situation, S_1 only predicts food in the presence of S_2, and for this reason S_2 is informative and becomes a conditioned reinforcer. These results, along with later experiments (e.g., Egger & Miller, 1963), suggest that a stimulus will become a conditioned reinforcer if it provides information about the occurrence of unconditioned reinforcement.

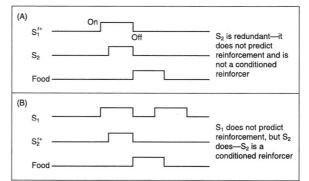

FIG. 10.5   Procedures and major results of an experiment using the extinction method to test for conditioned reinforcement. Based on a description of procedures as outlined in "Secondary reinforcement in rats as a function of information value and reliability of the stimulus," by M. D. Egger and N. E. Miller, 1962, *Journal of Experimental Psychology, 64*, 97–104.

Informativeness: Good News and Bad News

The informativeness of a stimulus should not depend on whether it is correlated with positive or negative events, because common sense would seem to tell us that bad news is just as informative as good news. Wyckoff (1952, 1969) designed an observing-response procedure to evaluate the strength of a conditioned reinforcer that predicted good or bad news. In this procedure, periods of reinforcement and extinction alternate throughout a session, but the contingencies are not signaled by S^Ds or S^Δs. The contingency is called a **mixed schedule of reinforcement**. A mixed schedule is the same as a multiple schedule, but without discriminative stimuli. Once the animal is responding on the mixed schedule, an observing response is added to the contingencies.

The **observing response** is a topographically different operant that functions to produce an S^D or S^Δ depending on whether reinforcement or extinction is in effect. In other words, an observing response changes the mixed schedule to a multiple schedule. Figure 10.6 shows the relationships among mixed, multiple, tandem, and chain schedules of reinforcement.

Wyckoff (1969) showed that pigeons would stand on a pedal to observe red and green colors associated with FI 30-s reinforcement or EXT 30 s. Before the birds had an observing response available, they pecked equally in the reinforcement and extinction phases, showing failure to discriminate between the schedules. When the observing

FIG. 10.6   The relationships among mixed, multiple, tandem, and chain schedules of reinforcement. These four schedules depend on whether an S^D is present or absent and whether unconditioned reinforcement occurs in one or all of the components.

response was added, the pigeons showed a high rate of pecking in the reinforcement phase and very low rates during extinction. Because the observing response was maintained, the results suggest that stimuli correlated with either reinforcement or extinction (good or bad news) became conditioned reinforcers.

Although Wyckoff's data are consistent with an information view of conditioned reinforcement, it is noteworthy that his pigeons only spent about 50% of the time making the observing response. One possibility is that the birds were observing the stimulus correlated with reinforcement (red color) but not the stimulus that signaled extinction (green color). In other words, the birds may have only responded for good news.

In fact, subsequent experiments by Dinsmoor, Brown, and Lawrence (1972) and by Killeen, Wald, and Cheney (1980) supported the good-news interpretation of conditioned reinforcement. Dinsmoor et al. (1972) trained pigeons to peck a key on a VI 30-s schedule of food reinforcement that alternated with unpredictable periods of extinction. The birds could peck another key to turn on a green light correlated with reinforcement and a red light correlated with extinction. That is, if reinforcement was in effect, an observing response turned on the green light, and if extinction was occurring, the response turned on the red light.

Observing responses were maintained when they produced information about both reinforcement and extinction. In the next part of the experiment, observing responses only produced the green light signaling reinforcement, or the red light associated with extinction. In this case, observing responses produced either good or bad news, but not both. When observing responses resulted in the green light correlated with reinforcement, the birds pecked at a high rate. In contrast, the pigeons would not peck a key that only produced a stimulus (red) signaling extinction. Thus, good news functions as conditioned reinforcement, but bad news does not.

The good-news conclusion is also supported by research using aversive, rather than positive, consequences. Badia, Harsh, Coker, and Abbott (1976) exposed rats to electric shocks. The shocks were delivered on several variable-time schedules, independent of the rats' behavior. During training, a light was always on and a tone occurred just before each shock. In Experiment 2 of their study, the researchers allowed the animals to press a lever that turned on the light for 1 min. During this time, if shocks were scheduled, they were signaled by a tone. In one condition, the light was never accompanied by a tone and shocks. That is, when the light was on the animal was completely safe from shocks. Other conditions presented more and more tones and shocks when the animal turned on the light. In these conditions, the light predicted less and less safety, and responding for the light decreased. In other words, the animals responded for a stimulus correlated with a shock-free period, but not for information about shock given by the tone signals (see also DeFran, 1972; Dinsmoor, Flint, Smith, & Viemeister, 1969; Mueller & Dinsmoor, 1986). Once again, conditioned reinforcement is based on good news but not on bad news.

Information, Reinforcement, and Human Observing Behavior

Stimuli Linked to Bad News and No News

The information and conditioned reinforcement accounts of observing behavior have been studied in humans. In a series of experiments, Fantino and Case (1983) had human participants make observing responses, but did not require responding for reinforcement (points worth 10 cents each). Sometimes points on a counter were arranged on a VT 60-s schedule, with a point presented once per minute on average. At other times, no points were given (EXT). That is, points were arranged on a mixed VT 60-s EXT schedule with periods of response-independent reinforcement (VT 60-s points) and periods of no reinforcement (EXT). The periods of points and no points alternated unpredictably, but participants could find out which period was in effect by responding on either of two levers. For the critical condition, observing responses on one lever produced a colored light (S−) on a V I60-s schedule only if a no-point (EXT) period was in effect. The light S− provided information (bad news) but had no reinforcement value. Responses on the other lever resulted in a different colored light (S^U, uncorrelated stimulus) on a VI 60-s schedule when periods of points were scheduled (VT 60 s), but also when periods of no points were in effect (EXT). The S^U light provided no information about the schedules of points and no points. Essentially, the critical conditions of the study offered participants a choice between information about bad news and uninformative "no news." As shown in Figure 10.7 (Experiment 2), choice proportions by 4 of 6 participants strongly favored the uninformative "no news" stimulus (average = 0.81) option. Contrary to an information (uncertainty-reduction) account, no one preferred observing the S correlated with bad news. Across three experiments, 19 of 22 participants preferred (0.70 average) to observe the uninformative "no news" stimulus.

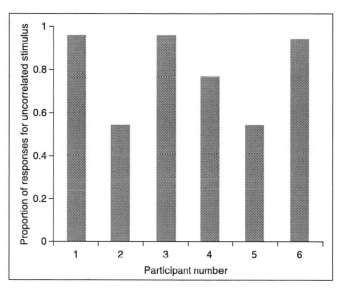

FIG. 10.7 Choice proportions for each of the six participants in Experiment 2 of Fantino and Case (1983). The data indicate that 4 of 6 participants strongly preferred to observe the uninformative no-news option compared with the informative bad-news alternative. The results are evidence that the information is not the critical factor for human observing. Based on data from E. Fantino and D. A. Case, 1983, "Human observing: Maintained by stimuli correlated with reinforcement but no extinction," *Journal of the Experimental Analysis of Behavior,* 18, 79–85.

Over a series of studies, a stimulus correlated with bad news (high information) did not maintain human observing, but one linked to "no news" (no information) did. Preference for the bad-news stimulus over the no-news stimulus occurred only when observing S− permitted more efficient responding for reinforcement—a finding that is inconsistent with the information hypothesis. That is, when observing information about bad news is linked to good news (reinforcement), people prefer to observe bad new information to uninformative "no news" (see Case, Fantino, & Wixted, 1985; Case & Fantino, 1989; Case, Ploog, & Fantino, 1990). Additionally, these studies consistently showed that a stimulus correlated with good news is highly preferred to one correlated with bad news, consistent with the findings of numerous animal experiments. Overall, the conditioned reinforcement view provided a systematic and consistent account of human observing behavior.

Preference for Bad News Over No News

In 1997, a series of experiments challenged the conditioned-reinforcement account of observing behavior, suggesting that humans actually prefer bad-news information (Lieberman, Cathro, Nichol, & Watson, 1997). In this study, participants could respond for a bad-news message or an uninformative no-news message while playing a lottery—pressing a button to have a computer (ERNIE) generate random numbers. After 50 button presses their best score would be saved by the computer and, after the study, the highest score of all the participants would win a monetary prize. To obtain information about how they were doing, participants could press either of two buttons. Each press (CRF) on one button produced a no-news, ambiguous message "ERNIE says you may win, but you may lose." Each press on the other button produced the no-news message most of the time, but sometimes the bad-news, informative message, which stated "A poor score. This one is not a winner." When each observing response was effective (CRF), participants preferred the bad-news option to the no-news alternative. A second experiment compared two groups of participants, one observing messages about periods of points and no points on CRF schedules, and another group observing messages about points on VI schedules, as in the experiment by Fantino and Case (1983). The results showed no preference for the no-news stimulus on the VI schedule, but a strong prefer-ence for the S−, bad-news message in the CRF group. A third experiment included a VI group that only had a few (30) observing responses to use, and the participants had to pay for additional observing responses (VI-cost condition). The group on the standard VI observing schedule was indifferent to the no-news and bad-news options, but the VI-cost group strongly preferred the bad-news information. Overall, the results provided consistent support for the **information account** of observing. People preferred the information about bad news to uninformative no-news.

Human Observing Maintained by Useful Information

Recently, Fantino and Silberberg (2010) acknowledged that a preference for bad-news information posed an apparent problem for the conditioned reinforcement account of human observing behavior. A series of five brief experiments investigated the role of good-news signals (S+), no-news stimuli (S^U), and signs of bad news (S−) for human observing behavior. Participants used a mouse to click response boxes on a computer screen to observe stimuli linked to earning occasional points worth a nickel. The points registered on the computer screen based on a mixed VT 30-s EXT schedule. In Experiment 1, the participant could click one box to sometimes see whether a point was going to register (colored pattern, S+) or could click another box to occasionally see if no points were going to register (color pattern, S−). The S+ and S− boxes were arranged to show colored patterns on two VI 30-s schedules. The participant received the good-news stimulus, S+ ("mean[ing] a nickel is coming soon") for an observing response only when the VT 30-s point schedule was actually going to pay off. She received the bad-news stimulus, S− ("mean[ing] a nickel is not coming soon") for a response only when the no-points (EXT) component of the mixed schedule was actually in effect. At other times, she received darkened boxes by responding to either the good-news or bad-news options. The participant was told that no matter which of the boxes she clicked, her responses would not affect the registration of points on the counter. The experimental results showed a consistent preference for good news over bad news, in accord with most previous studies. Also, using similar procedures, additional experiments compared a no-news stimulus, S^U ("mean[ing] a nickel is coming soon or a nickel is not coming soon") with a signal for bad news ("mean[ing] a nickel is not coming soon") when there was virtually no correlation between observing responses and periods of winning nickels. Contrary to the findings of Lieberman and colleagues, the participants showed a preference for observing the no-news stimulus, S^U, over bad news, S−, using VI schedules for observing responses, replicating the results of earlier experiments by Fantino and colleagues.

Fantino and Silberberg (2010) conducted critical experiments to show that only when observing S− is correlated with good news do participants prefer the bad-news option. Recall that observing in the study by Lieberman et al. (1997) occurred on CRF schedules. Assuming that points registered equally in the presence of the no-news and bad-news options, then each observing response for S− that did not produce a bad-news message was implicitly correlated with reinforcement (registration of points). Presumably, it was the implicit good news of points registering that maintained observing on the "bad news" option and the apparent preference for bad news in the experiments by Lieberman and colleagues. To test this analysis, Fantino and Silberberg arranged for each observing response to be effective (CRF or FR1) at producing stimulus patterns. For the no-news option, each observing response produced a patterned stimulus, S^U, uncorrelated with the components of the mixed schedule for winning nickels. However, each response to the bad-news box produced S− if and only if the EXT component of the mixed schedule was operative; at other times there was no stimulus change. That is, observing no stimulus change on the bad-news option was perfectly correlated with winning nickels. Under these contingencies, participants strongly preferred the bad-news option to the no-news alternative; they showed less preference for the bad-news option when the absence of a stimulus change was imperfectly correlated with winning nickels. Fantino and Silberberg suggest that the overall results from five experiments are in accord with a conditioned-reinforcement account of human observing behavior. They also indicate that the results of their experiments are compatible with the interpretation by Lieberman and colleagues that "humans do find information reinforcing, but that this preference depends on the utility of the information" (Lieberman et al., 1997, p. 20). Thus, information about good news is useful (reinforcing), but information about bad news only has utility if it is correlated with good news, and most of the time it is not.

FIG. 10.8 A woman keeping track of her stocks on the market. According to a conditioned reinforcement account, people who have a history of observing and successfully investing (good news) in the market are likely to keep close track of their stocks and portfolio. Those who have a history of observing and losing (bad news) on the market do not keep track of their investments on a daily basis. © Shutterstock.

In everyday life on campus, students who usually do well on mathematics exams quickly look up their marks on posted lists, while those who have done poorly wait for their grades to come in the mail. Seeing a grade is a conditioned reinforcer for students who are skilled at mathematics, but not for those who find the subject difficult. In another context, investors who usually make money on the stock market keep track of their portfolio (see Figure 10.8), but those who have been losing money may seldom look at how their investments are doing. For both students and investors, the conditioned reinforcing effects of good news maintain observing, but bad news does not.

DELAY REDUCTION AND CONDITIONED REINFORCEMENT

Fantino and Logan have reviewed the observing response studies and point out that:

> Only the more positively valued of two stimuli should maintain observing, since the less positive stimulus is correlated with an increase, not a reduction, in time to positive reinforcement (or a

reduction, not an increase, in time to an aversive event). . . . Conditioned reinforcers are those stimuli correlated with a reduction in time to reinforcement (or an increase in time to an aversive event).

(Fantino & Logan, 1979, p. 207)

This statement is based on Edmund Fantino's **delay-reduction hypothesis** (Fantino, 1969a). Stimuli closer in time to positive reinforcement, or further in time from an aversive event, are more effective conditioned reinforcers. Stimuli that signal no reduction in time to reinforcement (S^Δ) or no safety from an aversive event (S^{ave}) do not function as conditioned reinforcement. Generally, the value of a conditioned reinforcer is due to its delay reduction—that is, how close it is to reinforcement or how far it is from punishment.

Modern views of conditioned reinforcement are largely based on the concept of delay reduction (Fantino, 1969a; Squires & Fantino, 1971). The idea is to compare the relative value of two (or more) stimuli that are correlated with different amounts of time to reinforcement. To do this, a complex-choice procedure involving **concurrent-chain schedules** is used. On these schedules, an organism may choose between alternatives that signal different amounts of time to reinforcement.

Concurrent-Chain Schedules of Reinforcement

In Chapter 9, we discussed the analysis of choice based on *concurrent schedules of reinforcement*. We have also noted the importance of chain schedules for the study of conditioned reinforcement. These schedules allow a researcher to change the temporal location of a stimulus in relation to unconditioned reinforcement. For example, the terminal-link discriminative stimulus (S^D_2) on a chain VI 20 s VI 10 s is six times closer to unconditioned reinforcement than it is on a chain VI 20 s VI 60 s. This relation is shown in Figure 10.9. In terms of time, the terminal-link S^D that is nearer to unconditioned reinforcement should be a stronger conditioned reinforcer than one associated with a longer delay. Thus, the terminal-link S^D accompanying the VI 10-s schedule ought to be a more effective conditioned reinforcer than a discriminative stimulus correlated with VI 60 s.

For the effects of delay to be assessed, organisms must be able to choose between stimuli associated with different reductions in time to unconditioned reinforcement. For example, using a two-key choice procedure, a chain VI 20 s VI 10 s may be programmed on the left key and a chain VI 20 s VI 60 s on the right key.

FIG. 10.9 Comparison of chain VI 20 s VI 10 s with chain VI 20 s VI 60 s. Notice that the S^D closer to unconditioned reinforcement should be a more effective conditioned reinforcer.

This two-key concurrent-chains procedure is shown diagrammatically in Figure 10.10. Consider the situation in which responses to the left key are eventually reinforced with food. To start with, both left and right keys are illuminated with white lights. A bird makes left- and right-key pecks and after the left VI 20-s schedule times out, the first peck to the left key has two effects. The light on the right key goes out, and the VI 20-s schedule on that key stops timing. That is, the key becomes dark and inoperative. At the same time, the left key changes from white to a diamond pattern. In the presence of this pattern, pecking the left key is reinforced with food on a VI 10-s schedule. After unconditioned reinforcement, both left and right keys are again illuminated with white lights and the bird chooses between the two alternatives.

A similar sequence occurs when the right key times out and the bird pecks this key. The left key becomes dark and inoperative, and the right key changes from white to a dotted pattern. In the presence of this pattern, pecking the right key is reinforced with food on a VI 60-s schedule. Following reinforcement, the discriminative stimuli in the initial links of the two chains (left and right white keys) are in effect and the bird again chooses to enter one of the terminal links (left or right).

The patterned stimuli on the left and right keys have two functions. These

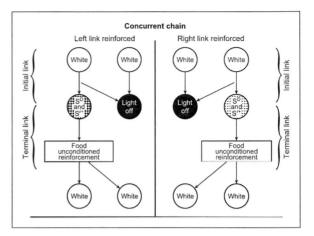

FIG. 10.10 A two-key concurrent-chain schedule of reinforcement. A chain VI 20 s VI 10 s is programmed on the left key, and a chain VI 20 s VI 60 s on the right.

stimuli are S^Ds that set the occasion for pecking for food in the terminal links of the two chain schedules. In addition, the patterned stimuli function as conditioned reinforcement for pecking one or the other of the white keys in the initial-links or choice phase of the experiment. That is, reinforcement for pecking in the choice phase is the onset of the stimuli (S^D and S^r) associated with unconditioned reinforcement in the terminal links. Because the bird is free to distribute pecks, the distribution of behavior in the initial links is a measure of the relative effectiveness of the two conditioned reinforcers.

Delay Reduction and Concurrent-Chain Schedules

Humans often respond on concurrent-chain schedules of reinforcement. A businessperson who frequently flies from Kansas City to Denver may call either Delta or American Airlines to book a ticket. Many people are trying to book flights, and the telephone lines to both companies are always busy. To contact an agent, the businessperson calls one airline and then the other. Eventually, one of the calls is successful, but both companies have recorded messages that state "All of the lines are busy at the moment—please hold until an agent is available." After the businessperson has waited for some time, an agent answers and the ticket is booked.

In this example, calling the two airlines is the choice phase. The length of time to complete a call and get the hold message (initial-link schedules) is determined by the number of telephone lines at each airline and the number of people phoning the companies. The recorded message is conditioned reinforcement for dialing that company. The amount of time waiting on hold to book a flight (terminal-link schedule) is a function of the number of available agents. Waiting in the terminal link is reinforced by booking the flight. The sequence is repeated the next time the businessperson has a meeting in Denver.

To predict how much more (or less) reinforcing it is to be placed on hold at Delta relative to American Airlines, it is useful to consider a situation in which the initial- and terminal-link schedules are known for each company. Suppose that, on average, the telephone lines of both companies are busy for 120 s before a call is successful. In other words, the initial links for Delta and American Airlines are similar to concurrent VI 120-s schedules. The terminal-link schedules are different for the two airlines. It takes an average of 30 s to talk to a Delta agent after being placed on hold. That is, the terminal link for Delta is similar to a VI 30-s schedule. After being placed on hold at American Airlines, it takes an average of 90 s to reach an agent, so that the terminal link for American Airlines is similar to a VI 90-s schedule. Thus, the sequence for booking a ticket at Delta is chain VI 120 s VI 30 s, and it is chain VI 120 s VI 90 s at American Airlines (see Advanced Section of this chapter for quantification of this example).

In this situation, Fantino's delay-reduction hypothesis predicts that the businessperson will prefer Delta to American Airlines. This is because more of the total time to reinforcement has elapsed when the person is placed on hold at Delta than with American. The conditioned reinforcement in this situation is getting the message "All of the lines are busy at the moment—please hold until an agent is available." After the message occurs, it is faster to book a ticket at Delta than at American. There has been relatively more reduction in delay to reinforcement when the Delta message occurs.

GENERALIZED CONDITIONED REINFORCEMENT

Formally, a **generalized conditioned reinforcer** is any event or stimulus that is associated with, or exchangeable for, many sources of unconditioned reinforcement. Generalized reinforcement does not depend on deprivation or satiation for any specific reinforcer. Skinner describes its effects in the following passage:

> A conditioned reinforcer is generalized when it is paired with more than one unconditioned reinforcer. The generalized reinforcer is useful because the momentary condition of the organism is not likely to be important. The operant strength generated by a single reinforcement is observed only under an appropriate condition of deprivation—when we reinforce with food, we gain control over the hungry man. But if a conditioned reinforcer has been paired with reinforcers appropriate to many conditions, at least one appropriate state of deprivation is more likely to prevail upon a later occasion. A response is therefore more likely to occur. When we reinforce with money, for example, our subsequent control is relatively independent of momentary deprivations.
>
> (Skinner, 1953, p. 77)

Generalized Social Reinforcement

A major source of generalized reinforcement is mediated by the behavior of other people. Social consequences such as praise, attention, status, and affection are powerful reinforcers for most people. Approval, attention, affection, and praise function as **generalized social reinforcement** for human behavior (Buckleitner, 2006; Kazdin & Klock, 1973; Kirby & Shields, 1972; Ruggles & LeBlanc, 1982; Vollmer & Hackenberg, 2001). In a classroom, a child's misbehavior may be followed regularly by attention, as when the teacher says "What are you doing out of your seat?" The teacher may complain that the student is an unmanageable child. However, the problem may concern the social reinforcement contingency between the student's misbehavior and the teacher's attention.

Misbehavior usually captures the teacher's attention because it is highly intense (even aggressive) activity. Attention is reinforcing to most children because it necessarily precedes other types of reinforcement from people. When attention is contingent on misbehavior, then misbehavior increases. The solution to the problem is not to change the child, but to alter the contingency of reinforcement. One possibility is to ignore misbehavior (extinction) and attend to the child at any time other than when he or she is misbehaving (differential reinforcement of other behavior, or DRO). "Catch them being good" is the operative phrase.

The importance of generalized social reinforcement involving approval and affection is recognized in the following passage from Skinner:

> Another person is likely to reinforce only that part of one's behavior of which he approves, and any sign of his approval therefore becomes reinforcing in its own right. Behavior which evokes a smile or the verbal response "That's right" or "Good" or any other commendation is strengthened. We use this generalized reinforcer to establish and shape the behavior of others, particularly in education. For example, we teach both children and adults to speak correctly by saying "That's right" when appropriate behavior is emitted.
>
> A still stronger generalized reinforcer is affection. It may be especially connected with sexual contact as an unconditioned reinforcer, but when anyone who shows affection supplies other kinds of reinforcement as well, the effect is generalized.
>
> It is difficult to define, observe, and measure attention, approval, and affection. They are not things but aspects of the behavior of others. Their subtle physical dimensions present difficulties not only for the scientist who must study them but also for the individual who is reinforced by them. If we do not easily see that someone is paying attention or that he approves or is affectionate, our behavior will not be consistently reinforced. It may therefore be weak, may tend to occur at the wrong time, and so on. We do not "know what to do to get attention or affection or when to do it." The child struggling for attention, the lover for a sign of affection, and the artist for professional approval show the persevering behavior which ... results from only intermittent reinforcement.
>
> (Skinner, 1953, pp. 78–79)

Skinner goes on to discuss the submissiveness of others as generalized reinforcement (see also Patterson, 1982, 2002). In an aggressive episode, two people use threats and possibly physical attack to control each other's behavior. Eventually, one of the combatants gives up, and this submissive behavior serves as reinforcement for the aggressive behavior of the other person. Giving up the argument often results in cessation of the attack by the aggressor, and this is reinforcement for the submissive behavior displayed by the other. Unfortunately, the contingencies of aggression and submission arrange for an indefinite escalation of conflict, which may inadvertently result in serious harm that is legally judged as assault or murder.

The contingencies of aggression may account for many instances of abuse involving children, partners, the elderly, and individuals incarcerated in prisons and mental hospitals. To the extent that these people are dependent on the benevolence of their parents, partners, or caretakers, they must give in to the demands of their keepers. Consider a woman who is unemployed, has few friends, and is married to a man who physically assaults her. When her husband becomes aggressive, she has little recourse other than submission. If she calls the police or tells a neighbor, she risks losing her home and income, and she may have learned that her husband will only become more angry. For these reasons, the husband's aggressive behavior is shaped to more extreme levels.

Occasionally, victims develop an emotional attachment to the people who mistreat them, sometimes called the Stockholm syndrome. This kind of affectionate behavior may be shaped as part of the aggressive episode. The contingencies could involve negative reinforcement, as when the aggressor's attack is reduced or removed by signs of affection from the victim. After some exposure to these contingencies, victims may even claim to love their abusers.

There are several steps that may be taken to reduce the incidence of victim abuse in our society. One solution involves the issue of control and countercontrol. To prevent abusive control, the victim must be able to arrange consequences that deter the actions of the aggressor. This *countercontrol* by victims is established when society provides agencies or individuals who monitor abusers and take action on behalf of the victims. Countercontrol may also involve passing laws to protect the rights of individuals who are in highly dependent situations. Another possibility is to teach alternative behavior in terms of negotiation and conflict resolution. Finally, a society that supports aggression as entertainment in sports, television, and movies should not be surprised at having high levels of violence in daily life.

Tokens, Money, and Generalized Reinforcement

Other conditioned reinforcers are economic in the sense of being exchangeable for goods and services. Awards, prizes, and scholarships support an enormous range of human activity. Perhaps the most important source of economic reinforcement is money. One way to understand the reinforcing effects of money is to view it as a type of token (coins or bills) exchangeable at a later time for a variety of goods and services.

FIG. 10.11   Token reinforcement and chimpanzee behavior. Reprinted with permission from Yerkes Regional Primate Research Center, Emory University.

Token reinforcement has been demonstrated in chimpanzees (Figure 10.11; see also Cowles, 1937). Chimpanzees *(Pan troglodytes)* were trained to exchange poker chips for raisins. After tokens and fruit were paired, the animals learned to select one of several patterns to get poker chips that were later exchanged for raisins. The animals collected several tokens and then went to another room, where they inserted the chips in a vending machine for raisins. Because the discriminative operant (pattern selection) was maintained, the chips were by definition conditioned reinforcers.

Another study (Wolfe, 1936) also showed that chimpanzees would tolerate a delay between getting a token and exchanging it for food. The animals earned white chips, which could be inserted into a vending machine that immediately delivered grapes. Inserting the chip into the machine was shaped by successive approximation. The experimenter placed a token partway into the vending slot, and any push by the chimpanzee caused the chip to drop, resulting in the delivery of a grape. This procedure continued until the animals started to retrieve the chips and insert them in the slot. Following this training, the animals were taught to pull a lever to get chips. At this point, access to the vending machine was delayed but the chimpanzees continued to work for tokens. Some animals even began to save their tokens much like people save money. When delays occurred after the chimpanzees had inserted the tokens into the vending machine, the reinforcing effectiveness of the tokens declined (the delay to reinforcement was increased, hence the delay-reduction hypothesis was supported). This suggests that the token bridged the interval between earning and spending, a conclusion supported by a recent review of token reinforcement by Hackenberg (2009, p. 262).

Experimental Analysis of Token Reinforcement

In the 1950s, Kelleher (1956, 1958) began the experimental analysis of token reinforcement, viewing the contingencies as a sequence of interconnected schedule components similar to second-order and chain schedules. **Token schedules** have three distinct components involving the token-production schedule, the exchange-production schedule, and the token-exchange schedule (Hackenberg, 2009). Thus, when we talk about token reinforcement, we are referring to three component schedules that form a higher-order sequence. Typically, one of the component schedules is varied while the other two components remain unchanged (held constant).

An experiment by Kelleher (1958) illustrates the experimental analysis of token reinforcement. Two chimpanzees were initially trained to press a lever on fixed-ratio (FR) and fixed-interval (FI) schedules of food reinforcement. Next, the chimps had to deposit poker chips in a receptacle for food when a window was illuminated, but not when it went dark (discriminated operant). When depositing of chips was well established, the animals were required to press a lever to obtain the poker-chip tokens. Both FR and FI schedules of token production were investigated using simple and multiple schedules. Overall, response patterns for tokens were similar to the break-and-run and scalloping patterns found on FR and FI schedules of food reinforcement.

Subsequently, Kelleher conducted a more in-depth analysis of FR schedules of token reinforcement with the same chimpanzees (No. 117 and No. 119). Responses in the presence of a white light produced tokens that could be exchanged for food at the end of the experimental session, as signaled by a red light. The chimps were required to obtain 60 tokens to produce an exchange period (exchange-production schedule FR 60), and each token could be traded for a food pellet (token exchange FR 1). The schedule of token production varied from FR 30 through to FR 125. Figure 10.12 shows the cumulative records of the final performances by the chimps on an FR 30 token-production schedule. The records show break-and-run patterns early in the session, but steady responding near the end when the chimps had collected nearly 60 tokens to be traded for food. Generally, the response patterns on FR token production showed bouts of responding and pausing typical of FR schedules— mirroring performance on FR schedules of food reinforcement.

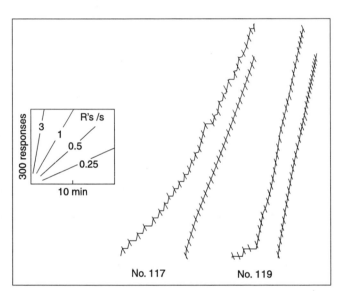

FIG. 10.12 Performance of two chimpanzees on an FR 30 schedule of token reinforcement. The cumulative records show the characteristic break-and-run pattern of FR schedules of food reinforcement early in the session, but a high steady rate of response as the period of token exchange approaches near the end of the session. This suggests that the requirements for token exchange (collecting a specified number of tokens) modulate token production behavior on the FR 30 schedule. From Kelleher, R. T., 1958, "Fixed-ratio schedules of conditioned reinforcement with chimpanzees," *Journal of the Experimental Analysis of Behavior, 1,* 281–289. © Society for the Experimental Analysis of Behavior. Published with permission.

The findings of Kelleher with regard to FR schedules of token production have been replicated with rats and pigeons using different types of tokens. These studies indicate that tokens function as conditioned reinforcers on schedules of reinforcement, but token reinforcement is more complicated than simple schedules (Hackenberg, 2009). Research by Bullock and Hackenberg (2006) showed that steady-state responding on the FR token-production schedule is modified by the requirements set by the exchange-production schedule (obtaining 2, 4, or 8 tokens before exchanging). Response rates decreased as the FR for token production increased, an effect that was exacerbated by high exchange-production requirements (FR 8 tokens for an exchange period). Thus, response rates on token-reinforcement schedules are jointly controlled by both the token-production and exchange-production schedules.

Additional research has investigated responding for tokens when the exchange-production schedule varied and the token-production and token-exchange FR schedules remained unchanged (see Foster, Hackenberg, & Vaidya, 2001). Fixed-ratio (FR) exchange-production schedules (number of tokens required for an exchange period) resulted in break-and-run patterns of responding for tokens, while VR schedules of exchange production eliminated pausing and produced higher overall response rates, similar to simple FR and VR schedules of food reinforcement. One possibility is that responding for tokens on the token-reinforcement schedule is a higher-order unit of behavior that is reinforced according to the requirements on the exchange-production schedule—as in second-order schedules of reinforcement. Hackenberg has summarized the overall findings:

> In sum, behavior under token reinforcement schedules is a joint function of the contingencies whereby tokens are produced and exchanged for other reinforcers. Other things being equal, contingencies in the later links of the chain exert disproportionate control over behavior. Token schedules are part of a family of sequence schedules that include second-order and extended chained schedules. . . . Token schedules can be used to create and synthesize behavioral units that participate in larger functional units under the control of other contingencies.
>
> (Hackenberg, 2009, p. 268)

The interdependence of the components of a token system (sequence of schedules) and the emergence of higher-order behavioral units, involving the production and exchange of other reinforcers, indicates that token research with animals may have relevance to research with humans using points and money as reinforcement.

Humans, Money, and Generalized Conditioned Reinforcement

For people, money is a form of token reinforcement that maintains an enormous diversity and amount of behavior. A major difference between the chimpanzees' tokens and money is that the latter is exchangeable for many different reinforcers. For this reason, money is a **generalized conditioned reinforcer**. Most behavioral experiments involving humans have used money as reinforcement. Money is relatively independent of momentary deprivation, is easily quantified, and is exchangeable for numerous goods and services outside of the laboratory.

Schedules of monetary reinforcement have been used to assess matching (see Chapter 9) and delay reduction with humans. Belke, Pierce, and Powell (1989) created a human-operant chamber, and people were required to pick up tokens from a dispenser and exchange them for 25¢ each. At first, a single token was exchanged for 25¢, then two tokens for 50¢, and then four tokens for $1. By extending the delay between earning and exchanging tokens, subjects learned to collect up to 40 tokens before trading them for $10.

In this experiment, there were no instructions and pressing left or right keys was shaped by monetary reinforcement. Various reinforcement schedules were then programmed to test matching, maximizing, and delay-reduction accounts of human choice and preference. Human performance on monetary schedules of reinforcement was better described by matching and maximizing models than by the delay-reduction equation. Relative rate of monetary reinforcement was the most important determinant of behavior in this situation (see Jackson & Hackenberg, 1996, on tokens used as substitutes for food with pigeons).

The applied advantage of money and tokens is that they are tangible objects that are observed easily, and their exchange value can be specified precisely. For this reason, a large amount of research has been conducted on experimental communities in which economic reinforcement is scheduled for effective patterns of behavior.

ON THE APPLIED SIDE: The Token Economy

One of the most important applications of behavior analysis is based on the use of tokens as generalized conditioned reinforcement. Tokens are arbitrary items such as poker chips, tickets, coins, checkmarks in a daily log, and stars or happy-face symbols given to students. To establish these objects as reinforcement, the applied researcher has a person exchange tokens for a variety of back-up reinforcers. A child may exchange five stars for a period of free play, a selection of toys, access to drawing materials, or an opportunity to use a LEGO™ set.

*A **token economy** is a set of contingencies or a system based on token (conditioned) reinforcement. That is, the contingencies specify when, and under what conditions, particular forms of behavior are reinforced with tokens. It is an economy in the sense that the tokens may be exchanged for goods and services much like money is in our economy. This exchange of tokens for a variety of back-up reinforcers ensures that the tokens become conditioned reinforcers.*

Systems of token reinforcement have been used to improve the behavior of psychiatric patients (Ayllon & Azrin, 1968), juvenile delinquents (Fixsen, Phillips, Phillips, & Wolf, 1976), pupils in remedial classrooms (Breyer & Allen, 1975), normal children in the home (Alvord & Cheney, 1994), and medical patients who must follow a plan of treatment (Carton & Schweitzer, 1996; Dapcich-Miura & Hovell, 1979). Token economies have also been designed for alcoholics, drug addicts, prisoners, nursing-home residents, and intellectually disabled people (Kazdin, 1977; see Dickerson, Tenhula, & Green-Paden, 2005, for a review of token-economy studies of the treatment of schizophrenia).

One of the first token systems was designed for psychiatric patients who lived in a large mental hospital. Schaefer and Martin (1966) attempted to modify the behavior of 40 female patients who were diagnosed as long-term schizophrenics. A general characteristic of these women was that they seemed to be disinterested in the activities and happenings on the ward. In addition, many of the women showed little interest in personal hygiene (i.e., they showed a low probability of washing, grooming, brushing their teeth, and so on). In general, Schaefer and Martin referred to this class of behavior as apathetic, and designed a token system to increase social and physical involvement by these patients.

The women were randomly assigned to a treatment or control group. Women in the control group received tokens no matter what they did (i.e., noncontingent reinforcement). Patients in the contingent reinforcement group obtained tokens that could be traded for a variety of privileges and luxuries. Tokens were earned for specific classes of behavior. These response classes were personal hygiene, job performance, and social interaction. For example, a patient earned tokens when she spoke pleasantly to others during group therapy. A social response such as "Good morning, how are you?" resulted in a ward attendant giving her a token and praising her effort. Other responses that were reinforced included personal hygiene, such as attractive use of cosmetics, showering, and generally maintaining a well-groomed appearance. Finally, tokens were earned for specified jobs, such as wiping tables and vacuuming carpets and furniture.

Notice that the reinforcement system encouraged behavior that was incompatible with the label "apathetic." A person who is socially responsive, well groomed, and who carries out daily jobs is usually described as being involved with life. To implement the program, general response classes such as personal hygiene had to be specified and instances of each class, such as brushing teeth or combing hair, had to be defined. Once the behavior was well defined, ward staff were trained to identify positive instances and deliver tokens for appropriate responses.

Over a 3-month period of the study, the ward staff counted instances of involved and apathetic behavior. Responses in each class of behavior—hygiene, social interaction, and work—increased for women in the contingent-token system, but not for patients who were simply given the tokens. Responses that were successful in the token economy were apparently also effective outside the hospital. Only 14% of the patients who were discharged from the token system returned to the hospital; this compared favorably with an average return rate of 28%.

Although Schaefer and Martin (1966) successfully maintained behavioral gains after the patients were discharged, not all token systems are equally effective (see Kazdin, 1983, for a review). Programs that teach social and life skills have lower return rates than those that do not. This presumably occurs because patients who are taught these skills can take better care of themselves and interact more appropriately with others. Of course, these operants are valued by members of the social community who reinforce and thereby maintain this behavior.

Token economies that gradually introduce the patient to the world outside the hospital also maintain behavior better than those programs with abrupt transitions from hospital to home. A patient on a token-economy ward may successively earn day passes, overnight stays, weekend release, discharge to a group home, and eventually a return to normal living. This gradual transition to everyday life has two major effects. Contrived reinforcement on the token system is slowly reduced or faded and, at the same time, natural consequences outside of the hospital are contacted. Second, the positive responses of patients are shifted from the relatively dense schedules of reinforcement provided by the token system to the more intermittent reinforcement of the ordinary environment. Designing token systems for transitions to settings outside the institution is a topic of considerable applied importance (Paul, 2006; Wakefield, 2006).

The popularity of the token economy has waned since the 1980s, but reviews of the evidence have resulted in pleas to reconsider its use (Dickerson et al., 2005; Matson & Boisjoli, 2009). With regard to children with intellectual disabilities and autism, there has been a preference for adopting new, untried treatments despite the evidence that token economies are highly effective at teaching a variety of intellectual and social skills. Recently, early-intervention programs for autism have targeted children too young to benefit from token programs, but older children with continuing behavioral problems could still benefit from a well-designed token economy (Matson & Boisjoli, 2009). With more call for evidence-based treatments in the autism community, it is likely that there will be a resurgence of token-economy programs in the near future.

ADVANCED SECTION: Quantification and Delay Reduction

Consider the example of the businessperson phoning Delta and American Airlines and how long it takes to get placed on hold at the two airlines (described in the section on

"Delay Reduction and Conditioned Reinforcement" earlier in this chapter). The average time to be placed on hold at both airlines is 120 s. If the person is dialing back and forth between Delta and American Airlines, the average time taken to get through is 120 s divided by the two choices, or 60 s (i.e., 120/2 = 60). This is because the initial-link schedules are simultaneously available and are both timing out.

Next, consider how long it takes to contact an agent once the businessperson has been placed on hold at one of the two airlines. In this case, the person is stuck on hold at one airline and can no longer dial the other company. The average time in the terminal links of the two chains is 30 s for Delta plus 90 s for American divided by the two links, or 60 s [i.e., (30 + 90)/2 = 60]. That is, over many bookings the person has sometimes waited 90 s for an American agent and at other times 30 s for a Delta agent. On average, the length of time spent waiting on hold is 60 s.

Based on the average times in the initial and terminal links (60 s + 60 s), the overall average total time, T, to book a flight is 120 s or 2 min. Given that it takes an average of T = 120 s to book a flight, how much will the businessperson prefer booking at Delta compared with American Airlines? Recall that it takes an average of 30 s to contact an agent at Delta and 90 s at American, after being placed on hold. This terminal-link time is represented as $t_{2\ DELTA}$ = 30 s, and $t_{2\ AMERICAN}$ = 90 s.

Of the average total time, 90 s have elapsed when the person is placed on hold at Delta ($T - t_{2\ DELTA}$ = 120 − 30 = 90 s). That is, the reduction in delay to reinforcement (booking a flight) is 90 s at Delta. The delay reduction at American is 30 s ($T - t_{2\ AMERICAN}$ = 120 − 90 = 30 s).

The greater the delay reduction at Delta relative to American Airlines, the greater the conditioned reinforcement value of Delta compared with American. This relation may be expressed as follows:

$$\frac{R_{DELTA}}{R_{DELTA} + R_{AMERICAN}} = \frac{T - t_{2\ DELTA}}{\left(T - t_{2\ DELTA}\right) + \left(T - t_{2\ AMERICAN}\right)}$$

$$= \frac{120 - 30}{\left(120 - 30\right) + \left(120 - 90\right)}$$

$$= \frac{90}{90 + 30}$$

$$= 0.75.$$

The R values represent responses or, in this example, the number of calls to Delta (R_{DELTA}) and American ($R_{AMERICAN}$), respectively. The relative number of calls made to Delta is equal to the relative reduction in time to book a flight (reinforcement). This time is calculated as the proportion of delay reduction at Delta to the total delay reduction. According to the calculation, 0.75 or 75% of the businessperson's calls will be directed to Delta Airlines.

Experimental Test of Delay Reduction

Edmund Fantino (Figure 10.13), a professor of psychology at the University of California, San Diego, first proposed and tested the delay-reduction analysis of conditioned reinforcement. He was trained in operant conditioning at Harvard University, where he worked in B. F. Skinner's laboratory and graduated with a PhD in 1964. After a brief stay at Yale University, he joined the faculty at San Diego and continued his research on the

FIG. 10.13   Edmund Fantino.
Reprinted with permission.

experimental analysis of choice. Fantino recounts his discovery of the delay-reduction hypothesis in the following passage:

> One of my first experiments at [San Diego], on choice behavior, was producing strange but consistent results in each of four pigeons. I was losing sleep over these results until one morning I awoke with the following hypothesis: Choice responses don't match rates of reinforcement of the outcomes but instead match the relative reduction in delay to reinforcement associated with these outcomes. This delay-reduction hypothesis then served to guide scores of experiments assessing its generality and limitations in areas such as choice, conditioned reinforcement, elicited responding, self-control, observing and experimental analogs of foraging decisions.
>
> (E. Fantino, personal communication, February 1992)

Fantino (1969a) proposed a general equation for preference on a concurrent-chain schedule that was based on delay reduction. Equation 10.1 is a generalized statement of the formula used to calculate preference for Delta and American Airlines.

$$\frac{R_L}{R_L + R_R} = \frac{T - t_2}{\left(T - t_{2L}\right) + \left(T - t_{2R}\right)} \tag{10.1}$$

In this equation, R_L and R_R represent the rate of response on the left and right initial links of a concurrent-chain schedule of reinforcement. The symbol T is the average time to reinforcement (see the airlines example for calculation). The time required in the left and right terminal links is represented by t_{2L} and t_{2R} in the equation. The equation states that relative rate of response is a function of relative reduction in time to unconditioned reinforcement.

The delay-reduction equation emphasizes conditioned reinforcement as a major determinant of choice. This is because the onset of the terminal-link S^D for each chain is correlated with a reduction in time to unconditioned reinforcement. This reduction is $T - t_{2L}$ for the left alternative and $T - t_{2R}$ for the right. Recall that the greater the reduction in time to unconditioned reinforcement signaled by a stimulus, the greater the conditioned-reinforcement value of that stimulus. The delay-reduction equation is a mathematical expression of this idea.

Fantino (1969a) designed an experiment to test the delay-reduction equation. The subjects were six pigeons who responded for food on concurrent-chain schedules of reinforcement. In this experiment, the terminal links were always set at $t_{2L} = 30$ s and $t_{2R} = 90$ s. Notice that for the left alternative the relative rate of unconditioned reinforcement is 0.75, and according to the matching law the birds should spend 75% of their time on the left key. The situation becomes more complex when initial-link schedules are varied. Fantino's experiment involved adding initial links to the VI 30-s and VI 90-s schedules. That is, he investigated concurrent-chain schedules with 30-s and 90-s terminal links. The schedules in the initial links were always the same for both alternatives, but the values of these schedules were varied over the course of the experiment. For example, in one condition the initial links were VI 30 s on the left and VI 30 s on the right. In another condition, the initial-link schedules were both VI 600 s. Other initial-link values between these two extremes were also investigated. The important question is what happens to the pigeons' preference for the shorter (VI 30-s) terminal link as time is increased in the first link of the chains.

Figure 10.14 shows the proportion of responses predicted by Equation 10.1 for the shorter (VI 30 s) terminal link as time is added equally to the initial links of the concurrent-chain schedule. When

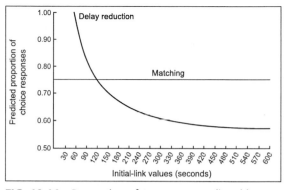

FIG. 10.14 Proportion of responses predicted by the delay-reduction equation is shown for the shorter (VI 30 s) terminal link, as time is added equally to the initial links of the concurrent-chain schedule. Adapted from "Choice and rate of reinforcement" by E. Fantino, *Journal of the Experimental Analysis of Behavior, 12*, 723–730. © 1969 Society for the Experimental Analysis of Behavior, Inc. Adapted with permission.

the schedules were chain VI 30 s VI 30 s on the left and chain VI 30 s VI 90 s on the right, the birds responded almost exclusively to the left alternative. When the chains were VI 120 s VI 30 s on the left and VI 120 s VI 90 s on the right, the pigeons showed response distributions close to matching (0.75 responses on the left). Finally, when time in the initial links was greatly increased to VI 600 s, the birds showed no preference for either alternative. As you can see in Figure 10.14, these results are in accord with the declining preference predicted by the delay-reduction equation.

A recent study by McDevitt & Williams (2010) confirmed the role of delay reduction in setting the relative value of terminal-link stimuli (conditioned reinforcers), but also found that the relative rate of conditioned reinforcement influenced choice behavior. Fantino and Romanowich (2007) argued that models of choice in concurrent-chain schedules do not require a term for rate of conditioned reinforcement, but these and other recent findings suggest that conditioned reinforcement rates may have to be included. However, the integration of the delay-reduction model with rate of conditioned reinforcement awaits further theoretical analysis.

CHAPTER SUMMARY

This chapter introduced the concept of conditioned reinforcement and some research to demonstrate the variables that determine its effectiveness. There are few unconditioned reinforcers, but when these biologically relevant events are correlated with previously ineffective stimuli, from light flashes to poker chips, these stimuli become capable of reinforcing behavior. Money is perhaps the most common and effective generalized conditioned reinforcer in human culture.

In order to demonstrate how conditioned reinforcers are studied, we described the use of chained schedules. Chain schedules involve stimuli that have more than one function (multiple functions). The discriminative stimulus sets the occasion for a response that can sometimes be reinforced, and a chain schedule shows that the S^D may also function as a conditioned reinforcer. The nearness in time of the conditioned stimulus to the unconditioned reinforcer is a critical factor in the delay-reduction account of conditioned reinforcement. Brain areas (the amygdala and nucleus accumbens) and neurochemicals (dopamine) participate in the regulation of behavior by contingencies of conditioned reinforcement. Organisms select the stimulus in a concurrent-chain procedure that reduces the time to reinforcement. In addition, we saw that the use of backward chaining to teach skills (building the chain backwards from the terminal reinforcer) is a very effective procedure. Finally, the text described the systematic use of conditioned reinforcers in the form of tokens in primates, including humans. Token systems are micro-examples of money economies, and these systems help to manage problems of human behavior in a variety of institutional settings.

KEY WORDS

Backward chaining

Chain schedule of reinforcement

Concurrent-chain schedule

Conditioned reinforcement

Conditioned reinforcer

Delay-reduction hypothesis

Discriminative-stimulus account of
   conditioned reinforcement

Established-response method

Generalized conditioned
   reinforcement

Generalized conditioned reinforcer

Generalized social reinforcement

Heterogeneous chain schedule

Homogeneous chain schedule

Information account of conditioned
   reinforcement

Mixed schedule of reinforcement

New-response method

Observing response

Second-order schedule

S–S account of conditioned
   reinforcement

Tandem schedule

Token economy

Token schedule of
reinforcement

Unconditioned reinforcer

ON THE WEB

www.youtube.com/watch?v=VPKmcT4lZDk&feature=related Ayumu, a young chimpanzee, has learned the order of the Arabic numerals, and outperforms humans on a short-term memory task. While the performance of Ayumu is amazing, it took several years of daily training to perfect. Try to figure out the contingencies using your basic principles of reinforcement, especially principles of matching to sample and conditioned reinforcement.

http://members.tripod.com/PoPsMin/classtokenecon.html This site focuses on the use of a token economy in classrooms with attention-deficit-disordered (ADD) children.

www.youtube.com/watch?v=nDdSUxi8X-o&feature=related This is a video of elementary use of clicker training with dogs. See if you can identify the basic principles of behavior and conditioned reinforcement that are used in clicker training.

www.youtube.com/watch?v=OGc8dFdQsJw This website describes how to use a token economy with autistic children.

BRIEF QUIZ

1. In the laboratory, when a clicking sound is followed by food, the clicking sound:

    (a) takes on a conditioned reinforcement function
    (b) will support an operant that produces it
    (c) can become an enduring reinforcing stimulus
    (d) is characterized by all of the above

2. Backward chaining involves:

    (a) teaching the initial component or link first
    (b) teaching the final component or link first
    (c) teaching from the middle to the last component or link
    (d) teaching the final component or link in random order

3. On a chain schedule of reinforcement, the longer the delay between the S^D and unconditioned reinforcement:

    (a) the greater the stimulus control
    (b) the less effective the S^D as a conditioned reinforcer
    (c) the greater the value of the unconditioned reinforcer
    (d) the less the value of the unconditioned reinforcer

4. In terms of good news and bad news, research suggests that:

    (a) stimuli correlated with positive or negative reinforcement maintain an observing response
    (b) stimuli correlated with punishment and extinction maintain an observing response
    (c) stimuli correlated with negative reinforcement and punishment maintain an observing response
    (d) stimuli correlated with positive reinforcement and extinction maintain an observing response

5. The behavior analysis of booking a flight on Delta or American Airlines illustrates:

    (a) how behavior is distributed on concurrent schedules of reinforcement
    (b) how behavior is distributed on concurrent-chain schedules of reinforcement
    (c) the role of delay reduction in choice situations
    (d) both (b) and (c)

6. According to Skinner (1953), a generalized conditioned reinforcer:

    (a) is extremely useful because it can be carried around and made contingent on behavior
    (b) is not very useful because it relies on the momentary deprivation/satiation of the organism
    (c) is produced by pairing a conditioned reinforcer with more than one unconditioned reinforcer
    (d) is produced by backward chaining of the unconditioned and conditioned reinforcers

7. Attention from other people is usually reinforcing for children because:

    (a) attention has preceded a variety of reinforcements from people
    (b) attention is needed for children to develop into emotionally healthy individuals
    (c) attention is around children all the time so they get used to it
    (d) attention is a fundamental necessity of life that children thrive on

8. Victims sometimes become emotionally attached to people who mistreat them. This could be due to:

    (a) punishment of affectionate behavior of the victim
    (b) negative reinforcement of affectionate behavior of the victim
    (c) longing for a real emotional attachment to the parents
    (d) a misplaced sexual drive that is directed at the abuser

9. The research on token reinforcement and chimpanzees shows:

    (a) token and food reinforcement are similar in maintaining behavior
    (b) tokens can bridge the interval between earning and spending
    (c) token reinforcement can maintain and train performance on discrimination tasks
    (d) all of the above

10. Systems of token reinforcement in humans have been used to improve the behavior of:

    (a) psychiatric patients
    (b) juvenile delinquents
    (c) normal children
    (d) medical patients
    (e) all of the above

Answers to Brief Quiz: 1, d (p. 294); 2, b (p. 296); 3, b (p. 298); 4, a (p. 304); 5, d (p. 310); 6, c (p. 310); 7, a (p. 311); 8, b (p. 311); 9, d (p. 312); 10, e (p. 315).

Correspondence Relations: Imitation and Rule-Governed Behavior

1. Inquire about contingencies of correspondence and human behavior.
2. Learn about spontaneous imitation in natural settings and the laboratory.
3. Investigate human imitation and mirror neurons.
4. Distinguish between generalized imitation and observational learning.
5. Learn about rule-governed and contingency-shaped behavior.
6. See how instructions affect sensitivity of behavior to contingencies.

People often do what others do. A child who observes his brother raid the cookie jar may engage in similar behavior—at least until they are both caught by their parent. Adults sometimes watch their teenagers' dancing and repeat aspects of these performances at a neighborhood party. Both of these examples involve **correspondence relations** between the demonstrated behavior and the replicated performance. Thus, correspondence involves a special type of stimulus control where the discriminative stimulus is behavior of an individual. In the case of social modeling, we may say that the behavior of one person sets the occasion for an equivalent response by the other.

CORRESPONDENCE AND HUMAN BEHAVIOR

There are other correspondence relations established by our culture. People look for and reinforce the correspondence between saying and doing, or more generally between past behavior and current actions (e.g., Lovaas, 1961; Matthews, Shimoff, & Catania, 1987; Paniagua & Baer, 1982; Risley & Hart, 1968; see also Lattal & Doepke, 2001 and Silva & Lattal, 2010, on correspondence as complex conditional discrimination). When a child promises to clean her room and actually does so, her parents are pleased, whereas failure to follow through on the promise may make the parents angry. A large part of socialization involves arranging social reinforcement for correspondence between what is said and what is done (see Luciano, Herruzo, & Barnes-Holmes, 2001, on generalized correspondence in children; see also Lima & Abreu-Rodrigues, 2010, on how "repeating what you said" contributes to generalized correspondence).

By the time a person is an adult, people expect consistency between spoken words and later performance. One kind of consistency that is upheld in social groups is between attitudes and behavior. A minister who preaches moral conduct and lives a moral life is valued; when moral words and moral deeds do not match, people become upset and act to correct the inconsistency. In such instances, what is said does not correspond adequately with what is done. Cognitive dissonance theory (Festinger, 1957; Gerard, 1994) predicted that people confronted with inconsistency (dissonance) between saying and doing would escape from it (dissonance reduction), thereby ensuring that attitudes matched behavior. Considerable research has supported this prediction. Behavior analysis helps to explain why people engage in dissonance reduction—pointing to the social contingencies that punish low correspondence between words and actions (see Egan, Santos, & Bloom, 2007, for an account of the origins of cognitive dissonance in children and monkeys).

Consistency is also important when people report on private internal events or happenings. In these cases, the correspondence is between the internal stimulation of the body, behavior, and the verbal report. The social community tries to establish accurate descriptions of private stimulation (see also Chapter 1). Successful training of such reports involves reinforcing self-descriptive statements such as "I feel angry" or "I am sick" in the presence of presumed private events. Because public cues and private events usually go together, people use external, public cues from behavior to train correspondence between internal stimulation and verbal reports (see Bem, 1972, on self-perception theory; see Egan, Bloom, & Santos, 2010, for an account of how the act of choosing (public cue) leads to preference in children and monkeys; see also Chapter 12). When a child is taught how to report being hurt, parents use crying, holding the wounded area, and physical damage to infer that she is actually in pain. Because the child's behavior and private stimulation of pain are (often) well correlated, she eventually reports "I am hurt" or other internal happenings, solely on the basis of the private stimulation. The private event (painful stimulation) comes to function as a discriminative stimulus for self-descriptive report.

A problem of privacy is also faced when the community must establish consistency between private social acts and the report of those actions. In this case, correspondence is between doing and saying (Baer & Detrich, 1990; Deacon & Konarski, 1987; Lubinski & Thompson, 1987; Okouchi & Songmi, 2004). During socialization, children are asked to report on their behavior in a variety of situations. A child who returns her empty plate to the kitchen may be asked if she ate her carrots. The response "Yes, I ate every last one" can be verified and reinforced for accuracy (see Paniagua, 1989, on lying in children as "do-then-report" correspondence).

This repertoire of doing and saying sometimes has serious implications in adult life. When an employee describes sexual harassment in the workplace, there is some attempt to check on the correspondence between what is reported and the actual happenings. This monitoring of doing and saying by the community is necessary to maintain the accuracy of witnesses' reports (see Critchfield & Perone, 1990, for reinforcement of accurate or truthful self-reports). The harassed person is questioned for explicit details, the accused is asked to give his or her story, and accounts by other people are used to ensure exactness of the reported events. Based on this inquiry, the community ensures reliable reports by victims and the punishment of sexual misconduct. Many aspects of legal trials involve procedures to check on and maintain correspondence between actions and recall. In the courtroom, a witness is asked to take a legal oath by swearing a solemn vow or an affirmation to tell the truth (see Figure 11.1). A witness who misleads the court by describing events and actions that did not occur is guilty of perjury and can be severely punished.

There is evidence that expressing one's feelings, saying and doing, and recalling actions and events are aspects of verbal behavior (Skinner, 1957). One important function of verbal behavior involves formulating and following rules, maxims, or instructions (Skinner, 1969). Rules may be analyzed as verbal stimuli that alter the responses of a listener. A doctor may state that "too much cholesterol increases the risk of heart attack," and the patient may then act by reducing or eliminating foods that have high cholesterol levels. Advice and other instructions regulate behavior because such rules usually guide effective action (i.e., health improves as a result of selecting low-cholesterol foods).

Based on personal experiences, people often describe contingencies (formulate rules) as speakers and then follow them as listeners (rule-governed). Bandura (1997) has outlined how self-efficacy rules (beliefs about one's ability to cope with situations and tasks) influence performance and achievement in life. Also, social psychologists have extensively studied the impact of self-rules on thinking and actions, but have relied on social cognitive explanations of this complex behavior (Kunkel, 1997). Behavior analysts insist that following rules, even self-generated rules, is behavior maintained by contingencies of reinforcement (Galizio, 1979; Hayes, 1989b). At the end of this chapter, we analyze the listener's actions as rule-governed *behavior*. The speaker's behavior in stating rules or describing contingencies is examined as verbal behavior in Chapter 12 of this book.

Initially, we describe the process of *observational learning* as a correspondence relationship. Learning by observation involves doing what others do (imitating), in which the performance of an observer or learner is regulated by the actions of a model (correspondence). Although modeling can produce a variety of effects (e.g., social facilitation, stimulus enhancement, and so on), **imitation**

FIG. 11.1   In a courtroom, a witness swears a solemn oath to tell the truth, the whole truth and nothing but the truth. Failure to comply with the oath, involving lack of correspondence between the testimony and the facts, is the crime of perjury, punished by imprisonment. © Shutterstock.

requires the learner to produce a novel response that could only occur by observing a model emit a similar response (Thorpe, 1963). This kind of social learning may arise from an innate capacity for spontaneous imitation from an early age (see "New Directions: Behavioral Neuroscience, Mirror Neurons, and Imitation" later in this chapter). More complex forms of observational learning involve contingencies that appear to build on this basic repertoire.

CORRESPONDENCE AND SPONTANEOUS IMITATION

Although doing what others do involves a large amount of social learning, this type of correspondence may have a biological basis. At the beginning of the 20th century, psychologists suggested that social organisms have an innate tendency to imitate the actions that they see or hear others perform (Baldwin, 1906; James, 1890; McDougall, 1908; Morgan, 1894). This assumption was largely based on observations that young infants seem to imitate the actions of an adult. McDougall (1908) indicated that, as early as 4 months of age, his child would stick out his tongue when an adult did the same.

Of course, 4-month-old infants already have a considerable history of interaction with their parents, and the observed tongue protrusion may simply be attributable to social conditioning. That is, parents and other people may have smiled and laughed when the infant imitated their responses. Presumably, these social consequences strengthen imitation by the child. Another possibility is that primate infants make a lot of mouth-opening and tongue-protruding responses, especially when they are aroused by some surprising event such as an adult face. In this case, the infant's tongue protrusions merely coincide with that of the adult model and are not true imitations. Although social conditioning and arousal are plausible, research with infants and animals is providing evidence for innate or spontaneous imitation. Furthermore, specialized neurons in the brains of primates have been discovered that may allow for early **innate imitation** by newborns, and more complex forms of imitation and observational learning (see "New Directions: Behavioral Neuroscience, Mirror Neurons, and Imitation" later in this chapter).

Spontaneous Imitation in Animals and Humans

Innate or **spontaneous imitation**, if real, is based on evolution and natural selection (a characteristic of the species) rather than experiences and contingencies during the lifetime of the individual. That is, imitation of others may be an important form of adaptive (functional) behavior (Davis, 1973; Hutchinson, 1981; Millard, 1979; Porter, 1910; Thorpe, 1963). This behavior may range from a few instinctive actions to a more generalized set of responses, depending on the species. In addition, imitation may occur only when the model is present, or it may be delayed for some time after the model has been removed. Such **delayed imitation** is often regarded as a more complex form, since it involves "remembering" the modeled stimulus, rather than direct stimulus control (see Courage & Howe, 2002, pp. 257–259, on cognitive development and delayed imitation; also see Chapter 8 of this book for a behavior analysis of remembering and forgetting that does not rely on concepts of memory and cognition).

There are ethological reports of imitation by animals and birds (e.g., Alcock, 1969; Fisher & Hinde, 1949; Kawai, 1965). Fisher and Hinde (1949) described how birds in a southern English village obtained milk by spearing the foil tops of bottles left on doorsteps. Eventually, this behavior spread to several species of birds throughout England, Wales, Scotland, and Ireland. It stretches the imagination to suppose that so many birds learned the same response on their own. One conclusion is that the behavior was acquired and transmitted through observation and imitation (see Dawson & Foss, 1965, for imitation of removal of container caps by budgerigars; see also Byrne, 2003, for a discussion of ethological observations in the great apes).

Japanese macaque monkeys also seem to pass on novel behavior by observational learning. A report by Kawai (1965) describes the social transmission of an innovative method of feeding. The researchers spread grains of wheat on a sandy beach where the troop often visited. Each monkey picked the grains from the sand and ate them one at a time. Then a young monkey began to separate the sand from the wheat more efficiently by tossing a handful of mixture into the water (see Figure 11.2). When this happened, the sand sank to the bottom and the wheat floated to the top. Using this technique, the monkey obtained more wheat with less effort. Other members of the troop observed this behavior and were soon imitating this new method of feeding. Kawai indicated that observational learning transmitted many other novel behaviors, including washing the sand off sweet potatoes and swimming in the ocean (see Ball, 1938, and Breuggeman, 1973, for a discussion of imitation by rhesus monkeys; see Bering, Bjorklund, & Ragan, 2000, for an account of delayed imitation by rhesus monkeys and orangutans; see also Custance, Whiten, Sambrook, & Galdikas, 2001, for a report of failure to observe imitation in the orangutan).

Although it seems likely that some birds, monkeys, and a few other species, such as African gray parrots (Moore, 1992), dolphins (Tayler & Saayman, 1973), infant rhesus macaques (Ferrari, Visalberghi, Pauker, Fogassi, Ruggiero, & Suomi, 2006), and mongooses (Muller & Cant, 2010) can imitate the novel responses of a model, these naturalistic studies are not sufficient to establish spontaneous imitation or to rule out alternative processes such as social facilitation (Zajonc, 1965), stimulus enhancement, or copying (Galef, 1988, pp. 15–16; Galef, 1990; Miklosi, 2007; see Zentall, 2006, for a review; see also Miller, Rayburn-Reeves, & Zentall, 2009, and Zentall,

FIG. 11.2 A Japanese macaque monkey is shown washing grain to eat. Monkeys were found to learn this behavior by observation of other monkeys in the troop. Photograph by Heather Angel of Natural Visions is published with permission.

2011, for a description of experimental control procedures to establish true imitation). Social animals have many experiences that may contribute to doing what others do. Therefore, it is not possible to be sure that the imitation was spontaneous (based on species history) rather than acquired (based on social learning). Only laboratory experiments can distinguish between acquired and spontaneous imitation.

IMITATION IN THE LABORATORY

Thorndike (1911) conducted the earliest experiment on spontaneous imitation. The experiment involved a cat getting out of what he called a puzzle box by observing the successful performance of others. A well-trained cat was placed in the box and an inexperienced cat was allowed to watch the performance from an adjacent cage. The experiment was a dismal failure. The observer cat was no better at getting out of the box than a naive animal. There was no improvement in learning regardless of the number of observational trials. Thorndike obtained similar negative results with chicks, dogs, and monkeys, and concluded that animals cannot learn by observation.

This conclusion stalled experiments on animal imitation for some time. Then Herbert and Harsh (1944) reported that cats could learn to solve manipulative problems by observation, if they observe mistakes as well as successful performances. Cats that observed both mistakes and correct responses by a model did better at problems than cats that only watched a skillful performance. When many alternative responses are available, seeing what does and does not work seemed to be necessary for observational learning (see Biederman & Vanayan, 1988, for an account of a similar effect with pigeons).

Around the same time, Warden and his associates (Warden & Jackson, 1935; Warden, Fjeld, & Koch, 1940) demonstrated imitation in rhesus monkeys. They trained monkeys by reinforcement to solve puzzles that opened doors to reveal hidden raisins. When this performance was well established, a naive monkey watched a trained animal obtain raisins. Observation of the model produced instantaneous solutions on 76% of the test trials. However, only the first instance of imitation could be described as spontaneous, since the discovery of the raisin would reinforce this behavior and increase its likelihood thereafter.

Spontaneous and Delayed Imitation in Pigeons

In fact, it is difficult to find an experiment that reliably demonstrates spontaneous imitation. This is because reinforcement of the observer's behavior always confounds the results. Based on this realization, Robert Epstein (1984) (Figure 11.3) designed an experiment to show spontaneous imitation with pigeons. The experimental procedures ensured that the observer was naive, and there were no programmed (or accidental) sources of reinforcement for imitative responses.

Figure 11.4 shows the subjects and apparatus that Epstein used. Some birds served as models, and others were observers. The observers had never been in a laboratory experiment, and none of them had ever eaten from a laboratory feeder. The model and observer pigeons could see one another through a clear partition that separated the chamber into left and right compartments. Each side had exactly the same configuration. Models were always placed in the left side of the chamber, where a feeder was filled with food. Observers were placed in the right side of the chamber, where the feeder never contained food. The modeled performance in various conditions was pecking or pushing a ball, pulling on a rope, or pecking a key. All of the models were trained by operant conditioning to emit the requisite performance for food reinforcement.

FIG. 11.3   Robert Epstein. Reprinted with permission.

FIG. 11.4   Subjects and apparatus used by Robert Epstein to study spontaneous imitation by pigeons. Adapted from "Spontaneous and deferred imitation in the pigeon," by R. Epstein, 1984, *Behavioural Processes*, 9, 347–352.

There were five conditions in the first experiment. During adaptation, a naive-observer bird was placed in the right side of the chamber. One object (a ping-pong ball, rope, or key) was situated in the left compartment but not available to the bird in the right chamber. After three sessions, the same object was added to the right chamber and the naive bird was placed alone in the chamber for three sessions of baseline. Next, the object was removed from the right chamber and the model bird was added. During exposure and adaptation to the model, the model engaged in the reinforced performance of pecking the ball, pulling the rope, or pecking the key, and the observer was exposed to this performance without the object for another three sessions. Following this phase, Epstein conducted a test for model-present imitation; he added the object to the observer's chamber while the model continued to demonstrate the performance. If the observer emitted the designated response at a higher rate than during baseline, this was declared to be evidence of direct spontaneous imitation. Finally, Epstein designed a test for model-absent imitation. The object remained present but the model was removed. If the observer responded to the object at a higher level than baseline, this was said to be evidence of delayed spontaneous imitation.

Of the four observer pigeons tested, all showed more responses (key, ball, or rope) with the model present than during baseline. Two of the birds demonstrated strong spontaneous imitation, but the effect was weaker for the other two pigeons. Birds that strongly imitated the model were found to continue this imitation even when the model was removed (i.e., model-absent imitation). The data suggested that delayed spontaneous imitation can occur in laboratory pigeons, but the results were inconsistent over subjects.

Epstein (1984) ran a second experiment that specifically focused on delayed spontaneous imitation. In this experiment he used only "peck the ball" as the imitative response. The same conditions were used as in the first experiment, but the model-present phase was omitted. Thus, the birds were never able to match their responses immediately to those of the model. The results for three new birds were clear. In each case, pecking the ball was higher after exposure to and removal of the model than during baseline. Spontaneous imitation occurred even after 24 h had elapsed between watching the model and the test for imitation.

Analysis of Epstein's Experiments

These experiments on direct and delayed spontaneous imitation are important. Experimental procedures ensured that the occurrence of imitation was not attributable to previous experience or current reinforcement. It therefore appears that spontaneous imitation is a real effect and is a form of phylogenetic behavior. Generally speaking, then, imitative behavior occurs because it has been important to the survival and reproduction of the species (i.e., contingencies of survival). In other words, organisms that imitated others were more likely to find food, avoid predators, and eventually produce offspring.

The phylogenetic basis of spontaneous imitation is a reasonable hypothesis. However, as Epstein notes, at least three aspects of the experiments suggest that some environmental experience is also necessary. The birds were raised in a colony and may have had social interactions that contributed to imitative performance. Pigeons that are isolated from birth may show smaller effects of exposure to a model (May & Dorr, 1968). In addition, the effects of food reinforcement may have contributed to the results. Although observers were never directly reinforced with food for imitation, they did see the models eat from the feeder. In fact, Epstein remarked that occasionally the naive bird would thrust its head into the feeder hole when the model did, even though it did not receive food. Finally, only one object was present in the right and left sides of the chamber. If three objects were available, would the observer peck or pull the one the model did, without training? Each of these aspects opposes a strong conclusion about the biological basis of spontaneous imitation in Epstein's experiments (see Zentall, 2006, 2011 for a discussion of a variety of alternative behavioral effects that are mistaken for imitation). Clearly, additional research is required.

There are other results, however, that point to an evolutionary basis for such behavior. The fact that pigeons showed imitation after a substantial delay is noteworthy, and deferred imitation has also been observed in Japanese quail (see also Dorrance & Zentall, 2001). In discrimination experiments, birds often have trouble remembering events (matching to sample) delayed by a few seconds. However, the birds in Epstein's second experiment showed imitation 24 h after the model had pecked the ball. And Japanese quail imitated treadle responses up to 30 min after the model's demonstration. The extended retention of such behavior is in accord with a biological account, suggesting the preparedness of these animals to imitate what others have done (Hinde & Stevenson-Hinde, 1973).

The experimental research by Epstein (1984) on imitation and delayed imitation in pigeons remains controversial, and imitation in rats is also in dispute (see Mitchell, Heyes, Gardner, & Dawson, 1999, for the effects of odor; see Ray, Gardner, & Heyes, 2000, for arguments against odor cues; see Zentall, 2006, for a review). Thus, Pear (2001, p. 96) argues on the basis of related research that stimulus enhancement, or pairing of a conspecific (member of a species) with the ping-pong ball, accounts for the apparent direct and delayed imitation by pigeons (recall, however, that Epstein used a ball, rope, and key). On the other hand, research using a two-action method of pecking or pressing a treadle supports Epstein's claim of spontaneous imitation by pigeons (Dorrance & Zentall, 2001; Kaiser, Zentall, & Galef, 1997; Zentall, Sutton, & Sherburne, 1996). Although there is no further research evidence of delayed imitation by pigeons, newer evidence indicates that pigeons can imitate a complex conditional discrimination (Dorrance, 2001), suggesting that delayed imitation is a possible interpretation of Epstein's results.

INFANT IMITATION RESEARCH

Spontaneous Imitation by Newborn Infants

There is evidence that spontaneous imitation occurs in human infants, almost from the moment of birth. Meltzoff and Moore (1977) were the first to report that 12- to 21-day-old infants can imitate the facial and hand movements of adult models. In these experiments, the imitative responses were tongue protrusion, mouth opening, lip protrusion, and sequential finger movement. The infants' facial gestures and modeled stimuli are illustrated in Figure 11.5.

Experiment 1 used three male and three female infants who ranged in age from 12 to 17 days. The experimenter presented a passive face to the infant for 90 s. Each infant was then shown four gestures (i.e., the modeled stimulus) in random order. The modeled stimulus was presented four times in a 15-s presentation period. An imitation-test period followed in which the experimenter resumed presenting a passive face and the infant was monitored for imitative responses. Each new gesture was followed by presenting a passive face for 70 s.

FIG. 11.5 Infants' facial gestures and modeled stimuli. From "Imitation and facial and manual gestures by human neonates," by A. N. Meltzoff and M. K. Moore, 1977, *Science, 198*, 75–78. © 1977 American Association for the Advancement of Science. Reprinted with permission.

The researchers made a videotape of the infants' behavior, and the segments were scored in random order by trained adult judges. For each segment, the judges were to order the four gestures from most likely to least likely in terms of imitation of the modeled stimulus. These judgments were collapsed to yes or no ratings of whether a particular gesture was the imitative response. In all cases, more yes judgments occurred when the gesture was imitative than when it was not.

Meltzoff and Moore (1977) designed a second experiment to correct some procedural problems with the first study. Six male and six female infants between 16 and 21 days old were used as subjects. The experiment began with the researcher inserting a pacifier into the infant's mouth and presenting a passive face for 30 s. A baseline period of 150 s followed in which the pacifier was removed, but the passive face continued to be presented. Next, the pacifier was reinserted in the infant's mouth and the researcher presented one of two gestures—mouth opening or lip protrusion. The modeled stimulus was presented until the infant had watched it for 15 s. The experimenter then stopped gesturing and resumed a passive face. At this point, the pacifier was removed and a 150-s response period or imitation test began, during which time the researcher maintained a passive face. Again, the pacifier was reinserted and the second gesture was presented in the same fashion.

The videotapes were scored in random order in terms of the frequency of tongue protrusion and mouth opening. Figure 11.6 shows the frequency of response during baseline and after exposure to the experimenter's gesture. When tongue protrusions were the modeled stimulus, the infant produced this response more frequently than during baseline. On the other hand, when mouth openings were the modeled stimulus, the infant frequently produced this response during the test period, but not tongue protrusions. These results suggest that babies are capable of spontaneous imitation of facial gestures (see Kuhl & Meltzoff, 1996, for a discussion of imitation of vocal speech sounds).

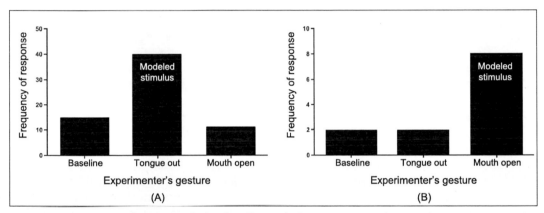

FIG. 11.6 Frequency of response during baseline and after exposure to the experimenter's gesture. In panel A the modeled stimulus is "tongue out" (protrusion) and the frequency of tongue protrusions by infants increases relative to baseline and to the control response of "mouth open." When the modeled stimulus is "mouth open" (panel B), the frequency of mouth opening by the infant increases relative to the control conditions. Adapted from "Imitation and facial and manual gestures by human neonates," by A. N. Meltzoff and M. K. Moore, 1977, *Science, 198,* 75–78.

In subsequent experiments, Meltzoff and Moore (1983) showed imitation of mouth opening and tongue protrusions in newborns that were 0.7 to 71 hours old. These results are in accord with Field, Woodson, Greenberg, and Cohen (1982), who reported imitation of mouth opening, mouth widening, and lip protrusion in infants who averaged 36 hours in age (see also Jacobson, 1979). More recently, human neonates between a few hours and a few days old showed spontaneous imitation of finger movements (Nagy, Compagne, Orvos, Pal, Molnar, Janszky et al., 2005), and auditory–oral matching of consonant sounds (early vocal imitation), behavior thought to be beyond newborn infants' capabilities (Chen, Striano, & Rakoczy, 2004). Notably, neonatal imitation has been reported for chimpanzees (*Pan troglodytes*), suggesting that an imitative capacity at birth is not unique to *Homo sapiens* (Bard, 2007).

Difficulties with Infant Imitation Research

The results of Meltzoff and Moore's experiments remain controversial (for reviews, see Anisfeld, 1996; Bjorklund, 1987; Jones, 2009). Hayes and Watson (1981) were unable to produce infant imitation despite careful attempts to follow the procedures described by Meltzoff and Moore (1977). In their second experiment, Hayes and Watson found that the pacifier could evoke mouth movements and that this, rather than the experimenter's presentation of the modeled gesture, may have produced the responses. If this is the case, infant imitation may simply be an artifact of the experimental procedures, although recent studies do not appear to have these problems (Chen et al., 2004; Nagy et al., 2005). Jacobson (1979) found that the imitative responses of infants could be elicited by nonspecific events. For example, tongue protrusion occurred when a pen was moved toward the infant's face (see Anisfeld, 1996, on infant behavior and innate releasers; see also Provine, 1989, on fixed-action patterns). And Jones (2006) found that an auditory stimulus (music) that substituted for the behavioral model increased tongue protrusions, indicating that these responses occur to "interesting distal stimuli."

Other problems concern measurement, restricted range of responses, and infant attention to the modeled stimulus. Meltzoff and Moore (1977) noted that infants' responses are not discrete or well formed each time they occur. This means that the response class is not clearly defined, and it is therefore difficult to obtain a reliable measure. Because the response class is unclear, coders who observe the modeled gesture may "see" the imitative response more frequently than other response forms (see Ullstadius, 2000, on variability in judgment of infant imitation). In addition, there are few experimentally useful infant behaviors for imitation research (Meltzoff & Moore, 1983), and these responses may have several determinants. Thus, facial movements may be determined by general arousal, be elicited by nonspecific events, or be imitations of a model. Research on finger movements (Nagy et al., 2005) and auditory–vocal imitation of consonants (Chen et al., 2004) suggests that restricted range of behaviors may no longer be a serious problem. Finally, it is difficult to keep the infant focused on the model. Because of this, researchers wait until the infant is "ready" before presenting the modeled stimulus. If experimenters match the model stimulus to infants' behavior, it may be that they are generating correspondence as an artifact (see also Jones, 1996, on oral exploration as an artifact). In other words, the experimenter accidentally imitates the infant instead of the infant imitating the experimenter's gesture (Field et al., 1982; Hayes & Watson, 1981; Jacobson, 1979).

Jones (2009) recently concluded that the widely accepted view of newborn infant imitation lacks supporting evidence. Newborns do match adult behaviors, but this matching is not true imitation. Tongue protrusions to adults by newborns—a well-replicated, apparently imitative behavior—are species-typical responses that occur to a range of stimuli across different sensory modalities (e.g., music). Also, early imitation studies do not rule out general arousal of species-typical responses as an alternative account for apparent newborn imitation. However, this conclusion is still in dispute, and the scientific community has not yet rejected the hypothesis of newborn infant imitation (e.g., Zentall, 2011).

Delayed Imitation by Human Infants

In 1988, Meltzoff reported on delayed imitation in 14-month-old infants (Meltzoff, 1988b). These infants were exposed to six modeled actions using different objects (e.g., an adult bending over and touching his or her head to an orange panel, causing a light to flash). One of the six actions had a zero probability of occurrence in spontaneous play. In the delayed-imitation condition, infants observed the modeled behavior but were not permitted to touch the objects, thereby preventing direct imitation of the model. Following a delay of 1 week, infants returned to the experimental setting and observers scored their imitation of the model's actions. Infants in the delayed-imitation condition emitted more target actions than infants in control groups who were not exposed to the modeled actions. There was also evidence for delayed imitation of the novel action even though the infants had never directly imitated this behavior at the time it was presented, a finding replicated by Barr and Hayne (1996).

A series of studies by Meltzoff (1988a, 1988b, 1988c) indicate that infants ranging in age from 9 to 24 months will imitate significantly more modeled actions than control groups over delays ranging from 24 h in the youngest infants to 4 months in the oldest. Additional research indicates that 14-month-old infants will show delayed imitation of behavior modeled on television after a 24-h delay. In the same study, the researchers found delayed imitation by infants of behavior modeled by an "expert" toddler performing a novel response after a 48-h delay and a change in context from the experimental situation to the home setting (Hanna & Meltzoff, 1993). The basic findings of the Meltzoff group have been replicated with 6- to 30-month-old infants by other researchers (for a review, see Courage & Howe, 2002). The use of "expert" children as models for disabled children in classroom settings has been adopted for such behaviors as toileting, block stacking, hand clapping, etc. (Bob Crow, personal communication).

Correspondence and Intermodal Mapping

Imitation in human newborns, if it exists, involves the infant observing a modeled gesture and responding with a set of muscle movements that correspond to the visual stimulus. The correspondence between the modeled stimulus and the form of response is a remarkable achievement, because the infant is unable to see its own face when it reproduces the facial gestures of the adult model (this has been called "opaque imitation" by Zentall, 2006, 2011).

Meltzoff and Moore (1999) refer to this process as "active intermodal mapping," where infants can monitor their facial movements through proprioceptive feedback and compare this felt activity to what they see. At the present time, there is no detailed evolutionary account of active intermodal mapping and spontaneous imitation (see Meltzoff, 1999, for a speculative account). The evidence is growing that mirror neurons in the brains of humans play a role in the capacity for observed goal-related actions of others, but this system does not seem to be well developed in neonates or even 6-month-old infants (Falck-Ytter, Gredeback, & van Hofsten, 2006). Thus, a definitive account of spontaneous imitation in newborn infants is not yet available.

NEW DIRECTIONS: Behavioral Neuroscience, Mirror Neurons, and Imitation

Some say that imitation is the highest form of flattery. Within the last decade, neurons in the ventral premotor area of the brain have been detected that respond when a primate sees someone doing something that the animal itself has done before. These so-called "mirror neurons" were active in macaque monkeys when the animals watched another monkey perform the same action that they had done themselves (Gallese, Fadiga, Fogassi, & Rizzolatti, 1996; Rizzolatti & Craighero, 2004). When a monkey engages in some action, neurons in its frontal lobe are active during the "doing," and a subset of these same neurons fire when the monkey just *watches* a model perform a similar response, even in newborn infant monkeys (Gross, 2006). The neurons fire as though the observer monkey was mirroring the movements of the model (see Figure 11.7). Located at the merger of the anterior dorsal visual stream into the motor cortex, mirror neurons have both motor and visual functions. Mirror neuron cells fire during action execution and

FIG. 11.7 The photograph (left) depicts modeling of tongue protrusions to a newborn rhesus monkey. The monkey's subsequent response (right) is an opaque imitation of the modeled stimulus. That is, the infant monkey is unable to see its own face when it reproduces the facial gestures of the adult human model. The mirror neuron system is implicated in this kind of intermodal mapping as well as other aspects of action understanding. Republished under common copyright from L. Gross, 2006, "Evolution of neonatal imitation," *PLoS Biology, 9,* 1484.

during the observation of the same action, coding both the motor act (grasping) and the action consequences (grasping for food or grasping to move an object). This core imitation circuit interacts with other neural systems related to visual, motor, and task-specific processing, but the key function is toward coding of the motor components of the model's performance, rather than visual representation of what is observed (Iacoboni, 2009).

Mirror-type cells, found in the human anterior cingulate, fire when a person is poked with a needle, but surprisingly they also fire when a patient watches someone else being poked. Some researchers have concluded that mirror neurons dissolve the distinction between "self" and "others," providing humans with the capacity for empathy and the ability to understand others better. Given the probability of mirror neurons existing in human infants, this could support the claims of those reporting infant facial imitation and active intermodal mapping (Meltzoff & Moore, 1999). However, the mirror circuits are largely underdeveloped in early infancy, requiring more interaction with the environment to organize into a functional mirror system (Coren, Ward, & Enns, 2004, pp. 453–455). Iriki (2006) suggests that the neural mechanisms for imitation also exist in lower primates, but that training (in tool use) is required for this capacity to become fully operational.

The impact of conditioning on the mirror neuron system (MNS) is a way of showing the plasticity of the mirror circuitry. The MNS usually supports automatic imitation of sensorimotor actions, but changes to the environmental contingencies result in adjustments by the mirror pathways. Research shows that nonmatching training can abolish or reverse the usual action-matching properties of the MNS (Ray & Heyes, 2011).

In one study, participants in a reaction-time task were trained to close their hands to hand-open stimuli, and to open their hands to hand-closed images (Heyes, Bird, Johnson, & Haggard, 2005). The results showed that nonmatching training eliminated automatic imitation. That is, participants no longer made automatic, faster hand-opening responses to the open stimulus than to the closed one. Another study trained nonmatching of finger abductions or movements of a finger away from the other digits (Catmur, Walsh, & Heyes, 2007). After training, the participants showed reverse imitation, producing abductions of the little finger to observed abduction movements of the index finger. The study also showed reverse responsiveness of the MNS using motor evoked potentials (MEPs), a common indicator of the mirror neuron system. Thus, after training in nonmatching, observed abductions of the index finger produced larger MEPs in the little finger muscle than in the muscle of the index finger itself. In addition, using functional magnetic resonance imaging (fMRI), researchers reversed the stronger MNS response to hand movements compared with movements of the foot (Catmur, Gillmeister, Bird, Liepelt, Brass, & Heyes, 2008). Participants were trained to make a hand response to a foot stimulus and a foot response to a hand stimulus. This training resulted in dominance of the foot over the hand in fMRI imaging responses of both the premotor and parietal areas of the mirror circuitry.

Together these studies show the neural plasticity of the MNS to modeling contingencies arranged along sensorimotor dimensions. When the contingencies require correspondence between the model stimulus (hand open) and the response of the observer (hand open), the MNS supports imitation. However, the MNS can support reverse imitation when the modeling contingencies require non-correspondence, as when people are given nonmatching training (hand-open model and hand-closed response). This plasticity of the MNS would allow people to use the observed behavior of others to face everyday challenges of social living. On some occasions people are reinforced for doing what others do, but sometimes doing the opposite of what others do is reinforced, as when one person pushes while another pulls. Thus one function of the MNS may relate to social coordination of individual action.

In fact the functions of mirror neurons are not entirely clear, but several possibilities have been postulated. **Autistic children** show a dysfunctional MNS that may help to explain some of their behavioral deficit (Oberman, Hubbard, McCleery, Altschuler, Ramachandran, & Pineda, 2005). Children with autism often fail to show empathy (recognizing the feelings of others), age-appropriate language skills (the mirror cells are near Broca's language area), or imitation of significant others (Iacobini, Woods, Brass, Bekkering, Mazziota, & Rizzolatti, 1999). These findings suggest that the MNS plays a central role in children's socialization and language learning. Furthermore, mirror neurons seem to enable observers to form action-understandings from others that do not strictly correspond to their own motor representations (Ferrari, Rozzi, & Fogassi, 2005).

A recent study by Repacholi and Meltzoff (2007) found that 18-month-old youngsters could regulate their imitation of an adult model on the basis of emotions expressed by a third party toward the model (angry or neutral). This kind of emotional eavesdropping by infants is what might be expected if the MNS allowed for action-understandings based on the emotional reactions of others. In adults, the act of imagining oneself swinging a golf club like Tiger Woods may activate the mirror circuits and improve one's own swing (Buccino, Vogt, Ritzl, Fink, Zilles, Freund et al., 2004), especially when accompanied by corrective feedback from hitting the ball (reinforcement). Observational learning (described later in this chapter) may therefore have its roots in the mirror neuron circuits of the human brain.

Analysis of Spontaneous and Delayed Imitation

Birds, apes, dolphins, and humans engage in imitation, delayed imitation, and opaque imitation (Zentall, 2011). The appearance of behavior similar to a model does not necessarily imply identical functions and mechanisms. That is, the evolution of spontaneous (and delayed) imitation in pigeons and quail, if real, probably resulted from different biological contingencies than those that led to this behavior in humans. For example, spontaneous imitation may be related to care taking in humans and to food gathering in birds. Any tendency to imitate, if reinforced, can promote such behavior in many subsequent settings. Only a detailed evolutionary analysis of behavior will provide an account that can be tested. Even with such experiments, it will be difficult to be certain about the adaptive advantage of spontaneous imitation for different species. However, supplementary studies from behavioral neuroscience should be helpful in unraveling the infant's capacity for innate imitation.

Another possibility is that there is no specialized capacity for spontaneous imitation. Ray and Heyes (2011) suggest that imitation is entirely acquired by associative learning and increased by reinforcement. Sources of correspondence learning used in infant imitation include direct self-observation, mirrored self-observation, synchronous action, acquired equivalence experience, and being imitated. Direct observation of one's actions is a common source of early correspondence learning as infants watch the movement of their limbs and actively match what they see. Older infants use mirrors and reflections to engage in a range of behaviors that serve as visual stimuli to repeat the corresponding actions, such as touching their nose or making a face. Synchronous actions involve the infant and caretaker responding in a similar manner to some event, as when they both open their mouths in response to the infant being fed by a spoon. In acquired equivalence experience, a stimulus is paired on some occasions with seeing an action, and on other occasions with the performance of the action (see Chapter 12 for a discussion of stimulus equivalence in the learning of language or verbal behavior). For example, a child hears the word "smile" on some occasions when she sees someone smiling and at other times when she herself is smiling, thereby establishing equivalence (the word "smile" = seeing a smile = smiling oneself).

Being imitated by others is the most prominent source of correspondence learning in infancy. Infants and caretakers spend much of the time in face-to-face social interaction, and 79% of the mother–infant interactions involve mothers imitating their infants' responses, increasing the opportunities for infants to do what they see and see what they do (see Chapter 12 on maternal imitation of the infant in the acquisition of language). Considering all the sources of correspondence learning and the progressive development of imitation throughout childhood, Ray and Heyes (2011) conclude that imitation is a completely ontogenetic achievement based on sensorimotor learning arising from a "richly imitiogenic sociocultural environment." That is, imitation is learned by contingencies arranged by the culture, rather than activated and maintained by innate neural or cognitive mechanisms.

A compromise position is that imitation by neonates is limited in range and is based on a rudimentary capacity to do what ones sees (Meltzoff & Moore, 1999), but later imitation is largely due to reinforcement and other ontogenetic experiences (Ray & Heyes, 2011). That is, imitation is the phenotypic outcome of an interaction of genes and environment. Skinner (1984b, p. 220) noted that only the first instance of any behavior is entirely attributable to genetic history. Thus, early imitation and delayed imitation by older human infants are probably less related to biology than to environmental experiences (see Tomasello, Savage-Rumbaugh, & Kruger, 1993, for a similar conclusion for chimpanzees and humans). Even so, there is no conclusive behavioral evidence showing that reinforcement history or associative sensorimotor learning accounts for delayed imitation by 6-week-old infants. Generalized imitation ("do what I do" generalized correspondence) can be established by reinforcement, but no one has yet shown this in 6-week-old infants. In fact, Horne and Erjavec (2007) could not obtain generalized imitation of empty-handed gestures in 11- to 18-month-old infants or manual gestures in 1- to 2-year-old youngsters (Erjavec, Lovett, & Horne, 2009).

Another aspect of delayed imitation by young infants is that they do not have to emit the novel actions of the model during the initial demonstration. That is, they merely observe the modeled stimulus and later show imitation in the absence of the model. Again, it is possible to provide an account of delayed imitation based on generalized imitation (see below), but whether this account can extend to 6-week-old infants is unknown. A reasonable assumption is that delayed imitation involves a capacity to reproduce the modeled actions in the absence of the model, as well as a reinforcement history that substantially builds on this biological capacity.

CORRESPONDENCE, GENERALIZED IMITATION, AND OBSERVATIONAL LEARNING

Operant Imitation and Generalized Imitation

It is possible to train imitation as an operant in a social contingency of reinforcement. The discriminative stimulus is the behavior of the model (S^D_{model}), the operant is a response that matches the modeled stimulus (R_{match}), and reinforcement is verbal praise (S^r_{social}). Matching the model is reinforced, while noncorrespondent responses are extinguished. These social contingencies are similar to the discrimination experiments involving matching to sample for primary reinforcement (see Chapter 8).

In fact, Miller and Dollard (1941) proposed that observational learning was simply a special case of operant discrimination involving matching to a modeled stimulus. If imitation is reinforced and nonimitation is extinguished, imitation of the model will increase. On the other hand, nonimitation occurs if imitation is extinguished and nonimitation is reinforced. In one study, Miller and Dollard (1941) showed that children who were reinforced for imitation of a leader repeated these actions more than children who did not receive reinforcement. This kind of leader–follower behavior has also been reported for rats and other animals (Hake, Donaldson, & Hyten, 1983).

Although **operant imitation** provides a straightforward account of observational learning, Bandura (1969) noted that the operant account may be limited to situations in which the observer sees the model, an imitative response immediately occurs, and reinforcement follows. In everyday life, there are occasions when imitation does not conform to this sequence. For example, suppose that a young child is seated in front of a television set watching *Sesame Street*, and she observes Kermit the Frog sing "It's not easy being green" for the first time. After watching Kermit's performance, the child turns off the television and goes to help her parent in the kitchen. The next day, the girl begins to sing Kermit's song. The child's performance approximates the puppet's song. She may not remember every word, but she has the basic tune. Notice that the girl has never before performed this sequence of responses. Because of this, reinforcement could not have strengthened her performance. Also, the child's imitative sequence occurred in the absence of the model; Kermit was not present when she imitated him. Finally, the girl's imitative performance was delayed; she sang the song the next day, not immediately after Kermit's demonstration.

The Kermit song example is typical of observational learning in everyday life, but it seems to defy an S^D: $R \rightarrow S^r$ interpretation. The imitative response is novel, and reinforcement for the song is (apparently) missing. In addition, the girl sings the song 1 day later with the model or S^D absent. Finally, Bandura (1969) noted that there is no account of the long delay between modeled performance and later imitation.

Although Bandura (1969, 1977, 1986) has argued against an operant account based on these difficulties, Donald Baer (Figure 11.8) and his associates provided a behavior analysis of imitation that handles each of the apparent challenges to the operant paradigm (Baer & Sherman, 1964; Baer, Peterson, & Sherman, 1967). The approach is called **generalized imitation**, and is based on operant principles of discrimination and generalization (see Glossary for complete definition).

FIG. 11.8   Donald Baer. Reprinted with permission.

The procedures of generalized imitation begin with simple reinforcement of correspondence or matching between the modeled performance (S^D model) and the imitative operant (R_{match}). The contingency requires the observer to perform the same action as the model. Reinforcement increases imitative behavior, while extinction makes it decrease. If a child is reinforced with praise for imitation of nonsense syllables by a puppet, this response will increase. When praise is withheld, imitation of the puppet declines (Baer & Sherman, 1964).

The actual discrimination procedures are shown in Figure 11.9, and involve several modeled stimuli (S^D) and multiple operants (R_{match}). The puppet's head nodding is an S^D for the child to nod her head and an S^Δ for saying nonsense syllables or opening and closing her mouth. When the puppet opens and closes its mouth, this is an S^D for similar behavior by the child and an S^Δ for the other two responses. In each case, what the model does sets the occasion for reinforcement of a similar response by the child; all other responses are extinguished. This training results in a *stimulus class of modeled actions* and an *imitative response class*. The child now imitates whichever of the three responses the model performs.

The next step is to test for generalization of the stimulus and response classes. Baer and Sherman (1964) showed that a new-modeled stimulus would set the occasion for a *novel imitative response*, without any further reinforcement. If the puppet began to press a lever, the child also imitated this performance, even though this response was never reinforced with praise. Thus, *generalized imitation* accounted for the appearance of novel imitative acts in children, even when these responses were never reinforced.

What about the absence of the discriminative stimulus and long delays? It is important to note that all instances of modeling and imitation involve the absence of the S^D before the imitative response occurs. That is, the model demonstrates the action (S^D presented), and after the demonstration (S^D removed) the imitative response is emitted. A contingency may be established that requires a delay of some time between the presentation of the discriminative stimulus and the imitative response (see

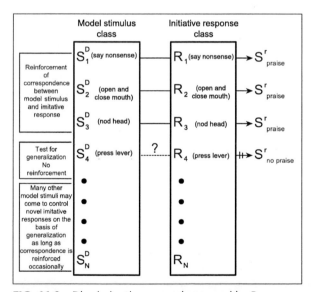

FIG. 11.9   Discrimination procedures used by Baer and Sherman to establish generalized imitation. After training several imitative responses, a test for generalization is given without reinforcement. Generalized stimulus (model) and response (imitation) classes are eventually formed on the basis of training the model-imitation exemplars. Based on a description of the contingencies in "Reinforcement control of generalized imitation in young children," by D. M. Baer and J. A. Sherman, 1964, *Journal of Experimental Child Psychology, 1,* 37–49.

Chapter 8 on delayed matching to sample). This is the same as when a pigeon pecks a key that matches the sample, but reinforcement depends on delaying the matching response by a few seconds. The delay between the offset of the sample stimulus and the occurrence of the matching response may be lengthened by successive approximation. Eventually, the pigeon may be accurate even after 20 s without seeing the sample.

Similarly, children may learn to delay their imitative responses. Adults may reinforce newborn infants when the baby mimics their behavior. As the child gets older, reinforcement of imitation depends on increasing delays between the modeled performance and the imitative response. If you tell a joke to someone, that person seldom repeats it in your presence. Immediate repetition of the joke does not reinforce the listener. Later the joke is told to another audience, whose laughter reinforces the imitative performance. In this way, social contingencies generate extensive delays between the model stimulus and the imitative response.

It is important to account for the maintenance of generalized imitation. One interpretation involves conditioned reinforcement. Baer and Sherman (1964) suggest that *similarity* becomes a conditioned reinforcer. When a child is taught to imitate, reinforcement occurs only if there is correspondence between the model's actions and the learner's performance. Since reinforcement depends on similarity, imitating others becomes a conditioned reinforcer. Thus, when it occurs, imitation is automatically reinforced (see Erjavec et al., 2009, for evidence against this interpretation).

Alternatively, generalized imitation may be maintained by intermittent reinforcement. Gewirtz (1971) indicated that there was no need to postulate similarity as a conditioned reinforcer. He noted that there is no way of separating similarity from the imitative behavior it is said to explain. Intermittent reinforcement for imitation may account for the persistence of generalized imitation. Occasional reinforcement of imitation would maintain the stimulus–response relationships. That is, occasionally imitating others pays off, as when a person learns to operate a computer by watching others.

Experiments on Generalized Imitation with Human Infants

Considerable research investigating generalized imitation has been done with children (Erjavec et al., 2009). However, most normal developing children have extensive repertoires of imitation before they participate in an experiment. This means that the best way to analyze the determinants of generalized imitation is to use normally developing infants who have more limited imitation histories. In several studies, infants between 9 and 18 months of age were found to pass generalized imitation tests for object-directed responses, vocalizations, and empty-handed gestures (Poulson & Kymmissis, 1998; Poulson, Kymmissis, Reeve, Andreatos, & Reeve, 1991; Poulson, Kyparissos, Andreatos, Kymmissis, & Parnes, 2002). However, new research with added controls reports no evidence for generalized imitation in infants around 1 to 2 years of age (Horne and Erjavec, 2007; Erjavec et al., 2009).

One of the most salient differences, in studies that support infant generalized imitation and those that do not, is testing for the imitative target behaviors before modeling and correspondence training begins. Studies that use novel imitative responses which are not already present in the infants' matching repertoire fail to find generalized imitation in infants. That is, after correspondence training these infants failed to show novel imitative responses to novel modeled stimuli. One possibility is that the infants did not have the requisite skills to match their behavior to the modeled stimulus. Thus, infants were given skills training on the target behaviors before exposure to the correspondence contingencies involving matching their gesture to the model. Even with skills training, infants failed to pass tests for generalized imitation (Horne & Erjavec, 2007). In an attempt to unravel the determinants of infant generalized imitation, Erjavec et al. (2009) increased the number of exemplars for correspondence training (the number of instances of matching to the model) to establish similarity as conditioned reinforcement (Baer & Deguchi, 1985). The results showed that infants would maintain matching to the model if some of the matches were intermittently reinforced (operant imitation), but even with training in multiple exemplars, infants did not pass tests for generalized imitation.

Up to this point, contingencies of correspondence as arranged in the laboratory have not produced generalized imitation in infants—suggesting that infants at this age may not have the ability to form higher-order (generalized) stimulus–response classes. Alternatively, training with multiple exemplars across many response topographies may be required—in other words, far more training than in these laboratory studies using only 12 exemplars. For example, Don Baer reported that it took several hundred instances of reinforced matching to establish generalized imitation in Marilla, a developmentally delayed child with no imitation skills (see "On the Applied Side: Training Generalized Imitation" in this chapter). Another possibility is that the emergence of generalized imitation requires verbal skills such as naming or labeling the modeled performance (as in "Do X"). If this is so, generalized imitation may increase with language acquisition and be related to the onset of observational learning in children.

ON THE APPLIED SIDE: Training Generalized Imitation

Donald Baer conducted the early research on generalized imitation and pioneered its application. Together with Montrose M. Wolf and Todd R. Risley at the University of Kansas (1965–2002), he founded the discipline of applied behavior analysis. He received numerous awards from the American Psychological Association and the Society for the Experimental Analysis of Behavior, served as an international distinguished professor, and was the Roy A. Roberts Distinguished Professor of Human Development at the University of Kansas. Don Baer died on 29 April 2002 while having lunch. He was known for his wit, intellectual brilliance, and advocacy on behalf of individuals with behavioral disabilities. In this section we learn about Baer's use of generalized imitation principles to teach imitation to a child with severe disabilities (Baer, Peterson, & Sherman, 1967).

Marilla was a profoundly retarded child who had never shown signs of imitating others. At 12 years old, she had a limited repertoire of responses that included grunting sounds, following simple commands like "Sit down," dressing and feeding herself, going to the washroom, and responses such as turning a knob or opening a door. Although the staff at Firecrest School had tried their best with Marilla, they were now convinced that the child was "just too dumb to learn anything." At this point, Baer and his associates used operant principles to teach generalized imitation to Marilla.

About an hour before lunch, Marilla was brought to a room containing a table and chairs. The training began when the teacher said "Do this," and raised his arm (S^D). Marilla simply stared at him and did not imitate the response. The same sequence was tried several times without success. On the next attempt, the teacher raised his arm and assisted Marilla in doing the same. After this sequence, Marilla received a spoonful of her lunch and at the same time the teacher said "Good." After several of these assisted trials, Marilla needed less and less help, and reinforcement only occurred when she lifted her arm by herself. Sometimes she raised her arm when the performance was not modeled (S^Δ); these responses were not *reinforced. With this training, Marilla acquired a simple response of raising her hand when the teacher said "Do this," and demonstrated the action (direct imitation).*

Other imitative responses, such as tapping a table and parts of the body with the left hand, were established by shaping and differential reinforcement. After seven examples had been taught, the teacher said "Do this," and tapped the arm of a chair. Marilla immediately made the same response although she had never been reinforced for doing so. This was the first instance of generalized imitation. A novel-modeling stimulus (tapping the arm of the chair) resulted in a new imitative response (Marilla tapping the arm of her chair).

As more instances of reinforced imitation were added to Marilla's repertoire, the percentage of novel imitations increased. Some of the responses were more important in everyday life, such as scribbling on paper, placing geometric forms in order, crawling under a table, and burping a doll. After 120 examples of reinforced imitation, the girl would immediately imitate new examples of modeled performance.

The basic idea of generalized imitation is that reinforcement of some members of the stimulus and response classes maintains the strength of all members—including novel imitations that have never been reinforced. To show the importance of reinforcement for Marilla's novel imitations, the contingency of reinforcement was changed. The teacher continued to model various actions, but Marilla was no longer reinforced for imitating. However, when she did anything except imitate, reinforcement occurred every 30 s. This differential reinforcement of other behavior (DRO) maintains the reinforcer in the setting, places imitation on extinction, and increases behavior that is incompatible with imitation. In less than 20 sessions, both reinforced and novel imitations declined to near-zero responses for each session. Clearly, generalized imitation was maintained by reinforcement.

Next, reinforcement for imitation was reinstated and generalized imitation was acquired again. At this point, the researcher began to teach sequences or chains of imitative performance to Marilla. For example, the teacher would raise his hand and stand up; reinforcement depended on Marilla imitating this two-response sequence. With small steps, the teacher was able to add more and more responses until Marilla could follow a seven-response sequence. Many of the sequences included novel imitative responses that had never been reinforced.

In the final phase of this project, Baer and his associates decided to add vocal responses to the imitative sequences. Since Marilla made grunting sounds, the teacher said, "Do this," rose from his chair, walked to the middle of the room, and said, "Ah." Marilla followed the sequence, but when it came to the vocal response she only made mouth movements. However, the facial expression was a good first approximation and was reinforced. Over time, closer and closer approximations occurred until Marilla completed the sequence with a well-expressed "Ah." Using fading, the teacher was able to get the girl to say "Ah" whenever he said "Do this," and demonstrated the vocal response.

Once the imitation of various sounds was well established, the teacher combined the sounds into words and, after about 20 h of vocal imitation, Marilla could imitate words like "Hi," "Okay," "Marilla," and the names of familiar objects. When generalized imitation of motor and vocal responses was well established, new male and female experimenters were used to extend the performance to new models. Now, any teacher could work with Marilla to broaden her skills and add to her behavioral repertoire. Once a sizable imitative repertoire is available, further learning occurs much more rapidly. Rather than teaching separate responses, a person can be shown what to do. This rapid learning of complex skills is necessary for getting along in the world.

The work of Baer et al. (1967) has important practical implications for learning-delayed people. What is less obvious is the theoretical value of this work. This research shows that complex human behavior may arise from relatively simple behavior principles operating in combination. One implication is that these same principles, when added to a possible cross-modal matching capacity (Meltzoff & Moore, 1999), account for the development of observational learning in everyday life.

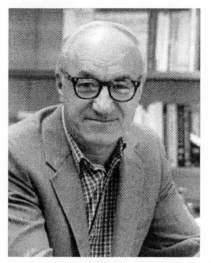

FIG. 11.10   Albert Bandura. Reprinted with permission.

Complex Observational Learning

Albert Bandura (Figure 11.10) worked on complex observational learning and self-regulatory processes for about 50 years, and is one of the most cited researchers in psychology. Currently, Dr. Bandura is Emeritus David Starr Jordan Professor of Social Sciences in Psychology at Stanford University. His work on observational learning, imitation, and aggression is discussed in the following section.

The Bobo Doll Experiment

Bandura (1965) designed an experiment to show a more complex form of learning by observation than generalized imitation. Children participated in this experiment on the imitation of aggressive behavior. As shown in Figure 11.11, each child watched a short film in which an adult demonstrated four distinctive aggressive actions

FIG. 11.11   Imitation of modeled aggression against a Bobo doll (from Bandura et al., 1963). After viewing a model hitting, jumping on, and verbally insulting a Bobo doll, male and female children also showed these imitative aggressive responses. Reprinted from "Imitation of film-mediated aggressive models," by A. Bandura, D. Ross, and S. A. Ross, 1969, *Journal of Abnormal and Social Psychology, 66,* 3–11. © 1969 Albert Bandura. Reprinted with permission.

toward an inflated Bobo doll (cf. Bandura, Ross, & Ross, 1963). Every aggressive action was accompanied by a unique verbal response. While sitting on the Bobo doll, the adult punched it in the face and said "Pow, right in the nose, boom, boom." In another sequence, the adult hit the doll with a mallet saying "Sockeroo, stay down." Also, the model kicked the Bobo doll and said "Fly away," and threw rubber balls at the doll while saying "Bang."

Some of the children saw the model rewarded by another adult, who supplied soda, a snack, and candies while saying "Strong champion." Other children saw the model receive negative consequences. The adult scolded and spanked the model for "picking on that clown," and warned him or her not to act that way again. A third group saw the modeled aggression, but no consequences were portrayed for the aggressive behavior.

When the film ended, a child was taken to a room that contained many toys, including a Bobo doll. The child was encouraged to play with the toys and was then left alone. The researchers watched through a one-way mirror and recorded instances of aggression and imitative aggression directed at the Bobo doll. Generally, there was a high frequency of imitative aggressive behavior toward the Bobo doll, and boys were more aggressive than girls.

Bandura (1965) also found that reward and punishment of the model's actions affected the imitation of aggression. Children who saw the model punished were less likely to imitate aggression than those who saw the model rewarded. Children who saw the model rewarded did not differ in imitative aggression from those who watched the model perform the actions without receiving social consequences. Importantly, this means that just seeing modeled aggression (no consequences) had about as much impact on imitation as observing violence being rewarded. Finally, Bandura offered an incentive to all the children if they could remember the actions of the model in the film. With this incentive, all three groups recalled the modeled aggression at about the same level. It seemed that all of the children had learned equally from the modeled aggression, but those who witnessed punishment of the model were less inclined to perform the aggressive sequences.

Social Cognitive Interpretation of Observational Learning in Children

Bandura (1986) argued that the difference between learning and performing modeled aggression requires a cognitive theory of **observational learning**. The observer pays attention to the modeled sequence, noting the arrangement of each action. The general information in the sequence must be coded and rehearsed, as when the child says "First sit on the Bobo, and then say the word 'pow.'" Once this abstract information is verbally coded and retained in memory, imitation is a matter of reproducing the component responses in the correct sequences. Of course the manifestations of these cognitive processes—coded, rehearsed, and remembered—are all overt behaviors.

However, complex behavior patterns cannot be learned by observation until the component skills have been mastered. It is impossible to fly a plane or do an inward one-and-a-half dive by mere observation. When the separate skills have been acquired, observing others can provide information on how to sequence complex performances, especially with corrective feedback. The golf instructor may show a person how to stand, hold the golf club, and swing at the ball. This demonstration could produce a sequencing of these responses, but the person may still not hit the ball well. It takes corrective feedback from the instructor and the trajectory of the ball to improve performance. Finally, the anticipated consequences of imitation determine whether an imitative response will occur. People who expect positive outcomes are likely to perform actions that they have witnessed, and those who expect negative consequences are less likely to imitate such actions.

Behavioral Interpretation of Observational Learning in Children

A behavioral interpretation of complex observational learning is that it may build on the processes of generalized imitation. As we have noted, generalized imitation provides an account of novel instances of imitation. From an operant perspective, imitation is most likely to occur in situations in which it was reinforced previously. Such behavior is unlikely to happen in situations in which it was extinguished, or in settings in which it was punished.

Suppose that Doug witnesses his brother, Barry, raiding the cookie jar before dinner. Barry is caught by his mother and sent to his room. Later, Doug steals a cookie, is also caught, and is sent to his room. Over time, such experiences teach the child a rule—"what happens to others can happen to me." Based on such a learning history, children show *differential imitation* based on modeled consequences. Doug avoids activities for which Barry has been punished, and imitates the rewarded actions of his brother. This kind of conditioning history provides a plausible account of Bandura's results concerning complex observational learning.

The learning and performance differences of the Bobo doll research may also be due to previous conditioning. When Bandura offered an incentive for recalling the modeled action, he presented a discriminative stimulus that increased the probability of this verbal behavior. For most children, it is likely that being promised a reward for recalling some action is a situation that has accompanied reinforcement in the past. That is, a child may be told "Mommy and Daddy will be proud of you if you can remember the alphabet," and the child is reinforced for reciting the ABCs. Many such instances result in a generalized tendency to recall events and actions when promised a reward. Given such a history and the incentive conditions that Bandura used, children in all three groups would show a high frequency of recalling what they have observed.

 # FOCUS ON: Rules, Observational Learning, and Self-Efficacy

Bandura has noted that observational learning in humans involves the discovery and use of abstract rules. In a dialogue with Richard Evans (1989), he stated:

> I began to develop the notion of modeling as a broad phenomenon that serves several functions. This conceptualization of modeling is concerned more with the observers' *extracting the rules* and structure of behavior, rather than copying particular examples they had observed. For example, in language learning, children are extracting the rules of how to speak grammatically rather than imitating particular sentences. Once they acquire the structure and the rules, they can use that knowledge to generate new patterns of behavior that go beyond what they've seen or heard. As they acquire the rules of language, they can generate sentences they have never heard. So modeling is a much more complex abstract process than a simple process of response mimicry.
>
> (Evans, 1989, p. 5)

From a behavioral perspective, "extracting the rules" is verbal operant behavior that describes the contingencies of reinforcement (Skinner, 1957, 1969). Both Skinner and Bandura agree about the importance of rules for human behavior, but they differ in terms of interpretation and philosophy.

Bandura (cited in Evans, 1989) talks about rules as cognitive events, and Skinner (1969) views them as verbal descriptions. For Skinner, following rules is behavior under the control of verbal stimuli. That is, statements of rules, advice, maxims, or laws are discriminative stimuli that set the occasion for behavior. Rules, as verbal descriptions, may affect observational learning. In this regard, Bandura's modeling experiments involve a number of distinct behavioral processes—including generalized imitation, descriptions of contingencies, and rule-governed behavior. Behavior analysts study each of these processes to understand how they may combine in complex forms of human behavior, including observational learning.

One kind of rule or description of contingency involves statements about oneself, such as "I am a competent person who can cope with this situation." This self-description can be contrasted with statements such as "I am an incompetent person who is unable to cope with this situation." Bandura (1997) refers to these kinds of responses as beliefs in self-efficacy, and provides evidence that these "cognitions" have a large impact on human behavior (see also Bandura & Locke, 2003, for evidence of the causal impact of self-efficacy beliefs).

From a behavior analysis view, statements of self-efficacy, as a class of verbal stimuli, can affect subsequent behavior (see the following section on "Rule-Governed Behavior"). For example, when confronted with the prospect of speaking to a large audience, John thinks (or states out loud) that he does not have the verbal skills to succeed, and estimates that his chances are only 40% for giving a well-organized, interesting, and clear presentation. Subsequently, he gives the talk and, as expected, performs at a low level. In this example, John's statement of self-efficacy describes a past history of behavior at speaking engagements (a rule). As a rule, the verbal stimulus sets up compliance as reinforcement (e.g., establishing operation). That is, for most people, stating and following rules (compliance) have resulted in generalized social reinforcement from a verbal community. Based on social conditioning for compliance, statements of self-efficacy often predict how a person will act in subsequent (similar) situations.

RULE-GOVERNED BEHAVIOR

A large part of human behavior is regulated by verbal stimuli. Verbal stimuli are the products of speaking, writing, signing, and other forms of verbal behavior (see Chapter 12). Rules, instructions, advice, and laws are verbal stimuli that affect a wide range of human action. The common property of these kinds of stimuli is that they describe the operating contingencies of reinforcement. The instruction "Turn on the computer and use the mouse to click the desired program in the menu" is a description of the behavior that must be executed to get a program running. Formally, rules, instructions, advice, and laws are **contingency-specifying stimuli**, describing the S^D: R $\rightarrow$ S^r relations of everyday life (Skinner, 1969).

The term **rule-governed behavior** is used when the listener's (or reader's) performance is regulated by contingency-specifying stimuli. According to this definition, a scientist shows rule-governed behavior when following specified procedures to make observations. People, as listeners, may generate their own rules when they speak. Travelers who read a map to get to their cabin might say to themselves "Take Interstate 5 and turn left at the first exit." The self-directions are verbal rules that describe the contingencies of reinforcement that result in getting to the cabin. In a classroom, a student may solve a set of mathematical problems by following the square-root rule. Rule-governed behavior is seen when a client follows the advice given by a counselor. When people obey the laws as expressed by posted speed limits, signs that say NO SMOKING, and proscriptions not to steal, the behavior is rule-governed.

Constructing and Following Rules

When solving a problem, people often make up or construct their own discriminative stimuli (response-produced stimuli). A person who has an important early-morning appointment may set an alarm clock for 6 a.m. Technically, setting the alarm is **precurrent behavior**, or an operant that precedes some other response. This behavior produces a discriminative stimulus that sets the occasion for getting up and going to the meeting. Thus, a major function of *precurrent behavior* is the **construction of S^{D}s** that regulate subsequent action.

FIG. 11.12   Illustration of how precurrent verbal behavior (or rules) functions as a discriminative stimulus regulating subsequent behavior (rule-governed behavior).

As shown in Figure 11.12, people may also construct discriminative stimuli through written words or spoken sounds (verbal stimuli). For example, a person may make a shopping list before going to the supermarket. Making a list is precurrent behavior, and the list is a discriminative stimulus for choosing groceries. Similarly, economical shoppers may say to themselves "Only buy products that are on sale." This verbal stimulus acts something like the grocery list in the previous example. As a rule, the verbal expression points to the relation between the stimuli, behavior, and reinforcement in the marketplace (see Taylor & O'Reilly, 1997, for a description of the use of self-instruction in shopping by people with mild learning disabilities). The words *on sale* identify a property of products that is correlated with saving money (reinforcement). The rule makes it easier to discriminate a good deal from a bad one, is easily recalled, and may be executed in any relevant situation.

Constructing discriminative stimuli and rules is important for a technological society. To improve mail delivery, zip codes are added to letters. When a person puts a zip code on a letter, the code is a verbal S^D that regulates sorting by postal employees. Letters are directed electronically throughout the postal system and arrive at an address specified by the code. Without such codes, mail is sorted at a much slower rate, and many letters get misdirected, lost, or returned.

Folk wisdom represents another example of constructing and following rules. The people who constructed the golden rule "Do unto others . . ." presumably did better in social relationships. When others transcribed the rule, it provided a guideline for successful interpersonal relationships to all who read it. Thus, a statement of wisdom is precurrent behavior that results in a verbal discriminative stimulus. The rule as an S^D regulates the subsequent behavior of the person. Once the rule is made public, it affects others as it did the originator.

Formal laws of government or religion may also involve constructing and following verbal discriminative stimuli (e.g., Norton, 2001). Laws of property rights probably developed from social contingencies. When someone stole another person's property, the victim and family usually retaliated. Eventually, the contingencies were described by rules such as "Thou shall not steal." Descriptions of the contingencies made it easier for people to avoid stealing. Once formulated and codified, the laws were stated by authorities and backed up by religious and legal sanctions. In this way, members of the group or culture conformed to the codified rules without risking exposure to the actual contingencies. "Be good or you will go to hell" may not be sufficient as a consequence for rule breaking, and the more immediate action of excommunication is invoked.

Although much human behavior is based on constructing and following rules, some contingencies seem to defy reliable description. An elite athlete may execute a skillful gold-medal-winning performance, but be unable to say exactly how it happened. A scientist may make an important discovery, yet be unable to advise others on how to be inventive. Creative artists and musicians produce interesting visual and auditory effects in ways that often cannot be stated. In all such cases, the interrelations of stimuli, responses, and reinforcements are so subtle that rules have not yet been described. In these situations, behavior is governed by exposure to the contingencies of reinforcement (contingency shaped) rather than being regulated by rules (rule governed).

Rule-Governed and Contingency-Shaped Behavior

People are said to solve problems either by discovery or by instruction. From a behavioral perspective, the difference is between the direct effects of contingencies (discovery) and the indirect effects of rules (instruction). When performance is attributed to direct exposure to reinforcement contingencies, behavior is said to be **contingency-shaped**. As previously noted, performance set up by constructing and following instructions (and other verbal stimuli) is termed *rule-governed behavior* (Catania, Matthews, & Shimoff, 1990; Hayes, 1989b).

Skinner (1969) illustrated the differences between contingency-shaped and rule-governed behavior in his analysis of a baseball player "catching the ball" and a naval commander "catching a satellite":

> The behavior of a baseball outfielder catching a fly ball bears certain resemblances to the behavior of the commander of a ship taking part in the recovery of a re-entering satellite. Both (the outfielder and commander) move about on a surface in a direction and with a speed designed to bring them, if possible, under a falling object at the moment it reaches the surface. Both respond to recent stimulation from the position, direction, and speed of the object, and they both take into account effects of gravity and friction. The behavior of the baseball player, however, has been almost entirely shaped by contingencies of reinforcement, whereas the commander is simply obeying rules derived from the available information and from analogous situations.
>
> (Skinner, 1969, p. 146)

Although behavior attributed to rules and that attributed to contingencies may occasionally look the same, the variables that affect performance are in fact quite different. One difference is motivational—reinforcement determines the rate of response (probability) for a given setting, while rules only affect how the response is executed (topography). Recall that a rule is a special kind of discriminative stimulus and that S^Ds affect behavior because they set the occasion for reinforcement. This means that *rule following itself must arise from contingencies of reinforcement*. The advice of a friend is taken only because such directions have been useful in the past. For example, a friend may have recommended a certain restaurant and you found it enjoyable. Based on these consequences, you are now more likely to follow your friend's advice, especially for dining.

Reinforcement for following the advice of others in various situations may establish a general tendency to do what others recommend. This kind of reinforcement history may underlie a *generalized susceptibility to social influence* (Orne & Evans, 1965). You probably know someone who is a sucker for a sales pitch. Many sales pitches are presented as advice, in the sense that a salesperson describes the benefits of owning a product. Often, however, the purchase results in more benefits to the seller than to the buyer. The television evangelist does not have a material product, but uses advice, promises, and threats of retribution to get people to send in money.

When directions are backed up with social punishment rather than natural consequences, they are called orders and commands (see Zettle & Hayes, 1982, on generalized compliance or *pliance* versus *tracking)*. Individuals follow orders, regardless of the particular commands, because they have been punished for disobedience (blind obedience). Of course, a generalized tendency for obedience often results in avoiding many aversive consequences in the world, as when a child is told "Don't play in the street" by a parent who has punished disobedience.

However, generalized obedience can be a problem. Governments can induce blind obedience in which a person harms another without regard to the moral consequences. In many countries, Amnesty International has documented the torture of political prisoners by guards and police. In these cases, obedience to authority becomes unquestioned and obviously results in serious harm or death to the victims (Milgram, 1974). The torture and abuse of Iraqi prisoners by some of the military guards (372nd Military Police Company of the United States) at Abu Ghraib prison probably involved generalized obedience to direct or implied orders from the Pentagon (as well as other behavioral processes). Figure 11.13 shows Dr. Stanley Milgram (left) with a shock panel that human participants from New Haven, Connecticut were ordered to use. The right-hand photograph shows an elderly man (learner) who was given the supposed shocks. Participants in the experiment delivered bogus shocks that they believed to be real. Many participants delivered the shocks even though the man complained of a heart problem. The tendency to obey the commands of the authority (the experimenter) outweighed the signs and sounds of distress from the elderly victim. Reicher, Haslam, and Smith (2012) described these competing contingencies in terms of participants' identification with the experimenter and the scientific community (reinforcement value of science), and the conflicting identification with the distress and harm inflicted on the learner and the general community he represents (reinforcement value of moral conduct). In the basic condition where the learner cries out in pain and asks to be set free at 150 V level, more than half of the participants continued to administer shocks to the highest level on the shock generator (450 V), and believed that the shocks might injure or kill the victim. The basic findings were

FIG. 11.13 Stanley Milgram's famous study of obedience to authority (Milgram, 1974) illustrates the impact of orders and commands on human behavior. Based on the experimenter's orders, subjects administered what they thought were increasingly severe electric shocks to a 59-year-old man who complained of a heart condition. (Left) Stanley Milgram with the shock generator used in the obedience experiment. (Right) Photograph of victim being strapped into the chair, from the film *Obedience* © 1965 by Stanley Milgram and distributed by Penn State Media Sales. Both photographs are reproduced with the permission of Alexandra Milgram.

replicated in 2006 with obedience rates only slightly lower than those found by Milgram 45 years earlier (Burger, 2009).

The importance of reinforcement contingencies in establishing and maintaining rule-following behavior is clearly seen with ineffective rules and instructions. One kind of rule that is likely to be weak is based on statistical analysis of contingencies. For example, it is unlikely that a person will give up smoking merely on the basis of the directive "Stop smoking—smoking causes cancer." The actual health consequences are too remote and the statistical chances of getting cancer too unlikely. Of course, smoking usually declines when a person gets cancer, but at this point it is too late. When rules describe delayed and improbable events, it is necessary to find other reasons to follow them.

In recent years, government reports about second-hand smoke and its effects have led some communities to classify public smoking as illegal. Towns and cities arrange fines and other penalties for failure to obey the no-smoking law. In this case, smokers follow the anti-smoking rule for reasons unrelated to smoking itself (i.e., social punishment). A similar effect is obtained when smoking is described as sinful or shameful and religious sanctions are used to promote compliance. Generally, social contingencies may be used to establish rule-following behavior when natural contingencies are too remote or improbable to be effective.

Baum (1995, 2005, pp. 167–171) emphasizes the importance of rules in terms of long-term contingencies between behavior and biological fitness. As a discriminative stimulus, the rule strengthens listeners' behavior that is reinforced in the short term by social contingencies, but the rule also enters into the long-term contingencies that enhance the listeners' fitness (reproductive success). For example, in following the rule "Do not smoke," the listener is reinforced by the speaker's consequences in the short term, but this behavior is also related to better health and longer reproductive years. When the rule is "internalized," the listener's behavior has switched from short- to long-term control. The fitness-enhancing consequences of long-term contingencies are health, resources, relationships, and reproduction. Baum's analysis of fitness and rule-governed behavior therefore integrates behavior-analysis explanations of human behavior with evolutionary theory and natural selection.

FOCUS ON: Instructions and Contingencies

In his discussion of rule-governed and contingency-shaped behavior, Skinner (1969) speculated that instructions might affect performance differently to the actual contingencies of reinforcement. One way to test this idea is to expose humans to reinforcement procedures that are accurately or inaccurately described by the experimenter's instructions. If behavior varies with the instructions while the actual contingencies remain the same, this would be evidence for Skinner's assertion (see Hackenberg & Joker, 1994, on correspondence between instructions and contingencies).

An early study by Lippman and Meyer (1967) showed that human performance on a fixed-interval schedule varied with instructions. When subjects were told that points (exchanged for money) would become available after a specific amount of time, their performance was characterized by a low rate of response, appropriate to the fixed interval. In contrast, subjects who were told that points depended on a certain number of responses produced a high and steady rate of response. In a similar kind of study, Kaufman, Baron, and Kopp (1966) placed subjects on a variable-interval (VI) schedule of reinforcement and told them that points were available on either a fixed-interval or a variable-ratio basis. Performance was more in accord with the experimental instructions than with the actual VI contingencies.

The fact that instructions, in these experiments, seem to override the actual contingencies has been used to argue against a reinforcement analysis of human behavior. Bandura (1971, 1974) linked instructions to modeling. He argued that both of these procedures activate subjects' expectations, which in turn affect subsequent behavior. This means that expected reinforcement, rather than actual contingencies, is the stronger determinant of human behavior. In addition, Dulany (1968) disputed the claim that instructions were complex discriminative stimuli. He argued that there was no evidence to show that instructions gain (or lose) control over behavior because of selective reinforcement.

FIG. 11.14   Mark Galizio. Reprinted with permission.

Mark Galizio (1979) (Figure 11.14) addressed both objections when he showed that following instructions is in fact a discriminative operant. In a series of important experiments, human subjects responded to avoid the loss of money. Subjects received a payment to attend experimental sessions, and they could turn a handle to avoid a loss of 5 cents from their earnings. When they turned the handle to the right, the onset of a red light and loss of money were postponed. Subjects were exposed to four different contingencies during a session. A change in the contingency was signaled by one of four amber lights. One condition had no losses, but the other three had costs scheduled every 10 s. For the conditions in which costs occurred, each response delayed the next loss for either 10, 30, or 60 s.

To vary instructional control, labels were placed above the amber lights that signaled each condition. When instructions were accurate, there were no discrepancies between the labels and the contingencies. Thus, the component in which each response postponed the loss for 10 s was labeled correctly as "10 s," as were the "30 s," "60 s," and "no loss" components.

Galizio (1979) also created conditions of inaccurate instructions in which the labels did not match the actual contingencies. In a no-contact condition, all of the components were changed to no losses, but the labels incorrectly described different response requirements. If subjects behaved in accord with the instructions, they made unnecessary responses, but there was no monetary loss. As you might expect, people followed the rules. For example, subjects turned the handle more when the label said "10 s" then when it said "60 s."

At this point, a contact condition was implemented in which losses occurred every 10 s in all components. The signs still read "10 s," "20 s," "60 s," and "no loss." In this situation, responding to the instructions produced considerable loss of earnings. Consider a person who turned the handle every 60 s but lost money every 10 s. Subjects quickly stopped following the instructions and responded in terms of the actual contingencies of reinforcement. Galizio (1979) explained the significance of these findings as follows:

> [In] the CONTACT condition, when instruction-following led to exposure to the loss contingency, instructional control was rapidly eliminated. The elimination of instruction-following persisted when the NO CONTACT condition was reinstated. This last finding is particularly important, since it shows that subject reactions to the instructions were irreversibly altered after exposure to the CONTACT condition. Subjects now "disbelieve" the instructions and

the schedule assumes control of behavior. But contact with schedule-instruction discrepancies is necessary for the elimination of instruction-following, not simply the existence of such a discrepancy. *Instruction-following is controlled by its consequences.*

(Galizio, 1979, p. 62)

Overall, the results of Galizio's experiments provide strong support for the view that instructional control is a form of rule-governed behavior (see also Buskist & Miller, 1986; Hayes, Brownstein, Haas, & Greenway, 1986; Horne & Lowe, 1993; Ribes & Martinez, 1998; Ribes & Rodriguez, 2001; see Hayes & Ju, 1997, and Plaud & Newberry, 1996, for applied implications of rule-governed behavior). In accord with numerous other experiments, subjects were found to rapidly acquire appropriate responses to the contingencies when instructed about how to behave. Importantly, the influence of instructions depended on the consequences of following these rules (see Svartdal, 1992). When the costs of rule-following behavior increased, people no longer followed the rules. Additional evidence showed that following instructions could be brought under stimulus control. Thus, people follow instructions in situations that lead to reinforcement, but not in situations that signal extinction or aversive consequences. Finally, Galizio showed that accurate instructions have reinforcing properties, a characteristic shared by simple discriminative stimuli. People not only respond to instructions but also seek out reliable descriptions of the contingencies.

Instructions about interval (or ratio) contingencies often occur in everyday life (see Luciano, 2000; Poppen, 1982). Students are given timetables, calendars, and outlines for lectures, due dates, examination periods, and official holidays. When instructions accurately describe contingencies, behavior is highly efficient. A professor who shows up at the stated time will have students who are punctual. And, as we have noted, reliable instructions are reinforcing; people seek out information about scheduled events, such as television programs and arrival–departure times of airlines.

Inaccurate instructions lead to several different effects. People will continue to follow misleading instructions when there is some benefit and little cost. Buses may never arrive as scheduled, but people continue to follow the listed times because the buses eventually show up. People may continue to follow inaccurate instructions because of social reinforcement. Students follow the rule "Go to class to get good grades." A few students who get satisfactory grades do not pay attention to the lectures, but they "put in time" in going to class. They follow the rule because their friends go to class, even though it has no effect on their grades. Unreliable instructions, however, are not followed if the rules lead to extinction or aversive consequences. When this occurs, people ignore the rule and act on the basis of the actual contingencies. Instructions to spend during periods of economic recession may be ignored as consumers contact the costs of buying (e.g., increasing debt, threats to basic essentials, etc.). Loss of consumer confidence may reflect the weakening of rule-governed behavior because of contact with the actual contingencies of the market (see Cullen, 1998, for a discussion of the problems with rules).

Rules as Function-Altering Events

Although the discriminative function (S^D) of rules is well established, several researchers (Malott, 1988; Michael, 1982a, 1983; Schlinger & Blakely, 1987) have argued that contingency-specifying stimuli have additional, and perhaps even more crucial, effects. Rules can act as **function-altering events**, altering the function of other stimuli, and thereby the strength of relations among these stimuli and behavior (Schlinger & Blakely,

1987). A passenger on an airplane is instructed to respond to a drop in cabin pressure by "placing the yellow oxygen mask over your mouth and breathing normally." The instruction is a *function-altering event* that sets up the "dangling yellow mask" as a discriminative stimulus for placing the mask on the face. In the absence of the rule, the dangling mask might occasion looking at it or asking for the stewardess (see Schmitt, 2001, for a discussion of rule following after a delay). The function-altering effect of the airline rule is shown when the passengers put on their masks only at the appropriate moment. Also, the probability of placing masks on faces is higher for those who are given the instruction.

Rules may alter the discriminative functions of stimuli in more complex ways, as when a person is given detailed instructions. An individual may be told "See George about buying the car, but if Craig is there don't make an offer." As a result of this verbal description, the listener emits a conditional discrimination: George is S^D for making an offer, and Craig is an S^Δ for this behavior. Notice that without the detailed instruction or rule, George and Craig may have no discriminative functions when buying a car.

Following Rules and Joint Control

In 1999, Barry Lowenkron gave a talk on "Joint control of rule following: An analysis of purpose" at the Annual Meeting of the Association for Behavior Analysis in Chicago (available at www.calstatela.edu/faculty/zlowenk/toc.html) (Lowenkron, 1999). The talk centered on how rules control behavior. That is, how do verbal statements of contingencies (rules) emitted at one time regulate behavior at a later time? Barry presented three problems for a behavior analysis of rules: first, *memory function* or how rules have effects after a delay; secondly, *recognition function* or how the event specified by a rule is known; and thirdly, *response function* or how the specified event occasions the specific response. In order to answer these questions without using the language of cognition and mental events, Lowenkron introduced the notion of **joint control** where two verbal stimuli exert stimulus control over a common verbal topography (Lowenkron, 2006).

Figure 11.15 depicts a task that involves joint control. The problem is for you to locate the number 103020 in the array at the top of the figure. This is a type of matching-to-sample problem with the array as the comparison. Try to do it now. Finding the correct sequence required joint control by verbal stimuli over the terminal verbal response "103020, I found it." Given the statement of the problem, you probably rehearsed or repeated the sequence to yourself (memory function) as you looked at the array of numbers to verbally identify the correct sequence (recognition function). The two verbal stimuli, repeating the required number and identifying that number in the array, jointly controlled the terminal verbal response "103020, I found it" (response function) (see Chapter 12 for

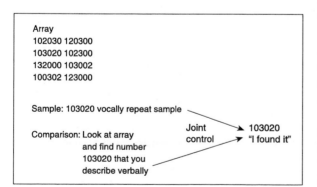

FIG. 11.15 Joint control by verbal stimuli. The two verbal stimuli—repeating the required number and identifying that number in the array—jointly control the terminal verbal response "103020, I found it" (response function). Based on "Joint control of rule following: An analysis of purpose," by B. Lowenkron, 1999, *Annual Meeting of the Association for Behavior Analysis, Chicago* (www.calstatela.edu/faculty/zlowenk/toc.html).

formal analysis of the verbal responses by the speaker; see Lowenkron, 2004, for an extension of this analysis to word–object meaning).

In another common example, you are getting ready for a birthday party and there is a cake in the oven. Your friend has to go to the store to buy some soft drinks and says to you "When the cake has risen, take it out of the oven" (rule). You are likely to repeat the rule ("better see if the cake is done") and check the cake as it is baking. Notice that the memory function of the rule is fulfilled by repetition or verbal rehearsal of the rule statement over time, not by a mental event or cognition. At some point, you repeat the rule to "check the cake," look in the oven, and verbally identify that "the cake has risen." The verbal stimulus "the cake has risen" fulfills the recognition function without reference to cognitive events. Rehearsal of the rule statement and verbally identifying that the cake has risen exert joint control over the terminal verbal response "the cake is done; take it out of the oven" and removal of the cake from the oven.

Notice that the form or topography of the terminal response is completely specified by your friend's statement of the rule—you say that the cake is done and take it out of the oven to comply with your friend's request (rule). Failure to follow the rules often results in social punishment, as people get upset when their instructions are not reinforced with compliance. Also, rules that are ignored usually have additional aversive consequences, such as ruined cakes and spoiled birthday parties (see Cerutti, 1989, on collateral consequences of rule following). As we have seen in this chapter, the contingencies of reinforcement ensure that we often follow the rules of others and the rules that we give to ourselves (self-generated rules). Thus, rule-governed behavior is operant behavior regulated by contingencies of reinforcement.

CHAPTER SUMMARY

In this chapter we have learned about correspondence relations, focusing on imitation and rule-governed behavior. Spontaneous imitation occurs in several species, including human infants, but the evidence is still controversial. The discovery of mirror neurons suggests that early imitation in infants and other primates is based on neural mechanisms that have been selected during our evolutionary history. It seems that operant imitation, generalized imitation, and complex observational learning build on a basic capacity for imitation. Observational learning seems to integrate imitation with rule-following behavior to produce behavior that is transmitted from one person to another and from one generation to the next. Rule-governed behavior concerns the effects of verbal stimuli on the behavior of the listener. That is, instructions (and other verbal stimuli) are products of the behavior of the speaker that regulate the behavior of the listener. We discovered that rules play a large and important role in the regulation of human behavior, not as mental events but as verbal descriptions of the contingencies. Rule-following behavior is maintained by social and collateral contingencies, but instructed behavior often appears to be insensitive to contingencies. However, when inaccurate rules generate behavior with high costs, people give up following the rules and respond to the actual contingencies. One way to understand rule-governed behavior is based on joint control where two verbal stimuli combine to control a common form of verbal response. In the next chapter, we shall examine contingencies of reinforcement that regulate the behavior of the speaker, or what Skinner (1957) called the analysis of verbal behavior.

KEY WORDS

Autistic children	Imitation
Construction of S^{D}s	Innate imitation
Contingency-shaped behavior	Joint control
Contingency-specifying stimuli	Observational learning
Correspondence relations	Operant imitation
Delayed imitation	Precurrent behavior
Function-altering event	Rule-governed behavior
Generalized imitation	Spontaneous imitation

ON THE WEB

www.pigeon.psy.tufts.edu/avc/zentall/default.htm On this website, Zentall and Akins address the issue of imitation in animals, including the evidence, function, and mechanisms. The distinction between apparent imitation and "true" imitation is one topic of interest.

www.ted.com/talks/susan_blackmore_on_memes_and_temes.html Susan Blackmore states that the basic unit of cultural transmission is the meme (after Richard Dawkins and *The Selfish Gene*). She studies memes (ideas that replicate from one person to another like a virus), and makes a bold new argument—that humanity has spawned a new kind of meme, the teme, which spreads and is maintained via technology such as the Internet.

BRIEF QUIZ

1. The relationship between saying and doing is formally a _____ relation.

   (a) cognitive consistency
   (b) correspondence
   (c) synergistic
   (d) dose–response

2. Imitation requires that the learner emits a _____ response that could only occur by observing a _____ emit a similar response.

   (a) significant; peer
   (b) operant; organism
   (c) novel; model
   (d) similar; conspecific

3. What did Thorndike (1911) conclude from imitation experiments with animals?

   (a) animals show amazing intelligence
   (b) animals can easily imitate another member of their species
   (c) animals do not show a capacity for intelligence
   (d) animals cannot learn by observation

4. The second experiment by Epstein (1984) concerned _____ _____ and showed that spontaneous imitation in pigeons occurred after _____had elapsed.

    (a) delayed imitation; 24 h
    (b) deferred matching; 48 h
    (c) delayed sampling; 24 h
    (d) deferred equivalence; 48 h

5. In the study (Experiment 1) of infant imitation by Meltzoff and Moore (1977), the researchers:

    (a) used 12- to 21-day-old infants
    (b) presented a passive face for 90 s
    (c) presented four gestures in random order
    (d) did all of the above

6. Both humans and pigeons seem to engage in spontaneous imitation. The appearance of similar behavior:

    (a) shows that humans and pigeons share much in common
    (b) shows identical functions of the behavior
    (c) shows that structure and function go together
    (d) shows none of the above

7. With regard to generalized imitation, which of the following statements are true?

    (a) generalized imitation is based on principles of social cognition
    (b) generalized imitation provides an account of imitation after a delay
    (c) generalized imitation is part of Bandura's cognitive theory
    (d) all of the above

8. To show the importance of _____for Marilla's _____ imitations, Don Baer changed the _____ of reinforcement.

    (a) stimulus control; immediate; contingency
    (b) stimulus control; spontaneous; quality
    (c) reinforcement; novel; contingency
    (d) reinforcement; immediate; quality

9. Rule-governed behavior involves:

    (a) control by contingency-specifying stimuli (verbal stimuli)
    (b) the effects of instructions on the behavior of the listener
    (c) the effects of advice given by a counselor
    (d) all of the above

10. Rule following is _____ regulated by _____ of reinforcement.

    (a) behavior; contingencies
    (b) cognitively; expectancies
    (c) mentally; contingencies
    (d) socially; expectancies

Answers to Brief Quiz: 1, b (p. 323); 2, c (p. 325); 3, d (p. 327); 4, a (p. 329); 5, d (p. 330); 6, d (pp. 335–336); 7, b (pp. 338–339); 8, c (p. 341); 9, d (p. 345); 10, a (p. 351).

Verbal Behavior

12

1. Identify the difference between language and verbal behavior.
2. Discover the operant functions of verbal behavior.
3. Investigate complex communication between pigeons based on operant conditioning.
4. See how reinforcement contingencies result in pigeons reporting "how they feel" on drugs.
5. Learn why the flag is a symbol of America by investigating the research on stimulus equivalence.

Humans are social animals. Most of the daily life of people takes place in the company of others. An important aspect of human social behavior involves what we do with words, as in speaking, writing, signing, and gesturing. Behavior analysts use the term *verbal behavior* to refer to this kind of human activity. In this chapter, verbal behavior is analyzed according to the same principles of behavior that have been used throughout this book. The analysis explores the role of contingencies of reinforcement in the regulation of verbal behavior.

In terms of behavior analysis, Lee (1981a) notes that language tends to obscure environment–behavior relationships. Language usually directs research attention to grammar, syntax, and unobservable mental representations and processes (structure), rather than to the objective conditions that influence the behavior of a speaker or writer (function). Catania (1998) has also noted that the "language of reference" implicitly proceeds from words to objects in the world. The possibility that environmental contingencies regulate our speaking and writing is usually not considered. Catania states:

> We also speak of language as if it were directed toward events or objects. We say that words or sentences refer to, deal with, speak of, call attention to, or are about things. The language of reference implicitly includes the direction from verbal behavior to environment. Everyday language doesn't include words that emphasize the opposite direction. What if our everyday language has prejudiced us about the ways in which our verbal behavior works? We hardly ever say that we utter nouns in the presence of relevant objects or that sentences are occasioned by relevant events. Instead, we say that words refer to objects or that sentences are about events. There are good reasons for these usages . . . [but] they may be misleading in an analysis of the behavior of speakers and listeners or readers and writers.
>
> (Catania, 1998, pp. 239–240)

LANGUAGE AND VERBAL BEHAVIOR

People usually use the term "language" when they talk about speaking and other forms of communication. Although some researchers argue that language is behavior (Baer & Guess, 1971), others use the term to refer to a set of linguistic habits (Hockett, 1958, 1968), while still others point to the underlying mental rules that are presumed to organize spoken and written words (e.g., Chomsky, 1957). Some view language as a cultural phenomenon that does not depend on individual behavior and mental rules (Sanders, 1974). Finally, language is said to consist of three main features involving vocabulary, syntax, and meaning (Erlich, 2000, p. 140). As you can see, there is little agreement on the definition of language. The most important implication of this confusion is that language may not be a useful concept for a natural-science approach to speaking (and other forms of verbal behavior).

To rectify these problems, Skinner (1957) introduced the term *verbal behavior*. This term helps to redirect attention to the operating contingencies. In contrast with the term *language*, **verbal behavior** deals with the performance of a speaker and the environmental conditions that establish and maintain such performance. That is, verbal behavior concerns the *function* of what we do with words that are spoken, written, or signed. Some of the functions of verbal behavior that have been researched include how we learn to talk about things and events in the world, how we learn to communicate our feelings and emotions, and how the listener's response to what we say shapes what we talk about.

FOCUS ON: Speaking and Evolution of the Vocal Tract

B. F. Skinner indicated that "verbal behavior does not evolve. It is the product of the verbal environment or what linguists call a language, and it is the verbal environment that evolves" (Skinner, 1986, p. 115). That is, the way in which people of a culture reinforce the verbal behavior of others changes over time, and modification of the social contingencies alters what people say. If biological evolution did not lead to mental rules of language, as is usually assumed (Dessalles, 2007, pp. 153–164), it is useful to ask what role it played in human speech and communication. In his 1986 paper on evolution and verbal behavior, Skinner speculated about the role of natural selection for vocal behavior or speaking. He stated:

> The human species took a crucial step forward when its vocal musculature came under operant control in the production of speech sounds. Indeed, it is possible that all the distinctive achievements of the species can be traced to that one genetic change. Other species behave vocally, of course, and the behavior is sometimes modified slightly during the lifetime of the individual. . . but. . . the principal contingencies have remained phylogenetic. . . . . Some of the organs in the production of speech sounds were already subject to operant conditioning. The diaphragm must have participated in controlled breathing, the tongue and jaw in chewing and swallowing, the jaw and teeth in biting and tearing, and the lips in sipping and sucking, all of which could be changed by operant conditioning. Only the vocal cords and pharynx seem to have served no prior operant function. The crucial step in the evolution of verbal behavior appears, then, to have been the genetic change that brought them under the control of operant conditioning and made possible the coordination of all of these systems in the production of speech sounds.
>
> (Skinner, 1986, p. 117)

Skinner's evolutionary analysis of the human anatomy allowing for vocal speech has been confirmed subsequently by research in acoustics, physiology, and anatomy. Although there is much controversy about the evolution of human speech, most scientists now agree on the "principles of physiology and the 'laws' of physical acoustics that determine the capabilities of the anatomy involved in the production of human speech" (Lieberman, Laitman, Reidenberg, & Gannon, 1992, p. 447).

Speech production occurs during the outward flow of air from the lungs. During expiration, normal breathing is substantially modified as the speaker takes more air into their lungs before producing a long sentence or phrase. This modification of breathing is often attributed to "planning ahead," but is quite consistent with operant control of the breathing system.

The human upper respiratory tract serves as the intersection for the breathing, swallowing, and vocalizing systems. Studies have shown that the position of the larynx in the neck determines the function of these intersecting tracts. In most mammals and nonhuman primates, the larynx is positioned high in the neck, ensuring mostly separate respiration and digestive tracts. One result of this location is that the production and variation of audible speech sounds are severely limited in mammals, including the great apes. Human infants retain the nonhuman primate and mammalian location of the larynx (upper neck, C3), and cannot make the vowel sounds [i], [u], and [a] that are present in adult speech. Over the first 2 to 3 years, the larynx of the child shows a developmental descent to the adult position (C6) in the neck. This descent is accompanied by other anatomical changes that dramatically alter the way children breathe and swallow. During this developmental period, neuromuscular control is extended within the larynx and pharynx, with changes beginning even before the decent of the larynx has occurred (see Laitman & Reidenberg, 1993).

Phonation, or the production of audible sources of speech sound, is made possible by the activity of the larynx involving the movement of the vocal folds or cords. Complex neuromuscular control ensures that the vocal folds are able to move inward before the onset of speech, and rapidly in and out for continued speech production. Rates of vocal fold movement can vary from 60 (in adult males) to 1500 (in children) open–close cycles per second. People can modulate their rate of vocal fold movement and airflow pattern by adjusting the tension of the muscles in the larynx and the alveolar air pressure; the effect is sustained and prolonged emission of sounds that are the basis of human speech (Lieberman et al., 1992).

The supralaryngeal vocal tract consists of both the oral and nasal airways that provide the phonetic quality of the sound (Figure 12.1). This tract serves as an acoustic filter (in much the same way as a pair of sunglasses filters light), suppressing the passage of sounds at particular frequencies but allowing passage of those at other frequencies. Formants are the maximal filtered frequencies produced by the speaker as determined by the shape, length, and volume of the vocal tract, an acoustically resonating system (Lieberman, 2007). For example, the vowels [i] and [u] in the words "see" and "sue" may have the same basic or fundamental frequency (e.g., 100 Hz), but different formant frequencies depending on variations in the vocal tract.

Clearly, the vocal apparatus of humans has the capability for fine-grain operant control of sound that can allow for varied vocal forms of verbal behavior (Skinner, 1957). During the course of human evolution, the breathing and digestive regions were modified from the two-tube system of our earliest hominid ancestors to the intersecting upper tracts that we have today. These changes would have involved substantial "restructuring in the respiratory, digestive and vocalizing patterns and would have occurred contemporaneously with parallel changes in central and peripheral neural control" (Lieberman et al., 1992). It is likely that many minor modifications of morphology had already appeared

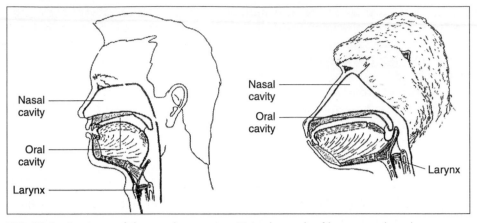

FIG. 12.1 Anatomy of the vocal apparatus. Voiced sounds of human and nonhuman primates involve vibration of the vocal folds of the larynx. Sound travels up the vocal tract where the oral and nasal cavities of the vocal tract act as a filter. This filter allows passage of acoustic energy at some frequencies and attenuates energy at other frequencies according to their size- and shape-specific transfer function. The sound radiated at the lips thus reflects the combined action of an acoustic source and a filter. The larynx lies lower in the vocal tract of the adult human compared with nonhuman primates or young children, creating a second large cavity (the pharynx) at the back of the mouth. Artwork is by Michael Graham. Taken from D. Rendall, J. R. Vokey and C. Nemeth, 2007, *Journal of Experimental Psychology: Human Perception and Performance. 33*, 1208–1219. Adapted with permission from the American Psychological Association.

in the genus *Homo* more than 1 million years ago. These modifications were further elaborated by natural selection and appeared as the integrated respiratory, upper digestive, and vocal tract of *Homo sapiens* approximately 500,000 years ago (see MacLarnon & Hewitt, 1999, 2004, on the evolution of human breath control; see also Kay, Cartmill, & Balow, 1998 and Takemoto, 2008, on the evolution of the human tongue). Specification of the selection pressures that favored such changes is a primary focus of research on the evolution of human speech (de Boer, 2005; Lieberman, 2007).

VERBAL BEHAVIOR: SOME BASIC DISTINCTIONS

Verbal behavior refers to the vocal, written, and signed behavior of a speaker, writer, or communicator. This behavior operates on the listener, reader, or observer, who arranges for reinforcement of the verbal performance in a particular setting. A woman who is hungry may ask a waiter for "the tossed green salad with the egg sandwich." The speaker's behavior affects the listener, who in turn supplies reinforcement (i.e., placing the meal on the table). A similar effect is produced if the woman writes her order on a piece of paper. In this case, the written words function like the spoken ones; the waiter reads the order and brings the meal. Verbal behavior therefore expands the ways that humans can produce effects on the world.

Verbal behavior allows us to affect the environment *indirectly* (Vargas, 1998). This contrasts with nonverbal behavior, which often results in direct and automatic consequences. When you walk toward an object, you come closer to it. If you lift a glass, there is a direct and automatic change in its position. Verbal behavior, on the other hand, only works through its effects on other people. To change the position of a lamp, the speaker says "Lift the blue lamp at the back of the room" to a listener who is inclined to respond. Notice that reinforcement of the verbal response is not automatic, since many conditions may affect what the listener does. The listener may not hear you, may be distracted, or may not understand you (i.e., they pick up the red lamp rather than the blue one). Generally, the social contingencies that regulate verbal behavior are complex, subtle, and highly flexible.

The Range of Verbal Behavior

Although verbal behavior is usually equated with speaking, vocal responses are only one of its forms. In addition to talking, a person emits gestures and body movements (signs) that indirectly operate on the environment through their effects on others. In most cultures, a frown sets the occasion for others to remove some aversive event, while a smile may signal the observer to behave in ways that produce positive reinforcement. In fact, frowns and smiles have such consistent and pervasive effects on others that some researchers have considered these gestures to be universal symbols (Ekman & Friesen, 1975; Rosenberg & Ekman, 1995).

Another kind of verbal behavior involves manual signing rather than speech sounds. In American Sign Language (ASL), the speaker produces arm and hand movements that are functionally similar to speech sounds. In this case, regulation of the listener's behavior is along a visual dimension. Deaf speakers may also acquire complex finger movements known as "finger spelling" that function like letters in the English alphabet. Figure 12.2 illustrates some of the basic manual movements of ASL and digital positions for finger spelling.

In the behavioral view, writing is verbal behavior that functions to regulate the behavior of a reader. Although written words and sentences have little formal similarity to spoken ones, the two modes of communication have equivalent functions. Recall that behavior analysts classify behavior in terms of its functions, and for this reason both writing and speaking are commonly categorized as *verbal operants*.

FIG. 12.2 Examples of American Sign Language (ASL) and finger-spelled letters. From *A Basic Vocabulary: American Sign Language for Parents and Children*, 1978, by T. J. O'Rourke, T. J. Publishers, Inc., Silver Spring, MD. © 1978, T. J. Publishers, Inc.

Speaking, Listening, and the Verbal Community

The behavior of the speaker (or writer) is functionally different from the behavior of the listener (or reader). That is, the conditions that regulate speaking are distinct from those that affect listening. In the field of psycholinguistics, the distinction between speaking and listening is often blurred by talking about language encoding and decoding. Since both are treated as aspects of language (i.e., the transmission of meaning), there is little attempt to analyze the separate functions of such behavior. In fact, Skinner (1969) used the term *rule-governed behavior* to describe the behavior of the listener and *verbal behavior* to specify the performance of the speaker. Of course, in any actual communication between two people, each person alternates as a speaker and a listener. The repertoires of behavior are, however, analytically distinct from Skinner's perspective.

Rule-governed behavior refers to the effects of words in the forms of instructions, advice, maxims, and laws on the listener's behavior (see Chapter 11). In this view, rules are seen as complex discriminative stimuli, and the principles that govern stimulus control also regulate the behavior of the listener. Although many behavior analysts have accepted this perspective, others have suggested that rule-governed behavior involves additional processes (see Parrott, 1987, for a discussion of these issues).

Regardless of one's view about the behavior of the listener, verbal behavior requires special attention because the consequences of verbal behavior are *mediated by the actions of others* (Vargas, 1998). The way a person speaks is shaped by the consequences supplied by the listener. A busy mother may not respond to the polite response of "Milk, please" by her child. However, a change in form to "Give me milk!" may induce compliance. Inadvertently, the mother is teaching her child to give commands in a loud voice. Subtle contingencies of reinforcement shape the style, dialect, tonal quality, and other properties of speaking.

The contingencies that regulate verbal behavior arise from the practices of people in the **verbal community**.These practices are part of the culture of the group, and they have evolved over time (Skinner, 1953). The practices of the verbal community therefore refer to the customary ways in which people reinforce the behavior of a speaker. In an English-speaking community, the speaker who substitutes "also" for "in addition" or "besides" is likely to be reinforced, especially if repetition is bothersome to the listener. When linguists analyze the grammar of a language, they state rules that describe the reinforcing practices of the verbal community. For example, the grammatical rule "i before e except after c" describes a requirement for reinforcement set by the community; the written word *received* is reinforced while *recieved* is not. Thus, verbal behavior is established and maintained by the reinforcing practices of the community, and these practices change based on cultural evolution. The analysis of cultural change in terms of verbal practices requires the integration of several fields of study, including anthropology, archeology, and linguistics, and is beyond the scope of this textbook.

Social Use of Words in a Verbal Community

In a mentalistic view of language, words are said to refer to things in the world. That is, words somehow have the power to represent, communicate, and express the world as perceived by the speaker. The speaker is said to encode by syntax (grammar) and semantics (meaning) the message or information that is transmitted by speech and decoded or comprehended by the listener. This information-transmission view of language has gained considerable popularity, especially in the age of computers and cellular communication.

Behavior analysts offer a completely different viewpoint, proposing that the social environment shapes the way in which we use words (Skinner, 1957; Guerin, 2003). That is, the way we talk and what we say are a function of social contingencies, involving effects or consequences arranged by members of a verbal community. If you yell at a rock or at the moon, it has no effect. On the other hand, when you yell "You're an idiot" at your partner there are usually observable social consequences, involving verbal counteraggression and disruption of the social relationship. Generally, we say things in ways that previously induced others to do something for us, compelled others to say things, elicited or occasioned people's attention, and influenced others to remain in social relationships with us. The long-range consequences of speech and word use reside in gaining access to the social and economic resources mediated by members of diverse verbal communities (Guerin, 2003), from close relationships in dating, mating, and families to friendship and collegial relationships of school, community, and workplace.

One of the ways in which words are used is to "establish facts," in the sense that our words correspond to events and objects in the everyday world. When words about the world correspond to actual happenings, people (or oneself) are likely to adopt and repeat those words, usually with conviction (response strength), and to act in ways consistent with the verbal description. In everyday language, a person who "believes" some statement of fact is likely to be persuaded by it. For example, if you can persuade a neighbor that you have a good reputation, this person may tell others about your standing in the community, do many things for you, and provide you with a variety of social and economic resources.

To establish facts and persuade others (or themselves), speakers use words to give accounts of their own or others' actions. A major emphasis of social psychology is attribution, or giving accounts and explanations of the actions of others and ourselves (Kelley, 1987). In the traditional view, attributions are cognitions generated by the perceiver in order to make sense of the world and predict what others will do in social interactions. However, Guerin (2003, p. 260) argues that attributions are not used to understand the social world, but are in fact verbal strategies or ways to persuade others (and oneself) with words, thereby gaining and maintaining access to social and economic resources. For example, an explanation or attribution of why Harry and Sally are fighting may attribute the cause to Harry's tendency to "sit on the couch" rather than look for employment ("Harry and Sally are fighting because Harry is lazy and a good-for-nothing")—an internal attribution to Harry's disposition. In contrast, an explanation of the conflict might involve giving an external attribution, describing the cause of fighting as the "lack of employment opportunities" in the job market and "the loss of income." A behavior analysis suggests that speakers will use a form of attribution (internal or external) to prevent challenges to their "factual" accounts and to maintain social credibility, rather than just to explain and understand the actions of others. Thus, a speaker who is talking to an audience (Sally's sister) predisposed against Harry is likely to provide an internal (dispositional) account of his actions; an audience predisposed toward Harry (his brother) would occasion an external (marketplace) attribution for the couple's dispute.

Control by the audience over the speaker's causal accounts of actions (internal vs. external) is clearly seen in the so-called self-serving bias, which attributes personal success to internal factors and failures to external sources. Research shows that people provide internal accounts of their own actions when they expect positive consequences from others. A pianist who gives an outstanding, gala performance may claim to television viewers that it was the outcome of her perseverance and dedication to music over a lifetime. Another pianist who gives a mediocre or dismal rendition of the musical work might point to aspects of the situation (an inattentive and restless audience) or context that disrupted her performance (external attribution). The internal attribution claims responsibility for the successful performance and positive social consequences from listeners; external attribution for failure weakens social responsibility, reducing blame and other negative social consequences. Overall, accounts or explanations of actions may be analyzed as the use of words by speakers (verbal behavior) shaped by the social consequences of listeners, or members of a verbal community (for a more complete analysis of speaker–listener conversation, see Guerin, 2003).

OPERANT FUNCTIONS OF VERBAL BEHAVIOR

In his book *Verbal Behavior*, Skinner (1957) presented a preliminary analysis of this kind of human activity. Although some linguists have treated Skinner's work as a behavioral theory of language, it is more likely that the book represents a set of testable hypotheses about verbal behavior (MacCorquodale, 1970). Skinner described verbal behavior in terms of the principles found in the operant laboratory. Such an analysis must ultimately be judged in terms of its adequacy. That is, it must deal with the facts of the speaker's behavior in natural settings and the experimental and observational evidence that supports or refutes such an account. In this section, the basic verbal classes are outlined using the distinctions made by Skinner (1957) as well as clarifications made by others (e.g., Michael, 1982b; Oah & Dickinson, 1989). Remember that the basic units or elements of verbal behavior would be combined, elaborated, and extended in any comprehensive account of speaking, talking, and communicating. How these basic units are integrated into actual complex speech requires continuing analysis and research, as found in the journal *The Analysis of Verbal Behavior*, published by the Association for Behavior Analysis International.

Functional Operant Units: Manding and Tacting

Verbal behavior may be separated into two broad operant classes, namely manding and tacting, based on the regulating conditions. These two operant classes involve the functions of getting what you want from others (manding) and making contact or reference to things and happenings in the world (tacting).

When you say "Give me the book," "Don't do that," "Stop," and so on, your words are regulated by motivational conditions—deprivation for the book, or another person doing something unpleasant. In behavior analysis, this verbal behavior is called manding. **Manding** refers to a class of verbal operants whose form is regulated by establishing operations (e.g., deprivation, aversive stimulation, etc.). The word manding comes from the common English word *commanding*, but commanding is only a small part of this operant class.

Everyday examples of manding include asking someone for a glass of water when you are thirsty, or requesting directions from a stranger when you are lost. Notice that specific reinforcement is made effective for manding by some establishing operation. A glass of water reinforces asking for it when you are deprived of water, and directions are reinforcement for requesting them when you are lost. Common forms of manding include speaking or writing orders, asking questions, requesting objects or things, giving flattering comments to others, and promoting commercial products (e.g., "Buy this detergent").

There is another major class of verbal operants. **Tacting** is defined as a class of verbal operants whose form is regulated by nonverbal discriminative stimuli (nonverbal S^D) and maintained by generalized conditioned reinforcement from the verbal community. A child is tacting when she says "The sun is orange" in the presence of the midday sun on a beach with her mother. In this example, the presence of the sun in the sky (and the relevant property of color) is a nonverbal S^D for tacting by the child. The operant class of tacting is maintained by generalized conditioned reinforcement from the verbal community (e.g., mother, father, teacher, and others), usually in the form of corrective feedback such as "Yes," "Right," and so on. The word *tacting* comes from the more familiar term *contacting*, and refers to verbal behavior that makes contact with events in the world (nonverbal S^Ds). Everyday examples of tacting include describing a scene, identifying objects, providing information about things or issues, and reporting on your own behavior and that of others.

Occasionally, it is difficult to distinguish between manding and tacting. A child who says "juice" in the presence of a glass of apple juice could mean "give juice" or "that is a glass of juice." If the response is equivalent to "give juice", it is functioning as manding (controlled by deprivation and the specific reinforcement of "getting juice"), but if the response is controlled by the nonverbal stimulus of the glass of juice, it is tacting. In another example, a person who says "I believe you have the sports page" may be tacting the nonverbal stimulus (the sports page), or manding specific reinforcement (getting the sports page). The issue is often resolved by the listener saying "Yes, I do" and continuing to read the paper. If the original response was manding, the listener's reply will not function as reinforcement (the sports page is not given). In this case, the speaker is likely to clarify the disguised manding by stating "May I please have the sports page!"

In a further example, a man who picks up his girlfriend for a date may say "Darling, you look beautiful tonight" (Figure 12.3). Again, *the form of response cannot distinguish manding from tacting*. If the man's verbal response is regulated by abstract properties of "beauty" (nonverbal S^D) of the woman, he is tacting. On the other hand, the verbal response could be regulated by deprivation for sexual reinforcement and, if so, the man is manding. Only an analysis and test of the relevant contingencies can distinguish between manding and tacting behavior. Thus, the woman could test the controlling contingencies by withholding sexual reinforcement—testing the veracity of her date's flattering remarks.

Many advertisements and television commercials are disguised manding, in the sense that the verbal responses of an announcer seem to

MO + S^D:	Verbal mand ———▶ S^r (specific)	
Deprivation for sexual reinforcement + Presence of female dating partner	Verbal response of male: "Darling, you look beautiful tonight"	Sexual reinforcement has resulted in the past

FIG. 12.3 An analytical diagram of manding sexual reinforcement on a date. The motivational operation (MO) of deprivation for sexual reinforcement plus the presence of the girlfriend as a discriminative stimulus (S^D) sets up the conditions for the man's response: "Darling, you look beautiful tonight." The verbal mand is maintained by a previous history of specific reinforcement (S^r sexual). Under different controlling conditions the same response could be a verbal tact of the girlfriend's "beauty" (a complex nonverbal discriminative stimulus). Notice that the form of response (what the man says) does not tell us whether the man is manding or tacting. Only an analysis of the controlling conditions for the verbal response can clarify its function—if the MO is withdrawn (sexual intercourse occurs) but the man still says she is "beautiful," the verbal response is likely to be a tact.

describe the benefits of the product (tacting), but are in fact requests to buy it (manding). A television actor dressed in a doctor's white coat states that "Xprin relieves pain and muscle ache" and is available at your local drug store. The verbal description of the product (relieves pain) suggests tacting by the speaker (actor), but there are manding (profit) aspects to the verbal behavior. Given these conflicting contingencies, listeners learn how to reveal the disguised manding of a speaker (testing the controlling variables), and speakers learn to conceal their obvious manding of a listener (making the verbal description of the product appear as tacting its benefits). Persuasion and attitude change may therefore be analyzed in terms of manding, tacting, and the interaction of speakers and listeners (Bem, 1965).

RESEARCH ON VERBAL BEHAVIOR: MANDING AND TACTING

Training of Verbal Operants

According to Skinner (1957), the basic classes of verbal behavior are functionally independent in the sense that the relations involved in manding are distinct from those that define tacting. This functional independence means that it is possible to teach manding and tacting as separate operant classes. It also implies that there is no basic ordering of the verbal repertoire; that is, it is not necessary to train manding in order to train tacting, or vice versa. In this section, research on basic verbal relations will be outlined and assessed in terms of **functional independence** of the response classes.

Manding Relations

Recall that the manding relation is defined by an establishing operation (EO) and specific reinforcement. An establishing procedure regulates the topography or form of manding behavior and sets up a specific consequence as reinforcement. To train manding, the most direct procedure is to manipulate an EO and reinforce the verbal response with the specified consequence. In the laboratory, establishing operations usually involve a history of deprivation for some event that functions as primary reinforcement (e.g., food).

Most human behavior, however, is regulated by conditioned reinforcement. To investigate the manding of conditioned reinforcement, Michael (1988) suggested the use of a **conditioned establishing operation (CEO)**. The procedure is called the blocked-response CEO, in which a response that usually occurs is blocked because of the temporary absence of a specific condition, stimulus, or event. For example, you may leave your seminar notes at home as you rush to the university. Because you cannot complete the behavioral sequence of giving a seminar presentation, obtaining the notes would function as reinforcement for making a telephone call to get them. The notes would not have a reinforcement function during a casual lunch with an old friend, because they are not necessary to this behavioral sequence. Whenever an event or stimulus is required to complete a behavior chain, withholding the event will establish it as reinforcement for operant behavior (see Michael, 2000, for a more extensive analysis).

Hall and Sundberg (1987) used the blocked-response CEO to train manding by deaf subjects. The first step was to teach a sequence or chain of responses. For example, a subject was taught to open a can of fruit with a can opener, to pour the contents into a bowl, and to eat it with a spoon. When the sequence was trained, the subject was given the items to complete the chain, except that one was missing. In this situation, the teacher reinforced a previously trained verbal response that specified the missing item (manding) by supplying the object. Since subjects came to emit such verbal responses, it appears that CEO and specific reinforcement are regulating conditions for manding behavior (see also Carroll & Hesse, 1987; Yamamoto & Mochizuki, 1988).

There are other studies of mand training that did not manipulate an establishing operation (Hung, 1980; Rogers-Warren & Warren, 1980; Savage-Rumbaugh, 1984; Simic & Bucher, 1980; Sundberg, 1985). In these studies, humans, apes, and pigeons were required to produce a response that specified a particular object (food items or toys). The objects were shown to the subject to evoke an appropriate manding response (EO). When the verbal response occurred, the object was given and this functioned as specific reinforcement.

For example, in the study by Savage-Rumbaugh (1984), chimpanzees were shown a number of food items. If the animal pointed to the corresponding symbol on a communication panel, the item was given as reinforcement. Chimpanzees readily acquired this kind of verbal behavior and even more complex symbolic communication (Savage-Rumbaugh, 1986; Savage-Rumbaugh & Lewin, 1994; Savage-Rumbaugh, Shanker, & Taylor, 1998). However, there is some question as to the exact regulating conditions. The food items may have functioned as discriminative stimuli that set the occasion for selecting the corresponding symbol key, in which case the chimpanzee was tacting rather than manding. Because the sources of control were complex, the behavior is best described as *impure manding* (i.e., it is attributable to the control exerted by the food items as discriminative stimuli and specific reinforcement).

In chimpanzee studies, pointing to a food symbol is regarded as manding, since it results in getting the item. Pointing at something is a type of manding in which the response topography or form (index finger extended) remains constant but the response is directed at different stimuli (banana, apple, etc.). This contrasts with human speech, in which the topography of the vocal response varies with the establishing operation and specific reinforcement (e.g., "give food" versus "give water"). Vocal manding facilitates discrimination by a listener (the form of response varies) and may therefore produce more rapid and precise compliance with manding. Although pointing to what you want is formally manding, saying what you want is much more effective—especially if the listener is in another room, or the object is out of sight.

Finally, manding can involve control of verbal behavior by contingencies of negative reinforcement. In a recent study, Yi, Christian, Vittimberga, and Lowenkron (2006) developed a program to increase the quality of life for three children with autism. The researchers taught the youngsters manding for the removal of non-preferred items. This negatively reinforced manding generalized to other untrained items as well.

Tacting Relations

To train tacting responses, a speaker must come to emit a verbal operant whose form depends on a nonverbal discriminative stimulus. A second requirement is that the operant class should be acquired and maintained by *nonspecific reinforcement*. Reinforcement is nonspecific if the reinforcer for one response exerts no stimulus control over the form of the next response. In animal studies, a response may qualify as tacting even if it is reinforced with food, as long as food reinforcement does not set the occasion for a subsequent verbal response or the selection of the next symbol. For example, a chimpanzee may be offered an apple, and when it selects the symbol key for apple it is given a piece of banana. The presentation of the banana cannot set the occasion for pressing the symbol for apple on the next trial.

Tact relations have been investigated with chimpanzees, in particular Kanzi the bonobo chimpanzee (Figure 12.4). Savage-Rumbaugh (1984) used pointing to symbol keys as the verbal response. When the experimenter displayed an item of food (apple), a response to the

FIG. 12.4   Kanzi the bonobo chimpanzee with his trainer, Sue Savage-Rumbaugh, currently at the Great Ape Trust, Des Moines, Iowa. Kanzi is shown with portable lexigram boards used to train tacting and other complex forms of verbal behavior. Published with permission of Sue Savage-Rumbaugh. © Bonobo Hope.

corresponding symbol on the lexigram board resulted in praise and the delivery of a different item of food (banana). That is, the item of food used as reinforcement always differed from the one on display.

In this situation, the display of an item of food was a nonverbal S^D that set the occasion for a response to the appropriate symbol key (tacting). Since reinforcement was nonspecific, the consequences of behavior could not regulate pointing to a particular symbol. That is, because the chimpanzee points to the apple symbol (in the presence of an apple) and is reinforced with a banana, we can be sure that the verbal response is tacting rather than manding.

Chimpanzees' symbol pointing came under the control of the displayed food items and therefore qualified as tacting. In this experiment, the *topography of the tact was the same* (i.e., pointing with the finger), but its location changed. In contrast, vocal tacting in human speech involves *changes in topography depending on the nonverbal stimulus* (i.e., "That's a chair" or "There's a table"). Finally, the delivery of a food item is probably not necessary, and generalized conditioned reinforcement (e.g., praise, acceptance, etc.) alone could be used to train tacting in both apes and human children (see Savage-Rumbaugh, Murphy, Sevcik, Brakke, Williams, & Rumbaugh, 1993; Savage-Rumbaugh, Shanker, & Taylor, 1998; see also Sundberg, 1996, for a behavioral analysis).

Researchers have also used pigeons to investigate tacting relations. Michael, Whitley, and Hesse (1983) attempted to train tacting based on changes in response topography. Pigeons received nonspecific reinforcement (food) that depended on a bird emitting a particular form of response in the presence of a nonverbal discriminative stimulus. For example, a thrust of the head was reinforced when a red ball was presented, and turning in a circle produced reinforcement when a blue ball was the discriminative stimulus. Functionally, this is equivalent to a child who says "That's a red coat" and "This is a brown coat" and is reinforced by acceptance of the description by the listener. Tacting in the pigeons was successfully established even though the contingencies required correspondence between the nonverbal stimulus and the form of the bird's response. A question that is left unanswered by this research is whether pigeons (or chimpanzees) can show generalization of a tacting relation. That is, without further training, would the respective responses for blue and red occur when the objects were triangles or squares rather than balls?

In terms of application, there are behavioral experiments with language-delayed humans that trained tacting as part of a more general program of language acquisition (Carroll & Hesse, 1987; Guess, 1969; Guess & Baer, 1973; Guess, Sailor, Rutherford, & Baer, 1968; Lamarre & Holland, 1985; Lee, 1981a). Carroll and Hesse (1987) investigated the effects of alternating between manding and tacting training. During manding training, a response to an object produced the item. When tacting was trained, the experimenter presented the objects as discriminative stimuli and provided praise as reinforcement for correct responses. Results indicated that subjects responded appropriately to the verbal contingencies, and that *manding training facilitated the acquisition of tacting*. That is, manding "Give cup" increased the acquisition of tacting "That's a cup." This latter finding is interesting because it suggests that under some conditions, manding and tacting are not independent classes of behavior (e.g., Sigafoos, Doss, & Reichle, 1989; Sigafoos, Reichle, Doss, Hall, & Pettitt, 1990). Apparently, these verbal operant relations may interrelate, as when parts of the response forms are shared (i.e., both involve the word "cup").

Experiments by LaMarre and Holland (1985) with typically developing children and by Lee (1981b) with language-delayed humans also concerned the acquisition of tacting (see also Partington, Sundberg, Newhouse, & Spengler, 1994, on tact training of an autistic child). In these experiments, one object was placed on the left and another on the right. The tact response was saying "On the right" or "On the left" depending on the position of the object. For example, the experimenter would prompt "Where is the dog?" The subject who answered "On the right" when the dog was on the right side of a flower received social praise as reinforcement. This type of training successfully established verbal responses that contacted the position of an object. In another version of tacting training, Guess (1969), Guess and Baer (1973), and Guess et al. (1968) trained verbal responses that contacted the quantity of an object. Speakers with language deficits were taught to emit the singular form of a noun when a single object was shown, and to emit the plural form if two identical items were presented.

In these experiments, correct responses produced food, rather than praise. Thus, the subject was presented with a single cup and saying "cup" rather than "cups" was reinforced with food. Food may be defined as nonspecific reinforcement in such studies, because it does not exert any stimulus control over the next verbal response "cup." In humans, both generalized conditioned reinforcement (e.g., praise) and nonspecific reinforcement (e.g., food in the preceding example) may be used to establish tacting to various features of the nonverbal environment (e.g., position of objects, quantity, etc.).

Overall, Skinner's description of the controlling variables for manding and tacting (Skinner, 1957) has been verified by research on a variety of animals, including primates, young children, and language-delayed humans. This research shows that manding is verbal behavior under the control of an establishing operation (EO) and specific reinforcement. In contrast, tacting is verbal behavior controlled by nonverbal discriminative stimuli and generalized reinforcement (or nonspecific reinforcement). The experimental analysis of manding and tacting has resulted in a technology of training verbal behavior in humans who do not show basic verbal skills (Sunberg & Michael, 2001). A basic question is whether these verbal classes (manding and tacting) are learned together or are acquired separately.

Functional Independence of Basic Verbal Classes

Skinner (1957) proposed the functional independence of manding and tacting response classes. That is, because the contingencies controlling these verbal responses are distinct, it should be possible to establish manding of an object or action without the speaker tacting it, and vice versa. Traditional cognitive or linguistic analysis does not make such distinctions, and would not predict that asking for something and identifying it by words arise from different contingencies of reinforcement set by the verbal community. For this reason, it is important to assess the research testing Skinner's functional independence hypothesis.

We have already seen that manding can emerge with tact training, and tacting sometimes appears along with the acquisition of manding—evidence seemingly contrary to Skinner's functional independence hypothesis. Also, in the everyday development of language, there is no indication that asking for things and identifying them develop separately in children. In fact, some behavior analysts argue that manding and tacting are necessarily interrelated by higher-order verbal skills involving derived stimulus relations (relational frames), or by higher-order naming relations (Barnes-Holmes, Barnes-Holmes, & Cullinan, 2000; Hayes, Barnes-Holmes, & Roche, 2001; Horne & Lowe, 1996).

Nonetheless, Lamarre and Holland (1985) demonstrated the functional independence of manding and tacting in children between 3 and 5 years old (Figure 12.5). As previously noted, the children were trained to respond "on the left" or "on the right" to identify the location of an object (tacting) or to ask the experimenter to place an object on the left or right of another one (manding). When tested under extinction conditions, children who were given tacting training did not show reliable evidence of manding, and those trained in manding failed to demonstrate tacting. That is, the training of one verbal operant did not result in the emergence of the other, demonstrating the functional independence of these verbal response classes. After finding this result for initial training, all of the children were trained to emit the verbal operant (manding or tacting) that had not been trained in the first phase of the study. Once the children had learned both manding and tacting, they were tested again for independence of function. Manding responses to left or right locations were now reversed, and tests were made for reversal of tacting; also, tacting to objects at these locations was reversed and tests were made for reversal of manding responses. Again, the results

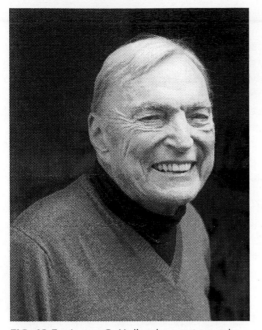

FIG. 12.5 James G. Holland, an esteemed researcher in behavior analysis. Jim Holland and his student, Jennifer Lamarre, conducted an experimental analysis of mand and tact response classes, providing support for Skinner's functional independence hypothesis (Skinner, 1957). Published with permission.

demonstrated functional independence of these verbal classes, even when the verbal response forms for manding and tacting were identical. The results clearly supported Skinner's functional independence hypothesis.

Subsequently, Petursdottir, Carr, and Michael (2005) used preschool children (aged from 2 years 6 months to 3 years 5 months) to systematically replicate and extend the findings of Lamarre and Holland (1985). Using stickers and praise as reinforcement, the researchers trained the children initially to complete two four-piece assembly tasks—constructing a cube and solving a puzzle. Next, they were trained to emit tacting responses to each of the four pieces of one task and to emit manding responses to the separate pieces of the other task, using arbitrary word forms. For example, Tristan received manding training first, followed by tacting training (other children received tacting training followed by manding training). With pieces of the puzzle hidden, Tristan had to correctly respond (manding) "boosha," "doso," "heeny," or "middy" to the question "What do you need?" Subsequently, Tristan had to correctly identify (tact) the four pieces of the cube by saying "chey," "noo," "sai," or "wa" when presented with each piece and the question "What is this?" Probe trials (tests) without reinforcement were used to assess the effects of training on the untrained response class (manding or tacting) for each child. Following manding training, 4 out of 4 children reliably emitted tacting responses on probe trials, but tacting training produced unreliable effects on tests for manding responses.

These findings differ from those of Lamarre and Holland (1985) in that the children showed transfer between verbal response classes, rather than complete functional independence. One possibility is that the contingencies differed between the two studies. The earlier study by Lamare and Holland (1985) required the children to emit verbal responses to an abstract stimulus property (location on the left or on the right), whereas the more recent study by Petursdottir et al. (2005) used a concrete stimulus (pieces of puzzles or cubes) to establish the requisite verbal behavior. For young children, transfer between manding and tacting might increase if the training stimuli were more concrete. In fact, when the stimulus properties were abstract, Twyman (1996) found functional independence of new manding and tacting responses to an abstract property (whole crayon) in educationally disabled children with existing manding and tacting responses. Another way to account for the differences in functional independence over studies relates to establishing operations. The earlier study by Lammare and Holland did not use an explicit establishing operation (EO) for manding training, but the assembly-task study did, using concealed pieces of the task as a specific EO. Differences in explicitness of the EO between studies would mean that children in the earlier location study (on the left of or on the right) were not trained in manding responses, whereas those in the assembly task were. If manding responses were not trained, there could be no transfer between manding and tacting response classes, leading Lamarre and Holland to the incorrect conclusion that there was functional independence.

Notably, the reinforcement histories of the children also differed between the two studies. When children have a relevant history of manding and tacting outside the laboratory, as would be the case for verbal responses involving objects (pieces of puzzle), these response classes would show more cross-transfer in an experimental setting. Without such a history, as with verbal responses related to abstract locations or other abstract stimulus properties, manding training would not result in transfer to tacting responses, and vice versa; the response classes would be independent.

A recent study on manual signing by typically developing infants suggests that, when reinforcement histories are controlled, transfer between manding and tacting responses does not occur (Normand, Machado, Hustyi, & Morely, 2011). The participants were three children between 8 and 15 months old, none of whom exhibited vocal language or manual signing before the study (one infant did occasionally gesture). To establish an explicit EO, manding training occurred at times when infants are usually hungry (e.g., after a nap or before dinner), or when an object (a rattle) was out of sight. Training for one infant involved emitting an informal sign for "apple sauce," bringing the open palm of one hand to the crown of the head (not formal ASL). Another infant was trained to emit a sign for "pears," bringing the palm of one hand to the nose. The target response for the third infant was an informal sign for "rattle," defined as one hand hitting the thigh with a double movement. Manding training involved social modeling of the sign and specific reinforcement of the infant's verbal response (sign) by delivery of the food or object. Test sessions were arranged to assess the acquisition of manding and the possible transfer between manding and tacting responses (echoic responses were also assessed). Tests for manding involved withholding the stimulus item (food or object) prior to a session, and following each target response (sign) with the presentation of the stimulus item (no model prompting). To assess tacting responses, the stimulus items were freely available to the infants for a period prior to and throughout the test session. In accord with the functional definition of tacting, brief verbal praise followed each signing response for these tests (other control conditions were also arranged, but are not discussed here).

Compared with baseline sessions without modeling and reinforcement, all of the infants emitted the target sign more during sign-training conditions. For test sessions, manding responses for the stimulus items were reliably observed for all infants, but none of them showed evidence of tacting the items. That is, the acquisition of manding responses (informal signing of items controlled by an explicit EO and specific reinforcement) did not increase the acquisition of tacting (informal signing of items and generalized reinforcement by praise). The infants in this study had no history of sign training before the study, and the verbal repertoires did not show transfer within the experiment, a result that is consistent with the findings of Lamarre and Holland (see also Nuzzolo-Gomez & Greer, 2004, on functional independence in children with autism/developmental disabilities who did not emit the target mands or tacts before training). At the present time, the functional independence of manding and tacting response classes is not completely resolved, but the weight of the evidence is tipping toward Skinner's hypothesis (Skinner, 1957) when reinforcement histories are controlled within the study.

ADDITIONAL VERBAL RELATIONS: INTRAVERBALS, ECHOICS, TEXTUALS, AND AUTOCLITICS

Intraverbal Relations

Other verbal responses also depend on discriminative stimuli. **Intraverbal behavior** is a class of verbal operants regulated by verbal discriminative stimuli. Verbal stimuli arise from verbal behavior;

a verbal response by a speaker ("one, two, three . . .") may be a stimulus for a subsequent verbal operant by the same speaker ("four"). When a verbal response ("Mary") exactly replicates the verbal stimulus (Say "Mary"), we may say that there is correspondence between them. In this case, the verbal behavior is defined as echoic (see below). However, intraverbal behavior has no point-to-point correspondence between the verbal stimulus ("jack, queen . . .") and the response ("king").

In a conversation by email or on the telephone, one person writes or says something and the other responds to the message. Katherine writes "I went shopping today" and Jason responds "What did you get?" Notice that there is no exact correspondence between the two responses, meeting the criterion of an intraverbal exchange. Our ability to answer questions, tell stories, describe events, solve problems, recall the past, and talk about the future depends on an extensive repertoire of intraverbal behavior.

In everyday language, thematically related words (or sentences) are examples of intraverbal behavior. For example, the verbal response "fish" to the spoken words "rod and reel" is an intraverbal operant; saying "water" in response to the written word "lake" is also intraverbal behavior. On the other hand, the person who says "water" to the spoken sound "water" is not showing intraverbal regulation; in this case, there is exact correspondence between the response and the stimulus, and the response is echoic.

FIG. 12.6   Learning the addition of numbers. This kind of instruction is involved in the acquisition of the intraverbal response "4" when the student is asked "What is 2 plus 2?" by her teacher. © Shutterstock.

Intraverbal training is part of our educational curriculum (see Figure 12.6). In elementary school, students are initially taught addition of numbers, as when a child says or writes the number "4" in response to the problem "2 + 2 equals . . ." An older child may recite the multiplication table, as in "5 × 5" equals "25." In this example, the verbal stimulus "5 × 5" exerts direct stimulus control over the response "25," and the relation is intraverbal. In contrast, a student who derives the answer "25" by adding five 5s, counting by 5s, or counting the cells in a 5 × 5 matrix is tacting the number or set of elements rather than emitting an intraverbal response. As you can see, the training of academic behavior in young children involves several verbal relations, including tacting and intraverbal behavior (see DeBaryshe & Whitehurst, 1986; Partington & Bailey, 1993).

Children and adults with language deficits may also benefit from intraverbal training (Sundberg, Endicott, & Eigenheer, 2000; Sundberg & Michael, 2001), and the number of empirical studies of intraverbal behavior has steadily increased over the past few years. In a recent study, Sundberg and Sundberg (2011) described the age-related changes in intraverbal behavior of 39 typically developing children (aged 23 to 61 months) and 71 autistic children (aged 35 months to 15 years), using an 80-item inventory. The inventory contains 8 sets or groups of intraverbal questions that are posed to the child and become increasingly more difficult, involving multiple sources of control within the question. For example, a Group 1 level question requires the child to emit a simple "fill in" response to "Twinkle, twinkle, little____," while a Group 8 level question asks "How is a car different from a bike?," requiring a complex verbal conditional discrimination. The child's exact response was recorded next to each question and subsequently scored as correct or erroneous by two individuals (over 90% reliable scoring). For typically developing children, the data showed that the intraverbal scores were correlated with age, with inventory scores generally increasing as the child became older. Also, the intraverbal scores of these typically developing children substantially improved after 3 years of age, and then rose toward the maximum score of 80 at 5 years of age. Errors by typically developing children often involved items requiring compound verbal conditional discrimination. Autistic children who scored at the same level as typically developing children (but not at the same age) made the same errors on the subtest, suggesting new intervention strategies for these youngsters.

Echoic Relations

When there is point-to-point correspondence between the stimulus and the response, verbal behavior may be classified as either echoic or textual, depending on the criterion of formal similarity. The contingencies of echoic behavior require formal similarity whereas the contingencies of textual behavior do not (see below). **Formal similarity** requires that the verbal stimulus and the product of the response be in the same mode (auditory, visual, etc.) and have exact physical resemblance (e.g., same sound pattern). An **echoic** is a class of verbal operants regulated by a verbal stimulus in which there is *correspondence and formal similarity* between the stimulus and the response. Saying "This is a dog" to the spoken stimulus "This is a dog" is an example of an echoic response in human speech. Generally, *echoic behavior is generalized imitation along a vocal dimension* (see Chapter 11 and Poulson et al., 1991).

Echoic behavior occurs at an early age in an infant's acquisition of speech. The child who repeats "dada" or "mama" to the same words uttered by a parent is showing echoic operant behavior. In this situation, any product of behavior (sound pattern of child) that closely replicates the verbal stimulus (modeled sound pattern) is reinforced (see Figure 12.7).

FIG. 12.7   A young mother interacting with her baby. An echoic response is trained when the mother says "mama" and the baby, intently looking at her lips, makes the approximation "ma" that is reinforced with smiles from the mother. Eventually, over time, the mother says "mama" and the child emits "mama" as an echoic response. © Shutterstock.

Although reinforcement appears to occur along a dimension of acoustical correspondence, the contingencies of echoic behavior are probably based more on the matching of phonetic units. Catania indicates that the learning of echoic behavior begins with the basic units of speech called phonemes. He explains:

> The significant dimensions of the units of speech called phonemes are more easily defined by articulations (position of the tongue, etc.) than by acoustic properties. . . . The interactions of articulation and

sounds are complex; for example, many English consonants (e.g., *p, b, d*) can't be produced unless accompanied by a vowel, and their acoustic properties vary as a function of context (e.g., the sounds of *l* and *k* are different in *lick* than in *kill*). Echoic behavior isn't defined by acoustic correspondence; it's defined by correspondences of the phonetic units.

(Catania, 1998, p. 241)

Coordinated movements of the child's larynx, tongue, and lips result in phonemes (e.g., "ma"), which replicate parts of adult speech ("ma . . . ma"). When articulations by the child correspond to those of the adult, the acoustical patterns also overlap. Adults who hear speech-relevant sounds ("ma") often provide social consequences (e.g., tickling, poking, etc.) that are paired with these acoustical patterns. On this basis, the duplication of speech sounds itself comes to function as automatic reinforcement for speech-relevant articulations by the child (Yoon & Bennett, 2000).

It is important to emphasize that echoic behavior is not simply the duplication of sounds. As a verbal operant, echoic performance is regulated by specific reinforcement contingencies based on articulation. Echoic contingencies in humans involve reinforcement by listeners of correspondence of basic speech units rather than the mere reproduction of sounds. These units begin as phonemes (i.e., the smallest sound units to which listeners react), expand to words, and eventually may include full phrases and sentences. In contrast, parrots and other birds duplicate the sounds that they hear (Pepperberg, 1981, 2000), but their behavior is not necessarily verbal in Skinner's sense (Skinner, 1957). Parrots will reproduce sounds or noises even when these responses produce no change in the behavior of the listener. For this reason an infant's speech is echoic behavior, but a parrot's "speech" is not.

Echoic contingencies are most prevalent during language acquisition. This means that an infant's vocalizations will have more echoic components than the speech of an adult. It also implies that adult speech will become more echoic when a person is learning to speak a second language. Thus, a Spanish teacher may demonstrate word pronunciation to a student who initially makes many errors in articulation. The teacher gives repeated examples, and the student is reinforced for correct pronunciation. After some practice and correction, the student's pronunciation becomes close to that of the teacher. Only when the speech units correspond is the student said to show competence in pronunciation of Spanish.

Textual Relations

Verbal behavior is textual when there is no formal similarity between the stimulus and the response. **Textual behavior** is defined as a class of verbal operants regulated by verbal stimuli where there is correspondence between the stimulus and the response, but no formal similarity. The most common example of textual behavior is reading out loud. The child looks at the text, which reads "See Dick see Jane," and emits the spoken words "See . . . Dick . . . see . . . Jane." In adult reading, the behavior is also textual but the "out loud" aspect is no longer emitted—the person reads silently so that the response is now a private event. Textual behavior is also observed when a secretary *takes dictation* from his or her boss. In this case, hearing the words "Dear Mr. Smith . . ." spoken by the boss sets the occasion for writing these words by the secretary. Again, correspondence between the stimulus and the response occurs, but there is no formal similarity.

Autoclitic Relations

The **autoclitic** is a form of verbal behavior that modifies the consequences produced by other verbal responses. It is verbal behavior used in conjunction with, and controlled by, primary verbal units, such as mands, tacts, and intraverbals. Skinner (1957) described five categories of autoclitic relations:

descriptive, qualifying, quantifying, manipulative, and relational (for a summary, see Howard & Rice, 1988). For example, descriptive autoclitics (e.g., I think, I doubt, I see, I hear) are used to further specify the control by a nonverbal stimulus over the speaker's tact. At a railway station, Paul says to Stephanie "*I see* the train is coming," adding "I see" to inform her that stimulus control over his tact "the train is coming" is visual rather than auditory. By adding the autoclitic to the tact, Paul provides more precise stimulus control over Stephanie's behavior (looking for the train), increasing the probability of generalized reinforcement ("Okay") from her. An in-depth coverage of autoclitic relations is beyond the scope of this textbook, and it is convenient for further analysis to collapse Skinner's five categories into two—autoclitic tacts and autoclitic mands (Peterson, 1978).

The defining property of autoclitic manding is that these verbal units are controlled by motivating operations (MO) that make it reinforcing for the speaker to modify the mand, thereby increasing stimulus control over the listener's behavior. If deprived of water, John may say "Get me some water" to his sister, Katherine. Alternatively, he may say "*Could you please* get me some water," with the first three words having no meaning (stimulus control) on their own, but functioning with the mand to increase the likelihood that his sister ("you") will comply. Thus, the autoclitic unit "Could you please . . ." is added to the mand, sharpening stimulus control over the listener's behavior (getting water) and increasing the probability of reinforcement for the speaker (receiving water). Many parts of speech that have no meaning on their own are added to the speaker's mands based on the practices of the verbal community.

As we mentioned earlier, autoclitics are used to modify the stimulus control exerted by the speaker's tact over the listener's response. Looking toward the gas gage, John says to his buddy George (the driver) "*I doubt* we are out of gas," as opposed to the response "*I'm sure* we are out of gas." For the listener, the words "I doubt" versus "I'm sure" control a conditional discrimination with respect to stopping for gas at the next station. You stop for gas if your buddy is "sure" that there is nothing left in the tank. For the speaker, the autoclitic is added as a verbal response under the stimulus control of the primary tact "We are out of gas," as indicated by the gauge pointer and the time since the last fill-up. That is, the speaker discriminates the strength (or weakness) of his own verbal behavior when saying "I'm sure" versus "I doubt." In a situation where you may be out of gas, the speaker must be able to tell whether saying "We are out of gas" is appropriate. The verbal community sets up the repertoire of "responding to one's own behavior," presumably because of the benefits that accrue to listeners (e.g., avoiding an empty gas tank) when speakers make such complex verbal discriminations.

A study by Howard and Rice (1988) is informative about the training involved in the early acquisition of autoclitic responses regulated by weak stimulus control of a primary tact. Four preschool children were initially trained to tact colors (red, yellow, and blue), geometric shapes (square, circle, and triangle) and alphabet letters (L, H, and M), using praise and "happy faces" exchanged for time with preferred activities (e.g., drawing a picture) as generalized reinforcement. Tact training involved the experimenter asking "What is this?," followed by presentation of a stimulus from one of the stimulus sets (colors, shapes, or letters) and the child identifying it with a verbal response (e.g., "red," "square," or "M"). Once 90% or more of the children's tacts were correct, they were trained to emit the autoclitic response "like" to weak stimulus control by the primary tact. The experimenter now presented the child with a distorted example of a stimulus from one set (e.g., red-like color) and asked "What is this?" If no autoclitic response occurred, the trainer modeled the correct response ("like red," "like square," or "like M"), withdrew the stimulus, and presented it again a few seconds later. Each stimulus set was trained separately until the children met a criterion of 90% or more correct. At this point autoclitic training continued, but probe trials were used to assess generalization of autoclitic responses (generalized response class). For probe trials, new distorted examples of stimuli from the three stimulus sets (never trained) were presented without reinforcement.

Although only one child completed all of the phases of the study, the overall results from probe trials showed that the children acquired the generalized autoclitic response, "like X," occasioned by weak stimulus control of the primary tact. Other findings showed that the ability to tact a stimulus is not sufficient to obtain autoclitic responses to distorted examples, and that training across multiple stimuli within sets must occur before a generalized response class or autoclitic frame ("like X") is formed. Howard and Rice (1988, pp. 57–58) noted that the "exact nature of the stimulus that evokes autoclitics of weakness" is difficult to specify. That is, "there is no particular characteristic of the nonverbal stimulus [that controls the tact] one can point to and say, 'It is this dimension [of the stimulus] which is controlling the autoclitic *like*.'" Given this problem, Howard and Rice argue that "it seems reasonable to assume that the speaker is reacting to some private stimulation related to the reduced tendency [low probability of response] to make the primary tact response."

Without a public stimulus to accompany the private stimulation of "response tendency," it is difficult to train descriptive autoclitics. In applied settings where the focus is on developing verbal behavior in children with autism, the complexity of training autoclitics is recognized. Behavior analysts recommend training a wide variety of primary verbal operants (mands, tacts, echoics, and intraverbals) to allow for "communication effectiveness" without direct training of "grammatical correctness" (Sundberg & Michael, 2001, p. 13). A broad range of primary verbal units would allow the autistic child to contact the natural contingencies of verbal community—adding grammatical correctness (autoclitics) to the child's verbal repertoire without direct instruction. An unfortunate implication of this view is that basic research on autoclitics has stalled, and applied studies have not clarified the contingencies for training each of Skinner's five classes of autoclitics. Overall, more basic and applied research is needed on contingencies of reinforcement and autoclitic behavior—a central component of Skinner's functional analysis of language (Skinner, 1957).

FOCUS ON: Higher-Order Verbal Classes and the Naming Relation

The basic units of verbal behavior are combined to form higher-order classes, allowing for the greater novelty and spontaneity in a child's language production. Previously, we described the emergence of generalized imitation as a higher-order operant class arising from reinforcement of numerous exemplars of modeling and imitation (see Chapter 11). Once a child has acquired generalized imitation, any new, modeled stimulus presented by an adult occasions a corresponding novel imitation by the child. Once established, general-ized imitation allows children to rapidly learn new forms of behavior from models—adding observational learning to the basic process of learning by successive approximation (see Chapter 4 on shaping). Catania described the basic features of such higher-order behavior classes. He states that:

> [a generalized operant class] includes within it other classes that can themselves function as operant classes (as when generalized imitation includes all component imitations that could be separately reinforced as subclasses). A higher-order class is sometimes called a generalized class, in the sense that contingencies arranged for some subclasses within it generalize to all the others. . . . Higher-order classes may be a source of novel behavior (e.g., as in generalized imitation of behavior the imitator had not seen before). *They also have the property that contingencies may operate differently on the higher-order class than on its component subclasses.* For example, if all instances of imitation are reinforced except those within one subclass (e.g., jumping whenever the model jumps), that subclass may not become differentiated from the higher-order class and so may change with the higher-order class rather than with the contingencies arranged for it (i.e., the imitation of jumping may not extinguish even though it is no longer reinforced). Control by the contingencies arranged

for the higher-order class rather than by those arranged for the subclasses defines these classes; the subclasses may then be said to be insensitive to the contingencies arranged for them. Higher-order classes of behavior are held together by the common consequences of their members.

(Catania, 1996, p. 278, emphasis added)

In a seminal article, Horne and Lowe (1996) proposed that naming something (object, place, or action) involves a generalized operant class that substantially expands the verbal repertoire of the child. Analytically, the **naming relation** or *the generalized class of naming* arises from verbal contingencies that integrate the echoic and tacting response classes of the child as speaker with the conditional discrimination behavior of the child as listener.

Seated on the floor, a mother may ask or instruct her child to point to the ball among the other toys, model and prompt pointing to the ball, and differentially reinforce pointing at the ball with praise and approval. That is, the mother in this episode is teaching the child to follow instructions—the basis of comprehension or listening. Within the same episode, the mother is likely to say "ball" while pointing to the ball and provide reinforcement for the child's echoing or repeating the mother's word. Notice that the social contingencies arranged by the mother require both listening and speaking by the child. The child as listener follows the mother's instruction, pointing to the ball. As the speaker, the child emits the word "ball" as an echoic response to a similar utterance by her mother. The naming relation also involves tacting training, as when the mother points to the ball and asks "What is this?," adding the prompt "Say, ball," and the child responds by saying the word "ball."

After extensive name training across various objects, we may say that the child knows the names of toys, such as ball, doll, and truck. That is, the child says "ball" (and not "doll" or "truck") when we hold up a ball and ask "What is this?" Also, we expect the child to look in the direction of the ball when we say "Where's the ball?," and to point at it, go to it, and pick it up if it is in sight. And when a new toy car is introduced, the mother may say "This is a car" and ask the child "What is this?" without further training. A child who answers "Car" to this question shows acquisition of the generalized verbal relation—a naming response has emerged without explicit reinforcement.

A variety of research studies with language-delayed children indicate that the naming relation arises from multiple exemplar instructions (MEI) (Greer, Stolfi, & Pistoljevic, 2007), involving rotation of the child's listener and speaker responses during training. After training to establish basic verbal units and listening, MEI alternates instruction to match with instruction to point and with instruction to tact, arranged in different sequences. For example, in the stimulus set of birds (parrot, canary, ostrich, cardinal, hummingbird), a child without naming capability may be shown pictures of birds and asked to "Match ostrich" by placing a target picture on top of the duplicate picture in the set. The child is then asked to "Point to parrot" among the set of five birds. This is followed by an opportunity to say "Humming-bird" (tact without prompt) in response to the presentation of a picture of a hummingbird, or tact the bird with the addition of a vocal antecedent "What is this?" For the set of gems (diamond, sapphire, ruby, amethyst, and emerald), the child may be asked to "Point to diamond," and then asked to "Match the amethyst," followed by an opportunity to tact a picture of the ruby, saying "Ruby" with or without the vocal prompt "What is this?"

One research question is whether this kind of MEI is required to establish the generalized class of naming, or whether single exemplar instruction (SEI) would also result in the higher-order verbal class (Greer et al., 2007). For SEI training, the child's listener and speaker responses are not rotated during instruction, but each learning unit (instructed matching to sample, instructed pointing to objects, and tacting of objects with and without vocal prompts) is trained separately in massed practice sessions. During training by either MEI or SEI, correct responses are reinforced (with tokens and praise) while incorrect responses by the child result in the trainer demonstrating the correct response (correction), repeating the vocal antecedent, and the child providing the accurate response (no tokens and praise).

The results showed that MEI training increased novel unreinforced listener and speaker components of naming. None of the children who were given SEI training showed emergent or novel naming, even though they received the same amount of training on the learning units. The data suggest that rotation of the speaker–listener components found in MEI training is required for the acquisition of naming in children who lack a naming repertoire (see Barnes-Holmes, Hayes, Barnes-Holmes, & Roche, 2002, for an alternative, post-Skinnerian interpretation of naming as a relational frame involving derived stimulus relations, bidirectionality, and combinatorial entailment). That is, through MEI instruction the child learns that listener and speaker responses go together, establishing the generalized verbal class of naming. The speaker–listener repertoires remain independent with SEI training, and there is no evidence of generalized naming with these procedures. Notably, children who did not initially learn generalized naming with SEI training subsequently showed naming of novel objects when retrained with the MSI protocol (see also Mahoney, Miguel, Ahearn, & Bell, 2011, on the use of motor responses (as opposed to vocal responses) in tact training and the emergence of naming and stimulus categorization in preschool children).

One possibility is that parents use unplanned multiple exemplar instruction to establish naming in typically developing children, as part of everyday language learning. Further research is required on the natural contingencies involved in the development of naming in children without language deficits.

ANALYSIS OF COMPLEX BEHAVIOR AND COMMUNICATION IN THE LABORATORY

Faced with the complexity of verbal behavior, many people find it hard to believe that basic behavior principles, such as stimulus control, shaping, and schedules of reinforcement, can eventually account for this kind of human activity. It is useful therefore to step back and consider the contingencies of complex behavior. Analysis of these contingencies convinced Skinner (1957) that operant principles could eventually provide a natural-science account of human language.

NOTE ON: Universal Grammar

Chomsky (1957, 1959) argued against behavior principles and for a system of mental rules underlying the speaker's performance. Schoneberger (2000) proposes that Chomsky now rejects his former ties to cognitivism; however, he still remains committed to universal grammar, deep structure, and an innate language-acquisition device. Recent studies by the linguistic anthropologist Daniel Everett (2012) cast doubt on universal grammar, based on 30 years of linguistic research on the Pirahã, a remote tribe in the Amazon jungle.

Everett indicates that the evolution of basic brain structures, culture, and the unique features of the Amazon jungle have shaped the Pirahã language.

Although there are many distinctions between the verbal behavior of humans and the complex behavior generated in pigeons, the laboratory analog identifies some of the basic contingencies that play a role in human language acquisition. In this section, we consider experimental procedures that result in pigeons showing conditional discriminations, symbolic communication, and communication of internal and private events. Many of these behaviors, if observed in humans, would be attributed to mental rules and processes rather than the contingencies of reinforcement that were known to produce them.

Let us begin with a fairly complex set of contingencies for pigeons. Consider a conditional-discrimination experiment described by Catania (1980b), in which a pigeon is placed in an operant chamber with left and right keys (Figure 12.8). Stimuli can be projected on the keys, and a light is situated in one corner of the response panel, allowing general illumination of the chamber (i.e., a houselight). The stimuli consist of circles with horizontal or vertical lines and triangles with similar angled lines (see the matrix in Figure 12.8). Centered below the keys is a feeder that provides food reinforcement depending on the prevailing conditions. When the houselight is ON, pecks to the left or right keys are reinforced according to line angle—horizontal or vertical (ON = peck by line angle). If the houselight is OFF, pecks to the keys produce food on the basis of form, circle, or triangle (OFF = peck by form). There are four possible arrangements of the two keys by line angle when the houselight is ON, and four other arrangements by form when the houselight is OFF. For each session the houselight is illuminated or not, and the four arrangements by line angle (or form) are presented in random order.

Figure 12.8 shows the contingencies based on whether the houselight is ON or OFF. During sessions when the houselight is ON, pecks to the left key are reinforced if the line angle projected on the two keys is horizontal (HORIZONTAL = peck left key) and pecking the right key is on extinction. When the line angle on the two keys is vertical, pecks to the right key produce food (VERTICAL = peck right key) and pecking the left key is on extinction. Notice that the form of the stimuli (triangles or circles) has no function when the houselight is ON or illuminated.

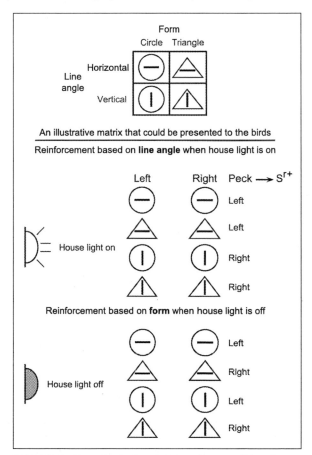

FIG. 12.8 Hypothetical experiment for conditional discrimination as described by Catania (1980b, p. 176). A matrix of possible shapes and line angles is portrayed. When the houselight is ON, reinforcement is based on line angle; the pigeon pecks left if the line angle is horizontal and pecks right if it is vertical. When the houselight is OFF, reinforcement is based on geometric form; the bird pecks left when the shape is a circle and pecks right when it is a triangle.

In contrast, when the houselight is OFF, key pecks are reinforced depending on form, and line angle no longer has a stimulus function. If circles are presented on the two keys, pecks to the left key are reinforced (CIRCLES = peck left key) and pecking the right key is on extinction. When triangles are projected on the keys, pecks to the right key produce food (TRIANGLES = peck right key) and pecking the left key is on extinction. Notice that the line angle (horizontal or vertical) has no function when the houselight is OFF.

Assuming that the bird's pecking is regulated by the appropriate stimuli, we may say that the performance demonstrates a **conditional discrimination**. Pecking the keys depends on line angle or form, conditional on the illumination of the houselight. These conditional relations among stimuli and responses are also observed in verbal behavior. A child provides the answer "five" when presented with a picture of five dimes and the question "How many coins?" When asked "What kind of coins are these?," the child will respond "dimes." This kind of verbal performance involves contingencies similar to the ones that produce conditional discrimination in the laboratory.

This does not mean that the pigeon's performance should be described as verbal. The laboratory procedure shows that nonverbal processes (conditional discrimination) may play a role in verbal behavior. In the pigeon experiments, the bird responded to angle and form only within the narrow context of the operant chamber. Verbal behavior in humans is not limited to specific situations or circumstances. You may also have noted that the bird's performance was maintained by food, and this is seldom the case with human verbal behavior. In addition, no audience responded to the performance and mediated reinforcement. In each of these respects, and perhaps others, the pigeon's behavior may be distinguished from human verbal performance. The point, however, is that conditional control by stimuli (e.g., four-term contingencies) is important in an analysis of human behavior, and this is especially so for verbal behavior.

Symbolic Communication in Animals

One implication of complex stimulus control in the laboratory is that animals exposed to such contingencies often acquire behavior that in humans is said to reflect mental or cognitive processes. That is, human communication is attributed to our expanded brain capacity and cognitive abilities. Behavior analysts offer an alternative to the mental capacity approach, arguing that symbolic communication is caused by special contingencies of reinforcement. To test this assumption, nonhuman organisms have been trained to emit verbal responses. In this research, one subject is designated the speaker and the other the listener. The roles of speaker and listener are used here to suggest the verbal exchange between two organisms—one which asks for and uses information (the listener), and the other who supplies it (the speaker).

The Jack and Jill Experiment

Epstein, Lanza, and Skinner (1980) first reported communication by pigeons in *Science* magazine. They wanted to show that language-like behavior could be generated in simple organisms by complex contingencies of reinforcement and, by implication, that human language could be generated by complex verbal contingencies.

The original experiment used discrimination procedures based on color; the illustrations in this textbook are in black and white, so for clarity we will substitute procedures based on geometric forms (e.g., triangles) rather than colors. The pigeons, called Jack and Jill, were placed in separate chambers with a clear Plexiglas partition between them (see Figure 12.9). In the original procedure, Jack was the listener and Jill was the speaker (see Epstein & Skinner, 1981, on the implications of training both birds as speaker and listener). The interrelationship between the behavioral sequences of the speaker and the listener defines the **interlocking contingencies** for the experiment. Following basic training for both birds to establish the respective operant chains, the interaction began when Jack pecked a key in his chamber that had the words *What form?* projected on it. When this happened, one of three forms—a triangle, circle, or square—was illuminated in Jill's chamber. Importantly, the form was hidden by a curtain and could not be seen by Jack (see Figure 12.9).

The speaker, Jill, thrust her head behind the curtain and looked at the geometric form projected on a disk. Following this, she pecked one of three symbol or letter keys, labeled with the letters T, C, or S (T = triangle, C = circle, S = square), that matched the form she had observed behind the curtain. When Jack looked into Jill's chamber, he saw which symbol key she had pecked. He then pecked his *Thank you* key that in turn operated Jill's feeder for a few seconds. Following this, Jack pecked one of three form keys in his chamber (i.e., triangle, circle, or square) that corresponded to the symbol (T, C, or S) selected by Jill. If Jack matched his form key to the symbol

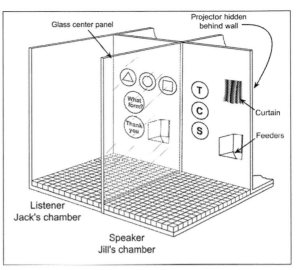

FIG. 12.9 Chambers and key arrangements for the Jack and Jill experiment as described in "Symbolic communication between two pigeons (*Columba livia domestica*)," by R. Epstein, R. P. Lanza, and B. F. Skinner, 1980, *Science, 207,* 543–545. For clarity, we have substituted geometric forms for color stimuli. The experiment involved communication between two pigeons. The curtain in Jill's chamber hides a projected geometric form (triangle, circle, or square). The letter or symbols correspond to the geometric forms (T = triangle, C = circle, and S = square). Jack matches geometric form (triangle, circle, or square) to the symbol key (T, C, or S) pecked by Jill. See text for a description of the contingencies.

pecked by Jill (e.g., if he pecked his triangle key when Jill had pecked her T symbol key), this response operated Jack's feeder for a few seconds. An incorrect response resulted in a short timeout. After 5 days of this interaction, the pigeons were accurate on more than 90% of the trials.

Formally, the experiment involved training pigeons in manding and tacting. Completion of the interaction sequence between the speaker and the listener defined a **social episode**. The role of the listener (Jack) required manding *What form?* His "question" is manding that is reinforced by Jill reporting the form she had observed behind the curtain. Jill "reports" her observation by pecking one of the three symbols or letter keys. This "report" by the speaker (Jill) allows the listener (Jack) to peck the corresponding geometric form on his panel. Because pecking the correct form is part of a sequence that leads to food, hiding the geometric shape from the listener may be viewed as a conditioned establishing operation (CEO, blocked-response procedure) in this experiment.

The speaker's sequence is also initiated when the listener pecks *What form?* In the presence of this verbal stimulus, the speaker must look at the form behind the curtain and "report" on the shape that she has seen. Pecking the correct symbol key is formally tacting in Skinner's classification of verbal behavior (Skinner, 1957). The symbolic response qualifies as tacting; a nonverbal aspect of the environment (the hidden color) controls the response that results in nonspecific reinforcement (i.e., the food supplied when the listener pecks *Thank you*). A nonspecific reinforcer is one that does not specify the topography of a subsequent tacting response. The speaker pecks T, C, or S and is reinforced with grain. The presentation of grain at the end of the listener–speaker interaction does not control which symbol the speaker pecks on the next trial.

Communication by pigeons maintained by food reinforcement is a demonstration that complex contingencies generate complex behavior, even in relatively simple organisms like pigeons. Of course, human verbal behavior involves sound production and infinite variations and combinations of phonemes and words. However, the verbal environment, composed of speakers from the verbal community, arranges intricate verbal contingencies that select the common forms and grammar of everyday speaking much as the contingencies of reinforcement did in the Jack and Jill demonstration.

Communication and Generalized Reinforcement

In human communication, tacting by a speaker almost never results in food reinforcement. It is therefore important to know whether animals will continue tacting when this behavior is supported by generalized conditioned reinforcement. An experiment by Lubinski and MacCorquodale (1984) with pigeons was designed to answer such a question. These researchers established a generalized reinforcer for the speaker by pairing a flashing light with the presentation of *both food and water*. On some days the pigeon was food deprived, and on other days it was deprived of water. Occasionally, the pigeon was deprived of both food and water. When food deprived, the bird could peck a key that operated a feeder. When the bird was thirsty, it could peck a different key to produce water. Importantly, responses for food or water were only effective when a light was flashing in the chamber. The flashing light functioned as a *generalized conditioned reinforcer* because it was associated with more than one source of primary reinforcement (food and water). Using the flashing light as reinforcement, Lubinski and MacCorquodale (1984) showed that tacting in pigeons would occur even when the only consequence was reinforcement from the "flashing light."

Research on nonhuman communication plays an important role in behavior analysis (for a review, see Lubinski & Thompson, 1993). Although human communication involves far more than the manding and tacting of symbols and forms, these nonhuman experiments point to the *basic elements* that underlie symbolic communication. This research also suggests that human communication may arise from the simultaneous interplay of relatively simple principles of behavior—in this case, shaping, fading, chaining, and discrimination procedures.

Reports of Private Events by Pigeons

One of the actions that is said to separate humans from other animals is the ability to report on internal states and feelings. Behaviorists maintain that humans do not have unique capabilities that give them self-awareness or special knowledge of themselves. Rather, behavior analysts suggest that self-description is something a person learns by interacting with others who ask questions about the person and their private events (e.g., "How do you feel?"). *It is only because of special verbal contingencies that a person acquires a repertoire of self-description* (Bem, 1965; Skinner, 1957).

As we have seen in earlier chapters, behavior analysts treat the internal and external happenings of an organism as *physical and functional* events. The only difference between the external environment and the one inside us is that internal events are *private*. This privacy means that *internal events are less accessible* to others and, as a result, it is more difficult for the verbal community to teach a person to describe internal events accurately.

When a verbal response is controlled by a nonverbal discriminative stimulus, this response is functionally defined as tacting. A person who has learned to describe the up-and-down flight of a butterfly may say "I have butterflies in my stomach" when upset or nervous. This response is analyzed as extended or *generalized tacting*—the person describes an upset stomach in the same way as a person describing the motion of a butterfly. This suggests that self-description is, in part, based on the verbal relations involved in tacting.

To set up a report on a private event (tacting), it is necessary to have a public event that is well correlated with this private happening. For example, a bump on the head and crying usually accompany painful private stimulation. A child who bumps her head and cries may occasion the response "Oh, you're hurt" by the parent. In this situation, the child is asked where it hurts and how she feels. The youngster is reinforced when she accurately reports "I hurt my head" and "It hurts a lot." Although parents use public events (bumps and crying) to train self-description, the public signs are usually well correlated with private stimulation (physical damage). Because of this correspondence, private stimulation eventually comes to regulate self-descriptive responses (e.g., "I am hurt") even in the absence of public signs such as crying.

The verbal relations that are presumed to set up a self-descriptive repertoire may be arranged in a laboratory (see Lubinski & Thompson, 1993). A pigeon is a useful organism on which to test these ideas, because pigeons are not usually able to describe themselves. Lubinski and Thompson (1987) therefore used pigeons that were trained to discriminate among the private stimulation produced by different drugs (S^D) and to "report" how they felt in each condition ($R_{tacting}$) for generalized conditioned reinforcement (S^r). *This is another example of communication in nonhuman organisms, but the experiment involves reporting on internal (private) drug effects rather than external events (S^Ds) such as triangles, circles, or squares.* Again, the internal effects of the drugs are treated as physical events that pigeons can discriminate, just as pigeons can discriminate among shapes projected on a key. Presumably, humans also discriminate among internal stimulations and are trained by the verbal community to report on these (physical) events. The basic point is that describing one's feelings and emotions is behavior controlled by the *interlocking contingencies* among speakers and listeners (the verbal community).

In the experiment by Lubinski and Thompson (1987), two pigeons were placed in separate chambers, as shown in Figure 12.10. One bird was the "mander" or listener and the other was the "tacter" or speaker, as in other studies of communication in pigeons described in this chapter. The first step was to develop a generalized reinforcer for the tacter. That is, pecking a key for food or a key for water was reinforced only when a blue light was flashing (as in the study by Lubinski & MacCorquodale, 1984). After this training, the tacting bird was given a drug that was a depressant, a stimulant, or a saline solution (salt water). Private stimulation consisted of the interoceptive effects produced by the different kinds of drugs or chemicals.

Again, after extensive training to establish the behavioral sequences, the interaction began with the mander (listener) pecking a *How do you feel?* key in its chamber. This response illuminated three keys in the tacter's (speaker's) chamber. Each key had a symbol—D for depressant, N for no drug, and Σ (sigma) for stimulant. The tacter had to peck a symbol key that corresponded to the drug which it had

FIG. 12.10 Chambers and key arrangements for the "mander" and "tacter" pigeons are shown for the experiment on communication of internal states by pigeons, as described in "An animal model of the interpersonal communication of interoceptive (private) states," by D. Lubinski and T. Thompson, 1987, *Journal of the Experimental Analysis of Behavior, 48*, 1–15. The symbols D, N, and Σ are equivalent to depressant, no drug, and stimulant, respectively. The symbols P, S, and C are equivalent to phenobarbital, saline, and cocaine, respectively. The flashing light is generalized conditioned reinforcement for the behavior of the "tacter" bird. See text for a description of the contingencies.

received (D after an injection of phenobarbital, N after saline, or Σ after cocaine). When this occurred, a sample disk was illuminated in the mander's chamber with the symbol reported by the tacter (Σ), and at the same time a *Thank you* key was illuminated. Pecks to the *Thank you* key by the manding bird activated a flashing blue light in the tacter's chamber. The tacting bird could then receive food or water by pecking the corresponding keys.

The interaction ended with the mander pecking one of three comparison keys that matched the sample (D, N, or Σ) reported by the tacting bird. The mander's three keys had the letters P, S, or C on them (P for phenobarbital, S for saline, and C for cocaine). If the symbol N (no drug) was the sample (i.e., the tacting bird had pecked the N key), pecking the S key for saline resulted in food reinforcement for the mander. Reinforcement also occurred if the mander pecked its P key for pentobarbital when D (depressant) was the sample, or pecked the C key for cocaine when Σ (stimulant) was the sample. Notice that this experiment is similar to those in which pigeons reported on hidden forms or symbols. The interesting twist on the procedure is that the tacting bird reports an internal and private drug state ("I am on a stimulant" = Σ). The mander, on the other hand, indicates her "understanding the feeling" by matching the symbol for the drug to the sample (i.e., pecking the C key for cocaine).

Although these complex behavioral sequences took a long time to train, eventually the tacter's "reports" and the mander's "comprehensions" were highly accurate, exceeding 90% reliability. At this point, Lubinski and Thompson (1987) conducted additional experiments on the communication of internal events, in order to extend the findings to human behavior. In a test for generalization, the researchers substituted the drug Dexedrine (d-amphetamine) for cocaine and Librium (chlordiazpoxide) for pentobarbital. Although Dexedrine and Librium differ chemically and pharmacologically from cocaine and pentobarbital, both share pharmacological properties with these agents. *The generalization tests showed that accurate reporting of drug effects occurred even when the same bird was given a different depressant and stimulant.* This finding suggested that the tacting response (i.e., pecking the symbol key that corresponded to the drug effect) had generalized to a class of drugs with common chemical effects. In addition, the experiments showed that *accurate tacting of the drug effects could be maintained by generalized conditioned reinforcement* (as would be the case in human reports of internal states). In this case, the tacting bird was satiated on food and water, and the only result of the report was the blue flashing light. Even though the number of tacting responses declined, the pigeon was still highly reliable at reporting on the internal effects of the drugs.

The research on private events by Lubinski and Thompson (1987) is an important step in the analysis of verbal behavior and self-description. The contingencies arranged by the researchers resulted in a complex sequence of behavior between two pigeons. *When birds are exposed to verbal contingencies that are presumed to operate in human behavior, they begin to act something like humans—reporting on how they feel to one another* (Lubinski & Thompson, 1993).

Self-reference in humans is trained through the socialization practices of the community (Bem, 1965). People in different parts of the world (e.g., India) are able to contact and describe internal events that are usually unavailable to North Americans. These people receive religious and educational training that makes them more "aware" of themselves. Although mystical and mentalistic explanations have been given for such abilities, contingencies of reinforcement provide a scientific account of this kind of human behavior.

SYMBOLIC BEHAVIOR AND STIMULUS EQUIVALENCE

For most Americans, the flag is a significant symbol. When we see the flag, we may think of the United States, mother, and apple pie. This suggests that symbolic behavior involves the training of

stimulus equivalence. The presentation of one class of stimuli (e.g., flags) sets the occasion for responses made to other stimulus classes (e.g., countries). This seems to be what we mean when we say that the flag stands for, represents, or signifies our country. Equivalence relations such as these are an important aspect of human behavior. For example, when teaching a child to read, spoken words (names of animals) are trained to visual stimuli (pictures of animals) and then to written symbols (written words for animals). Eventually, the written word is then said to stand for (or mean) the actual object, in the same sense that a flag stands for a country. In this section, we shall examine the behavior analysis of equivalence relations as a scientific account of symbolic activity and meaning.

Basic Equivalence Relations

When stimulus class A is shown to be interchangeable with stimulus class B (if A = B then B = A), we may say that the organism shows **symmetry** between the stimulus classes. Symmetry is only one form of equivalence relation. A more elementary form of equivalence is called **reflexivity**. In this case, an A to A relation (A = A) is established so that, given the color red on a sample key, the organism responds to the comparison key with the identical color (red). A child who is given a picture of a cat and then finds a similar picture in a set of photographs is showing reflexivity (identity matching).

Reflexivity and symmetry are basic logical relations of mathematics. A child who is presented with the number 1 shows reflexivity when she points to 1 in an array of numbers {2,3,1,4,5}. The same child shows symmetry if, when given the number 2, she selects the set {X, X} rather than {X} or {X, X, X}, and when given {X, X} she selects 2 from the array {3,2,1,5,4}.

There is one other equivalence relation in mathematics. This is the relation of **transitivity**. If the written numbers one, two, and three are equivalent to the arithmetic numbers 1, 2, and 3, and these arithmetic numbers are equivalent to sets {X}, {X, X}, and {X, X, X}, it logically follows that one, two, and three are equivalent to sets {X}, {X, X}, and {X, X, X}. That is, if A = B and B = C, then A = C (transitivity).

Experimental Analysis of Equivalence Relations

Although equivalences are logically required by mathematics, it is another thing to show that such relations govern the behavior of organisms. In terms of behavior, three stimulus classes (A, B, and C) are called equivalent when an organism has passed tests for reflexivity, symmetry, and transitivity (Sidman & Tailby, 1982). Thus, after equivalence training in early reading, the spoken sound "Say 'cat'," the word CAT, and the picture of a cat acquire equivalence of function for a young child (Figure 12.11).

A complete experiment for stimulus equivalence consists of both identity and symbolic matching procedures. In **identity matching**, the researcher presents a sample stimulus (e.g., a triangle) and two options (e.g., triangle or circle). The organism is reinforced for choosing the triangle option that corresponds to the triangle sample (i.e., matching to sample). **Symbolic matching** involves presenting one class of stimuli (e.g., geometrical forms) as the sample and another set of stimuli (e.g., different line angles) as the options. Reinforcement depends on an arbitrary relation (e.g., triangle = horizontal, flag = country). After the reinforced relations are trained, tests are made for each kind of equivalence relation. *The question is whether reflexivity, symmetry, and transitivity occur without further training.* To make this clear, identity and symbolic matching

FIG. 12.11 A mother teaching an equivalence relation in early reading. After training by many examples through parent and child interaction, the sound of the spoken word, "Say cat," the word CAT, and the picture of a cat acquire equivalence in function. This is the beginning of early reading. Stimulus equivalence (reflexivity, symmetry, and transitivity) seems to underlie much of human language and complex symbolic behavior. © Shutterstock.

are training procedures that allow for stimulus equivalence, but the procedures do not guarantee it. We shall describe such an experiment in a step-by-step manner.

Figure 12.11 shows the identity-matching procedures used to show reflexivity. The training involves identity matching for line angles or geometric forms by a pigeon. The bird is presented with three keys that may be illuminated as shown in the two displays (Display A or B). For each display, two sets alternate on the three keys. A set includes a sample key and two option keys. For the sake of clarity, in our example the option (side key) that matches the sample is always shown on the left of the displays, and the nonmatching option is on the right. *In real experiments, of course, the position of the matching stimulus varies from trial to trial, eliminating any left or right bias.* A peck on the sample key illuminates the option keys, and pecks to the matching key produce food and the next sample. Pecks to the nonmatching key are not reinforced and lead to the next trial (i.e., the next sample).

Reflexivity

Reflexivity or generalized identity matching may be shown using this identity-matching procedure. In Display A (angle match) of Figure 12.12, the sample key presents a line angle (horizontal). When the pigeon pecks the sample key, horizontal and vertical stimuli are presented on the side keys (matching and nonmatching). Pecks to the horizontal matching key are reinforced with food, while pecks to the vertical nonmatching key are not. The next trial may present Display B (angle match). Now the sample is a vertical line. If the bird pecks the vertical line matching key, it receives food, but pecks to the horizontal line nonmatching key are extinguished. Based on this training and many more matching-to-sample trials, the bird learns to identify line angles (identity matching).

Similar procedures may be used to train identity matching based on geometric form. In Display A (form match) in Figure 12.12, the form display is based on triangles and circles. When Display A is in effect, the sample key is illuminated with a triangle. Pecks to the sample produce the two options—triangle and circle. Pecks to the key that matches the sample are reinforced, while pecks to the nonmatching geometric form are placed on extinction. A new trial may result in Display B (form match). In this case, the sample is a circle. When the bird pecks the sample, two options are presented on the side keys (circle and triangle). Pecks to the key with a circle produce food, but pecks to the key with a triangle are extinguished. Using these procedures, the pigeon learns to identify geometric forms.

Reflexivity is shown by *a test for generalization of identity matching*. A test for reflexivity would involve testing for generalization of identity matching based on the training of matching to sample based on angle and form. For example, a bird trained to identity match to angle and form could be tested with colors (green or red) as the sample and comparison stimuli. A bird that pecks to the color that matches the sample, *without specific training* on colors, shows reflexivity or generalized identity matching. Lowenkron (1998) showed that many instances of generalized identity matching involved the training of joint stimulus control in the sense that two stimuli come to regulate a common response topography.

Symmetry

Figure 12.13 shows the procedures used to train symbolic matching and the tests for symmetry. These procedures are implemented only after a bird has shown identity matching. For example, symbolic matching occurs if the bird is trained to discriminate geometric shapes on the basis of angles (angle-to-form discrimination). **Symmetry** occurs if the bird can pass *a test for reversal* (form-to-angle discrimination) *without further training*.

This procedure is shown by the angle-to-form display in Figure 12.13 (Display

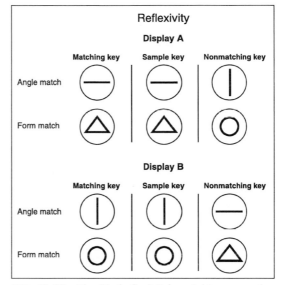

FIG. 12.12   Identity (reflexivity) matching procedures used to establish reflexivity in pigeons, as described by Catania (1984). First, train matching to angles using the *angle match* arrangements in Displays A and B (top). Next, train matching to form using the *form match* arrangements in Displays A and B (bottom). Finally, test for reflexivity or generalized identity matching using color matching displays (not shown). See text for a description of the contingencies.

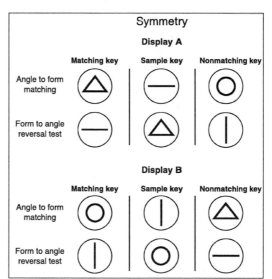

FIG. 12.13   Symbolic matching procedures used to train and test for symmetry in pigeons, as described by Catania (1984). First, train angle-to-form matching (angle = form) using the arrangements of Displays A and B (top). Next, test for reversal or symmetry (form = angle) using the form-to-angle arrangements of Displays A and B (bottom). See text for a description of the contingencies.

A). Pecks to the horizontal sample illuminate the side options—a triangle or a circle. In the presence of the horizontal-line sample, pecks to the triangle are reinforced while pecks to the circle are not. When Display B is presented, the sample is the vertical line and pecks to the circle are reinforced while pecking the triangle is on extinction.

Once the matching of angle to geometric form is well established, a **reversal test** (form to angle) is conducted without any further reinforcement. In a reversal test of Display A, the bird is presented with a triangle as the sample and the question is whether it pecks the side key with the horizontal line. Because horizontal = triangle was trained, the bird shows symmetry if it pecks the horizontal comparison key when presented with a triangle sample (triangle = horizontal). Similarly, because vertical = circle was trained, symmetry is shown if the bird pecks the vertical side key of Display B when the circle is presented as the sample (circle = vertical). In everyday language, the bird responds as if the horizontal line stands for triangle and as if the vertical line means circle. The percentage of "correct" responses during the test (without reinforcement) is the usual measure of symbolic performance on this symmetry task.

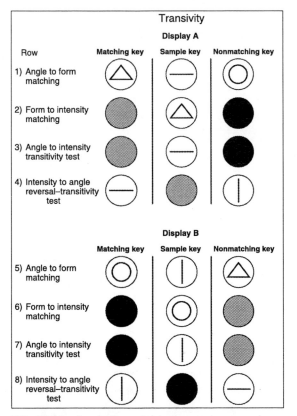

FIG. 12.14   Symbolic matching procedures used to establish and test for transitivity in pigeons, as described by Catania (1984). First, train angle-to-form matching (angle = form) using the arrangements in rows 1 and 5 of Displays A and B. Next, train form-to-intensity matching (form = intensity) using the arrangements in rows 2 and 6 of Displays A and B. Following training, conduct a transitivity test (angle = intensity) using the arrangements in rows 3 and 7 of Displays A and B. Finally, conduct reversal–transitivity tests (intensity = angle) using the arrangements in rows 4 and 8 of Displays A and B. See text for a description of the contingencies.

Transitivity

Figure 12.14 illustrates the procedures that may be used to train and test a pigeon for transitivity. These procedures would be used only if a bird had passed the tests for reflexivity and symmetry. Rows 1 and 5 of Displays A and B of the figure present the angle-to-form (symbolic matching) procedures for symmetry that were described earlier (horizontal = triangle; vertical = circle). To test for transitivity, the pigeon is trained to produce an additional discrimination. Rows 2 and 6 of Displays A and B illustrate this training. The pigeon is reinforced for matching a geometric form to intensity of illumination on the option keys—darker or lighter key. For example, in row 2 of Display A, pecking the lighter option key is reinforced when a triangle is the sample (triangle = lighter) and pecking the darker key is not reinforced; also, row 6 of Display B shows that pecking the darker key produces food when a circle is the sample (circle = darker) while pecking the lighter option is on extinction.

Notice that the bird is trained such that horizontal = triangle and vertical = circle (rows 1 and 5) and has shown reversal on tests of symmetry. Given this performance, if triangle = lighter and circle = darker (rows

2 and 6), then the following relations could occur without explicit training on transitivity tests: horizontal = lighter, and lighter = horizontal (rows 3 and 4); also vertical = darker, and darker = vertical (rows 7 and 8). These tests would establish transitivity in the pigeon, showing that the bird responds to the set of line angles as it does to the set of geometric forms, and responds to the set of geometric forms as it does to the set of light intensities (A = B = C). This performance would be similar to that of a person who responds to the written word "dog" in the same way as they do to a picture of a dog or the spoken word "dog." The stimuli are said to be equivalent because they regulate the same operant class. Lowenkron (1998) proposed that many instances of *joint stimulus control* (equivalence between stimuli) of response forms underlie human language-related performances involving both logical (relative size and distance) and semantic (word meaning) relations.

NEW DIRECTIONS: Behavioral Neuroscience and Derived Conceptual Relations

Neuroscientists are searching for the brain mechanisms that support the behavior of language use. Major theories about concept formation difficulties often make use of stimulus equivalence operations as a basis for inferring the acquisition of new knowledge. For example, when stimulus class A is shown to be interchangeable with stimulus class B we say that the two classes show equivalence (symmetry) or that the person has formed a concept. Reinforcing behavior that is under the control of distinct sets of arbitrary conditional relations will result in the appearance of new *derived* relations.

Much is known behaviorally about the formation of equivalence relations, but the brain mechanisms and neural networks underlying this ability are not known. Recently, researchers have applied functional neuroimaging of the brain of conscious humans to reveal the neural systems involved in trained and derived conceptual relations (Schlund, Hoehn-Saric, & Cataldo, 2007; Schlund, Cataldo, & Hoehn-Saric, 2008). Research of this nature promises to clarify the neurobiological substrates of behavior that are usually taken to indicate conceptual and other higher cognitive processes.

Using a matching-to-sample task (MTS), human participants were trained to form conditional relations within stimulus classes (Schlund et al., 2007). That is, the participants were asked to respond to sample and comparison symbols and learn the symbolic equivalences. This type of conditional responding is suspected to recruit specific frontal-parietal and frontal-subcortical brain networks central to higher cognitive functioning. A neuroimaging procedure called functional magnetic resonance imaging (fMRI) allowed the researchers to correlate blood-oxygen-level activation in areas of the brain with the behavioral discriminations for individual participants.

Responding to both conditional and derived relations activated similar regions of the brain, but the magnitude was greater for trained relations in frontal areas of the brain (see Dickins, Singh, Roberts, Burns, Downes, Jimmieson et al., 2001, on involvement of the dorsolateral prefrontal cortex, a part of the brain related to semantic processing in language). The researchers also observed predominantly right hemisphere activation, suggesting that the complex conditional responding in this type of task (MTS) is mediated more by nonverbal than by verbal processes. A subsequent study showed that transitive relational responses activate the anterior hippocampus in the medial temporal lobe (memory areas), but symmetrical relations increase blood-oxygen flow to the parahippocampus (memory encoding area), as well as the frontal and parietal lobe regions (Schlund et al., 2008). The common activation of these frontal and medial-temporal regions appears to support conditional responding to both directly trained relations and the derived emergent relations. It is also the case that the frontal area of the brain is often where injuries occur as a result of automobile accidents. This brain region is not critical for life, and therefore victims of such injuries often survive, but are frequently cognitively impaired. Rehabilitation efforts for these victims might be improved by the combined results from neuroimaging and behavioral research. More research is required to better isolate the motor and neural functions of equivalence class formation and to specify more precisely the sensory and motivational aspects of derived conceptual behavior.

Research on Equivalence Relations

Murray Sidman and his colleagues established the basic procedures to assess equivalence relations in both human and nonhuman subjects (Sidman, Rauzin, Lazar, Cunningham, Tailby, & Carrigan, 1982; Sidman & Tailby, 1982). These methods help to eliminate alternative hypotheses for failure to observe emergent equivalence relations (symmetry and transitivity) in different species. To ensure that animals have the prerequisite repertoires for equivalence class formation, baseline training is given for A to A (color to color) and B to B (geometric shape to geometric shape) identity discriminations and for A to B (color to shape) discriminations, involving matching of a sample to a set of comparisons. An evaluation is then made of the animal's ability to make successive discriminations among all samples and simultaneous discriminations among all comparisons (Saunders & Spradlin, 1989). The method also includes probe tests for reflexivity, symmetry, and transitivity, as well as unreinforced probe trials within an ongoing baseline of reinforced trials. If probes do not show emergent or untrained relations (e.g., symmetry), then performance on baseline trials is used to assess any decline in the basic (A–A, B–B, or A–B) relations necessary for equivalence class formation. Finally, the rate of reinforcement on baseline trials is thinned to reduce the discrimination of nonreinforcement on probe trials. With this procedure, a failure to find emergent relations is unlikely, due to discriminated extinction on probe trials.

Using these standardized methods, Sidman and colleagues (1982) reported that monkeys and baboons could not pass tests for equivalence that were easily passed by children, even children with developmental delay (see Carr, Wilkinson, Blackman, & McIlvane, 2000). It seems that nonhuman subjects lacked critical experiences (e.g., multiple exemplar training, control of location variables, and generalized identity matching) that are naturally arranged by the environment of humans. Subsequently, a limited number of nonhuman studies claimed that animals could pass tests for reflexivity, symmetry, and transitivity (McIntire, Cleary, & Thompson, 1987; Vaughn, 1988) or symmetry and transitivity (D'Amato, Salmon, Loukas, & Tomie, 1985; Richards, 1988). These studies are controversial, as some researchers assert that the animals did not demonstrate generalized relations—all of the relations were directly trained (e.g., Hayes, 1989a; Saunders, 1989). Also, in nonhuman research there is some question as to whether the pigeon (or ape) is picking out the key that matches the sample or is merely doing *exclusion*, rejecting the nonmatching option (Carrigan & Sidman, 1992).

A recent review of symmetry in nonhuman animals identified 24 studies in species ranging from rats to chimpanzees, but the overall results were equivocal, with about 55% of the studies showing mixed or strong evidence of emergent relations (Lionello-DeNolf, 2009). Two studies in sea lions (Rocky and Rio, described in Chapter 8 in the section on "Discrimination of Identity") showed clear evidence of symmetry and transitivity, a result attributed to the animals' history of multiple exemplar training and the use of multiple S- comparison stimuli during training (Kastak,

FIG. 12.15 Rio the California sea lion. Colleen Kastak and Ronald J. Schusterman raised and trained Rio at the Pinniped Cognition & Sensory Systems Laboratory in Santa Cruz, CA. Rio is shown during training of the A–B relation (given CRAB choose TULIP) and the B–C relation (given TULIP choose RADIO). The third photograph in this sequence shows a test for one of the four C–A emergent relationships, illustrating both symmetry and transitivity (given RADIO choose CRAB). © Dr. Colleen Reichmuth of the Institute of Marine Sciences, University of California, Santa Cruz. Reprinted with permission.

Schusterman, & Kastak, 2001; Schusterman & Kastak, 1993). Figure 12.15 shows Rio during training of the A–B relation (given CRAB choose TULIP) and the B–C relation (given TULIP choose RADIO). The third photograph in this sequence shows the test for one of the four C–A emergent relationships, illustrating both symmetry and transitivity (given RADIO choose CRAB). Another study reported unambiguous evidence of symmetry in pigeons. These experiments used successive matching to sample to control for variation in stimulus location and intermixed sessions of A–B with A–A and B–B identity training to control for temporal placement of the stimulus as either a sample or a comparison (Frank & Wasserman, 2005). Follow-up experiments showed that pigeons which were given similar training, but without the intermixed sessions of identity training, did not show emergent symmetry on probe trials. Also, pigeons that were initially trained only with arbitrary matching trials did not show symmetry on probe trials, but subsequently demonstrated emergent symmetry when intermixed identity training was added to the baseline-training trials.

We noted the role of multiple exemplar instruction in the naming relation, and the evidence suggests that multiple exemplar training (MET) is a critical feature for the emergence of symbolic equivalence classes in nonhuman animals. Exactly why training with multiple exemplars works is not well understood, but it probably relates to reduced control by *where and when* a stimulus appears. MET ensures that samples and comparisons appear in multiple locations, allowing for the generalization among stimuli over locations. In addition, MET reduces control by the temporal location of the sample and comparison stimuli. That is, on training trials samples always appear first and comparisons second, a temporal feature that gains control of behavior and interferes with equivalence learning. One possibility is that the intermixed sessions of identity training that were used for pigeons showing emergent symmetry also reduce control by irrelevant temporal and spatial features of sample and comparison stimuli. Further research using MET-type procedures with numerous training trials should eventually reveal how to reliably establish equivalence classes and emergent relations in nonhuman animals.

Stimulus Equivalence and Application

At the applied level, stimulus equivalence training has been helpful to those who lack reading skills, and in the development of educational curricula based on derived stimulus relations (for a review, see Rehfeldt, 2011). Researchers have used developmentally delayed people who could pass a reflexivity test (identity matching) but, before training, failed to show symmetry or transitivity

(Sidman & Cresson, 1973; Sidman, Cresson, & Wilson-Morris, 1974; see also Lazar, 1977). These subjects were given training in symbolic matching. They were presented with one of 20 spoken names and asked to select the corresponding picture from a comparison set (A = B training). Next, the subjects were trained to select printed words from a set when given one of the 20 names (A = C training). After both training procedures, subjects displayed four untrained relations without further training—two symmetry and two transitivity relations. Subjects showed B to A and C to A reversals—when given a picture they emitted the corresponding name, and when given a printed word they said it. In addition, subjects showed two transitivity relations. When given a picture (e.g., of a car, boy, dog, etc.), subjects selected the corresponding printed word (B = C), and when given the printed word, they selected the corresponding picture (C = B).

During training the subjects were presented with three stimulus classes that contained 20 elements in each class (spoken words, pictures, and written words). Forty instances of symbolic matching were reinforced (spoken words = pictures, and spoken words = written words). Tests revealed that 80 new instances of correspondence were established indirectly from training (B = A, C = A, B = C, and C = B).

As you can see, the reinforcement of symbolic matching resulted in a preliminary form of reading by these individuals. The limits on this training have not been established, but it seems obvious that equivalence relations make up a large part of human education (mathematics, science, reading, etc.). Equivalence classes are not the same as discriminative stimuli, because S^Ds cannot be exchanged for the responses they occasion. Clearly, equivalence relations define symbolic performance and are an important part of the experimental analysis of verbal behavior (see Sidman, 1994).

One problem with this conclusion is a modest literature showing that reinforcement is not necessary for the emergence of equivalent stimulus functions (Minster, Elliffe, & Muthukumaraswany, 2011). The idea is that stimulus–stimulus (S–S) correlation, the degree to which one stimulus goes together with another (e.g., sight of dog with word "dog"), is the basic determinant of emergent stimulus relations, not reinforcement contingencies as required by Sidman (2000). Several reports support this conclusion (e.g., Smeets, Barnes-Holmes, & Nagel, 2000). In fact, Minster et al. (2011) designed an experiment with humans to include conditions where stimulus relations were correlated during training, but explicitly placed on operant extinction. They found that emergent stimulus relations were established by the environmental stimulus–stimulus correlations alone. This means that reinforcement contingencies and S–S correlations each produce similar outcomes. Since reinforcement contingencies always contain S–S correlations, it may be that S–S correlation is the driving force behind equivalence and derived-stimulus learning. For training symbolic behavior, explicit reinforcement may not be as critical as arranging correlations among common stimulus features (e.g., a real dog, a picture of a dog, and the word "dog").

ON THE APPLIED SIDE: Three-Term Contingencies and Natural Speech

At the most basic level, behavior analysts suggest that the acquisition of verbal behavior is governed by contingencies of reinforcement. An important question is whether humans arrange verbal contingencies in their everyday interactions. Evidence of operant contingencies in casual speech is important for a comprehensive account of verbal behavior. When observational research shows natural dependencies between speakers and listeners, we can be more confident that our understanding of speaking (and writing) is not an artifact of laboratory procedures. Also, evidence of verbal contingencies without explicit control by an experimenter suggests that laboratory findings may eventually have general applicability. For both of these reasons, the analysis by Moerk (1990) of contingency patterns in mother–child verbal episodes is an important contribution to the analysis of verbal behavior.

Data, Transcripts, and Findings

The data are based on a reanalysis of the verbal interactions between a child named Eve and her mother. The original observations were collected by Roger Brown (1973) as part of a larger study of mother–child interaction. Eve and her mother were observed in their home during everyday activities. When the study began, Eve was 18 months old, and she was 28 months old at the end of the research. Brown collected numerous samples of verbal interaction between Eve and her mother over this 10-month period. Moerk selected all odd-numbered samples and analyzed 2 h of transcribed audio recording for each of these samples.

Moerk and two trained research assistants coded the transcripts. Observational categories included verbal behavior emitted by both mother and child (Eve). For example, sentence expansion involved the mother adding syntactic elements to her child's utterance (e.g., Eve says "see boy" and her mother says "You see the boy"), while sentence reduction occurred when Eve omitted elements that were originally present in her mother's speech (e.g., mother says "Give the toy to mommy" and Eve says "Give toy mum"). The research focuses on the arrangement of such verbal utterances in mother–child–mother interactions.

Moerk (1990) found that many different mother–child–mother verbal sequences ended with maternal reinforcement. Reinforcement was defined as feedback from the mother that confirmed that Eve's utterance was linguistically acceptable (e.g., "Yes," "Right," "OK," and so on). A sequence that often occurred was the mother saying a new or rare word (model) that was repeated by Eve (imitation) and followed by her acceptance by the mother (reinforcement). Another three-term pattern involved the mother repeating what she had just said, Eve emitting an approximation to this utterance, and her mother ending the sequence with words of acceptance.

The findings indicate that three-term contingencies (maternal verbal stimulus, child verbal imitation, and maternal reinforcement) characterized many of the verbal episodes of early language learning, and are compatible with Skinner's functional analysis of verbal behavior (see also Moerk, 2000).

ADVANCED SECTION: A Formal Analysis of Manding and Tacting

In his book *Verbal Behavior*, Skinner (1957) discusses the formal differences in behavior regulation between manding and tacting. In this section on advanced issues, we explore the social contingencies that establish and maintain these two classes of verbal behavior. The contingencies are somewhat complex, and diagrams of the interrelationship of the speaker and listener help to depict the controlling variables.

The Manding Relation

Figure 12.16 is a formal analysis of the manding relation. A *social episode* involves the social interaction of speaker and listener. The line through the middle of the diagram separates the speaker's events and actions from those of the listener. Each person

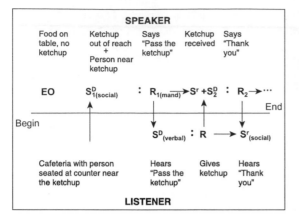

FIG. 12.16 Analysis of the manding relation between speaker and listener, based on Skinner (1957). The man who needs ketchup is analyzed as the speaker, and another customer is the listener. EO = establishing operation; S^D = discriminative stimulus; R = operant; S^r = reinforcement. See text for a description of the verbal contingencies.

completes a behavioral sequence or chain ($S^D: R \rightarrow S^r + S^D: R \rightarrow S^r \ldots$), and social interaction involves the intermingling of these chains or the *interlocking contingencies* (examine this in Figure 12.16). In the diagram of a social episode, an arrow ($\rightarrow$ horizontal or vertical) means "produces or causes"; thus, a verbal response by one person may cause an event, condition, or stimulus for the behavior of the other person (vertical arrow). That is, the verbal behavior of one person functions as a stimulus and/or consequence in the behavior chain of the other person. Also, within the behavioral sequences of each individual, the verbal operants produce effects or consequences (horizontal arrow) supplied by the behavior of the other person (check this out).

In the example shown in Figure 12.16, we assume that two people are seated at a counter in a cafeteria. Dinner is placed in front of the speaker, but the ketchup is out of reach and situated near the other person or listener. In this context, the presence of food on the table is an *establishing operation* (EO) for behavior that has produced ketchup in the past (see Michael, 1982a; 1993; see also Chapter 2). The EO also makes getting ketchup a reinforcing event in this situation.

In addition to the EO, the speaker's manding response ("Pass the ketchup") in Figure 12.16 is regulated by the presence of ketchup near the listener (S^D_1 for speaker). The first vertical arrow, passing from the listener's side of the interaction (operant chain) to the speaker's side, shows the causal effect of the listener. If there were no other people in the restaurant, it is likely that the speaker would get out of his or her seat and get the ketchup. The presence of a listener increases the probability that the speaker will say "Pass the ketchup" rather than get it him- or herself. This means that the listener functions as part of the discriminative stimulus (S^D_1) in this social episode. Together, the out-of-reach ketchup and the presence of the listener (S^D_1) set the occasion for (:) a verbal response (R_1) by the speaker.

The speaker's verbal response (R_1) of "Pass the ketchup" affects the listener as a stimulus. The causal effect of the speaker's behavior on the listener is shown as a vertical downward arrow from R_1 (speaker) to the listener's side of the interaction (operant chain). The words "Pass the ketchup" uttered by the speaker are a verbal stimulus for the listener (S^D_1) that sets the occasion for (:) the listener to pass the ketchup (R_1 for listener). In this social episode, the listener's response of passing the ketchup (R_1 for listener) is reinforcement for the speaker's verbal operant (S^r_1 for speaker). Because the speaker's verbal response ("Pass the ketchup") produces specific reinforcement (getting the ketchup) from the listener, the verbal operant is formally manding. As previously stated, *manding* is a verbal behavior that is set up by an establishing operation (out-of-reach ketchup) and maintained by specific reinforcement (getting the ketchup) mediated by the listener's behavior.

In this situation, the listener's response of passing the ketchup has **multiple functions** for the speaker's behavior ($S^r_1 + S^D_2$ for speaker). Passing the ketchup not only functions as reinforcement for manding, but it also functions as a discriminative stimulus for the next response by the speaker. That is, the same event (the listener giving the ketchup) can have several causal effects on the speaker. Based on the discriminative function of the listener's behavior (S^D_2 for speaker), getting the ketchup sets the occasion for (:) the speaker saying "thank you," a verbal response (R_2 for speaker) that serves as generalized conditioned reinforcement for the listener's behavior (S^r_1 for listener). The "thank you" response also serves as the ending point for this social episode, releasing the listener from obligations with respect to the speaker.

The Tacting Relation

Figure 12.17 is a formal analysis of the tacting relation. As with the manding relation, the verbal episode involves the interlocking contingencies of a speaker and a listener. In this example, the speaker is a student and the listener is a teacher. The social episode begins in a classroom with the teacher showing pictures of objects to a young student.

When a picture of a red ball is displayed, this event causes (horizontal arrow) the teacher to say "What color?" (Figure 12.17). The teacher's question (R_1) produces a verbal stimulus to the student (vertical arrow upward). In this situation, the student's answer depends on *both* the nonverbal stimulus of the red ball ($S^D_{1\ speaker}$) and the teacher's question ($S^D_{2\ speaker}$). Notice that the student will give a different answer if the question is "What shape?"

FIG. 12.17 Analysis of the tacting relation between speaker and listener, based on Skinner (1957). Both the student and the teacher emit verbal behavior during the social episode, but tacting by the student (speaker) is the focus of the analysis. S^D = discriminative stimulus; R = operant; S^r = reinforcement. See text for a description of the verbal contingencies.

The student's answer of "red" is formally tacting ($R_{1\ speaker}$) because the operant is regulated by the nonverbal stimulus (redness of ball). In this example, the student's tacting produces a verbal stimulus ($S^D_{1\ listener}$) for the teacher that may or may not *correspond* to the specified physical property of the ball ($S^D_{2\ listener}$). If the student's answer of "red" corresponds to the color of the ball, the teacher's question "What color?" is reinforced ($S^r_{1\ listener}$). Notice how the speaker and listener complete individual operant chains (e.g., $S^D: R \rightarrow S^r + S^D: R \rightarrow S^r \ldots$) that are *interlocking*, in the sense that the behavior of each person causes stimulation and reinforcement for the behavior of the other.

In terms of analysis, the teacher's question "What color is the ball?" is manding. This verbal response is reinforced by correspondence between the student's tacting and the actual color of the object. When correspondence occurs, this condition sets the occasion for the teacher saying ($R_{2\ listener}$) "Yes" and turning to the next picture (noncorrespondence may lead to repeating the question, perhaps in a different way). The teacher's verbal response ("Yes") produces generalized conditioned reinforcement ($S^r_{1\ speaker}$) for the student's tacting and functions to maintain the operant class.

Finally, it is useful to compare the tacting and manding relations. As we have seen in the teacher–student example, the form or topography of tacting depends on an appropriate nonverbal stimulus. The redness of the ball regulated the student's verbal response. In contrast, manding depends on an establishing operation (EO) such as deprivation. The dinner without ketchup regulated asking for it. Generalized conditioned reinforcement (acceptance, praise, etc.) serves to maintain the operant class of tacting. In contrast, specific reinforcement related to an establishing operation (getting the ketchup) maintains the operant class of manding.

CHAPTER SUMMARY

People talk to each other, and in different countries they use different languages. It seems clear that this ability is usually learned in childhood, and according to the principles that govern other operant behavior. However, evidence suggests that the vocal apparatus and its neuromuscular features may have evolutionary origins allowing for extensive and complex production and control of speech sounds. Skinner defined speaking, writing, and gesturing as verbal behavior, and proposed an analysis in his book of that name. This analysis begins with a description of the function of language as established by the reinforcing practices of the verbal community. Manding and tacting are two broad classes of verbal operant behavior. Manding is a verbal form regulated by establishing operations and specific reinforcement. Tacting is a form regulated by nonverbal discriminative stimuli and maintained by generalized conditioned reinforcement. A verbal interaction between two people may involve manding, tacting, and many other verbal response classes (e.g., intraverbals) regulated by verbal stimuli. The Jack and Jill pigeon study demonstrated some of the basic contingencies involved in communication. The study illustrated the effects of training manding and tacting repertoires in birds as an animal model for communication by humans. Pigeons have also been trained to report on their internal states, or "feelings", by the interlocking contingencies among speakers and listeners. Finally, symbolic behavior and stimulus equivalence were discussed as examples of "higher-order" activities involving verbal operants. The equivalence relations of reflexivity, symmetry, and transitivity were shown to extend from formal mathematics to the control of behavior. Stimulus classes exist when organisms have passed tests for these three relationships. Verbal behavior is possibly the most complex of human activities, and its intricacies continue to engender much research and behavior analysis.

KEY WORDS

Autoclitic (verbal behavior)

Conditional discrimination

Conditioned establishing operation
  (CEO)

Echoic behavior

Formal similarity

Functional independence

Identity matching

Interlocking contingencies

Intraverbal behavior

Manding

Multiple functions

Naming relation

Reflexivity

Reversal test

Social episode

Stimulus equivalence

Symbolic matching

Symmetry

Tacting

Textual behavior

Transitivity

Verbal behavior

Verbal community

ON THE WEB

www.ted.com/talks/deb_roy_the_birth_of_a_word.html MIT researcher Deb Roy wanted to understand how his infant son learned language—so he wired up his house with video cameras to catch every moment (with exceptions) of his son's life, then parsed 90,000 hours of home video to watch "gaaaa" slowly turn into "water." This is astonishing, data-rich research with deep implications for how we learn verbal behavior.

www.youtube.com/watch?v=QKSvu3mj-14 This is an excerpt from *Cognition and Creativity* by Robert Epstein and B. F. Skinner. The clip introduces basic conditioning and then goes on to present the Jack and Jill study of communication in pigeons. See if you can analyze how Epstein and Skinner got pigeons to show such complex "verbal" behavior.

www.youtube.com/watch?v=dBUHWoFnuB4 This film features research and life with Kanzi, a bonobo chimpanzee, and Dr. E. Sue Savage-Rumbaugh at the Georgia State University Language Research Center in Atlanta, GA.

BRIEF QUIZ

1. _____introduced the term verbal behavior to deal with the _____ of the speaker.

   (a) Chomsky; transformational grammar
   (b) Skinner; performance
   (c) Crick; conscience
   (d) Pavlov; conditioned responses

2. According to the behavioral or functional account, sign language, gestures, and body movements are instances of:

   (a) nonverbal communication
   (b) message transmission
   (c) verbal behavior
   (d) culture and tradition

3. One kind of conditioned establishing operation (CEO) called the _____ involves withholding an object or item necessary to complete a behavioral sequence.

   (a) no item method
   (b) absent object technique
   (c) interrupted item method
   (d) blocked response

4. When a verbal response depends on a verbal discriminative stimulus, the verbal relations are:

   (a) manding
   (b) tacting
   (c) intraverbal
   (d) textual

5. In echoic behavior, when _____ by the child correspond to those of the adult, the _____ patterns also overlap.

   (a) sounds; temporal
   (b) phonemes; reverberation
   (c) speech; phoneme
   (d) articulations; acoustical

6. When pecking the keys is based on line angle or form depending on the state of the houselight (on/off), we can say that the pigeon shows:

   (a) simple discrimination
   (b) conditional discrimination
   (c) simple generalization
   (d) generalized discrimination

7. A response such as "I have butterflies in my stomach" can be analyzed as: _____.

   (a) generalized tacting
   (b) generalized manding
   (c) formal manding
   (d) formal tacting

8. When reinforcement is based on matching of geometric forms to different line angles, the procedure is called:

   (a) identity matching
   (b) matching to sample
   (c) transitivity matching
   (d) symbolic matching

9. If a picture of a dog, the spoken word "dog," and the written word DOG all regulate the same behavior, we say that the stimulus classes are:

   (a) overlapping
   (b) the same
   (c) equivalent
   (d) confounded

10. **ADVANCED SECTION:** In terms of interlocking contingencies, a vertical arrow (downward) from the speaker's operant chain to that of the listener indicates that:

    (a) the speaker's behavior causes stimulation and/or reinforcement for the listener's behavior
    (b) the listener is causally motivated to behave as the speaker requests
    (c) the speaker is motivated to produce a condition for the listener
    (d) the interaction between the speaker and the listener is mutually beneficial and anticipated

Answers to Brief Quiz: 1, b (p. 358); 2, c (p. 361); 3, d (p. 366); 4, c (pp. 371–372); 5, d (p. 374); 6, b (p. 380); 7, a (p. 382); 8, d (p. 387); 9, c (p. 389); 10, a (p. 394)

Applied Behavior Analysis

13

1. Read about applied behavior analysis, its methods, and data recording.
2. Investigate contingency management of drug abstinence.
3. Discover the ABC program for the treatment of autistic behavior.
4. Study activity anorexia and the treatment of human anorexia.
5. Focus on the problem of conditioning, overeating, and obesity.
6. Explore the MammaCare behavioral program for the detection of breast cancer.

The experimental analysis of behavior is a science that easily lends itself to application. This is because the focus of the discipline is on those environmental events that directly alter the behavior of individual organisms. Almost half a century ago (e.g., Dollard & Miller, 1950; Skinner, 1953), behavior analysts suggested that since operant and respondent principles regulate behavior in the laboratory, they probably affect human and nonhuman behavior in the everyday world. Thus, principles of behavior can be used to change socially significant human conduct. Based on this assumption, Skinner's second book, *Walden Two* (Skinner, 1948), is a novelized description of a utopian society based on behavior principles. At least two communities developed utilizing many of the principles of *Walden Two*: Twin Oaks in the Eastern USA and Los Horcones near Hermosillo, Mexico (Fishman, 1991; McCarty, 2012).

Principles of behavior change have been used to improve the performance of university students (Martin, Pear, & Martin, 2002; Moran & Malott, 2004; Pear & Crone-Todd, 1999), increase academic skills (Alberto & Troutman, 2006; Sulzer-Azaroff, 1986), teach developmentally delayed and autistic children self-care (Langone & Burton, 1987; McGaha-Mays & Hcflin, 2011), reduce phobic reactions (Jones & Friman, 1999; Shabani & Fisher, 2006), persuade children and adult drivers to wear seat belts (Sowers-Hoag, Thyer, & Bailey, 1987; Van Houten, Malenfant, Reagan, Sifrit, Compton, & Tenenbaum, 2010), encourage drivers to obey stop signs (Austin, Hackett, Gravina, & Lebbon, 2006), prevent occupational injuries (Geller, 2006, 2011), prevent gun play in children (Miltenberger, Gatheridge, Satterlund, Egemo-Helm, Johnson, Jostad et al., 2005), and help individuals stop substance abuse (Donohue, Karmely, & Strada, 2006; Higgins, Silverman, & Heil, 2007). Behavioral interventions have had an impact on clinical psychology, medicine, counseling, job effectiveness, sports training, and environmental protection. Applied experiments have ranged from investigating the behavior of psychotic individuals to analyzing (and altering) contingencies of entire institutions (see Kazdin, 2000). Thus, principles of behavior derived from experimental and applied research have wide-scale applicability because the world actually operates according to these principles.

CHARACTERISTICS OF APPLIED BEHAVIOR ANALYSIS

Behavioral principles, research designs, observational techniques, and methods of analysis transfer readily to an applied science. When this is done to improve performance or solve social problems, the technology is called applied behavior analysis (Baer et al., 1968). Thus, **applied behavior analysis** or behavioral engineering is a field of study that focuses on the application of the principles, methods, and procedures of the science of behavior. Because applied behavior analysis is a wide field of study, it cannot be characterized by a single definition. Nonetheless, several features in combination distinguish applied behavior analysis as a unique discipline.

Concentration on Research

Behavior therapists and applied researchers are committed to a scientific analysis of human behavior. What a person does and the events that govern behavior are objectively identified. In this regard, operant and respondent conditioning are assumed to regulate most human activity regardless of how verbal behavior, generalized imitation, equivalence relationships, and physiology complicate the analysis. Although behavior principles have been widely applied to human behavior, these principles are also broadly used in the management of nonhuman behavior, such as that in pets (Friedman, Edling, & Cheney, 2006; www.Behaviorworks.org), zoo animals (Markowitz, 1981), and livestock (Provenza, Villalba, Cheney, & Werner, 1998; www.Behave.net).

Applied behavior analysis involves two major areas of research which entail the application of operant and respondent principles to improve human behavior. A good deal of literature has documented the success of this enterprise (see the *Journal of Applied Behavior Analysis* from its beginning in 1968 for many examples). Thousands of experiments and applications have shown how basic conditioning principles can be used in a variety of complex settings. Problems that are unique to the applied context have been addressed, and treatment packages that are designed for the modification of behavior have been described and evaluated (see Martin & Pear, 2010).

Another set of studies have not focused directly on behavior change, but are a part of applied behavior analysis and are currently discussed as translational research (Mace & Critchfield, 2010). Such investigations are involved with an analysis of everyday human behavior and have long-range implications for improving the human condition. For example, studies that investigate environmental factors that produce cooperation, competition, successful teaching, and coercive family dynamics often identify basic principles of complex human interaction (Dymond & Critchfield, 2002; Epling & Pierce, 1986). Researchers in this area of applied behavior analysis are attempting to specify the contingencies that produce social problems (Lamal, 1997).

Behavior is the Primary Focus

Applied behavior analysts focus on the observable behavior of people and other animals in non-laboratory settings. Behavior is not considered to be an expression of inner agencies or causes such as personality, cognition, and attitude. Marital difficulties, children who are out of control, public littering, phobic reactions, poor performance in exams, excessive energy use, and negative self-descriptions are analyzed as problems of behavior. Interventions for these and other problems are directed at changing environmental events to improve behavior.

Of course, people think, feel, and believe a variety of things associated with what they do. Individuals who are experiencing difficulty in life may have unusual thoughts and feelings. A depressed person may feel worthless and think that nobody likes him or her. The same person does not spend much time visiting friends, going to social events, or engaging in the usual activities of life. A behavioral intervention for this problem would probably focus on increasing the person's activity, especially social interaction. The individual may be asked to set goals for completing various tasks, and reinforcement is arranged when they are accomplished. When people become more socially involved, physically active, and complete daily tasks, they do not describe themselves as depressed. In this and many more cases, a change in reinforcement or the density of reinforcement of daily activities produces a change in feelings and cognition (Cautela, 1984, 1994).

A Case Study

In some cases, what a person says about his or her feelings and thoughts may be treated as verbal operant behavior that requires change (see Chapter 12). Tammi was an 8-year-old girl who was diagnosed as neurotic by a physician who saw her in his general practice. She was referred to a behavior analyst (Frank Epling) for evaluation and treatment.

It turned out that when she was 6 years old, Tammi had witnessed a gruesome farm accident in which her brother was killed. The girl frequently talked about killing herself and joining her brother in heaven. She had also deliberately cut herself with a kitchen knife on two occasions. Her parents were asked to record the circumstances that preceded and followed these episodes and the number of times they occurred.

Tammi had cut herself on two occasions since her brother's death, but had not done so during the past year. Talking about suicide had, however, increased, and she did this about three times a week. This talk usually took place during the evening meal when both parents were present. She did not talk about dying to her older siblings or to other people. Quite naturally, these episodes upset her mother and father and they routinely attempted to "calm her down and reason with her" when they occurred.

This information suggested stimulus control (parents present) and (unintentional) reinforcement by parental attention. After the mother and father had been taught a few simple principles of extinction, they withheld social reinforcement when talk about suicide occurred. The parents were instructed to avoid eye contact, make no comment, and if possible turn away from Tammi when she talked about killing herself. They were also told that extinction would probably produce an initial increase in the form and frequency of the behavior. In other words, Tammi would temporarily get worse (extinction burst), but a rapid improvement could be expected to follow. At the end of 5 weeks and at a 6-month follow-up, talk of killing herself had decreased to zero and she had not cut herself again.

The Importance of Conditioning

This discussion should make it clear that problem behavior may, in most cases, be understood in the same fashion as any other behavior. Principles of conditioning are neutral with respect to the form and frequency of behavior. Maladaptive, annoying, or dangerous responses may be inadvertently produced by environmental contingencies, just like more positive responses to life events.

Consider an institutional setting in which three staff nurses are in charge of 20 disabled children. The nurses are busy, and as long as the children behave they are left alone. This natural response to a strenuous work schedule may, for some children, result in deprivation for adult attention. When one of the children accidentally hits their head and is hurt, very likely a staff member rushes over and comforts the child. It is possible that head hitting will increase in frequency because it has been reinforced by contingent attention (e.g., Lovaas & Simmons, 1969). Of course, when people are injured they cannot be ignored. One way to deal with such a conundrum would be to provide plenty of social reinforcement for appropriate play, academic activities, ward chores, self-hygiene, and so on. This tactic is called **differential reinforcement of other behavior**, or **DRO** (e.g., Hammond, Iwata, Fritz, & Dempsey, 2011; Lindberg, Iwata, Kahng, & DeLeon, 1999). In the preceding example, the procedure would strengthen responses that are incompatible with self-injury and reduce deprivation for adult attention. Another useful strategy is **differential reinforcement of alternative behavior**, or **DRA**, which targets a specific alternative response for reinforcement (see Petscher, Rey, & Bailey, 2009, for a review in the context of developmental disabilities).

Although much human behavior is a function of contingencies of reinforcement, biological factors also produce behavior change. A person who has experienced a stroke, a child with fetal alcohol syndrome, an individual in the later stages of Alzheimer's disease, or an adult suffering from Huntington's chorea may emit responses that are a function of brain damage, toxic agents, disease, and genetics. However, even when this is the case, principles of conditioning can often be used to improve behavior (see Epling & Pierce, 1990, pp. 452–453).

Direct Treatment of Problem Behavior

Applied behavior analysts usually focus directly on the environmental events that generate and maintain behavior. Typically, target behavior and the events that precede and follow those responses are counted for several days. During this baseline, treatment is withheld so that a later change in behavior can be evaluated. This assessment also provides information about stimulus control (events that precede the behavior) and contingencies of reinforcement (events that follow behavior) that maintain responses.

Following a baseline period of assessment, a behavioral plan of action may be negotiated between the behavior therapist, the client, and concerned others (see, for example, Azrin, McMahon, Donahue, Besalel, Lapinski, Kogan et al., 1994 for a treatment program aimed at drug abuse). This plan usually includes a statement of target responses, consequences that follow different actions, and long-term goals. In many cases, a detailed **behavioral contract** is drawn up that objectively specifies what is expected of the client and the consequences that follow behavior (Hall & Hall, 1982). Figure 13.1 outlines the major principles of behavioral contracts. At a minimum, the behavior analyst should clearly identify the problem behavior, and the contract should specify in a straight-forward transparent manner the reinforcement for meeting behavioral objectives, the people who provide reinforcement, and the contingencies of reinforcement.

Applied behavior analysts do not typically focus on what has been called the "therapeutic process." This is because they do not place much faith in talking about problems to relieve stress or develop insight. They prefer to arrange contingencies of reinforcement to alter behavior problems. Although this is the case, Dr. Steven Hayes at the University of Nevada in Reno is a behavior analyst who has recognized the importance of rule-governed behavior in a therapeutic setting. From his perspective, talking is a form of social influence that may be used to change the client's actions. That is, instructions and other verbal stimuli may directly alter the probability of behavior (see Hayes, 1987; Zettle & Hayes, 1982). Today, most applied behavior analysts prefer direct contingency management. Others, however, are investigating the practical importance of instructions, rules, and therapeutic advice ("if it hurts when you do that, then don't do that"; see Hayes, 1989b)—verbal stimuli maintained by more remote contingencies of social reinforcement.

```
                      A GUIDE TO BEHAVIORAL CONTRACTING

  1.  Specify the target behavior.

  2.  Describe the behavior in a way that an observer may count or time.

  3.  Collect baseline data on the frequency of response or time spent responding.

  4.  Identify consequences that may be used to increase desired behavior (positive and
      negative reinforcers).

  5.  Find people who will monitor the behavior and provide the consequences.

  6.  Write the contract in clear statements of behavior and consequences (e.g., if you do
      "X" then you receive "Y").

  7.  Collect data on frequency of response or time spent responding and compare with
      baseline level.

  8.  Modify the contract if the desired behavior does not increase (e.g., try different
      consequences).

  9.  Gradually remove arbitrary consequences and replace them with natural
      reinforcers—rewrite the contract and monitor the behavior.

  10. Plan for generalization—implement the contract in a variety of settings.
```

FIG. 13.1   The steps in writing a behavioral contract. Based on the book, *How to Negotiate a Behavioral Contract*, by R. V. Hall and M. C. Hall, 1982, H. & H. Enterprises, Lawrence, KS.

Programming for Generality

In terms of direct treatment of problem behavior, applied behavior analysts are also concerned with the generality of behavior change (Baer, 1982; Stokes & Baer, 1977). That is, researchers attempt to ensure that their interventions produce lasting changes in behavior that occur in all relevant settings. As noted in Chapter 8, when organisms are reinforced in the presence of a particular stimulus, they typically produce a gradient of generalization that falls on both sides of the discriminative stimulus. Rather than rely on the organism to generalize automatically in an appropriate manner, the applied behavior analyst often attempts to program for generality (i.e., teach it directly).

Generality of behavior change involves three distinct processes: stimulus generalization, response generalization, and behavior maintenance (Martin & Pear, 2010). Behavior change has generality if the target response(s) occurs in a variety of situations, spreads to other related responses, and persists over time. Stimulus generalization occurs when the person responds similarly to different situations (e.g., a person greets one friend as she does another). **Response generalization** occurs when a target response is strengthened and other similar responses increase in frequency (e.g., a child who is reinforced for building a house out of Lego® may subsequently arrange the pieces in many different ways). **Behavior maintenance** refers to how long a new behavior persists after the original contingencies are removed (e.g., an anorexic man who is taught to eat properly shows long-lasting effects of treatment if he maintains adequate weight for many years).

Donald Baer (see Chapter 11 and generalized imitation) emphasized the importance of training behavioral generality, and provided the following illustration:

Suppose that a client characterized by hypertension has been taught systematic progressive relaxation techniques on the logic that the practice of relaxation lowers blood pressure a clinically significant amount, at least during the time of relaxation, and that the technique is such that relaxation can be practiced during all sorts of everyday situations in which the client encounters the kinds of stress that would raise blood pressure if self-relaxation did not pre-empt that outcome. Suppose that the relaxation technique has been taught in the clinician's office, but is to be used by the client not only there, but in the home, at work, and recreation settings in which stress occurs. Thus, generalization of the technique across settings, as well as its maintenance after clinical treatment stops, is required.

(Baer, 1982, p. 207)

To program generality of behavior change, Baer (1982) suggests a variety of procedures that affect stimulus and response generalization and behavior maintenance. First, stimulus generalization of relaxation (or any other behavior) is promoted when the last few training sessions are given in situations that are as similar as possible to everyday settings. Second, when relaxation training is done in a variety of different contexts, such as different rooms with different therapists and at different times of day, stimulus generalization increases. Finally, a therapist who trains relaxation in the presence of stimuli that elicit hypertension in everyday life is programming for stimulus generalization.

Response generalization is increased when the client is taught a variety of ways to obtain the same effect. For example, to relax and reduce her blood pressure, the client may be taught meditation, progressive muscle relaxation, and controlled breathing. In addition, a person may be taught to produce new forms of response, as when the therapist says "Try to find new ways of relaxing and reducing your blood pressure" and reinforces novel responses.

Behavior change may be programmed to last for many years if operant responses contact sources of reinforcement outside of the therapeutic setting. Applied behavior analysts who teach their clients skills that are reinforced by members of the social community are programming for behavior maintenance. This sort of programming has been called **behavior trapping** because, once learned, the new behavior is "trapped" by natural contingencies of reinforcement (e.g., Durand, 1999; Hansen & Lignugaris/Kraft, 2005; Stokes, Fowler, & Baer, 1978).

Focus on the Social Environment

From a behavioral point of view, it is the physical environment and social system that require change, not the person. James Holland, Emeritus Professor at the University of Pittsburgh, highlighted this issue when he stated:

Our contingencies are largely programmed in our social institutions and it is these systems of contingencies that determine our behavior. If the people of a society are unhappy, if they are poor, if they are deprived, then it is the contingencies embodied in institutions in the economic system, and in the government, which must change. It takes changed contingencies to change behavior.

(Holland, 1978, p. 170)

Behavior-change programs are usually more circumscribed in their focus than Holland recommends (but see Chapter 14 for a discussion of cultural design). Applied behavior analysts have seldom been in a position to change institutional contingencies. They have targeted more local contingencies involving family and community. In the case of Tammi, the social contingencies for talking about suicide were located in the family. When her parents stopped attending to such talk, she stopped saying that she wanted to kill herself. The focus of the intervention was on the family system rather than Tammi's neurosis.

Most behavior-change programs attempt to identify and alter significant variables that maintain target responses. As we have said, these variables are usually in the person's social environment. For this reason, treatment programs are often conducted in schools, hospitals, homes, prisons, and the community at large (see Glenwick & Jason, 1980; Jason, 1998; Lamal, 1997; Mattaini & McGuire, 2006). Parents, teachers, friends, coworkers, bosses, partners, and others typically control significant sources of reinforcement that maintain another person's behavior. These individuals are often involved and instructed in how to change contingencies of reinforcement to alter a client's behavior. This is especially relevant with interactions in a family where the "problem" is the child's behavior but the solution is changing the parents' contingency management (Latham, 1994).

RESEARCH STRATEGIES IN APPLIED BEHAVIOR ANALYSIS

In Chapter 2, we discussed A–B–A–B reversal designs for operant research. For single-subject research, basic or applied, the A–B–A–B reversal design has the highest level of **internal validity**— ruling out most extraneous factors. While a reversal design is always preferred, there are practical and ethical difficulties that restrict its use in applied settings.

In natural settings, behavior is often resistant to a reversal procedure. For example, using contingencies of reinforcement to increase socially acceptable playing may alter a child's shyness. If the reinforcement procedure is now withdrawn, the child will probably continue playing with other children (the point of the intervention). This may occur because the shy child's behavior is maintained by the social reinforcement she now receives from playmates. In other words, the child's behavior is trapped by other sources of reinforcement. While this is a good result for the child, it is not a useful outcome in terms of inference and research design. This is because the applied analyst cannot be absolutely sure that the original improvement in behavior was caused by his or her intervention.

Another difficulty with the reversal design in applied settings is that it requires the withdrawal of a reinforcement procedure that was probably maintaining improved behavior. For example, a psychiatric patient may be restrained with leather cuffs to prevent him from biting his arms. A DRO procedure is implemented and arm biting is substantially reduced, to a point at which the cuffs are no longer necessary. Although we cannot be sure that the DRO contingency caused the reduction in self-injury, it would be inadvisable to remove the contingency only to show that it was effective. Thus, the A–B–A–B reversal design is sometimes inappropriate for ethical reasons.

Multiple Baseline Designs

To solve the problems raised by the reversal design, applied behavior analysts have developed other single-subject designs. A **multiple baseline design** demonstrates experimental control and helps to eliminate alternative explanations for behavior change (Christ, 2007). There are three major types of multiple baseline designs as first described by Hall, Cristler, Cranston, and Tucker (1970). These designs are a **multiple baseline across settings,** a **multiple baseline across subjects,** and a **multiple baseline across behaviors.**

FIG. 13.2   The multiple baseline design across stimulus conditions. From "Teachers and parents as researchers using multiple baseline designs," by R. V. Hall, C. Cristler, S. S. Cranston, and B. Tucker, 1970, *Journal of Applied Behavior Analysis, 3,* 247–255. © 1970 Society for the Experimental Analysis of Behavior. Reprinted with permission.

Multiple Baseline Across Settings

In this design, a reinforcement procedure is applied in one situation but is withheld in other settings. When behavior only changes in the situation where it is reinforced, then the contingency is applied to the same response in another setting. Hall and his associates used this design in a modification of children's tardiness in getting to class after recess or lunch (Hall et al., 1970).

Figure 13.2 shows the multiple baselines across settings used by Hall et al. (1970). The researchers used what they called a "patriots chart" to modify lateness after lunch and after morning and afternoon recess. Children in the fifth grade who were on time for class had their names posted on the chart—an intervention that was easy and low cost to the teacher. As you can see, punctuality improved when the chart was posted. Notice that the chart was first posted after lunchtime, but it was not introduced following morning or afternoon recess. The number of students who were late for class after lunch declined from about eight to less than two. This was not the case for the recess periods; the number of students who were tardy after recess remained at four or five. Next, the researchers continued to post the patriots chart after lunch, but they added the chart following the morning recess. When this occurred, all of the students were on time for class following both lunch and morning recess. Finally, when the chart was also posted following the afternoon recess, all of the students were on time for all of the class periods. The multiple baseline across settings demonstrates an effect of the intervention by staggering the introduction of the independent variable over time and settings (see also Alberto, Heflin, & Andrews, 2002).

Multiple Baseline Across Participants

A similar logic is used when an intervention is progressively introduced to different participants who exhibit similar target behavior (see Iwata, Pace, Kalsher, Cowdery, & Cataldo, 1990, Study 2, on the use of this design to assess modification of self-injurious behavior). In Experiment 2, Hall et al. (1970) attempted to improve three students' scores on French quizzes. Modification involved a requirement to stay after school for tutoring if the student scored below a C grade on a quiz. The contingency was first introduced to Dave, then to Roy, and finally to Debbie. Figure 13.3 indicates that Dave's quiz performance dramatically improved when the contingency was applied. The other students also showed improvement only after the contingency went into effect. All of the students received grades of C or better when contingency management was used to improve their performance in the French class.

Multiple Baseline Across Behaviors

A multiple baseline design across behaviors is used when a reinforcement procedure is applied progressively to several operants. In this case, the subject, the setting, and the consequences remain

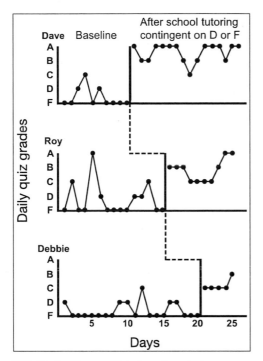

FIG. 13.3 The multiple baseline design across subjects. From "Teachers and parents as researchers using multiple baseline designs," by R. V. Hall, C. Cristler, S. S. Cranston, and B. Tucker, 1970, *Journal of Applied Behavior Analysis, 3,* 247–255. © 1970 Society for the Experimental Analysis of Behavior. Reprinted with permission.

the same, but different responses are sequentially modified. Hall et al. (1970) provided an example of this design with a 10-year-old girl when they modified her after-school reading, work on a Campfire honors project, and practicing of the clarinet. The girl had to spend at least 30 min on an activity or else she had to go to bed early. She had to go to bed 1 min earlier for every minute less than 30 min she spent on an activity. As you can see from Figure 13.4, practicing the clarinet was modified first, and time spent playing the instrument increased from about 15 to 30 min. Next, both practicing the clarinet and working on the Campfire project were targeted, and both performances were at about 30 min. Finally, reading for book reports was modified and all three target responses occurred for 30 min. The avoidance contingency seems to be effective because each behavior changes when the contingency is introduced, but not before.

Multiple baseline and A–B–A–B reversal designs are the most frequently used research methods in applied behavior analysis. There are, however, many variations of these basic designs that may be used to increase internal validity or to

deal with specific problems in the applied setting (e.g., Carr & Burkholder, 1998). Often the basic designs are combined in various ways to be certain that the effects are due to the independent variable. In fact, Hall et al. (1970) used a reversal phase in their experiment on tardiness and the patriots chart, but for reasons of clarity this was not shown in Figure 13.2. There are many other designs that are useful in a given situation. A changing criterion design involves progressive increases (or decreases) in the performance criterion for reinforcement. For example, a hyperactive child is reinforced for spending progressively more time on academic work. At first the child may be required to spend 3 min working quietly, then 5 min, then 10 min, and so on. The child's

FIG. 13.4 The multiple baseline design across behaviors. From "Teachers and parents as researchers using multiple baseline designs," by R. V. Hall, C. Cristler, S. S. Cranston, and B. Tucker, 1970, *Journal of Applied Behavior Analysis, 3,* 247–255. © 1970 Society for the Experimental Analysis of Behavior. Reprinted with permission.

behavior is measured at each level of the criterion. A research example of this design is given in the section on self-control in this chapter (see also Belles & Bradlyn, 1987).

Issues of Measurement in Applied Behavior Analysis

It is relatively easy to define objectively an operant in the laboratory. Responses are often defined by electrical switch closures, and there is no dispute about their occurrence. When responses occur, computers and other electronic equipment record them. In the applied setting, definition and measurement of the behavior is much more difficult, especially when parents, teachers, and psychologists are used to identify problem behavior. In this regard, Kazdin has made the point that:

> Identification of the target behavior may appear to be a relatively simple task. In a given setting (e.g., the home, school, or work place), there is general agreement as to the "problems" of the clients whose behaviors need to be changed and as to the general goals of the program. Global or general statements of behavioral problems are usually inadequate for actually beginning a behavior modification program. For example, it is insufficient to select as the goal alteration of aggressiveness, learning deficits, speech, social skills, depression, psychotic symptoms, self-esteem, and similar concepts. Traits, summary labels, and personality characteristics are too general to be of much use. Moreover, definitions of the behaviors that make up such general labels may be idiosyncratic among different behavior change agents (parents, teachers, or hospital staff). The target behaviors have to be defined explicitly so that they can actually be observed, measured, and agreed upon by individuals administering the program.
>
> (Kazdin, 1989, p. 54)

Kazdin goes on to discuss three criteria for an adequate response definition (see also Johnston & Pennypacker, 1993). The first criterion is *objectivity*. This means that the response definition should refer to observable features of behavior in clearly specified situations. *Clarity* of definition is another requirement. This means that the description of the response can be read and then clearly restated by a trained research assistant or observer. Finally, the definition should be *complete* in the sense that all instances of the behavior are distinguished from all non-occurrences. Thus, a troublesome student may be objectively defined as one who talks without permission when the teacher is talking, and who is out of their seat without permission during a lesson. The definition is clear in that it is easily understood and may serve as a basis for actual observation. Completeness is also shown, since only these two responses are instances of the troublesome behavior class, and any other responses are not.

This definition of response assumes that there is a problem with the student's performance, not the teacher's judgment. The applied behavior analyst must be sensitive to the possibility that the teacher is too critical of the student. It is possible that many students talk without permission and leave their seats during lessons. The teacher, however, only gets upset when Anna is running about or talking during instruction. In this case, response definition may be accurate and modification successful, but the intervention is unfair. Applied behavior analysts must constantly be aware of whether they are part of the solution or part of the problem (Holland, 1978). If the problem lies with the teacher, it is his or her behavior that requires change.

Recording Behavior

Once a suitable response has been defined, the next step is to record the behavior when it occurs. The simplest tactic is to record every instance of the response. Practically, this strategy may be very time-consuming and beyond the resources of most applied behavior analysts. One alternative is to count each instance of behavior only during a certain period of the day (e.g., lunch, recess, first class in the morning, and so on). This method of observation is called event recording for specified periods.

Another strategy is to select a block of time and divide the block into short, equal intervals. This is called **interval recording**. For example, a 30-min segment of a mathematics class may be divided into 10-s segments. Regardless of the number of responses, if the behavior occurs in a given 10-s segment, then the observer records it as a single event. One way in which this could

FIG. 13.5 Interval recording method used in behavioral observation and measurement.

be done is to have an observer wear a headset connected to a cassette tape recorder that plays a tape that beeps every 10 s. When the target behavior occurs, the observer records it on a piece of paper divided into segments that represent the 10-s intervals (see Figure 13.5). After each beep, the observer moves to the next interval.

Time sampling is another method of recording used in applied behavior analysis. This technique samples behavior over a long time scale, with observations made at specified times throughout the day. For example, a patient on a psychiatric ward may be observed every 30 min, as a nurse does the rounds, and instances of psychotic talk are recorded. Again, the issue is whether the target behavior is occurring at the time of the observation, not how many responses are made.

When behavior is continuous, **duration recording** is the preferred method of observation. Continuous behavior involves responses such as watching television, riding a bicycle, sitting in a chair, and so on. When behavior is continuous rather than discrete, an observer may use a stopwatch to record the duration of occurrence. When the person is sitting in a chair the watch is timing, and when the person does something else the watch is stopped.

Reliability of Observations

No matter what method of recording behavior is used, **reliability of observation** is a critical issue. Briefly, reliability of observation involves the amount of agreement among observers who independently record the same response. For example, two observers may sit at the back of a classroom and use 10-s intervals to record the occurrence of Jessica's out-of-seat behavior. After 30 min of observation, each researcher has recorded 180 intervals of 10 s. One way to assess reliability is to count the number of times both observers agree that the behavior did or did not occur within an interval. This can be accomplished by video recording the participant during an observation period and then having two observers score the responses later from the tape. Reliability is usually calculated as the percentage agreement between observers, and ranges from zero to 100%. Generally, applied behavior analysts strive for reliability of greater than 80%.

CONTINGENCY MANAGEMENT AND SUBSTANCE ABUSE

Addiction to drugs, alcohol, and cigarettes is a major health problem in the USA. Estimates by the National Institutes of Health indicate that addiction to drugs costs our society over half a trillion dollars each year, exceeding the costs of all other major medical illnesses (Silverman, Roll, & Higgins, 2008). The indirect costs in terms of early deaths and destroyed lives are immeasurable. Given the devastating impact of drug addiction, the federal government has invested large sums of money to find effective treatment programs. One highly effective intervention, called **contingency management (CM)**, uses operant principles to arrange contingencies to increase abstinence from drug use, to promote adherence to taking prescribed medication, and to increase retention in treatment programs (Higgins & Katz, 1998; Higgins & Petry, 1999; Higgins, Delaney, Budney, Bickel, Hughes, & Foerg, 1991).

NOTE ON: Contingency Management and Online Help Resources

In this chapter, we emphasize the evidenced-based research on contingency management, drug dependence, and addiction. However, there have been other important advances in the use of contingency management, especially in the use of online help resources. These resources have not been evaluated for effectiveness by controlled trials, but are noted here as interesting advances in the use of new technologies to assist in the delivery of contingency management interventions.

> If you ever had a New Year's resolution you didn't keep, there's help for you. An online contingency management program, *Stickk.com*, is an example of a website designed to help people achieve their personal behavioral goals—goals that seldom are realized. Behavioral economists at Yale University developed *Stickk.com* to allow you to define your behavioral objectives, set up a contract and have the option of naming a referee to enforce it. As part of the contract, you can choose to set a penalty for failing to reach your target. The penalty could merely be emailing your failure to a list of friends (or enemies), or paying some of your hard-earned cash as a backup. You can make a commitment to paying the money to anyone you want, including an "anti-charity," which for a liberal could be giving the money to the Republican Party. The more money you put on the line, the better you do, according to an analysis by *Stickk.com* of 125,000 contracts over the past three years. The likelihood of success for people who don't make a commitment of some kind is only 29%, but it rises to 59% if you designate a referee, and to 71.5% if you make a monetary commitment. A contract that includes both a referee and a financial investment has about an 80% success rate.
>
> (John Tierney, Be It Resolved, *The New York Times Sunday Review*, 5 January 2012)

One problem with the *Stickk.com* program and other "self-help" websites is the use of punishment. If you fail to reach your goal, you lose money and it goes to an organization you cannot stand. This can work to generate avoidance, but it does not generate a pleasant outcome for goal attainment. Commitment of money is a good strategy, as money is usually an effective consequence. However, we would recommend refunding the deposit for achieving one's goal and recruiting friends and colleagues to provide positive social support. Another strategy is to reinforce alternative behavior by altering one's lifestyle—a procedure often overlooked by self-help websites.

Those who have body weight and obesity problems might want to try another online website. One online treatment program offers the opportunity to sign up for weight-loss challenges. The website, *HealthyWage.com*, arranges challenges and contests that allow participants to win money for losing body weight (see also *Gym-pact.com* and *Dietbet.com*). The company indicates that it receives financial support from insurers, health services and hospitals, food companies, and the government. These agencies donate money in the belief that paying incentives for people to lose weight costs less than paying for the healthcare of an obese population.

The *HealthyWage.com* website offers three challenges that involve different require-ments, betting and payoffs. Here we describe the most basic challenge. The 10% challenge allows you to bet money on losing weight; you double your money for losing 10% of your weight in 6 months. At registration, you pay $100 and if you lose 10% of your weight in 6 months, the company pays you $200. Your starting and ending weights must be verified (by a health club or physician), and you are required to give weekly reports of your weight on the website. We should note that betting on your ability to lose weight is not the best way to manage body weight over a lifetime. Also, the effectiveness of this and other weight loss challenges has not yet been established by independent clinical trials, but online contingency management is an up-and-coming method of delivering individual treatment for those plagued by problems of being overweight or obese (see also "Behavior Management of the Obesity Crisis" in Chapter 14).

Reinforcement of Abstinence

Contingency management (CM) has been widely applied to promote abstinence from drug use and abuse. Typically, drug users are required to provide urine specimens several times a week, and the samples are screened for evidence of drug use. Notice that the use of urine specimens allows for an objective assessment of drug use outside the clinic; verbal reports of use by drug addicts are unreli-able and often fabricated to appease the inquiries of treatment staff. When urine samples are nega-tive for drug use (drug free), clients receive reinforcement consisting of take-home doses of methadone, increased privileges at the treatment clinic, money, and vouchers exchangeable for retail goods. In voucher-based CM programs, the value of the vouchers increases as the client shows longer and longer periods of abstinence. Presentation of urine samples that indicate drug use results in withholding of vouchers (no reinforcement) and, in some programs, the purchasing value of vouchers is reduced, or the client temporarily loses their take-home privileges (punishment).

One way to assess the effectiveness of the voucher-exchange contingency of CM is to compare it with the standard *community reinforcement approach (CRA)*, which has been shown to be one of the most effective programs in the treatment of alcohol and drug addiction (Hendrik, Boulogne, van Tulder, van den Brink, De Jong, & Kerkhof, 2004), but an approach without specific contingencies for abstinence. CRA is based on the assumption that environmental contingencies, especially social and economic ones, play a central role in the regulation of drug and alcohol use (Hunt & Azrin, 1973). Consequently, CRA uses social, recreational, familial, and vocational reinforcement contingencies to support a drug-free lifestyle.

In a recent treatment study of cocaine dependence in Spain, Steve Higgins and his colleagues randomly assigned cocaine users to CRA and CRA-plus-vouchers conditions (Garcia-Fernandez, Secades-Villa, Garcia-Rodriguez, Sanchez-Hervas, Fernandez-Hermida, & Higgins, 2011). The CRA involved five training components: drug avoidance skills, lifestyle change, relationship counseling, other substance abuse, and other psychiatric problems. The components of the CRA were applied individually to vocational counseling, lifestyle change, relationship counseling, and other psychiatric problems, while the rest of the components were applied in group therapy sessions (Budney & Higgins, 1998). In the CRA condition, urine specimens were collected twice a week and participants were informed of their urinalysis results immediately after submitting their specimens. However, users did not receive vouchers for remaining drug free. Cocaine patients in the CRA-plus-vouchers condition were also informed of their urinalysis results, but urine samples were taken three times a week and the program added vouchers contingent on abstinence.

The voucher program used points valued at 35 cents each; the first drug-free test earned 10 points, with a 5-point increase for each subsequent and consecutive negative sample. Patients also earned a 40-point bonus for three consecutive drug-free tests. Failure to submit a sample or a positive test for cocaine set the value back to the initial 10 points, but submission of three consecutive negative tests returned the value to its level before the reset. Points could not be lost once they had been earned. Participants on this point system earned an average of about $900 over a 12-week period. After this initial period, on a random basis, only half of the specimens collected twice a week earned points, and patients now earned about $750 on average. Points were exchangeable for vouchers that allowed patients to purchase a variety of goods and services appropriate to a drug-free lifestyle.

The results of the study are shown in Figure 13.6. The percentage of drug-free tests was 80% on average for the CRA condition, but 97% for the CRA with added vouchers (panel A)—a 17% improvement over the standard behavioral program. Panel B shows that 93% of the patients in the CRA-plus-vouchers group remained abstinent for 4 weeks, compared with 53% in the CRA condition. At 12 weeks, 72% of the patients in the CRA-plus-vouchers program remained drug free, compared with 38% in the CRA condition (Petry, Martin, Cooney, & Kranzler, 2000 reported similar percentages of abstinence from alcohol at 8 weeks, using opportunities to win prizes as reinforcement). Approximately 38% of the patients in the CRA-plus-vouchers group succeeded in remaining drug free throughout the entire 24 weeks of the study, compared with 35% of the patients in CRA condition. Notably, both behavioral programs (CRA and CRA plus vouchers) after 6 months attained substantially higher percentages of abstinence than usual-care and 12-step programs (AA philosophy) for cocaine abuse (0–20%; Hendrik et al., 2004). In one study, a 12-step program achieved only 5% abstinence at the end of 4 months of treatment (Higgins, Budney, Bickel, Hughes, Foerg, & Badger, 1993).

Figure 13.6 (panel B) also indicates that the initially high effectiveness of the voucher exchange contingency diminished over the 24-week period of treatment. One possibility is that the switch from 3-weekly urine tests to 2-weekly specimens with random testing weakened control of abstinence by the voucher program. Participants made less money ($900 vs. $750) when urine samples were reduced and random testing began (weeks 13 to 24), even though the maximum amount of

FIG. 13.6 Graph portraying the major findings of a Spanish study of contingency management (CM) of cocaine addiction, conducted by Steve Higgins and associates. Panel A shows that the percentage of negative urine samples (abstinence) is greater with the Community Reinforcement Approach (CRA) with added voucher-based CM than without the vouchers. Panel B shows that the percentage of patients who are drug free after 4 and 12 weeks is higher with CRA plus vouchers than with CRA alone. After 24 weeks, CRA and CRA plus vouchers have a similar percentage of patients who are drug free, indicating that the voucher program did not maintain abstinence in the long term. Graphs are based on findings reported by Garcia-Fernandez, Secades-Villa, Garcia-Rodriguez, Sanchez-Hervas, Fernandez-Hermida, & Higgins (2011).

possible earnings increased (from $1400 to $2200). These results indicate that it is difficult to maintain the large treatment gains offered by voucher-based contingency management and to keep patients drug free once the CM procedure is removed. New research on choice as melioration (Heyman, 2009; Kurti & Dallery, 2012) and self-control as discounting (Madden & Bickel, 2009; see Chapter 9) may be helpful in designing CRA and CM programs to maintain long-term abstinence and to arrange environmental contingencies for a drug-free lifestyle.

Cessation of Smoking during Pregnancy

Contingency management has been extended to the treatment of other socially important problems. Smoking during pregnancy is the leading preventable cause of poor pregnancy outcomes in the USA, causing serious immediate and longer-term negative effects for mothers and their offspring. CM and financial incentives are an evidence-based method for promoting abstinence from cigarette smoking during pregnancy, especially for economically disadvantaged mothers, who have the highest smoking rates. Higgins and colleagues conducted a review of the studies in which pregnant women earned vouchers exchangeable for retail items contingent on biochemically verified abstinence from recent smoking (Higgins, Washio, Heil, Solomon, Gaalema, Higgins et al., 2012). Results from six controlled trials with economically disadvantaged pregnant smokers support the efficacy of a voucher-based CM program for increasing smoking abstinence rates before the birth of the infant and early postpartum. In addition, results from three randomized trials provide evidence that the CM intervention improves fetal growth, mean birth weight, percentage of low-birth-weight deliveries, and breastfeeding duration. The systematic use of CM has promise as a way of promoting smoking cessation among economically disadvantaged pregnant and recently postpartum women, and as a treatment to improve childbirth outcomes.

Evaluation of Contingency Management and Substance Abuse

Quantitative reviews of substance abuse disorders show that CM outperforms other interventions, including cognitive–behavioral therapy (Dutra, Stathopoulou, Basden, Leyro, Powers, & Otto, 2008; Lussier, Heil, Mongeon, Badger, & Higgins, 2006; Prendergast, Podus, Finney, Greenwell, & Roll, 2006). Given the strong evidence of its effectiveness, it is noteworthy that community-based treatment providers are not using the "better mousetrap" (Roll, Madden, Rawson, & Petry, 2009). It might be easy to blame the providers of drug-abuse treatment for their ignorance of CM or judgmental bias, but behavior analysts insist that "the subject [is] always right" (Skinner, 1948, p. 240). Thus, the behavior of the providers (those who adopt the CM technology) requires analysis (Roll et al., 2009).

One possibility is that providers of treatment are not familiar with behavioral principles, CM technology, and behavioral language such as "contingency" and "management." Most treatment providers are trained with a clinical focus, using predominantly cognitive theories. These non-specialists may be "turned off" when a component of the treatment package that makes sense in terms of behavior principles seems to be impractical for a clinical setting (who has time to monitor the target behavior?). Decisions to adopt a new technology instead of a less effective treatment also involve assessment of economic costs and benefits. When there are substantial costs to implementing a treatment program, the benefits of adopting the new technology must be considerable and immediate. However, the implementation of a CM treatment often results in immediate costs for the adopters, and delayed signs of benefit for drug-using clients.

In terms of immediate costs, clinical staff are required to conduct regular drug tests that involve wage and material costs for collecting samples, testing specimens, and recording results. Most providers indicate that they could afford to conduct tests once a week, but effective CM programs require repeated drug testing several times a week, a component of treatment that makes CM unacceptable to many clinicians. Voucher-based interventions also have costs related to the use of monetary reinforcement. Providers indicate that $50 a month per client is a feasible cost, but research shows that effective CM interventions spend about $50 a week, a cost that is impractical for many clinical settings. Adoption of CM treatment thus depends on identifying high-valued reinforcements at low cost that can effectively compete with drug reinforcers. Few, if any, have been identified to date—suggesting that vouchers for abstinence are a necessary expense in the treatment of substance abuse.

Ultimately, the amount of money available for treatment of substance abuse (and CM interventions) depends on cultural values and social contingencies (Lamal, 1997). Evidence indicates that drug-abuse treatments provide positive economic returns to society (Cartwright, 2000), and are far less expensive than placing substance users in prisons (Chandler, Fletcher, & Volkow, 2009). However, a large sector of the American public condemns the use of drugs as immoral and criminal conduct, deserving of punishment by imprisonment. Based on this public sentiment, prisons in the USA are more overcrowded with drug offenders than those in any other nation (Bewley-Taylor, Hallam, & Allen, 2009). Until there is a shift toward rehabilitation relative to deterrence by punishment, government funding of CM drug treatment is likely to remain inadequate, subverting widespread clinical adoption of this effective behavioral technology.

BEHAVIOR ANALYSIS IN EDUCATION

Behavior principles have been applied in a wide variety of educational settings (Sulzer-Azaroff, 1986; West & Young, 1992). University students have shown better academic performance after being taught with Fred Keller's personalized system of instruction (PSI), either in the classroom (Cook, 1996; Keller, 1968; Kulik, Kulik & Cohen, 1980) or with computers (Pear, Schnerch, Silva, Svenningsen, & Lambert, 2011; Springer & Pear, 2008). In addition, learning has been accelerated, both for elementary-school children and for university students learning English with computers, by precision teaching (Cuzzocrea, Murdaca, & Oliva, 2011; Lindsley, 1972). Athletic performance has been improved by applying behavior principles to physical education (Colquitt, Pritchard, & McCollum, 2011; Martin & Hrycaiko, 1983; Pocock, Foster, & McEwan, 2010). Autistic children have benefited from the teaching of social and living skills (Lovaas, 1987; Maurice, 1993). These are just a few of the many applications of behavior principles to education. In this section we focus on two examples, but there are many more educational applications than are reported here, including programmed learning (Skinner, 1968), direct instruction (Engelmann & Carnine, 1982), and interteaching (Boyce & Hineline, 2002).

From a behavioral viewpoint, the ideal "teacher" is a personal tutor who knows all the topic information and all the appropriate behavioral science (i.e., shaping, chaining, reinforcement schedules, establishing operations, etc.), and who keeps accurate track of student performance, delivering immediate reinforcement for maximum effectiveness. Our culture is getting close to creating such an individual in the form of a personal computer. Artificial intelligence and robotics will soon produce personal tutors, perhaps before the next edition of this textbook is published.

For the moment, Headsprout® is an online and computer-based early reading program that demonstrates the use of new technology to deliver educational services to parents and children. This program effectively teaches young children the basic skills and strategies for successful reading. In the Headsprout system, children learn to read with positive reinforcement, discovering that letters and sounds go together to make words, the words make sentences, and sentences make stories. The children go on to learn that stories convey meaning and can be read either to extract information or just for fun and pleasure. Basic skills and strategies for reading are acquired in an exciting "learn-by-doing" manner, involving the instruction and mastery of skills such as phonemic awareness (sounds go with words), print awareness, phonics, sounding out, segmenting, and blending (using sound elements to decode words). Additional programmed instruction teaches vocabulary development, reading fluency, and reading comprehension.

The success of Headsprout is based on four teaching fundamentals. First, the instructional program arranges the reading material so that children succeed (high rate of reinforcement). Second, children practice and learn the material until they master the skill or strategy. Third, the skill is practiced and reinforced until the child is able to consistently, quickly, and accurately perform it (fluency). Finally, the child is given cumulative reviews of skills and strategies to improve retention and transfer their reading skills to material outside of the program (Layng, Twyman & Stikeleather, 2004). When parents purchase Headsprout Early Reading package (40 episodes), they are sent a package containing a progress map to track their child's progress, stickers to place on the map after the child has mastered an episode, and story books to read at designated points in the program. Overall, Headsprout is an example of effective behavioral technology that is currently being used to teach basic reading to many American children.

A Personalized System of Instruction

The traditional lecture method that is used to instruct college and university students has remained largely unchanged for thousands of years. A teacher stands in front of a number of students and talks about his or her area of expertise. There are variations on this theme—students are encouraged to participate in discussion, to discover new facts on their own, to reach conclusions by being led through a series of questions, and to be active rather than passive learners. During lectures, various forms of logic are used to arrive at conclusions, and classroom demonstrations are arranged. Basically, the lecture method of instruction is the same as it has always been, but presenting material is not equivalent to teaching the subject matter.

Fred Keller recognized that the lecture method of college teaching was inefficient and in many cases a failure. He reasoned that anyone who had acquired the skills needed to attend college was capable of successfully mastering most or all college courses. Some students might take longer than others to acquire expertise in a course, but the overwhelming majority of students would be able to do so eventually. If behavior principles were to be taken seriously, there were no bad students, only bad teachers.

In a seminal article, titled "Good-bye, teacher . . .," Fred Keller outlined a college teaching method based on principles of operant conditioning (Keller, 1968). Keller called his teaching method a **personalized system of instruction (PSI)**. The method has also been called the "Keller Plan" (Sherman, Ruskin, & Semb, 1982). Basically, PSI courses are organized such that students move through the course at their own pace. Some students may finish the course within a few weeks, whereas others require a semester or longer.

Course material is broken down into many small units of reading and (if required) laboratory assignments. Students earn points (conditioned reinforcement) for completing unit tests and lab assignments. Mastery of the lab assignments and unit tests is required. If test scores are not close to perfect, the test (usually in a different form) is taken again. The assignments and tests build on one another, so they must be completed in order. Undergraduate proctors are recruited to assist with running the course. These individuals tutor students and mark unit tests and laboratory assignments. Proctors are "chosen for [their] mastery of the course content and orientation, for [their] maturity of judgment, for [their] understanding of the special problems that confront . . . beginner[s], and for [their] willingness to assist [with the course]" (Keller, 1968, p. 81). Lectures and class demonstrations are an optional privilege; students may or may not attend them. Lectures are scheduled once the majority of students in the class have passed a sufficient number of unit tests to indicate that they are ready to appreciate the lectures; no exams are based on these lectures. The course instructor designs the course, makes up the tests, delivers the optional lectures, adjudicates disputes, and oversees the course.

Comparison studies have evaluated student performance on PSI courses against performance of students given computer-based instruction, audio-tutorials, traditional lecture-based teaching, visual-based instruction, and other programmed instruction methods. College students instructed by PSI outperformed students taught by these other methods when given a common final exam (for a review, see Lloyd & Lloyd, 1992). Despite this positive outcome, logistical problems in organizing PSI courses, teaching to mastery level (most students get an A for the course), and allowing students more time than the allotted semester to complete the course have worked against the wide adoption of PSI in universities and colleges (Binder & Watkins, 1989).

Precision Teaching

Ogden Lindsley extended the method of free operant conditioning to humans, emphasizing Skinner's dictum to focus on rate of response (Lindsley, 1972, 1991). In what became known as **precision teaching**, Lindsley (1990a, 1990b) devised a method of systematic instruction that encouraged students and teachers to target specific behaviors, to count, time, and graph them, and to revise instructional procedures based on the charted data (see also Binder, 2010). As an instructional system, precision teaching has four guiding principles: a focus on directly observable behavior, rate as the basic behavioral measure, the charting of behavior on a Standard Celeration Chart, and "the learner knows best."

In terms of the *focus on behavior*, precision teaching involves translating learning tasks into concrete, directly observable behaviors that can be counted, timed, and recorded. Private behavior, such as silent reading, must be made public. A child, Sally, who is poor at silent reading might be asked to read out loud so that counts of the number of correct words can be obtained (a measure of so-called "decoding" skills). To assess her comprehension skills, the teacher might provide a list of questions to Sally after she has silently read a passage from a book. Following this, the teacher would count the number of correct answers that Sally made on the quiz.

Once behavior is defined, the rate of behavior is used as the basic measure of learning (or performance). The rate is the average number of correct responses during the period of assessment, or *counts per minute*. The use of rate of correct responses (frequency/time) focuses instruction on **fluency** involving accuracy *and* high frequency. When a performance becomes fluent, the behavior is retained for longer, persists during long periods on the task, is less affected by distractions, and is more likely to be available in new learning situations (i.e., to combine with other well-learned behaviors) (see Binder, 1996; West & Young, 1992).

Next, *the rate is plotted* on a Standard Celeration Chart, allowing the teacher and student to observe improvement in the target behavior for each week (Figure 13.7). The degree of acceleration (or deceleration) is a useful measure of learning in academic settings. In this regard, West and Young stated:

> When data are plotted on the standard celeration chart, learning is generally represented by a straight or nearly straight line. The value of the slope of the line which best fits the distribution of values

[plotted rates over days] on a logarithmic scale is thought of as an 'index of learning.' The steeper the slope, the faster the learning is; the flatter the slope, the slower the learning is.

(West & Young, 1992, p. 132)

The whole idea of precision teaching is to improve learning in a way that is objective and quantifiable. Teachers and students work out plans for improvement, implement the instructional procedures, and assess the effects of the interventions.

The general rule is that *the learner knows best*. That is, if a student is progressing according to the instructional plan, then the program is appropriate for that student. In contrast, if the targeted behavior for a student shows low **celeration**, the program needs to be changed. In other words, precision teaching requires that we alter the teaching strategy rather than blame the student (e.g., by assuming that "John is stupid"). That is, the student is always "right" and, in the context of low improvement, new instructional procedures are required to improve learning and performance (Carnine, 1995; see also *Behavior and Social Issues*, Special Section: What Works in Education, 1997, 7, 1–68).

Precision teaching is a cost-effective technology (according to a survey by Albrecht, cited in Lindsley, 1991) that has been successfully applied to teach learners ranging from the developmentally

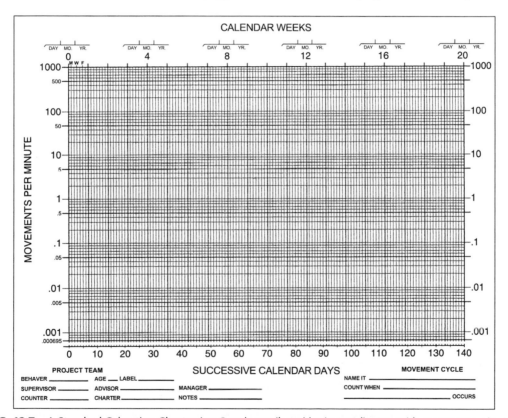

FIG. 13.7 A Standard Celeration Chart using 6-cycle semilogarithmic coordinates, with counts per minute (rate of target behavior) on the y-axis and calendar days on the x-axis. Using this 6-cycle scale, a student whose rate of spelling targeted words increased from 2 to 4 words a minute per week would appear the same as another student whose rate increased from 20 to 40 words a minute in the same period. The students show the same proportional amount of improvement. When the charted rate doubles from one week to the next, we say that it is accelerating at "times 2." When the charted rate is reduced by half from one week to the next, we say that it is decelerating at "divided by 2." A straight line drawn from the lower left corner to the upper right corner of the Standard Celeration Chart has an angle of 30°. This represents a times 2 change in behavior per week—the objective of accelerating precision teaching interventions.

delayed to university graduate students (White, 1986). Binder and Watkins (1990) reported on a precision teaching program conducted in Great Falls, Montana in the early 1970s. Over a 4-year period, teachers at Sacajawea elementary school added 20–30 min of precision teaching to their regular curriculum. On the Iowa Test of Basic Skills, the students who were given precision teaching improved between 19 and 40 percentile points compared with other students in the district. More generally, improvements of two or more grade-levels per year of instruction are commonly observed in precision teaching classrooms (e.g., West, Young, & Spooner, 1990), and significant learning gains are achieved for developmentally delayed and autistic students (Fischer, Howard, Sparkman, & Moore, 2010; Holding, Bray, & Kehle, 2010; Johnson and Layng, 1994). These instructional gains have been attributed to the effects of rate building on fluent performance, a conclusion that has been challenged. Experimental studies of the learning gains from precision teaching have not ruled out the effects of practice and high rates of reinforcement as the critical factors, rather than the arrangement of instructional material designed to alter response rate and fluency (Chase, Doughty, & O'Shields, 2005; Doughty, Chase, & O'Shields, 2004; but see Binder, 2004 and Kubina, 2005, for counterarguments).

Although highly successful in promoting rapid and fluent learning, precision teaching remains only a small part of mainstream education. In what Skinner (1984a) called *The Shame of American Education*, he indicated that most educational problems "could be solved if students learned twice as much in the same time and with the same effort" (p. 947). This is exactly what precision teaching is all about. The problem, said Skinner, is that theories of human behavior based on humanism and developmental and cognitive psychology are most often taught in schools of education, but teaching/learning based on these theories is often ineffective. In his solution, Skinner pointed to several steps that needed to be taken to advance the educational system: (1) be clear about what is to be taught, (2) teach first things first, in an ordered sequence of progression, (3) stop making all students advance at essentially the same pace, and (4) program the subject matter—a good program of instruction guarantees a great deal of successful action.

In the end, the problem of American education rests with our culture. Skinner stated that "a culture that is not willing to accept scientific advances in the understanding of human behavior, together with the technology that emerges from these advances, will eventually be replaced by a culture that is" (Skinner, 1984a, p. 953). The survival of the American way of life depends on education of the young. The question is, are American people willing to adopt and promote a scientific approach to effective education?

APPLICATIONS OF BEHAVIOR PRINCIPLES

Training Self-Control

In applied behavior analysis, **self-control** techniques may be taught to clients, who are then better able to manage their own behavior. One common technique for self-control is called self-reinforcement. Belles and Bradlyn (1987) conducted an interesting study to modify the behavior of a heavy smoker by arranging self-reinforcement and self-punishment over the telephone. The client was a 65-year-old man who lived 200 miles away from the clinic. The researchers arranged a treatment program with the client and his wife. For each day that he smoked less than a specified number of cigarettes, he added $3 to a savings fund that was used to buy items that he wanted. When he exceeded the agreed number of cigarettes, he had to send a $25 check to the therapist, who donated the money to a charity that was unacceptable to the

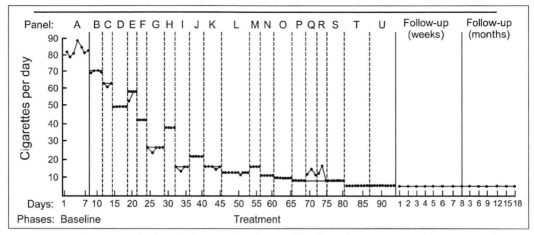

FIG. 13.8 A changing criterion design used in the modification of excessive smoking. From "The use of the changing criterion design in achieving controlled smoking in a heavy smoker," by D. Belles and A. S. Bradlyn, 1987, *Journal of Behavior Therapy and Experimental Psychiatry*, 18, 77–82. © 1987 Elsevier, Ltd. Published with permission.

client. His wife verified the number of cigarettes he smoked each day by unobtrusively monitoring his behavior.

A **changing criterion design** was used to evaluate the effectiveness of the self-control procedure (see Gast, 2010, pp. 383–389, for a complete description of the advantages and limitations of this design). In this design, the criterion for the number of cigarettes smoked each day was progressively lowered over 95 days. The effects of self-reinforcement are shown if the subject meets or falls below the criterion set by the researchers. Figure 13.8 shows the effects of the treatment. A horizontal line shows the target level for each period, indicating that the client generally matched his behavior to this criterion. Notice that although the criterion generally decreased, the researchers occasionally set a value higher than a previous phase and the client's behavior changed in accord with the contingencies. After 81 days on the program, the client's cigarette consumption had declined from about 85 to 5 cigarettes each day. At this point, he was satisfied with his progress and said that he wanted to remain at this level. Follow-up reports on his smoking over 18 months showed that he continued to smoke only 5 cigarettes a day.

Behavior Analysis in the Treatment of Autism

Autistic children show an early lack of social interaction with parents, other family members, and peers. For example, these children often resist being held and may have a tantrum if picked up or hugged. When autistic children get older they may be mistakenly thought to be deaf because they do not talk or even establish eye contact when spoken to. These children often show repeated stereotyped patterns of behavior such as rocking back and forth, spinning a top, wiggling their fingers in front of their eyes, and so on. More than 85% of autistic children fail to speak at an age when other children are highly verbal. The long-term outcome for this disorder is grim; the overwhelming majority of such children require extended care and supervision (Ghezzi, Williams, & Carr, 1999).

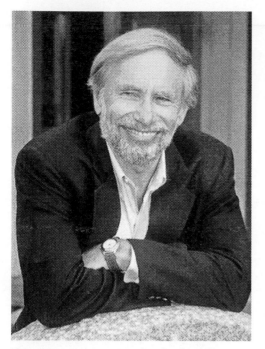

FIG. 13.9 Ivar Lovaas, who developed the applied behavior analysis and early intensive behavioral intervention approach to the treatment of autism. Lovaas Institute. Published with permission.

The late Ivar Lovaas (Figure 13.9), professor at the University of California at Los Angeles, researched and developed the applied behavior analysis (ABA) and treatment of autism from the 1960s onward (Lovaas, 1966, 1977, 1987; McEachin, Smith, & Lovaas; 1993). Lovaas (1977, 1987) described an **early intensive behavioral intervention (EIBI)** in which youngsters are given 40 or more hours each week of behavioral intervention designed to increase social behavior, teach speaking and communication, and eliminate self-stimulation and aggressive behavior. Most of the treated autistic children showed significant improvement in their daily functioning. Incredibly, after 2 years of EIBI treatment of autistic children less than 30 months old, 50% of these youngsters were later indistinguishable from normal school-children. No other treatment of autistic children has produced such dramatic improvement (Foxx, 2008; Lovaas, 1993; Maurice, 1993; Schopler & Mesibov, 1994).

Recently, a meta-analysis of studies has supported the effectiveness of ABA-based early intervention programs (Peters-Scheffer, Didden, Korzillius, & Sturmey, 2011; but see Warren, McPheeters, Sathe, Foss-Feig, Glasser, & Veenstra-VanderWeele, 2011, for a discussion of reservations and methodological concerns). An evidence-based review panel of the New York Department of Health concluded that of 18 types of interventions for autism, only ABA combined with EIBI was effective, whereas auditory integration therapy, facilitated communication, floor time, sensory integration therapy, touch therapy, music therapy, hormones, vitamin therapies, and special diets were not recommended (Foxx, 2008). Furthermore, the National Research Council of the United States set out guidelines for effective educational programs for autism, and only ABA with EIBI met or exceeded these standards (Figure 13.10).

Effective Educational Programs for Autism
US National Research Council

- Early entry into intervention
- Intensive instructional programming (25 or more hours a week, 5 or more days a week, 12 months a year)
- One-to-one or small-group instruction to achieve clearly defined individualized goals
- Specialized training by discrete trials and incidental teaching
- Systematic and individualized instruction
- Focus on development of spontaneous social communication, adaptive skills, appropriate behaviors, play skills, and cognitive and academic skills

---

FIG. 13.10 Summary of the guidelines for an effective program in the treatment of autism as set out by the National Research Council of the United States. Extracted from Foxx (2008).

NEW DIRECTIONS: Autism, Mirror Neurons, and Applied Behavior Analysis

Autism is a multiply determined and multiply expressed disorder that has become alarmingly prevalent. The source of the disordered behaviors labeled as autism is not clear, but the treatment of choice is EIBI by skilled behavior analysts (Charlop-Christy & Kelso, 1997; Ghezzi, Williams, & Carr, 1999; Foxx, 2008). Because of its unknown etiology and often extraordinary behavioral manifestations, people are desperate to try different treatments and to promote a variety of possible causes.

The definition of autism is almost exclusively based on behavior, primarily in terms of deficits such as poor eye contact, little communication skill, noncompliance, and lack of social play (Klin, Chawarska, Rubin, & Volkmar, 2004; Volkmar, Carter, Grossman, & Klin, 1997). The autistic child looks normal but does not show age-appropriate behavior, especially social behavior. There is a set of molecular pathways that are abnormally expressed in the brain of autistic people (Voineagu, Wang, Johnston, Lowe, Tian, Horvath et al., 2011), and genetic mutations associated with autism (Sanders, Murtha, Gupta, Murdoch, Raubeson, Willsey et al., 2012), but at present the causal evidence is not definitive.

The discovery of the "mirror neuron" system (see Chapter 11) and its lack of development in autistic children suggest that these youngsters may benefit from intensive behavioral training in generalized imitation (Baer et al., 1967) and other forms of visual discrimination training. The mirror system allows the observer to process information about self-performed actions and, using the same system, to understand the actions, emotions, and intentions of others (Oberman & Ramachandran, 2007). The integration of behavioral neuroscience with applied behavioral interventions could greatly enhance the understanding and treatment of childhood autism (see Thompson, 2007, pp. 429–430). One possibility is that intensive early training is effective for up to 50% of autistic children with intact neural systems because it organizes and activates the mirror neural system in the developing child, as Iriki (2006) suggests is the case for lower primates.

Obviously neural mechanisms are altered during early experience, and the immature nervous system is especially sensitive to environmental influences during **maturation** and development. Thompson (2007) recently suggested that "early differential reinforcement of discriminative responding [by autistic children] to visual images of hand and arm movements may promote gene expression in the mirror neuron system" (p. 437). EIBI has produced lasting modifications of autistic behavior in some children, and it is possible that interventions aimed at priming the mirror neuron system (e.g., training to discriminate the actions and emotions modeled by others) could be even more effective.

Unfortunately, there is a subgroup of autistic children who do not benefit from 30 or more hours of weekly behavioral treatment (Thompson, 2007, p. 429). Modern neural imaging could help to demarcate autistic children who are unable to form synapses in the brain (especially the mirror neuron areas) and profit from EIBI. However, these individuals could be treated by alternative behavioral procedures designed for their specific deficits and excesses.

FIG. 13.11   Dr. Joseph Morrow and Brenda Terzich, the founders of Applied Behavioral Consultants (ABC) and the ABC schools for treatment of autism. Published with permission.

The ABC Approach to Autism

Because the Lovaas treatment approach is highly effective, Dr. Joe Morrow and Brenda Terzich (Figure 13.11) started a business devoted to behavioral intervention for autism, Applied Behavior Consultants (ABC), in Sacramento, California. Initially, ABC used the treatment package described by Lovaas, but now the program is supplemented by other work in the field. The Picture Exchange Communication System (PECS) developed by Andy Bondy is used for children who have problems with vocalization (Bondy and Frost, 1994), and the Verbal Behavior approach by Mark Sundberg is included to establish functional verbal responses, which are so necessary for communication (Barbera, 2007).

The co-founder of ABC, Brenda Terzich, also made valuable additions to the treatment of autism, designing and implementing a programmed generalization model called R.E.A.L. (Recreating Environment to Accelerate Learning). The R.E.A.L. generalization program aids in the transfer and maintenance of learned skills from a highly structured training situation to the child's everyday environment (home, school, and community). In this extended ABA-based program, parents are taught the necessary behavioral skills for training their child. The treatment package includes specific intervention strategies for accomplishing behavioral outcomes. For example, the children are reinforced for making eye contact when the teacher talks to them. Appropriate life skills, such as eating meals with utensils, dressing oneself, and personal hygiene (i.e., brushing teeth, combing hair, etc.), are reinforced with tokens and social approval. Verbal skills, including manding and tacting, are also targets for behavior change. ABC staff members monitor progress and, if necessary, advise program changes.

In 1994, Morrow and Terzich started a communication-based private school for children diagnosed as autistic. At the ABC school, autistic children receive individualized behavioral training for about 5 h a day, 218 days per year. The emphasis at the school is on verbal and academic behavior as well as on social skills (Bondy, 1996; Bondy & Frost, 1994). A primary objective of the program is to move children from the ABC school to public schools (either general or special education) within 2 years. To accomplish this, ABC uses a five-step program that guides the progression of lessons from discrete trials learning to the ultimate transfer of the control of social behavior to the verbal community, including the child's peer group (Morrow, Terzich, & Williamson, 2002).

Level 1 of the program involves discrete trials procedures in which the teacher presents a stimulus and the response by the child is reinforced (or corrected). The training at this level also includes training generalization of subskills to new situations, trainers, and variations within the standard teaching setting. At level 2, the teaching is focused on stimulus generalization. That is, once the child masters an appropriate response in the presence of a specific S^D (level 1), the teacher varies properties of the S^D while maintaining the appropriate response. The S^D may be "What am I doing?" and hand waving by the teacher, and the child is reinforced for saying "You're waving your hand." At level 2 the teacher may say "I'm doing what?" or "Hey, what's happening here?" (varying the S^D), and reinforcement remains contingent on the response "You're waving your hand." At level 3, the training emphasizes maintaining learned concepts and skills. The training ensures that the child demonstrates generalization of skills when lessons are changed from one location or time to another. Level 3 training also involves programmed environmental distractions, similar to everyday interruptions in a classroom (building behavioral momentum, as described by Nevin & Grace, 2000). The child is taught to maintain accurate responding in the face of these random interruptions.

At level 4, children are taught "splinter skills." A child may be able to use the toilet and to dress herself, but be unable to select the clothes to wear. In the classroom, a child may be able to write on a piece of paper when instructed by the teacher, but be unable to get a piece of paper on her own. Formally, the training at this level is focused on completion of extended behavior chains or sequences. The final level of the program, level 5, is focused on the training and generalization of social skills (greetings, reciprocity, and empathy) that will be necessary to interact with others in everyday settings (e.g., classroom, playground, and home). For example, the child is taught to discriminate between greeting his or her parents and saying hello to a playmate. Training at level 5 also ensures that this kind of social skill is maintained in a variety of appropriate settings.

How successful is this kind of behavioral program? Well, at the time of admission to the program, 57% of the autistic children have no speech. After 1 year, all of the children are manding (e.g., requesting, asking for, and asking questions) vocally, or by sign language, or by a picture exchange communication system (PECS) (Figure 13.12; see also Chapter 12 on manding).

What about transition from the behavioral program to regular classrooms? The first thing to note is that almost no children move from traditional, nonbehavioral treatment programs to public school classrooms (Lovaas, 1987). Over the first 4 years of ABC's school operation, 71 children had completed all five levels of behavioral training and had made the move to regular education classrooms. Of the 31 children who were aged 6 years or more (eldest group) on admission to the ABC school, none made successful transitions to public education classrooms. Of the 25 children who were aged between 4 and 6 years at admission (middle group), only 8% made a successful transition. When the children's age at admission was 4 years or less (youngest group), 40% moved into the public education system and did not return to ABC. The unpublished data indicate that intensive behavioral intervention is most successful for younger children.

The findings at the ABC school substantiate recommendations by Maurice, Green, and Luce (1996) concerning intensive behavioral treatment of autism. Their manual indicates that intensive behavioral programs work best when children are less than 5 years of age (the younger the better), the program includes at least 30 h of treatment per week, and children continue in the program for at least 2 years. Under these conditions, even very

FIG. 13.12 Brenda Terzich, a behavioral technician, and a child using the Picture Exchanged Communication System (PECS) at the ABC school for autism in Sacramento, CA. PECS is a behavioral technology developed by Andy Bondy that allows the non-vocal child to communicate with others, and acquire a basic verbal repertoire of manding and tacting. Published with permission.

low-functioning children make large behavioral gains. In 2005, ABC began a center-based infant-toddler (birth to 3 years old) development program for children who exhibit autism-like behaviors and are at risk for a diagnosis of autism spectrum disorder. As part of this very early intensive behavioral intervention, parents participate in an 8-week training program focused on behavior principles, involving consistency, reinforcement, and making their actions contingent on the desired behavior.

Because of the success of and subsequent demand for in-home and center-based behavioral treatment, ABC currently has 500 or more employees and has opened in-home ABA programs and behavioral schools in China, Portugal, and Bahrain. ABC is also disseminating behavioral technology for autism throughout Europe, Asia, and Africa. In 2006, the Association for Behavior Analysis International recognized the significant contribution of Dr. Joe Morrow (cofounder of ABC) to the field with the distinguished award for "Outstanding Contributions to the International Dissemination of Behavior Analysis."

Since the program started in 1987, more than 3000 autistic children have been treated by ABC's behavioral technology. Each of these children has received about 40 h a week of one-on-one behavior therapy over a period of several years. ABC has been able to reach such a large number of autistic children because of their emphasis on training parents to work with these youngsters (rather than directly providing therapy themselves). Although time-consuming, early intensive behavior intervention has rescued many children from an otherwise isolated and impoverished life. Happily, this intervention is also much more cost-effective than providing a lifetime of supervision or institutionalization. The state of California has recognized both of these facts and provides most, or all, of the money for the program.

Video Modeling, Mobile Technology, and Autism

In Chapter 11, we saw that modeling, imitation, and observational learning were critical to the rapid acquisition of human behavior, especially for those with developmental disabilities and autism (see "On the Applied Side: Training Generalized Imitation" in that chapter). People with autism and other learning difficulties are now able to access video modeling (VM), which is a video demonstration by a model of an integrated sequence of skills to perform some task, and video prompting (VP), which is a video of a model showing the separate steps or components of a task, using new mobile technology (Ayres & Langone, 2005). This includes portable DVD players, laptop computers, and personal digital assistants (PDA), as well as the popular iPod, iPad, and iPhone. For many autistic people, using these devices is highly reinforcing, as it allows them to obtain self-generated information about living and life skills, and to fit into the wider community that endorses the use of such technology (Bereznak, Ayres, Mechling, & Alexander, 2012).

In a study of video self-prompting and mobile technology, Bereznak et al. (2012) used iPhones to teach vocational and daily living skills to three male high school students with autism spectrum disorder. The students were taught to use the devices to access video prompting of the steps to use a washing machine, a microwave to make noodles, and a photocopying machine. For example, to use the washing machine, a task analysis defined the following steps or components: turn dial to setting for regular wash, pull dial to start running water, open the door, take cap off detergent, pour detergent into washer, put cap back on detergent, put detergent on counter, put clothes in the washer, close the door. After instruction in how to use an iPhone to watch a training video, the student was situated before a washing machine, given the iPhone showing play, forward, and rewind buttons, and told to "touch play to start doing the wash." The student now touched the play feature and a single word appeared on the screen describing the step, followed by the video presentation with an audio description for the first step. At the end of each step, the video displayed a stop sign, which set the occasion for the student to press the pause button. After hitting the pause button, the student was asked to imitate the behavior shown on the video clip. Incorrect responses (not matching to the video model) were blocked and corrected, while the correct response received a schedule of verbal praise, such as "nice job turning the dial."

The results indicated an immediate effect of video prompting on each targeted skill (using a washing machine, making noodles, and photocopying) across the three students, indicating that an iPhone can serve as an effective self-prompting device to teach daily living and vocational skills to adolescent students with autism spectrum disorder. One hidden benefit is that self-prompting on an iPhone is a valued behavior in America, indicating to others some degree of autonomy and self-determination. Thus, behavior principles along with mobile technology may generate self-regulation of actions (not just rote learning), giving the person with autism spectrum disorder greater independence and intrinsic motivation.

CAUSES AND PREVENTION OF BEHAVIOR PROBLEMS

In recent years, behavior analysts have focused attention on the factors that produce behavior problems. Animal models of disordered behavior have been developed that provide insight into the causes of problem behavior involving depression, anorexia, and other psychiatric disorders (see Epling & Pierce, 1992; Keehn, 1986; Seligman & Maier, 1967). Other researchers have been concerned with promoting behavior related to physical health. The area of **behavioral medicine** is a multidisciplinary field that includes behavior-change programs targeted at health-related activities such as following special diets, self-examination for early symptoms of disease, exercising, taking medicine, stopping smoking, and other health issues (Friman, Finney, Glasscock, Weigel, & Christophersen, 1986; Gellman & Turner, 2012; Pomerleau, 1979). The idea is that many health problems may be prevented or treated by integrating knowledge about biological, genetic, and behavioral risk factors.

Anorexia Nervosa and Activity Anorexia

A young woman goes on a severe diet and continues to the point of starvation. How can this person be anything but mentally disturbed? In fact, *anorexia nervosa* is currently classified as a neurotic disorder by psychiatrists and psychologists (American Psychiatric Association, 2000). Mental illness and disturbed cognitions are suggested by the many symptoms that accompany willful starvation (see Garner & Desai, 2000, for a multidimensional analysis). These symptoms include fear of being fat, obsessive food rituals, distorted body image, and disturbed self-perception.

Notably, modern psychiatry has reinforced the view that cognitive and mental events cause abnormal human behavior. This is convincing to people, because unusual thoughts often accompany bizarre behavior. Although these thoughts may occur and are associated with disturbed eating, this evidence is not sufficient to claim that they are causes. One reason for the association may be that anorexics learn to label their emotional states and behavior in accord with the expectations of therapists, family, and friends.

The numerous and varied symptoms of anorexia also arise from starvation itself (Epling & Pierce, 1992; Keys, Brozek, Henschel, Mickelsen, & Taylor, 1950). Keys et al. (1950) observed many of the symptoms of anorexia nervosa in psychologically healthy men who participated in a study of forced starvation. Symptoms similar to those found in anorexia nervosa developed as the men lost weight. On psychological tests the men became neurotic (a few scored in the psychotic range), they were obsessed with food, some became bulimic (excessive overeating), and so on. Importantly, these symptoms *followed* rather than preceded starvation—suggesting that they were not the causes of anorexia.

Physical Activity and Anorexia

Clinical reports of anorexia nervosa have viewed excessive physical activity as an interesting but unimportant symptom of the syndrome. For example, Feighner, Robins, Guze, Woodruff, Winokur, and Munoz (1972) have described diagnostic criteria that include periods of overactivity as one of six possible secondary symptoms. In the traditional view, activity is secondary because it is simply a way that the anorectic burns off calories. That is, physical activity reflects the patient's desire to lose weight.

   Although this interpretation is widely accepted, there is evidence that it is wrong. Excessive physical activity appears central to many cases of human self-starvation (Epling & Pierce, 1992). The evidence for the importance of activity comes from a variety of sources. Controlled experiments with animals have shown that physical activity can make an animal give up eating when food is relatively abundant (Epling & Pierce, 1984, 1988). Research with humans has also suggested a link between excessive activity and self-starvation (Davis, Kennedy, Ravelski, & Dionne, 1994; Davis, 1999; Davis & Kaptein, 2006), viewing anorexia as similar to obsessive-compulsive disorder (OCD). Beumont and his colleagues asked 25 anorexics to identify their symptoms and the order of occurrence (Beumont, Booth, Abraham, Griffiths, & Turner, 1983). Of the 28 reported symptoms, only manipulating food servings and increased sports activity were present in all patients. Generally, the ordering of the symptoms indicated that changes in dieting and food intake were followed by increased physical activity. Many other studies have documented excessive physical activity in anorexic patients (see Epling, Pierce, & Stefan, 1983; Meyer, Taranis, Goodwin, & Haycraft, 2011), but have not related "exercise" to food-related search or travel when food is depleted. An animal model of activity anorexia clarifies the interrelationships between food intake, body weight, and food-related locomotion and physical activity (Epling & Pierce, 1992).

Anorexia in Animals

The process of **activity anorexia** begins when rats are fed a single daily meal and are allowed to run on an activity wheel. It is important to note that the size of the meal is more than adequate for survival. Also, animals are not forced to exercise on the wheel. They can choose to remain in an attached cage or just lie in the wheel. In fact, the animals start running, and this activity increases daily because of the time-limited, one-meal-a-day food schedule (Epling & Pierce, 1996b).

   As shown in Figure 13.13, wheel running rapidly increases to excessive levels. An adolescent rat may run up to 20 km a day at the peak. Ordinarily, these animals would run less than 1 km a day. This excessive activity is surprising

FIG. 13.13 Excessive running and reduction of food intake by an adolescent rat, reported in "A theory of activity-based anorexia," by W. F. Epling, W. D. Pierce, and L. Stefan, 1983, *International Journal of Eating Disorders, 3*, 27–46. Reprinted with permission.

because the animal is expending many more calories than it is consuming. For this reason, the activity is life-threatening.

A more startling effect is that food intake remains drastically reduced as running becomes excessive. As you can see, at the end of 1 week (Figure 13.13) the animal is eating very little. The rat is giving up eating despite increasing energy expenditure through wheel running. If this process is allowed to continue, the animal dies of starvation. The drop in running on the last day occurs because the rat is too weak to continue.

Reinforcement Values of Eating and Running

In Chapter 7, we discussed the interrelations of eating and running (Pierce, Epling, & Boer, 1986). Recall that the research evidence indicates that rats will work more for an opportunity to run on a wheel as food deprivation increases. The animals bar pressed many more times for 60 s of wheel running as their body weight declined. In addition, rats pressed a lever for food less when they had run on a wheel the night before a food session. This effect occurred even though the animals had several hours of rest before being placed in the operant chamber. The overall findings suggest that the reinforcing effectiveness of physical activity increased as a function of food deprivation. Also, the reinforcement value of eating food decreased when preceded by a bout of physical activity. These two reinforcement relations provide a behavioral account of the activity anorexia cycle (see Chapter 7 for a discussion of the biological basis of these reinforcement relationships).

Activity-Induced Taste Aversion

The suppression of eating during activity anorexia also involves conditioned taste aversion (CTA), although evidence suggests that CTA does not explain the activity anorexia cycle (Sparkes, Grant, & Lett, 2003). **Activity-induced taste aversion** occurs when a distinctive taste becomes a conditioned stimulus (CS) that is followed by the physiological consequences of wheel running, the unconditioned stimulus (US). Lett and Grant (1996) were the first to test the hypothesis that CTA is induced by physical activity. In their experiment, rats were exposed to flavored liquids that were paired or unpaired with wheel running. Compared with control rats that remained in their home cages, experimental rats drank less of the flavor paired with wheel running—the rats showed CTA induced by wheel running. Subsequent research has replicated the basic effect, ruled out mere novelty of the wheel as the basis for the original finding, and extended the CTA effect to food stimuli (Heth, Inglis, Russell, & Pierce, 2001; Nakajima, Hayashi, & Kato, 2000; Salvy, Pierce, Heth, & Russell, 2003).

Dr. Sarah Salvy is a behavioral and social scientist with RAND Corporation and former associate professor in the Department of Pediatrics at SUNY (Buffalo). Early in her career, Sarah worked with David Pierce (coauthor of this textbook) on her doctoral research at the University of Alberta. Her studies show that CTA induced by wheel running can be eliminated by pre-exposure to the wheel running US (Salvy, Pierce, Heth, & Russell, 2002; also see Heth & Pierce, 2007, on pre-exposure to a novel food). This result is consistent with habituation effects and a respondent conditioning account of CTA induced by wheel running. Her research also indicated that CTA is related more to the contingency between a distinctive taste and wheel running than to the intensity of the physical activity. That is, the association between taste and the physiological effects of wheel running is more important than the "dose" level of physical activity.

Using a backward conditioning procedure in which the taste CS followed the wheel US, Salvy was the first to obtain evidence for conditioned taste preference (CTP) (Salvy, Heth, Pierce, &

Russell, 2004). This finding suggests a bivalent effect of wheel running similar to drugs such as morphine. That is, wheel running conditions either CTA or CTP depending on its temporal location (before or after) relative to the CS-taste. Other researchers have subsequently established the bivalent effects of wheel running (Dobek, Heth, & Pierce, 2012; Hughes & Boakes, 2008). Salvy's work on taste conditioning induced by wheel running constitutes significant "bridging experiments" linking respondent conditioning, activity anorexia, and human anorexia in everyday life.

 # FOCUS ON: Conditioned Overeating and Childhood Obesity

Taste conditioning plays a role in the development of obesity as well as anorexia. Families that provide children with calorie-wise foods and drinks may inadvertently contribute to overeating and childhood obesity, according to recent research using respondent conditioning to induced overeating (Davidson & Swithers, 2004; Pierce, Heth, Owczarczyk, Russell, & Proctor, 2007; Swithers & Davidson, 2008; Swithers, Doerflinger, & Davidson, 2006). The researchers found that food with low calories or artificial sweeteners disrupted the body's capacity to regulate energy intake—resulting in overeating and weight gain. The findings help to explain why increasing numbers of children and adults in North America lack the ability to regulate energy intake.

Pierce et al. (2007) suggest that being able to match calorie intake with the body's need involves the ability to learn that the food tastes predict the amount of calories ingested (see also Swithers & Davidson, 2008). Thus, both obese-prone and lean juvenile rats are prepared to learn that particular tastes signal caloric energy. Based on this associative learning, the use of calorie-wise foods may undermine the body's natural ability to regulate food intake and weight. In this way, diet foods and drinks could lead to **conditioned overeating** and obesity in children, which is especially a problem for obese-prone individuals.

Early experiences can teach young rats that specific food flavors are useful for predicting the energy content of foods. Subsequently, the animals use food tastes to determine the body's need for calories. When food flavors have been associated with low caloric energy, as with diet foods and drinks, juvenile rats eat more than their bodily need after ingesting a nutritious snack or pre-meal containing that flavor. Overall, the research shows that young rats overeat and gain weight when the taste of food has been associated with low energy content.

Obesity is a significant risk factor for both type 2 diabetes and cardiovascular disease, and is an increasing major health problem in North America and Europe. In this regard, it is important to note that the food industry generates an extensive variety of products some of which offer attractive tastes but have little or no caloric energy. In fact, it has become commonplace for people to eat calorie-wise foods and drinks or add artificial sweeteners rather than consume less of high-energy foods (i.e., small servings). Given the ubiquity of the "diet craze," many children may learn that the taste of food often predicts low energy value. Youngsters with such a dietary history may not effectively regulate their caloric intake over the course of a day—overeating at dinner, by failing to compensate for intake of palatable high-calorie snack foods during and after school. The best strategy, according to the researchers, is to keep diet foods away from youngsters and give them smaller portions of regular foods to avoid weight gain and obesity (Pierce et al., 2007).

Humans and Anorexia

The seemingly willful starvation of animals exposed to activity anorexia appears similar to cases of human anorexia. For humans, social reinforcement can increase the tendency to diet or exercise. An individual, especially a girl or woman, may learn to combine stringent dieting with excessive exercising in order to escape or avoid criticism for being overweight or to gain approval for being slim and fit (see Pierce & Epling, 1997, for an analysis of the social contingencies). The type and intensity of dieting and exercise are initially regulated by the reactions of other people to the change in body shape and size.

Once social reinforcement has encouraged food restriction, especially in the context of increasing exercise, the activity anorexia cycle would be initiated. When the process starts, the person may become trapped by the activity–food reduction cycle. People put themselves on diets for a variety of reasons. All diets do not generate excessive activity. The type, severity, and pattern of diet are important factors contributing to physical activity. For example, many anorexics change their meal pattern from several meals to one per day. This change in the number of meals may be important in generating activity anorexia (Kanarek & Collier, 1978).

Mandrusiak (2002) conducted a productive experiment in our laboratory at the University of Alberta. Using a foraging model, rats had to press a procurement lever to produce food on a second lever (the meal lever). Mandrusiak wanted to find out whether rats would self-starve without any imposed food restriction by the experimenter. The findings indicate that rats "choose" to starve when the procurement cost of meals is high (the number of responses required to gain an opportunity to eat a meal) and an opportunity for physical activity is available. Basically, the high cost of meals drives down the number of eating bouts per day (to one meal a day). Interestingly, the amount of food consumed during the meal does not compensate for the reduction in the number of eating bouts (no energy balance). The rat literally places itself on a restricted food schedule.

When self-imposed food restriction is combined with the opportunity for physical activity, the activity anorexia cycle is initiated and the animal will eventually die. The foraging model is another animal analog for human self-starvation (see also Belke, Pierce, & Duncan, 2006, for a behavioral economic model of activity anorexia). In humans, the cost of taking meals could include social contingencies based on appearance or alternative sources of reinforcement involving work, family, or school (Pierce & Epling, 1997). As the social costs of eating increase, people would self-impose food restriction and become physically active. The result would be that some people would inadvertently initiate the activity anorexia cycle.

Assessment, Treatment, and Prevention

The activity anorexia model has important practical implications. In their book, *Solving the Anorexia Puzzle: A Scientific Approach*, Epling and Pierce (1992) outline the criteria for assessment, treatment, and prevention of activity anorexia. In terms of assessment, the primary criteria involve a history of low and declining food intake, a history of excessive physical activity, and psychological symptoms that follow rather than precede weight loss. Epling and Pierce (1992) recommend treatment based on traditional behavior-modification programs for anorexia nervosa combined with family therapy, but treatment is directed at the responses that comprise the activity–anorexia cycle. For example, contingencies are arranged to stop excessive dieting and exercise. In addition, patients are taught how to eat and how to discriminate between moderate and excessive levels of exercise. A program that incorporates some of these features began in Sweden and is now available in San Diego, CA. The program, called the Mandometer Clinic for Eating Disorders, focuses on retraining of normal eating levels and restriction of physical activity. In addition the program has been evaluated for effectiveness by a randomized controlled trial, and 93% of the treated patients remained in remission after 1 year (Berg, Brodin, Lindberg, & Sodersten, 2002; Zandian, Ioakimidis, Bergh, & Sodersten, 2007).

Prevention of activity anorexia involves changing the sociocultural conditions that promote excessive dieting and exercising. Medical doctors are in the best position to call attention to the role of diet and exercise in the onset and maintenance of eating disorders. Self-help groups concerned with eating disorders may have members who recognize the biobehavioral processes involved in self-starvation. These groups can play an important role in preventing onset and relapse of activity anorexia. A second major function of self-help groups is education and social change. The groups may send speakers to schools, public meetings, and professional conferences. These groups may also lobby physicians, government agencies, private organizations, and public companies. Because of this active and organized involvement, self-help groups may be the most important source of prevention for activity anorexia.

ON THE APPLIED SIDE: MammaCare— Detection and Prevention of Breast Cancer

Over 250,000 American women developed breast cancer in 2010. The disease killed almost 40,000 women in 2009. Every woman is a potential victim, and about 12% of women will develop breast cancer at some time in their life. In addition to loss of life, victims of breast cancer often undergo surgery that may physically and emotionally disable them.

At present, doctors do not know how to prevent breast cancer, but early detection significantly improves a woman's chances of survival. Importantly, the victims of the disease are themselves almost always the first ones to detect the tumor. In most cases, however, women only detect the tumor after the cancer has reached an advanced stage. Regular and proficient self-examination by young women could substantially improve the detection of small tumors.

Surprisingly, a Canadian study by Baxter (2001) based on a summary of the literature concluded that teaching breast self-examination (BSE) to women aged 40–49 years has no benefits (in terms of detection of tumors or lowering death rates) and is actually harmful because women are constantly going to doctors based on false readings that result in increased tests for benign biopsies. This assessment is echoed by the U.S. Preventive Services Task Force (USPSTF), which recommends that women should not learn BSE (Nelson, Tyne, Naik, Bougatsos, Chan, & Humphrey, 2009). These conclusions about BSE are controversial (Larkin, 2001), with the American Cancer Society saying that it is a matter of individual choice, the American Medical Association recommending it with no age limits, and the USPSTF recommending that BSE should not be used (Allen, Van Groningen, Barksdale, & McCarthy, 2010). At the moment, women are best advised to consult with their family physician about BSE as a method to assist in cancer detection.

Often BSE programs use pamphlets, posters, and films to teach the requisite skills, but these educational aids alone are not enough, and are not effective. In a clinical trial of 266,064 Chinese women, some women were randomly assigned to receive intensive instruction in BSE and others did not receive instruction. Intensive instruction in BSE did not reduce mortality from breast cancer (Thomas, Gao, Ray, Wang, Allison, Chen et al., 2002). There is reason to believe, however, that a strict behavioral approach to BSE would fare much better—but a controlled clinical trial of the behavioral approach has not been conducted, and is unlikely in the near future (Saslow, Hannan, Osuch, Alciati, Baines, Barton et al., 2004).

In this section, we outline a rigorous behavioral technology of BSE for women to use at home to detect small irregularities in breast tissue. The behavioral approach relies on detection by touch, but fingers and feel alone cannot distinguish between cancerous lesions and benign tumors—a biopsy of the lump is necessary for diagnosis. Women who use the "fingers and feel" technology would identify small lumps and report them to a physician, who would make the decision about obtaining a biopsy. Here we describe the behavioral technology for BSE and how to obtain this training. In addition to BSE, we address the extension of the behavioral technology to a computer-based system for clinical breast examination (CBE) funded by the National Science Foundation (NSF), teaching clinicians how to perform clinical breast exams to detect lumps and save lives (National Science Foundation, 2011).

The MammaCare Program

Dr. Henry S. Pennypacker (Figure 13.14) and his associates at the University of Florida developed a strict behavioral program, which they called MammaCare, to teach women effective self-examination of their breasts (Hall, Adams, Stein, Stephenson, Goldstein, & Pennypacker, 1980; Pennypacker, Bloom, Criswell, Neelakantan, Goldstein, & Stein, 1982). He began to work on this program because:

> *Like many before me, I took a degree in classical experimental psychology and began an academic career. I rapidly became uncomfortable with the hypocrisy inherent in my position: I was an "expert" in learning using none of my expertise in my work. My interest turned to education at all levels, partly because of the critical role it plays in the survival and evolution of the culture and partly because it looked like an easy place to make a contribution. How wrong I was! . . . [W]ith hindsight . . . I have a better understanding of the problems we face and general strategies needed to solve them. MammaCare is a step in that direction.*
>
> *(H. S. Pennypacker, personal communication, 22 February 1989)*

*The **MammaCare program** is based on the assumption that women are often unable to detect small tumors simply because they have not been trained to do so. The pressure receptors of the fingertips allow for subtle discrimination of surface contour (e.g., from smooth to bumpy), as is clearly demonstrated by blind people who read Braille. It follows that women may be trained to detect small lesions in the breast related to cancerous tumors. An effective program must teach women to tell the difference between small tumors and the normal lumpiness of the breast itself.*

FIG. 13.14   Dr. Henry S. Pennypacker, of MammaCare, who conducted much of the research on breast self-examination (BSE) by palpation and search, using silicone breast models to train this skillful and complex behavior. Published with permission.

Components of MammaCare

An initial step involves discrimination training. The patient is trained to use the tactile sensors of the pads of her middle three fingers to discriminate lesions of varying size and texture from ordinary nodules in the breast. This training is accomplished with a series of silicone breast models, progressively increasing in difficulty of detection, that have been developed to match the physical properties of real breast tissue (Bloom, Criswell, Pennypacker, Catania, & Adams, 1982; Hall et al., 1980). A woman uses her fingers to palpate (examine by touch) the breast model to detect lumps of different size and hardness, located at various depths, and varying in lateral mobility. Detection of lumps functions as reinforcement that maintains searching for and reporting on irregularities in the breast tissue.

Once the patient is able to detect small lumps (e.g., with a diameter of 0.3 mm) with her fingertips, she is taught additional palpation and search skills (Saunders, Pilgram, & Penny-packer, 1986). A vertical strips pattern of search is used because it gives greater success in detection when compared with concentric circles or radial spokes patterns (Saunders et al., 1986). The target of these procedures is to ensure that a woman's fingers contact a maximum volume of breast tissue during self-examination. In this phase, the woman learns palpation and search on her own breast while being carefully evaluated by a trained professional. A patient must be at least 95% proficient before leaving the training center. This level of proficiency helps to ensure that self-examination techniques become an integrated skill that may be practiced monthly as recommended.

A final component of the program ensures maintenance of self-examination by reinforced practice. After MammaCare training, each woman is given a take-home kit which contains a breast model that is matched to the firmness and nodularity of her own breast tissue. This breast model is used to update the patient's tactile skill just before she carries out the monthly self-examination. The practice model contains five small tumor simulations that the patient can find only if she performs the examination correctly. Based on this reinforced practice, a woman who finds nothing unusual during a breast examination can be almost certain that there was nothing there to detect.

Effectiveness of the Program

Women who learn the MammaCare method of breast self-examination are able to detect lesions as small as 0.3 mm in diameter. This compares favorably with the average tumor that women discover by accident, measuring 3.6 cm in diameter (the size of a ping pong ball). It also compares well with conventional BSE, in which women detect tumors in the 2.0-cm range. Evidence also shows that training in self-examination improves detection in actual breast tissue (Pennypacker et al., 1982, pp. 109–110). The effectiveness of a behavioral system of BSE lies in the fact that the program directly teaches women what to feel for and how to search their breasts thoroughly. The value of the behavioral approach is that it allows for early detection of minute breast lumps in women who are asymptomatic and are younger than 40 years of age, when mammograms are recommended (Saslow et al., 2004).

The MammaCare program is now available to a greater number of women at a lower cost at training centers in the USA and Europe (for further information, write to The MammaCare Corporation, 930 NW 8th Ave., Gainesville, FL 32601, or visit www.mammacare.com). A woman uses the breast models to master the self-examination skills, and is asked to perform a portion of the breast exam in the presence of a trained professional instructor, who corrects any problems.

Clinical Breast Examination and the P.A.D. Simulator-Trainer

The MammaCare system has other applications. One of these is to teach physicians and other health professionals the palpation method of clinical breast examination (CBE) to a certified level of performance (Pennypacker, Naylor, Sander, & Goldstein, 1999; Trapp, Kottke, Viekrant, Kaur, & Sellers, 1999). With the support of the National Science Foundation, Mark Goldstein (founder and Chairman of MammaCare Corporation) developed the CBE simulator-trainer (see Figure 13.15). The trainer uses the Palpation Assessment and Training Device (P.A.D.) as well as a computer-based system to provide visual feedback and instruction by "Hally," a computer-generated female voice (after the HAL computer from the science-fiction movie 2001: A Space Odyssey). The P.A.D. simulator-trainer uses electronic sensors and computer feedback, but is based on the same shaping and stimulus control procedures that characterized the original MammaCare training method (see video at www.nsf. gov/news/news_summ.jsp?cntn_id=122294). Four breast models of increasing complexity are placed sequentially on the P.A.D. as clinicians are trained to palpate the breast, search for subtle breast abnormalities, and transfer this learning to breast examinations of actual patients.

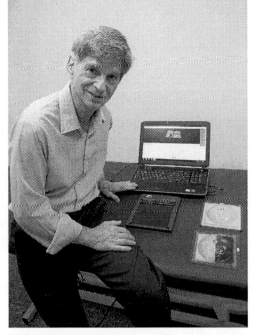

FIG. 13.15   Mark Goldstein, the founder and Chairman of MammaCare Corporation. Dr. Goldstein is shown with the P.A.D. simulator-trainer used to train clinical breast examination (CBE) by physicians and other health professionals. Published with permission.

Figure 13.16 shows the CBE simulator-trainer with a breast model situated on the P.A.D. and the visual feedback presented on the computer screen. The tactile sensors (transducers) of the P.A.D. locate and register each palpation at more than 1000 levels of pressure within a spatial resolution of 3 mm. The instructional software records and interprets the sensitivity and specificity of the clinician's performance as computer-generated feedback shapes, and confirms their palpation and search skills. The CBE simulator/trainer produces and records the complete repertoire of examination skills, including breast lesion detection, tissue coverage, search pattern completeness, and performance of the required range of palpation pressures—allowing for CBE standard certification of the clinician.

The MammaCare system for breast self-examination (BSE) and certified clinical breast examination (CBE) represents a state-of-the-art development in behavioral technology. Laboratory-based principles of operant conditioning have been systematically extended to an analysis of the detection of lesions in breast tissue. The analysis indicated that the critical operant behavior of palpation could be rigorously defined, allowing for the design of programmed contingencies of reinforcement. The programmed contingencies are used to train the requisite behavior of palpation and searching of breast tissue, systematically shaping performance of increasing complexity. Refinement of the contingencies in applied settings has

FIG. 13.16 A series of realistic breast models are placed on the Palpation Assessment and Training Device (P.A.D.), which is integrated with computer software to provide visual feedback (via a computer screen) on the trainee's palpation and search for lesions or tumors. The National Science Foundation helped to fund the development of this behavioral technology used at 23 Veterans Administration Hospitals in the United States. Dr. Mark Goldstein, the founder and Chairman of MammaCare Corporation, provided the photograph and conducted much of the research on the P.A.D. system of clinical breast examination. Published with permission.

allowed for the development of the CBE simulator-trainer, bringing together behavior principles, behavior technology, and computer-based systems to aid in the battle against breast cancer and improve the survival of women.

CHAPTER SUMMARY

This chapter has presented many examples of applied behavior analysis. Issues of observer reliability, irreversibility of treatment and multiple baseline designs, and fluency and rate as dependent measures were highlighted. We emphasize a focus on behavior and its functions, such as gaining attention for self-abusive behavior. The behavioral approach to therapy involves direct interventions on the problem behavior by manipulating the environment, as illustrated by voucher-based contingency management of drug abuse and addiction. Applied behavior analysts reject appeals to cognitive processes in favor of changing the world in which people live.

Several systematic educational programs were described that have shown profound improvements in student achievement. For decades, precision teaching and PSI have produced superior pupil progress, but these approaches are largely ignored in mainstream education. Applications of behavior principles have also been used to educate autistic children, helping many of them to enter the regular educational system. Private schools and programs such as the ABC school have flourished by producing positive behavior improvement.

The eating disorder of anorexia has been the subject of extensive behavior analysis using the animal model of activity anorexia. Much has come from this work, leading to specific recommendations for treating and preventing this dangerous human condition. We also reviewed new research on conditioned overeating and its implications for childhood obesity. Finally, we described a program for self-detection of breast cancer and clinical breast examination by physicians and health-care professionals. This successful venture illustrates the use of behavior principles in health and medicine, indicating that applied behavior analysts are making important contributions to human welfare.

KEY WORDS

Activity anorexia

Activity-induced taste aversion

Applied behavior analysis

Behavior maintenance

Behavior trapping

Behavioral contract

Behavioral medicine

Celeration

Changing criterion design

Conditioned overeating

Contingency management

Differential reinforcement of alternative
    behavior (DRA)

Differential reinforcement of other
    behavior (DRO)

Duration recording

Early intensive behavioral intervention
(EIBI)

Fluency

Internal validity

Interval recording

Maturation

MammaCare program

Maturation

Multiple baseline design (across behaviors;
    across settings; across subjects)

Personalized system of instruction (PSI)

Precision teaching

Reliability of observation

Response generalization

Self-control

Time sampling

ON THE WEB

www.bacb.com Do you want to become a certified behavior analyst? Go to this website to get more information on the steps and examinations involved. The Behavior Analyst Certification Board is a nonprofit corporation established as a result of credentialing needs identified by behavior analysts, state governments, and consumers of behavior analysis services.

www.mammacare.com To find out more about the behavioral approach to breast self-examination or clinical breast examination, go to the MammaCare website.

www.nsf.gov/news/news_summ.jsp?cntn_id=122294 The National Science Foundation funded the P.A.D. simulator-trainer for clinical breast examination by clinicians. This video describes the development of this behavioral technology by Mark Goldstein and the scientists at Mamma-Care, and how it is being used to save lives by providing training in palpation and search of breast tissue.

http://rsaffran.tripod.com/aba.html This website contains a collection of Internet resources for parents of children with autism and related disorders, based on applied behavior analysis. It provides help in finding service providers and private schools, and information about parental experiences, intervention principles, and much more.

www.abcreal.com This website provides more information about the ABC school of autism and Applied Behavioral Consultants, Inc. It also has a video presentation of the treatment program based on early intensive behavioral intervention, PECS, and the verbal behavior approach.

www.iaba.com This is the website of the Institute for Applied Behavior Analysis in southern California, which offers behavioral management services, and supported educational and employment services to people with developmental disabilities.

 BRIEF QUIZ

1. Applied behavior analysis is a field of study that focuses on the application of the _____, methods, and procedures of the science of behavior.

    (a) equations
    (b) principles
    (c) research
    (d) findings

2. In terms of a behavioral contract, the details usually specify:

    (a) what is expected of the client
    (b) the level of attention required
    (c) the consequences that follow behavior
    (d) both (a) and (c)

3. What is behavior trapping?

    (a) the fact that animal behavior leads to trapping by hunters
    (b) Don Baer got trapped by a behavioral contingency
    (c) new behavior is trapped by the natural contingencies
    (d) an attempt to overcome the traps that our behavior causes

4. Which of the following are multiple baseline designs?

    (a) multiple baseline across stimulus condition
    (b) multiple baseline across subjects
    (c) multiple baseline across behaviors
    (d) all of the above

5. In the treatment of drug use and addiction, contingency management involves:

    (a) the use of fading medical testing
    (b) the use of vouchers contingent on abstinence
    (c) the use of contingent attention
    (d) the use of reinforcement of alternative behavior

6. Fred Keller wrote a seminal article on college teaching called _____.

   (a) "Farewell to college education"
   (b) "Good-bye, teacher . . ."
   (c) "Keller on teaching"
   (d) "So long to higher education"

7. Belles and Bradlyn (1987) conducted a stop smoking study using a _____ design.

   (a) multiple baseline across subjects
   (b) A–B–A–B reversal
   (c) changing criterion
   (d) factorial

8. Level 1 of the ABC school program for autistic children involves:

   (a) teaching of "splinter skills" to able students
   (b) teaching of stimulus generalization to those who are advanced
   (c) training and generalization of social skills, especially with parents
   (d) discrete trials of stimulus, response, and reinforcement

9. In conditioned taste aversion induced by wheel running, _____ is the US and _____ is the CS.

   (a) wheel running; distinctive flavor
   (b) distinctive flavor; wheel running
   (c) wheel running; drug
   (d) drug; distinctive taste

10. Which of the following is a component of the MammaCare system for breast self-examination?

    (a) discrimination training
    (b) finger-tip utilization
    (c) palpation and search skills
    (d) both (a) and (c)

Answers to Brief Quiz: 1, b (p. 400); 2, d (p. 402); 3, c (p. 404); 4, d (p. 405); 5, b (p. 411); 6, a (p. 415); 7, c (p. 419); 8, d (p. 422); 9, a (p. 427); 10, d (p. 432).

Three Levels of Selection: Biology, Behavior, and Culture

14

1. Explore evolution, natural selection, and contingencies of survival.
2. Learn about the genetic and operant control of behavior in the marine snail, *Aplysia*.
3. Discover how operant conditioning furthered the survival and reproductive success of organisms, including humans.
4. Find out how the operant regulation of verbal behavior contributed to the transmission of cultural practices.
5. Inquire about innovation and cultural evolution based on variation and selection at the behavioral and cultural levels.

Behavioral researchers have suggested that **selection by consequences** is the operating principle for biology, behavior, and culture (e.g., McDowell, 2004; Pierce & Epling, 1997; Skinner, 1981). It is a general form of causation that goes beyond the push–pull mechanistic Newtonian model of physics (Hull, Langman, & Glen, 2001). In terms of biology (level 1), selection by consequences involves natural selection or the selection of genes based upon reproductive success. At the level of behavior (level 2), selection by consequences is described by the principle of reinforcement—the selection of operant behavior by the effects that it produces. A third level of selection occurs in terms of culture (level 3 or cultural selection). Cultural practices (ways of doing things) are selected by macro-level consequences for the group involving greater efficiency, lower costs, and higher likelihood of survival.

In this chapter, selection by consequences is examined at the genetic, behavioral, and cultural levels (see Figure 14.1). In showing the parallels

CONTINGENCY OF SURVIVAL

Ecological environment $\bullet$ Genotype $\longrightarrow$ Benefits/costs for reproduction

[In a specific habitat, species characteristics resulting from differences in genotype produce more (or less) reproductive success—process is natural selection]

CONTINGENCY OF REINFORCEMENT

Situation $\vdots$ Operant $\longrightarrow$ Reinforcement/ punishment

[In a specific situation, a particular response from an operant class produces reinforcement (or extinction) that increases (or decreases) the rate of occurrence of the operant—process is reinforcement]

METACONTINGENCY

Technological environment $\bullet$ Cultural practice $\longrightarrow$ Benefits/costs for survival of group

[In a specific technological environment, a particular kind of cultural practice produces outcomes for the group that increase (or decrease) the practice—process of cultural selection]

FIG. 14.1 Selection by consequences operates at three levels: biology, behavior, and culture.

among these different levels, behavior analysts seek to integrate the study of behavior with biology on the one hand and the social sciences on the other. The attempt is not to reduce behavior to biology, or culture to behavior. Rather, it is to show the common underpinnings of all life science in terms of the extension and elaboration of basic principles.

LEVEL 1: EVOLUTION AND NATURAL SELECTION

The evolutionary history of a species, or **phylogeny**, is the outcome of natural selection. Darwin (1859) showed how organisms change in accord with this principle (Figure 14.2). Based on a thorough analysis of life forms, Darwin concluded that reproductive success was the underlying basis of evolution. That is, individuals with more children pass on a greater number of their characteristics to the next generation.

Darwin noticed structural differences among members of sexually reproducing species. Except for identical (monozygotic) twins, individuals in the population vary in their physical features. Thus, birds like the thrush show variation in color of plumage, length of wings, and thickness of beak. Based on differences in their features, some individuals in a population are more successful than others at surviving and producing offspring. Differences in reproductive success occur when certain members of a species possess attributes that make them more likely to survive and reproduce in a given environment. Generally, individuals with features that meet the survival requirements of a habitat produce more offspring than others. As the number of descendants with those features increases, the genetic traits of these individuals are more frequently represented in the population. If there is a fecundity (surplus) of individuals produced and there exists even small variability between individuals, those with the most fit characteristics will be selected and hence multiply. This process of differential reproduction is called **natural selection**, and the change in the genetic make-up of the species is **evolution**.

FIG. 14.2   Charles Darwin in his later years. Darwin discovered the principle of natural selection. Reprinted with permission from the Archives of the History of American Psychology, Center for the History of Psychology, The University of Akron.

Contingencies of Survival

From a behavioral viewpoint, natural selection involves **contingencies of survival** (Skinner, 1986). The habitat or environment inadvertently sets requirements for survival of individuals. Members of a species who exhibit features and behavior appropriate to the contingencies survive and reproduce. Those with less appropriate characteristics have fewer offspring and their genetic line may become extinct. Natural selection therefore occurs as particular organisms satisfy (or fail to satisfy) the contingencies of survival.

An important implication of a contingency analysis of evolution is that the requirements for survival and reproductive success may change gradually or suddenly. For example, during the time of the dinosaurs, the collision of a large asteroid with the earth may have drastically changed climate, fauna, and temperature of the planet in a very brief time (e.g., Alvarez, 1982; Alvarez, Alvarez, Asaro, &

Michel, 1980; Alvarez, Asaro & Michel, 1980; Alvarez, Asaro, Michel, & Alvarez, 1982). Given these changes in environmental contingencies, dinosaurs could not survive. However, the smaller mammals, which possessed features more appropriate to the new habitat, survived and reproduced. Changes in the contingencies due to large-scale disasters may, therefore, occasionally favor characteristics that have advantages in a changed environment. This would occur even though these characteristics may have been a disadvantage in the past (see Gould, 1989, 2002, for a punctuated-equilibrium view of evolution; see Dawkins, 1976, 1996, 2004, for a discussion of gradual genetic selection).

Phenotype, Genotype, and Environment

Evolutionary biologists distinguish between phenotype and genotype. An organism's **phenotype** refers to all the characteristics observed during the lifetime of an individual. For example, an individual's size, color, and shape are anatomical aspects of phenotype. Behavioral features include taste preferences, aggressiveness, shyness, and so on. Different phenotypic attributes of individuals may or may not reflect underlying genetic variation.

The **genotype** refers to the actual genetic make-up of the organism. Some observable characteristics are largely determined by genotype, while other features are strongly influenced by experience. However, as shown in Figure 14.3, most result from an interaction between genes and environment. Thus, the height of a person is attributable to both genes and nutrition. Evolution only occurs when the phenotypic differences among individuals are based on differences in genotype. If differences in height or other features did not result from genetic differences, selection for tallness (or shortness) could not occur. This is because there would be no genes for height to pass on to the next generation. People who engage in bodybuilding by lifting weights and taking steroids may substantially increase their muscle size (phenotype), but this characteristic will not be passed on to their children; it is not heritable. Natural selection can only work when there are genes that underlie physical features.

Sources of Genetic Variation

There are two major sources of heritable genetic variation: sexual recombination of existing genes and mutation. Genetic differences among individuals arise from sexual reproduction. This is because the blending of male and female genes produces an enormous number of random combinations. Although sexual recombination produces variation, the number of genetic combinations is constrained by the existing pool of genes. In other words, there is a finite number of genes in a population, and this determines the amount of variation caused by sexual reproduction.

Mutation occurs when the genetic material (e.g., genes or chromosomes) of an individual changes. These changes are accidents that affect the genetic code carried by an ovum or sperm. For example, naturally occurring background radiation may alter a gene site, or a chromosome may break during the formation of sex cells or gametes. Such mutations are passed on to offspring, who display new characteristics. In most instances, mutations produce physical features that work against an organism's survival and reproductive success.

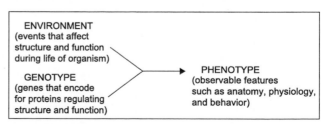

FIG. 14.3 Phenotype is a product of genotype and environment.

However, on rare occasions mutations produce traits that improve reproductive success. The importance of mutation is that it is the source of new genetic variation. All novel genetic differences are ultimately based on mutation.

Natural selection depends on genetic variation based on sexual recombination and mutation. Genes code for proteins, which in turn regulate embryonic development and structural form. This means that differences in genes result in phenotypic differences in the structure (e.g., size and form of the brain) and physiology (e.g., release of hormones) of organisms. Selection occurs when specific genes underlying these phenotypic features contribute to fitness. Individuals with such characteristics have more offspring, ensuring that their genes occur at a higher frequency in the next generation.

GENETIC REGULATION OF BEHAVIOR

Behavioral Rigidity

As we have noted, the behavior of organisms is always a phenotypic expression of genes and environment. Genes closely regulate some behavioral characteristics, and in such instances the environment plays a subsidiary role. For example, in some species, defense of territory occurs as a ritualized sequence of behavior called a fixed-action pattern (e.g., Tinbergen, 1951). The sequence or chain is set off by a specific stimulus, and the component responses are repeated almost identically with each presentation of the stimulus (see Chapter 3). The behavior pattern is based on a "genetic blueprint", and the environment simply initiates the sequence.

For example, the male stickleback fish will aggressively defend its territory from male intruders during the mating season. The fish shows a fixed sequence of threatening actions that are elicited by the red underbelly of an intruding male. Tinbergen (1951) showed that this fixed-action pattern occurred even to cigar-shaped pieces of wood that had a red patch painted on the bottom (see Chapter 3). In addition, he showed that a male intruder with its red patch hidden did not evoke the threatening sequence. Generally, the male stickleback is genetically programmed to carry out the attack sequence given a specific stimulus at a particular moment in time.

FOCUS ON: Genetic Control of a Fixed-Action Pattern

Richard Scheller, a geneticist at Stanford University and currently vice president of Research and Development at Genentech, and Richard Axel, a biochemist at the Howard Hughes Medical Institute and University Professor at Columbia University, reported on the genetic control of a complex behavioral sequence. Scheller and Axel (1984) used recombinant DNA technology to isolate a subset of gene locations that control the egg-laying sequence of the marine snail (*Aplysia*).

Recombinant DNA technology is beyond the scope of this book, but the important thing is that these procedures can be used to identify gene sites that encode for specific neuropeptides. In the experiment by Scheller and Axel (1984), the researchers isolated a set of gene sites that coordinated the release of several peptides. These chemicals caused neurological changes that invariably produced the egg-laying sequence (see also Hermann, de Lange, Pieneman, ter Maat, & Jansen, 1997, on genetic control of egg-laying in the great pond snail, *Lymnaea stagnalis*).

Using techniques of genetic manipulation, Scheller and Axel were able to "turn on" the gene sites that controlled a complex and integrated sequence of behavior. In this sequence, the snail first contracts the muscles of the reproductive duct and expels a string of egg cases. Next, the animal grasps the egg string in its mouth and waves its head, behavior that typically functions to remove eggs from the duct. It then attaches the tangle of string to a solid surface. This behavioral sequence is shown in Figure 14.4. The fixed-action pattern was activated in an unmated snail by direct manipulation of the egg-laying hormone (ELH) gene.

The DNA sequences that control egg laying may play an important role in other aspects of this animal's behavior. For example, the genetic material that encodes for head-waving behavior may be duplicated and appear in other genes that regulate feeding (Sossin, Kirk, & Scheller, 1987). In this regard, Scheller and Axel suggested:

FIG. 14.4   The egg-laying sequence of the marine snail (*Aplysia*). The sequence involves (1) expelling a string of egg cases, (2) grasping the egg string by the mouth, (3) waving the head to draw the string out of the duct, and (4) affixing a triangle of string to a solid substance. This behavior was elicited by genetic procedures that activated the gene coding for egg-laying hormone (ELH) and other peptides associated with egg-laying behavior. Reproduced from "How genes control innate behavior," by R. H. Scheller and R. Axel, 1984, *Scientific American, 250*, 54–62. © 1984 Estate of Ikuyo Tagawa Garbar. Reprinted with permission.

> The same peptide may be incorporated in several different precursors encoded by different genes. Consider head waving in *Aplysia*. A characteristic waving of the snail's head takes place during feeding as well as during egg laying. The same peptide or peptides could elicit the same behavioral component (head waving) in two very different contexts. To this end the head-waving peptide (or peptides) may be encoded in some other gene—one implicated in feeding behavior—as well as the ELH gene. In this way complex behaviors could be assembled by the combination of simple units of behavior, each unit mediated by one peptide or a small number of peptides.
>
> (Scheller & Axel, 1984, p. 62)

When environments were stable and predictable, the replication of the same DNA sequence in a new genetic context may be one way in which organisms evolved complex behavior (see also the role of gonadotropin-releasing hormone (GnRH) in the control of complex behavior and locomotion of *Aplysia*, but not in its reproduction; Sun & Tsai, 2011). This solution involves using the same genetic code in different combinations. Although a high level of behavioral complexity may be achieved in this manner, the resulting behavior is tightly controlled by the underlying genetic context.

Some forms of animal communication are strongly influenced by genotype. For example, the waggle dance of the honey bee is a highly ritualized sequence of behavior, under genetic control (Johnson,

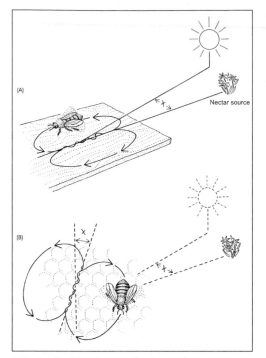

FIG. 14.5   The dance of a honey bee illustrates a phylogenetic form of communication in animals. When the bee returns from a nectar source, the dance begins with the insect waggling its abdomen. The number of waggles and direction of movement control the flight pattern of other bees that observe the performance. The orientation of the food source, relative to the current position of the sun, is also indicated by the waggle dance. From *Animal Behavior: An Evolutionary Approach*, p. 207, by J. Alcock, 1989, Sinauer Associates, Sunderland, MA. © 1989 Sinauer Associates, Inc. Reprinted with permission.

Oldroyd, Barron, & Crozier, 2002), that guides the travel of other bees (see Figure 14.5) (Frisch, 1967), and varies with the particular habitats in which honey bees evolved (Dornhaus & Chittka, 2004). After abundant foraging, a bee returns to the hive and begins to dance while other bees observe the performance in the hive in the dark. Subsequently, the bees that observe the dance fly directly to the foraging area in a so-called beeline. However, stimulus control by the waggle dance is not entirely rigid, as experienced successful foragers follow dances just briefly, perhaps to confirm that the flowers are still yielding forage (Biesmeijer & Seeley, 2005).

The position of the sun with respect to food plays an important role in determining the initial dance. A bee may dance for several hours, and during this time the dance changes. These behavioral changes occur as the position of the sun with respect to food is altered by the rotation of the earth. That is, the bee's dancing corrects for the fact that the sun rises and falls over the course of a day.

The survival value of the dance relates to increased food supply for the hive. One problem is accounting for the occurrence of the dance before other bees responded to it—that is, before the dance had survival value. Presumably, the distance and direction that bees traveled had some effect on their behavior. Signs of fatigue and phototropic movements may have varied with distance and the position of the sun when they returned.

Bees that evolved sensitivity to what others did could respond to these aspects of behavior—relying on genes that coded for specific neurochemicals. Over time, natural selection favored variations in phototropic (and other) movements that made honey-bee dancing more effective. Foraging bees would dance in conspicuous ways that allowed other bees to travel more accurately to the food source (for a similar analysis, see Skinner, 1986, p. 116).

Fixed-action patterns and the communication of bees are examples of behavior that is predominantly regulated by genes and is usually termed species-specific. In both instances, complex sequences of behavior are activated by specific stimuli and carried out in a highly ritualized manner. As shown in Figure 14.6, this form of behavior regulation was selected when the habitat of an animal was relatively stable and predictable.

Behavioral Flexibility

When organisms were faced with unpredictable and changing environments, natural selection favored **behavioral flexibility**—that is, adjusting one's behavior on the basis of past experience (alternatively, behavioral flexibility may have allowed for radiation and exploitation of novel environments; Leal & Powell, 2012). In this case, genes played a subsidiary role, coding for general processes of learning. These processes allowed an organism to adjust to changing environmental requirements throughout its life span (see Davies, Krebs, & West, 2012, pp. 18–20, on phenotypic or behavioral plasticity related to climate change and breeding times). Flexibility of behavior in turn contributed to the reproductive success of the organism. Skinner noted the reproductive advantage of behavioral flexibility:

> Reproduction under a much wider range of conditions became possible with the evolution of two processes through which individual organisms acquired behavior appropriate to novel environments. Through respondent (Pavlovian) conditioning, responses paired in advance by natural selection could come under the control of new stimuli. Through operant conditioning, new responses could be strengthened (reinforced) by events which immediately followed them.
>
> (Skinner, 1984b, p. 477)

In other words, respondent and operant conditioning are processes that are themselves genetically determined.

There is evidence for the selection of conditioning. Hirsch and McCauley (1977) showed that the blowfly, *Phormia regina*, could be classically conditioned and that the process of conditioning was heritable. Blowflies can be trained to extend their proboscis (or snout) whenever water is applied to their feet, if they are given sugar that is paired with foot wetting. Even though this conditioned reflex is learned, the process of establishing the reflex can be modified dramatically by artificial selection. Flies varied in the number of elicited responses to the conditioned stimulus on trials 8–15, and were assigned a conditioning score between 0 and 8. Subjects with higher conditioning scores were selected and mated with each other, as were subjects with lower scores. A control group of flies was mated independent of their conditioning scores.

As shown in Figure 14.7, over seven generations, flies selected for conditioning showed increasingly more conditioned responses on test trials than their ancestors. When conditioning was selected against, each generation of flies showed less conditioned responses than the previous population. Flies that were mated regardless of conditioning scores (control) did not show a change over generations. At the end of seven generations, there was no overlap in the distribution of conditioning scores for the three groups— indicating that selection resulted in three separate populations of flies.

The experiment by Hirsch and McCauley (1977) demonstrates that conditioning of a specific reflex has a range of variability. Based on this variation, selection can enhance the process of conditioning or eliminate it for distinct behavioral units. From a behavioral view, contingencies of survival continually mold the degree of behavioral flexibility of organisms—extending (or removing) the process of conditioning to a wide range of responses (see also Lofdahl, Holliday, & Hirsch, 1992, on selective breeding of excitatory conditionability in the fruit fly, *Drosophila melanogaster*).

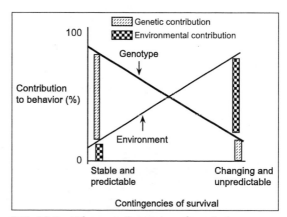

FIG. 14.6 When contingencies of survival are relatively stable and predictable, genetic regulation of behavior is predominant (e.g., fixed-action patterns) and the environment plays a subsidiary role. As contingencies of survival become more uncertain, the role played by the environment and conditioning increases, while direct genetic regulation of behavior declines.

The presence of genetic variation for learning ability in animals opens the way for experiments asking how and under what ecological conditions improved conditioning should evolve. Mery and Kawecki (2002) investigated the experimental evolution of learning ability in *Drosophila melanogaster*. Over 51 generations, experimental populations of flies were exposed to conditions favoring associative conditioning of oviposition substrate choice (choice of a medium—pineapple vs. orange—on which to lay eggs). Flies that learned to associate a chemical stimulus (quinine) with a particular substrate, and still avoided this medium several hours after the stimulus had been removed, were selected for breeding. After 15 generations of selection, the experimental populations showed a marked ability to avoid laying eggs on substrates that had contained the quinine stimulus several hours earlier. The improved conditioned avoidance was also observed when the flies were faced with a choice between novel substrates. Generally, the study demonstrates that these behavioral changes are caused by artificial selection for rate of learning and retention of the avoidance response following removal of the aversive stimulus (better remembering). One implication is that natural selection would produce similar changes in conditioning ability and response retention in the everyday world of organisms.

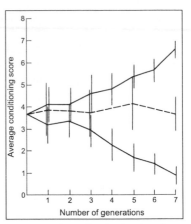

FIG. 14.7   Artificial selection for respondent conditioning in the blowfly, *Phormia regina*, reported by Hirsch and McCauley (1977). Flies mated for high-conditioning scores (solid upward-sloping line) showed more conditioned responses over generations than flies that were randomly paired (broken line). Other flies that were mated on the basis of low-conditioning scores (solid downward-sloping line) did progressively worse than their ancestors. From "Successful replication of, and selective breeding for, classical conditioning in the blowfly (*Phorma regina*)," by J. Hirsch and L. McCauley, 1977, *Animal Behaviour, 25*, 784–785. © 1977 Elsevier. Reprinted with permission.

Evolution, Behavioral Flexibility, and Body Form

The Cambrian explosion of animal life around 530 million years ago is probably the most spectacular diversification in evolutionary history (Figure 14.8), and there is evidence for the hypothesis that one of the key factors driving this great diversification in life forms was associative learning (Ginsburg & Jablonka, 2010). According to the hypothesis, the evolution of associative learning required only small modifications

FIG. 14.8   A depiction of the Cambrian explosion around 530 million years ago, involving the relatively rapid appearance of the major animal phyla (divisions) as found in the fossil record. Evidence indicates that until around 580 million years ago, most organisms were simple cells living in colonies. Then, over a period of about 70 to 80 million years, the rate of evolution increased exponentially and the diversity of life forms began to approximate those of today. Photograph by D. W. Miller. Published with permission.

in already evolved neural mechanisms. Once the basic conditioning mechanisms appeared on the evolutionary scene, associative learning enabled animals to exploit new niches, promoted new types of behavior related to predation, and led to adaptive responses fixed through genetic accommodation processes. Ginsburg and Jablonka explained that:

> Organisms with . . . associative learning had an enormous selective advantage: they were able to adapt ontogenetically to a variety of biotic and abiotic environments and to use new resources. Their learnt behaviors guided where and how they looked for food and protection, how they sought mates, how they reacted to predators and to competitors, and were fundamental to the construction of the niches that they and their offspring inhabited. . . . For example, if an animal learnt that food is usually available in a particular area and consequently it tended to stay and reproduce there, its offspring would have the same learning environment and learning opportunities. Natural selection would then favor any physiological or morphological features that improved adaptation to this learning environment. The explosion of new behaviors and new ecological opportunities that followed the evolution of associative learning would have been accompanied by an explosion of new, matching, morphological adaptations.
>
> (Ginsburg & Jablonka, 2010, p. 15)

Thus, one possibility is that natural selection for associative learning drove the evolution of animal morphology or body forms, a proposition contrary to the traditional biological view that form determines function (learning).

LEVEL 2: SELECTION BY REINFORCEMENT

The evolution of operant behavior allowed variation and selection to work throughout the lifetime of an organism. Many organisms evolved genetic programs that coded for operant processes. For some species, natural selection ensured that operant processes were extended to more and more aspects of behavior. Individuals who inherited an extensive capacity for operant conditioning could adjust to complex and changing, often social, situations on the basis of behavioral consequences. Selection by reinforcement therefore became a major mode of adaptation (Glenn & Field, 1994).

Evolution and Behavioral Dynamics

McDowell (2010) outlined an evolutionary theory of behavioral dynamics built on the idea that behavior is selected by its consequences. The theory uses three rules—a selection rule, a reproduction rule, and a mutation rule—to generate expected adaptive behavior in single and concurrent operant situations. Predictions of the theory are then compared with the distribution of responses by live animals (e.g., pigeons). To implement the theory, each behavior in the population of potential behaviors is represented by a 10-bit string of 0s and 1s, extending from [0000000000] to [1111111111]. The 10-bit string is the behavior's *genotype* that can be decoded into a decimal integer between 0 (all 0s) and 1023 (all 1s) that identifies the particular behavior and is conceptually its *phenotype*. In a random draw of 100 potential behaviors from the population of permissible phenotypes (0 to 1023), only a particular range or set of values would succeed in generating reinforcement. For example, all behaviors in the range 513 to 641 (operant class) could potentially operate a lever to produce reinforcement, although each behavior (e.g., phenotype 523) is unique in its topography or some other property.

Once a randomly selected behavior is emitted, a new population of potential behaviors is generated using 100 pairs of parent behaviors. For example, a father behavior might be the integer 235

[0011101011] and the mother behavior could be the integer 115 [0001110011]. The method of choosing parents depends on whether the emitted behavior was reinforced. If the emitted behavior is reinforced, the parent behaviors are chosen in accord with the theory's *selection rule* (not outlined here). If the emitted behavior is not reinforced, parent behaviors are chosen at random. After the parent behaviors have been chosen, each mother–father pair is mated in accord with a *reproduction rule* yielding a child behavior 123 [**0001111011**] with a 10-bit string composed of bits (0s and 1s) taken from the father behavior (in bold type) and other bits taken from the mother behavior. *Mutation* may also occur, as when the child behavior phenotype 123 is changed to 115 by a random change in the 7th bit from 1 to 0 yielding the string [0001110011]. Using the three rules of selection, reproduction, and mutation, the evolutionary theory is used to generate the adaptive behavior of a virtual (computer-generated) organism that can be compared with the actual behavior of organisms in operant settings. Other aspects of the theory and its implementation are beyond the scope of this book.

McDowell's evolutionary theory of behavioral dynamics fits quantitatively with the behavior of live organisms adapting to operant contingencies. The rules of the evolutionary theory when implemented on a computer generate behavioral output consistent with modern matching theory (e.g., generalized matching equation; see Chapter 9), suggesting that steady-state matching may be a higher-level outcome of Darwinian rules operating in dynamic behavioral systems (McDowell & Popa, 2010). One issue is how to tie the theory of adaptive behavior to Darwinian principles at the level of neural mechanisms. Referring to Edelman's theory of selection of neuronal groups (Edelman, 1987, 2007), McDowell noted that:

> The bit, the bit sequence, the bit string, and the bit string class [of my theory] are realized in [Edelman's theory] as a neuron, a synapse, a neuronal group, and a collection of degenerate neuronal groups [all having the same function]. In addition, the action of selection, which is carried out formally by the parental selection function in the [evolutionary theory of behavior dynamics] is realized in [Edelman's theory] by the operation of diffuse value systems [such as the dopamine pathways] in the brain that alter synaptic strengths or thresholds.
>
> (McDowell, 2010, p. 364)

One future possibility is that Darwinian principles may allow for a more comprehensive theory of brain function and behavior—a unified theory based on Skinner's notion of selection by consequences.

Selection for Operant Processes

Glenn (1991) noted the biological advantage of operant processes and selection by behavioral consequences:

> The instability of local environments and what might be considered a limit on behavioral complexity in genetic programs appears to have given rise to a less cumbersome and more rapid sort of variation and selection. Instead of building thousands of complex behavioral relations into DNA, evolution built a few programs for behavioral processes that allowed changing environments to build behavior repertoires "as needed" during the lifetime of individuals. A relatively small change in a bit of DNA could result in profound changes in the possibility for ontogenetic adaptability if that change involved a gene for a behavioral process. All that was required as a first step was genetically uncommitted activity and susceptibility of that activity to selection by behavioral consequences.
>
> (Glenn, 1991, p. 43)

The evolution of operant conditioning, a range of uncommitted behavior, and susceptibility to certain kinds of reinforcement resulted in a second level of selection. Behavioral selection supplemented and extended selection at the biological level (i.e., natural selection).

FOCUS ON: Operant Regulation in the Marine Snail, *Aplysia*

An example of how behavioral selection supplements the genetic control of behavior is seen in the marine snail, *Aplysia* (Figure 14.9) (see "Focus On: Genetic Control of a Fixed-Action Pattern" in this chapter). This simple organism serves as a model system for investigating the role of operant processes in the regulation of feeding (Brembs, Lorenzetti, Reyes, Baxter, & Byrne, 2002; see also operant conditioning by heat in the fruit fly (*Drosophila melanogaster*) related to the *ignorant* gene, the role of the behavior-initiating neuron in operant conditioning of the great pond snail (*Lymnaea stagnalis*), and evidence in the fruit fly that operant and respondent conditioning are distinct, involving two largely separate molecular processes; Brembs, 2003, 2008, 2011). Intact, freely behaving snails with extracellular electrodes in the buccal ganglia were observed during food ingestion. Recorded neural activity that accompanied eating was delivered contingent on spontaneous biting (no food present), and biting increased during the session and even occurred at some level when tested 24h later. These observations were taken as evidence of operant learning (biting reinforced by the eating-related neural activity), and also of "memory" of that behavior (reoccurrence some time later) in the intact animal.

Subsequently, the buccal ganglia neural network was removed from trained subjects and its sensitivity to depolarizing current compared with networks taken from non-trained and yoked controls. Differential activity indicated that buccal motor patterns became ingestion-like as a result of training. Finally, one cell called B51, which is active during feeding (and could be the site of operant "memory"), was isolated and received a brief puff of dopamine contingent upon depolarization and membrane changes. There was a significant decrease in this cell's threshold compared with control cells, indicating an operant reinforcement effect at the cellular level. That is, the contingent dopamine served to differentially alter the cell's activity so that it produced ingestion-like motor patterns.

The research on operant conditioning of *Aplysia* at the cellular, neural network, and behavioral levels shows the universal nature of *selection by consequences*. Clearly, the neural network activity and single-cell activity are modifiable by the effects of what happens when they are activated. As in any operant, the consequences at the neural and cellular levels affect the reoccurrence of the neuronal activity, and thereby contribute to the regulation of feeding in

FIG. 14.9 Photograph of the marine snail, *Aplysia*, used to study the role of operant processes in the regulation of feeding. Intact, freely behaving snails with extracellular electrodes in the buccal ganglia were observed during food ingestion. Recorded neural activity that accompanied eating was delivered contingent on spontaneous biting (no food present), and biting increased during the session, and even occurred at some level when tested 24 hours later. Common access provided by Wikimedia.

Aplysia. In addition, the work on *Aplysia* illustrates the continuum of behavioral regulation based on both genetic and environmental influences. That is, analysis of egg laying and feeding by *Aplysia* suggests regulation of behavior by gene-activated hormones and neurotransmitters combined with operant conditioning at the cellular level.

Operant Selection and Extinction

The unit of selection at the behavioral level is the operant. The operant is a functional unit of behavior. At the neurocellular level, operants involve increased activation, integration, and consolidation of neurons. Thus, the neuron is the physical unit on which behavioral selection works (see Chapter 4 on conditioning the neuron; see also Donahoe, 2002 and Guerra & Silva, 2010, on neural networks and neural analysis of conditioning). An operant is composed of response forms that make contact with the environment, an operant class. Response forms vary from moment to moment, and some variations change the environment in ways that increase those forms (selection by consequences). A child who manipulates a rubber duck in the bathtub may inadvertently squeeze it in ways that produce a squeaking sound. If the sound functions as reinforcement, the operant of squeezing the squeaking duck increases over time. Recall that reinforcers are defined not by what they are (squeaking rubber duck) but by their effect on behavior.

If few (or no) response variations are reinforced, the operant decreases and the process is extinction. That is, all members of an operant class cease to exist when they no longer result in reinforcement. The sound device in the toy duckling may break, and squeezing it in different ways no longer has the characteristic effect. Over time, the child will squeeze the rubber duck less and less as the operant undergoes extinction.

Extinction not only eliminates operants but also generates behavioral variation. Greater variation in the behavior increases an individual's chances of contacting the prevailing contingencies. In the bathtub, the child may push the broken rubber duck under the water, emitting a response that has never occurred before. The effect of this behavior may be to generate bubbles on the surface that, in turn, reinforce the child's behavior.

A more profound example of extinction and behavioral variation concerns people trying new ways of doing things when old ways no longer work (or do not work well). Thomas Edison's invention of the electric light bulb involved behavioral variation and selection. To generate electric light, Edison collected and tested a variety of materials to produce an effective lamp filament (Etzkowitz, 1992, p. 1005). He was known as the trial-and-error inventor, but a better description of his performance is "trial and success." Invention occurs when novel forms of response (trying different filaments) are generated by extinction and the appropriate response (using a tungsten filament) has been selected by the prevailing contingencies of reinforcement (effective and efficient light). Creativity, originality, or invention can be defined as nonrepetitive perseverance, and control by operant contingencies contributes to such behavior.

Susceptibility to Reinforcement

Contingencies of reinforcement resemble contingencies of survival (Skinner, 1986). Many animals eat and copulate simply because these responses have contributed to survival and reproduction. Male black widow spiders copulate and are then eaten by their mates. For these animals, copulating only had survival value for the species—passing on the genetic code even though the individual dies following the act. Other organisms evolved sensory systems that allowed food and sexual contact to reinforce behavior. That is, an animal whose actions resulted in sexual contact was more likely to act that way again. At this point, organisms had two redundant reasons for eating and copulating—survival of the species and reinforcement.

When food and sexual contact became reinforcing, new forms of behavior, indirectly related to eating and copulating, could be established. Animals could acquire new ways of finding, gathering, and processing foods based on reinforcement. Similarly, sexual reinforcement could establish and maintain a diversity of actions. These include looking at erotic objects, seeking out sexual partners, attracting a desirable mate, and performing a variety of sexual responses (e.g., genital contact with parts of body, position of intercourse).

Susceptibility to reinforcement may sometimes depend on the species and the particular behavior. Species-specific reinforcement is also shown by the fact that chaffinches (*Fringilla coelebs*) will peck a disk for food, but will not peck for contingent presentation of bird song. However, the same bird will step on a perch for species-specific song, suggesting the biological preparedness of the response–reinforcer relationship (Hinde & Stevenson-Hinde, 1973; see also Chapter 7).

Primates may also be susceptible to species-specific reinforcement. The work of Harlow and Zimmerman (1959) on mother–infant attachment suggests that "contact comfort" may function as reinforcement for infants staying close to and preferring their mothers. Infants who only received food reinforcement from their mothers did not show strong attachment behavior. These findings again suggest that the response–reinforcer relationship is biologically prepared.

Organisms that are susceptible to reinforcement may acquire behavior that is not adaptive (Pierce & Epling, 1988). One paradoxical byproduct of selection for operant conditioning is that people behave in ways that have distinct biological costs. Humans choose foods that are not healthful and engage in sexual behavior that is not related to procreation. In addition, conditioned reinforcement ensures that people come to value objects and events that are unrelated to survival and reproduction. Conditioned reinforcement may shape behavior that decreases reproductive success. People learn to use birth control, love adopted children, risk their lives to help others, risk their lives to kill others, and some even kill themselves. (We are not making a value judgment about these activities; the point is that these behaviors do not obviously contribute to reproductive success.) The point is that susceptibility to reinforcement has been adaptive, but this sensitivity may generate behavior that has no adaptive value.

NEW DIRECTIONS: Evolution, Environment, and the Obesity Crisis

Obesity is usually viewed clinically as a body weight disorder related to diabetes, metabolic syndrome, and heart disease. In contrast to this medical view, an evolutionary analysis indicates that genotype (genetic makeup) may be related to an animal's survival of food-related challenges ("thrifty gene theory"; Neel, 1962). From this perspective, obesity has resulted from variation in genotype (obese-prone or lean-prone) combined with an environment offering free access to high-calorie, energy-dense foods. One possibility is that the obese-prone genotype is nonadaptive—resulting from a coincidence of genetic drift (change in gene frequency of a population based on random mating of parents) and the high-energy foods of modern humans (Speakman, 2008). Alternatively, the obese-prone geno-type may be a consequence of adaptation, and obesity is a phenotypic expression of an interaction between genotype (obese-prone vs. lean-prone) and environment (high-energy/low-energy food supply).

David Pierce (coauthor of this textbook) and his associates proposed an adaptive hypothesis that the obese-prone genotype confers an advantage under conditions of unpredictable changes in food supply—allowing for storage and conservation of energy and increased foraging during periods of food depletion (Diane, Pierce, Heth, Russell, Richard, & Proctor, 2011; Pierce, Diane, Heth, Russell, & Proctor, 2010). In the laboratory, rats on food restriction with the opportunity to (wheel) run show activity anorexia, a vicious cycle of suppressed food intake, declining body weight and escalating wheel activity leading to starvation and death—the *AA challenge* (see Chapter 13). One test of the evolutionary hypothesis of obesity is to expose obese-prone rats to the AA chal-lenge to see if this genotype would survive under famine-like conditions.

Obese-prone (cp/cp) JCR:LA-cp rats lack the ObR leptin receptor, eliminating control by leptin, a major hormone for regulation of energy intake and energy expenditure. In a free-feeding environment, cp/cp (obese-prone) rats show over-eating, excessive body weight gain, and pronounced inactivity leading to obesity, metabolic syndrome, and cardiac failure in adult animals. That is, obese-prone rats adapt poorly to an environment of unlimited, high-energy food supply. In contrast, JCR:LA-cp lean-prone (+/?) rats with free access to food eat moderately, maintain a healthy body weight, and remain physically active into adulthood. These rats adapt well to a food-abundant environment. However, studies of the AA challenge indi-cate that lean-prone rats do not survive, reaching the starvation criterion (75% of body weight) in 3 to 5 days. Would juvenile obese-prone rats (without obesity) outlast their lean-prone counterparts in the AA situation? To answer this question, obese-prone (cp/cp) and lean-prone (+/?) rats aged 35–40 days (see Figure 14.10) were exposed to the AA challenge (1.5 h of food access and 22.5 h of access to running wheels), and measures of behavior and metabolism were obtained.

The findings supported the adaptive hypothesis of obesity. Juvenile obese-prone (cp/cp) rats gained a survival advantage over lean-prone (+/?) rats when confronted with the food restriction, wheel-running challenge. Young obese-prone rats survived approximately twice as long as lean-prone juveniles, even though their initial body weight did not differ before the challenge (Figure 14.11, left). Food intake by obese-prone rats was similar to that by lean-prone animals for the AA period, but body composition measures indicated that juvenile obese-prone rats conserved fat mass while lean-prone rats had depleted fat reserves, a finding that was confirmed by metabolic measures.

During food restriction, the daily wheel running of juvenile cp/cp rats was similar to that of lean-prone juveniles, but the young cp/cp rats maintained this pace for more days and covered three times the distance (Figure 14.11, right). Other evidence showed less physiological stress in the obese-prone rats compared with the lean-prone animals, allowing for extensive daily travel. In the natural world, the obese-prone genotype would have adaptive value, allowing animals to search for food over larger distances and increasing the likelihood of contact with a stable food source.

The evidence suggests that having an obese-prone genotype is deleterious when food is abundant, but is adaptive when food is scarce and food-related travel is

FIG. 14.10 The phenotypic development of JCR:LA-cp male rats from weanling pups to adulthood in a free feeding environment. Lean-prone rats (+/?) of this strain eat moderately, remain physically active, and maintain a trim body weight. Obese-prone (cp/cp) rats are characterized by overeating, pronounced inactivity, and excessive gains in body weight. In the study, both lean-prone and obese-prone rats (35–40 days old) were exposed to the AA challenge of 1.5 hours of access to food and 22.5 hours of access to running wheels—testing the evolutionary hypothesis that an obese-prone genotype allows for survival during periods of unpredictable food shortages and food-related travel. Photographs provided by Dr. Spencer Proctor, Director of the Cardiovascular Diseases Laboratory, The Alberta Institute of Diabetes, University of Alberta, Edmonton, Alberta, Canada. Dr. James C. Russell of the Faculty of Medicine (retired) at the University of Alberta developed the JCR:LA-cp strain as an animal model for obesity, heart disease, and the metabolic syndrome.

FIG. 14.11 Results of the experiment exposing lean-prone and obese-prone rats to the AA challenge (1.5 hours of access to food and 22.5 hours of access to running wheels). The left side of the graph shows the number of days the rats lasted in the AA challenge, indicating that obese-prone rats lasted about twice as long as their lean-prone counterparts. The right side of the graph shows the results for wheel running in the AA challenge. Obese-prone rats travelled about three times the distance travelled by lean-prone animals during the AA challenge—behavior that would increase the likelihood of contact with a food source in the natural environment. The overall results indicate that an obese-prone genotype had survival value when animals were faced with unpredictable food shortages and famines. From Pierce, W. D., Diane, A., Heth, C. D., Russell, J. C., & Proctor, S. D., 2010, "Evolution and obesity: Resistance of obese-prone rats to a challenge of food restriction and wheel running," *International Journal of Obesity, 34*, 589–592.

initiated. Additional research (Diane et al., 2011) shows that experience with food restriction and an obese-prone genotype combine to further increase survival in the AA challenge. Thus, both genotype and food environment contributed to survival during unpredictable food shortages, requiring extended food-related travel. However, in our current food-rich environment, an obese-prone genotype that favors overconsumption and conservation of fat reserves is not an advantage.

Behavior Management of the Obesity Crisis

One implication of the research on obese-prone rats and the AA challenge is that modification of the food environment, especially for obese-prone children, is a necessary step toward solving the obesity crisis in America. As the rising medical costs of obesity have effects on the public purse, more political and social policies are expected to regulate the food industry and advertising of food products (see Centre for Science in the Public Interest news release on mandating nutrition information on menus of chain-restaurants, Ottawa, Canada, 8 May 2012; http://cspinet.org/canada/pdf/ontario.newsrelease.menulabelling.may8-2012.pdf). These large-scale changes could alter community and family contingencies supporting children's high consumption of energy-dense, fattening foods.

Childhood obesity may also be tackled by behavioral interventions targeted at nursery and school-age children. Pauline Horne and Fergus Lowe, behavior analysts at Bangor University in the UK, have developed the Food Dude Healthy Eating Program (http://food-dudes.co.uk/prog_over.htm) to instill healthy food choices in the nation's children. The program is based on social modeling and reinforcement principles. One part of the program involves schoolchildren watching DVDs of the adventures of Food Dudes, who are "cool" superhero children battling the Junk Punks to save the Life Force. The Junk Punks weaken the Life Force by depriving the world of fruit and vegetables. The Food Dudes gain special powers by eating fruit and vegetables, and are able to thwart the scheming of the Junk Punks. The purpose of the Food Dude series of DVDs is to use principles of modeling and imitation to increase the schoolchildren's consumption of fruit and vegetables at meals and snack time, both at school and at home. Food Dude Rewards (stickers and Food Dude prizes) are also part of the program. When children initially select and eat fruit and vegetables, they receive Food Dude Rewards and soon come to enjoy the taste of these foods, allowing the rewards to be gradually phased out. In a recent study with pre-school children, the researchers concluded that:

> The modeling and rewards intervention proved to be a powerful means of producing lasting increases in young children's snack-time consumption of fruit and vegetables . . . [and] despite the fact that there were never any reward contingencies [at lunch-time] . . . the effects of the snack-time intervention generalized strongly to a different time of day and a different meal context. . . . [At follow-up] there were large and significant increases in lunchtime consumption [of fruits and vegetables].
> (Horne, Greenhalgh, Erjavec, Lowe, Viktor, & Whitaker, 2011, pp. 382–383)

The Food Dudes program for prevention of childhood obesity has spread throughout the schools of the UK and Ireland, and there are indications that other countries, including Canada and the USA, are interested in developing programs based on the success of the Bangor model.

Another necessary step toward solving the obesity crisis is to design and implement behavior management programs for overweight adults in America. Research shows that behavior-focused techniques which are effective in treating autism, stuttering, and substance abuse (see Chapter 13) may also be effective in managing weight and preventing weight gain (Freedman, 2011). Studies show that recording calories, eating patterns, exercise, and body weight is essential. In addition, setting modest, achievable, step-by-step goals helps to shape an active lifestyle, and joining a support group such as a runners' club or a virtual group of dieters increases the chances of success. Overall, there are a variety of behavioral strategies to help solve the obesity crisis in America even as we await advances in the control of metabolic processes related to body weight (e.g., brown fat, and making white fat cells burn energy rather than store it; Spiegelman, 2008; Zielinska, 2012).

EVOLUTION, REINFORCEMENT, AND VERBAL BEHAVIOR

Social Signals

As we noted earlier, a honey bee signals the location of food by dancing in ways that affect the travel of other bees. This form of communication involves a high degree of genetic regulation. Genes, as we have seen, code for the general behavioral processes known as respondent and operant conditioning. Once these learning capacities evolved, signaling could be acquired on the basis of an organism's interaction with the environment.

Skinner explained the acquisition of human gestures in terms of selection by consequence and susceptibility to aversive stimulation. He analyzed the contingencies as follows:

> One person can stop another by placing a hand on his chest, and if the person who is stopped finds the contact aversive, he will stop on later occasions before contact is made. The movement of the arm and hand changes from a practical response to a gesture. Once that happened, the topography can change until it would have little or no physical effect.
>
> The gesture that means "Come here" is another example. It presumably originated as practical pulling, but became effective as a gesture when people who were pulled moved quickly to avoid physical contact. The topography of the gesture still varies with distance, possibly because of visibility, but also as if some practical work remained to be done: When the parties are far apart, the whole arm is moved; when they are fairly near, only the forearm; and when they are close, only a hand or a finger.
>
> (Skinner, 1986, pp. 116–117)

For Skinner, gesturing is behavior that results from social contingencies of reinforcement. A social contingency involves the behavior of two (or more) people who arrange stimuli and reinforcement for each other's actions.

The person who sees a surprising sight may pull a companion toward the view and be reinforced by their friend's reactions to the sight (see Figure 14.12). On later occasions, a pulling motion may occur before the companion is within reach. The friend may avoid being dragged to the sight by coming when the pulling motion is first made. The reinforcement contingencies composed of each person's behavior establish and maintain this social episode.

FIG. 14.12   How pulling a person to see a sight may have evolved into the gesture of pulling the arm toward the body (Frank Epling on the left and David Pierce on the right, the original authors of this textbook).

Although social contingencies are clearly involved in human signs and gestures, other processes may play an important role. The research on stimulus equivalence discussed in Chapter 12 is relevant to signs and gestures (Dickins & Dickins, 2001). Humans easily distinguish equivalent stimulus classes, but other organisms do not. Gestures and signs may stand for or be equivalent to other stimulus classes. A smile, the spoken words "good job," and the gesture for "OK" (thumb and index finger make an O) become equivalent when they have a similar effect on behavior. Equivalence relations depend on discrimination of reflexivity (A = A and B = B), symmetry (if A = B then B = A), and transitivity (if A = B and A = C, then B = C). Complex transitivity relations seem to involve evolution of species-specific capacities for discrimination as well as general behavioral processes such as operant conditioning.

Humans readily generate and respond to iconic or representational signs when there is a requirement to communicate but speaking is not possible (Kuschel, 1973; Meissner & Philpott, 1975). For example, Brown (1986) recounts a study that compared severely deaf children with a normal hearing group (Goldin-Meadow & Morford, 1985). Parents who refused to sign to them because they believed that signing would retard vocal speech raised the deaf children. Each of the 10 deaf children independently acquired a similar repertoire of iconic signs. Presumably, some particular ways of signing were more effective than others in altering the behavior of the parents. The hearing children also showed iconic signing that gradually diminished as vocal speech increased. This later finding suggests that speech has some advantages over gestures and iconic signs when speakers and listeners have normal hearing (Goldin-Meadow & Wagner, 2005).

Corballis (1999, 2003) reviewed several perspectives dealing with the probable evolution of language from manual gestures, hand to mouth. He indicated that with the emergence of the genus *Homo* and their increased brain size and adequate vocal apparatus, contingencies could have further promoted the development of speech and language. In this regard, it is useful to provide a behavior analysis of the evolution of speech sounds.

Vocal and Speech Sounds

Natural selection must have been important in the evolution of vocalization and speech sounds. Compared with gestures and iconic signs, sounds can affect a listener's behavior when it is too dark to see, others are out of sight, or no one is looking at the speaker. Spoken sounds are also an advantage to speakers whose hands are full—whether they are warding off prey or holding weapons to attack an enemy. Skinner noted additional benefits of speech sounds over gestures:

> There are special advantages, however, in large operant repertoires, especially the enormous variety of available speech sounds. Gestures are not as conspicuously different as speech sounds and hence are fewer in number, and the sounds one produces are more like the sounds one hears than gestures are like the gestures one sees (because they are seen from a different point of view). One learns to

gesture through movement duplication, but to speak through product duplication, which is more precise.

(Skinner, 1986, p. 117)

Most of the organs that allowed for speech sounds probably evolved for other reasons (see Chapter 12). The diaphragm was used in breathing, the tongue and jaws were involved in eating, and the lips could take in water by sucking and sipping. The vocal cords and pharynx did not play a direct role in survival, but may have evolved in social species that could benefit from the calls and cries of others (see Blumstein & Armitage, 1997, on social alarms in marmots).

There were probably several other important steps in the evolution of human speech. One involved the extension of operant processes to a range of speech-relevant behavior. Each organ that contributed to speech was initially reflexive—the organism responding to specific stimulation. Survival must have been better served when operant processes supplemented reflexive behavior. An organism could breathe as a reflex elicited by high levels of circulating carbon dioxide, or it could hold its breath to avoid a predator. Based on natural selection, more and more speech-relevant behavior came under the control of its consequences. Compared with the great apes, humans made an evolutionary leap when the vocal apparatus was supplied with nerves (i.e., innervated) for operant regulation.

The step to operant regulation of the vocal musculature is not sufficient to account for speech. Evolution must also have resulted in the coordination of all the systems involved in the production of speech. The great apes have complete operant control of their hands but have not developed a sophisticated system of signs or gestures. Children show early iconic signing that shifts toward spoken words as more and more speech is acquired. Both iconic signing and spoken words require that the speaker and listener respond to abstract stimulus relations along several dimensions. Thus, neural coordination of speech probably built on, and added to, specialized capacities for discrimination involving the visual, auditory, and motor systems. In less technical terms, humans evolved systems for symbolic behavior, and these systems were eventually integrated with those of speech (Pierce & Epling, 1988).

Speech sounds are a large pool of uncommitted behavior. This behavior is spontaneously emitted at high frequency but plays no direct role in survival (Skinner, 1984b). From a behavioral view, wide variation in spontaneous speech sounds allows for selection of vocal operants by reinforcement supplied by listeners. Thus, Osgood (1953) found that an infant's babbling included all of the speech sounds that make up the different languages of the world. Vocal responses similar to the verbal community increase, while dissimilar speech drops out of the repertoire (Irwin, 1948, 1952). One possibility is that a child's speech sounds are shaped toward adult forms by reinforcement of successive approximations.

Goldstein, King, and West (2003) manipulated mothers' reactions to infants' vocalizations and found that phonological aspects of babbling increase with contingent social stimulation from mothers (reinforcement), but not with noncontingent maternal behavior. Social shaping by reinforcement creates rapid shifts in infant vocalization to more advanced speech sounds. Interestingly, bird song of juvenile male cowbirds is shaped toward mature forms used in mating by subtle reactions of females called wing strokes (West & King, 1988). Thus, social shaping by reinforcement may be a general mechanism for the development of adult vocal forms of communication across diverse species.

Verbal Behavior

The evolution of operant processes, the coordination of speech systems, and a large variety of uncommitted speech sounds allowed for the regulation of vocal operants by others. A person in an

English-speaking community learns to speak in accord with the verbal practices of the community. That is, the way a person speaks is shaped by the reinforcement practices of others. On a specific occasion, the community provides reinforcement for certain ways of speaking and withholds reinforcement or supplies aversive stimulation for other unacceptable responses. In this manner, the individual conforms to the customary practices of the community and, in so doing, contributes to the perpetuation of the culture.

Verbal behavior (see Chapter 12) allows people to coordinate their actions. When people observe rules, take advice, heed warnings, and follow instructions, their behavior is rule governed. Rule-governed behavior (see Chapter 11) allows people to profit from what others say. If a fellow camper reports that a bear is near your tent, you can move the tent to a different camping site. A student looking for a good course may benefit from the advice of another student. In these examples, the listener or person who responds to the verbal report avoids an aversive event (the bear) or contacts positive reinforcement (a good course). Children are taught to follow advice and instructions. Parents and others provide simple verbal stimuli that set the occasion for reinforcement of the child's compliance. In this way, the child is taught to listen to what others say.

As we have noted, listeners benefit from the verbal reports of others. For this reason, listeners are inclined to reinforce the person who provides useful instructions. In a verbal community, people are taught to express their appreciation for the advice received from others. For example, in an English-speaking community, people say "Thank you" and other variations of this response when given directions, advice, or instructions. These verbal responses by the listener reinforce the behavior of the speaker.

Verbal behavior evolved (level 2) in the sense that particular ways of speaking were more or less effective in regulating the behavior of listeners within a verbal community. Response variation ensured that many ways of speaking were tried and more and more people adopted successful combinations of speech sounds.

Speaking by Whistling

How people speak depends on the verbal contingencies of reinforcement. Ecological and geographic aspects of the environment (topography of the terrain) alter verbal contingencies in the sense that listeners cannot reinforce the verbal responses of speakers when they cannot hear and understand what is being said. Under these conditions, new ways of speaking and listening should evolve, and this is what happened on La Gomera, one of the Canary Islands in the Atlantic off the coast of North Africa (Classe, 1957; see also Wilken, 1979, on whistle speech in Mexico).

The island has a harsh terrain consisting of high mountain peaks and low ravines, gorges, and valleys, which separate the hamlets of the Gomeros, a Spanish-speaking people (Figure 14.13). A short distance of 500 yards may take an hour or so to walk on the rough paths, which are not much more than goat trails. To say the least, communication over a distance has been a central problem to people on the island. Long ago the Gomeros began to use a whistled speech, which allowed them to speak to each other over extended distances across the disjoined landscape. The language is called "silbo" (Spanish for "whistle"), and it is not just a signal system but is considered to be a version of the Spanish language. Whistled Spanish uses fingers positioned in the mouth to facilitate the whistle and articulation by the tongue to produce verbal responses, as in ordinary speech. Its main utility is that the whistles can be heard and clearly understood over great distances—much further than shouting in everyday Spanish. On a good day without wind, a listener more than a mile away can understand the silbo Spanish of the speaker. A skillful silbador can whistle messages that travel 3 miles or more, and the record is said to be up to 8 miles (see Meyer, 2007, for further analysis of whistled languages).

Speaking by whistling shows that verbal behavior evolves and adapts to the contingencies of reinforcement (level 2 selection). In the everyday world of Spanish speakers, talking with words

FIG. 14.13 (Left) The rugged landscape of La Gomera that favored the use of whistle speech or *silbo* by the islanders. (Right) A Gomera woman using her fingers and articulation of the tongue to whistle in Spanish. The major function of whistled speech is that it can be clearly heard and understood by villagers several miles away, thus overcoming the communication obstacles caused by the disjointed terrain of the island. From Classe, A., 1957, "The whistled language of La Gomera," *Scientific American, 196*, 111–120. Published with permission from the Nature Publishing Group.

allows for reinforcement by listeners. For the Gomeros, the rugged landscape has altered the usually verbal contingencies, and whistling Spanish has evolved as a way of solving the problem. The customary way of speaking, by means of words or whistles, refers to the common linguistic practices of a verbal community—the common standards for speech (a grammar). These verbal practices served as the underlying basis for a third level of selection, namely the selection and evolution of cultural practices.

LEVEL 3: SELECTION AND EVOLUTION OF CULTURE

The evolution of operant processes and verbal behavior allowed for the emergence of human culture. Sigrid Glenn (1988, 1989; see also Lloyd, 1985) proposed a behavior analysis of culture that builds on the works of Skinner (1953) and anthropologist Marvin Harris (1979). Although social scientists often talk about culture as the ideas and values of a group, a behavioral viewpoint suggests that a culture involves the usual ways of acting and speaking in a community. These customary forms of behavior (customs, mores, etc.) are the cultural practices of the group.

Cultural Practice

From a behavioral perspective, cultural practices involve the interlocking operant behavior of many people—the members of a culture. Each person's behavior provides stimulation and reinforcement for the actions of others. A **cultural practice** is therefore defined in terms of interlocking social contingencies—where the behavior of each person supports the behavior of other members of the community. The pattern of behavior that arises from the interlocking contingencies is the type of practice (e.g., what people do in that culture).

This view of culture suggests that what people do in a particular community is determined by the function of a practice. The ancient Romans adopted military tactics that were highly effective in most battles. For example, Roman soldiers would form a close body of men, called a phalanx, and interlock their shields as a common barrier against the enemy. Although there are many ways to conduct a battle, this military maneuver became popular because of its effectiveness. In other words, what people in a particular culture do is a function of the previous benefits and costs of that practice. With changes in technology (the products of a culture), the phalanx and the interlocking of shields became obsolete—the costs in terms of casualties and lost battles increased relative to the benefits.

Cultural practices are functionally similar to operants. Both operants and cultural practices are selected by consequences (Lamal, 1997). Thus, a cultural practice increases when people have benefited from it. The practice of making water jars involves alternative sets of interlocking operants that result in a common outcome. One person gathers clay, another person makes the pot, and a consumer trades something for the jar. The common outcome of such a practice is greater efficiency in transporting and storing water. There are many ways of storing and transporting water, including shells, hollow leaves, woven baskets, clay pots, and indoor plumbing. The cultural form that predominates (e.g., plumbing) reflects the basic processes of selection by consequences. In terms of selection, operants are selected by contingencies of reinforcement and cultural practices are selected by metacontingencies (see, for example, Norton, 1997, on geographic practices, rule-governed behavior, and metacontingencies).

Metacontingencies and Cultural Practices

Dr. Sigrid Glenn (Figure 14.14) at the University of North Texas made an important contribution to the behavior analysis of culture when she first described the metacontingencies of cultural practices. **Metacontingencies** refer to contingent relations between cultural practices and the effects of those practices for the group (Glenn, 1988, 2004; see Vichi, Andery, & Glenn, 2009, for experimental evidence of metacontingency). For example, competence in science is important for people who live in a technologically advanced culture. Scientific research produces a range of benefits for the general society. These include better medicine, more productive crop yields, new and better building materials, more efficient and longer-lasting appliances, and superior regulation of human behavior. Thus, a positive metacontingency exists between educational practices that increase scientific competence and long-term benefits to the group. This analysis suggests that teaching methods that promote science were selected, while alternative methods of education declined in popularity.

Metacontingency implies that there will be an increase in those forms of education that result in more and better trained students of science, but this may not occur. In complex cultures such as the USA, competing (or concurrent) metacontingencies may mean that the "best" educational practice is not selected. A less than optimal form of scientific education may prevail for some time because teaching science is only part of the function of education. For example, the manifest function of education is to teach

FIG. 14.14   Sigrid Glenn. Published with permission.

reading, writing, and arithmetic. The hidden or latent function of schooling includes keeping people out of the workforce and categorizing them into high-, medium-, and low-status groups based on educational attainment. Thus, the form of education that predominates is one that has produced the most overall benefit to the community, group, or society. If the relative outcomes of an educational practice resulting in low scientific competence exceed those of a system that yields high scientific achievement, then the less adequate educational practice will predominate in the culture (see Lamal & Greenspoon, 1992, on metacontingencies and the US Congress; see also Lamal, 1997).

FOCUS ON: Depleting Resources, Punishment, and Communication

One problem faced by people in complex social–ecological systems is the use and misuse of limited resources involving forests, pastures, air, energy, fisheries, and water systems (see Platt, 1973, for a discussion of other kinds of *social traps*, or social dilemmas). In his classic article on "The Tragedy of the Commons," Hardin (1968) described the dilemma arising from the contingencies regulating the use of a public grazing area for cows called the "Commons." Farmers are free to use the commons to feed cows and increase profit (immediate individual gain), but the more cows they feed the faster the grazing area is depleted (given a fixed rate of resource repletion), until there is no grass left and no more farming (long-term loss to users of the resource). Notice that this kind of social problem involves the *interlocking operant behavior of multiple individuals* each making repeated choices between short-term and long-term contingencies of reinforcement (see Chapter 9 on choice and self-control for similar contingencies at the individual level of analysis). Hardin's analysis suggested that individuals acting independently and pursuing their own self-interest would eventually deplete the limited resource, even when it is not in anyone's long-term interest to do so. In America today, burning of fossil fuels and pollution is an example of the limited-resource dilemma. Each user (or company) can dump the waste products from burning oil and gas from cars and households into the atmosphere for a short-term gain, but this practice depletes the air quality and raises the global temperature—long-term effects that are in no one's best interest.

Experimental Analysis of Common Resource Dilemmas

In the laboratory, it is possible to arrange the basic contingencies of common resource dilemmas and experimentally analyze the conditions leading to overuse of resources and to solving this problem of human behavior. In an early study, resource dilemmas were arranged by schedules of reinforcement with immediate and delayed consequences (Brechner, 1977). Student participants in groups of three could respond individually for points exchanged toward class credit. Every 10 responses (FR 10) added one point to the student's total (individual short-term benefit), but subtracted a point from a common pool of points that replenished at a fixed rate (long-term cost to users of the resource). If the three participants responded for points faster than the replenishment rate, the pool would deplete and the experiment would end before the students could obtain the maximum class credit. The researcher also varied the maximum size of the pool and the opportunity for the students to communicate. The results indicated that less efficient resource management (replenishment of points in the pool) occurred when the pool was small and the participants could not communicate (this research on resource dilemmas is related to experiments on social cooperation and exchange; for a review, see Fehr & Gintis, 2007).

The effects of communication and costly punishment (using punishment at a personal cost) on resource management were recently investigated with a computer simulation of the common resource problem (Janssen, Holahan, Lee, & Ostrom, 2010). The experimental environment involved five participants (resource users) gathering tokens (the resource) from a common pool of tokens (stars) distributed over a computer-simulated grid of cells. Participants collected tokens from the pool by pressing the arrow keys to move their avatars around the screen, and pressed the space bar to collect each token (worth 2 cents) during each decision period. The resource rapidly depleted when everyone gathered tokens for themselves as quickly as possible without considering the long-term effects on all the resource users; participants who pursued only immediate reinforcement sat looking at a dark screen not making any money. On the other hand, if participants restrain themselves by maintaining 50% of the tokens on the screen, they could triple their earnings. In periods when punishment was allowed, participants could subtract two tokens from another user at the cost of one of their own tokens, as long as they had funds in their account (costly punishment). Written communication, when allowed, involved text messages in a "chat room" before a decision period. Each experimental condition consisted of three consecutive 4-min periods of costly punishment (P), communication (C), or a combination of both (CP), and three consecutive 4-min periods when neither communication nor punishment (NCP) was allowed.

When the experiment started with NCP, the participants depleted the resource (pool of tokens) within about 90 s, showing that without punishment and communication the participants responded in terms of immediate reinforcement, as expected by Hardin's analysis of the "tragedy of the commons." In contrast, an opportunity to communicate reduced the rate of collecting tokens by each group member and increased the pool of tokens (and profit) for all. Participants' messages in C periods focused on the timing and location of the tokens. A common message was to refrain from gathering tokens for a set length of time, to allow the resource to regenerate. When participants started the game with C periods, the amount of earnings did not drop off when participants were no longer able to communicate, upholding their prior agreements.

When P without communication was introduced after NCP (or at the start of the experiment), gross earnings dropped, as the contingency of punishment was not specific without a preceding verbal stimulus. That is, removal of tokens (punishment) without prior messages did not stipulate what behavior produced the loss—collecting too many tokens, gathering tokens in a particular location, collecting tokens in a specific pattern, or moving the avatar too quickly on the screen. For P phases, participants did not use punishment in half of the periods when it was allowed. Without communication, they were reluctant to punish token gathering by others based on the threat of retaliation. When participants in P conditions did use punishment to control token collecting, going too fast or having too many tokens were given as reasons, which was consistent with the record of punishment events.

Interestingly, communication with punishment (CP) did not lead to as long-lasting cooperative behavior as communication without punishment (C). It appears that the use of punishment erodes prior cooperative agreements, which are then less likely to persist when punishment and communication are withdrawn. For CP periods, the main reason participants gave for punishing others, when they did so, was for not following the agreements. In addition to using costly punishment, participants in CP periods would use messages to scold others who were viewed as free riders, taking advantage of the increased tokens in the pool but not contributing themselves.

These experiments confirm that people will reluctantly use punishment to manage the uncooperative behavior of others, even when it is costly for them to do so (costly punishment). However, the use of punishment without communication does not solve the common resource dilemma, and leads to large individual losses in the long term. When communication is allowed, the users make agreements to manage common resources, increase their overall gains, and continue to make gains even when communication is no longer available (notably, learning to negotiate agreements is not analyzed in these studies, and the contingencies of this complex verbal behavior require additional experimental analysis). These gains are not sustained when punishment is used and communication is withdrawn, presumably because punishment erodes interpersonal trust (counting on others to do their part or contribute their fair share). At the practical level, conservation of limited resources may not improve as a result of imposing social and economic sanctions on users, even when communication is possible. However, negotiation and agreements among the parties (communication) may be helpful to resource management, especially if individual users and the group benefit in the long term (see also Molm, Takahashi, & Peterson, 2000, for an experimental analysis of risk and trust in social exchange).

ORIGIN, TRANSMISSION, AND EVOLUTION OF CULTURAL PRACTICES

Cultural practices arise and are transmitted over generations. Galef and Allen (1995) showed how diet preferences could be established, diffused, and socially transmitted by rats. Founder colonies of four rats were taught an arbitrary food preference. Subsequently, members of the colonies were slowly replaced with naive rats that had no food preferences. The food preference was still maintained in the third generation of replacements, although none of these animals had received the original training. Thus, a food practice established by arbitrary non-social contingencies was transmitted and maintained by implicit social contingencies of the group.

Another example comes from a story about animals in a zoo enclosure. A troop of baboons was provided with a choice between a preferred food (bananas) and a less appetizing laboratory chow (Pierce, 1991). As expected, the baboons consistently chose to eat bananas. Following a baseline period, the researchers established a negative reinforcement contingency for eating the less preferred food. Whenever any animal approached the bananas, the entire colony was drenched with water from a fire hose that was used to clean the enclosure. After exposure to this contingency, the troop attacked any member that approached the bananas. Eventually, all members of the troop were exclusively eating the less preferred chow and avoiding cold showers.

The researchers then removed the reinforcement contingency—approaching and eating the bananas no longer resulted in being soaked with water. As you might expect, the group did not test the operating contingencies and continued to attack any member that went toward the preferred food. At this point, the contingencies had established a *cultural taboo* that was highly resistant to change. Thus, social contingencies and observational learning contributed to the maintenance of the food taboo even though the original negative reinforcement contingencies had long since been removed.

Harris (1974) has provided a functional analysis of the origin and transmission of many human cultural practices. To illustrate, in India the cow is deified and many Hindus do not eat beef. This was not always the case—when the last ice age ended the peoples of Northern India raised and ate cattle, sheep, goats, and many agricultural products. Cattle, however, have some advantages other than just providing a source of meat; they may be easily herded and trained to pull plows or carts.

The population density increased greatly in the Ganges River valley, and by 300 BC the people of the valley had destroyed the trees surrounding the river. As a result, the risk of drought increased and farms decreased in size. Small farms have little space for animals, but draft animals were essential for working the land and transporting agricultural products. Cows provided traction, milk, and meat, but the farmer who ate his cow lost milk production and a working animal. Thus, the people of India faced a social trap involving the immediate benefit of eating beef and the long-term loss of the cows' other advantages.

A cost–benefit analysis suggests that it was better to keep a cow than to eat it. To avoid this social trap, the cow was deified and eating beef became a cultural taboo. The Hindu community has maintained this practice right up to modern times. Other cultures have food taboos that may be analyzed in terms of the function of cultural practices. Until very recently, Catholics did not eat meat on Fridays, many Islamic and Jewish people will not eat pork, and Chinese people despise cow's milk (Harris, 1974; see Kangas, 2007, on Marvin Harris's cultural materialism and its ties to behavior analysis; see also Ward, 2006, for an experimental analysis of Harris's cultural materialism).

Cultural Evolution

Cultural evolution presumably begins at the level of the individual where technological effects reinforce variation in individual behavior. An inventor may discover a new way of making a wheel, a farmer finds a food crop that produces higher yields, and a teacher may find a novel way to teach reading. A culture is said to evolve when the community adopts these innovations.

Adoption of innovations depends on the metacontingencies facing the group. For example, a new food crop with higher yield is selected when the metacontingencies favor increased grain production. This could occur when a community is impoverished or when higher-yielding crops support the feeding of domestic animals used for work or consumption. Higher-yield crops may not be selected when food is overly abundant, when increased grain supply leads to problems of storage, or when a new crop attracts pests that spread disease.

Adoption of Novel Behavior

A troop of Japanese macaques on Koshima Island is well known for its innovations and traditions (Kawamura, 1959). In one example, an infant female called Imo began to wash sweet potatoes to remove the grit. This behavior was later observed in Imo's playmates and her mother, who taught it to another offspring. Imo was also among the first to take up swimming and to throw wheat kernels on the water. Throwing wheat on the water removed the sand that was mixed with the kernels, because the sand sank and the kernels floated. Both of these practices were eventually adopted by the entire troop (Tomasello, 2009; Whiten & Boesch, 2001; see Whiten, McGuigan, Marshall-Pescini, & Hopper, 2009, on social learning, imitation, and chimpanzee culture; see also Whiten, Hinde, Laland & Stringer, 2011, for an overview of the evidence for continuity between nonhuman and human culture).

Transfer of Cultural Practices to a New Situation

How would an American eat Sushi if she had never observed anyone use chopsticks before? She would probably follow the customary practice of North American culture and use a fork (Call & Tennie, 2009). Gruber and colleagues presented two adjacent troops of chimpanzee with a problem equivalent to eating Sushi. The researchers drilled holes at two depths into wooden logs, and filled them with honey (Gruber, Muller, Strimling, Wrangham, & Zuberbuhler, 2009). The chimps could extract the honey from the shallow hole with their fingers, but had to use a tool to remove the honey from the deeper hole. One group traditionally used leaves to remove liquid from holes, while the other group commonly used sticks. The two chimpanzee groups applied their customary "table manners" to the problem of eating the honey— one group used leaves to get at the honey, while the other group used sticks (Figure 14.15). Preference for sticks or leaves was consistent within each group, matching the chimpanzees' natural foraging techniques in other situations. The evidence indicates that chimpanzee groups use their traditional cultural practice to solve a new feeding problem, an example of transfer of a practice from one situation to another (but see Gruber, Reynolds, & Zuberbuhler, 2010, for a discussion of the continuing debate on chimpanzee culture).

FIG. 14.15 Chimpanzees from a troop that uses sticks to extract substances from cracks and holes. In the study, the chimps were given logs in which there were two holes filled with honey, one shallow and the other deeper. The animals could extract the honey from shallow holes with their fingers, but had to use a tool to get the honey from deeper holes. One group traditionally used leaves to remove liquid from holes, while the other group commonly used sticks. The two chimpanzee groups applied their customary "table manners" to the problem of eating the honey—one group used leaves to get at the honey, while the other group used sticks. Originally published by Josep Call and Claudio Tennie, 2009, "Animal culture: chimpanzee table manners?" *Current Biology, 19*, R981–R983. Republished with permission of the Max Planck Institute for Evolutionary Anthropology.

Persistence of Cultural Practices

A common observation is that cultural practices in humans often remain unchanged over many generations, even when these customs make no sense. A practice may persist for many years because the members of the group who engage in it (e.g., do not kill cows for food) fail to contact a change in the metacontingencies (e.g., the cost of cows is rising relative to their benefits). At the individual level, a person conforms to the taboo because the social contingencies arranged by the group (religious proclamations and sanctions) avert contact with the positive reinforcement contingency (e.g., eating beef is good).

Cultural practices may also persist when the metacontingencies are stable and the current practices are sufficient to meet the contingencies. For centuries, the only way that books were manufactured was by having scribes make written copies. As a cultural practice, copying books by hand allowed for more standardized transmission of knowledge than that by word of mouth. Better methods of food preparation, house construction, agriculture, waste disposal, and transportation could be described in a common manner and passed from one generation to another. Thus, written transcription satisfied the metacontingencies for passing on social knowledge, but it was not the only way to reproduce books. The advent of the printing press allowed for an alternative form of book duplication that was less costly in time and effort, more productive, and much faster. Thus, transcription by hand was eventually made obsolete by the invention of the printing press, but for a while both forms of the practice were used for duplication of social knowledge. In fact, transcription by hand is still used today, although it is done infrequently and for specialized purposes (e.g., translation of a work from one language to another). In unstable, rapidly changing environments, people learn about many ways of doing things that are retained in the culture (persistence of social knowledge), but they select among a few, less persistent forms of behavior that have resulted in high payoffs (Rendell, Boyd, Enquist, Feldman, Fogarty, & Laland, 2011).

A final point is that an innovation such as the printing press often determines whether a culture remains static or dynamic. Individual inventions produce variation in cultural practices in much the same way that genetic mutations produce changes in species characteristics. That is, new forms of individual behavior (e.g., designing and making can openers) are generated by aversive contingencies or extinction (satisfying a need). These novel behaviors and products (can openers) are occasionally adopted by others and propagated as ways of meeting the metacontingencies (efficient storage and access to food with low risk of disease). Generally, variation in form and selection by consequences operate at different levels—producing both individual innovation and cultural evolution.

CHAPTER SUMMARY

This chapter provides many examples of how selection by consequences can operate at various levels of analysis. Our point has been that adaptive behaviors that provide benefits can lead to changes at the genetic, behavioral, and cultural levels. Selection is a universal process and, although we for the most part restrict our analysis to the behavior of organisms, such a process has much greater range. The application of contingency analysis has proved useful in accounting for many diverse observations, from changes in conditioning ability in flies, to acquisition of verbal behavior in humans, to the creation and maintenance of cultural dietary taboos. Alternative forms of explanation for these observations have not proved as helpful as assuming and applying the unifying concept of selection by consequences. A scientific approach to behavior based on selection is not only possible, but is ongoing and substantiated by thousands of research studies. The findings from these explorations have led to further questions about the regulation of behavior in more complex and widespread areas. The next step is the full integration of behavior analysis and neuroscience within a common framework based on evolution and selection.

KEY WORDS

Behavioral flexibility	Metacontingencies
Contingencies of survival	Mutation
Cultural evolution	Natural selection
Cultural practice	Phenotype
Evolution	Phylogeny
Genotype	Selection by consequences

ON THE WEB

www.ucmp.berkeley.edu/history/evolution.html This website explores the theory of evolution and the history of evolutionary thought.

http://en.wikipedia.org/wiki/Richard_Dawkins Go to Wikipedia and explore the contributions and controversies of Richard Dawkins on evolution, especially his dispute with religion.

http://videolectures.net/yaleeeb122f07_stearns_lec33/ Evolution, behavior, and game theory have implications for solving problems such as the Tragedy of the Commons discussed in this chapter. Take a look at the lecture by Dr. Stephen Stearns at Yale University to learn more about this subject.

http://news.sciencemag.org/sciencenow/2008/06/04-04.html Observe a video clip of the waggle dance of bees and explore new research on dialects of bees' communication in the hive at Science Now. Although the dance involves genetic control of behavior, learning plays a role in this fascinating ritual of bees.

www.youtube.com/watch?v=PgEmSb0cKBg The whistle speech of La Gomera Island, silbo, is a form of Spanish that has been passed down over the centuries to handle the problem of communication at a distance in the rugged, disjointed landscape of the island. Take a look!

BRIEF QUIZ

1. The single common principle operating at the level of biology, behavior, and culture is:

   (a) selection by design
   (b) survival of the fittest
   (c) phylogenetic contingencies
   (d) selection by consequences

2. Natural selection involves:

   (a) differential reproduction
   (b) genetic variation
   (c) reproductive diversity
   (d) ontogenetic adaptation

3. At what levels does selection by consequences occur?

   (a) cultural
   (b) biological
   (c) behavioral
   (d) all of the above

4. Two major sources of genetic variation are mutations and:

   (a) phenotypic genes
   (b) sexual recombination
   (c) random novelty
   (d) social pressure

5. Egg laying in *Aplysia* is an example of:

   (a) genetic control of behavior
   (b) environmental control of behavior
   (c) basic instincts
   (d) released action patterns

6. The behavior of invertebrates such as *Aplysia* is totally:

    (a) controlled by genes
    (b) learned
    (c) reflexive
    (d) none of the above

7. Operant behaviors are selected by:

    (a) chromosomes
    (b) consequences
    (c) choice
    (d) cognitions

8. The ability to have one's behavior strengthened by reinforcement is:

    (a) learned
    (b) heritable
    (c) determined
    (d) disadvantageous

9. Social signaling:

    (a) is mostly genetically regulated in bees
    (b) is mostly due to reinforcement contingencies in humans
    (c) may involve stimulus equivalence in humans
    (d) all of the above

10. What allowed for the emergence of human culture?

    (a) evolution of operant processes
    (b) evolution of verbal behavior
    (c) social signaling by bees
    (d) both (a) and (b)

Answers to Brief Quiz: 1, d (p. 439); 2, a (p. 440); 3, d (p. 439); 4, b (p. 442); 5, a (p. 442); 6, d (p. 450); 7, b (p. 448); 8, b (p. 448); 9, d (pp. 444, 455–456); 10, d (p. 459).

Glossary

A–B–A–B design. This is the most basic single-subject research design. Also called a *reversal design*, it is ideally suited to show that specific features of the environment regulate an organism's behavior. The A-phase, or baseline, is used to measure behavior before the researcher introduces an environmental change. During baseline, the experimenter takes repeated measures of the behavior under study, and this establishes a criterion against which any changes (attributed to the independent variable) may be assessed. Following the baseline phase, an environmental condition is changed (B-phase) and behavior is measured repeatedly. If the independent variable, or environmental condition, has an effect, then the behavioral measure (dependent variable) will change (i.e., increase or decrease). Next, the baseline phase is reintroduced (A) and behavior is again measured. Since the treatment is removed, behavior should return to baseline levels. Finally, the independent variable is introduced again and behavior is reassessed (B). According to the logic of the design, behavior should return to a level observed in the initial B-phase of the experiment. This second application of the independent variable helps to ensure that the behavioral effect is caused by the manipulated condition.

Abolishing operation (AO). In contrast to the establishing operation, an abolishing operation (AO) decreases the effectiveness of behavioral consequences, and momentarily reduces behavior that has resulted in those consequences in the past. Thus, providing frequent social attention for a period (*noncontingent* attention) functions as an abolishing operation. That is, a period of noncontingent attention subsequently decreases the effectiveness of attention as a social reinforcer, and reduces self-injurious behavior maintained by adult attention.

Absolute stimulus control. When operants are regulated by the physical properties of one stimulus (e.g., color or hue), this is called absolute stimulus control. See also **relative stimulus control**.

Activity anorexia. Following a period of food restriction, physical activity suppresses food intake and declining body weight increases activity. This negative feedback loop is called activity anorexia in rats, and a similar cycle occurs in many anorexic patients.

Activity-induced taste aversion. Conditioned taste aversion (avoidance) that occurs when a novel food or liquid taste is followed by wheel running. The conditioned stimulus (CS), taste, is conditioned as an aversive stimulus when associated with the neurophysiological effects of wheel running (unconditioned stimulus, US).

Ad libitum weight. The body weight of an organism that has free access to food 24 h a day.

Adjunctive behavior. Also called interim behavior. On interval schedules of reinforcement, or time-based delivery of food, organisms often show excessive behavior within the interreinforcement interval. For example, rats may drink up to three times their usual daily water intake (polydipsia) over a 1-h session. This behavior immediately follows reinforcement and is a side effect of periodic food delivery.

Ainslie–Rachlin principle. A principle which states that reinforcement value decreases as the delay between making a choice and obtaining the reinforcer increases. The principle predicts preference reversal when a delay precedes the choice between a small, immediate reward and a large, deferred reinforcer. That is, at some time prior to the choice the large, deferred reinforcer becomes more valued than the small, immediate reward.

Anticipatory contrast. The schedule of reinforcement following the target component (B) in a sequence of schedules (A → B → C) generates strong contrast that increases as training progresses. The strong contrast effect is called anticipatory contrast to distinguish it from the weak elicited responding by the preceding schedule.

Applied behavior analysis. A branch of behavior analysis that uses behavior principles to solve practical problems such as the treatment of autism or improvement of teaching methods. Applied behavior analysis is also referred to as behavioral engineering.

Associative strength. During respondent conditioning, the term associative strength is used to describe the relation between the conditioned stimulus (CS) and the magnitude of the conditioned response (CR). In general, associative strength increases over conditioning trials and reaches some maximum level.

Assumption of generality. This assumption implies that the effects of contingencies of reinforcement extend over species, reinforcement, and behavior. For example, a fixed-interval schedule is expected to produce the scalloping pattern for a pigeon pecking a key for food and a child who is solving mathematics problems for teacher approval, all other things being equal.

Autistic children. This term refers to children who show an early lack of social interaction with parents, other family members, and peers. For example, these children often resist being held, and may have a tantrum if picked up or hugged. When autistic children get older they may be mistaken as deaf because they do not talk or establish eye contact when spoken to. These children often show repeated stereotyped patterns of behavior such as rocking back and forth, spinning a top, wiggling their fingers in front of their eyes, and so on.

Autoclitic (verbal behavior). A form of verbal behavior that modifies the consequences produced by other verbal responses. It is verbal behavior used in conjunction with, and controlled by, primary verbal units such as mands, tacts, and intraverbals. Skinner (1957) described five categories of autoclitic relations: descriptive, qualifying, quantifying, manipulative, and relational.

Autoshaping. A respondent conditioning procedure that generates skeletal responses. For example, a key light is turned on for a few seconds before grain is presented to a pigeon. After several pairings of the key light and grain, the bird begins to peck the key. This effect was first reported as autoshaping—an automatic way to teach pigeons to key peck.

Aversive stimulus. An event or stimulus that an organism escapes or avoids.

Avoidance. See **negative reinforcement**.

Backward chaining. A procedure used to train a chained performance. The basic idea is to first train behavior that is closest to primary reinforcement; once responding is established, links in the chain are added that are further and further from primary reinforcement. Each link in the chain is reinforced by the S^D, which is also a conditioned reinforcer signaling the next component in the sequence.

Backward conditioning. In the respondent procedure of backward conditioning, the unconditioned stimulus (US) comes on before the conditioned stimulus (CS). The general consensus has been that backward conditioning is unreliable, and many researchers question whether it occurs at all. There is evidence that backward conditioning can occur when the CS has biological significance (e.g., the sight of a predator).

Baseline. The base rate of behavior against which an experimental manipulation is measured. An uncontrolled baseline is the rate of an operant before any known conditioning. A controlled baseline (e.g., the rate of response on a variable-interval 60-s schedule) may be established to assess the effects of an experimental manipulation (e.g., presentation of intermittent shocks).

Baseline sensitivity. The phenomenon whereby a low dose of a drug can cause substantial changes in baseline behavior. More generally, a behavioral baseline that varies with small increases in the independent variable is said to show sensitivity.

Behavior. Everything that an organism does, including covert actions such as thinking.

Behavior analysis. A comprehensive experimental approach to the study of the behavior of organisms. Primary objectives are the discovery of principles and laws that govern behavior, the extension of these principles over species, and the development of an applied technology.

Behavior analysts. Researchers and practitioners of behavior analysis.

Behavior maintenance. The length of time for which a new behavior persists after the original contingencies have been removed (e.g., an anorexic patient who is taught to eat properly shows long-lasting effects of treatment if he maintains adequate weight for many years).

Behavior system. A species-specific set of responses elicited by a particular unconditioned stimulus (US). That is, for each species there is a behavior system related to procurement of food, another related to obtaining water, and yet another for securing warmth.

Behavior trapping. The teaching of new behavior that, once established, is "trapped" by natural contingencies of reinforcement—the contingencies of everyday life.

Behavioral contract. A behavioral plan of action that is negotiated between a client, a child, or a partner and concerned others. The plan usually includes a statement of target responses, consequences that follow different actions, and long-term goals. The contract objectively specifies what is expected of the person in terms of behavior and the consequences that follow.

Behavioral contrast. Contrast refers to an inverse relationship between the response rates for two components of a multiple schedule—as one goes up, the other goes down. There are two forms of contrast: positive and negative. Positive contrast occurs when the rate of response in an *unchanged* component of a multiple schedule *increases* with a decline in behavior in the other schedule. Negative contrast occurs when the rate of response in an *unchanged* component of a multiple schedule *decreases* with an increase in behavior in the other component.

Behavioral dynamics. An area of research that attempts to analyze schedule effects in terms of a few basic processes. Behavioral dynamics requires a high level of mathematical sophistication. Both linear and nonlinear calculus is used to model the behavioral impact of schedules of reinforcement. If performance on schedules can be reduced to a small number of fundamental principles, then reasonable interpretations may be made about any particular arrangement of the environment. Also, it should be possible to predict more precisely behavior based on knowledge of the operating contingencies and the axioms that govern reinforcement schedules.

Behavioral economics. The use of economic concepts (price, substitute commodity, etc.) and principles (e.g., marginal utility) to predict, control, and analyze the behavior of organisms in choice situations.

Behavioral flexibility. When organisms were faced with unpredictable and changing environments, natural selection favored those individuals whose behavior was flexible—adjusting on the basis of past experience. In this case, genes played a subsidiary role coding for general processes of learning. These processes allowed an organism to adjust to changing environmental requirements throughout its life span. Flexibility of behavior in turn contributed to the reproductive success of the organism.

Behavioral medicine. Behavior-change programs that target health-related activities such as following special diets, self-examination for early symptoms of disease, exercising, taking medicine, and so on. In many instances, the idea is that problems of behavior that affect health may be prevented before treatment is necessary.

Behavioral neuroscience. A scientific area that integrates the science of behavior (behavior analysis) with the science of the brain (neuroscience). Areas of interest include the effects of drugs on behavior (behavioral pharmacology), neural imaging and complex stimulus relations, choice and neural activity, and the brain circuitry of learning and addiction.

Behavioral variability. The tendency of an animal to emit variations in response form in a given situation. The range of behavioral variation is related to the animal's capabilities based on genetic endowment, degree of neuroplasticity, and previous interactions with the environment. Behavioral variability in a shaping procedure allows for selection by reinforcing consequences, and is analogous to the role of genetic variability in natural selection.

Behaviorism. The scientific philosophy of behavior analysis.

Bias. For the generalized matching equation, bias is indicated by variation in the value of k from 1. Generally, bias is produced by some unknown asymmetry between the alternatives on a concurrent schedule that affects preference over and above the relative rates of reinforcement.

Biological context. The evolutionary history and biological status of an organism, which are part of the context for specific environment–behavior interactions.

Blocking. In respondent compound conditioning, a conditioned stimulus (CS) that has been associated with an unconditioned stimulus (US) blocks a subsequent CS–US association. A CS_1 is paired with a US until the conditioned response reaches maximum strength. Following this conditioning, a second stimulus or CS_2 is presented at the same time as the original CS_1, and both are paired with the US. On test trials, the original CS_1 elicits the conditioned response (CR) but the second stimulus or CS_2 does not.

Break and run. A pattern of response, seen on a cumulative record, that occasionally develops on fixed-interval schedules. There is a long postreinforcement pause (PRP) followed by a brief burst of responses that result in reinforcement.

Breakpoint. The highest ratio value completed on a progressive ratio (PR) schedule of reinforcement.

Celeration. A term used in precision teaching to denote two kinds of behavior change: acceleration and deceleration. Acceleration occurs when the rate of target behavior (frequency/time) is increasing over days, while deceleration involves decreasing rate over this period. A graph of the rates over days allows for evaluation of behavior change and revision of the instructional components based on the observed celeration (change in rate over days).

Chain schedule of reinforcement. Two or more simple schedules (CRF, FI, VI, FR, or VR), each of which is presented sequentially and signaled by a discriminative stimulus (S^D). Only the final or terminal link of the chain results in primary reinforcement. See also **homogeneous** and **heterogeneous chain schedules**.

Change in associative strength. A factor that affects the increment in associative strength on any one trial; the change in associative strength is the difference between the present strength of the conditioned stimulus (CS) and its maximum possible value.

Change in level (from baseline to treatment). One of the inspection criteria for visual assessment of behavior change, the change in level is the difference in the average (response rate or percentage) from baseline to treatment.

Changeover delay (COD). A control procedure that is used to stop rapid switching between alternatives on concurrent schedules of reinforcement. The COD contingency stipulates that responses do not have an effect immediately following a change from one schedule to another. After switching to a new alternative, a brief time is required before a response is reinforced. For example, if an organism has just changed to an alternative schedule that is ready to deliver reinforcement, there is a brief delay before a response is effective. As soon as the delay has elapsed, a response is reinforced. The COD contingency operates in both directions whenever a change is made from one alternative to another.

Changeover response. On a concurrent schedule, a changeover is a response that an organism emits when it switches from one alternative to another. See also **Findley procedure**.

Changing criterion design. A research design primarily used in applied behavior analysis. The rate of target behavior is progressively changed to some new criterion (up or down). For example, the criterion for the number of cigarettes a person smokes each day could be progressively lowered over several months. The effects of the independent variable are shown if the subject meets or falls below the criterion for any set of days (e.g., the criterion is 20 cigarettes for week 3, but changes to 10 by week 6).

Choice. From a behavioral view, choice is the distribution of operant behavior among alternative sources of reinforcement (e.g., concurrent schedules of reinforcement).

Coercion. Coercion is defined as the "use of punishment and the threat of punishment to get others to act as we would like, and to our practice of rewarding people just by letting them escape from our punishments and threats" (Sidman, 2001, p. 1). That is, coercion involves the basic contingencies of punishment and negative reinforcement.

Commitment response. Some behavior emitted at a time prior to the choice point that eliminates or reduces the probability of impulsive behavior. For example, a student who invites a classmate over to study on Friday night (commitment response) ensures that she will "hit the books" and give up the option of partying when the choice point arrives.

Compound stimuli. In respondent conditioning, two (or more) conditioned stimuli (e.g., tone and light) called a compound are presented together and acquire the capacity to evoke a single conditioned response (e.g., salivation).

Concurrent-chains schedule. Two or more chain schedules that are simultaneously available. See also **chain schedule of reinforcement** and **concurrent schedules of reinforcement**.

Concurrent schedules of reinforcement. Two or more schedules of reinforcement (e.g., FR, VR, FI, VI) that are simultaneously available. Each alternative is associated with a separate schedule of reinforcement, and the organism is free to distribute behavior to the schedules.

Conditional discrimination. A differential response to stimuli that depends on the stimulus context (a four-term contingency of reinforcement). Consider a matching-to-sample experiment in which a bird has been trained to match to triangles and squares based on the sample stimulus. To turn this experiment into a conditional-discrimination task, a house light is inserted that may be turned on or off. The bird is required to match to the sample when the house light is on and to choose the noncorresponding stimulus when the house light is off. Conditional matching to sample involves simultaneous discrimination of three elements in a display. The animal must respond to geometric form depending on the sample, to the correspondence or noncorrespondence of the comparison stimuli, and to the condition of the house light (on/off). See also **matching to sample**.

Conditioned aversive stimulus (S^{ave}). An aversive stimulus based on a history of conditioning. See **aversive stimulus**.

Conditioned establishing operation (CEO). An establishing operation that depends on a history of reinforcement for completing a behavioral sequence or chain. One procedure is called the blocked-response CEO, in which a response that usually occurs is blocked because of the temporary absence of a specific condition, stimulus, or event. For example, you may leave your seminar notes at home as you rush to the university. Because you cannot complete the behavioral sequence of giving a seminar presentation, obtaining the notes would function as reinforcement for making a telephone call to get them. The notes would not have a reinforcement function during a casual lunch with an old friend because they are not necessary to this behavioral sequence. Whenever an event or stimulus is required to complete a behavior chain, withholding the event will establish it as reinforcement for operant behavior.

Conditioned inhibition. In respondent conditioning, when a CS$^+$ is presented repeatedly without the US (extinction), the conditioned stimulus is said to acquire increasing amounts of inhibition, in the sense that its presentation suppresses the response.

Conditioned overeating. A procedure that involves pairing a food taste (salt or sweet) with low caloric energy. When high-energy foods with tastes that have predicted low calorie content are consumed, juvenile rats overeat at their regular meals. The basic effect is that diet foods can cause overeating in children as an unintended side effect of taste conditioning.

Conditioned place preference (CPP). A procedure in which the conditioned stimulus (CS) is a particular place or location and the sweet-flavored solution is the unconditioned stimulus (US). The solution is given in one distinct chamber (stripes) but not in another (white), and the animal shows a preference by a choice test for the location paired with the solution.

Conditioned reflex. See **conditioned response** and **conditioned stimulus**.

Conditioned reinforcement. The presentation of a conditioned reinforcer and the subsequent increase in rate of the operant that produced it.

Conditioned reinforcer. An event or stimulus that has acquired its effectiveness to increase operant rate on the basis of an organism's life or ontogenetic history.

Conditioned response (CR). An arbitrary stimulus, such as a tone, is associated with an unconditioned stimulus that elicits reflexive behavior (e.g., food elicits salivation). After several pairings, the stimulus is presented alone. If the stimulus now elicits a response (tone now evokes salivation), the response to the tone is called a conditioned response (CR).

Conditioned stimulus (CS). An arbitrary stimulus, such as a tone, is associated with an unconditioned stimulus that elicits reflexive behavior (e.g., food elicits salivation). After several pairings, the stimulus is presented alone. If the stimulus now elicits a response (tone elicits salivation), it is called a conditioned stimulus (CS).

Conditioned-stimulus function. An event or stimulus that has acquired its function to elicit a response on the basis of respondent conditioning. When a tone is followed by food in the mouth, the tone becomes a conditioned stimulus (CS) for salivation.

Conditioned suppression. In conditioned suppression, a previously conditioned stimulus (e.g., tone, light, etc.) is paired with an aversive unconditioned stimulus (US) such as an electric shock. After several pairings, the original CS becomes a conditioned aversive stimulus (CS^{ave}). Once the CS^{ave} has been conditioned, its onset suppresses ongoing operant behavior. A rat may be trained to press a lever for food. After a stable rate of response is established, the CS^{ave} is introduced. When this occurs, the animal's lever pressing is suppressed.

Conditioned taste aversion (CTA). A sweet-flavored liquid may function as a conditioned stimulus (CS) in taste-aversion conditioning, and drug-induced sickness (e.g., using lithium chloride) may serve as the unconditioned stimulus (US). After repeated pairings of the flavor or taste with the drug, the animal shows avoidance of the sweet-flavored solution.

Conditioned taste preference. When a taste or flavor CS is repeatedly associated with an appetitive US such as the sweetness of sugar, in a choice test, animals prefer the solution with the CS-taste.

Conditioned withdrawal. When a conditioned stimulus (CS) that accompanies drug use is presented, people are said to have "cravings" and this respondent process is called conditioned withdrawal. The CS elicits reactions that are ordinarily countered by the unconditioned stimulus (US). However, when the US is not delivered and the conditioned response occurs, people experience withdrawal. A heroin addict can have her withdrawal symptoms immediately terminated by a heroin injection. If you are accustomed to having a cigarette after a meal, the craving that you experience can be alleviated with a smoke.

Construction of S^Ds. When solving problems, people make up or construct their own discriminative stimuli. A person who has an important early-morning appointment may set an alarm clock for 6.00 a.m. Technically, setting the alarm is precurrent behavior, or an operant that precedes some other response or performance. That is, setting the alarm is behavior that results in the alarm ringing at 6.00 a.m., setting the occasion for getting up and going to the meeting. A major function of precurrent behavior is the construction of S^Ds that regulate subsequent action. See also **precurrent behavior**.

Context for conditioning The ontogenetic and phylogenetic histories of an organism, including its current physiological status as well as contextual events or stimuli that are present when conditioning occurs are the context for conditioning.

Context of behavior. This refers to the fact that environment–behavior relationships are always conditional—depending on other circumstances.

Contextual stimuli. In terms of operant and respondent conditioning, contextual stimuli are uncontrolled sights, sounds, smells, etc. that are the background for conditioning. These stimuli are conditioned at the same time that behavior is strengthened.

Contingencies of survival. The contingencies (in the sense of "if–then" requirements) that result in differential reproduction or natural selection. The habitat or ecological environment sets requirements for the survival of individuals and their genes. Members of a species who exhibit features and behavior appropriate to the contingencies survive and reproduce, and those with less appropriate characteristics have fewer offspring. Natural selection (differential reproduction) therefore occurs as particular organisms satisfy (or fail to satisfy) the contingencies of survival.

Contingency (respondent). In respondent conditioning, contingency refers to a correlation between the conditioned stimulus (CS) and the unconditioned stimulus (US). Rescorla (1972) suggested that a positive correlation between the CS and the US, rather than the mere pairing of these stimuli, is necessary for conditioning. For operant conditioning, see **contingency of reinforcement**.

Contingency of reinforcement. A definition of the relationship between the occasion, the operant class, and the consequences that follow the behavior (e.g., $S^D: R \rightarrow S^r$). We change the contingencies by altering one of the components and observing the effect on behavior. For example, a researcher may change the rate of reinforcement for an operant in a given situation. In this case, the $R \rightarrow S^r$ component is manipulated while the $S^D: R$ component is held constant. Contingencies of reinforcement can include more than three terms, as in conditional discrimination (e.g., four-term relations); also, the effectiveness of reinforcement contingencies depends on motivational events called establishing operations (e.g., deprivation and satiation).

Contingency management. A highly effective behavioral intervention that uses operant principles to arrange contingencies to promote desired behavior. In the context of drug abuse, contingency management (CM) is used to increase abstinence from drug use, to promote adherence to taking prescribed medication, and to increase retention in treatment programs.

Contingency-shaped behavior. Operant behavior that is directly under the control of contingencies of reinforcement, as opposed to rule-governed behavior.

Contingency-specifying stimuli. A technical term for verbal stimuli that regulate the behavior of listeners. Rules, instructions, advice, maxims, and laws are contingency-specifying stimuli in the sense that the verbal stimulus describes an actual contingency of reinforcement of everyday life. See **rule-governed behavior**.

Contingent response. In the response-deprivation hypothesis, the contingent response is the activity obtained by making the instrumental response, as in the contingency if activity A occurs (instrumental response) then the opportunity to engage in activity B (contingent response) occurs.

Continuous recording. A tactic used in applied behavior analysis for assessing the rate of target behavior. Each instance of behavior is counted during certain periods of the day (e.g., lunch, recess, first class in the morning, and so on).

Continuous reinforcement. When each response produces reinforcement (e.g., each lever press produces food), the schedule is called continuous reinforcement (CRF).

Controlling stimulus (S). Any stimulus or event that changes the probability of operant behavior. There are three kinds of controlling stimuli: S^D, S^Δ, and S^{ave}. An S^D increases the probability of response, and an S^Δ makes responding less likely. An S^{ave} may increase or decrease the likelihood of operant behavior, depending on the operating contingency.

Correlation. As used in respondent conditioning, the percentage of conditioning trials in which the conditioned stimulus (CS) is followed by the unconditioned stimulus (US), and the percentage of trials in which the CS is not followed by the US. See also **contingency**.

Correspondence relations. Survival or reinforcement contingencies that select for equivalence, matching, or similarity between (1) the behavior of a model and an observer, as in imitation, (2) what a person says and what is done (say–do correspondence), (3) what is done and what is said (do–say correspondence), (4) private stimulation and the verbal report (describing emotions), and (5) an instruction or rule and what is done (rule-governed behavior).

CS-pre-exposure effect. An alternative term for latent inhibition.

Cultural evolution. This begins at the level of the individual, when its technological effects reinforce behavior. For example, an inventor may discover a new way of making a wheel, a farmer may find a food crop that produces higher yields, and a teacher may find a novel way to teach reading. A culture is said to evolve when the community adopts these innovations and the practice (e.g., using a higher-yield type of wheat) is passed on from one generation to the next.

Cultural practice. A cultural practice is defined in terms of interlocking social contingencies—where the behavior of each person supports the behavior of other members of the community. The pattern of behavior that arises from the interlocking contingencies is the type of practice (i.e., what people do in that culture).

Culture. Culture is usually defined in terms of the ideas and values of a society. However, behavior analysts define culture as all the conditions, events, and stimuli arranged by other people that regulate human action.

Cumulative record. A real-time graphical representation of operant rate. Each response produces a constant upward increment on the y-axis, and time is indexed on the x-axis. The faster the rate of response, the steeper the slope or rise of the cumulative record. See also **cumulative recorder**.

Cumulative recorder. A laboratory instrument that is used to record the frequency of operant behavior in real time (rate of response). For example, paper is drawn across a roller at a constant speed, and each time a lever press occurs a pen steps up one increment. When reinforcement occurs, the same pen makes a downward deflection. Once the pen reaches the top of the paper, it resets to the bottom and starts to step up again. See also **cumulative record**.

Delay discounting. Delay discounting involves deciding between small, immediate rewards and large, delayed ones. If you are watching your weight, you often have to choose between the immediate reinforcement from a piece of chocolate cake or the long-term reinforcement of body weight loss and improved health. If you are like most of us, you find yourself eating the cake and forgoing the weight loss. That is, the large benefit in the future is devalued or discounted.

Delay-reduction hypothesis. Stimuli that signal a decrease in time to positive reinforcement, or an increase in time to an aversive event, are more effective conditioned reinforcers. Generally, the value of a conditioned reinforcer is attributed to its delay reduction—how close it is to reinforcement or how far it is from punishment.

Delayed conditioning. A respondent conditioning procedure in which the conditioned stimulus (CS) is presented a few seconds before the unconditioned stimulus (US) occurs.

Delayed imitation. Imitation of the modeled stimulus after a delay and in the absence of the model or modeled stimulus. Delayed imitation is considered to require more cognitive abilities than direct imitation (i.e., it involves remembering the modeled stimulus).

Delayed matching to sample. On a matching-to-sample task, the comparison stimuli are presented some time after the sample stimulus is turned off. See also **matching to sample**.

Demand curve. A mathematical curve showing how consumption decreases with price. When consumption of a commodity (reinforcer) rapidly decreases with price, the commodity is said to be *elastic*. Luxury items (e.g., a European vacation) are highly elastic, being sensitive to price. Consumption of necessities (e.g., groceries) does not change much with price and is said to be *inelastic*.

Dependent variable. The variable that is measured in an experiment, commonly called an effect. In behavior analysis, the dependent variable is a measure of the behavior of an organism. One common dependent variable is the rate of occurrence of an operant (e.g., the rate of lever pressing for food).

Deprivation operation. The procedure of restricting access to a reinforcing event. Withholding an event or stimulus increases its effectiveness as a reinforcer.

Differential reinforcement. In *discrimination procedures*, differential reinforcement involves reinforcement in the presence of one stimulus (S^D) but not in other settings (S^Δ). The result is that the organism comes to respond when the S^D is presented and to show a low probability of responding in settings that have not resulted in reinforcement (S^D). A differential response in S^D and S$^\Delta$ situations is called discrimination, and an organism that shows this differential response is said to discriminate the occasion for reinforcement.

Differential reinforcement may be based on a property of operant behavior and in this case results in *response differentiation*. For example, when reinforcement is based on short interresponse times or IRTs (2–5 s), the distribution of IRTs becomes centered around short intervals. A change in the contingencies to reinforce longer IRTs (20–25 s) produces a new distribution centered around long intervals. See **response differentiation**.

Differential reinforcement of alternative behavior (DRA). In applied behavior analysis, the undesirable behavior is placed on extinction while alternative behavior, which is incompatible with the undesirable response, is reinforced. This differential reinforcement procedure often results in an increase in alternative, desirable behavior and a decrease in the undesirable response.

Differential reinforcement of other behavior (DRO). Reinforcement for any behavior other than a target operant. For example, after a period of time the applied behavior analyst delivers reinforcement for any behavior other than "getting out of seat" in a classroom. The target behavior is on extinction and any other behavior is reinforced.

Differential response. When an organism makes a response in one situation but not in another, we say that the animal discriminates between the situations or makes a differential response.

Direct replication. Repeating the procedures and measures of an experiment with several subjects of the same species (e.g., pigeons). If each pigeon is exposed to a fixed-interval 30-s schedule of food reinforcement, and each bird shows a scalloping pattern of pecking the key (i.e., a low rate of response following reinforcement that increases to a high rate at the moment of reinforcement), then the experimental procedures show direct replication.

Discounting curve. After obtaining 7 or 8 indifference points over the range of the delays, the indifference point at each delay is plotted on a graph and a mathematical curve is fitted to the points, called the discounting curve (see Delay discounting).

Discriminated avoidance. Avoidance behavior that is emitted to a warning stimulus. For example, a dog stops barking when its owner shouts "Shut up!"

Discriminated extinction. A low rate of operant behavior that occurs as a function of an S$^\Delta$. For example, the probability of putting coins in a vending machine with an "out of order" sign on it is very low.

Discrimination. When an organism makes a differential response to two or more stimuli (or events), we can say that the animal discriminates between them. This process is called discrimination.

Discrimination index (I_D). This index compares the rate of response in the S^D component with the sum of the rates in both S^D and S$^\Delta$ phases.

$$I_D = (S^D \text{ rate})/(S^D \text{ rate} + S^\Delta \text{ rate})$$

The measure is a proportion that varies between 0.00 and 1.00. Using the I_D measure, when the rates of response are the same in the S^D and S$^\Delta$ components, the value of I_D is 0.50, indicating no discrimination. When all responses occur during the S^D phase, the S$^\Delta$ rate is zero and I_D is 1. Thus, a discrimination index of 1 indicates a perfect discrimination and maximum stimulus control of behavior. Intermediate values of the index signify more or less control by the discriminative stimulus.

Discriminative function. When an organism's behavior is reinforced, those events that reliably precede responses come to have a **discriminative function**. These events are said to *set the occasion* for behavior and are called discriminative stimuli. Discriminative stimuli acquire this function because they predict (have been followed by) reinforcement.

Discriminative stimulus (S^D). An event or stimulus that precedes an operant and sets the occasion for operant behavior (antecedent stimulus).

Discriminative-stimulus account of conditioned reinforcement. The hypothesis that it is necessary for a stimulus to be an S^D in order for it to be a conditioned reinforcer. This hypothesis has been largely discounted, and the weight of the evidence supports the delay-reduction hypothesis of Fantino (1969b). See **delay-reduction hypothesis**.

Displacement behavior. This behavior is observed in the natural environment and is characterized as irrelevant, incongruous, or out of context. That is, the behavior of the animal does not make sense given the situation, and the displaced responses do not appear to follow from immediately preceding behavior. Like **adjunctive behavior**, displacement responses arise when consummatory activities such as eating are interrupted or prevented.

Duration recording. When behavior is continuous, duration recording is a method of observation. An observer may use a stopwatch or other timing device to record the duration of behavior. When a person is sitting in a chair, the watch is timing, and when the person leaves the chair, the watch is stopped.

Early intensive behavioral intervention (EIBI). Lovaas (1977, 1987) described an early intensive behavioral intervention (EIBI) in which youngsters are given 40 or more hours each week of behavioral intervention designed to increase social behavior, to teach speaking and communication, and to eliminate self-stimulation and aggressive behavior. Most autistic children showed significant improvement in their daily functioning as a result of EIBI. See **intensive behavioral intervention**.

Echoic behavior. When there is point-to-point correspondence between the stimulus and the response, verbal behavior may be classified as echoic. A further requirement is that the verbal stimulus and the echoic response must be in the same mode (auditory, visual, etc.) and show exact physical resemblance (e.g., the same sound pattern). An echoic is a class of verbal operants regulated by a verbal stimulus in which there is correspondence and topographic similarity between the stimulus and the response. Saying "This is a dog" to the spoken stimulus "This is a dog" is an example of an echoic response in human speech.

Elicited (behavior). Respondent (CR) and reflexive (UR) behavior is elicited in the sense that the behavior is made to occur by the presentation of a stimulus (CS or US).

Emitted (behavior). Operant behavior is emitted in the sense that it occurs at some probability in the presence of a discriminative stimulus, but the S^D does not force its occurrence.

Emotional response. A response such as "wing flapping" in birds that occurs with the change in contingencies from reinforcement to extinction. One common emotional response is called aggression (attacking another organism or target).

Environment. The functional environment is all of the events and stimuli that affect the behavior of an organism. This includes events "inside the skin," such as thinking, hormonal changes, and pain stimulation.

Errorless discrimination. In errorless discrimination, the trainer does not allow the organism to make mistakes by responding to the extinction stimulus (S^Δ). Initially S^D and S^Δ are very different, but differences between the stimuli are gradually reduced as training progresses. The procedure eliminates the emotional behavior generated by extinction with other discrimination-training methods. For example, pigeons flap their wings in an aggressive manner and work for an opportunity to attack another bird during the presentation of the S^Δ on a multiple schedule. This behavior does not occur when errorless discrimination is used in training.

Escape. See **negative reinforcement**.

Established-response method. In terms of conditioned reinforcement, an operant that produces unconditioned reinforcement is accompanied by a distinctive stimulus, just prior to reinforcement. When responding is well established, extinction is implemented but half of the subjects continue to get the stimulus that accompanied unconditioned reinforcement. The other subjects undergo extinction without the distinctive stimulus. Generally, subjects with the stimulus present respond more than the subjects who do not get the stimulus associated with unconditioned reinforcement. This result is interpreted as evidence for the effects of conditioned reinforcement.

Establishing operation. Formally, an establishing operation is defined as any change in the environment that alters the effectiveness of some stimulus or event as reinforcement and simultaneously alters the momentary frequency of the behavior that has been followed by that reinforcement. Thus, an establishing operation has two major effects: it increases the momentary effectiveness of reinforcers supporting operant behavior, and it increases the momentary probability of operants that have produced such reinforcement. For example, the most common establishing operation is deprivation for primary reinforcement. This procedure has two effects. First, food becomes an effective reinforcer for any operant that produces it. Second, behavior that has previously resulted in getting food becomes more likely.

Evolution. In terms of biology, the change in the genetic make-up of the species as observed in the expressed characteristics of its members.

Experimental analysis of behavior. The method of investigation most commonly used in behavior analysis. The method involves breaking down complex environment–behavior relations into component principles of behavior. The analysis is verified by arranging experimental procedures that reveal the underlying basic principles and controlling variables. This involves intensive experimentation with a single organism over an extended period, rather than statistical assessment of groups exposed to experimental treatments.

External validity. The extent to which experimental findings generalize to other behaviors, settings, reinforcers, and populations—that is, whether the cause-and-effect relationship found in an experiment occurs at different times and places, when the original conditions are in effect.

Extinction. The procedure of extinction involves the breaking of the contingency between an operant and its consequence. For example, bar pressing followed by food reinforcement no longer produces food. As a behavioral process, extinction refers to a decline in the frequency of the operant when an extinction procedure is in effect. In both instances, the term extinction is used correctly. See **Reactive measurement**.

Extinction burst. A rapid burst of responses when an extinction procedure is first implemented.

Extinction stimulus (S^Δ). An S^Δ (pronounced S-delta) is a stimulus that sets the occasion for a decrease in operant responses. For example, an "out of order" sign on a vending machine decreases the probability of putting money in the machine. See **S-delta**.

Extraneous sources of reinforcement (R_e). All nonprogrammed sources of reinforcement that regulate alternative behavior—reducing the control of behavior on a specified schedule of reinforcement. Extraneous sources of reinforcement include any unknown contingencies that support the behavior of the organism. For example, a rat that is pressing a lever for food on a particular schedule of reinforcement could receive extraneous reinforcement for scratching, sniffing, and numerous other behaviors. The rate of response for food will be a function of the programmed schedule as well as the extraneous schedules controlling other behavior. In humans, a student's mathematical performance will be a function of the schedule of correct solutions as well as extraneous reinforcement for other behavior from classmates or teachers, internal neurochemical processes, and changes to the physical/chemical environment (e.g., the smell of food drifting from the cafeteria). See also **quantitative law of effect**.

Facultative behavior. Collateral behavior generated by properties of a schedule of reinforcement. See also **adjunctive behavior**.

Fading. The transfer of stimulus control from one value of a stimulus to another. This is done by gradually changing a controlling stimulus from an initial value to some designated criterion.

Findley procedure. An experimental method used to present concurrent schedules in the operant laboratory. Separate schedules are programmed on a single key, and the organism may switch schedules (and associated S^Ds) by making a response on a changeover key.

First-order conditioning. In first-order respondent conditioning, an apparently neutral stimulus is paired with an unconditioned stimulus (US). When this occurs, the control of the response to the US is transferred to the neutral stimulus, which is now called a conditioned stimulus (CS).

Fixed action pattern (FAP). A sequence or chain of behavior set off by a specific stimulus. The component responses are repeated almost identically with each presentation of the stimulus. Fixed action patterns are based on a "genetic blueprint," and the environment simply initiates the sequence. For example, the male stickleback fish will aggressively defend its territory from male intruders during the mating season. The fish shows a fixed sequence of threatening actions that are elicited by the red underbelly of an intruding male.

Fixed interval (FI). A schedule of reinforcement in which an operant is reinforced after a fixed amount of time has passed. For example, on a fixed-interval 90-s schedule (FI 90), one bar press after 90 s results in reinforcement. Following reinforcement, another 90-s period goes into effect, and after this time has passed, another response will produce reinforcement.

Fixed ratio (FR). A response-based schedule of reinforcement that delivers reinforcement after a fixed number of responses have been made. For example, on a fixed ratio of 10 (FR 10), the organism must make 10 responses per reinforcement.

Fluency. In precision teaching, the use of rate (frequency/time) focuses instruction on *fluency* or accuracy *and* high frequency. When a performance becomes fluent, the behavior is retained for longer, persists during long periods on the task, is less affected by distractions, and is more likely to be available in new learning situations (i.e., to combine with other well-learned behaviors).

Force of response. Reinforcement can be made contingent on the force or magnitude of response. Force or magnitude is a property or dimension of behavior.

Formal similarity. A term used in verbal behavior to define echoic behavior. Formal similarity requires that the verbal stimulus and the product of the response are in the same mode (auditory, visual, etc.) and show exact physical resemblance (e.g., the same sound pattern).

Free operant method. A method in which an organism may repeatedly respond over an extensive period of time. The organism is "free" to emit many responses or none at all. More accurately, responses can be made without interference by the experimenter (as in a trials procedure).

Function-altering event. Verbal stimuli such as rules and instructions can alter the function of other stimuli and, thereby, the strength of relations among stimuli and behavior. For example, an instruction about what to do in an airline emergency can establish stimulus control by a "dangling yellow mask" over the behavior of "placing the mask over your face and breathing normally,"

Functional analysis. An analysis of behavior in terms of its products or consequences. Functionally, there are two basic types of behavior: operant and respondent. The term *respondent* defines behavior that increases or decreases because of the presentation of a stimulus (or event) that precedes the response. Such behavior is said to be elicited, in the sense that it reliably occurs when the stimulus is presented. There is a large class of behavior that does not depend on an eliciting stimulus. This behavior is described as *emitted*, and spontaneously occurs at some frequency. When emitted behavior is strengthened or weakened by the events that follow the response, it is called *operant* behavior. Thus, operants are emitted responses that increase or decrease depending on the consequences they produce.

Functional independence. A term used in verbal behavior to describe the independence of the operant classes of manding and tacting. Formally, each operant class is controlled by separate contingencies of reinforcement; training in manding relations would not necessarily affect the training in tacting relations, or vice versa.

Generality. An experimental result has generality when it is observed in different environments, organisms, and so on. For example, the principle of reinforcement generalizes over species, settings, responses, and reinforcers. In a pigeon, the peck-for-food relationship depends on the establishing operation of deprivation for food in the immediate past. For humans, who have an extensive capacity for operant conditioning, going to a soda machine to get a cold drink on a hot afternoon is an effective contingency. In both examples, establishing operations and reinforcement are the operating principles.

Generalization gradient (operant). Generalization occurs when an organism responds to values of the S^D (or fewer responses to the S^Δ) that were not trained during acquisition. A generalization gradient is the function (graph) that relates values of the S^D (intensity of light) to a measure of response strength (operant rate).

Generalization gradient (respondent). Generalization occurs when an organism shows a conditioned response (CR) to values of the conditioned stimulus (CS) that were not trained during acquisition. A generalization gradient is the function (graph) that relates values of the CS (loudness of tone) to a measure of response strength (amount of CR).

Generalized conditioned reinforcement. A reinforcement procedure using a generalized conditioned reinforcer such as money that may be exchanged for many other reinforcers (goods and services) and is relatively independent of momentary level of deprivation for any particular reinforcer such as food.

Generalized conditioned reinforcer. A conditioned reinforcer that is backed up by many other sources of reinforcement. Money is a good example of a generalized conditioned reinforcer. Cash may be exchanged for a wide variety of goods and services. Human behavior is regulated by generalized reinforcement, involving social attention, approval, and affection.

Generalized imitation. A reinforcement procedure used to teach the generalized response and stimulus classes "do as I do." The procedure involves reinforcement of correspondence between modeled performance and imitative operants. After training a number of exemplars, a novel modeled stimulus is presented without reinforcement and a new imitative response occurs that matches the modeled performance. Generalized imitation involves both stimulus generalization of the class of modeled stimuli and response generalization of the class of imitative responses.

Generalized matching law. Proportion equations such as $B_a/(B_a + B_b) = R_a/(R_a + R_b)$ describe concurrent performance when alternatives differ only in rate of reinforcement. However, in complex environments, other factors also contribute to choice and preference. These factors arise from the biology and environmental history of the organism. For example, sources of error may include different amounts of effort for the responses, qualitative differences in reinforcement such as food versus water, a history of punishment, a tendency to respond to the right alternative rather than the left, and sensory capacities.

To include these and other conditions within the matching law, it is useful to express the law in terms of ratios rather than proportions (i.e., $B_a/B_b = R_a/R_b$). When relative rate of response matches relative rate of reinforcement, the ratio equation is simply a restatement of the proportional form of the matching law. A generalized form of the ratio equation may, however, be used to handle the situation in which unknown factors influence the distribution of behavior. These factors produce systematic departures from ideal matching, but may be represented as two constants (parameters) in the generalized matching equation.

$$B_a/B_b = k(R_a/R_b)^a$$

In this form, the matching equation is known as the generalized matching law. The coefficient k and the exponent a are values that represent two sources of error for a given experiment. When these parameters are equal to 1, the equation is the simple ratio form of the matching law. See also **matching law.**

Generalized social reinforcement. A generalized conditioned reinforcer that is also a social reinforcer increases or maintains operant behavior. Praise is a social reinforcer backed up by many sources of reinforcement. See also **generalized conditioned reinforcer.**

Genotype. The genetic make-up of the organism. Some observable characteristics are largely determined by genotype, other features are strongly influenced by experience, but most result from an interaction of genes and environment. Thus, the height of a person is attributable to both genes and nutrition.

Habituation. Habituation occurs when an unconditioned stimulus (US) repeatedly elicits an unconditioned response (UR). The frequent presentation of the US produces a gradual decline in the magnitude of the unconditioned response. When the UR is repeatedly elicited it may eventually fail to occur at all.

Heterogeneous-chain schedule. A heterogeneous chain requires different responses for each link of the chain schedule. Dog trainers make use of heterogeneous chains when they teach complex behavioral sequences to their animals. When going for a walk, a seeing-eye dog stops at intersections, moves forward when the traffic is clear, pauses at a curb, avoids potholes, and finds the way home. Each of these different responses is occasioned by specific stimuli and results in conditioned reinforcement. See also **chain schedule of reinforcement**.

History of reinforcement. The reinforcement contingencies that an organism has been exposed to during its lifetime, including the changes in behavior due to such exposure.

Homeostasis. Claude Bernard proposed the concept of stability of the "milieu intérieur" in 1885. Subsequently, Walter Cannon coined the term "homeostasis" in 1926 to describe the tendency of a system to remain stable and to resist change. In terms of a biological system, homeostasis refers to the regulation of the system by negative feedback loops. For example, the body maintains a temperature within a very fine tolerance. If the environment warms up or cools down, physiological mechanisms (sweating or shivering) involving the sympathetic and parasympathetic nervous systems are activated to reduce the drift from normal body temperature. Homeostasis involves self-regulation to maintain an internal environment in a stable or constant condition by means of multiple dynamic equilibrium adjustments.

Homogeneous-chain schedule. Operant chains are classified as homogeneous when the topography or form of response is similar in each link of the schedule—for example, a bird pecks the same key in each component of the chain. Each link in the schedule produces a discriminative stimulus for the next link, and the S^D is also a conditioned reinforcer for the behavior that produces it. See also **chain schedule of reinforcement**.

Hyperbolic discounting equation. A delay discounting equation by Mazur (1987) that shows a hyperbolic decay:

$$V_d = \frac{A}{1 + kd}$$

In the equation, we are predicting discounted values, V_d, of the reinforcer. The amount of the reinforcer, A, is $100,000 in our example, and the value, d, is the delay—the variable on the x-axis. The value k is called the *discounting rate*, which must be estimated to fit a curve to the indifference points (data) obtained from the experiment.

Hypothetical construct. An unobservable event or process that is postulated to occur and that is said to explain behavior. For example, Freud's mental device "ego" is a hypothetical construct that is used to explain self-gratifying behavior. In cognitive psychology, terms such as "cognitive representation" or "mental imagery" are hypothetical terms that are said to explain the behavior of knowing and observing the world. From a behavioral perspective, the difficulty is that the mental constructs are easily invented, are inferred from the behavior they are said to explain, and are inherently unobservable with direct observation. That is, there is no objective way of obtaining information about such events except by observing the behavior of people or other organisms.

Identity matching. In identity matching or discrimination, the researcher presents a sample stimulus (e.g., vertical line) and two side-key options (e.g., vertical line and horizontal line). The organism is reinforced for selecting the comparison stimulus that corresponds to the sample (e.g., pecking the side key with a vertical line when the sample is a vertical line). See also **matching to sample**.

Imitation. True imitation requires that the learner emits a novel response that could only occur by observing a model emit a similar response.

Immediacy of change (baseline to treatment). When visually inspecting behavioral data, we assume that the cause of a change in behavior must immediately precede the change. In behavior analysis, immediacy is assessed using the last three data points of the baselines and the first three data points for the treatment phases. Immediacy of change is also assessed from the treatment phase to the return to baseline. For the high-impact results, the change in the dependent variable is almost immediate with the changes in the independent variable (baseline to treatment, or treatment to baseline).

Immediate causation. Refers to the kind of mechanism studied by physics and chemistry; the "billiard ball" sort of process where we try to isolate a chain of events that directly result in some effect. For example, chemical reactions are explained by describing molecular interactions. In the study of behavior, an immediate causal explanation might refer to the physiology and biochemistry of the organism.

Impulsive behavior. When a person (or other animal) selects the smaller, immediate payoff over the larger, delayed benefits, we may say that the person shows impulsive behavior.

Independent variable. The variable that is manipulated, changed, or controlled in an experiment, commonly called a cause. In behavior analysis, it is a change in the contingencies of reinforcement, the arrangement of events that precede and follow the behavior of an organism (e.g., changing the rate of reinforcement).

Information account of conditioned reinforcement. A hypothesis which suggests that a stimulus becomes a conditioned reinforcer if it provides information about the occurrence of primary reinforcement. This notion has been largely discounted and replaced by the delay-reduction hypothesis of Fantino (1969b). See also **delay-reduction hypothesis**.

Innate imitation. See **spontaneous imitation**.

Instinctive drift. Species-characteristic behavior that becomes more and more invasive during operant training.

Instrumental response. In the response-deprivation hypothesis, the instrumental response is the behavior that produces the opportunity to engage in some activity.

Intensive behavioral intervention. A term used in the treatment of autistic behavior where the child is given targeted or planned interventions for behavioral excesses and deficits of 30 or more hours each week. This kind of programmed behavioral intervention is most effective with children under 4 years of age.

Interim behavior. See **adjunctive behavior**.

Interlocking contingencies. In social episodes involving manding and tacting, each person (speaker and listener) completes a behavioral sequence or chain ($S^D: R \rightarrow S^r + S^D: R \rightarrow S^r \ldots$), and the verbal relations involve the intermingling of these chains or the interlocking contingencies. In an interlocking contingency the behavior of one person causes stimulation and reinforcement for the behavior of the other, and vice versa.

Intermittent reinforcement effect. See **partial reinforcement effect**.

Intermittent reinforcement schedule. A schedule programmed so that some rather than all operants are reinforced. In other words, an intermittent schedule is any schedule of reinforcement other than continuous reinforcement (CRF). See **partial reinforcement effect**.

Internal validity. When many extraneous variables are ruled out by an experimental design, the research has high internal validity. That is, changes in the dependent variable may be reasonably attributed to changes in the independent variable (cause $\rightarrow$ effect). Internal validity is the minimum requirement for all experiments.

Interreinforcement interval (IRI). The time between any two reinforcers. Research shows that the postreinforcement pause (PRP) is a function of the IRI. As the time between reinforcements becomes longer, the PRP increases. On fixed-interval (FI) schedules the PRP is approximately half of the IRI. For example, on an FI 300-s schedule (in which the time between reinforcements is 300 s), the average PRP will be 150 s. On fixed-ratio (FR) schedules, the evidence indicates similar control by the IRI: as the ratio requirement increases, the PRP becomes longer. See **postreinforcement pause (PRP)**.

Interresponse time (IRT). The time between any two responses. The interresponse time may be treated as a conditionable property of operant behavior; for example, the IRTs on a variable-interval (VI) schedule of reinforcement are much longer than those on a variable-ratio (VR) schedule. VI schedules are said to differentially reinforce long IRTs, while VR schedules differentially reinforce short interresponse times.

Interval recording. A measurement strategy used in applied behavior analysis to assess the rate of target behavior. A block of time is selected and divided into short equal intervals, and if the target behavior occurs it is recorded once in an appropriate time bin. For example, a 30-min segment of mathematics class may be divided into 10-s bins. Regardless of the number of responses, if the behavior occurs in a given 10-s segment, then the observer records it as a single event.

Interval schedules. Schedules of reinforcement based on the passage of time and one response after that time has elapsed.

Intraverbal behavior. A class of verbal operants regulated by verbal discriminative stimuli. In everyday language, thematically related words (or sentences) are examples of intraverbal relations. For example, the verbal response "fish" to the spoken words "rod and reel" is an intraverbal response; saying "water" to the written word LAKE is also intraverbal behavior. Thus, intraverbal relations arise from verbal behavior itself. A previous verbal response by a speaker is a stimulus for a subsequent verbal operant.

In-vitro reinforcement. A method used to investigate reinforcement in the neuron. It involves increasing calcium bursts or firings by injection of dopamine agonists or other agents.

Joint control. The notion that two verbal stimuli exert stimulus control over a common verbal topography. When finding the correct sequence of numbers in an array, repeating the required number and identifying that number in the array jointly control the terminal verbal response "[number]—I found it."

Latency. The time from the onset of one event to the onset of another (e.g., the time it takes a rat to reach a goal box after it has been released in a maze).

Latent inhibition. A term used to denote that an animal's learning of the CS–US relation is reduced or inhibited by pre-exposure of the CS, revealed by an acquisition test following the conditioning phase.

Law of effect. As originally stated by Thorndike, this law refers to stamping in (or out) some response. For example, a cat opened a puzzle-box door more rapidly over repeated trials. Currently the law is stated as the principle of reinforcement—operants may be followed by consequences that increase (or decrease) the probability or rate of response.

Law of intensity–magnitude. As the intensity of an unconditioned stimulus (US) increases, so does the magnitude or size of the unconditioned response (UR).

Law of latency. As the intensity of the unconditioned stimulus (US) increases, the latency (time to onset) of the unconditioned response (UR) decreases.

Law of the threshold. At very weak intensities a stimulus will not elicit a response, but as the intensity of the eliciting stimulus increases there is a point at which the response is evoked. That is, there is a point below which no response is elicited and above which a response always occurs.

Learned helplessness. This involves exposing an animal to inescapable and severe aversive stimulation (shocks). Eventually the animal gives up and stops attempting to avoid or escape the situation. Next, an escape response that under ordinary circumstances would be acquired easily is made available, but the animal does not make the response. The organism seems to give up and become helpless when presented with inescapable aversive stimulation.

Learning. The acquisition, maintenance, and change of an organism's behavior as a result of life-time events (the ontogeny of behavior). In everyday language, the word "learning" is often used to refer to transitional changes in behavior (e.g., from not knowing to knowing one's ABC), but conditions that maintain behavior in a steady state are also part of what we mean by learning (e.g., continuing to recite the alphabet).

Limited hold. A contingency where the reinforcer is available for a set time after an interval schedule has timed out. Adding a limited hold to a variable-interval (VI) schedule increases the rate of responding by reinforcing short interresponse times (IRTs).

Log-linear matching equation. To write the matching law as a straight line, we may write the log-linear equation:

$$\log(B_a/B_b) = \log k + [a \times \log(R_a/R_b)].$$

Notice that in this form, $\log(B_a/B_b)$ is the y variable and $\log(R_a/R_b)$ is the x variable. The constants a and $\log k$ are the slope and intercept, respectively. See **generalized matching law**.

Magazine training. A procedure that involves following the click of the feeder (stimulus) with the presentation of food (reinforcement). For example, a rat is placed in an operant chamber and a microcomputer periodically turns on the feeder. When the feeder is turned on, it makes a click and a food pellet falls into a cup. Because the click and the appearance of food are associated in time you would, after training, observe a typical rat staying close to the food magazine, quickly moving toward it when the feeder is operated. See **conditioned reinforcer**.

MammaCare. A behavioral program that is used to teach women effective self-examination of their breasts.

Manding. The word manding comes from the common English word *commanding*, but commanding is only part of this operant class. Manding is a class of verbal operants whose form is regulated by establishing operations (e.g., deprivation, aversive stimulation, etc.) and specific reinforcement. When you say "Give me the book," "Don't do that," "Stop," and so on, your words are regulated by motivational conditions or establishing operations (e.g., deprivation for the book, or by another person doing something unpleasant). The establishing operation (no ketchup) regulates the topography of manding ("Give ketchup") and ensures that a particular event functions as specific reinforcement (getting ketchup).

Matching law. When two or more concurrent-interval schedules are available, the relative rate of response matches (or equals) the relative rate of reinforcement. More generally, the matching law states that the distribution of behavior between (or among) alternative sources of reinforcement is equal to the distribution of reinforcement for these alternatives. See **relative rate of response** and **relative rate of reinforcement**.

Matching to sample. A procedure that is used to investigate recognition of stimuli. For example, a pigeon may be presented with three keys. A triangle or sample stimulus is projected onto the center key. To ensure that the bird attends to the sample, the pigeon is required to peck the sample key. When this happens, two side keys are illuminated with a triangle on one and a square on the other, called the comparison stimuli. If the bird pecks the comparison stimulus that corresponds to the sample, this behavior is reinforced and leads to the presentation of a new sample. Pecks to the noncorresponding stimulus result in extinction and the next trial. See **identity matching** and **discrimination**.

Maturation. One source of internal invalidity in experiments. The term refers to biological or psychological processes that change over time (e.g., aging, development). If these maturational changes occur at the same time as the manipulation of the independent variable, they (rather than the experimental treatment) could be responsible for the findings. See also **internal validity**.

Maximization. In this economic view of behavior, humans and other animals are like organic computers that compare their behavioral distributions with overall outcomes and eventually stabilize on a response distribution that maximizes overall rate of reinforcement. See **melioraton** as an alternative view.

Maximum associative strength. In the Rescorla–Wagner model, a conditioned stimulus (CS) can acquire only so much control over a conditioned response (CR). This is the maximum associative strength for the CS. Thus, a tone (CS) that is paired with 1 g of food will have maximum associative strength when conditioned salivation (the conditioned response, CR) to the tone is about the same amount as the unconditioned salivation (unconditioned response, UR) elicited by the food (US). That is, a US elicits a given magnitude of the UR. This magnitude sets the upper limit for the CR. The CS cannot elicit a greater response than the one produced by the US.

Mechner notation. A notation system that describes the independent variables that produce operant behavior. That is, Mechner notation is a set of symbols for programming schedules of reinforcement arranged in the laboratory.

Melioration. An explanation of how organisms come to produce matching on concurrent schedules of reinforcement. In contrast to overall maximizing of reinforcement, Herrnstein (1982) proposed a process of melioration (doing the best at the moment). Organisms, he argued, are sensitive to fluctuations in the momentary rates of reinforcement rather than to long-term changes in overall rates of reinforcement.

Metacontingencies. The contingent relations among cultural practices and the effects of those practices for the group. For example, competence in science is important for people who live in a technologically advanced culture. Scientific research produces a range of benefits for the general society. These include better medicine, more productive crop yields, new and better building materials, more efficient and longer-lasting appliances, and superior regulation of human behavior. Thus, a positive metacontingency exists between educational practices that increase scientific competence and long-term benefits to the group.

Mixed schedule of reinforcement. Two or more basic schedules (CRF, FR, FI, VI, VR) presented sequentially in which each link ends with primary reinforcement (or in some cases extinction) and the component schedules are not signaled by discriminative stimuli. In other words, a mixed schedule is the same as an unsignaled multiple schedule. See **multiple schedule**.

Modal action pattern (MAP). The behavioral flexibility of seemingly fixed action patterns. The major topographic features of these reflex combinations may appear similar across individuals and situations, but there are numerous idiosyncratic differences. For example, all robins (*Turdus americanus*) build nests that appear very similar in construction. However, it is clear they do not all build in the same location, or use the same materials. There is great individual variation in all phases of nest construction, suggesting modification by the environment (ontogeny).

Molar account or perspective. Molar accounts of behavior on schedules of reinforcement or punishment are concerned with large-scale factors that regulate responding over a long period of time. For example, the average time between reinforcers for an entire session and the overall reduction in shock frequency are molar-level variables.

Molecular account or perspective. Molecular accounts of behavior on schedules of reinforcement or punishment focus on small moment-to-moment relationships between behavior and its consequences. For example, the time between any two responses (the interresponse time) and the response–shock interval (R–S) are molecular-level variables.

Motivating operation. To capture both the establishing and abolishing effects of events that precede reinforced behavior (or punishment), it is useful to introduce a more inclusive concept. The motivating operation (MO) refers to any event that alters the reinforcement effectiveness of behavioral consequences and changes the frequency of behavior maintained by those consequences.

Multiple baseline across behaviors. A multiple baseline research design across behaviors is used when a reinforcement procedure is applied progressively to several operants. In this case, the subject, setting, and consequences remain the same, but different responses are modified sequentially.

Multiple baseline across stimulus conditions. In this research design, a reinforcement procedure is applied in one situation but is withheld in other settings. When behavior changes in the situation where it is reinforced, the contingency is applied to the same response in another setting.

Multiple baseline across subjects. A research design in which an intervention is introduced progressively for different subjects who exhibit similar target behavior. The same behavior (e.g., stealing) is first modified for subject 1, and baselines are collected for subjects 2 and 3. Next, the behavior of subject 2 is changed while the rate of target behavior for subjects 1 and 3 continues to be assessed. Finally, the treatment procedure is applied to subject 3.

Multiple baseline design. A class of research designs used primarily in applied behavior analysis. See **multiple baseline across behaviors, multiple baseline across stimulus conditions**, and **multiple baseline across subjects**.

Multiple functions (of stimuli). A given event or stimulus, such as a student saying "The ball is red," can have several functions in the control of behavior (e.g., $S^r + S^D$). For example, the response can function as reinforcement for the teacher's question "What color is the ball?" and at the same time function as a discriminative stimulus for the teacher saying "Yes."

Multiple schedule. Two or more basic schedules (CRF, FR, FI, VI, VR) presented sequentially, each link ending with primary reinforcement (or in some cases extinction); the component schedules are signaled by discriminative stimuli. In other words, a multiple schedule is the same as a chain schedule, but each link produces primary reinforcement. See **chain schedule of reinforcement**.

Mutation. Mutation occurs when the genetic material (e.g., genes or chromosomes) of an individual changes. These changes are accidents that affect the genetic code carried by an ovum or sperm. For example, naturally occurring background radiation may alter a gene site, or a chromosome may break during the formation of sex cells or gametes. Such mutations are passed on to offspring, who display new characteristics.

Naming relation. Horne and Lowe (1996) proposed that naming something (an object, place, or action) involves a generalized operant class that substantially expands the verbal repertoire of the child. Analytically, the naming relation or the *generalized class of naming* arises from verbal contingencies that integrate the echoic and tacting response classes of the child as speaker with the conditional discrimination behavior of the child as listener.

Natural selection. The differential reproduction of the members of a species and their genetic endowment. Based on a thorough analysis of life forms, Darwin concluded that reproductive success was the underlying basis of evolution. That is, individuals with more offspring pass on a greater number of their characteristics (genes) to the next generation.

Negative automaintenance. Birds are autoshaped to peck a key, but in negative automaintenance food is not presented if the bird pecks the key. This is also called an omission procedure or training, because food reinforcement is omitted if key pecking occurs.

Negative contrast. See **behavioral contrast**.

Negative punishment. A contingency that involves the removal of an event or stimulus following behavior that has the effect of decreasing the rate of response. The negative punishment procedure requires that behavior (watching television) is maintained by positive reinforcement (entertaining programs) and the reinforcer is removed (TV turned off) if a specified response occurs (yelling and screaming). The probability of response is reduced by the procedure.

Negative reinforcement. A contingency where an ongoing stimulus or event is removed (or prevented) by some response (operant) and the rate of response increases. If it is raining, opening and standing under an umbrella removes the rain and maintains the use of the umbrella on rainy days. When operant behavior increases by removing an ongoing event or stimulus, the contingency is called *escape*. The contingency is called *avoidance* when the operant increases by preventing the onset of the event or stimulus. Both escape and avoidance involve negative reinforcement.

Negative reinforcer. Any event or stimulus that increases the probability (rate of occurrence) of an operant that removes or prevents it. See also **negative reinforcement**.

Neuroplasticity. Alterations of neurons and neural interconnections during a lifetime by changes in environmental contingencies.

New-response method for conditioned reinforcement. First, a nonreinforcing stimulus is associated with a reinforcing event (sound of feeder is followed by food), and after this procedure the stimulus (sound of feeder) is shown to increase the frequency of some operant behavior.

Nondiscriminated avoidance. A procedure used to train avoidance responding in which no warning stimulus is presented (also called Sidman avoidance). See also **negative reinforcement**.

Observational learning. From a social cognitive viewpoint, the observer pays attention to the modeled sequence, noting the arrangement of each action. The general information in the sequence must be coded and rehearsed. Once this abstract information is retained in memory, imitation is a matter of reproducing the component responses in the correct sequences. From a behavioral perspective, observational learning involves the integration of generalized imitation, rule-governed behavior, and verbal behavior. Each of these components is addressed separately in behavior analysis.

Observing response. A topographically different operant that functions to produce an S^D or S^Δ depending on whether reinforcement or extinction is in effect. In other words, an observing response changes a mixed schedule of reinforcement to a multiple schedule. See **mixed schedule of reinforcement** and **multiple schedule**.

Omission procedure (or training). See **negative automaintenance**.

Ontogenetic. Each organism has a unique life history (ontogeny) that contributes to its behavior. Ontogenetic changes in behavior are caused by events that occur over the lifetime of an individual. Ontogenetic history builds on species history (phylogeny) to determine when, where, and what kind of behavior will occur at a given moment. See also **phylogenetic**.

Ontogenetic selection. The selection of operant behavior during the lifetime of an organism. The process involves operant variability during periods of extinction and selection by contingencies of reinforcement. An organism that alters its behavior (adaptation) on the basis of changing life experiences is showing ontogenetic selection. In this ontogenetic form of adaptation, the topography and frequency of behavior increase when reinforcement is withheld (increase in operant variability). These behavioral changes during extinction allow for the selection of behavior by new contingencies of reinforcement. For example, a wild rat that has been exploiting a compost heap may find that the homeowner has covered it. In this case, the rat emits various operants that may eventually uncover the food. The animal may dig under the cover, gnaw a hole in the sheathing, or search for some other means of entry. A similar effect occurs when food in the compost heap is depleted and the animal emits behavior that results in getting to a new food patch. In the laboratory, this behavior is measured as an increase in the topography and frequency of bar pressing as the schedules of reinforcement change.

Operant. An operant is behavior that operates on the environment to produce a change, effect, or consequence. These environmental changes select the operant appropriate to a given setting or circumstance. That is, particular responses increase or decrease in a situation as a function of the consequences that they produced in the past. Operant behavior is said to be emitted (rather than elicited) in the sense that the behavior may occur at some frequency before any known conditioning.

Operant aggression. Aggressive behavior that is reinforced (increased) by the removal of an aversive event arranged by another member of the species. See also **negative reinforcement**.

Operant chamber. A laboratory enclosure or box used to investigate operant conditioning. An operant chamber for a rat is a small, enclosed box that typically contains a lever with a light above it and a food magazine or cup connected to an external feeder. The feeder delivers a small food pellet when electronically activated.

Operant class. A class or set of responses that vary in topography but produce a common environmental consequence or effect. The response class of turning on the light has many variations in form (turn on the light with the left index finger, or with the right one, or with the side of the hand, or by saying to someone "Please turn on the light").

Operant conditioning. An increase or decrease in operant response as a function of the consequences that have followed the response.

Operant imitation. Imitative behavior that is controlled by its consequences. See **imitation**.

Operant level. The rate of an operant before any known conditioning (e.g., the rate of key pecking before a peck–food contingency has been established).

Operant rate. See **rate of response**.

Operant variability. Operant behavior becomes increasingly more variable as extinction proceeds. From an evolutionary view, it makes sense to try different ways of acting when something no longer works. That is, behavioral variation increases the chances that the organism will reinstate reinforcement or contact other sources of reinforcement, increasing the likelihood of its survival and reproduction.

Overcorrection. A positive punishment procedure that uses "restitution" to reduce or eliminate destructive or aggressive behavior. Overcorrection may also involve *positive practice*, requiring the violator to intensively practice an overly correct form of the action.

Overmatching. In the generalized matching equation, a value of *a* greater than 1 indicates that changes in the response ratio (B_a/B_b) are larger than changes in the ratio of reinforcement (R_a/R_b). This outcome occurs because relative behavior increases faster than predicted from relative rate of reinforcement. See also **generalized matching law**.

Overshadowing. This effect occurs when a compound stimulus is used as the conditioned stimulus (CS) in a respondent conditioning experiment. For example, a light + tone (CS) may be presented at the same time and be associated with an unconditioned stimulus (US) such as food. The most *salient* property of the compound stimulus comes to regulate exclusively the conditioned response. Thus, if the tone is more salient than the light, only the tone will elicit salivation.

Paradoxical effects of punishment. This refers to the evidence that response-produced shock resembles some of the effects of positive reinforcement (FI scalloping). However, the shocks do not actually function as positive reinforcement.

Partial reinforcement effect. Partial (or intermittent) reinforcement schedules generate greater resistance to extinction than continuous reinforcement (CRF). The higher the rate of reinforcement the greater the resistance to change; however, the change from CRF to extinction is discriminated more rapidly than between intermittent reinforcement and extinction.

Peak shift. A shift that occurs in the peak of a generalization gradient away from an extinction (S^{Δ}) stimulus. See **generalization gradient**.

Permanence of punishment. This refers to a debate as to whether punishment by itself, without additional procedures such as extinction or reinforcement of alternative behavior, can permanently eliminate undesirable behavior.

Personalized system of instruction (PSI). A teaching method based on principles of operant conditioning and designed by Fred Keller (Keller, 1968). Keller called his teaching method a personalized system of instruction (PSI). Basically, PSI courses are organized such that students move through the course at their own pace and are reinforced for completing small course units.

Phenotype. The anatomical and behavioral characteristics that are observed during the lifetime of an individual. For example, the individual's size, color, and shape are anatomical aspects of phenotype. Behavioral features include taste preferences, aggressiveness, and shyness. Different phenotypic attributes of individuals may or may not reflect underlying genetic variation.

Phylogenetic. Behavior relations that are based on the genetic endowment of an organism, and that are present on the basis of species history. Behavior that aids survival or procreation is often (but not always) unlearned. This is because past generations of organisms that engaged in such behavior survived and reproduced. These animals passed on to the next generation the characteristics (via genes) that allowed similar behavior. Thus, species history provides the organism with a basic repertoire of responses that are evoked by environmental conditions. See also **ontogenetic behavior**.

Phylogeny. The species history of an organism.

Placebo effect. The effect of an inert substance such as a sugar pill on the "physiological well-being" of a patient. That is, patients who are treated with sugar pills show improvements relative to a no-treatment control group.

Polydipsia. Polydipsia or excessive drinking is adjunctive behavior induced by the time-based delivery of food. For example, a rat that is working for food on an intermittent schedule may drink as much as half its body weight during a single session. This drinking occurs even though the animal is not water deprived. See also **adjunctive behavior**.

Positive contrast. See **behavioral contrast**.

Positive punishment. A procedure that involves the presentation of an event or stimulus following behavior that has the effect of decreasing the rate of response. For example, a child is given a spanking for running into the street, and as a result the probability of the behavior is decreased.

Positive reinforcement. A contingency that involves the presentation of an event or stimulus following an operant that increases the rate of response.

Positive reinforcer. Any stimulus or event that increases the probability (rate of response) of an operant when presented.

Postreinforcement pause (PRP). The pause in responding that occurs after reinforcement on some intermittent schedules (e.g., FR, FI).

Power law for matching. See **generalized matching law**.

Precision teaching. In what became known as *precision teaching*, Ogden Lindsley devised a method of systematic instruction that encouraged students and teachers to target specific behaviors, to count, time, and graph them, and to revise instructional procedures based on the charted data. The use of the Standard Celeration Chart for graphing change in response rate over days is a prominent feature of this teaching method.

Precurrent behavior. Operant behavior that precedes a current response. Precurrent behavior often functions to establish stimulus control over subsequent operant behavior, as when a person sets the alarm for 6.00 a.m. (precurrent behavior) to ensure stimulus control by the clock over waking up and going to an appointment or job (current behavior). In this example, both the precurrent and current behavior are maintained by the reinforcement contingency (i.e., avoiding the consequences of being late). When precurrent behavior is private, as in thinking about chess moves, the behavior provides S^D control over the actual movement of the chess pieces. Thinking about chess moves and actual moves are maintained by the contingency of reinforcement, involving gaining a momentary advantage and ultimately winning the game. See **construction of S^Ds**.

Preference. When several schedules of reinforcement are available concurrently, one alternative may be chosen more frequently than others. When this occurs, we say that the organism shows a preference for that alternative.

Preference for choice. When equated for differential outcomes, humans and other animals show a preference for options that allow them to make choices compared with options that limit or restrict the opportunity to choose.

Preference reversal. The change in value of a reinforcer as a function of time to the choice point (as in self-control). For example, people make a commitment to save their money (monthly deduction at the bank) rather than spend it because the value of saving is greater than that of spending when far from the choice point (getting paid). At the choice point, spending is always higher in value than saving the money. See **Ainslie–Rachlin principle**.

Premack principle. A higher-frequency behavior will function as reinforcement for a lower-frequency behavior.

Preparedness. Some relations between stimuli, and between stimuli and responses, are more likely because of phylogenetic history. This phenomenon has been called preparedness. For example, a bird that relies on sight for food selection would be expected to associate the appearance of a particular food item with illness, but rats that select food on the basis of taste quickly make a flavor–illness association.

Preratio pause. The number of responses (ratio size) required and the magnitude of the reinforcer have both been shown to influence the postreinforcement pause (PRP). Calling this pause a "post"-reinforcement event accurately locates the pause, but it is the ratio size that actually controls it. Hence, many researchers refer to the PRP as a preratio pause. See **postreinforcement pause (PRP)**.

Primary aversive stimulus. An aversive stimulus that has acquired its properties as a function of species history. See **aversive stimulus**.

Primary laws of the reflex. These include the law of the threshold, the law of intensity–magnitude, and the law of latency. These laws govern the US $\rightarrow$ UR relationship.

Private behavior. Behavior that is only accessible to the person who emits it (e.g., thinking).

Probability of response.   The probability that an operant will occur on a given occasion (measured as the rate of response).

Progressive ratio schedule. A schedule in which the number of responses (ratio) increases (or decreases) after reinforcement. For example, a pigeon on an increasing progressive ratio may be required to make 2 responses for access to food, then 4, 8, 16, 32, and higher ratios. In a foraging model, the increasing progressive ratio schedule simulates a depleting patch of food.

Punisher. A stimulus that decreases the frequency of an operant that produces it.

Punishment. As a procedure, punishment involves following an operant with a punisher. Usually, the operant is maintained by positive reinforcement so that punishment is superimposed on a baseline of positive reinforcement. Punishment also refers to a decrease in operant behavior when followed by a punisher or when reinforcement is withdrawn contingent on responding. See **positive punishment** and **negative punishment**.

Punishment debate. This concerns the arguments and evidence for and against the use of punishment to control self-injurious and aggressive behavior in positive behavioral support programs.

Quantitative law of effect. This law states that the absolute rate of response on a schedule of reinforcement is a hyperbolic function of rate of reinforcement on the schedule relative to the total rate of reinforcement (both scheduled and extraneous reinforcement). That is, as the rate of reinforcement on the schedule increases, the rate of response also rises, but eventually further increases in the rate of reinforcement produce less and less of an increase in the rate of response (hyperbolic). Also, the rise in rate of response with increasing rate of reinforcement is modified by extraneous sources of reinforcement (R_e). Extraneous reinforcement reduces the rate of response on the reinforcement schedule. One implication is that control of behavior by a schedule of reinforcement is weakened by sources of extraneous reinforcement.

   A proportional matching equation is one mathematical expression of the quantitative law of effect. The equation relates absolute response and reinforcement rates, using alternative sources of reinforcement as the context. The equation may be derived from a restatement of the proportional matching law, and is written as $B_a/(B_a + B_e) = R_a/(R_a + R_e)$. In this equation, B_e refers to all behavior directed to extraneous sources of reinforcement, and R_e represents these sources.

The term B_a represents rate of response on the programmed schedule, and R_a is the rate of scheduled reinforcement.

Range of variability (in assessment). Changes in level produced by the treatment must be assessed in relation to the visual inspection of the range of variability of the dependent variable. The range of variability is the difference between the highest and lowest values of the dependent measures in the baseline and treatment phases of the experiment.

Rate of response (operant rate). The number of responses that occur in a given interval. For example, a bird may peck a key for food 2 times per second, or a student may do math problems at the rate of 10 problems per hour.

Ratio schedule. A response-based schedule of reinforcement that is set to deliver reinforcement following a prescribed number of responses. The ratio specifies the number of responses for each reinforcer.

Ratio strain. A disruption of responding that occurs when a ratio schedule is increased rapidly. For example, if faced with a change in the schedule from continuous reinforcement to the large fixed-ratio value, an animal will probably show ratio strain in the sense that it pauses for longer and longer after reinforcement. This occurs because the time between successive reinforcements contributes to the postreinforcement pause (PRP). The pause gets longer as the interreinforcement interval (IRI) increases. Because the PRP makes up part of the interval between reinforcements and is controlled by it, the animal eventually stops responding. Thus, there is a negative feedback loop between increasing PRP length and the time between reinforcements (IRI). See **postreinforcement pause (PRP)** and **interreinforcement interval (IRI)**.

Reaction chain. Reaction chains are phylogenetic sequences of behavior. An environmental stimulus sets off behavior that produces stimuli that set off the next set of responses in the sequence; these behaviors produce the next set of stimuli, and so on. Presenting stimuli that prompt responses ordinarily occurring in the middle part of the sequence will start the chain at that point rather than at the beginning. Reaction chains are like consecutive sets of reflexes where the stimulus that elicits the next response in the sequence is produced by the previous reflex.

Reactive measurement. Reactive measurement limits the generality of a treatment (or intervention) to situations where the dependent variable is being measured or counted. For example, a person in a weight-control program (treatment) may lose weight just because they are weighed daily by a researcher. Daily weighing may focus attention on being overweight, and the program is only effective under these conditions. See **external validity**.

Reflex. When an unconditioned stimulus elicits an unconditioned response (US → UR), the relationship is called a reflex.

Reflexive aggression. Aggression elicited by the presentation of an aversive stimulus or event. Reflexive aggression is elicited by an aversive unconditioned stimulus such as a shock in the presence of another member of the species, and in humans it may involve conditioned aversive stimuli such as the verbal stimulus "You idiot!" (respondent aggression). Reflexive aggression is also called pain-elicited aggression.

Reflexivity. This involves responding to a one-to-one relationship (A = A) between stimulus classes. For example, a pigeon is presented with the color red on a sample key and the bird responds to a comparison key with the identical color (red). A child who is given a picture of a cat and then finds a similar picture in a set of photographs is showing reflexivity. See also **identity matching**.

Reinforcement. An increase in the rate of operant behavior as a function of its consequences. Reinforcement also refers to the procedure of presenting a reinforcing event when a response occurs.

Reinforcement efficacy. Most of the applied research on progressive ratio (PR) schedules uses the giving-up point or breakpoint as a way of measuring reinforcement efficacy or effectiveness, especially of drugs like cocaine. The breakpoint for a drug indicates how much operant behavior the drug will sustain at a given dose. If the breakpoints for two drugs are different, we can say that the drug with the higher breakpoint has greater reinforcement efficacy.

Reinforcement function. Any event (or stimulus) that follows a response and increases its frequency is said to have a reinforcement function. If an infant's babbling increases due to touching by the mother, we can say that maternal touching has a reinforcement function.

Reinstatement (of behavior). The recovery of behavior when the reinforcer is presented alone (response independent) after a period of extinction. In an operant procedure, reinstatement involves reinforcement of a response followed by extinction. After extinction, response-independent rein-forcement is arranged and the opportunity to respond is removed (using retractable levers). This is followed by tests that reinstate the opportunity to respond (response levers available).

Relative rate of reinforcement. When two or more sources of reinforcement are available (as on a concurrent schedule), the relative rate of reinforcement refers to the rate of reinforcement deliv-ered on one alternative divided by the sum of the rates of reinforcement from all sources of reinforcement. Relative rate of reinforcement is a measure of the distribution of reinforcement between or among alternatives.

Relative rate of response. When two or more sources of reinforcement are available (as on a concur-rent schedule), the relative rate of response refers to the rate of response on one alternative divided by the sum of the response rates on all alternatives. Relative rate of response is a measure of the distribution of behavior between or among alternative sources of reinforcement.

Relative stimulus control. The responding of an organism to differences between two or more stimuli. For example, a pigeon may be trained to peck in the presence of the larger of two triangles rather than to the absolute size of a triangle. See also **absolute stimulus control**.

Relativity of punishment. The Premack principle states that a lower-frequency operant will punish a higher-frequency behavior. For example, when wheel running is a lower-frequency operant, drinking is punished when followed by wheel running. In contrast, drinking is reinforced by wheel running when running in a wheel is a higher-frequency operant. According to the Premack principle, we cannot make an absolute statement about whether wheel running is a punisher or a reinforcer for drinking.

Reliability of observation. In applied behavior analysis, reliability of observation involves the amount of agreement among observers who independently record the same behavior. One way to assess reliability is to count the number of times two observers agree that a target behavior did (or did not) occur. This can be expressed as a percentage agreement that ranges from 0 to 100%. Generally, applied behavior analysts strive for reliability of greater than 80%.

Remembering. The verb "remembering" (or "forgetting") is used to refer to the effect of some event on behavior after the passage of time (as opposed to the noun "memory," which seems to refer to a mental representation stored in the brain). According to White (2002), remembering is not so much a matter of looking back into the past or forward into the future as it is of *making choices at the time of remembering*.

Remote causation. Involves explaining a phenomenon by pointing to remote events that made it likely. Thus, the causal explanation of a species characteristic (e.g., size, coloration, exceptional vision, etc.) involves the working of natural selection on the gene pool of the parent population. An evolu-tionary account of species coloration, for example, would involve showing how this characteristic improved the reproductive success of organisms in a given ecological environment. That is, natural selection for coloration explains the current frequency of the characteristic in the population.

Repertoire (of behavior). All of the behavior that an organism is capable of emitting on the basis of species and environmental history.

Replication (of results). Replication of results is used to enhance both the internal and external validity of an experiment. If the results replicate over time and place, it is likely that the original findings were due to the experimental variable and not to extraneous conditions (internal validity). Replication also establishes that the findings have generality in the sense that the effects are not limited to specific procedures, behaviors, or species (external validity). See also **direct replication** and **systematic replication**.

Rescorla–Wagner model. The basic idea of the Rescorla–Wagner model of respondent conditioning is that a conditioned stimulus acquires a limited amount of associative strength on any one trial. The term *associative strength* describes the relation between the conditioned stimulus (CS) and the magnitude of the conditioned response (CR). In general, associative strength increases over conditioning trials and reaches some maximum level. A given CS can acquire only so much control over a CR. This is the maximum associative strength for the CS. Thus, a tone (CS) paired with 1 gram of food will have maximum associative strength when conditioned salivation (CR) has the same strength as unconditioned salivation (unconditioned response, UR) elicited by the gram of food (unconditioned stimulus, US). The magnitude of the UR to the US sets the upper limit for the CR. The CS cannot elicit a greater response (CR) than the one produced by the US.

Resistance to extinction. The perseverance of operant behavior when it is placed on extinction. Resistance to extinction is substantially increased when an intermittent schedule of reinforcement has been used to maintain behavior. See **partial reinforcement effect**.

Respondent. This refers to behavior that increases or decreases by the presentation of a conditioned stimulus (CS) that *precedes* the conditioned response (CR). We say that the presentation of the CS regulates or controls the respondent (CR). Respondent behavior is elicited, in the sense that it reliably occurs when the CS is presented. The notation system used with elicited behavior is CS → CR. The CS causes (arrow) the CR.

Respondent acquisition. The procedure of pairing the conditioned stimulus (CS) with the unconditioned stimulus (US) over trials when the respondent level for the CS is near zero. It also refers to the increase in magnitude of the conditioned response (CR) when the respondent level for the CS is near zero.

Respondent conditioning. This occurs when an organism responds to a new event based on a history of pairing with a biologically important stimulus. The Russian physiologist Ivan Pavlov discovered this form of conditioning at the turn of the century. He showed that dogs salivated when food was placed in their mouths. This relationship between the food stimulus and salivation is called a reflex, and it occurs because of the animal's biological history. When Pavlov rang a bell just before feeding the dog, it began to salivate at the sound of the bell. In this way, new features (sound of bell) controlled the dog's respondent behavior (salivation). Thus, presenting stimuli together in time (typically conditioned stimulus and then unconditioned stimulus) is the procedure for respondent conditioning. If a conditioned stimulus comes to regulate the occurrence of a conditioned response, respondent conditioning has occurred.

Respondent discrimination. This occurs when an organism shows a conditioned response to one stimulus but not to other similar events. A discrimination procedure involves positive and negative conditioning trials. For example, a positive trial occurs when a CS⁺ such as a 60-dB tone is followed by an unconditioned stimulus such as food. On negative trials, a 40-dB tone is presented (CS⁻) but not followed by food. Once a differential response occurs (salivation to 60 dB but not to 40 db), we may say that the organism discriminates between the tones.

Respondent extinction. The procedure of respondent extinction involves the presentation of the conditioned stimulus without the unconditioned stimulus after acquisition has occurred. As a behavioral process, extinction refers to a decline in the strength of the conditioned response when an extinction procedure is in effect. In both instances, the term extinction is used correctly.

Respondent generalization. This occurs when an organism shows a conditioned response to values of the conditioned stimulus that have not been trained. For example, if a tone of 375 Hz is followed by food, a dog will salivate at maximum level when this tone is presented. However, the animal may salivate to other values of the tone. As the tone differs more and more from 375 Hz, the conditioned response decreases in magnitude.

Respondent level. The baseline level (magnitude) of the conditioned response (CR) to the conditioned stimulus (CS) before any known conditioning has taken place. For example, the amount of salivation (CR) to a tone (CS) before the tone has been paired with food in the mouth is usually zero (no salivation).

Response chain. A sequence of discriminative stimuli and responses in which each response produces a change in the stimulus controlling behavior. Once established, each S^D in the chain has two functions—as a conditioned reinforcer for the response that produced it, and as a discriminative stimulus for the next response in the sequence.

Response class. All the forms of the performance that have a similar function (e.g., putting on a coat to keep warm). In some cases, the responses in a class show close physical resemblance, but this is not always the case. For example, saying "Please open the door" and physically opening the door are members of the same response class if both result in an open door.

Response cost. A negative punishment procedure in which conditioned reinforcers (tokens) are removed contingent on behavior, and the behavior decreases.

Response-deprivation hypothesis. The principle that organisms work to gain access to activities that are restricted or withheld (deprivation), presumably to reinstate equilibrium or free-choice levels of behavior. This principle is more general than the Premack principle, predicting when any activity (high or low in rate) will function as reinforcement.

Response differentiation. When reinforcement is contingent on some difference in response properties, that form of response will increase. For example, the force or magnitude of response can be differentiated; if the contingencies of reinforcement require a forceful or vigorous response in a particular situation, then that form of response will predominate. In another example, when reinforcement is based on short interresponse times or IRTs (2–5 s), the distribution of IRTs becomes centered on short intervals. Changing the contingencies to reinforce longer IRTs (20–25 s) produces a new distribution centered on long intervals. See **differential reinforcement**.

Response generalization. This occurs when a target response is strengthened and other similar responses increase in frequency (e.g., a child who is reinforced for building a house out of Lego™ may subsequently arrange the pieces in many different ways).

Response hierarchy. The differences in relative frequency or probability of different responses in a free-choice or baseline setting. For a rat, the probability of eating, drinking, and wheel running might form a hierarchy, with eating occurring most frequently and wheel running least often.

Response–shock interval (R–S). On an avoidance schedule, the time from a response that postpones shock to the onset of the aversive stimulus, assuming that another response does not occur. See also **shock–shock interval (S–S)**.

Resurgence. After a period of reinforcement, the increase in behavioral variability or topography during extinction.

Retention interval. The time between the offset of the sample stimulus and the onset of the comparison stimuli.

Reversal test. Once the matching of angle to geometric form is well established, a reversal test (form to angle) is conducted without any further reinforcement. In a reversal test, the bird is presented with a triangle as the sample, and the question is whether it pecks the side key with the horizontal line. Because horizontal = triangle was trained, the bird shows symmetry if it pecks the horizontal comparison key when presented with a triangle sample (triangle = horizontal). Similarly, because vertical = circle was trained, symmetry is shown if the bird pecks the vertical side key when the circle is presented as the sample (circle = vertical). In everyday language, the bird responds as if the horizontal line stands for triangle and as if the vertical line means circle. The percentage of "correct" responses during the test (without reinforcement) is the usual measure of symbolic performance on this reversal test.

Rule-governed behavior. The effects of contingency-specifying stimuli on the listener's behavior. When instructions, rules, advice, maxims, and laws regulate operant behavior, the behavior is said to be rule-governed. Control by instructions can make operant behavior insensitive to the operating contingencies of reinforcement.

Run of responses. A fast burst of responding. For example, after the postreinforcement pause on a fixed-ratio schedule, an organism will rapidly emit the responses required by the ratio.

Salience. The symbol S in the Rescorla–Wagner equation is a constant that varies between 0 and 1, and may be interpreted as the salience (e.g., dim light versus bright light) of the conditioned stimulus (CS) based on the sensory capacities of the organism. The constant S (salience) is estimated after conditioning and determines how quickly the associative strength of the CS rises to its maximum. That is, a larger salience coefficient makes the associative strength of the CS rise more quickly to its maximum

Satiation. Repeated presentations of a reinforcer weaken its effectiveness, and for this reason the rate of response declines. Satiation refers to this effect, and the repeated presentation of a reinforcer is called a satiation operation.

Scalloping. The characteristic pattern of response seen on a cumulative record produced by a fixed-interval schedule. There is a pause after reinforcement, then a few probe responses, and finally an increasingly accelerated rate of response to the moment of reinforcement.

Schedule of reinforcement. In relation to responses, a schedule of reinforcement is the arrangement of the environment in terms of discriminative stimuli and behavioral consequences. Mechner notation describes these behavioral contingencies. See **Mechner notation**.

Schedule-induced behavior. See **adjunctive behavior**.

Science of behavior. See **behavior analysis**.

S-delta (S$^\Delta$). When an operant does not produce reinforcement, the stimulus that precedes the operant is called an S-delta (S$^\Delta$). In the presence of an S-delta, the probability of emitting an operant declines. See **Extinction stimulus**.

Second-order conditioning. Second-order conditioning involves pairing two conditioned stimuli (CS$_1$ + CS$_2$), rather than a conditioned and unconditioned stimulus (CS + US). Pavlov (1927/1960) conducted the early experiments on second-order conditioning. The tick of a metronome was paired with food, and the sound of the metronome came to elicit salivation. Once the ticking sound reliably elicited salivation, Pavlov paired it with the sight of a black square (CS$_1$ + CS$_2$). Following several pairings of the metronome beat with the black square, the sight of the black square elicited salivation.

Second-order schedule of reinforcement. Two (or more) schedules of reinforcement in which completion of the requirements of one schedule is reinforced according to the requirements of a second schedule.

Selection by consequences. From a behavioral viewpoint, the principle of causation for biology, behavior, and culture is selection by consequences. With regard to biology, mutation and sexual reproduction ensure a range of variation in genes that code for the features of organisms. Some physical attributes of the organisms, coded by genes, meet the requirements of the environment. Organisms with these adaptive features survive and reproduce, passing on their genes to the next generation (phylogenetic). Organisms without these characteristics do not reproduce as well and therefore their genes are less represented in the subsequent generations. Natural selection is a form of selection by consequences that occurs at the biological level.

Selection by consequences has been extended to the level of behavior as the principle of reinforcement. Operant behavior is an expressed characteristic of many organisms, including humans. Organisms with an extensive range of operant behavior adjust to new environmental situations on the basis of the consequences that follow behavior. This kind of selection occurs over the lifetime of the individual (ontogenetic), and behavior change is a form of evolution. Brain neurons are probably the units selected at the behavioral level; the interplay of neurons allows for behavior to be passed on from one moment to the next (transmitted). The process of the selection and change of operant behavior is analogous to evolution and natural selection at the genetic level. Reinforcement is therefore an ontogenetic process that extends selection by consequences to the level of behavior.

A third level of evolution and selection occurs at the cultural level (cultural selection). The unit of selection at this level is the cultural practice or meme (Dawkins, 1976). A cultural practice involves the interlocking behavior of many people. As with operant behavior itself, cultural practices vary in form and frequency. Different ways of doing things are more or less successful in terms of efficiency, productivity, and survival of group members. Generally, group-level outcomes or effects (metacontingencies) increase or decrease the rate of adoption and transmission of practices in the population. The fit between current practices and new ways of doing things (e.g., technology) plays a role in the adoption and transmission of innovations by the group. Although an innovative technology or method may be more efficient, it may also be more costly to change from traditional to new ways of doing things.

Self-control. From a behavioral perspective, self-control occurs when a person emits a response that affects the probability of subsequent behavior—giving up immediate gains for greater long-term benefits, or accepting immediate costs for later rewards. When people (and other organisms) manage their behavior in such a way that they choose the more beneficial long-term consequences, they are said to show self-control.

Sexual selection. The increased reproductive success of genes that code for attributes or behavior that is attractive (having a stimulus function) to the opposite sex. Individuals with these features and underlying genes have increased chances of copulation and bearing more offspring compared with those who lack such attractiveness.

Shaping. The method of successive approximation or shaping may be used to establish a response. This method involves the reinforcement of closer and closer approximations to the final performance. For example, a rat may be reinforced for standing in the vicinity of a lever. Once the animal is reliably facing the lever, a movement of the head toward the bar is reinforced. Next, closer and closer approximations to pressing the lever are reinforced. Each step of the procedure involves reinforcement of closer approximations and nonreinforcement of more distant responses. Many novel forms of behavior may be shaped by the method of successive approximation.

Shock–shock interval (S–S). The scheduled time between shocks using an avoidance procedure. It is the time from one shock to the next if the avoidance response does not occur. See also the **response–shock interval (R–S)**.

Sidman avoidance. See **nondiscriminated avoidance**.

Sign tracking. Approaching a sign (or stimulus) that signals a biologically relevant event. For example, dogs are required to sit on a mat and a stimulus that signals food is presented to the animals. When the food signal is presented, the dogs approach the stimulus and make food-soliciting responses to it.

Simultaneous conditioning. A respondent conditioning procedure in which the conditioned stimulus (CS) and unconditioned stimulus (US) are presented at the same moment. Compared with delayed conditioning, simultaneous conditioning produces a weaker conditioned response (CR).

Simultaneous discrimination. In simultaneous discrimination, the S^D and S^Δ are presented at the same time, and the organism is reinforced for responding to the relative properties of one or the other. For example, a pigeon may be presented with two keys, both illuminated with white lights, but one light is brighter than the other. The bird is reinforced for pecking the dimmer of the two keys. Pecks to the other key are placed on extinction. After training, the pigeon will peck the darker of any two keys. See also **relative stimulus control**.

Single-subject research. Experimental research that is concerned with discovering principles and conditions that govern the behavior of single or individual organisms. Each individual's behavior is studied to assess the impact of a given experimental variable. In behavioral research, a change in the contingencies of reinforcement is assessed for each bird, rat, or human (e.g., changing the schedule of reinforcement, the operant, or the discriminative stimuli).

Social disruption. A negative side effect of punishment in which the person who delivers punishment and the context become conditioned aversive stimuli. Individuals will attempt to escape from or avoid the punishing person or setting.

Social episode. A social episode involves the interlocking contingencies between speaker and listener, as when a customer asks the waiter for a napkin and is given it (manding). The episode begins with the customer spilling her coffee (establishing the napkin as reinforcement) and ends when the waiter provides the napkin (reinforcement) and the customer says "Thank you."

Spontaneous imitation. Innate imitation based on evolution and natural selection (a characteristic of the species) rather than experiences during the lifetime of the individual. See **imitation** and **generalized imitation**.

Spontaneous recovery (operant). After a period of extinction, an organism's rate of response may be close to operant level. After some time, the organism is again placed in the setting and extinction is continued. Responding initially recovers, but over repeated sessions of extinction the amount of recovery decreases. Repeated sessions of extinction eliminate stimulus control by extraneous features of the situation, and eventually "being placed in the setting" no longer occasions the operant.

Spontaneous recovery (respondent). An increase in the magnitude of the conditioned response (CR) after respondent extinction has occurred and time has passed. A behavioral analysis of spontaneous recovery suggests that the relationship between conditioned stimulus (CS) and CR is weakened by extinction, but the context or features of the situation elicit some level of the conditioned response. During respondent conditioning, many stimuli not specified by the researcher as the CS, but present in the experimental situation, come to regulate behavior.

S–S account of conditioned reinforcement. The hypothesis that it is necessary for a stimulus to be paired with primary reinforcement to become a conditioned reinforcer. This hypothesis has been largely discounted, and the weight of the evidence supports the delay-reduction hypothesis of Fantino (1969b). See **delay-reduction hypothesis**.

Steady-state performance. Schedule-controlled behavior that is stable and does not change over time. For example, after an extensive history on VI 30 s, a rat may press a lever at approximately the same rate day after day.

Stimulus class. Stimuli that vary across physical dimensions but have a common effect on behavior belong to the same stimulus class.

Stimulus control. A change in operant behavior that occurs when either an S^D or S^Δ is presented. When an S^D is presented, the probability of response increases, and when an S^Δ is given, operant behavior has a low probability of occurrence.

Stimulus equivalence. This involves the presentation of one class of stimuli (e.g., flags) that occasions responses to other stimulus classes (e.g., countries). This seems to be what we mean when we say that the flag stands for, represents, or signifies our country. Equivalence relations such as these are an important aspect of human behavior. For example, when teaching a child to read, spoken words (names of animals) are trained to visual stimuli (pictures of animals) and then to written symbols (written words for animals). Eventually, the written word is said to stand for the actual object, in the same sense that a flag stands for a country.

Stimulus function. When the occurrence of an event changes the behavior of an organism, we may say that the event has a stimulus function. Both respondent and operant conditioning are ways to create stimulus functions. During respondent conditioning, an arbitrary event such as a tone comes to elicit a particular response, such as salivation. Once the tone is effective, it is said to have a conditioned-stimulus function for salivation. In the absence of a conditioning history, the tone may have no specified function and does not affect the specified behavior.

Stimulus generalization. Stimulus generalization occurs when an operant reinforced in the presence of a specific discriminative stimulus is also emitted in the presence of other stimuli. The process is called stimulus generalization because the operant is emitted to new stimuli that presumably share common properties with the discriminative stimulus.

Stimulus substitution. When a conditioned stimulus (e.g., light) is paired with an unconditioned stimulus (e.g., food), the conditioned stimulus is said to substitute for the unconditioned stimulus. That is, food evokes salivation and by conditioning the light elicits similar behavior.

Structural approach. In the structural approach, behavior is classified in terms of its form or topography. For example, many developmental psychologists are interested in the intellectual growth of children. These researchers often investigate what a person does at a given stage of development. The structure of behavior is emphasized because it is said to reveal the underlying stage of intellectual development. See also **functional analysis**.

Substitutability. This term is used to denote that a change in price of one reinforcer alters the consumption of a second reinforcer, holding income constant. For some commodities, consumption decreases with price, but consumption of a second commodity increases. The two commodities are said to be *substitutes*. For example, butter and margarine are substitutes if a change in the price of butter results in more consumption of margarine. Beverages such as Coke and Pepsi are another example of substitutes. Other commodities are *independents*. As the price of one commodity increases and its consumption decreases, the consumption of a second commodity does not change. For example, your consumption of gasoline is independent of the price of theatre tickets. A third way in which commodities are related is as *complements*. As the price of one commodity increases and its consumption decreases, consumption of the other commodity also decreases. For example, when the price of hot dogs increases and you eat less of them, your consumption of hot-dog buns, relish, etc. also decreases.

Successive approximation. See **shaping**.

Successive discrimination. A procedure that is used to train differential responding. The researcher arranges the presentation of S^D and S^Δ so that one follows the other. For example, a multiple schedule is programmed so that a red light signals variable-interval food reinforcement; this is followed by a green light that indicates extinction is in effect.

Superstitious behavior. Behavior that is accidentally reinforced. For example, a parent may inadvertently strengthen aggressive behavior when a child is given his or her allowance just after fighting with a playmate. Switching from one alternative to another may be accidentally reinforced on a concurrent schedule if the alternative schedule has a reinforcement setup. In this case, the organism is accidentally reinforced for a change from one schedule to another.

Symbolic matching. In a matching-to-sample task, symbolic matching involves the presentation of one class of stimuli as the sample (geometrical forms) and another set of stimuli (different line angles) as the comparisons. Reinforcement depends on an arbitrary relationship (triangle = vertical).

Symmetry. When stimulus class A is shown to be interchangeable with stimulus class B (if A = B then B = A), we may say that the organism shows symmetry between the stimulus classes. After training a form-to-angle discrimination (triangle = vertical), a reversal test is conducted without reinforcement using line angles as the sample and geometric shapes as the comparisons (vertical = triangle). An organism that passes the reversal test is said to demonstrate symmetry of angles and forms. See also **reversal test**.

Systematic replication. Refers to increasing the generality of an experimental finding by conducting other experiments in which the procedures are different but are logically related to the original research. An experiment is conducted with rats to find out what happens when food pellets are presented contingent on lever pressing. The observation is that lever pressing increases when followed by food pellets. In a systematic replication, elephants step on a treadle to produce peanuts. The observation is that treadle pressing increases. Both experiments are said to show the effects of positive reinforcement contingencies on operant behavior. See also **direct replication**.

Tacting. A class of verbal operants whose form is regulated by specific nonverbal discriminative stimuli. For example, a child may see a cat and say "kitty." The word *tacting* comes from the more familiar term *contact*. Tacting is verbal behavior that makes contact with the environment. In common parlance we say that people make reference to the world (language of reference), but in behavior analysis the world (stimuli) controls the verbal response class of tacting.

Tandem schedule. Two or more basic schedules (CRF, FR, FI, VI, VR) presented sequentially in which only the final link ends with primary reinforcement (or in some cases extinction) and the component schedules are not signaled by discriminative stimuli. In other words, a tandem schedule is the same as an unsignaled chain schedule.

Taste aversion learning. When a distinctive taste (e.g., flavored liquid) is paired with nausea or sickness induced by a drug, X-ray, or even physical activity, the organism shows suppression of intake of the paired flavor.

Temporal pairing. In respondent conditioning, the pairing of the conditioned and unconditioned stimuli in time.

Terminal behavior. On a schedule of reinforcement, as the time for reinforcement gets close, animals engage in activities related to the presentation of the reinforcer. For example, a rat will orient toward the food cup.

Textual behavior. A class of verbal operants regulated by verbal stimuli where there is correspondence between the stimulus and the response, but no topographical similarity. The most common example of textual behavior is reading out loud. The child looks at the text *See Dick, see Jane* and emits the spoken words "See Dick, see Jane." The stimulus and response correspond, but the stimulus is visual and the response is vocal.

Time sampling. A method of recording used mostly in applied behavior analysis. Behavior is sampled over a long time scale. The idea is to make observations at specified times throughout the day. For example, a patient on a psychiatric ward may be observed every 30 min, as a nurse does the rounds, and instances of psychotic talk are recorded.

Timeout from avoidance. Negative reinforcement of behavior that terminates, prevents, or postpones the avoidance contingencies of work or life. We value holidays, leaves of absence, and other periods that temporarily suspend or remove the everyday "shocks" and behavioral requirements that pervade our lives.

Timeout from positive reinforcement. A negative punishment procedure in which the wrongdoer loses access to positive reinforcement for a specified period of time for engaging in the undesirable behavior.

Token economy. A reinforcement system based on token reinforcement; the contingencies specify when, and under what conditions, particular forms of behavior are reinforced. The system is an economy in the sense that tokens may be exchanged for goods and services, in much the same way as money is in our economy. This exchange of tokens for a variety of back-up reinforcers ensures that the tokens are conditioned reinforcers. Token economies have been used to improve the behavior of psychiatric patients, juvenile delinquents, pupils in remedial classrooms, medical patients, alcoholics, drug addicts, prisoners, nursing home residents, and developmentally delayed people.

Token schedule of reinforcement. Token schedules of reinforcement have three distinct components involving the token-production schedule, the exchange-production schedule, and the token-exchange schedule (Hackenberg, 2009). Thus, when we talk about token reinforcement, we are referring to three component schedules that form a higher-order sequence. Typically, one of the component schedules is varied while the other two components remain unchanged (held constant).

Tolerance (to a drug). When more of a drug (unconditioned stimulus) is needed to obtain the same drug effects (unconditioned response), we talk about drug tolerance. In respondent conditioning, the counteractive effects to conditioned stimuli are major components of drug tolerance.

Topography. The physical form or characteristics of the response (e.g. the way that a rat presses a lever with the left paw, the hind right foot, etc.). The topography of response is related to the contingencies of reinforcement in the sense that the form of response can be broadened or restricted by the contingencies. The contingency of reinforcement may require only responses with the left paw rather than any response that activates the microswitch—under these conditions left paw responses will predominate. Generally, topography or form is a function of the contingencies of reinforcement.

Trace conditioning. A respondent conditioning procedure in which the conditioned stimulus (CS) is presented for a brief period and after some time has elapsed the unconditioned stimulus (US) occurs. Generally, as the time between the CS presentation and the occurrence of the US increases, the conditioned response becomes weaker. When compared with delayed conditioning, trace conditioning is not as effective.

Transition-state performance. The instability of behavior generated by a change in contingencies of reinforcement. For example, when continuous reinforcement contingencies are changed to FR 10, the pattern of response is unstable during the transition. After prolonged exposure to the FR contingency, the performance eventually stabilizes into a regular or characteristic pattern. See also **steady-state performance**.

Transitivity. An organism shows transitivity when it responds to stimulus class A as it does to stimulus class C or A = C after training that A = B and B = C. For example, if the written words *one, two*, and *three* are equivalent to the arithmetic numbers 1, 2, and 3, and the words and these arithmetic numbers are equivalent to sets {X}, {X, X}, and {X, X, X}, then it logically follows that the words *one, two*, and *three* are equivalent to sets {X}, {X, X}, and {X,X, X}—the relationship is transitive. An organism is said to show transitivity when it passes tests for transitivity after training for symbolic matching of stimulus class A (angles) to stimulus class B (geometric forms), and stimulus class B (geometric forms) to stimulus class C (intensity of illumination).

Trend (in baseline). A systematic decline or rise in the baseline values of the dependent variable. A drift in baseline measures can be problematic when the treatment is expected to produce a change in the same direction as the trend.

Trial-and-error learning. A term coined by Thorndike (1898, 1911), which he used to describe the results of his puzzle-box and maze-learning experiments. Animals were said to make fewer and fewer errors over repeated trials, learning by trial and error.

Two-key procedure. On a concurrent schedule of reinforcement, the alternative schedules are presented on separate response keys.

Unconditioned reinforcer. A reinforcing stimulus that has acquired its properties as a function of species history. Although many reinforcers, such as food and sex, are general over species, other reinforcers, such as the song of a bird or the scent of a mate, are specific to a species. Behavior analysis, evolutionary biology, and neuroscience are necessary to describe, predict, and control the behavior regulated by unconditioned reinforcement.

Unconditioned response (UR). All organisms are born with a set of reflexes (US → UR). These relationships are invariant and biologically based. The behavior elicited by the unconditioned stimulus (US) is called the unconditioned response (UR).

Unconditioned stimulus (US). All organisms are born with a set of reflexes (US → UR). These relationships are invariant and biologically based. The eliciting event for the reflex is called the unconditioned stimulus (US).

Undermatching. In the generalized matching equation, the exponent *a* takes on a value less than 1. This result is described as undermatching, and it occurs when changes in the response ratio are less than changes in the reinforcement ratio. The effect is interpreted as low sensitivity to the programmed schedules of reinforcement. See also **generalized matching law**.

US-pre-exposure effect. A procedure in which animals are first given repeated exposures to the unconditioned stimulus (US) by itself and then a series of CS → US pairings (conditioning). Compared with animals given pairings with a novel US, those familiar with the US (pre-exposed) show weaker and slower conditioning on the acquisition test.

Variable interval (VI). A schedule of reinforcement in which one response is reinforced after a variable amount of time has passed. For example, on a VI 30-s schedule, the time to each reinforcement changes but the average time is 30 s.

Variable ratio (VR). A response-based schedule of reinforcement in which the number of responses required for reinforcement changes after each reinforcer. The average number of responses is used to index the schedule. For example, a rat may press a lever for reinforcement 50 times, and then 150, 70, 30, and 200 times. Adding these response requirements for a total of 500 and then dividing by the number of separate response runs (5) yields the schedule value, VR 100.

Verbal behavior. The vocal, written, and gestural performances of a speaker, writer, or communicator. This behavior operates on the listener, reader, or observer, who arranges for reinforcement of the verbal performance. Verbal behavior only has indirect effects on the environment. This contrasts with nonverbal behavior, which usually results in direct and automatic consequences. When you walk toward an object, you come closer to it. Verbal behavior, on the other hand, works through its effects on other people. To change the position of a lamp, the speaker states "Lift the lamp at the back of the room" to a listener who is inclined to respond. Although verbal behavior is usually equated with speaking, vocal responses are only one of its forms. For example, a person may emit gestures and body movements that indirectly operate on the environment through their effects on others. A frown sets the occasion for others to remove some aversive event, while a smile may signal the observer to behave in ways that produce positive reinforcement.

Verbal community. The contingencies that regulate verbal behavior arise from the practices of people in the verbal community. The verbal community refers to the customary ways that people reinforce the behavior of the speaker. These customary ways or practices have evolved as part of cultural evolution. The study of the semantics and syntax of words and sentences (linguistics) describes the universal and specific contingencies arranged by the verbal community. In the behavioral view, language does not reside in the mind but in the social environment of the speaker.

References

Abramson, L. Y., Seligman, M. E. P., & Teasdale, J. D. (1978). Learned helplessness in humans: Critique and reformulation. *Journal of Abnormal Psychology, 87*, 49–74.

Ader, R., & Cohen, N. (1981). Conditioned immunopharmacologic responses. In R. Ader (Ed.), *Psychoneuro-immunology* (pp. 281–319). New York: Academic Press.

Ader, R., & Cohen, N. (1985). CNS–immune system interactions: Conditioning phenomena. *Behavior and Brain Sciences, 8*, 379–394.

Ader, R., & Cohen, N. (1993). Psychoneuroimmunology: Conditioning and stress. *Annual Review of Psychology, 44*, 53–85.

Afifi, T. O., Mota, N. P., Dasiewicz, P., MacMillan, II. L., & Sareen, J. (2012). Physical punishment and mental disorders: Results from a nationally representative sample. *Pediatrics*. Online publication July 2: doi/10.1542/peds.2011–2947.

Ainslie, G. W. (1974). Impulse control in pigeons. *Journal of the Experimental Analysis of Behavior, 21*, 485–489.

Ainslie, G. W. (1975). Specious reward: A behavioral theory of impulsiveness and impulse control. *Psychological Bulletin, 82*, 463–496.

Ainslie, G. W. (2005). Précis of breakdown of will. *Behavioral and Brain Sciences, 28*, 635–673.

Alberto, P. A. & Troutman, A. C. (2006). *Applied behavior analysis for teachers* (7th ed.). Upper Saddle River, NJ: Pearson.

Alberto, P. A., Heflin, L. J., & Andrews, D. (2002). Use of the timeout ribbon procedure during community-based instruction. *Behavior Modification. 26*, 297–311.

Alcock, J. (1969). Observational learning in three species of birds. *Ibis, 11*, 308–321.

Alferink, L.A., Crossman, E.K., & Cheney, C. D. (1973). Control of responding by a conditioned reinforcer in the presence of free food. *Animal Learning and Behavior, 1*, 38–40.

Allen, C. M. (1981). On the exponent in the "generalized" matching equation. *Journal of the Experimental Analysis of Behavior, 35*, 125–127.

Allen, T. L., Van Groningen, B. J., Barksdale, D. J., & McCarthy, R. (2010). The breast self-examination controversy: What providers and patients should know. *Journal for Nurse Practitioners, 6*, 444–451.

Alsiö, J., Nordenankar, K., Arvidsson, E., Birgner, C., Mahmoudi, S., Halbout, B. et al. (2011). Enhanced sucrose and cocaine self-administration and cue-induced drug seeking after loss of VGLUT2 in midbrain dopamine neurons in mice. *Journal of Neuroscience, 31*, 12593–12603.

Alvarez, L. W. (1982). Experimental evidence that an asteroid impact led to the extinction of many species 65 million years ago. *Proceedings of the National Academy of Sciences, 80*, 627–642.

Alvarez, L. W., Alvarez, W., Asaro, F., & Michel, H. V. (1980). Extraterrestrial cause for the Cretaceous–Tertiary extinction. *Science, 208*, 1095–1108.

Alvarez, L. W., Asaro, F., & Michel, H. V. (1980). Extraterrestrial cause for the Cretaceous–Tertiary extinction—Experimental results and theoretical interpretation. *Science, 206*, 1095–1108.

Alvarez, W., Asaro, F., Michel, H. V., & Alvarez, L. W. (1982). Iridium anomaly approximately synchronous with terminal Eocene extinction. *Science, 216*, 886–888.

Alvord, J. R., & Cheney, C. D. (1994). *The home token economy*. Cambridge, MA: Cambridge Center for Behavioral Studies.

Amat, J., Aleksejev, R. M., Paul, E., Watkins, L. R., & Maier, S. F. (2010). Behavioral control over shock blocks behavioral and neurochemical effects of later social defeat. *Behavioural Neuroscience, 165*, 1031–1038.

Amat, J., Baratta, M. V., Paul, E., Bland, S. T., Watkins, L. R., & Maier, S. F. (2005). Medial prefrontal cortex determines how stressor controllability affects behavior and dorsal raphe nucleus. *Nature Neuroscience, 8*, 365–371.

American Psychiatric Association (2000). *Diagnostic and Statistical Manual of Mental Disorders, Fourth Edition, Text Revision (DSM-IV-TR)*. Washington, DC: American Psychiatric Association.

Anderson, C. A., Buckley, K. E., & Carnagey, N. L. (2008). Creating your own hostile environment: A laboratory examination of trait aggressiveness and the violence escalation cycle. *Personality and Social Psychology Bulletin, 34*, 462–473.

Anderson, C. D., Ferland, R. J., & Williams, M. D. (1992). Negative contrast associated with reinforcing stimulation of the brain. *Society for Neuroscience Abstracts, 18*, 874.

Anderson, N. D., & Craik, F. I. (2006). The mnemonic mechanisms of errorless learning. *Neuropsychologica, 44*, 2806–2813.

Andre, J., Albanos, K., & Reilly, S. (2007). C-fos expression in the rat brain following lithium chloride-induced illness. *Brain Research, 1135*, 122–128.

Anger, D. (1956). The dependence of interresponse times upon the relative reinforcement of different interresponse times. *Journal of Experimental Psychology, 52*, 145–161.

Anisfeld, M. (1996). Only tongue protusion modeling is matched by neonates. *Developmental Review, 16*, 149–161.

Anrep, G. V. (1920). Pitch discrimination in a dog. *Journal of Physiology, 53*, 367–385.

Antonitis, J. J. (1951). Response variability in the white rat during conditioning, extinction, and reconditioning. *Journal of Experimental Psychology, 42*, 273–281.

Appel, J. B. (1961). Punishment in the squirrel monkey *Saimiri sciurea*. *Science, 133*, 36.

Appel, J. B., & Peterson, N. J. (1965). Punishment: Effects of shock intensity on response suppression. *Psychological Reports, 16*, 721–730.

Arantes, J. & Machado, A. (2011). Errorless learning of a conditional temporal discrimination. *Journal of the Experimental Analysis of Behavior, 95*, 1–20.

Arbuckle, J. L., & Lattal, K. A. (1988). Changes in functional response units with briefly delayed reinforcement. *Journal of the Experimental Analysis of Behavior, 49*, 249–263.

Arcediano, F., & Miller, R. R. (2002). Some constraints for models of timing: A temporal coding hypothesis perspective. *Learning and Motivation, 33*, 105–123.

Arwas, S., Rolnick, A., & Lubow, R. E. (1989). Conditioned taste aversion in humans using motion-induced sickness as the US. *Behavior Research and Therapy, 27*, 295–301.

Association for Behavior Analysis International (2010). *Statement on restraint and seclusion*. www.abainternational.org/ABA/statements/RestraintSeclusion.asp

Ator, N. A. (1991). Subjects and instrumentation. In I. H. Iverson & K. A. Lattal (Eds.), *Experimental analysis of behavior: Part 1* (pp. 1–62). New York: Elsevier.

Austin, J., Hackett, S., Gravina, N., & Lebbon, A. (2006). The effects of prompting and feedback on drivers' stopping at stop signs. *Journal of Applied Behavior Analysis, 39*, 117–121.

Autor, S. M. (1960). *The strength of conditioned reinforcers as a function of frequency and probability of reinforcement*. Unpublished doctoral dissertation. Cambridge, MA: Harvard University.

Ayllon, T., & Azrin, N. H. (1968). *The token economy: A motivational system for therapy and rehabilitation*. New York: Appleton-Century-Crofts.

Ayres, K. M., & Langone, J. (2005). Intervention and instruction with video for students with autism: A review of the literature. *Education and Training in Developmental Disabilities, 40*, 183–196.

Azar, B. (2002). Pigeons as baggage screeners, rats as rescuers. *Monitor On Psychology, 33*, 42–44.

Azrin, N. H. (1956). Effects of two intermittent schedules of immediate and nonimmediate punishment. *Journal of Psychology, 42*, 3–21.

Azrin, N. H. (1958). Some effects of noise on human behavior. *Journal of the Experimental Analysis of Behavior, 1*, 183–200.

Azrin, N. H. (1959). Punishment and recovery during fixed ratio performance. *Journal of the Experimental Analysis of Behavior, 2*, 303–305.

Azrin, N. H. (1960). Effects of punishment intensity during variable-interval reinforcement. *Journal of the Experimental Analysis of Behavior, 3*, 123–142.

Azrin, N. H., & Holz, W. C. (1961). Punishment during fixed interval reinforcement. *Journal of the Experimental Analysis of Behavior, 4*, 343–347.

Azrin, N. H., & Holz, W. C. (1966). Punishment. In W. K. Honig (Ed.), *Operant behavior: Areas of research and application* (pp. 380–447). New York: Appleton-Century-Crofts.

Azrin, N. H., Hake, D. F., & Hutchinson, R. R. (1965). Elicitation of aggression by a physical blow. *Journal of the Experimental Analysis of Behavior, 8*, 55–57.

Azrin, N. H., Holz, W. C., & Hake, D. (1963). Fixed-ratio punishment. *Journal of the Experimental Analysis of Behavior, 6*, 141–148.

Azrin, N. H., Hutchinson, R. R., & Hake, D. F. (1963). Pain-induced fighting in the squirrel monkey. *Journal of the Experimental Analysis of Behavior, 6*, 620.

Azrin, N. H., Hutchinson, R. R., & Hake, D. F. (1966). Extinction-induced aggression. *Journal of the Experimental Analysis of Behavior, 9*, 191–204.

Azrin, N. H., Hutchinson, R. R., & Sallery, R. D. (1964). Pain aggression toward inanimate objects. *Journal of the Experimental Analysis of Behavior, 7*, 223–228.

Azrin, N. H., McMahon, P. T., Donahue, B., Besalel, V., Lapinski, K. J., Kogan, E. et al. (1994). Behavioral therapy for drug abuse: A controlled treatment outcome study. *Behavior Research and Therapy, 32*, 857–866.

Baars, B. J. (1986). *The cognitive revolution in psychology.* New York: The Guilford Press.

Badia, P., Harsh, J., Coker, C. C., & Abbott, B. (1976). Choice and the dependability of stimuli that predict shock and safety. *Journal of the Experimental Analysis of Behavior, 26*, 95–111.

Baer, D. M. (1981). A flight of behavior analysis. *The Behavior Analyst, 4*, 85–91.

Baer, D. M. (1982). The role of current pragmatics in the future analysis of generalization technology. In R. B. Stuart (Ed.), *Adherence, compliance and generalization in behavioral medicine* (pp. 192–212). New York: Brunner/Mazel.

Baer, D. M., & Deguchi, H. (1985). Generalized imitation from a radical-behavioral viewpoint. In S. Reiss, & R. Bootzin (Eds.), *Theoretical issues in behavior therapy* (pp. 179–217). New York: Academic Press.

Baer, D. M., & Detrich, R. (1990). Tacting and manding in correspondence training: Effects of child selection of verbalization. *Journal of Experimental Analysis of Behavior, 54*, 23–30.

Baer, D. M., & Guess, D. (1971). Receptive training of adjectival inflections in mental retardates. *Journal of Applied Behavior Analysis, 4*, 129–139.

Baer, D. M., & Sherman, J. A. (1964). Reinforcement control of generalized imitation in young children. *Journal of Experimental Child Psychology, 1*, 37–49.

Baer, D. M., Peterson, R. F., & Sherman, J. A. (1967). The development of imitation by reinforcing behavioral similarity to a model. *Journal of the Experimental Analysis of Behavior, 10*, 405–416.

Baer, D. M., Wolf, M. M., & Risley, T. R. (1968). Some current dimensions of applied behavior analysis. *Journal of Applied Behavior Analysis, 1*, 91–97.

Baker, A. G. (1976). Learned irrelevance and learned helplessness: Rats learn that stimuli, reinforcers, and responses are uncorrelated. *Journal of Experimental Psychology: Animal Behavior Processes, 2*, 130–141.

Baker, A. G., Steinwald, H., & Bouton, M. E. (1991). Contextual conditioning and reinstatement of extinguished instrumental responding. *The Quarterly Journal of Experimental Psychology Section B: Comparative and Physiological Psychology, 43*, 199–218.

Baker, T. B., & Tiffany, S. T. (1985). Morphine tolerance as habituation. *Psychological Review, 92*, 78–108.

Baldwin, J. M. (1906). *Mental development, methods, and processes.* New York: Macmillan.

Ball, J. (1938). A case of apparent imitation in a monkey. *Journal of Genetic Psychology, 52*, 439–442.

Bandura, A. (1965). Influence of models' reinforcement contingencies on the acquisition of imitative responses. *Journal of Personality and Social Psychology, 1*, 589–595.

Bandura, A. (1969). *Principles of behavior modification.* New York: Holt, Rinehart, & Winston.

Bandura, A. (1971). Vicarious and self-reinforcement processes. In R. Glaser (Ed.), *The nature of reinforcement* (pp. 228–278). New York: Academic Press.

Bandura, A. (1974). Behavior theory and the models of man. *American Psychologist, 29*, 859–869.

Bandura, A. (1977). *Social learning theory.* Englewood Cliffs, NJ: Prentice-Hall.

Bandura, A. (1986). *Social foundations of thought and action: A social cognitive theory.* Englewood Cliffs, NJ: Prentice-Hall.

Bandura, A. (1997). *Self-efficacy: The exercise of control.* New York: Freeman.

Bandura, A., & Locke, E. (2003). Negative self-efficacy and goal effects revisited. *Journal of Applied Psychology, 88*, 87–99.

Bandura, A., Ross, D., & Ross, S. A. (1963). Imitation of film-mediated aggressive models. *Journal of Abnormal and Social Psychology, 66*, 3–11.

Barbera, M. L. (2007). *The verbal behavior approach: How to teach children with autism and related disorders.* London, UK: Jessica Kingsley Publishers.

Bard, K. (2007). Neonatal imitation in chimpanzees (*Pan troglodytes*) tested with two paradigms. *Animal Cognition, 10*, 233–242.

Barker, L. M., Best, M. R., & Domjan, M. (Eds.) (1977). *Learning mechanisms in food selection.* Waco, TX: Baylor University Press.

Barlow, G. W. (1968). Ethological units of behavior. In D. Ingle (Ed.), *The central nervous system and fish behavior* (pp. 217–237). Chicago: University of Chicago Press.

Barnes-Holmes, D., Barnes-Holmes, Y., & Cullinan, V. (2000). Relational frame theory and Skinner's Verbal Behavior: A possible synthesis. *The Behavior Analyst, 23*, 69–84.

Barnes-Holmes, Y., Hayes, S., Barnes-Holmes, D., & Roche, B. (2002). Relational frame theory: A post-skinnerian account of human language and cognition. *Advances in Child Development and Behavior, 28*, 101–138.

Barnet, R. C., & Miller, R. R. (1996). Second-order excitation mediated by a backward conditioned inhibitor. *Journal of Experimental Psychology: Animal Behavior Processes, 22*, 279–296.

Baron, A. (1991). Avoidance and punishment. In I. H. Iverson & K. A. Lattal (Eds.), *Experimental analysis of behavior: Part 1* (pp. 171–217). New York: Elsevier Science.

Baron, A., & Galizio, M. (1983). Instructional control of human operant behavior. *The Psychological Record, 33*, 495–520.

Baron, A., & Galizio, M. (2005). Positive and negative reinforcement: Should the distinction be preserved? *The Behavior Analyst, 28*, 85–95.

Baron, A., & Galizio, M. (2006). The distinction between positive and negative reinforcement: Use with care. *The Behavior Analyst, 29*, 141–151.

Baron, R. A., & Richardson, D. R. (1993). *Human aggression.* New York: Plenum Press.

Baron, R. A., Russell, G. W., & Arms, R. L. (1985). Negative ions and behavior: Impact on mood, memory, and aggression among Type A and Type B persons. *Journal of Personality and Social Psychology, 48*, 746–754.

Barr, R., & Hayne, H. (1996). The effect of event structure on imitation in infancy: Practice makes perfect? *Infant Behavior and Development, 19*, 253–257.

Baum, W. M. (1965). An automated apparatus for the avoidance training of rats. *Psychological Reports, 16*, 1205–1211.

Baum, W. M. (1969). Paradoxical effect of alcohol on the resistance to extinction of an avoidance response in rats. *Journal of Comparative and Physiological Psychology, 69*, 238–240.

Baum, W. M. (1974a). Choice in free-ranging wild pigeons. *Science, 185*, 78–79.

Baum, W. M. (1974b). On two types of deviation from the matching law: Bias and undermatching. *Journal of the Experimental Analysis of Behavior, 22*, 231–242.

Baum, W. M. (1979). Matching, undermatching, and overmatching in studies of choice. *Journal of the Experimental Analysis of Behavior, 32*, 269–281.

Baum, W. M. (1983). Studying foraging in the psychological laboratory. In R. L. Mellgren (Ed.), *Animal cognition and behavior* (pp. 253–278). New York: North-Holland.

Baum, W. M. (1992). In search of the feedback function for variable-interval schedules. *Journal of the Experimental Analysis of Behavior, 57*, 365–375.

Baum, W. M. (1993). Performance on ratio and interval schedules of reinforcement: Data and theory. *Journal of the Experimental Analysis of Behavior, 59*, 245–264.

Baum, W. M. (1995). Rules, culture, and fitness. *The Behavior Analyst, 18*, 1–21.

Baum, W. M. (2001). Molar versus molecular as a paradigm clash. *Journal of the Experimental Analysis of Behavior, 75*, 338–341.

Baum, W. M. (2002). From molecular to molar: a paradigm shift in behavior analysis. *Journal of the Experimental Analysis of Behavior, 78*, 95–116.

Baum, W. M. (2005). *Understanding behaviorism: Behavior, culture and evolution*. Malden, MA: Blackwell.

Baum, W. M. (2010). Dynamics of choice: A tutorial. *Journal of the Experimental Analysis of Behavior, 94*, 161–174.

Baum, W. M., & Rachlin, H. C. (1969). Choice as time allocation. *Journal of the Experimental Analysis of Behavior, 12*, 861–874.

Baxter, M. G., & Murray, E. A. (2002). The amygdala and reward. *Nature Reviews Neuroscience, 3*, 563–573.

Baxter, N. (for the Canadian Task Force on Preventive Health Care) (2001). Preventive health care, 2001 update: Should women be routinely taught breast self-examination to screen for breast cancer? *Canadian Medical Association Journal, 164*, 1837–1846.

Belke, T. W., & Pierce, W. D. (2009). Body weight manipulation, reinforcement value and choice between sucrose and wheel running: A behavioral economic analysis. *Behavioural Processes, 80*, 147–156.

Belke, T. W., Pierce, W. D., & Duncan, I. D. (2006). Reinforcement value and substitutability of sucrose and wheel running: Implications for activity anorexia. *Journal of the Experimental Analysis of Behavior, 86*, 97–109.

Belke, T. W., Pierce, W. D., & Powell, R. A. (1989). Determinants of choice for pigeons and humans on concurrent-chains schedules of reinforcement. *Journal of the Experimental Analysis of Behavior, 52*, 97–109.

Belles, D., & Bradlyn, A. S. (1987). The use of the changing criterion design in achieving controlled smoking in a heavy smoker: A controlled case study. *Journal of Behavior Therapy and Experimental Psychiatry, 18*, 77–82.

Bem, D. J. (1965). An experimental analysis of self-persuasion. *Journal of Experimental Social Psychology, 1*, 199–218.

Bem, D. J. (1972) Self-perception theory. In L. Berkowitz (Ed.), *Advances in experimental social psychology: Volume 6* (pp. 1–62). New York: Academic Press.

Bem, D. (2011). Feeling the future: Experimental evidence for anomalous retroactive influences on cognition and affect. *Journal of Personality and Social Psychology, 100*, 407–425.

Benbassat, D., & Abramson, C. I. (2002). Errorless discrimination learning in simulated landing flares. *Human Factors and Aerospace Safety, 2*, 319–338.

Bereznak, S., Ayres, K. M., Mechling, L. C., & Alexander, J. L. (2012). Video self-prompting and mobile technology to increase daily living and vocational independence for students with autism spectrum disorders. *Journal of Developmental and Physical Disabilities, 24*, 269–285.

Berg, C., Brodin, U., Lindberg, G., & Sodersten, P. (2002). Randomized controlled trial of a treatment for anorexia and bulimia nervosa. *Proceedings of the National Academy of Sciences, 99*, 9486–9491.

Bergvall, U. A., & Balogh, A. C. V. (2008). Consummatory simultaneous positive and negative contrast in fallow deer: Implications for selectivity. *Mammalian Biology, 74*, 236–239.

Bergvall, U. A., Rautio, P., Luotola, T., & Leimar, O. (2007). A test of simultaneous and successive negative contrast in fallow deer foraging behavior. *Animal Behaviour, 74*, 395–402.

Bering, J. M., Bjorklund, D. F., & Ragan, P. (2000). Deferred imitation of object-related actions in human-reared juvenile chimpanzees and orangutans. *Developmental Psychobiology, 36*, 218–232.

Berkowitz, L., & Donnerstein, E. (1982). External validity is more than skin deep: Some answers to criticism of laboratory experiments. *American Psychologist, 37*, 245–257.

Bernard, C. (1927). *An introduction to the study of experimental medicine*. New York: Macmillan (original work published in 1865).

Bernstein, I. L., Wilkins, E. E., & Barot, S. K. (2009). Mapping conditioned taste aversion associations through patterns of c-Fos expression. In S. Reilly & T. R. Schachtman (Eds.), *Conditioned taste aversion* (pp. 328–340). New York: Oxford.

Bertaina-Anglade, V., La Rochelle, C. D., & Scheller, D. K. (2006). Antidepressant properties of rotigotine in experimental models of depression. *European Journal of Pharmacology, 548*, 106–114.

Berton, O., McClung, C., DiLeone, R.J., Krishnan, V., Renthal, W., Russo, S. J. et al. (2006). Essential role of BDNF in the mesolimbic dopamine pathway in social defeat stress. *Science, 311*, 864–868.

Besson, A., Privat, A. M., Eschalier, A., & Fialip, J. (1999). Dopaminergic and opiodergic mediations of tricyclic antidepressants in the learned helplessness paradigm. *Pharmacology, Biochemistry, and Behavior, 64*, 541–548.

Beumont, A. L., Booth, S. F., Abraham, D. A., Griffiths, D. A., & Turner, T. R. (1983). Temporal sequence of symptoms in patients with anorexia nervosa: A preliminary report. In P. L. Darby, P. E. Garfinkel, D. M. Garner, & D. V. Coscina (Eds.), *Anorexia nervosa: Recent developments in research* (pp. 129–136). New York: Alan R. Liss.

Bewley-Taylor, D., Hallam, C., & Allen, R. (2009). *The incarceration of drug offenders: An overview*. Oxford, UK: The Beckley Foundation Drug Policy Programme. http://idpc.net/publications/2009/06/incarceration-drug-offenders-overview-beckley-briefing-16

Bickel, W. K., Odum, A. L., & Madden, G. J. (1999). Impulsivity and cigarette smoking: Delay discounting in current, never, and ex-smokers. *Psychopharmacology, 146*, 447–454.

Biederman, G. B., & Vanayan, M. (1988). Observational learning in pigeons: The function of quality of observed performance in simultaneous discrimination. *Learning and Motivation, 19*, 31–43.

Bierley, C., McSweeney, F. K., & Vannieuwkerk, R. (1985). Classical conditioning of preferences for stimuli. *Journal of Consumer Research, 12*, 316–323.

Biesmeijer, J. C., & Seeley, T. D. (2005). The use of waggle dance information by honey bees throughout their foraging careers. *Behavioral Ecology and Sociobiology, 59*, 133–142.

Bijou, S., & Baer, D. M. (1978). *Behavior analysis of child development*. Englewood Cliffs, NJ: Prentice-Hall.

Binder, C. (1996). Behavioral fluency: Evolution of a new paradigm. *The Behavior Analyst, 19*, 163–197.

Binder, C. (2004). A refocus on response-rate measurement: Comment on Doughty, Chase, and O'Shields. *The Behavior Analyst, 27*, 281–286.

Binder, C. (2010). Building fluent performance: Measuring response rate and multiplying response opportunities. *Behavior Analyst Today, 11*, 214–225.

Binder, C., & Watkins, C. L. (1989). Promoting effective instructional methods: Solutions to America's educational crisis. *Future Choices, 1*, 33–39.

Binder, C., & Watkins, C. L. (1990). Precision teaching and direct instruction: Measurably superior instructional technology in schools. *Performance Improvement Quarterly, 3*, 74–96.

Bitterman, M. E., Menzel, R., Fietz, A., & Schafer, S. (1983). Classical conditioning of the proboscis extension in honeybees (*Apis mellifera*). *Journal of Comparative Psychology, 97*, 107–119.

Bjork, D. W. (1993). *B. F. Skinner: A life*. New York: Basic Books.

Bjorklund, D. F. (1987). A note on neonatal imitation. *Developmental Review, 7*, 86–92.

Blass, E. M., Ganchrow, J. R., & Steiner, J. E. (1984). Classical conditioning in newborn humans 2–48 hours of age. *Infant Behavior and Development, 7*, 223–235.

Blenkush, N. A., von Heyn, R. E., & Israel, M. L. (2007). *The effect of contingent skin shock on treated and untreated problem behaviors*. Retrieved from www.judgerc.org/effectsofshock.html

Bloom, H. S., Criswell, E. L., Pennypacker, H. S., Catania, A. C., & Adams, C. K. (1982). Major stimulus dimensions determining detection of simulated breast lesions. *Perception and Psychophysics, 32*, 251–260.

Blough, D. S. (1957). Spectral sensitivity in the pigeon. *Journal of the Optical Society of America, 47*, 827–833.

Blough, D. S. (1959). Delayed matching in the pigeon. *Journal of the Experimental Analysis of Behavior, 2*, 151–160.

Blough, D. S. (1966). The reinforcement of least-frequent interresponse times. *Journal of the Experimental Analysis of Behavior, 9*, 581–591.

Blough, D. S. (1982). Pigeon perception of letters of the alphabet. *Science, 218*, 397–398.

Blumstein, D. T., & Armitage, K. B. (1997). Alarm calling in yellow-bellied marmots: 1. The meaning of situationally variable alarm calls. *Animal Behaviour, 53*, 143–171.

Boakes, R. A., & Nakajima, S. (2009). Conditioned taste aversions based on running or swimming. In S. Reilly & T. R. Schachtman (Eds.), *Conditioned taste aversion: Behavioral and neural processes* (pp. 159–178). New York: Oxford University Press.

Bolles, R. C. (1970). Species-specific defense reactions and avoidance learning. *Psychological Review, 77*, 32–48.

Bolles, R. C. (1979). *Learning theory*. New York: Holt, Rinehart & Winston.

Bondy, A. (1996). *The pyramid approach to education: An integrative approach to teaching children and adults with autism*. Cherry Hill, NJ: Pyramid Education Consultants, Inc.

Bondy, A., & Frost, L. (1994). The picture exchange communication system. *Focus on Autistic Behavior, 9,* 1–19.

Borden, R. J., Bowen, R., & Taylor, S. P. (1971). Shock setting behavior as a function of physical attack and extrinsic reward. *Perceptual and Motor Skills, 33,* 563–568.

Boren, J. J. (1961). Resistance to extinction as a function of the fixed ratio. *Journal of Experimental Psychology, 4,* 304–308.

Borrero, J. C., & Vollmer, T. R. (2002). An application of the matching law to severe problem behavior. *Journal of Applied Behavior Analysis, 35,* 13–27.

Bouton, M. E. (2004). Context and behavioral processes in extinction. *Learning and Memory, 11,* 485–494.

Bouton, M. E., & Swartzentruber, D. (1991). Sources of relapse after extinction in Pavlovian and instrumental learning. *Clinical Psychology Review, 11,* 123–140.

Bower, G. H., & Hilgard, E. R. (1981). *Theories of learning.* Englewood Cliffs, NJ: Prentice-Hall.

Boyce, T. E., & Hineline, P. N. (2002). Interteaching: A strategy for enhancing the user-friendliness of behavioral arrangements in the college classroom. *The Behavior Analyst, 25,* 215–226.

Bradshaw, C. M., & Szabadi, E. (1988). Quantitative analysis of human operant behavior. In G. Davey & C. Cullen (Eds.), *Human operant conditioning and behavior modification* (pp. 225–259). New York: John Wiley & Sons.

Bradshaw, C. M., Ruddle, H. V., & Szabadi, E. (1981). Studies of concurrent performance in humans. In C. M. Bradshaw, E. Szabadi, & C. F. Lowe (Eds.), *Quantification of steady-state operant behavior* (pp. 79–90). Amsterdam: Elsevier/North-Holland.

Brandon, P. K., & Houlihan, D. (1997). Applying behavior theory to practice: An examination of the behavioral momentum metaphor. *Behavioral Interventions, 12,* 113–131.

Bratcher, N. A., Farmer-Dougan, V., Dougan, J. D., Heidenreich, B. A., and Garris, P. A. (2005). The role of dopamine in reinforcement: Changes in reinforcement sensitivity induced by D1-type, D2-type, and non-selective dopamine receptor agonists. *Journal of the Experimental Analysis of Behavior, 84,* 371–399.

Bray, S., & O'Doherty, J. (2007). Neural coding of reward-prediction error signals during classical conditioning with attractive faces. *Journal of Neurophysiology, 97,* 3036–3045.

Brechner, K. C. (1977). An experimental analysis of social traps. *Journal of Experimental Social Psychology, 13,* 552–564.

Breland, K., & Breland, M. (1961). The misbehavior of organisms. *American Psychologist, 16,* 681–684.

Brembs, B. (2003). Operant conditioning in invertebrates. *Current Opinion in Neurology, 13,* 710–717.

Brembs, B. (2008). Operant learning of *Drosophila* at the torque meter. *Journal of Visualized Experiments, 16,* 731.

Brembs, B. (2011). Spontaneous decisions and operant conditioning in fruit flies. *Behavioural Processes, 87,* 157–164.

Brembs, B., Lorenzetti, F. D., Reyes, F. D., Baxter, D. A., & Byrne, J. H. (2002). Operant reward learning in *Aplysia*: Neuronal correlates and mechanisms. *Science, 296,* 1706–1708.

Breuggeman, J. A. (1973). Parental care in a group of free-ranging rhesus monkeys. *Folia Primatologica, 20,* 178–210.

Breyer, N. L., & Allen, G. L. (1975). Effects of implementing a token economy on teacher attending behavior. *Journal of Applied Behavior Analysis, 8,* 373–380.

Brody, H. (2000). *The placebo response.* New York: Harper Collins.

Brooks, D. C., & Bouton, M. E. (1993). A retrieval cue for extinction attenuates spontaneous recovery. *Journal of Experimental Psychology: Animal Behavior Processes, 19,* 77–89.

Brown, J. L., Krantz, P. J., McClannahan, L. E., & Poulson. C. L. (2008). Using script fading to promote natural environment stimulus control of verbal interactions among youths with autism. *Research in Autism Spectrum Disorders, 2,* 480–497.

Brown, P. L., & Jenkins, H. M. (1968). Auto-shaping of the pigeon's key-peck. *Journal of the Experimental Analysis of Behavior, 11,* 1–8.

Brown, R. (1973). *A first language: The early stages.* Cambridge, MA: Harvard University Press.

Brown, R. (1986). *Social psychology: The second edition.* New York: Free Press.

Browne, C., Stafford, K., & Fordham, R. (2006). The use of scent-detection dogs. *Irish Veterinary Journal, 59,* 97–104.

Brownstein, A. J., & Pliskoff, S. S. (1968). Some effects of relative reinforcement rate and changeover delay in response-independent concurrent schedules of reinforcement. *Journal of the Experimental Analysis of Behavior, 11*, 683–688.

Bruce, S. & Muhammad, Z. (2009). The development of object permanence in children with intellectual disability, physical disability, autism and blindness. *International Journal of Disability, Development and Education, 56*, 229–246.

Bruzek, J. I., Thompson, R. H., & Peters, L. C. (2009). Resurgence of infant caregiving responses. *Journal of the Experimental Analysis of Behavior, 92*, 327–343.

Buccino, G., Vogt, S., Ritzl, A., Fink, G. R., Zilles, K., Freund, H. J. et al. (2004). Neural circuits underlying imitation learning of hand actions: An event-related fMRI study. *Neuron, 42*, 323–334.

Buckleitner, W. (2006). Relationship between software design and children's engagement. *Early Education and Development, 17*, 489–505.

Buckley, K. B. (1989). *Mechanical man: John Broadus Watson and the beginnings of behaviorism*. New York: The Guilford Press.

Budney, A.J., & Higgins, S.T. (1998). *National Institute on Drug Abuse Therapy Manuals for Drug Addiction: Manual 2. A Community Reinforcement Approach: Treating Cocaine Addiction* (NIH Publication No. 98-4309). Rockville, MD: US Department of Health and Human Services.

Bullock, C. E., & Hackenberg, T. D. (2006). Second-order schedules of token reinforcement with pigeons: Implications for unit price. *Journal of the Experimental Analysis of Behavior, 85*, 95–106.

Bullock, C., & Myers, T. W. (2009). Stimulus–food pairings produce stimulus-directed touch-screen responding in cynomolgus monkeys (*Macaca fascicularis*) with or without a positive response contingency. *Journal of the Experimental Analysis of Behavior, 92*, 41–55.

Burger, J. M. (2009). Replicating Milgram: Would people still obey today? *American Psychologist, 64*, 1–11.

Bushell, D., Jr., & Burgess, R. L. (1969). Characteristics of the experimental analysis. In R. L. Burgess & D. Bushell, Jr. (Eds.), *Behavioral sociology: The experimental analysis of social processes* (pp. 145–174). New York: Columbia University Press.

Buske-Kirschbaum, A., Kirschbaum, C., Stierle, H., Jabaij, L., & Hellhammer, D. (1994). Conditioned manipulation of natural killer (NK) cells in humans using a discriminative learning protocol. *Biological Psychology, 38*, 143–155.

Buskist, W. F., & Miller, H. L. (1986). Interaction between rules and contingencies in the control of fixed-interval performance. *The Psychological Record, 36*, 109–116.

Byrne, D. (1971). *The attraction paradigm*. New York: Academic Press.

Byrne, R. W. (2003). Imitation as behavior parsing. *Philosophical Transactions of the Royal Society B: Biological Sciences, 358*, 529–536.

Call, J., & Tennie, C. (2009). Animal culture: Chimpanzee table manners? *Current Biology, 19*, R981–R983.

Cameron, J., & Pierce, W. D. (1994). Reinforcement, reward and intrinsic motivation: A meta-analysis. *Review of Educational Research, 64*, 363–423.

Cameron, J., & Pierce, W. D. (2002). *Rewards and intrinsic motivation: Resolving the controversy*. Westport, CT: Bergin & Garvey.

Cameron, J., Banko, K., & Pierce, W. D. (2001). Pervasive negative effects of rewards on intrinsic motivation: The myth continues. *The Behavior Analyst, 24*, 1–44.

Cameron, J., Pierce, W. D., Banko, K. M., & Gear, A. (2005). Achievement-based rewards and intrinsic motivation: A test of cognitive mediators. *Journal of Educational Psychology, 97*, 641–655.

Carnine, D. (1995). Rational schools: The role of science in helping education become a profession. *Behavior and Social Issues, 5*, 5–19.

Carr, D., Wilkinson, K. M., Blackman, D., & McIlvane, W. J. (2000). Equivalence classes in individuals with minimal verbal repertoires. *Journal of the Experimental Analysis of Behavior, 74*, 101–114.

Carr, E. G., & McDowell, J. J. (1980). Social control of self-injurious behavior of organic etiology. *Behavior Therapy, 11*, 402–409.

Carr, J. E., & Burkholder, E. O. (1998). Creating single-subject design graphs with Microsoft Excel™. *Journal of Applied Behavior Analysis, 31*, 245–251.

Carrigan, P. F., Jr., & Sidman, M. (1992). Conditional discrimination and equivalence relations: A theoretical analysis of control by negative stimuli. *Journal of the Experimental Analysis of Behavior, 58*, 183–204.

Carroll, M. E. (1993). The economic context of drug and non-drug reinforcers affects acquisition and maintenance of drug-reinforced behavior and withdrawal effects. *Drug and Alcohol Dependence, 33*, 201–210.

Carroll, M. E., Lac, S. T., & Nygaard, S. L. (1989). A concurrently available nondrug reinforcer prevents the acquisition of decreases in the maintenance of cocaine-reinforced behavior. *Psychopharmacology, 97*, 23–29.

Carroll, R. J., & Hesse, B. E. (1987). The effects of alternating mand and tact training on the acquisition of tacts. *The Analysis of Verbal Behavior, 5*, 55–65.

Carton, J. S., & Schweitzer, J. B. (1996). Use of a token economy to increase compliance during hemodialysis. *Journal of Applied Behavior Analysis, 29*, 111–113.

Cartwright, W. S. (2000). Cost–benefit analysis of drug treatment services: Review of the literature. *Journal of Mental Health Policy and Economics, 3*, 11–26.

Carvalho, L. S., Knott, B., Berg, M. L., Bennett, A. T. D., & Hunt, D. M. (2010). Ultraviolet-sensitive vision in long-lived birds. *Proceedings of the Royal Society B: Biological Sciences, 278*, 107–114.

Case, D. A., & Fantino, E. (1989). Instructions and reinforcement in the observing behavior of adults and children. *Learning and Motivation, 20*, 373–412.

Case, D. A., Fantino, E., & Wixted, J. (1985). Human observing: Maintained by negative information stimuli only if correlated with improved response efficiency. *Journal of the Experimental Analysis of Behavior, 54*, 185–199.

Case, D. A., Ploog, B. O., & Fantino, E. (1990). Observing behavior in a computer game. *Journal of the Experimental Analysis of Behavior, 54*, 185–199.

Catania, A. C. (1966). Concurrent operants. In W. K. Honig (Ed.), *Operant behavior: Areas of research and application* (pp. 213–270). Englewood Cliffs, NJ: Prentice-Hall.

Catania, A. C. (1973). The concept of the operant in the analysis of behavior. *Behaviorism, 1*, 103–116.

Catania, A. C. (1975). Freedom and knowledge: An experimental analysis of preference in pigeons. *Journal of the Experimental Analysis of Behavior, 24*, 89–106.

Catania, A. C. (1980a). Freedom of choice: A behavioral analysis. In G. H. Bower (Ed.), *The psychology of learning and motivation, Volume 14* (pp. 97–145). New York: Academic Press.

Catania, A. C. (1980b). Autoclitic processes and the structure of behavior. *Behaviorism, 8*, 175–186.

Catania, A. C. (1984). *Learning.* Englewood Cliffs, NJ: Prentice-Hall.

Catania, A. C. (1996). Natural contingencies in the creation of naming as a higher-order behavior class. *Journal of the Experimental Analysis of Behavior, 65*, 276–279.

Catania, A. C. (1998). *Learning.* Englewood Cliffs, NJ: Prentice-Hall.

Catania, A. C. (2008). The *Journal of the Experimental Analysis of Behavior* at zero, fifty, and one hundred. *Journal of the Experimental Analysis of Behavior, 89*, 111–118.

Catania, A. C., & Harnard, S. (1988). *The selection of behavior.* New York: Cambridge University Press.

Catania, A. C., & Reynolds, G. S. A. (1968). A quantitative analysis of the responding maintained by interval schedules of reinforcement. *Journal of the Experimental Analysis of Behavior, 11*, 327–383.

Catania, A. C., & Sagvolden, T. (1980). Preference for free choice over forced choice in pigeons. *Journal of the Experimental Analysis of Behavior, 34*, 77–86.

Catania, A. C., Matthews, B. A., & Shimoff, E. H. (1990). Properties of rule-governed behaviour and their implications. In D. E. Blackman & H. Lejeune (Eds.), *Behaviour analysis in theory and practice: Contributions and controversies* (pp. 215–230). Hillsdale, NJ: Lawrence Erlbaum Associates.

Cate, C. T., & Rowe, C. (2007). Biases in signal evolution: Learning makes a difference. *Trends in Ecology and Evolution, 22*, 380–387.

Catmur, C., Gillmeister, H., Bird, G., Liepelt, R., Brass, M., & Heyes, C. (2008) Through the looking glass: counter-mirror activation following incompatible sensorimotor learning. *European Journal of Neuroscience, 28*, 1208–1215.

Catmur, C., Walsh, V., & Heyes, C. (2007). Sensorimotor learning configures the human mirror system. *Current Biology, 17*, 1527–1531.

Cautela, J. R. (1984). General level of reinforcement. *Journal of Behavior Therapy and Experimental Psychiatry, 15*, 109–114.

Cautela, J. R. (1994). General level of reinforcement II. Further elaborations. *Behaviorology, 2*, 1–16.

Cerutti, D. (1989). Discrimination theory of rule-governed behavior. *Journal of the Experimental Analysis of Behavior, 51,* 251–259.

Chance, P. (1999). Thorndike's puzzle boxes and the origins of the experimental analysis of behavior. *Journal of the Experimental Analysis of Behavior, 72,* 433–440.

Chandler, R. K., Fletcher, B. W., & Volkow, N. D. (2009). Treating drug abuse and addiction in the criminal justice system. *Journal of the American Medical Association, 301,* 183–190.

Charlop-Christy, M. H. & Kelso, S. E. (1997). *How to treat the child with autism: A guide to treatment at the Claremont Autism Center.* Claremont, CA: Marjorie H. Charlop-Christy.

Charnov, E. L. (1976). Optimal foraging: The marginal value theorem. *Theoretical Population Biology, 9,* 129–136.

Chase, P. N., Doughty, S. S., & O'Shields, E. (2005). Focus on response rate is important but not sufficient: A reply. *The Behavior Analyst, 28,* 163–168.

Chen, X., Striano, T., & Rakoczy, H. (2004). Auditory–oral matching behavior in newborns. *Developmental Science, 7,* 42–47.

Cheney, C. D., & Eldred, N. L. (1980). Lithium-chloride-induced aversions in the opossum (*Didelphis virginiana*). *Physiological Psychology, 8,* 383–385.

Cheney, C., & Epling, W. F. (1968). *Running wheel activity and self-starvation in the white rat.* Unpublished manuscript. Cheney, WA: Department of Psychology, Eastern Washington State University.

Cheney, C. D. & Tam, V. (1972). Interocular transfer of a line tilt discrimination without mirror-image reversal using fading in pigeons. *Journal of Biological Psychology, 14,* 17–20.

Cheney, C. D., Bonem, E., & Bonem, M. (1985). Changeover cost and switching between concurrent adjusting schedules. *Behavioural Processes, 10,* 145–155.

Cheney, C. D., DeWulf, M. J., & Bonem, E. J. (1993). Prey vulnerability effects in an operant simulation of foraging. *Behaviorology, 1,* 23–30.

Cheney, C., van der Wall, S. B., & Poehlmann, R. J. (1987). Effects of strychnine on the behavior of Great Horned Owls and Red-Tailed Hawks. *Journal of Raptor Research, 21,* 103–110.

Cheng, J. & Feenstra, M. G. P. (2006). Individual differences in dopamine efflux in nucleus accumbens shell and core during instrumental learning. *Learning and Memory, 13,* 168–177.

Cheng, K., & Spetch, M. L. (2002). Spatial generalization and peak shift in humans. *Learning and Motivation, 33,* 358–389.

Cheng, T. D., Disterhoft, J. F., Power, J. M., Ellis, D. A., & Desmond, J. E. (2008). Neural substrates underlying human delay and trace eyeblink conditioning. *Proceedings of the National Academy of Sciences, 105,* 8108–8113.

Cherek, D. R. (1982). Schedule-induced cigarette self-administration. *Pharmacology, Biochemistry, and Behavior, 17,* 523–527.

Chillag, D., & Mendelson, J. (1971). Schedule-induced airlicking as a function of body-weight in rats. *Physiology and Behavior, 6,* 603–605.

Chomsky, N. (1957). *Syntactic structures.* The Hague: Mouton.

Chomsky, N. (1959). Review of B. F. Skinner's verbal behavior. *Language, 35,* 26–58.

Christ, T. J. (2007). Experimental control and threats to internal validity of concurrent and nonconcurrent multiple baseline designs. *Psychology in the Schools, 44,* 451–459.

Ciano, P. D. (2008). Drug seeking under a second-order schedule of reinforcement depends on dopamine D_3 receptors in the basolateral amygdala. *Behavioral Neuroscience, 122,* 129–139.

Classe, A. (1957). The whistled language of La Gomera. *Scientific American, 196,* 111–120.

Cohen, D., Nisbett, R. E., Bowdle, B. F., & Schwarz, N. (1996). Insult, aggression, and the southern culture of honor: An "experimental ethnography." *Journal of Personality and Social Psychology, 70,* 945–960.

Cohen, P. S. (1968). Punishment: The interactive effects of delay and intensity of shock. *Journal of the Experimental Analysis of Behavior, 11,* 789–799.

Cohn, S. L. (1998). Behavioral momentum: The effects of the temporal separation of rates of reinforcement. *Journal of the Experimental Analysis of Behavior, 69,* 29–47.

Cole, R. P., & Miller, R. R. (1999). Conditioned excitation and conditioned inhibition acquired through backward conditioning. *Learning and Motivation, 30,* 129–156.

Colquitt, G., Pritchard, T., & McCollum, S. (2011). The personalized system of instruction in fitness education. *Journal of Physical Education, Recreation and Dance, 82,* 1–58.

Conger, R., & Killeen, P. (1974). Use of concurrent operants in small group research. *Pacific Sociological Review, 17*, 399–416.

Cook, D. (1996). Reminiscences: Fred S. Keller: An appreciation. *Behavior and Social Issues, 6*, 61–71.

Cooper, J. O., Heron, T. E., & Heward, W. L. (2007). *Applied behavior analysis* (2nd ed.). Upper Saddle River, NJ: Pearson.

Corballis, M. C. (1999). The gestural origins of language. *American Scientist, 87*, 138–145.

Corballis, M. C. (2003). From mouth to hand: Gesture, speech, and the evolution of right-handedness. *Behavioral and Brain Sciences, 26*, 199–208.

Coren, S., Ward, L. M., & Enns, J. T. (2004). *Sensation and perception* (6th ed.). Hoboken, NJ: John Wiley & Sons.

Cornu, J. N., Cancel-Tassin, G., Ondet, V., Girardet, C., & Cussenot, O. (2011). Olfactory detection of prostate cancer by dogs sniffing urine: A step forward in early diagnosis. *European Urology, 59*, 197–201.

Courage, M. L., & Howe, M. L. (2002). From infant to child: The dynamics of cognitive change in the second year of life. *Psychological Bulletin, 129*, 250–277.

Courtney, K. & Perone, M. (1992). Reduction in shock frequency and response effort as factors in reinforcement by timeout from avoidance. *Journal of the Experimental Analysis of Behavior, 58*, 485–496.

Cowles, J. T. (1937). Food-tokens as incentive for learning by chimpanzees. *Comparative Psychology Monographs, 14*, 1–96.

Critchfield, T. S. (2011). Translational contributions of the experimental analysis of behavior. *The Behavior Analyst, 34*, 3–17.

Critchfield, T. S., & Perone, M. (1990). Verbal self-reports as a function of speed, accuracy, and reinforcement of the reported performance. *The Psychological Record, 40*, 541–554.

Crossman, E. K., Trapp, N. L., Bonem, E. J., & Bonem, M. K. (1985). Temporal patterns of responding in small fixed-ratio schedules. *Journal of the Experimental Analysis of Behavior, 43*, 115–130.

Cullen, C. (1998). The trouble with rules. *The Psychologist, 11*, 471–475.

Cumming, W. W. (1966). A bird's eye glimpse of men and machines. In R. Ulrich, T. Stachnik, & J. Mabry (Eds.), *Control of human behavior* (pp. 246–256). Glenview, IL: Scott Foresman & Co.

Custance, D. M., Whiten, A., Sambrook, T., & Galdikas, B. (2001). Testing for social learning in the "artificial fruit" processing of wildborn orangutans (*Pongo pygmaeus*), Tanjung Puting, Indonesia. *Animal Cognition, 4*, 305–313.

Cuzzocrea, F., Murdaca, A. M., & Oliva, P. (2011). Using precision teaching method to improve foreign language and cognitive skills in university students. *International Journal of Digital Literacy and Digital Competence, 2*, 50–60.

D'Amato, M. R., Salmon, D. P., Loukas, E., & Tomie, A. (1985). Symmetry and transitivity of conditional relations in monkeys (*Cebus apella*) and pigeons (*Columba livia*). *Journal of the Experimental Analysis of Behavior, 44*, 35–47.

Dale, R. H. I. (2008). The spatial memory of African elephants (*Loxodonta africana*): Durability, interference, and response biases. In N. K. Innis (Ed.), *Reflections on adaptive behavior: Essays in honor of J. E. R. Staddon*, (pp. 143–170). Cambridge, MA: MIT Press.

Daniels, A. C., & Daniels, J. E. (2004). *Performance management: Changing behavior that drives organizational effectiveness* (4th ed.). Atlanta, GA: Performance Management Publications.

Dapcich-Miura, E. & Hovell, M. F. (1979). Contingency management of adherence to a complex medical regimen in elderly heart patients. *Behavior Therapy, 10*, 193–201.

Darley, J. M., Glucksberg, S., & Kinchla, R. A. (1991). *Psychology*. Englewood Cliffs, NJ: Prentice-Hall.

Darwin, C. (1859). *On the origin of species by means of natural selection*. London: John Murray.

Davidson, T. L., & Swithers, S. E. (2004). A Pavlovian approach to the problem of overeating. *International Journal of Obesity, 28*, 933–935.

Davies, N. B., Krebs, J. R., & West, S. A. (2012). *An introduction to behavioral ecology*. West Sussex, UK: Wiley-Blackwell.

Davis, C. (1999). Excessive exercise and anorexia nervosa: Addictive and compulsive behaviors. *Psychiatric Annals, 29*, 221–224.

Davis, C., & Kaptein, S. (2006). Anorexia nervosa with exercise: A phenotype with close links to obsessive-compulsive disorder. *Psychiatric Research, 142*, 209–217.

Davis, C., Kennedy, S. H., Ravelski, E., & Dionne, M. (1994). The role of physical activity in the development and maintenance of eating disorders. *Psychological Medicine, 24*, 957–967.

Davis, C., Kennedy, S. H., Ralevski, E., Dionne, M., Brewer, H., Neitzert, C. et al. (1995). Obsessive compulsiveness and physical activity in anorexia nervosa and high-level exercising. *Journal of Psychosomatic Research, 39*, 967–976.

Davis, J. M. (1973). Imitation: A review and critique. In P. P. G. Bateson & P. H. Klopfer (Eds.), *Perspectives in ethology, Volume 1* (pp. 43–72). New York: Plenum Press.

Davison, M. C. (1969). Preference for mixed-interval versus fixed-interval schedules. *Journal of the Experimental Analysis of Behavior, 12*, 247–252.

Davison, M. C. (1972). Preference for mixed-interval versus fixed-interval schedules: Number of component intervals. *Journal of the Experimental Analysis of Behavior, 17*, 169–176.

Davison, M. C. (1981). Choice between concurrent variable-interval and fixed-ratio schedules: A failure of the generalized matching law. In C. M. Bradshaw, E. Szabadi, & C. F. Lowe (Eds.), *Quantification of steady-state operant behaviour* (pp. 91–100). Amsterdam: Elsevier/North-Holland.

Davison, M. C., & Ferguson, A. (1978). The effect of different component response requirements in multiple and concurrent schedules. *Journal of the Experimental Analysis of Behavior, 29*, 283–295.

Davison, M. C., & Hunter, I. W. (1976). Performance on variable-interval schedules arranged singly and concurrently. *Journal of the Experimental Analysis of Behavior, 25*, 335–345.

Davison, M. C., & Jenkins, P. E. (1985). Stimulus discriminability, contingency discriminability, and schedule performance. *Animal Learning and Behavior, 13*, 147–162.

Davison, M. C., & McCarthy, D. (1988). *The matching law: A research review*. Hillsdale, NJ: Lawrence Erlbaum Associates.

Dawkins, R. (1976). *The selfish gene*. London: Oxford University Press.

Dawkins, R. (1996). *Climbing Mount Improbable*. New York: W. W. Norton.

Dawkins, R. (2004). *The ancestor's tale: A pilgrimage to the dawn of evolution*. Boston, MA: Houghton Mifflin.

Dawson, B. V. & Foss, B. M. (1965). Observational learning in budgerigars. *Animal Behaviour, 13*, 470–474.

Deacon, J. R., & Konarski, E. A., Jr. (1987). Correspondence training: An example of rule-governed behavior? *Journal of Applied Behavior Analysis, 20*, 391–400.

DeBaryshe, B. D., & Whitehurst, G. J. (1986). Intraverbal acquisition of semantic concepts by preschoolers. *Journal of Experimental Child Psychology, 42*, 169–186.

De Boer, B. (2005). Evolution of speech and its acquisition. *Adaptive Behavior, 13*, 281–292.

De Brugada, I., Hall, G., & Symonds, M. (2004). The US-preexposure effect in lithium-induced flavor-aversion conditioning is a consequence of blocking by injection cues. *Journal of Experimental Psychology: Animal Behavior Processes, 20*, 58–66.

deCharms, R. C., Maeda, F., Glover, G., Ludlow, D., Pauly, J. M., Soneji, D. et al. (2005). Control over brain activation and pain learned by using real-time functional MRI. *Proceedings of the National Academy of Sciences of the United States of America, 102*, 18626–18631.

Deci, E. L., Koestner, R., & Ryan, R. M. (1999). A meta-analytic review of experiments examining the effects of extrinsic rewards on intrinsic motivation. *Psychological Bulletin, 125*, 627–668.

DeFran, R. H. (1972). *Reinforcing effects of stimuli paired with schedules of aversive control*. Unpublished doctoral dissertation. Bowling Green, OH: Bowling Green State University.

De Houwer, J., Thomas, S., & Baeyens, F. (2001). Association learning of likes and dislikes: A review of 25 years of research on human evaluative conditioning. *Psychological Bulletin, 127*, 853–869.

Deitz, S. M. (1978). Current status of applied behavior analysis: Science versus technology. *American Psychologist, 33*, 805–814.

Derenne, A. & Baron, A. (2002). Preratio pausing: effects of an alternative reinforcer on fixed- and variable-ratio responding. *Journal of the Experimental Analysis of Behavior, 77*, 273–282.

Derenne, A., Richardson, J. V., & Baron, A. (2006). Long-term effects of suppressing the preratio pause. *Behavioural Processes, 72*, 32–37.

Dessalles, J. L. (2007). *Why we talk: The evolutionary origins of language*. New York: Oxford University Press.

De Villiers, P. (1977). Choice in concurrent schedules and a quantitative formulation of the law of effect. In W. K. Honig & J. E. R. Staddon (Eds.), *Handbook of operant behavior* (pp. 233–287). Englewood Cliffs, NJ: Prentice-Hall.

DeWall, C. N., Twenge, J. M., Gitter, S. A., & Baumeister, R. F. (2009). It's the thought that counts: The role of hostile cognition in shaping aggressive responses to social exclusion. *Journal of Personality and Social Psychology*, *96*, 45–59.

Dews, P. B. (1963). Behavioral effects of drugs. In S. M. Farber & R. H. L. Wilson (Eds.), *Conflict and creativity* (pp. 138–153). New York: McGraw-Hill.

Dews, P. B. (1969). Studies on responding under fixed-interval schedules of reinforcement: The effects on the pattern of responding of changes in requirements at reinforcement. *Journal of the Experimental Analysis of Behavior*, *12*, 191–199.

Diane, A., Pierce, W. D., Heth, C. D., Russell, J. C., Richard, D., & Proctor, S. D. (2011). Feeding history and obese-prone genotype increase survival of rats exposed to a challenge of food restriction and wheel running. *Obesity*, *20*, 1787–1795.

DiCara, L. V. (1970). Learning in the autonomic nervous system. *Scientific American*, *222*, 30–39.

Dickerson, F. B., Tenhula, W. N., & Green-Paden, L. D. (2005). The token economy for schizophrenia: Review of the literature and recommendations for future research. *Schizophrenia Research*, *75*, 405–416.

Dickins, D. W., Singh, K. D., Roberts, N., Burns, P., Downes, J. J., Jimmieson, P. et al. (2001). An fMRI study of stimulus equivalence. *NeuroReport: Brain Imaging*, *12*, 405–411.

Dickins, T. E., & Dickins, D. W. (2001). Symbols, stimulus equivalence and the origins of language. *Behavior and Philosophy*, *29*, 221–244.

Dinsmoor, J. A. (1951). The effect of periodic reinforcement of bar-pressing in the presence of a discriminative stimulus. *Journal of Comparative and Physiological Psychology*, *44*, 354–361.

Dinsmoor, J. A. (1952). A discrimination based on punishment. *Quarterly Journal of Experimental Psychology*, *4*, 27–45.

Dinsmoor, J. A. (1977). Escape, avoidance, punishment: Where do we stand? *Journal of the Experimental Analysis of Behavior*, *28*, 83–95.

Dinsmoor, J. A. (2001a). Stimuli inevitably generated by behavior that avoids electric shock are inherently reinforcing. *Journal of the Experimental Analysis of Behavior*, *75*, 311–333.

Dinsmoor, J. A. (2001b). Still no evidence for temporally extended shock-frequency reduction as a reinforcer. *Journal of the Experimental Analysis of Behavior*, *75*, 367–378.

Dinsmoor, J. A., Brown, M. P., & Lawrence, C. E. (1972). A test of the negative discriminative stimulus as a reinforcer of observing. *Journal of the Experimental Analysis of Behavior*, *18*, 79–85.

Dinsmoor, J. A., Flint, G. A., Smith, R. F., & Viemeister, N. F. (1969). Differential reinforcing effects of stimuli associated with the presence or absence of a schedule of punishment. In D. P. Hendry (Ed.), *Conditioned reinforcement* (pp. 357–384). Homewood, IL: Dorsey Press.

Dixon, P. D., Ackert, A. M., & Eckel, L. A. (2003). Development of, and recovery from, activity-based anorexia in female rats. *Physiology and Behavior*, *80*, 273–279.

Dobek, C., Heth, C. D., & Pierce, W. D. (2012). Bivalent effects of wheel running on taste conditioning. *Behavioural Processes*, *89*, 36–38.

Dollard, J., & Miller, N. E. (1950). *Personality and psychotherapy*. New York: McGraw-Hill.

Donahoe, J. W. (2002). Behavior analysis and neuroscience. *Behavioural Processes*, *57*, 241–259.

Donohue, B. C., Karmely, J., & Strada, M. J. (2006). Alcohol and drug abuse. In M. Hersen (Ed.), *Clinician's handbook of child behavioral assessment* (pp. 337–375). San Diego, CA: Elsevier Academic Press.

Donovan, W. I. (1981). Maternal learned helplessness and physiologic response to infant crying. *Journal of Personality and Social Psychology*, *40*, 919–926.

Donovan, W. J. (1978). Structure and function of the pigeon visual system. *Physiological Psychology*, *6*, 403–437.

Dornhaus, A., & Chittka, L. (2004). Why do bees dance? *Behavioral Ecology and Sociobiology*, *55*, 395–401.

Dorrance, B. R. (2001). Imitative learning of conditional discriminations in pigeons. *Dissertation Abstracts International: Section B: The Sciences & Engineering, 61(11-B)*, No. 6169.

Dorrance, B. R., & Zentall, T. R. (2001). Imitative learning in Japanese quail depends on the motivational state of the observer at the time of observation. *Journal of Comparative Psychology*, *115*, 62–67.

Dos Santos, C. V., Gehm, T., & Hunziker, M. H. L. (2010). Learned helplessness in the rat: Effect of response topography in a within-subject design. *Behavioural Processes*, *86*, 178–183.

Dotto-Fojut, K. M., Reeve, K. F., Townsend, D. B., & Progar, P. R. (2011). Teaching adolescents with autism to describe a problem and request assistance during simulated vocational tasks. *Research in Autism Spectrum Disorders, 5*, 826–833.

Doughty, S. S., Chase, P. N., & O'Shields, E. (2004). Effects of rate building on fluent performance: A review and commentary. *The Behavior Analyst, 27*, 7–23.

Dove, L. D. (1976). Relation between level of food deprivation and rate of schedule-induced attack. *Journal of the Experimental Analysis of Behavior, 25*, 63–68.

Doyle, T. A., & Samson, H. H. (1988). Adjunctive alcohol drinking in humans. *Physiology and Behavior, 44*, 775–779.

Draganski, B., Gaser, C., Busch, V., Schuierer, G., Bogdahn, U., & May, A. (2004). Neuroplasticity: Changes in grey matter induced by training. *Nature, 427*, 311–312.

Dube, W. V., & McIlvane, W. J. (2001). Behavioral momentum in computer-presented discriminations in individuals with severe mental retardation. *Journal of the Experimental Analysis of Behavior, 75*, 15–23.

Ducharme, J. M., & Worling, D. E. (1994). Behavioral momentum and stimulus fading in the acquisition and maintenance of child compliance in the home. *Journal of Applied Behavior Analysis, 27*, 639–647.

Dulany, D. E. (1968). Awareness, rules, and propositonal control: A confrontation with S–R behavior theory. In T. Dixon & D. Horton (Eds.), *Verbal behavior and behavior theory* (pp. 340–387). New York: Prentice Hall.

Durand, V. M. (1999). Functional communication training using assistive devices: Recruiting natural communities of reinforcement. *Journal of Applied Behavior Analysis, 32*, 247–267.

Dutra, L., Stathopoulou, G., Basden, S. L., Leyro, T. M., Powers, M. B., & Otto, M. W. (2008). A meta-analytic review of psychosocial interventions for substance use disorders. *American Journal of Psychiatry, 165*, 179–187.

Dworkin, B., & Miller, N. (1986). Failure to replicate visceral learning in the acute curarized rat preparation. *Behavioral Neuroscience, 100*, 299–314.

Dwyer, D. M., & Boakes, R. A. (1997). Activity-based anorexia in rats as failure to adapt to a feeding schedule. *Behavioral Neuroscience, 111*, 195–205.

Dymond, D., & Critchfield, T. S. (2002). A legacy of growth: Human operant research in *The Psychological Record*, 1980–1999. *The Psychological Record, 52*, 99–108.

Eckerman, D. A., & Lanson, R. N. (1969). Variability of response location for pigeons responding under continuous reinforcement, intermittent reinforcement, and extinction. *Journal of the Experimental Analysis of Behavior, 12*, 73–80.

Edelman, G. M. (1987). *Neural Darwinism: The theory of neuronal group selection*. New York: Basic Books.

Edelman, G. M. (2007). Learning in and from brain-based devices. *Science, 318*, 1103–1105.

Egan, L. C., Bloom, P., & Santos, L. R. (2010). Choice-induced preferences in the absence of choice: Evidence from a blind two-choice paradigm with young children and capuchin monkeys. *Journal of Experimental Social Psychology, 46*, 204–207.

Egan, L. C., Santos, L. R., & Bloom, P. (2007). The origins of cognitive dissonance: Evidence from children and monkeys. *Psychological Science, 18*, 978–983.

Egger, M. D., & Miller, N. E. (1962). Secondary reinforcement in rats as a function of information value and reliability of the stimulus. *Journal of Experimental Psychology, 64*, 97–104.

Egger, M. D., & Miller, N. E. (1963). When is reward reinforcing? An experimental study of the information hypothesis. *Journal of Comparative and Physiological Psychology, 56*, 132–137.

Eibl-Eibesfeldt, I. (1975) *Ethology: The biology of behavior*. New York: Holt, Rinehart and Winston.

Eisenberger, R., & Cameron, J. (1996). The detrimental effects of reward: Myth or reality? *American Psychologist, 51*, 1153–1166.

Eisenberger, R., & Shanock, L. (2003). Rewards, intrinsic motivation, and creativity: A case study of conceptual and methodological isolation. *Creativity Research Journal, 15*, 121–130.

Ekman, P., & Friesen, W. V. (1975). *Unmasking the face*. Englewood Cliffs, NJ: Prentice-Hall.

Ellison, G. D. (1964). Differential salivary conditioning to traces. *Journal of Comparative and Physiological Psychology, 57*, 373–380.

Elsmore, T. F., & McBride, S. A. (1994). An eight-alternative concurrent schedule: Foraging in a radial maze. *Journal of the Experimental Analysis of Behavior, 61*, 331–348.

Engelmann, S., & Carnine, D. W. (1982). *Theory of instruction: Principles and application.* New York: Irvington.

Engle, B. T. (1993). Autonomic behavior. *Experimental Gerontology, 28,* 499–502.

Epling, W. F., & Pierce, W. D. (1983). Applied behavior analysis: New directions from the laboratory. *The Behavior Analyst, 6,* 27–37.

Epling, W. F., & Pierce, W. D. (1984). Activity-based anorexia in rats as a function of opportunity to run on an activity wheel. *Nutrition and Behavior, 2,* 37–49.

Epling, W. F., & Pierce, W. D. (1986). The basic importance of applied behavior analysis. *The Behavior Analyst, 9,* 89–99.

Epling, W. F., & Pierce, W. D. (1988). Activity-based anorexia: A biobehavioral perspective. *International Journal of Eating Disorders, 7,* 475–485.

Epling, W. F., & Pierce, W. D. (1990). Laboratory to application: An experimental analysis of severe problem behaviors. In A. C. Repp, & N. N. Singh (Eds.), *Perspectives on the use of nonaversive and aversive interventions for persons with developmental disabilities* (pp. 451–464). Sycamore, IL: Sycamore Publishing Co.

Epling, W. F., & Pierce, W. D. (1992). *Solving the anorexia puzzle: A scientific approach.* Toronto: Hogrefe & Huber.

Epling, W. F., & Pierce, W. D. (Eds.) (1996a). *Activity anorexia: Theory, research, and treatment.* Mahwah, NJ: Lawrence Erlbaum Associates, Inc.

Epling, W. F., & Pierce, W. D. (1996b). An overview of activity anorexia. In Epling, W. F., & Pierce, W. D. (Eds.), *Activity anorexia: Theory, research, and treatment* (pp. 1–4). Mahwah, NJ: Lawrence Erlbaum Associates, Inc.

Epling, W. F., Pierce, W. D., & Stefan, L. (1983). A theory of activity-based anorexia. *International Journal of Eating Disorders, 3,* 27–46.

Epstein, R. (1983). Resurgence of previously reinforced behavior during extinction. *The Behavior Analyst Letters, 3,* 391–397.

Epstein, R. (1984). Spontaneous and deferred imitation in the pigeon. *Behavioural Processes, 9,* 347–354.

Epstein, R. (1985). Extinction-induced resurgence: Preliminary investigation and possible application. *Psychological Record, 35,* 143–153.

Epstein, R., & Skinner, B. F. (1981). The spontaneous use of memoranda by pigeons. *Behavior Analysis Letters, 1,* 241–246.

Epstein, R., Lanza, R. P., & Skinner, B. F. (1980). Symbolic communication between two pigeons (*Columba livia domestica*). *Science, 207,* 543–545.

Erjavec, M., Lovett, V. E., & Horne, P. J. (2009). Do infants show generalized imitation of gestures? II. The effects of skills training and multiple exemplar matching training. *Journal of the Experimental Analysis of Behavior, 91,* 355–376.

Erlich, P. R. (2000). *Human natures: Genes, cultures, and the human prospect.* New York: Penguin.

Ernst, A. J., Engberg, L., & Thomas, D. R. (1971). On the form of stimulus generalization curves for visual intensity. *Journal of the Experimental Analysis of Behavior, 16,* 177–180.

Estes, W. K. (1944). An experimental study of punishment. *Psychological Monographs, 57* (Serial No. 3).

Estes, W. K., & Skinner, B. F. (1941). Some quantitative properties of anxiety. *Journal of Experimental Psychology, 29,* 390–400.

Ettinger, R. H., & McSweeney, F. K. (1981). Behavioral contrast and responding during multiple food–food, food–water, and water–water schedules. *Animal Learning and Behavior, 9,* 216–222.

Etzkowitz, H. (1992). Inventions. In E. F. Borgatta & M. L. Borgatta (Eds.), *Encyclopedia of sociology, Volume 2* (pp. 1004–1005). New York: Macmillan.

Evans, R. I. (1989). *Albert Bandura, the man and his ideas—a dialogue.* New York: Praeger.

Everett, D. L. (2012). *Language: The cultural tool.* New York: Pantheon.

Falck-Ytter, T., Gredeback, G., & von Hofsten, C. (2006). Infants predict other people's action goals. *Nature Neuroscience, 9,* 878–879.

Falk, J. L. (1961). Production of polydipsia in normal rats by an intermittent food schedule. *Science, 133,* 195–196.

Falk, J. L. (1964). Studies on schedule-induced polydipsia. In M. J. Wayner (Ed.), *Thirst: First international symposium on thirst in the regulation of body water* (pp. 95–116). New York: Pergamon Press.

Falk, J. L. (1969). Schedule-induced polydipsia as a function of fixed interval length. *Journal of the Experimental Analysis of Behavior, 9*, 37–39.

Falk, J. L. (1971). The nature and determinants of adjunctive behavior. *Physiology and Behavior, 6*, 577–588.

Falk, J. L. (1977). The origin and functions of adjunctive behavior. *Animal Learning and Behavior, 5*, 325–335.

Falk, J. L. (1994). Schedule-induced behavior occurs in humans: A reply to Overskeid. *Psychological Record, 44*, 45–63.

Falk, J. L. (1998). Drug abuse as adjunctive behavior. *Drug and Alcohol Dependence, 52*, 91–98.

Falk, J. L., D'Mello, K., & Lau, C. E. (2001). Two procedures establishing preference for oral cocaine and lidocane solutions which do not use an associative history with a reinforcer. *Behavioral Pharmacology, 12*, 117–123.

Falk, J. L., & Lau, C. E. (1997). Establishing preference for oral cocaine without an associative history with a reinforcer. *Drug and Alcohol Dependence, 46*, 159–166.

Fantino, E. (1965). Some data on the discriminative stimulus hypothesis of secondary reinforcement. *Psychological Record, 15*, 409–414.

Fantino, E. (1967). Preference for mixed- versus fixed-ratio schedules. *Journal of the Experimental Analysis of Behavior, 10*, 35–43.

Fantino, E. (1969a). Choice and rate of reinforcement. *Journal of the Experimental Analysis of Behavior, 12*, 723–730.

Fantino, E. (1969b). Conditioned reinforcement, choice, and the psychological distance to reward. In D. P. Hendry (Ed.), *Conditioned reinforcement* (pp. 163–191). Homewood, IL: Dorsey Press.

Fantino, E. (1977). Conditioned reinforcement: Choice and information. In W. K. Honig & J. E. R. Staddon (Eds.), *Handbook of operant behavior* (pp. 313–339). Englewood Cliffs, NJ: Prentice-Hall.

Fantino, E. (2008). Choice, conditioned reinforcement, and the Prius effect. *The Behavior Analyst, 31*, 95–111.

Fantino, E., & Case, D. A. (1983). Human observing: Maintained by stimuli correlated with reinforcement but not extinction. *Journal of the Experimental Analysis of Behavior, 18*, 79–85.

Fantino, E., & Logan, C. A. (1979). *The experimental analysis of behavior: A biological perspective.* San Francisco, CA: W. H. Freeman.

Fantino, E. & Romanowich, P. (2007). The effect of conditioned reinforcement rate on choice: A review. *Journal of the Experimental Analysis of Behavior, 87*, 409–421.

Fantino, E., & Silberberg, A. (2010). Revisiting the role of bad news in maintaining human observing behavior. *Journal of the Experimental Analysis of Behavior, 93*, 157–170.

Fawcett, T. W., McNamara, J. M., & Houston, A. (2012). When is it adaptive to be patient? A general framework for evaluating delayed rewards. *Behavioural Processes, 89*, 128–136.

Fehr, E., & Gintis, H. (2007). Human motivation and social cooperation: Experimental and analytical foundations. *Annual Review of Sociology, 33*, 43–64.

Feighner, J. P., Robins, E., Guze, S. B., Woodruff, R. A., Winokur, G., & Munoz, R. (1972). Diagnostic criteria for use in psychiatric research. *Archives of General Psychiatry, 26*, 57–63.

Feldman, M. A. (1990). Balancing freedom from harm and right to treatment for persons with developmental disabilities. In A. C. Repp & N. N. Singh (Eds.), *Perspectives on the use of nonaversive and aversive interventions for persons with developmental disabilities* (pp. 261–271). Sycamore, IL: Sycamore Publishing Co.

Ferrari, P. F., Rozzi, S., &. Fogassi L (2005). Mirror neurons responding to observation of actions made with tools in monkey ventral premotor cortex. *Journal of Cognitive Neuroscience, 17*, 212–226.

Ferrari, P. F., Visalberghi, E., Pauker, A., Fogassi, L., Ruggiero, A., & Suomi, S. J. (2006). Neonatal imitation in rhesus macaques. *PLoS Biology, 4*, 1501–1508.

Ferster, C. B. (2000). Schedules of reinforcement with Skinner. *Journal of the Experimental Analysis of Behavior, 77*, 303–311.

Ferster, C. B., & Appel, J. B. (1961). Punishment of S^{Δ} responding in matching to sample by time out from positive reinforcement. *Journal of the Experimental Analysis of Behavior, 4*, 45–56.

Ferster, C. B., & Skinner, B. F. (1957). *Schedules of reinforcement.* New York: Appleton-Century-Crofts.

Ferster, C. B., Culbertson, S., & Boren, M. C. P. (1975). *Behavior principles.* Englewood Cliffs, NJ: Prentice-Hall.

Festinger, L. (1957). *A theory of cognitive dissonance.* Stanford, CA: Stanford University Press.

Field, T, M., Woodson, R., Greenberg, R., & Cohen, D. (1982). Discrimination and imitation of facial expressions by neonates. *Science, 218*, 179–181.

Fields, R. D. (2009). *The other brain*. New York: Simon & Schuster.

Filby, Y., & Appel, J. B. (1966). Variable-interval punishment during variable-interval reinforcement. *Journal of the Experimental Analysis of Behavior, 9*, 521–527.

Findley, J. D. (1958). Preference and switching under concurrent scheduling. *Journal of the Experimental Analysis of Behavior, 1*, 123–144.

Finger, B. C., Dinan, T. G., & Cryan, J. F. (2010). Progressive ratio responding in an obese mouse model: Effects of fenfluramine. *Neuropharmacology, 59*, 619–626.

Fiorillo, C. D., Tobler, P. N., and Schultz, W. (2003). Discrete coding of reward probability and uncertainty by dopamine neurons. *Science, 299*, 1898–1902.

Fischer, J. L., Howard, J. S., Sparkman, C. R., & Moore, A. G. (2010). Establishing generalized syntactical responding in young children with autism. *Research in Autism Spectrum Disorders, 4*, 76–88.

Fischer, S. M., Iwata, B. A., & Worsdell, A. S. (1997). Attention as an establishing operation and as reinforcement during functional analyses. *Journal of Applied Behavior Analysis, 30*, 335–338.

Fisher, J., & Hinde, C. A. (1949). The opening of milk bottles by birds. *British Birds, 42*, 347–357.

Fisher, W. W., & Mazur, J. E. (1997). Basic and applied research on choice responding. *Journal of Applied Behavior Analysis, 30*, 387–410.

Fishman, S. (1991). The town B. F. Skinner boxed. *Health, 5*, 50–60.

Fiston, K. (2010). The free-energy principle: A unified brain theory? *Nature Reviews Neuroscience, 11*, 127–138.

Fixsen, D. L., Phillips, E. L., Phillips, E. A., & Wolf, M. M. (1976). The teaching-family model of group home treatment. In W. E. Craighead, A. E. Kazdin, & M. J. Mahoney (Eds.), *Behavior modification: Principles, issues, and applications* (pp. 310–320). Boston, MA: Houghton Mifflin.

Flory, R. K. (1969). Attack behavior as a function of minimum inter-food interval. *Journal of the Experimental Analysis of Behavior, 12*, 825–828.

Foreman, A. M. (2009). *Negative reinforcement by timeout from avoidance: The roles of shock-frequency reduction and response-effort reduction*. Masters of Science Thesis. Morgantown, WV: Department of Psychology, Eberly College of Arts and Sciences, West Virginia University.

Foster, T. A., Hackenberg, T. D., & Vaidya, M. (2001). Second-order schedules of token reinforcement with pigeons: Effects of fixed- and variable-ratio exchange schedules. *Journal of the Experimental Analysis of Behavior, 76*, 159–178.

Foxx, R. M. (2008). Applied behavior analysis treatment of autism: The state of the art. *Child and Adolescent Psychiatric Clinics of North America, 17*, 821–834.

Foxx, R. M., & Azrin, N. H. (1972). Restitution: A method of eliminating aggressive-disruptive behavior of retarded and brain damaged patients. *Behavior Research and Therapy, 10*, 15–27.

Foxx, R. M., & Azrin, N. H. (1973). The elimination of autistic self-stimulatory behavior by overcorrection. *Journal of Applied Behavior Analysis, 6*, 1–14.

Frank, A. J., & Wasserman, E. A. (2005). Associate symmetry in the pigeon after successive matching-to-sample training. *Journal of the Experimental Analysis of Behavior, 84*, 147–165.

Freedman, D. H. (2011). How to fix the obesity crisis. *Scientific American, 304*, 40–47.

Friedman, S. G., Edling, T., & Cheney, C. D. (2006). The natural science of behavior. In G. J. Harrison and T. L. Lightfoot (Eds.), *Clinical avian medicine* (pp. 46–59). Palm Beach, FL: Spix.

Friman, P. C., Finney, J. W., Glasscock, S. T., Weigel, J. W., & Christophersen, E. R. (1986). Testicular self-examination: Validation of a training strategy for early cancer detection. *Journal of Applied Behavior Analysis, 19*, 87–92.

Frisch, K. von (1967) *The dance language and orientation of bees*. Cambridge, MA: Harvard University Press.

Galef, B. G. (1988). Imitation in animals: History, definition, and interpretation of data from the psychological laboratory. In T. R. Zentall & B. G. Galef, Jr. (Eds.), *Social learning: Psychological and biological perspectives* (pp. 3–28). Hillsdale, NJ: Lawrence Erlbaum Associates.

Galef, B. G. (1990). Necessary and sufficient conditions for communication of diet preferences by Norway rats. *Animal Learning and Behavior, 18*, 347–351.

Galef, B.G. Jr., & Allen, C. (1995). A new model system for studying behavioural traditions in animals. *Animal Behaviour, 50*, 705–717.

Galizio, M. (1979). Contingency-shaped and rule-governed behavior: Instructional control of human loss avoidance. *Journal of the Experimental Analysis of Behavior, 31*, 53–70.

Gallese, V., Fadiga, L., Fogassi, L., & Rizzolatti, G. (1996). Action recognition in the premotor cortex. *Brain, 119*, 593–609.

Garcia, J., & Koelling, R. A. (1966). Relation of cue to consequence in avoidance learning. *Psychonomic Science, 4*, 123–124.

Garcia-Fernandez, G., Secades-Villa, R., Garcia-Rodriguez, O., Sanchez-Hervas, E., Fernandez-Hermida, J., & Higgins, S. T. (2011). Adding voucher-based incentives to community reinforcement approach improves outcomes during treatment for cocaine dependence. *American Journal on Addictions, 20*, 456–461.

Gardner, E. T., & Lewis, P. (1976). Negative reinforcement with shock-frequency increase. *Journal of the Experimental Analysis of Behavior, 25*, 3–14.

Garner, D. M., & Desai, J. J. (2000). Eating disorders. In M. Hersen & A. S. Bellack (Eds.), *Psychopathology in adulthood* (2nd ed.) (pp. 419–441). Needham Heights, MA: Allyn & Bacon.

Garner, D. M., Garfinkel, P. E., Stancer, H. C. & Moldofsky, H. (1976). Body image disturbances in anorexia nervosa and obesity. *Psychosomatic Medicine, 38*, 327–336.

Gast, D. L. (2010). *Single subject research methodology in behavioral sciences*. New York: Routledge.

Geen, R. G. (1968). Effects of frustration, attack, and prior training in aggressiveness upon aggressive behavior. *Journal of Personality and Social Psychology, 9*, 316–321.

Geiger, B., & Fischer, M. (2006). Will words ever harm me? Escalation from verbal to physical abuse in sixth-grade classrooms. *Journal of Interpersonal Violence, 21*, 337–357.

Geller, E. S. (2006). Occupational injury prevention and applied behavior analysis. In A. C. Gielen, D. A. Sleet & R. J. DiClemente (Eds.), *Injury and violence prevention: Behavioral science theories, methods, and applications* (pp. 297–322). San Francisco, CA: Jossey-Bass.

Geller, E. S. (2011). Psychological science and safety: Large-scale success at preventing occupational injuries and fatalities. *Current Directions in Psychological Science, 20*, 109–114.

Geller, I., & Seifter, J. (1960). The effects of meprobamate, barbiturates, d-amphetamine and promazine on experimentally induced conflict in the rat. *Psychopharmacologia, 1*, 482–492.

Geller, I., Kulak, J. T., Jr., & Seifter, J. (1962). The effects of chlordiazepoxide and chlorpromazine on punished discrimination. *Psychopharmacologia, 3*, 374–385.

Gellman, M., & Turner, J. R. (2012). *Encyclopedia of behavioral medicine*. New York: Springer Publishing.

Gendall, K. A., Kaye, W. H., Altemus, M., McConaha, C. W., & La Via, M. C. (1999) Leptin, neuropeptide Y, and peptide YY in long-term recovered eating disorder patients. *Biological Psychiatry, 46*, 292–299.

Gerard, H. B. (1994). A retrospective review of Festinger's A Theory of Cognitive Dissonance. *Psychological Critiques, 39*, 1013–1017.

Gershoff, E. T. (2002). Corporal punishment by parents and associated child behaviors and experiences: A meta-analytic and theoretical review. *Psychological Bulletin, 128*, 539–579.

Gewirtz, J. L. (1971). The roles of overt responding and extrinsic reinforcement in "self-" and "vicarious-reinforcement" phenomena and in "observational learning" and imitation. In R. Glaser (Ed.), *The nature of reinforcement* (pp. 279–309). New York: Academic Press.

Ghezzi, P., Williams, W. L., & Carr, J. (1999). *Autism: Behavior analytic perspectives*. Reno, NV: Context Press.

Ginsburg, S., & Jablonka, E. (2010). The evolution of associative learning: A factor in the Cambrian explosion. *Journal of Theoretical Biology, 266*, 11–20.

Giurfa, M. (2007). Behavioral and neural analysis of associative learning in the honeybee: A taste from the magic well. *Journal of Comparative Physiology A, 193*, 801–824.

Glazer, H. I., & Weiss, J. M. (1976a). Long-term interference effect: An alternative to "learned helplessness." *Journal of Experimental Psychology: Animal Behavior Processes, 2*, 202–213.

Glazer, H. I., & Weiss, J. M. (1976b). Long-term and transitory interference effects. *Journal of Experimental Psychology: Animal Behavior Processes, 2*, 191–201.

Gleeson, S. (1991). Response acquisition. In I. H. Iverson & K. A. Lattal (Eds.), *Experimental analysis of behavior: Part 1* (pp. 63–86). New York: Elsevier.

Glenn, S. S. (1988). Contingencies and metacontingencies: Toward a synthesis of behavior analysis and cultural materialism. *The Behavior Analyst, 11*, 161–179.

Glenn, S. S. (1989). Verbal behavior and cultural practices. *Behavior Analysis and Social Action, 7*, 10–14.

Glenn, S. S. (1991). Contingencies and metacontingencies: Relations among behavioral, cultural, and biological evolution. In P. A. Lamal (Ed.), *Behavioral analysis of societies and cultural practices* (pp. 39–73). New York: Hemisphere.

Glenn, S. S. (2004). Individual behavior, culture, and social change. *The Behavior Analyst, 27*, 133–151.

Glenn, S. S., & Field, D. P. (1994). Functions of the environment in behavioral evolution. *The Behavior Analyst, 17*, 241–259.

Glenwick, D., & Jason, L. (1980). *Behavioral community psychology: Progress and prospects*. New York: Praeger.

Goetz, E. M., & Baer, D. M. (1973). Social control of form diversity and the emergence of new forms in children's blockbuilding. *Journal of Applied Behavior Analysis, 6*, 209–217.

Goldin-Meadow, S., & Morford, M. (1985). Gesture in early child language: Studies of deaf and hearing children. *Merrill-Palmer Quarterly, 31*, 145–176.

Goldin-Meadow, S., & Wagner, S. M. (2005). How our hands help us learn. *Trends in Cognitive Sciences, 9*, 234–241.

Goldsmith, T. H. (2006). What birds see. *Scientific American, 295*, 68–75.

Goldsmith, T. H., & Butler, B. K. (2005). Color vision of the budgerigar (*Melopsittacus undulates*): Hue matches, tetrachromacy, and intensity discrimination. *Journal of Comparative Physiology A: Neuroethology, Sensory, Neural, and Behavioral Physiology, 191*, 933–951.

Goldstein, M. H., King, A. P., & West, M. J. (2003). Social interaction shapes babbling: Testing parallels between birdsong and speech. *Proceedings of the National Academy of Sciences, 100*, 8030–8035.

Gollub, L. R. (1991). The use of computers in the control and recording of behavior. In I. H. Iverson & K. A. Lattal (Eds.), *Experimental analysis of behavior: Part 2* (pp. 155–192). New York: Elsevier.

Gollub, L. R. (1958). *The chaining of fixed-interval schedules*. Unpublished doctoral dissertation. Cambridge, MA: Harvard University.

Gollub, L. R. (1977). Conditioned reinforcement: Schedule effects. In W. K. Honig & J. E. R. Staddon (Eds.), *Handbook of operant behavior* (pp. 288–312). Englewood Cliffs, NJ: Prentice-Hall.

Gonnerman, J. (2007). *School of Shock*, 19 August 2007. www.motherjones.com/politics/2007/08/school-shock

Gonzalez, R. C., Gentry, G. V., & Bitterman, M. E. (1954). Relational discrimination of intermediate size in the chimpanzee. *Journal of Comparative and Physiological Psychology, 47*, 385–388.

Gott, C. T., & Weiss, B. (1972). The development of fixed-ratio performance under the influence of ribonucleic acid. *Journal of the Experimental Analysis of Behavior, 18*, 481–497.

Gould, S. J. (1989). *Wonderful life*. New York: W. W. Norton.

Gould, S. J. (2002). *The structure of evolutionary theory*. Cambridge, MA: Harvard University Press.

Grant, D. S. (1975). Proactive interference in pigeon short-term memory. *Journal of Experimental Psychology: Animal Behavior Processes, 1*, 207–220.

Grant, D. S. (1981). Short-term memory in the pigeon. In N. E. Spear & R. R. Miller (Eds.), *Information processing in animals: Memory mechanisms* (pp. 227–256). Hillsdale, NJ: Lawrence Erlbaum Associates.

Green, D. M., & Swets, J. A. (1966). *Signal detection theory and psychophysics*. New York: John Wiley & Sons.

Green, L., & Freed, D. E. (1993). The substitutability of reinforcers. *Journal of the Experimental Analysis of Behavior, 60*, 141–158.

Green, L., Fisher, E. B., Perlow, S., & Sherman, L. (1981). Preference reversal and self control: Choice as a function of reward amount and delay. *Behavior Analysis Letters, 1*, 43–51.

Green, L., Fry, A. F., & Myerson, J. (1994). Discounting of delayed rewards: A life-span comparison. *Psychological Science, 5*, 33–36.

Greene, W. A., & Sutor, L. T. (1971). Stimulus control of skin resistance responses on an escape-avoidance schedule. *Journal of the Experimental Analysis of Behavior, 16*, 269–274.

Greer, R. D., Stolfi, L., & Pistoljevic, N. (2007). Emergence of naming in preschoolers: A comparison of multiple and single exemplar instruction. *European Journal of Behavior Analysis, 8*, 109–131.

Griggio, M., Hoi, H., & Pilastro, A. (2010). Plumage maintenance affects ultraviolet colour and female preference in the budgerigar. *Behavioural Processes, 84*, 739–744.

Gross, L. (2006). Evolution of neonatal imitation. *PLOS Biology, 4*, e311. doi:10.1371/journal.pbio.0040311.

Gruber, T., Muller, M. N., Strimling, P., Wrangham, R., & Zuberbuhler, K. (2009). Wild chimpanzees rely on cultural knowledge to solve an experimental honey acquisition task. *Current Biology, 19*, 1806–1810.

Gruber, T., Reynolds, V., & Zuberbuhler, K. (2010). The knowns and unknowns of chimpanzee culture. *Communicative and Integrative Biology, 3*, 221–223.

Guerin, B. (2003). Language use as social strategy: A review and an analytic framework for the social sciences. *Review of General Psychology, 7*, 251–298.

Guerra, L. G., & Silva, M. T. (2010). Learning processes and the neural analysis of conditioning. *Psychology and Neuroscience, 3*, 195–208.

Guess, D. (1969). A functional analysis of receptive language and productive speech: Acquisition of the plural morpheme. *Journal of Applied Behavior Analysis, 2*, 55–64.

Guess, D., & Baer, D. M. (1973). An analysis of individual differences in generalization between receptive and productive language in retarded children. *Journal of Applied Behavior Analysis, 6*, 311–329.

Guess, D., Helmstetter, E., Turnbull, H. R., & Knowlton, S. (1986). *Use of aversive procedures with persons who are disabled: An historical review and critical analysis* (Monograph No. 2). Seattle, WA: The Association for Persons with Severe Handicaps.

Guess, D., Sailor, W., Rutherford, G., & Baer, D. M. (1968). An experimental analysis of linguistic development: The productive use of the plural morpheme. *Journal of Applied Behavior Analysis, 1*, 297–306.

Guillette, L. M., Farrell, T. M., Hoeschele, M., Nickerson, C. M., Dawson, M. R., & Sturdy, C. B. (2010). Mechanisms of call note-type perception in black-capped chickadees (*Poecile atricapillus*): Peak shift in a note-type continuum. *Journal of Comparative Psychology, 124*, 109–115.

Gully, K. J., & Dengerink, H. A. (1983). The dyadic interaction of persons with violent and nonviolent histories. *Aggressive Behavior, 7*, 13–20.

Gustafson, R. (1989). Frustration and successful vs. unsuccessful aggression: A test of Berkowitz' completion hypothesis. *Aggressive Behavior, 15*, 5–12.

Guttman, A. (1977). Positive contrast, negative induction, and inhibitory stimulus control in the rat. *Journal of the Experimental Analysis of Behavior, 27*, 219–233.

Guttman, N., & Kalish, H. I. (1956). Discriminability and stimulus generalization. *Journal of Experimental Psychology, 51*, 79–88.

Hackenberg, T. D. (2009). Token reinforcement: A review and analysis. *Journal of the Experimental Analysis of Behavior, 91*, 257–286.

Hackenberg, T. D., & Joker, V. R. (1994). Instructional versus schedule control of humans' choices in situations of diminishing returns. *Journal of the Experimental Analysis of Behavior, 62*, 367–383.

Haggbloom, S. J. (2002). The 100 most eminent psychologists of the 20th century. *Review of General Psychology, 6*, 139–152.

Hake, D. F., Donaldson, T., & Hyten, C. (1983). Analysis of discriminative control by social behavioral stimuli. *Journal of the Experimental Analysis of Behavior, 39*, 7–23.

Hall, D. C., Adams, C. K., Stein, G. H., Stephenson, H. S., Goldstein, M. K., & Pennypacker, H. S. (1980). Improved detection of human breast lesions following experimental training. *Cancer, 46*, 408–414.

Hall, G. (2009). Preexposure to the unconditioned stimulus in nausea-based aversion learning. In S. Reilly & T. R. Schachtman (Eds.), *Conditioned taste aversion: Behavioral and neural processes* (pp. 58–73). New York: Oxford University Press.

Hall, G., & Sundberg, M. L. (1987). Teaching mands by manipulating conditioned establishing operations. *The Analysis of Verbal Behavior, 5*, 41–53.

Hall, R. V., & Hall, M. C. (1982). *How to negotiate a behavioral contract*. Lawrence, KS: H. & H. Enterprises.

Hall, R. V., Cristler, C., Cranston, S. S., & Tucker, B. (1970). Teachers and parents as researchers using multiple baseline designs. *Journal of Applied Behavior Analysis, 3*, 247–255.

Hammack, S. E., Cooper, M. A., & Lezak, K. R. (2012). Overlapping neurobiology of learned helplessness and conditioned defeat: Implications for PTSD and mood disorders. *Neuropharmacology, 62*, 565–575.

Hammer, M. & Menzel, R. (1998). Multiple sites of associative odor learning as revealed by local brain micro-injections of octopamine in honeybees. *Learning and Memory, 5*, 146–156.

Hammond, J. L., Iwata, B. A., Fritz, J. N., & Dempsey, C. M. (2011). Evaluation of fixed momentary DRO schedules under signaled and unsignaled arrangements. *Journal of Applied Behavior Analysis, 44*, 69–81.

Hanna, E., & Meltzoff, A. N. (1993). Peer imitation by toddlers in laboratory, home and day care contexts: Implications for social learning and memory. *Developmental Psychology, 29*, 701–710.

Hansen, S. D., & Lignugaris/Kraft, B. (2005). Effects of a dependent group contingency on the verbal interactions of middle school students with emotional disturbance. *Behavioral Disorders, 30*, 170–184.

Hanson, H. M. (1959). Effects of discrimination training on stimulus generalization. *Journal of Experimental Psychology, 58*, 321–334.

Hardin, G. (1968). The tragedy of the commons. *Science, 162*, 1243.

Harlow, H. F., & Zimmerman, R. R. (1959). Affectional responses in the infant monkey. *Science, 130*, 421–432.

Harper, D. N., & McLean, A. P. (1992). Resistance to change and the law of effect. *Journal of the Experimental Analysis of Behavior, 57*, 317–337.

Harris, M. (1974). *Cows, pigs, wars, and witches*. New York: Vintage Books.

Harris, M. (1979). *Cultural materialism*. New York: Random House.

Harris, S., Sheth, S. & Cohen, M. (2007). Functional neuroimaging of belief, disbelief, and uncertainty. *Annals of Neurology, 63*, 141–147.

Harrison, J. M. (1991). Stimulus control. In I. H. Iversion & K. A. Lattal (Eds.), *Experimental Analysis of Behavior: Part 1* (pp. 251–300). Amsterdam: Elsevier Science.

Hasazi, J. E. & Hasazi, S. E. (1972). Effects of teacher attention on digit-reversal behavior in an elementary school child. *Journal of Applied Behavior Analysis, 5*, 157–162.

Hastad, O., Ernstdotter, E., & Odeen, A. (2005). Ultraviolet vision and foraging in dip and plunge birds. *Biological Letters, 1*, 306–309.

Hausmann, F., Arnold, K. E., Marshall, N. J., & Owens, I. P. F. (2003). Ultraviolet signals in birds are special. *Proceedings of the Royal Society B, 270*, 61–67.

Havermans, R. C., Salvy, S., & Jansen, A. (2009). Single-trial exercise-induced taste and odor aversion learning in humans. *Appetite, 53*, 442–445.

Haw, J. (2008). Random-ratio schedules of reinforcement: The role of early wins and unreinforced trials. *Journal of Gambling Issues, 21*, 56–67.

Hayes, L. A. & Watson, J. S. (1981). Neonatal imitation: Fact or artifact. *Developmental Psychology, 17*, 655–660.

Hayes, S. C. (1987). A contextual approach to therapeutic change. In N. Jacobson (Ed.), *Psychotherapists in clinical practice: Cognitive and behavioral perspectives* (pp. 329–383). New York: Guilford Press.

Hayes, S. C. (1989a). Nonhumans have not yet shown stimulus equivalence. *Journal of the Experimental Analysis of Behavior, 51*, 385–392.

Hayes, S. C. (1989b). *Rule-governed behavior: Cognition, contingencies, and instructional control*. New York: Plenum Press.

Hayes, S. C., & Ju, W. (1997). The applied implications of rule-governed behavior. In W. T. O'Donohue (Ed.), *Learning and behavior therapy* (pp. 374–391). Needham Heights, MA: Allyn & Bacon.

Hayes, S. C., Barnes-Holmes, D., & Roche, B. (2001). *Relational frame theory: A post-Skinnerian account of human language and cognition*. New York: Plenum.

Hayes, S. C., Brownstein, A. J., Haas, J. R., & Greenway, D. E. (1986). Instructions, multiple schedules, and extinction: Distinguishing rule-governed from schedule-controlled behavior. *Journal of the Experimental Analysis of Behavior, 46*, 137–147.

Hayes, S. C., Rincover, A., & Solnick, J. V. (1980). The technical drift of applied behavior analysis. *Journal of Applied Behavior Analysis, 13*, 275–285.

Hearst, E. (1961). Resistance-to-extinction functions in the single organism. *Journal of the Experimental Analysis of Behavior, 4*, 133–144.

Hearst, E., & Jenkins, H. M. (1974). *Sign tracking: The stimulus–reinforcer relation and directed action*. Austin, TX: The Psychonomic Society.

Heath, R. G. (1963). Electrical self-stimulation of the brain in man. *American Journal of Psychiatry, 120*, 571–577.

Heil, S. H., Johnson, M. W., Higgins, S. T., & Bickel, W. K. (2006). Delay discounting in currently using and currently abstinent cocaine-dependent outpatients and non-drug-using matched controls. *Addictive Behaviors, 31*, 1290–1294.

Heinemann, E. G., & Chase, S. (1970). On the form of stimulus generalization curves for auditory intensity. *Journal of Experimental Psychology, 84*, 483–486.

Heinrich, B., & Bugnyar, T. (2007). Just how smart are ravens? *Scientific American, 296*, 64–71.

Hendrik, G. R., Boulogne, J. J., van Tulder, M. W., van den Brink, W., De Jong, C. A. J., & Kerkhof, A. J. F. M. (2004). A systematic review of the effectiveness of the community reinforcement approach in alcohol, cocaine and opioid addiction. *Drug and Alcohol Dependence, 74*, 1–13.

Hendry, D. P. (1969). *Conditioned reinforcement.* Homewood, IL: Dorsey Press.

Herbert, J. J., & Harsh, C. M. (1944). Observational learning by cats. *Journal of Comparative Psychology, 37*, 81–95.

Herman, R. L., & Azrin, N. H. (1964). Punishment by noise in an alternative response situation. *Journal of the Experimental Analysis of Behavior, 7*, 185–188.

Hermann, P. M., de Lange, R. P. J., Pieneman, A. W., ter Maat, A., & Jansen, R. F. (1997). Role of neuropeptides encoded on CDCH-1 gene in the organization of egg-laying behavior in the pond snail, *Lymnaea stagnalis. Journal of Neurophysiology, 78*, 2859–2869.

Herrnstein, R. J. (1961a). Stereotypy and intermittent reinforcement. *Science, 133*, 2067–2069.

Herrnstein, R. J. (1961b). Relative and absolute strength of responses as a function of frequency of reinforcement. *Journal of the Experimental Analysis of Behavior, 4*, 267–272.

Herrnstein, R. J. (1964a). Aperiodicity as a factor in choice. *Journal of the Experimental Analysis of Behavior, 7*, 179–182.

Herrnstein, R. J. (1964b). Secondary reinforcement and the rate of primary reinforcement. *Journal of the Experimental Analysis of Behavior, 7*, 27–36.

Herrnstein, R. J. (1970). On the law of effect. *Journal of the Experimental Analysis of Behavior, 13*, 243–266.

Herrnstein, R. J. (1974). Formal properties of the matching law. *Journal of the Experimental Analysis of Behavior, 21*, 159–164.

Herrnstein, R. J. (1979). Acquisition, generalization, and reversal of a natural concept. *Journal of Experimental Psychology: Animal Behavior Processes, 5*, 116–129.

Herrnstein, R. J. (1982). Melioration as behavioral dynamicism. In M. L. Commons, R. J. Herrnstein, & H. Rachlin (Eds.), *Quantitative analyses of behavior: Volume 2. Matching and maximizing accounts of behavior* (pp. 433–458). Cambridge, MA: Ballinger.

Herrnstein, R. J. (1997). Melioration as behavioral dynamics. In H. Rachlin & D. I. Laibson (Eds.), *The matching law: Papers in psychology and economics by Richard J. Herrnstein* (pp. 74–99). Cambridge, MA: Harvard University Press.

Herrnstein, R. J., & de Villiers, P. A. (1980). Fish as a natural category for people and pigeons. In G. H. Bower (Ed.), *The psychology of learning and motivation, Volume 14* (pp. 60–95). New York: Academic Press.

Herrnstein, R. J., & Hineline, P. N. (1966). Negative reinforcement as shock frequency reduction. *Journal of the Experimental Analysis of Behavior, 9*, 421–430.

Herrnstein, R. J., & Loveland, D. H. (1964). Complex visual concept in the pigeon. *Science, 146*, 549–551.

Herrnstein, R. J., & Loveland, D. H. (1975). Maximizing and matching on concurrent ratio schedules. *Journal of the Experimental Analysis of Behavior, 24*, 107–116.

Herrnstein, R. J., & Prelec, D. (1997). Melioration: A theory of distributed choice. In H. Rachlin & D. I. Laibson (Eds.), *The matching law: Papers in psychology and economics by Richard J. Herrnstein* (pp. 274–292). Cambridge, MA: Harvard University Press.

Herrnstein, R. J., Loveland, D. H., & Cable, C. (1976). Natural concepts in pigeons. *Journal of Experimental Psychology: Animal Behavior Processes, 2*, 285–302.

Heth, C. D. (1976). Simultaneous and backward fear conditioning as a function of number of CS–UCS pairings. *Journal of Experimental Psychology: Animal Behavior Processes, 2*, 117–129.

Heth, C. D., & Pierce, W. D. (2007). The role of pre-exposure to novel food tastes in activity-based conditioned taste avoidance. *Learning and Motivation, 38*, 35–43.

Heth, D. C., Inglis, P., Russell, J. C., & Pierce, W. D. (2001). Conditioned taste aversion induced by wheel running is not due to novelty of the wheel. *Physiology and Behavior, 74*, 53–56.

Heyes, C. M., Bird, G., Johnson, H., & Haggard, P. (2005). Experience modulates automatic imitation. *Cognitive Brain Research, 22*, 233–240.

Heyman, G. M. (2009). *Addiction: A disorder of choice*. Cambridge, MA: Harvard University Press.

Higgins, S. T., & Katz, J. L. (1998). *Cocaine abuse: Behavior, pharmacology, and clinical applications*. San Diego, CA: Academic Press.

Higgins, S. T., & Petry, N. M. (1999). Contingency management: Incentives for sobriety. *Alcohol Research and Health, 23*, 122–127.

Higgins, S. T., Bickel, W. K., & Hughes, J. R. (1994). Influence of an alternative reinforcer on human cocaine self-administration. *Life Sciences, 55*, 179–187.

Higgins S. T., Budney A. J., Bickel, W. K., Hughes, J., Foerg, F., & Badger, G. J. (1993). Achieving cocaine abstinence with a behavioral approach. *American Journal of Psychiatry, 150*, 763–769.

Higgins, S. T., Delaney, D., Budney, A., Bickel, W., Hughes, J., & Foerg, F. (1991). A behavioral approach to achieving initial cocaine abstinence. *American Journal of Psychiatry, 148*, 1218–1224.

Higgins, S. T., Silverman, K., & Heil, S. H. (2007). *Contingency management in substance abuse treatment*. New York: The Guilford Press.

Higgins, S. T., Washio, Y., Heil, S. H., Solomon, L. J., Gaalema, D. E., Higgins, T. M. et al. (2012). Financial incentives for smoking cessation among pregnant and newly postpartum women. *Preventive Medicine, 55* (Suppl.), S33–S40.

Hilgard, E. R., & Marquis, D. G. (1961). *Conditioning and learning*. New York: Appleton (original work published in 1940).

Hinde, R. A., & Stevenson-Hinde, J. (1973). *Constraints on learning: Limitations and predispositions*. New York: Academic Press.

Hineline, P. N. (1970). Negative reinforcement without shock reduction. *Journal of the Experimental Analysis of Behavior, 14*, 259–268.

Hineline, P. N. (1977). Negative reinforcement and avoidance. In W. K. Honig & J. E. R. Staddon (Eds.), *Handbook of operant behavior* (pp. 364–414). Englewood Cliffs, NJ: Prentice-Hall.

Hineline, P. N. (1984). Aversive control: A separate domain? *Journal of the Experimental Analysis of Behavior, 42*, 495–509.

Hinson, R. E., Poulos, C. X., & Cappell, H. (1982). Effects of pentobarbital and cocaine in rats expecting pentobarbital. *Pharmacology, Biochemistry, and Behavior, 16*, 661–666.

Hiroto, D. S., & Seligman, M. E. P. (1975). Generality of learned helplessness in man. *Journal of Personality and Social Psychology, 31*, 311–327.

Hirsch, J., & McCauley, L. (1977). Successful replication of, and selective breeding for, classical conditioning in the blowfly (*Phorma regina*). *Animal Behaviour, 25*, 784–785.

Hockett, C. F. (1958). *A course in modern linguistics*. New York: Macmillan.

Hockett, C. F. (1968). *The state of the art*. The Hague: Mouton.

Hodgetts, R. M. (1997). Discussing incentive compensation with Donald Hastings of Lincoln Electric. *Compensation and Benefits Review, 29*, 60–66.

Hodos, W. (1961). Progressive ratio as a measure of reward strength. *Science, 134*, 943–944.

Hogg, C., Neveu, M., Stokkan, K., Folkow, L., Cottrill, P., Douglas, P. et al. (2011). Arctic reindeer extend their visual range into the ultraviolet. *Journal of Experimental Biology, 214*, 2014–2019.

Holding, E., Bray, M. A., & Kehle, T. J. (2010). Does speed matter? A comparison of the effectiveness of fluency and discrete trial training for teaching noun tables to children with autism. *Psychology in the Schools, 48*, 166–188.

Holland, J. G. (1978). Behaviorism: Part of the problem or part of the solution? *Journal of Applied Behavior Analysis, 11*, 163–174.

Hollerman, J. R., & Schultz, W. (1998). Dopamine neurons report an error in temporal prediction of reward during learning. *Nature Neuroscience, 1*, 304–309.

Hollis, J. H. (1973). "Superstition": The effects of independent and contingent events on free operant responses in retarded children. *American Journal of Mental Deficiency, 77*, 585–596.

Holt, D. D., Green, L., & Myerson, J. (2003). Is discounting impulsive? Evidence from temporal and probability discounting in gambling and non-gambling college students. *Behavioural Processes, 31*, 355–367.

Horne, P. J., & Erjavec, M. (2007). Do infants show generalized imitation of gestures? *Journal of the Experimental Analysis of Behavior, 87*, 63–88.

Horne, P. J., & Lowe, C. F. (1993). Determinants of human performance on concurrent schedules. *Journal of the Experimental Analysis of Behavior, 59*, 29–60.

Horne, P. J., & Lowe, C. F. (1996). On the origins of naming and other symbolic behavior. *Journal of the Experimental Analysis of Behavior, 65*, 185–241.

Horne, P. J., Greenhalgh, J., Erjavec, M., Lowe, C. F., Viktor, S., & Whitaker, C. J. (2011). Increasing preschool children's consumption of fruit and vegetables: A modeling and rewards intervention. *Appetite, 56*, 375–385.

Horner, R. H., Carr, E. G., Strain, P. S., Todd, A. W., & Reed, H. K. (2002). Problem behavior interventions for young children with autism: A research synthesis. *Journal of Autism and Developmental Disorders, 32*, 423–446.

Horner, R. H., Day, H. M., & Day, J. R. (1997). Using neutralizing routines to reduce problem behavior. *Journal of Applied Behavior Analysis, 30*, 601–614.

Hothersall, D. (1990) *History of psychology*. New York: McGraw-Hill.

Houston, A. (1986). The matching law applies to wagtails' foraging in the wild. *Journal of the Experimental Analysis of Behavior, 45*, 15–18.

Howard, J. & Rice, D. (1988). Establishing a generalized autoclitic repertoire in preschool children. *The Analysis of Verbal Behavior, 6*, 45–60.

Huffington Post (2012). *Judge Rotenberg Center Trial: Tape shows teen being shocked 31 times* (graphic video) (www.huffingtonpost.com/2012/04/12/judge-rotenberg-center-trial_n_1420633.html?view=print&comm_ref=false); *Fox Under Cover: Rotenberg Settlement* (www.myfoxboston.com/story/17735846/fox-undercover-rotenberg-settlement).

Hughes, S. C., & Boakes, R. A. (2008). Flavor preferences produced by backward pairing with wheel running. *Journal of Experimental Psychology: Animal Behavior Processes, 34*, 283–293.

Hull, D. L., Langman, R. E., & Glenn, S. S. (2001). A general account of selection: Biology, immunology, and behavior. *Behavioral and Brain Sciences, 24*, 511–573.

Hung, D. (1980). Training and generalization of "yes" and "no" as mands in two autistic children. *Journal of Autism and Developmental Disorders, 10*, 130–152.

Hunt, G. M., & Azrin, N. H. (1973). A community-reinforcement approach to alcoholism. *Behavior Research and Therapy, 11*, 91–104.

Hunt, H. F., & Brady, J. V. (1955). Some effects of punishment and intercurrent anxiety on a simple operant. *Journal of Comparative and Physiological Psychology, 48*, 305–310.

Hursh, S. R. (1991). Behavioral economics of drug self-administration and drug abuse policy. *Journal of the Experimental Analysis of Behavior, 56*, 377–393.

Hursh, S. R., Galuska, C. M., Winger, G., & Woods, J. H. (2005). The economics of drug abuse: A quantitative assessment of drug demand. *Molecular Interventions, 5*, 20–28.

Hursh, S. R., Navarick, D. J., & Fantino, E. (1974). "Automaintenance": The role of reinforcement. *Journal of the Experimental Analysis of Behavior, 21*, 112–124.

Hutchinson, G. E. (1981). Random adaptation and imitation in human evolution. *American Scientist, 69*, 161–165.

Hutchinson, R. R. (1977). By-products of aversive control. In W. K. Honig & J. E. R. Staddon (Eds.), *Handbook of operant behavior* (pp. 415–431). Englewood Cliffs, NJ: Prentice-Hall.

Hutchinson, R. R., Azrin, N. H., & Hunt, G. M. (1968). Attack produced by intermittent reinforcement of a concurrent operant response. *Journal of the Experimental Analysis of Behavior, 11*, 489–495.

Iacoboni, M. (2009). Neurobiology of imitation. *Current Opinion in Neurobiology, 19*, 661–665.

Iacoboni, M.,Woods, R. P., Brass, M., Bekkering, H., Mazziota J. C., & Rizzolatti. G. (1999). Cortical mechanisms of human imitation. *Science, 286*, 2526–2528.

Inman, D. & Cheney, C. (1974). Functional variables in fixed ratio pausing with rabbits. *The Psychological Record, 24*, 193–202.

Iriki, A. (2006). The neural origins and implications of imitation, mirror neurons and tool use. *Current Opinion in Neurobiology,16*, 660–667.

Irwin, O. C. (1948). Infant speech: Development of vowel sounds. *Journal of Speech and Hearing, 13*, 31–34.

Irwin, O. C. (1952). Speech development in the young child: 2. Some factors related to the speech development of the infant and the young child. *Journal of Speech and Hearing, 17,* 209–279.

Ishaq, F. S. (Ed.) (1991). *Human behavior in today's world.* New York: Praeger.

Israel, M. L. (undated). *Aversives at JCR: A better alternative to the use of drugs, restraint, isolation, warehousing, or expulsion in the treatment of severe problem disorders. Summary statement on JCR and the aversives controversy.* Canton, MA: Judge Rotenberg Center (www.judgerc.org).

Israel, M. L., Blenkush, N. A., von Heyn, R. E., & Rivera, P. M. (2008). Treatment of aggression with behavioral programming that includes supplementary contingent skin-shock. *Journal of Behavior Analysis of Offender and Victim Treatment and Prevention, 1,* 119–166.

Iwata, B. A., Pace, G. M., Kalsher, M. J., Cowdery, G. E., & Cataldo, M. F. (1990). Experimental analysis and extinction of self-injurious escape behavior. *Journal of Applied Behavior Analysis, 23,* 11–27.

Jackson, K. & Hackenberg, T. D. (1996). Token reinforcement, choice, and self-control in pigeons. *Journal of the Experimental Analysis of Behavior, 66,* 29–49.

Jackson, R. L., Alexander, J. H., & Maier, S. F. (1980). Learned helplessness, inactivity, and associative deficits: Effects of inescapable shock on response choice escape learning. *Journal of Experimental Psychology: Animal Behavior Processes, 6,* 1–20.

Jacobson, S. W. (1979). Matching behavior in the young infant. *Child Development, 50,* 425–430.

Jaffe, Y., Shapir, N., & Yinon, Y. (1981). Aggression and its escalation. *Journal of Cross-Cultural Psychology, 12,* 21–36.

James, W. (1890). *Principles of psychology.* New York: Holt, Rinehart & Winston.

Janssen, M. A., Holahan, R., Lee, A., & Ostrom, E. (2010). Lab experiments for the study of social-ecological systems. *Science, 328,* 613–617.

Jason, L. A. (1998). Tobacco, drug, and HIV preventive media interventions. *American Journal of Community Psychology, 26,* 151–187.

Jenkins, H. M., Barrera, F. J., Ireland, C., & Woodside, B. (1978). Signal-centered action patterns of dogs in appetitive classical conditioning. *Learning and Motivation, 9,* 272–296.

Jenkins, W. O., & Stanley, J. C. (1950). Partial reinforcement: a review and critique. *Psychological Bulletin, 47,* 193–234.

Johnson, K. (2010). Scientists and soldiers solve a bee mystery. *The New York Times, 6 October,* 11–21.

Johnson, K. R., & Layng, T. V. J. (1994). The Morningside Model of generative instruction. In R. Gardner III, D. M. Sainato, J. O. Cooper, T. E. Heron, W. L. Heward, J. Eshleman et al. (Eds.), *Behavior analysis in education: Focus on measurably superior instruction* (pp. 173–197). Monterey, CA: Brooks/Cole.

Johnson, R. N., Oldroyd, B. P., Barron, A. B., & Crozier, R. H. (2002). Genetic control of honey bee (*Apis mellifera*) dance language: Segregating dance forms in a backcrossed colony. *Journal of Heredity, 93,* 170–173.

Johnston, J. M., & Pennypacker, H. S. (1993). *Strategies and tactics of human behavioral research.* Hillsdale, NJ: Lawrence Erlbaum Associates.

Jonas, G. (1973). *Visceral learning: Toward a science of self-control.* New York: Viking Press.

Jones, K. M., & Friman, P. C. (1999). A case study of behavioral assessment and treatment of insect phobia. *Journal of Applied Behavior Analysis, 32,* 95–98.

Jones, S. S. (1996). Imitation or exploration? Young infants' matching of adults' oral gestures. *Child Development, 67,* 1952–1969.

Jones, S. S. (2006). Exploration or imitation? The effect of music on 4-week-old infants' tongue protrusions. *Infant Behavior and Development, 29,* 126–130.

Jones, S. S. (2009). The development of imitation in infancy. *Philosophical Transactions of the Royal Society B: Biological Sciences, 364,* 2325–2335.

Juujaevari, P., Kooistra, L., Kaartinen, J., & Pulkkinen, L. (2001) An aggression machine. V: Determinants in reactive aggression revisited. *Aggressive Behavior, 27,* 430–445.

Kaiser, D. H., Zentall, T. R., & Galef, B. G., Jr. (1997). Can imitation in pigeons be explained by local enhancement together with trial-and-error learning? *Psychological Science, 8,* 459–460.

Kamin, L. J. (1969). Predictability, surprise, attention, and conditioning. In B. A. Campbell & R. M. Church (Eds.), *Punishment and aversive behavior* (pp. 279–296). New York: Appleton-Century-Crofts.

Kanarek, R. B., & Collier, G. (1978). Patterns of eating as a function of the cost of the meal. *Physiology and Behavior, 23,* 141–145.

Kandel, E. R. (2006). *In search of memory*. New York: W. W. Norton & Co.

Kangas, B. D. (2007). Cultural materialism and behavior analysis. *The Behavior Analyst, 30*, 37–47.

Karsina, A., Thompson, R. H., & Rodriguez, N. M. (2011). Effects of a history of differential reinforcement on preference for choice. *Journal of the Experimental Analysis of Behavior, 95*, 189–202.

Kastak, C. R., Schusterman, R. J., & Kastak, D. (2001). Equivalence classification by California sea lions using class specific reinforcers. *Journal of the Experimental Analysis of Behavior, 76*, 131–158.

Kastak, D., & Schusterman, R. J. (1994). Transfer of visual identity matching to sample in two California seal lions (*Zalophus californianus*). *Animal Learning and Behavior, 22*, 427–435.

Kaufman, A., Baron, A., & Kopp, R. E. (1966). Some effects of instructions on human operant behavior. *Psychonomic Monograph Supplements, 11*, 243–250.

Kawai, M. (1965). Newly acquired pre-cultural behavior of the natural troop of Japanese monkeys on Koshima Islet. *Primates, 6*, 1–30.

Kawamura, S. (1959). The process of sub-culture propagation among Japanese macaques. *Primates, 2*, 43–60.

Kay, R. F., Cartmill, M., & Balow, M. (1998). The hypoglossal canal and the origin of human vocal behavior. *Proceedings of the National Academy of Sciences, 95*, 5417–5419.

Kazdin, A. E. (1977). *The token economy: A review and evaluation*. New York: Plenum Press.

Kazdin, A. E. (1983). Failure of persons to respond to the token economy. In E. B. Foa & P. M. G. Emmelkamp (Eds.), *Failures in behavior therapy* (pp. 335–354). New York: John Wiley & Sons.

Kazdin, A. E. (1989). *Behavior modification in applied settings* (4th ed.). Belmont, CA: Brooks/Cole.

Kazdin, A. E. (2000). *Behavior modification in applied settings* (6th ed.). Belmont, CA: Wadsworth.

Kazdin, A. E., & Klock, J. (1973). The effect of nonverbal teacher approval on student attentive behavior. *Journal of Applied Behavior Analysis, 6*, 643–654.

Keehn, J. D. (1986). *Animal models for psychiatry*. London: Routledge & Kegan Paul.

Keehn, J. D., & Jozsvai, E. (1989). Induced and noninduced patterns of drinking by food-deprived rats. *Bulletin of the Psychonomic Society, 27*, 157–159.

Keith-Lucas, T., & Guttman, N. (1975). Robust single-trial delayed backward conditioning. *Journal of Comparative and Physiological Psychology, 88*, 468–476.

Kelleher, R. T. (1956). Intermittent conditioned reinforcement in chimpanzees. *Science, 124*, 679–680.

Kelleher, R. T. (1958). Fixed-ratio schedules of conditioned reinforcement with chimpanzees. *Journal of the Experimental Analysis of Behavior, 1*, 281–289.

Kelleher, R. T. (1966). Conditioned reinforcement in second-order schedules. *Journal of the Experimental Analysis of Behavior, 9*, 475–485.

Kelleher, R. T., & Gollub, L. R. (1962). A review of positive conditioned reinforcement. *Journal of the Experimental Analysis of Behavior, 5*, 543–597.

Kelleher, R. T., Fry, W., & Cook, L. (1959). Inter-response time distribution as a function of differential reinforcement of temporally spaced responses. *Journal of the Experimental Analysis of Behavior, 2*, 91–106.

Keller, F. S. (1968). "Good-bye, teacher . . ." *Journal of Applied Behavior Analysis, 1*, 79–89.

Keller, F. S. (1977). *Summers and sabbaticals*. Champaign, IL: Research Press.

Kelley, H. H. (1987). Attribution in social interaction. In E. E. Jones, D. E. Kanouse, H. H. Kelley, R. E. Nisbett, S. Valins, & B. Weiner (Eds.), *Attribution: Perceiving the causes of behavior*, (pp. 1–26). Hillsdale, NJ: Lawrence Erlbaum Associates.

Kempermann, G., Gast, D., & Gage, W. B. (2002). Neuroplasticity in old age: Sustained five-fold induction of hippocampal neurogenesis by long-term environmental enrichment. *Annals of Neurology, 52*, 135–143.

Keys, A., Brozek, J., Henschel, A., Mickelsen, O., & Taylor, H. L. (1950). *The biology of human starvation*. Minneapolis, MN: University of Minnesota Press.

Khalili, J., & Cheney, C. D. (1969). Development and maintenance of FR escape with titrated reinforcement. *Psychonomic Science, 15*, 10–11.

Khalili, J., Daley, M. F., & Cheney, C. D. (1969). A titration procedure for generating escape behavior. *Behavior Research Methods and Instrumentation, 6*, 293–294.

Killeen, P. R. (1992). Mechanics of the animate. *Journal of the Experimental Analysis of Behavior, 57*, 429–463.

Killeen, P. R., Posadas-Sanchez, D., Johansen, E. B., & Thraikill, E. A. (2009). Progressive ratio schedules of reinforcement. *Journal of Experimental Psychology: Animal Behavior Processes, 35*, 35–50.

Killeen, P. R., Wald, B., & Cheney, C. (1980). Observing behavior and information. *The Psychological Record*, *30*, 181–190.

Kimmel, E., & Kimmel, H. D. (1963). Replication of operant conditioning of the GSR. *Journal of Experimental Psychology*, *65*, 212–213.

Kimmel, H. D. (1974). Instrumental conditioning of autonomically mediated responses in human beings. *American Psychologist*, *29*, 325–335.

King, L. E., Douglas-Hamilton, I., & Vollrath, F. (2011). Beehive fences as effective deterrents for crop-raiding elephants: Field trials in northern Kenya. *African Journal of Ecology*, *49*, 431–439.

Kintsch, W. (1965). Frequency distribution of interresponse times during VI and VR reinforcement. *Journal of the Experimental Analysis of Behavior*, *8*, 347–352.

Kirby, F. D., & Shields, F. (1972). Modification of arithmetic response rate and attending behavior in a seventh-grade student. *Journal of Applied Behavior Analysis*, *5*, 79–84.

Klin, A., Chawarska, K., Rubin, E., & Volkmar, F. (2004). Clinical assessment of young children at risk for autism. In R. DelCarmen-Wiggins & A. Carter (Eds.), *Handbook of infant, toddler and preschool mental health assessment* (pp. 311–336). New York: Oxford University Press.

Knikou, M., Angeli, C. A., Ferreira, C. K., & Harkema, S. J. (2009). Flexion reflex modulation during stepping in human spinal cord injury. *Experimental Brain Research*, *196*, 341–351.

Kobayashi, S., Schultz, W., & Sakagami, M. (2010). Operant conditioning of primate prefrontal neurons. *Journal of Neurophysiology*, *103*, 1843–1855.

Kohler, W. (1927). *The mentality of apes* (2nd revised ed., E. Winter, trans.). London: Routledge & Kegan Paul.

Komar, I. (1983). *Living a dream: A documentary study of the Twin Oaks community*. Norwood, PA: Norwood Editions.

Kram, M. L., Kramer, G. L., Ronan, P. J., Steciuk, M. & Petty, F. (2002). Dopamine receptors and learned helplessness in the rat: an autoradiographic study. *Progress in Neuropsychopharmacology and Biological Psychiatry*, *26*, 639–645.

Kratochwill, T. R., Hitchcock, J., Horner, R. H., Levin, J. R., Odom, S. L., Rindskopf, D. M. et al. (2010). Single-case designs technical documentation. Retrieved from What Works Clearinghouse website (http://ies.ed.gov/ncee/wwc/pdf/wwc_scd.pdf).

Krebs, J. R., & Davies, N. B. (Eds.) (1978). *Behavioural ecology: An evolutionary approach*. Oxford: Blackwell Scientific Publications.

Kubina, R. M. Jr. (2005). The relations among fluency, rate building, and practice. A response to Doughty, Chase, and O'Shields (2004). *The Behavior Analyst*, *28*, 73–76.

Kuhl, P. K., & Meltzoff, A. N. (1996). Infant vocalizations in response to speech: Vocal imitation and developmental change. *Journal of the Acoustical Society of America*, *100*, 2425–2438.

Kulik, C. C., Kulik, J. A., & Cohen, P. A. (1980). Instructional technology and college teaching. *Teaching of Psychology*, *7*, 199–205.

Kunkel, J. H. (1997). The analysis of rule-governed behavior in social psychology. *The Psychological Record*, *47*, 698–716.

Kurti, A. N., & Dallery, J. (2012). Review of Heyman's addiction: A disorder of choice. *Journal of Applied Behavior Analysis*, *45*, 229–240.

Kuschel, R. (1973). The silent inventor: The creation of a sign language by the only deaf mute on a Polynesian island. *Sign Language Studies*, *3*, 1–28.

Kushner, M. (1970). Faradic aversive control in clinical practice. In C. Neuringer & J. Michael (Eds.), *Behavior modification in clinical psychology* (pp. 26–51). New York: Appleton-Century-Crofts.

Laitman, J. T., & Reidenberg, J. S. (1993). Specializations of the human upper respiratory and upper digestive systems as seen through comparative and developmental anatomy. *Dysphagia*, *8*, 318–325.

Lamal, P. A. (Ed.) (1997). *Cultural contingencies: Behavior analytic perspectives on cultural practices*. Westport, CT: Praeger.

Lamal, P. A., & Greenspoon, J. (1992). Congressional metacontingencies. *Behavior and Social Issues*, *2*, 71–81.

Lamarre, J., & Holland, J. G. (1985). The functional independence of mands and tacts. *Journal of the Experimental Analysis of Behavior*, *43*, 5–19.

Lane, H. (1961). Operant control of vocalizing in the chicken. *Journal of the Experimental Analysis of Behavior, 4*, 171–177.

Langer, E., Djikic, M., Pirson, M., Madenci, A., & Donohue, R. (2010). Believing is seeing: Using mindlessness (mindfully) to improve visual acuity. *Psychological Science, 21*, 661–666.

Langone, J., & Burton, T. A. (1987). Teaching adaptive behavior skills to moderately and severely handicapped individuals: Best practices for facilitating independent living. *Journal of Special Education, 21*, 149–165.

Laraway, S., Snycerski, S., Michael, J., & Poling, A. (2003). Motivating operations and terms to describe them: Some further refinements. *Journal of Applied Behavior Analysis, 36*, 407–414.

Larkin, M. (2001). Breast self examination does more harm than good, says task force. *Lancet, 357*, 2109.

Lasiter, P. S. (1979). Influence of contingent responding on schedule-induced activity in human subjects. *Physiology and Behavior, 22*, 239–243.

Latham, G. (1994). *The power of positive parenting*. North Logan, UT: P&T.

Lattal, K. A. (1984). Signal functions in delayed reinforcement. *Journal of the Experimental Analysis of Behavior, 42*, 239–253.

Lattal, K. A., & Doepke, K. J. (2001). Correspondence as conditional stimulus control: Insights from experiments with pigeons. *Journal of Applied Behavior Analysis, 34*, 127–144.

Lattal, K. A., & Ziegler, D. R. (1982). Briefly delayed reinforcement: An interresponse time analysis. *Journal of the Experimental Analysis of Behavior, 37*, 407–416.

Lattal, K. A., Reilly, M. P., & Kohn, J. P. (1998). Response persistence under ratio and interval reinforcement schedules. *Journal of the Experimental Analysis of Behavior, 70*, 165–183.

LaVigna, G. W., & Donnellan, A. W. (1986). *Alternatives to punishment: Solving behavior problems with non-aversive strategies*. New York: Irvington.

Layng, T. V. J., Twyman, J. S., & Stikeleather, G. (2004). Selected for success: How *Headsprout Reading Basics™* teaches beginning reading. In D. J. Moran & R. W. Malott (Eds.), *Evidence-based educational methods* (pp. 171–195). San Diego, CA: Elsevier Inc.

Lazar, R. (1977). Extending sequence-class membership with matching to sample. *Journal of the Experimental Analysis of Behavior, 27*, 381–392.

Leaf, R. C. (1965). Acquisition of Sidman avoidance responding as a function of S–S interval. *Journal of Comparative and Physiological Psychology, 59*, 298–300.

Leal, M., & Powell, B. J. (2012). Behavioural flexibility and problem-solving in a tropical lizard. *Biological Letters, 8*, 28–30.

Lee, R., Sturmey, P., & Fields, L. (2007). Schedule-induced and operant mechanisms that influence response variability: A review and implications for future investigations. *The Psychological Record, 57*, 429–455.

Lee. V. L. (1981a). Prepositional phrases spoken and heard. *Journal of the Experimental Analysis of Behavior, 35*, 227–242.

Lee, V. L. (1981b). Terminological and conceptual revision in the experimental analysis of language development: Why? *Behaviorism, 9*. 25–53.

Leotti, L. A., & Delgado, M. R. (2011). The inherent reward of choice. *Psychological Science, 22*, 1310–1318.

Lerman, D. C., & Vorndran, C. M. (2002). On the status of knowledge for using punishment: Implications for treating behavior disorders. *Journal of Applied Behavior Analysis, 35*, 431–464.

Lerman, D. C., Iwata, B. A., & Wallace, M. D. (1999). Side effects of extinction: Prevalence of bursting and aggression during the treatment of self-injurious behavior. *Journal of Applied Behavior Analysis, 32*, 1–8.

Lerman, D. C., Iwata, B. A., Zarcone, J. R., & Ringdahl, J. (1994). Assessment of stereotypic and self-injurious behavior as adjunctive responses. *Journal of Applied Behavior Analysis, 27*, 715–728.

Lett, B. T., & Grant, V. L. (1996). Wheel running induces conditioned taste aversion in rats trained while hungry and thirsty. *Physiology and Behavior, 59*, 699–702.

Lett, B. T., Grant, B. L., Byrne, M. J., & Koh, M. T. (2000). Pairings of a distinctive chamber with the after-effect of wheel running produce conditioned place preference. *Appetite, 34*, 87–94.

Lewis, M. (2010). *The big short: Inside the doomsday machine*. New York: W. W. Norton & Company.

Lewis, P., Gardner, E. T., & Hutton, L. (1976). Integrated delays to shock as negative reinforcement. *Journal of the Experimental Analysis of Behavior, 26*, 379–386.

Li, B., Piriz, J., Mirrione, M., Chung, C., Proulx, C. D., Schulz, D. et al. (2011). Synaptic potentiation onto habenula neurons in the learned helplessness model of depression. *Nature, 470*, 535–539.

Lieberman, D. A., Cathro, J. S., Nichol, K., & Watson, E. (1997). The role of S– in human observing behavior: Bad news is sometimes better than no news. *Learning and Motivation, 28*, 20–42.

Lieberman, P. (2007). The evolution of human speech: Its anatomical and neural bases. *Current Anthropology, 48*, 39–66.

Lieberman, P., Laitman, J. T., Reidenberg, J. S., & Gannon, P. J. (1992). The anatomy, physiology, acoustic and perception of speech: Essential elements in analysis of the evolution of human speech. *Journal of Human Evolution, 23*, 447–467.

Lima, E. L., & Abreu-Rodrigues, J. (2010). Verbal mediating responses: Effects on generalization of say–do correspondence and noncorrespondence. *Journal of Applied Behavior Analysis, 43*, 411–424.

Lindberg, J. S, Iwata, B. A., Kahng, S., & DeLeon, I. G. (1999). DRO contingencies: An analysis of variable-momentary schedules. *Journal of Applied Behavior Analysis, 32*, 123–135.

Lindsley, O. R. (1972). From Skinner to precision teaching: The child knows best. In J. B. Jordan & L. S. Robbins (Eds.), *Let's try something else kind of thing: Behavioral principles of the exceptional child* (pp. 1–11). Arlington, VA: The Council for Exceptional Children.

Lindsley, O. R. (1990a). Our aims, discoveries, failures, and problem. *Journal of Precision Teaching, 7*, 7–17.

Lindsley, O. R. (1990b). Precision teaching: By teachers for children. *Teaching Exceptional Children, 22*, 10–15.

Lindsley, O. R. (1991). Precision teaching's unique legacy from B. F. Skinner. *Journal of Behavioral Education, 1*, 253–266.

Lionello-DeNolf, K. M. (2009). The search for symmetry: 25 years in review. *Learning and Behavior, 37*, 188–203.

Lippman, L. G., & Meyer, M. E. (1967). Fixed-interval performance as related to instructions and to the subject's vocalizations of the contingency. *Psychonomic Science, 8*, 135–136.

Lloyd, K. E. (1985). Behavioral anthropology: A review of Marvin Harris' *Cultural Materialism*. *Journal of the Experimental Analysis of Behavior, 43*, 279–287.

Lloyd, K. E., & Lloyd, M. E. (1992). Behavior analysis and technology in higher education. In R. P. West & L. A. Hamerlynck (Eds.), *Designs for excellence in education: The legacy of B. F. Skinner* (pp. 147–160). Longmont, CO: Sopris West, Inc.

Lofdahl, K. L., Holliday, M., & Hirsch, J. (1992). Selection for conditionability in *Drosophila melanogaster*. *Journal of Comparative Psychology, 106*, 172–183.

Logue, A. W. (1979). Taste aversion and the generality of the laws of learning. *Psychological Bulletin, 86*, 276–296.

Logue, A. W. (1985). Conditioned food aversion learning in humans. In N. S. Braveman & P. Bronstein (Eds.), *Experimental assessments and clinical applications of conditioned food aversions* (pp. 316–329). New York: New York Academy of Sciences.

Logue, A. W. (1988). A comparison of taste aversion learning in humans and other vertebrates: Evolutionary pressures in common. In R. C. Bolles & M. D. Beecher (Eds.), *Evolution and learning* (pp. 97–116). Hillsdale, NJ: Lawrence Erlbaum Associates.

Logue, A. W., Pena-Correal, T. E., Rodriguez, M. L., & Kabela, E. (1986). Self-control in adult humans: Variation in positive reinforcer amount and delay. *Journal of the Experimental Analysis of Behavior, 46*, 159–173.

Lohrman-O'Rourke, S., & Zirkel, P. A. (1998). The case law on aversive interventions for students with disabilities. *Exceptional Children, 65*, 101–123.

Long, J. (2009). *Paradoxical effects of shock: The role of shock intensity and interresponse times followed by shock*. Dissertation submitted to Eberly College of Arts and Sciences at West Virginia University, Morgantown, WV.

Lovaas, O. I. (1961). Interaction between verbal and nonverbal behavior. *Child Development, 32*, 329–336.

Lovaas, O. I. (1966). A program for the establishment of speech in psychotic children. In J. K. Wing (Ed.), *Early childhood autism* (pp. 115–144). Elmsford, NY: Pergamon.

Lovaas, O. I. (1977). *The autistic child: Language development through behavior modification*. New York: Irvington.

Lovaas, O. I. (1987). Behavioral treatment and normal educational and intellectual functioning in young autistic children. *Journal of Consulting and Clinical Psychology, 55*, 3–9.

Lovaas, O. I. (1993). The development of a treatment-research project for developmentally disabled and autistic children. *Journal of Applied Behavior Analysis, 26*, 617–630.

Lovaas, O. I., & Simmons, J. Q. (1969). Manipulation of self-destruction in three retarded children. *Journal of Applied Behavior Analysis, 2*, 143–157.

Lowe, F. C. (1979). Determinants of human operant behavior. In M. D. Zeiler & P. Harzem (Eds.), *Reinforcement and the organization of behaviour* (pp. 159–192). New York: John Wiley & Sons.

Lowe, F. C., Beasty, A., & Bentall, R. P. (1983). The role of verbal behavior in human learning: Infant performance on fixed-interval schedules. *Journal of the Experimental Analysis of Behavior, 39*, 157–164.

Lowenkron, B. (1998). Some logical functions of joint control. *Journal of the Experimental Analysis of Behavior, 69*, 327–354.

Lowenkron, B. (1999). Joint control of rule following: An analysis of purpose. *Annual Meeting of the Association for Behavior Analysis*, May 1999, Chicago.

Lowenkron, B. (2004). Meaning: A verbal behavior account. *The Analysis of Verbal Behavior, 20*, 77–97.

Lowenkron, B. (2006). Joint control and the selection of stimuli from their description. *The Analysis of Verbal Behavior, 22*, 129–151.

Lubinski, D., & MacCorquodale, K. (1984). "Symbolic communication" between two pigeons (*Columba livia*) without unconditioned reinforcement. *Journal of Comparative Psychology, 98*, 372–380.

Lubinski, D., & Thompson, T. (1987). An animal model of the interpersonal communication of interoceptive (private) states. *Journal of the Experimental Analysis of Behavior, 48*, 1–15.

Lubinski, D., & Thompson, T. (1993). Species and individual differences in communication based on private states. *Behavioral and Brain Science, 16*, 627–680.

Lubow, R. E. (1974). High-order concept formation in the pigeon. *Journal of the Experimental Analysis of Behavior, 21*, 475–483.

Lubow, R. E. (2009). Conditioned taste aversion and latent inhibition: A review. In S. Reilly & T. R. Schachtman (Eds.), *Conditioned taste aversion: Behavioral and neural processes* (pp. 37–57). New York: Oxford University Press.

Lubow, R.E., & Moore, A.U. (1959). Latent inhibition: The effect of non-reinforced preexposure to the conditioned stimulus. *Journal of Comparative and Physiological Psychology, 52*, 415–419.

Lucas, G. A., Deich, J. D., & Wasserman, E. A. (1981). Trace autoshaping: Acquisition, maintenance, and path dependence at long trace intervals. *Journal of the Experimental Analysis of Behavior, 36*, 61–74.

Luciano, M. C. (1986). Acquisition, maintenance, and generalization of productive intraverbal behavior through transfer of stimulus control procedures. *Applied Research in Mental Retardation, 7*, 1–20.

Luciano, M. C. (2000). Applications of research on rule-governed behavior. In J. C. Leslie & D. Blackman (Eds.), *Experimental and applied analysis of human behavior* (pp. 181–204). Reno, NV: Context Press.

Luciano, M. C., Herruzo, J., & Barnes-Holmes, D. (2001). Generalization of say–do correspondence. *The Psychological Record, 51*, 111–130.

Luiselli, J. K., Ricciardi, J. N., & Gilligan, K. (2005). Liquid fading to establish milk consumption by a child with autism. *Behavioral Interventions, 20*, 155–163.

Lukas, K. E., Marr, M. J., & Maple, T. L. (1998). Teaching operant conditioning at the zoo. *Teaching of Psychology, 25*, 112–116.

Lussier, J. P., Heil, S. H., Mongeon, J. A., Badger, G. J., & Higgins, S. T. (2006). A meta-analysis of voucher-based reinforcement therapy for substance use disorders. *Addiction, 101*, 192–203.

MacCorquodale, K. (1970). On Chomsky's review of Skinner's *Verbal Behavior. Journal of the Experimental Analysis of Behavior, 13*, 83–99.

Mace, F. C. (1996). In pursuit of general behavioral relations. *Journal of Applied Behavior Analysis, 29*, 557–563.

Mace, F. C., & Critchfield, T. S. (2010). Translational research in behavior analysis: Historical traditions and imperative for the future. *Journal of the Experimental Analysis of Behavior, 93*, 293–312.

Mace, F. C., Neef, N. A., Shade, D., & Mauro, B. C. (1994). Limited matching on concurrent schedule reinforcement of academic behavior. *Journal of Applied Behavior Analysis, 27*, 585–596.

Machado, A. (1989). Operant conditioning of behavioral variability using a percentile reinforcement schedule. *Journal of the Experimental Analysis of Behavior, 52,* 155–166.

Machado, A. (1992). Behavioral variability and frequency dependent selection. *Journal of the Experimental Analysis of Behavior, 58,* 241–263.

Machado, A. (1997). Increasing the variability of response sequences in pigeons by adjusting the frequency of switching between two keys. *Journal of the Experimental Analysis of Behavior, 68,* 1–25.

Mackenzie-Keating, S., & McDonald, L. (1990). Overcorrection: Reviewed, revisited and revised. *The Behavior Analyst, 13,* 39–48.

MacLarnon, A., & Hewitt, G. (1999). The evolution of human speech: The role of enhanced breathing control. *American Journal of Physical Anthropology, 109,* 341–363.

MacLarnon, A. M., & Hewitt, G. P. (2004). Increased breathing control: Another factor in the evolution of human language. *Evolutionary Anthropology, 13,* 181–197.

Macphail, E. M. (1968). Avoidance responding in pigeons. *Journal of the Experimental Analysis of Behavior, 11,* 629–632.

Madden, G. J., & Bickel, W. K. (Eds.). (2010). *Impulsivity: The behavioral and neurological science of discounting.* Washington, DC: American Psychological Association.

Madden, G. J., & Johnson, P. S. (2010). A delay-discounting primer. In G. J. Madden & W. K. Bickel (Eds.), *Impulsivity: The behavioral and neurological science of discounting* (pp. 11–38). Washington, DC: American Psychological Association.

Madden, G. J., Peden, B. F., & Yamaguchi, T. (2002). Human group choice: Discrete-trial and free-operant tests of the ideal free distribution. *Journal of the Experimental Analysis of Behavior, 78,* 1–15.

Madden, G. J., Petry, N. M., Badger, G. J., & Bickel, W. K. (1997). Impulsive and self-control choices in opioid-dependent patients and non-drug-using control participants: Drug and monetary rewards. *Experimental and Clinical Psychopharmacology, 5,* 256–262.

Mahoney, A. M., Miguel, C., Ahearn, W. H., & Bell, J. (2011). The role of common motor responses in stimulus categorization by preschool children. *Journal of the Experimental Analysis of Behavior, 95,* 237–262.

Maier, S. F. (1970). Failure to escape traumatic electric shock: Incompatible skeletal-motor responses or learned helplessness. *Learning and Motivation, 1,* 157–169.

Maier, S. F., & Seligman, M. E. P. (1976). Learned helplessness: Theory and evidence. *Journal of Experimental Psychology: General, 105,* 3–46.

Maier, S. F., Albin, R. W., & Testa, T. J. (1973). Failure to learn to escape in rats previously exposed to inescapable shock depends on nature of the escape response. *Journal of Comparative and Physiological Psychology, 85,* 581–592.

Maier, S. F., Seligman, M. E. P., & Solomon, R. L. (1969). Pavlovian fear conditioning and learned helplessness. In B. A. Campbell & R. M. Church (Eds.), *Punishment and aversive behavior* (pp. 299–342). New York: Appleton-Century-Crofts.

Maki, W. S., & Hegvik, D. K. (1980). Directed forgetting in pigeons. *Animal Learning and Behavior, 8,* 567–574.

Malott, R. W. (1988). Rule-governed behavior and behavioral anthropology. *The Behavior Analyst, 11,* 181–203.

Mandrusiak, M. (2002). *Activity anorexia induced by increased procurement cost of meals and opportunity for physical activity.* Honors thesis submitted to the Faculty of Science, Department of Psychology, University of Alberta.

Markowitz, H. (1981). *Behavioral enrichment in the zoo.* New York: Van Nostrand Reinhold.

Markowitz, H., Schmidt, M., Nadal, L., & Squier, L. (1975). Do elephants ever forget? *Journal of Applied Behavior Analysis, 8,* 333–335.

Marr, M. J. (1992). Behavior dynamics: One perspective. *Journal of the Experimental Analysis of Behavior, 57,* 249–266.

Marsh, G., & Johnson, R. (1968). Discrimination reversal learning without "errors." *Psychonomic Science, 10,* 261–262.

Martens, B. K., Lochner, D. G., & Kelly, S. Q. (1992). The effects of variable-interval reinforcement on academic engagement: A demonstration of matching theory. *Journal of Applied Behavior Analysis, 25,* 143–151.

Martin, G., & Pear, J. (2006). *Behavior modification: What it is and how to do it* (8th ed.). Upper Saddle River, NJ: Prentice-Hall.

Martin, G., & Pear, J. (2010). *Behavior modification: What it is and how to do it* (9th ed.). Upper Saddle River, NJ: Prentice-Hall.

Martin, G. L., & Hrycaiko, D. (1983). *Behavior modification and coaching: Principles, procedures and research*. Springfield, IL: Charles C. Thomas.

Martin, T. L., Pear, J. J., & Martin, G. L. (2002) Feedback and its effectiveness in a computer-aided personalized system of instruction course. *Journal of Applied Behavior Analysis, 35*, 427–430.

Martinez, E. (2010). DA: Kevin and Elizabeth Schatz killed daughter with "religious whips" for mispronouncing word. CBSNEWS, *Crimesider*, 22 February. www.cbsnews.com/8301-504083_162-6009742-504083.html

Masaki, T. & Nakajima, S. (2008). Forward conditioning with wheel running causes place aversion in rats. *Behavioural Processes, 79*, 43–47.

Masserman, J. H. (1946). *Principles of dynamic psychiatry*. Philadelphia, PA: Saunders.

Matson, J. L., & Boisjoli, J. A. (2009). The token economy for children with intellectual disability and/or autism: A review. *Research in Developmental Disabilities, 30*, 240–248.

Matson, J. L., & Taras, M. E. (1989). A 20-year review of punishment and alternative methods to treat problem behaviors in developmentally disabled persons. *Research in Developmental Disabilities, 10*, 85–104.

Mattaini, M. A., & McGuire, M. S. (2006). Behavioral strategies for constructing nonviolent cultures with youth: A review. *Behavior Modification, 30*, 184–224.

Matthews, B. A., Shimoff, E., & Catania, A. C. (1987). Saying and doing: A contingency-space analysis. *Journal of Applied Behavior Analysis, 20*, 69–74.

Matthews, L. R., & Temple, W. (1979). Concurrent schedule assessment of food preference in cows. *Journal of the Experimental Analysis of Behavior, 32*, 245–254.

Maurice, C. (1993). *Let me hear your voice*. New York: Knopf.

Maurice, C., Green, G., & Luce, S. C. (1996). *Behavioral intervention for young children with autism—A manual for parents and professionals*. Sarasota, FL: Pro-Ed.

May, J. G., & Dorr, D. (1968). Imitative pecking in chicks as a function of early social experience. *Psychonomic Science, 11*, 109–129.

Mazur, J. E. (1983). Steady-state performance on fixed-, mixed-, and random-ratio schedules. *Journal of the Experimental Analysis of Behavior, 39*, 293–307.

Mazur, J. E. (1987). An adjusting procedure for studying delayed reinforcement. In M. L. Commons, J. E. Mazur, J. A. Nevin & H. Rachlin (Eds.), *Quantitative analyses of behavior. Volume 5. The effect of delay and of intervening events on reinforcement value* (pp. 55–73). Hillsdale, NJ: Lawrence Erlbaum Associates.

McAndrew, F. T. (2009). The interacting roles of testosterone and challenges to status in human male aggression. *Aggression and Violent Behavior, 14*, 330–335.

McCarty, K. F. (2012). *Twin Oaks: A case study of an intentional egalitarian community*. Capstone Collection. Paper 2494. http://digitalcollections.sit.edu/capstones/2494

McDevitt, M. A. & Williams, B. A. (2010). Dual effects on choice of conditioned reinforcement frequency and conditioned reinforcement value. *Journal of the Experimental Analysis of Behavior, 93*, 147–155.

McDonald, J. S. (1988). Concurrent variable-ratio schedules: Implications for the generalized matching law. *Journal of the Experimental Analysis of Behavior, 50*, 55–64.

McDougall, W. (1908). *An introduction to social psychology*. London: Methuen.

McDowell, J. J. (1981). On the validity and utility of Herrnstein's hyperbola in applied behavior analysis. In C. M. Bradshaw, E. Szabadi & C. F. Lowe (Eds.), *Quantification of steady-state operant behaviour* (pp. 311–324). Amsterdam: Elsevier/North-Holland.

McDowell, J. J. (1982). The importance of Herrnstein's mathematical statement of the law of effect for behavior therapy. *American Psychologist, 37*, 771–779.

McDowell, J. J. (1988). Matching theory in natural human environments. *The Behavior Analyst, 11*, 95–109.

McDowell, J. J. (2004). A computational model of selection by consequences. *Journal of the Experimental Analysis of Behavior, 81*, 297–317.

McDowell, J. J. (2010). Behavioral and neural Darwinism: Selectionist function and mechanism in adaptive behavior dynamics. *Behavioural Processes, 84*, 358–365.

McDowell, J. J., & Caron, M. L. (2010). Bias and undermatching in delinquent boys' verbal behavior as a function of their level of deviance. *Journal of the Experimental Analysis of Behavior, 93*, 471–483.

McDowell, J. J., & Popa, A. (2010). Toward a mechanics of adaptive behavior: Evolutionary dynamics and matching theory statics. *Journal of the Experimental Analysis of Behavior, 94*, 242–260.

McDowell, J. J., & Wixted, J. T. (1986). Variable-ratio schedules as variable-interval schedules with linear feedback loops. *Journal of the Experimental Analysis of Behavior, 46*, 315–329.

McEachin, J. J., Smith, T., & Lovaas, O. I. (1993). Long-term outcome for children with autism who received early intensive behavioral treatment. *American Journal on Mental Retardation, 97*, 359–372.

McGaha-Mays, N., & Heflin, L. J. (2011). Increasing independence in self-care tasks for children with autism using self-operated auditory prompts. *Research in Autism Spectrum Disorders, 5*, 1351–1357.

McGinnis, M. A., Houchins-Juarrez, N., McDaniel, J. L., & Kennedy, C. H. (2010). Abolishing and establishing operation analyses of social attention as positive reinforcement for problem behavior. *Journal of Applied Behavior Analysis, 43*, 119–123.

McIntire, K. D., Cleary, J., & Thompson, T. (1987). Conditional relations by monkeys: Reflexivity, symmetry, and transitivity. *Journal of the Experimental Analysis of Behavior, 47*, 279–285.

McSweeney, F. K., Ettinger, R. A., & Norman, W. D. (1981). Three versions of the additive theories of behavioral contrast. *Journal of the Experimental Analysis of Behavior, 36*, 285–297.

McSweeney, F. K., Melville, C. L., & Higa, J. (1988). Positive behavioral contrast across food and alcohol reinforcers. *Journal of the Experimental Analysis of Behavior, 50*, 469–481.

McSweeney, F. K., Murphy, E. S., & Kowal, B. P. (2003). Dishabituation with component transitions may contribute to the interactions observed during multiple schedules. *Behavioural Processes, 64*, 77–89.

McSweeney, F. K., & Weatherly, J. N. (1998). Habituation to the reinforcer may contribute to multiple-schedule behavioral contrast. *Journal of the Experimental Analysis of Behavior, 69*, 199–221.

Mechner, F. (1959). A notation system for the description of behavioral procedures. *Journal of the Experimental Analysis of Behavior, 2*, 133–150.

Mechner, F. (2010). Chess as a behavioral model for cognitive skill research: Review of *Blindfold Chess* by Eliot Hearst and John Knott. *Journal of the Experimental Analysis of Behavior, 94*, 373–386.

Meech, R. W. (2008). Non-neural reflexes: Sponges and the origins of behaviour. *Current Biology, 18*, R70–R72.

Meissner, M., & Philpott, S. B. (1975). The sign language of sawmill workers in British Columbia. *Sign Language Studies, 9*, 291–308.

Mellitz, M., Hineline, P. N., Whitehouse, W. G., & Laurence, M. T. (1983). Duration reduction of avoidance sessions as negative reinforcement. *Journal of the Experimental Analysis of Behavior, 40*, 57–67.

Meltzoff, A. N. (1988a). Imitation of televised models by infants. *Child Development, 59*, 1221–1229.

Meltzoff, A. N. (1988b). Infant imitation after a 1-week delay: Long-term memory for novel acts and multiple stimuli. *Developmental Psychology, 24*, 470–476.

Meltzoff, A. N. (1988c). Infant imitation and memory: Nine-month-olds in immediate and deferred tests. *Child Development, 59*, 217–225.

Meltzoff, A. N. (1999). Born to learn: What infants learn from watching us. In N. Fox & J. G. Worhol (Eds.), *The role of early experience in infant development* (pp. 1–10). Skillman, NJ: Pediatric Institute Publications.

Meltzoff, A. N., & Moore, M. K. (1977). Imitation of facial and manual gestures by human neonates. *Science, 198*, 75–78.

Meltzoff, A. N., & Moore, M. K. (1983). Newborn infants imitate adult facial gestures. *Child Development, 54*, 702–709.

Meltzoff, A. N., & Moore, M. K. (1999). Resolving the debate about early imitation. In A. Slater & D. Muir (Eds.), *Reader in developmental psychology* (pp. 151–155). Oxford: Blackwell Science.

Mendelson, J., & Chillag, D. (1970). Schedule-induced air licking in rats. *Physiology and Behavior, 5*, 535–537.

Mery, F., & Kawecki, T. J. (2002). Experimental evolution of learning ability in fruit flies. *Proceedings of the National Academy of Sciences, 22*, 14274–14279.

Meyer, C., Taranis, L., Goodwin, H., & Haycraft, E. (2011). Compulsive exercise and eating disorders. *European Eating Disorders Review, 19*, 174–189.

Meyer, D. R., Cho, C., & Wesemann, A. F. (1960). On problems of conditioning discriminated lever-press avoidance responses. *Psychological Review, 67*, 224–228.

Meyer, J. (2007). Acoustic strategy, phonetic comparison and perceptive cues of whistled languages. *HAL Archives*, halshs-00133192, version 1. http://halshs.archives-ouvertes.fr/halshs-00133192

Meyer, L. H., & Evans, I. M. (1989). *Non-aversive intervention for behavior problems: A manual for home and community*. Baltimore, MD: Paul H. Brookes.

Michael, J. L. (1975). Positive and negative reinforcement, a distinction that is no longer necessary: Or a better way to talk about bad things. *Behaviorism*, *3*, 33–44.

Michael, J. L. (1980). Flight from behavior analysis. *The Behavior Analyst*, *3*, 1–24.

Michael, J. L. (1982a). Distinguishing between discriminative and motivational functions of stimuli. *Journal of the Experimental Analysis of Behavior*, *37*, 149–155.

Michael, J. L. (1982b). Skinner's elementary verbal relations: Some new categories. *The Analysis of Verbal Behavior*, *1*, 1–3.

Michael, J. (1983). Evocative and repertoire-altering effects of an environmental event. *The Analysis of Verbal Behavior*, *2*, 19–21.

Michael, J. L. (1988). Establishing operations and the mand. *The Analysis of Verbal Behavior*, *6*, 3–9.

Michael, J. L. (1993). Establishing operations. *The Behavior Analyst*, *16*, 191–206.

Michael, J. L. (2000). Implications and refinements of the establishing operation concept. *Journal of Applied Behavior Analysis*, *33*, 401–410.

Michael, J. L., Whitley, P., & Hesse, B. E. (1983). The pigeon parlance project. *The Analysis of Verbal Behavior*, *1*, 6–9.

Miklosi, A. (2007). The ethological analysis of imitation. *Biological Reviews*, *74*, 347–374.

Milenberger, R. G., & Fuqua, R. W. (1981). Overcorrection: A review and critical analysis. *The Behavior Analyst*, *4*, 123–141.

Milgram, S. (1974). *Obedience to authority*. New York: Harper & Row.

Millard, W. J. (1979). Stimulus properties of conspecific behavior. *Journal of the Experimental Analysis of Behavior*, *32*, 283–296.

Millenson, J. R. (1967). *Principles of behavioral analysis*. New York: Macmillan.

Miller, H. C., Rayburn-Reeves, R., & Zentall, T. R. (2009). Imitation and emulation by dogs using a bidirectional control procedure. *Behavioural Processes*, *80*, 109–114.

Miller, H. L., & Loveland, D. H. (1974). Matching when the number of response alternatives is large. *Animal Learning and Behavior*, *26*, 106–110.

Miller, J. R., Lerman, D. C., & Fritz, J. N. (2010). An experimental analysis of negative reinforcement contingencies for adult-delivered reprimands. *Journal of Applied Behavior Analysis*, *43*, 769–773.

Miller, N. E. (1951). Learnable drives and rewards. In S. S. Stevens (Ed.), *Handbook of experimental psychology* (pp. 435–472). New York: John Wiley & Sons.

Miller, N. E. (1960). Learning resistance to pain and fear: Effects of overlearning, exposure, and rewarded exposure in context. *Journal of Experimental Psychology*, *60*, 137–145.

Miller, N. E. (1969). Learning of visceral and glandular responses. *Science*, *163*, 434–445.

Miller, N. E., & Banuazizi, A. (1968). Instrumental learning by curarized rats of a specific visceral response, intestinal or cardiac. *Journal of Comparative and Physiological Psychology*, *65*, 1–7.

Miller, N. E., & Carmona, A. (1967). Modification of a visceral response, salivation in thirsty dogs, by instrumental training with water reward. *Journal of Comparative and Physiological Psychology*, *63*, 1–6.

Miller, N. E., & DiCara, L. (1967). Instrumental learning of heart rate changes in curarized rats: Shaping and specificity to discriminative stimulus. *Journal of Comparative and Physiological Psychology*, *63*, 12–19.

Miller, N. E., & Dollard, J. (1941). *Social learning and imitation*. New Haven, CT: Yale University Press.

Miller, N. E., & Dworkin, B. R. (1974). Visceral learning: Recent difficulties with curarized rats and significant problems for human research. In P. A. Obrist, A. H. Black, J. Brener & L. V. DiCara (Eds.), *Cardiovascular psychophysiology: Current issues in response mechanisms, biofeedback and methodology* (pp. 295–331). Chicago, IL: Aldine.

Miltenberger, R. G., Gatheridge, B. J., Satterlund, M., Egemo-Helm, K. R., Johnson, B. M., Jostad, C. et al. (2005) Teaching safety skills to children to prevent gun play: An evaluation of *in situ* training. *Journal of Applied Behavior Analysis*, *38*, 395–398.

Minshawl, N. F. (2008). Behavioral assessment and treatment of self-injurious behavior in autism. *Child and Adolescent Psychiatric Clinics of North America*, *17*, 875–886.

Minster, S. T., Elliffe, D., & Muthukumaraswamy, S. D. (2011). Emergent stimulus relations depend on stimulus correlation and not on reinforcement contingencies. *Journal of the Experimental Analysis of Behavior, 95*, 327–342.

Misanin, J. R., Goodhart, M. G., Anderson, M. J., & Hinderliter, C. F. (2002). The interaction of age and unconditioned stimulus intensity on long-trace conditioned flavor aversion in rats. *Developmental Psychobiology, 40*, 131–137.

Mitchell, C. J., Heyes, C. M., Gardner, M. R., & Dawson, G. R. (1999). Limitations of a bidirectional control procedure for the investigation of imitation in rats: Odor cues on the manipulandum. *Quarterly Journal of Experimental Psychology. B, Comparative and Physiological Psychology, 52B*, 193–202.

Mitchell, D., Kirschbaum, E. H., & Perry, R. L. (1975). Effects of neophobia and habituation on the poison-induced avoidance of exteroceptive stimuli in the rat. *Journal of Experimental Psychology: Animal Behavior Processes, 104*, 47–55.

Modaresi, H. A. (1990). The avoidance barpress problem: Effects of enhanced reinforcement and an SSDR-congruent lever. *Learning and Motivation, 21*, 199–220.

Moerk, E. L. (1990). Three-term contingency patterns in mother–child verbal interactions during first-language acquisition. *Journal of the Experimental Analysis of Behavior, 54*, 293–305.

Moerk, E. L. (2000). *The guided acquisition of first language skills*. Stamford, CT: Ablex Publishing.

Molm, L. D., Takahashi, N., & Peterson, G. (2000). Risk and trust in social exchange: An experimental test of a classical proposition. *American Journal of Sociology, 105*, 1396–1427.

Moore, B. R. (1992). Avian movement imitation and a new form of mimicry: Tracing the evolution of a complex form of learning. *Behaviour, 122*, 231–263.

Moore, J. (2000). Thinking about thinking and feeling about feeling. *The Behavior Analyst, 23*, 45–56.

Moore, J. (2003). Some further thoughts on the pragmatic and behavioral conception of private events. *Behavior and Philosophy, 31*, 151–157.

Moran, D. J., & Malott, R. W. (2004). *Evidence-based educational methods*. San Diego, CA: Elsevier Academic Press.

Morgan, C. L. (1894). *An introduction to comparative psychology*. London: W. Scott.

Morgan, D., Carter, C., DuPree, J. P., Yezierski, R. P., & Vierck, C. J., Jr. (2008). Evaluation of prescription opioids using operant-based pain measures in rats. *Experimental and Clinical Psychopharmacology, 16*, 367–375.

Morgan, L., & Neuringer, A. (1990). Behavioral variability as a function of response topography and reinforcement contingency. *Animal Learning and Behavior, 18*, 257–263.

Morris, E. K. (1988). Contextualism: The world view of behavior analysis. *Journal of Experimental Child Psychology, 46*, 289–323.

Morris, E. K. (1992). The aim, progress, and evolution of behavior analysis. *The Behavior Analyst, 15*, 3–29.

Morrow, J. E., Terzich, B. J., & Williamson, P. N. (2002). *Behavior analytic treatment of autism in a private school*. Invited address, Ohio State University's Third Focus on Behavior Analysis in Education Conference, September 2002.

Morse, W. H. (1966). Intermittent reinforcement. In W. K. Honig (Ed.), *Operant behavior: Areas of research and application* (pp. 52–108). New York: Appleton-Century-Crofts.

Morse, W. H., & Kelleher, R. T. (1977). Determinants of reinforcement and punishment. In W. K. Honig, & J. E. R. Staddon (Eds.), *Handbook of operant behavior* (pp. 174–200). Englewood Cliffs, NJ: Prentice-Hall.

Moseley, J. B., O'Malley, K., Petersen, N. J., Menke, T. J., Brody, B. A., Kuykendall, D. H. et al. (2002). A controlled trial of arthroscopic surgery for osteoarthritis of the knee. *New England Journal of Medicine, 347*, 81–88.

Moser, E., & McCulloch, M. (2010). Canine scent detection of human cancers: A review of methods and accuracy. *Journal of Veterinary Behavior: Clinical Applications and Research, 5*, 145–152.

Mueller, K. L., & Dinsmoor, J. A. (1986). The effect of negative stimulus presentations on observing-response rates. *Journal of the Experimental Analysis of Behavior, 46*, 281–291.

Mueller, M. M., Palkovic, C. M., & Maynard, C. S. (2007). Errorless learning: Review and practical application for teaching children with pervasive developmental disorders. *Psychology in the Schools, 44*, 691–700.

Muller, C. A., & Cant, M. A. (2010). Imitation and traditions in the wild banded mongooses. *Current Biology*, *20*, 1171–1175.

Muller, P. G., Crow, R. E., & Cheney, C. D. (1979). Schedule-induced locomotor activity in humans. *Journal of the Experimental Analysis of Behavior*, *31*, 83–90.

Murphy, M. S., & Cook, R. G. (2008). Absolute and relational control of a sequential auditory discrimination by pigeons (*Columba livia*). *Behavioural Processes*, *77*, 210–222.

Myers, D. L., & Myers, L. E. (1977). Undermatching: A reappraisal of performance on concurrent variable-interval schedules of reinforcement. *Journal of the Experimental Analysis of Behavior*, *25*, 203–214.

Myers, J. L. (1958). Secondary reinforcements: A review of recent experimentation. *Psychological Bulletin*, *55*, 284–301.

Myers, R. D., & Mesker, D. C. (1960). Operant conditioning in a horse under several schedules of reinforcement. *Journal of the Experimental Analysis of Behavior*, *3*, 161–164.

Myerson, J., & Hale, S. (1984). Practical implications of the matching law. *Journal of Applied Behavior Analysis*, *17*, 367–380.

Nader, M. A., & Woolverton, W. L. (1992). Effects of increasing response requirement on choice between cocaine and food in rhesus monkeys. *Psychopharmacology*, *108*, 295–300.

Nagy, E., Compagne, H., Orvos, H., Pal, A., Molnar, P., Janszky, I. et al. (2005). Index finger movement imitation by human neonates: Motivation, learning and left-hand preference. *Pediatric Research*, *58*, 749–753.

Nakajima, S., Hayashi, H., & Kato, T. (2000). Taste aversion induced by confinement in a running wheel. *Behavioural Processes*, *49*, 35–42.

Naqvi, N., Rudrauf, D., Damasio, H., & Bechara, A. (2007). Damage to the insula disrupts addiction to cigarette smoking. *Science*, *315*, 531–534.

National Science Foundation (2011). Press Release 11–248. Mark Goldstein discusses and demonstrates MammaCare. www.nsf.gov/news/news_videos.jsp?cntn_id=122294&media_id=71492&org–SF

Neal, D. T., Wood, W., & Quinn, J. M. (2006). Habits—A repeat performance. *Current Directions in Psychological Science*, *15*, 198–202.

Neel, J. V. (1962). Diabetes mellitus: A "thrifty" genotype rendered detrimental by "progress"? *American Journal of Human Genetics*, *14*, 353–362.

Nelson, H. D., Tyne, K., Naik, A., Bougatsos, C., Chan, B., & Humphrey, L. (2009). Screening for breast cancer: An update for the U.S. Preventive Services Task Force. *Annals of Internal Medicine*, *151*, 727–737.

Nergardh, R., Ammar, A., Brodin, U., Bergstrom, J., Scheurink, A., & Sodersten, P. (2007). Neuropeptide Y facilitates activity-based anorexia. *Psychoneuroendocrinology*, *32*, 493–502.

Neuringer, A. (2004). Reinforced variability in animals and people. *American Psychologist*, *59*, 891–906.

Neuringer, A. (2009). Operant variability and the power of reinforcement. *The Behavior Analyst Today*, *10*, 319–343.

Neuringer, A. J. (1986). Can people behave "randomly?" The role of feedback. *Journal of Experimental Psychology: General*, *115*, 62–75.

Neuringer, A. J. (2002). Operant variability: Evidence, function, and theory. *Psychonomic Bulletin and Review*, *9*, 672–705.

Nevin, J. A. (1974). Response strength in multiple schedules. *Journal of the Experimental Analysis of Behavior*, *21*, 389–408.

Nevin, J. A. (1988). Behavioral momentum and the partial reinforcement effect. *Psychological Bulletin*, *103*, 44–56.

Nevin, J. A. (1992). An integrative model for the study of behavioral momentum. *Journal of the Experimental Analysis of Behavior*, *57*, 301–316.

Nevin, J. A., & Grace, R. C. (2000). Behavior momentum and the law of effect. *Behavioral and Brain Sciences*, *23*, 73–130.

Nevin, J. A., Grace, R. C., Holland, S., & McLean, A. P. (2001). Variable-ratio versus variable-interval schedules: Response rate, resistance to change, and preference. *Journal of the Experimental Analysis of Behavior*, *76*, 43–74.

Nonacs, P. (2001). State-dependent behavior and the marginal value theorem. *Behavioral Ecology*, *12*, 71–83.

Norman, W. D., & McSweeney, F. K. (1978). Matching, contrast, and equalizing in the concurrent lever-press responding of rats. *Journal of the Experimental Analysis of Behavior*, *29*, 453–462.

Normand, M. P., Machado, M. A., Hustyi, K. M., & Morely, A. J. (2011). Infant sign training and functional analysis. *Journal of Applied Behavior Analysis*, *44*, 305–314.

Norton, W. (1997). Human geography and behavior analysis: An application of behavior analysis to the explanation of the evolution of human landscapes. *The Psychological Record*, *47*, 439–460.

Norton, W. (2001). Following rules in the intermontaine West: 19th-century Mormon settlement. *The Behavior Analyst*, *24*, 57–73.

Notterman, J. M. (1959). Force emission during bar pressing. *Journal of Experimental Psychology*, *58*, 341–347.

Nuzzolo-Gomez, R., & Greer, R. D. (2004). Emergence of untaught mands and tacts of novel adjective–object pairs as a function of instructional history. *The Analysis of Verbal Behavior*, *20*, 63–67.

Oah, S., & Dickinson, A. M. (1989). A review of empirical studies of verbal behavior. *The Analysis of Verbal Behavior*, *7*, 53–68.

Oberman, L. M., & Ramachandran, V. S. (2007). The stimulating social mind: The role of the mirror neuron system and simulation in the social and communicative deficits of autism spectrum disorders. *Psychological Bulletin*, *133*, 310–327.

Oberman, L. M., Hubbard, E. M., McCleery, J. P., Altschuler, E. L., Ramachandran, V. S., & Pineda, J. A. (2005). EEG evidence for mirror neuron dysfunction in autism spectrum disorders. *Cognitive Brain Research*, *24*, 190–198.

O'Brien, R. M., & Simek, T. C. (1983). A comparison of behavioral and traditional methods for teaching golf. In G. L. Martin & D. Harycaiko (Eds.), *Behavior modification and coaching: Principles, procedures, and research* (pp. 175–183). Springfield, IL: Charles C. Thomas.

Odum, A. L. (2011a). Delay discounting: trait variable? *Behavioural Processing*, *83*, 1–9.

Odum, A. L. (2011b). Delay discounting: I'm a k, you're a k. *Journal of the Experimental Analysis of Behavior*, *96*, 427–439.

Odum, A. L., & Baumann, A. A. L. (2010). Delay discounting: State and trait variable. In G. J. Madden & W. K. Bickel (Eds.), *Impulsivity: The behavioral and neurological science of discounting* (pp. 39–66). Washington, DC: American Psychological Association.

Odum, A. L., Ward, R. D., Barnes, C. A., & Burke, K. A. (2006) The effects of delayed reinforcement on variability and repetition of response sequences. *Journal of the Experimental Analysis of Behavior*, *86*, 159–179.

O'Heare, J. (2009). *On the permanence of punishment*. www.jamesoheare.com/weblog/permanenceofpunish.html

O'Kelly, L. E., & Steckle, L. C. (1939). A note on long enduring emotional responses in rats. *Journal of Psychology*, *8*, 125–131.

Okouchi, H. & Songmi, K. (2004). Differential reinforcement of human self-reports about schedule performance. *The Psychological Record*, *54*, 461–478.

Olds, J., & Milner, P. (1954). Positive reinforcement produced by electrical stimulation of the septal area and other regions of the rat brain. *Journal of Comparative and Physiological Psychology*, *47*, 419–428.

O'Leary, M. R., & Dengerink, H. A. (1973). Aggression as a function of the intensity and pattern of attack. *Journal of Experimental Research in Personality*, *7*, 61–70.

Oorsouw, W. M. W. J., Israel, M. L., von Heyn, R. E., & Duker, P. C. (2008). Side effects of contingent shock treatment. *Research in Developmental Disabilities*, *29*, 513–523.

Orlando, R., & Bijou, S. W. (1960). Single and multiple schedules of reinforcement in developmentally retarded children. *Journal of the Experimental Analysis of Behavior*, *3*, 339–348.

Orne, M. T., & Evans, F. J. (1965). Social control in the psychology experiment: Antisocial behavior and hypnosis. *Journal of Personality and Social Psychology*, *1*, 189–200.

Osborne, J. G. (2002). Response-contingent water misting. *Encyclopedia of Psychotherapy*, *2*, 553–560.

Osgood, C. E. (1953). *Method and theory in experimental psychology*. New York: Oxford University Press.

Overmier, J. B., & Seligman, M. E. P. (1967). Effects of inescapable shock upon subsequent escape and avoidance responding. *Journal of Comparative and Physiological Psychology*, *63*, 28–33.

Overskeid, G. (1992). Is any human behavior schedule-induced? *The Psychological Record*, *42*, 323–340.

Page, S., & Neuringer, A. J. (1985). Variability is an operant. *Journal of Experimental Psychology: Animal Behavior Processes*, *11*, 429–452.

Paloyelis, Y., Asherson, P., Mehta, M. A., Faraone, S. V., & Kunts, J. (2010). DAT1 and COMT effects on delay discounting and trait impulsivity in male adolescents with attention deficit/hyperactivity disorder and healthy controls. *Neuropsychopharmacology, 35,* 2414–2426.

Paniagua, F. A. (1989) Lying by children: Why children say one thing, do another? *Psychological Reports, 64,* 971–984.

Paniagua, F. A., & Baer, D. M. (1982). The analysis of correspondence as a chain reinforceable at any point. *Child Development, 53,* 786–798.

Papachristos, E. B., & Gallistel, C. R. (2006). Autoshaped head poking in the mouse: A quantitative analysis of the learning curve. *Journal of the Experimental Analysis of Behavior, 85,* 293–308.

Papini, M. R., & Bitterman, M. E. (1990). The role of contingency in classical conditioning. *Psychological Review, 97,* 396–403.

Park, R. D. (2002). Punishment revisited—science, values, and the right question: Comment on Gershoff (2002). *Psychological Bulletin, 128,* 596–601.

Parker, L. A. (2003). Taste avoidance and taste aversion: Evidence for two different processes. *Learning and Behavior, 31,* 165–172.

Parkinson, J. A., Crofts, H. S., McGuigan, M., Tomic, D. L., Everitt, B. J., & Roberts. A. C. (2001). The role of the primate amygdala in conditioned reinforcement. *Journal of Neuroscience, 21,* 7770–7780.

Parrott, L. J. (1987). Rule-governed behavior: An implicit analysis of reference. In S. Modgil & C. Modgil (Eds.), *B. F. Skinner: Consensus and controversy* (pp. 265–276). New York: Falmer Press.

Partington, J. W., & Bailey, J. S. (1993). Teaching intraverbal behavior to preschool children. *Analysis of Verbal Behavior, 11,* 9–18.

Partington, J. W., Sundberg, M. L., Newhouse, L., & Spengler, S. M. (1994). Overcoming an autistic child's failure to acquire a tact repertoire. *Journal of Applied Behavior Analysis, 27,* 733–734.

Patterson, G. R. (1976) The aggressive child: Victim and architect of a coercive system. In E. J. Mash, L. A. Hamerlynck, & L. H. Hendy (Eds.), *Behavior modification and families* (pp. 269–316). New York: Brunner/Mazel.

Patterson, G. R. (1982). *Coercive family processes.* Eugene, OR: Castalia.

Patterson, G. R. (2002). Etiology and treatment of child and adolescent antisocial behavior. *The Behavior Analyst Today, 3,* 133–144.

Paul, G. L. (2006). Myth and reality in Wakefield's assertions regarding Paul and Lentz (1977). *Behavior and Social Issues, 15,* 244–252.

Pauley, P. J. (1987). *Controlling life: Jacques Loeb and the engineering ideal in biology.* New York: Oxford University Press.

Pavlov, I. P. (1960). *Conditioned reflexes: An investigation of the physiological activity of the cerebral cortex* (G. V. Anrep, trans.). New York: Dover (original work published in 1927).

Pear, J. J. (1985). Spatiotemporal patterns of behavior produced by variable-interval schedules of reinforcement. *Journal of the Experimental Analysis of Behavior, 44,* 217–231.

Pear, J. J. (2001) *The science of learning.* Philadelphia, PA: Psychology Press.

Pear, J. J., & Crone-Todd, D. E. (1999). Personalized system of instruction in cyberspace. *Journal of Applied Behavior Analysis, 32,* 205–209.

Pear, J. J., Schnerch, G. L., Silva, K. M., Svenningsen, L., & Lambert, J. (2011). Web-based computer-aided personalized system of instruction. *New Directions for Teaching and Learning, 128,* 85–94.

Pedersen, W. C., Gonzales, C., & Miller, N. (2000). The moderating effect of trivial triggering provocation on displaced aggression. *Journal of Personality and Social Psychology, 78,* 913–927.

Pennypacker, H. S., Bloom, H. S., Criswell, E. L., Neelakantan, P., Goldstein, M. K., & Stein, G. H. (1982). Toward an effective technology of instruction in breast self-examination. *International Journal of Mental Health, 11,* 98–116.

Pennypacker, H. S., Naylor, L., Sander, A. A., & Goldstein, M. K. (1999). Why can't we do better breast examinations? *Nurse Practitioner Forum, 10,* 122–128.

Pepperberg, I. M. (1981). Functional vocalizations by an African gray parrot (*Psittacus erithacus*). *Zeitschrift fur Tierpsychologie, 58,* 193–198.

Pepperberg, I. M. (2000). *The Alex studies: Cognitive and communicative abilities of grey parrots.* Cambridge, MA: Harvard University Press.

Perin, C. T. (1942). Behavior potentiality as a joint function of the amount of training and the degree of hunger at the time of extinction. *Journal of Experimental Psychology, 30*, 93–113.

Perone, M. (1991). Experimental design in the analysis of free-operant behavior. In I. H. Iverson & K. A. Lattal (Eds.), *Experimental analysis of behavior: Part 1* (pp. 135–172). New York: Elsevier.

Perone, M., & Galizio, M. (1987). Variable interval schedules of timeout from avoidance. *Journal of the Experimental Analysis of Behavior, 47*, 97–113.

Peterson, C., & Seligman, M. E. P. (1984). Causal explanations as a risk factor for depression: Theory and evidence. *Psychological Review, 91*, 347–374.

Peterson, G. B. (2004). A day of great illumination: B.F. Skinner's discovery of shaping. *Journal of the Experimental Analysis of Behavior, 82*, 317.

Peterson, G. B., Ackil, J. E., Frommer, G. P., & Hearst, E. S. (1972). Conditioned approach and contact behavior toward signals for food or brain-stimulation reinforcement. *Science, 177*, 1009–1011.

Peterson, N. (1978). *An introduction to verbal behavior.* Grand Rapids, MI: Behavior Associates Inc.

Peters-Scheffer, N., Didden, R., Korzilius, H., & Sturmey, P. (2011). A meta-analytic study on the effectiveness of comprehensive ABA-based intervention programs for children with autism spectrum disorders. *Research in Autism Spectrum Disorders, 5*, 60–69.

Petry, N. M., & Madden, G. J. (2010). Discounting and pathological gambling. In G. J. Madden & W. K. Bickel (Eds.), *Impulsivity: The Behavioral and Neurological Science of Discounting* (pp. 273–294). Washington, DC: American Psychological Association.

Petry, N. M., Martin, B., Cooney, J. L., & Kranzler, H. R. (2000). Give them prizes, and they will come: Contingency management for treatment of alcohol dependence. *Journal of Consulting and Clinical Psychology, 68*, 250–257.

Petscher, E. S., Rey, C., & Bailey, J. S. (2009). A review of empirical support for differential reinforcement of alternative behavior. *Research in Developmental Disabilities, 30*, 409–425.

Petursdottir, A. I., Carr, J. E., & Michael, J. (2005). Emergence of mands and tacts of novel objects among preschool children. *The Analysis of Verbal Behavior, 21*, 59–74.

Pierce, W. D. (1991). Culture and society: The role of behavioral analysis. In P. A. Lamal (Ed.), *Behavioral analysis of societies and cultural practices* (pp. 13–37). New York: Hemisphere.

Pierce, W. D. (2001). Activity anorexia: Biological, behavioral, and neural levels of selection. *Behavioral and Brain Sciences, 24*, 551–552.

Pierce, W. D., & Cameron, J. (2002). A summary of the effects of reward contingencies on interest and performance. *The Behavior Analyst Today, 3*, 221–228.

Pierce, W. D., & Epling, W. F. (1980). What happened to analysis in applied behavior analysis? *The Behavior Analyst, 3*, 1–9.

Pierce, W. D., & Epling, W. F. (1983). Choice, matching, and human behavior: A review of the literature. *The Behavior Analyst, 6*, 57–76.

Pierce, W. D., & Epling, W. F. (1988). *Biobehaviorism: Genes, learning and behavior* (Working Paper No. 88-5). Edmonton, Alberta: Center for Systems Research, University of Alberta.

Pierce, W. D., & Epling, W. F. (1991). Activity anorexia: An animal model and theory of human self-starvation. In A. Boulton, G. Baker, & M. Martin-Iverson (Eds.), *Neuromethods: Animal models in psychiatry 1: Volume 18* (pp. 267–311). Clifton, NJ: Humana Press.

Pierce, W. D., & Epling, W. F. (1997). Activity anorexia: The interplay of culture, behavior, and biology. In P. A. Lamal (Ed.), *Cultural contingencies: Behavior analytic perspectives on cultural practices* (pp. 53–85). Westport, CT: Praeger.

Pierce, W. D., Epling, W. F., & Boer, D. P. (1986). Deprivation and satiation: The interrelations between food and wheel running. *Journal of the Experimental Analysis of Behavior, 46*, 199–210.

Pierce, W. D., Epling, W. F., & Greer, S. M. (1981). Human communication and the matching law. In C. M. Bradshaw, E. Szabadi, & C. F. Lowe (Eds.), *Quantification of steady-state operant behaviour* (pp. 345–352). Amsterdam: Elsevier/North Holland Biomedical Press.

Pierce, W. D., Diane, A., Heth, C. D., Russell, J. C., & Proctor, S. D. (2010). Evolution and obesity: Resistance of obese-prone rats to a challenge of food restriction and wheel running. *International Journal of Obesity, 34*, 589–592.

Pierce, W. D., Heth, C. D., Owczarczyk, J., Russell, J. C., & Proctor, S. D. (2007). Overeating by young obese-prone and lean rats caused by tastes associated with low energy foods. *Obesity, 15*, 1069–1079.

Pierrel, R., Sherman, G. J., Blue, S., & Hegge, F. W. (1970). Auditory discrimination: A three-variable analysis of intensity effects. *Journal of the Experimental Analysis of Behavior, 13*, 17–35.

Pietras, C. J., & Hackenberg, T. D. (2005). Response-cost punishment via token loss with pigeons. *Behavioural Processes, 69*, 343–356.

Pitts, R. C., & Malagodi, E. F. (1996). Effects of reinforcement amount on attack induced under a fixed interval schedule in pigeons. *Journal of the Experimental Analysis of Behavior, 65*, 93–110.

Platt, J. (1973). Social traps. *American Psychologist, 28*, 641–651.

Platt, J. R. (1979). Interresponse-time shaping by variable-interval-like interresponse-time reinforcement contingencies. *Journal of the Experimental Analysis of Behavior, 31*, 3–14.

Plaud, J. J. (1992). The prediction and control of behavior revisited: A review of the matching law. *Journal of Behavior Therapy and Experimental Psychiatry, 23*, 25–31.

Plaud, J. J., & Newberry, D. E. (1996). Rule-governed behavior and pedophilia. *Sexual Abuse: Journal of Research and Treatment, 8*, 143–159.

Pliskoff, S. S., & Brown, T. G. (1976). Matching with a trio of concurrent variable-interval schedules of reinforcement. *Journal of the Experimental Analysis of Behavior, 25*, 69–74.

Pocock, T. L., Foster, M., & McEwan, J. S. (2010). Precision teaching and fluency: The effects of charting and goal-setting on skaters' performance. *Journal of Behavioral Health and Medicine, 1*, 93–118.

Poling, A. (1978). Performance of rats under concurrent variable-interval schedules of negative reinforcement. *Journal of the Experimental Analysis of Behavior, 30*, 31–36.

Poling, A., Edwards, T. L., Weeden, M., & Foster, T. M. (2011). The matching law. *The Psychological Record, 61*, 313–322.

Poling, A., Nickel, M., & Alling, K. (1990). Free birds aren't fat: Weight gain in captured wild pigeons maintained under laboratory conditions. *Journal of the Experimental Analysis of Behavior, 53*, 423–424.

Poling, A., Weetjens, B., Cox, C., Beyene, N. W., Bach, H., & Sully, A. (2011). Using trained pouched rats to detect land mines: Another victory for operant conditioning. *Journal of Applied Behavior Analysis, 44*, 351–355.

Pomerleau, O. F. (1979). Behavioral medicine: The contribution of the experimental analysis of behavior to medical care. *American Psychologist, 34*, 654–663.

Poppen, R. (1982). The fixed-interval scallop in human affairs. *The Behavior Analyst, 5*, 127–136.

Porter, J. H., Brown, R. T., & Goldsmith, P. A. (1982). Adjunctive behavior in children on fixed interval food reinforcement schedules. *Physiology and Behavior, 28*, 609–612.

Porter, J. P. (1910). Intelligence and imitation in birds: A criterion of imitation. *American Journal of Psychology, 21*, 1–71.

Poulos, C. X., Wilkinson, D. A., & Cappell, H. (1981). Homeostatic regulation and Pavlovian conditioning intolerance to amphetamine-induced anorexia. *Journal of Comparative and Physiological Psychology, 95*, 735–746.

Poulson, C. L., & Kymmissis, E. (1998). Generalized imitation in infants. *Journal of Experimental Child Psychology, 46*, 324–336.

Poulson, C. L., Kymmissis, E., Reeve, K. F., Andreatos, M., & Reeve, L. (1991). Generalized vocal imitation in infants. *Journal of Experimental Child Psychology, 51*, 267–279.

Poulson, C. L., Kyparissos, N., Andreatos, M., Kymmissis, E., & Parnes, M. (2002). Generalized imitation within three response classes in typically developing infants. *Journal of Experimental Child Psychology, 81*, 341–357.

Powell, R. W. (1968). The effect of small sequential changes in fixed-ratio size upon the post-reinforcement pause. *Journal of the Experimental Analysis of Behavior, 11*, 589–593.

Powers, R., Cheney, C. D., & Agostino, N. R. (1970). Errorless training of a visual discrimination in preschool children. *The Psychological Record, 20*, 45–50.

Prangnell, S. J. (2009). Behavioural interventions for self-injurious behaviour: A review of recent evidence (1998–2008). *British Journal of Learning Disabilities, 38*, 259–270.

Prelec, D. (1984). The assumptions underlying the generalized matching law. *Journal of the Experimental Analysis of Behavior, 41*, 101–107.

Premack, D. (1959). Toward empirical behavioral laws: 1. Positive reinforcement. *Psychological Review, 66*, 219–233.

Premack, D. (1962). Reversability of the reinforcement relation. *Science, 136*, 235–237.

Premack, D. (1971). Catching up with common sense or two sides of a generalization: Reinforcement and punishment. In R. Glaser (Ed.), *The nature of reinforcement* (pp. 121–150). New York: Academic Press.

Prendergast, M., Podus, D., Finney, J., Greenwell, L., & Roll, J. (2006). Contingency management for treatment of substance use disorders: A meta-analysis. *Addiction, 101*,1546–1560.

Provenza, F. D., Lynch, J. J., & Nolan, J. V. (1994). Food aversion conditioned in anesthetized sheep. *Physiology and Behavior, 55*, 429–432.

Provenza, F. D., Villalba, J. J., Cheney, C. D., & Werner, S. J. (1998). Self-organization of foraging behavior: From simplicity to complexity without goals. *Nutrition Research Review, 11*, 199–222.

Provine, R. R. (1989). Contagious yawning and infant imitation. *Bulletin of the Psychonomic Society, 27*, 125–126.

Pryor, K. W. (1999). *Don't shoot the dog.* New York: Bantum.

Pryor, K. W., Haag, R., & O'Reilly, J. (1969). The creative porpoise: Training for novel behavior. *Journal of the Experimental Analysis of Behavior, 12*, 653–651.

Rachlin, H. (1969). Autoshaping of key pecking in pigeons with negative reinforcement. *Journal of the Experimental Analysis of Behavior, 12*, 521–531.

Rachlin, H. (1970). *Introduction to modern behaviorism.* San Francisco, CA: W. H. Freeman.

Rachlin, H. (1974). Self-control. *Behaviorism, 2*, 94–107.

Rachlin, H. (1992). Diminishing marginal value as delay discounting. *Journal of the Experimental Analysis of Behavior, 57*, 407–415.

Rachlin, H. (2000). *The science of self-control.* Cambridge, MA: Harvard University Press.

Rachlin, H. & Green, L. (1972). Commitment, choice and self-control. *Journal of the Experimental Analysis of Behavior, 17*, 15–22.

Rachlin, H., & Laibson, D. I. (Eds.) (1997). *The matching law: Papers in psychology and economics by Richard J. Herrnstein.* Cambridge, MA: Harvard University Press.

Rachlin, H., Green, L., Kagel, J. H., & Battalio, R. C. (1976). Economic demand theory and psychological studies of choice. In G. H. Bower (Ed.), *The psychology of learning and motivation: Volume 10* (pp. 129–154). New York: Academic Press.

Rachlin, H. R., Raineri, A., & Cross, D. (1991). Subjective probability and delay. *Journal of the Experimental Analysis of Behavior, 55*, 233–244.

Rankin, C. H., Abrams, T., Barry, R. J., Bhatnagar, S., Clayton, D. F. et al. (2009). Habituation revisited: An update and revised description of the behavioral characteristics of habituation. *Neurobiology of Learning and Memory, 92*, 135–138.

Ray, E., & Heyes, C. (2011). Imitation in infancy: The wealth of the stimulus. *Developmental Science, 14*, 92–105.

Ray, E. D., Gardner, M. R., & Heyes, C. M. (2000). Seeing how it's done: Matching conditions for observer rats (*Rattus norvegicus*) in bidirectional control. *Animal Cognition, 3*, 147–157.

Razran, G. (1949). Stimulus generalization of conditioned responses. *Psychological Bulletin, 46*, 337–365.

Reed, P. (2007). Response rate and sensitivity to the molar feedback function relating response and reinforcement rate on VI+ schedules of reinforcement. *Journal of Experimental Psychology: Animal Behavior Processes, 33*, 428–439.

Reed, P., Soh, M., Hildebrandt, T., DeJongh, J., & Shek, W. Y. (2000). Free-operant performance on variable interval schedules with a linear feedback loop: No evidence for molar sensitivities in rats. *Journal of Experimental Psychology: Animal Behavior Processes, 26*, 416–427.

Rehfeldt, R. A. (2011). Toward a technology of derived stimulus relations: An analysis of articles published in the *Journal of Applied Behavior Analysis*, 1992–2009. *Journal of Applied Behavior Analysis, 44*, 109–119.

Reicher, S. D., Haslam, S. A., & Smith, J. R. (2012). Working toward the experimenter: Reconceptualizing obedience within the Milgram paradigm as identification-based followership. *Perspectives on Psychological Science, 7*, 315–324.

Reilly, S. & Schachtman, T. R. (Eds.). (2009). *Conditioned taste aversion.* New York: Oxford University Press.

Rendell, L., Boyd, R., Enquist, M., Feldman, M. W., Fogarty, L., & Laland, K. N. (2011). How copying affects the amount, evenness and persistence of cultural knowledge: Insights from the social learning strategies tournament. *Philosophical Transactions of the Royal Society B, 366*, 1118–1128.

Repacholi, B. M., & Meltzoff, A. N. (2007). Emotional eavesdropping: Infants selectively respond to indirect emotional signals. *Child Development, 78*, 503–521.

Rescorla, R. A. (1966). Predictability and number of pairings in Pavlovian fear conditioning. *Psychonomic Science, 4*, 383–384.

Rescorla, R.A. (2006). Stimulus generalization of excitation and inhibition. *Quarterly Journal of Experimental Psychology, 59*, 53–63.

Rescorla, R. A., & Wagner, A. R. (1972). A theory of Pavlovian conditioning: Variations in the effectiveness of reinforcement and nonreinforcement. In A. H. Black & W. F. Prokasy (Eds.), *Classical conditioning II: Current research and theory* (pp. 64–69). New York: Appleton-Century-Crofts.

Revusky, S. H., & Bedarf, E. W. (1967). Association of illness with prior ingestion of novel foods. *Science, 155*, 219–220.

Revusky, S. H., & Garcia, J. (1970). Learned associations over long delays. In G. H. Bower (Ed.), *The psychology of learning and motivation: Advances in research and theory. Volume 4* (pp. 1–84). New York: Academic Press.

Reynolds, G. S. (1961a). An analysis of interactions in a multiple schedule. *Journal of the Experimental Analysis of Behavior, 4*, 107–117.

Reynolds, G. S. (1961b). Behavioral contrast. *Journal of the Experimental Analysis of Behavior, 4*, 57–71.

Reynolds, G. S. (1963). Some limitations on behavioral contrast and induction during successive discrimination. *Journal of the Experimental Analysis of Behavior, 6*, 131–139.

Reynolds, G. S. (1966a). *A primer of operant conditioning.* Glenview, IL: Scott Foresman & Co.

Reynolds, G. S. (1966b). Discrimination and emission of temporal intervals by pigeons. *Journal of the Experimental Analysis of Behavior, 9*, 65–68.

Rhodes, G. (2006). The evolutionary psychology of facial beauty. *Annual Review of Psychology, 57*, 199–226.

Ribes, E. M., & Martinez, C. (1998). Second-order discrimination in humans: The roles of explicit instructions and constructed verbal responding. *Behavioural Processes, 42*, 1–18.

Ribes, E. M., & Rodriguez, M. E. (2001). Correspondence between instructions, performance, and self-descriptions in a conditional discrimination task: The effects of feedback and type of matching response. *Psychological Record, 51*, 309–333.

Richards, R. W. (1988) The question of bidirectional associations in pigeons' learning of conditional discrimination tasks. *Bulletin of the Psychonomic Society, 26*, 577–579.

Richardson, J. V., & Baron, A. (2008). Avoidance of timeout from response-independent food: Effects of delivery rate and quality. *Journal of the Experimental Analysis of Behavior, 89*, 169–181.

Risley, T. R., & Hart, B. (1968). Developing correspondence between the nonverbal and verbal behavior of preschool children. *Journal of Applied Behavior Analysis, 1*, 267–281.

Rizley, R. C., & Rescorla, R. A. (1972). Associations in second-order conditioning and sensory preconditioning. *Journal of Comparative and Physiological Psychology, 81*, 1–11.

Rizzolatti, G., & Craighero, L. (2004). The mirror-neuron system. *Annual Review of Neuroscience, 27*, 169–192.

Roane, H. S. (2008). On the applied use of progressive-ratio schedules of reinforcement. *Journal of Applied Behavior Analysis, 41*, 155–161.

Roberts, A. C., Reekie, Y., & Braesicke, K. (2007). Synergistic and regulatory effects of orbitofrontal cortex on amygdala-dependent appetitive behavior. *Annals of the New York Academy of Sciences, 1121*, 297–319.

Rogers-Warren, A., & Warren, S. (1980). Mands for verbalization: Facilitating the display of newly trained language in children. *Behavior Modification, 4*, 361–382.

Roll, J. M., & Higgins. S. T. (2000). A within-participant comparison of three different schedules of reinforcement of drug abstinence using cigarette smoking as an exemplar. *Drug and Alcohol Dependence, 58*, 103–109.

Roll, J. M., Higgins, S. T., & Badger, G. J. (1996). An experimental comparison of three different schedules of reinforcement of drug abstinence using cigarette smoking as an exemplar. *Journal of Applied Behavior Analysis, 29*, 495–505.

Roll, J. M., Madden, G. J., Rawson, R., & Petry, N. M. (2009). Facilitating the adoption of contingency management for the treatment of substance use disorders. *Behavior Analysis in Practice, 2*, 4–13.

Rosenberg, E. L., & Ekman, P. (1995). *Motivation and Emotion, 19*, 111–138.

Roth, W. J. (2002). Teaching dolphins to select pictures in response to recorded dolphin whistles with few errors. *Dissertation Abstracts International: Section B: The Sciences & Engineering, 62 (10-B)*, No. 95008.

Routtenberg, A., & Kuznesof, A. W. (1967). Self-starvation of rats living in activity wheels on a restricted feeding schedule. *Journal of Comparative and Physiological Psychology, 64*, 414–421.

Rozin, P., & Kalat, J. (1971). Adaptive specializations in learning and memory. *Psychological Review, 78*, 459–486.

Rubene, D., Hastad, O., Tauson, R., Wall, H., & Odeen, A. (2010). The presence of UV wavelengths improves the temporal resolution of the avian visual system. *Journal of Experimental Biology, 213*, 3357–3363.

Ruggles, T. R., & LeBlanc, J. M. (1982). Behavior analysis procedures in classroom teaching. In A. S. Bellack, M. Hersen, & A. E. Kazdin (Eds.), *International handbook of behavior modification and therapy* (pp. 959–996). New York: Plenum Press.

Salamone, J. D., Correa, M., Mingote, C. S., & Weber, S. M. (2003). Nucleus accumbens dopamine and the regulation of effort in food-seeking behavior: Implications for studies of natural motivation, psychiatry, and drug abuse. *Journal of Pharmacology and Experimental Therapeutics, 305*, 1–8.

Salvy, S. J., Heth, D. C., Pierce, W. D., & Russell, J. C. (2004). Conditioned taste aversion induced by wheel running: Further evidence on wheel running duration. *Behavioural Processes, 66*, 101–106.

Salvy S., Mulick J. A., Butter E., Bartlett R. K., & Linscheid T. R. (2004). Contingent electric shock (SIBIS) and a conditioned punisher eliminate severe head banging in a preschool child. *Behavioral Interventions, 19*, 59–72.

Salvy, S., Pierce, W. D., Heth, C.D., & Russell, J. C. (2002). Pre-exposure to wheel running disrupts taste aversion conditioning. *Physiology and Behavior, 76*, 51–56.

Salvy, S. J., Pierce, W. D., Heth, D. C., & Russell, J. C. (2003). Wheel running produces conditioned food aversion. *Physiology and Behavior, 80*, 89–94.

Salvy, S. J., Pierce, W. D., Heth, D. C., & Russell, J. C. (2004). Taste avoidance induced by wheel running: Effects of backward pairings and robustness of conditioned taste aversion. *Physiology and Behavior, 82*, 303–308.

Sanders, G. A. (1974). Introduction. In D. Cohen (Ed.), *Explaining linguistic phenomena* (pp. 1–20). Washington, DC: Hemisphere.

Sanders, S. J., Murtha, M. T., Gupta, J. D., Murdoch, J. D., Raubeson, M. J., Willsey, A. J. et al. (2012). *De novo* mutations revealed by whole-exome sequencing are strongly associated with autism. *Nature, 485*, 237–241.

Sargisson, R. J., & White, K. G. (2001). Generalization of delayed matching-to-sample performance following training at different delays. *Journal of the Experimental Analysis of Behavior, 75*, 1–14.

Saslow, D., Hannan, J., Osuch, J., Alciati, M. H., Baines, C., Barton, M. et al. (2004). Clinical breast examination: Practical recommendations for optimizing performance and reporting. *CA: A Cancer Journal for Clinicians, 54*, 327–344.

Saunders, K. J. (1989). Naming in conditional discrimination and stimulus equivalence. *Journal of the Experimental Analysis of Behavior, 51*, 379–384.

Saunders, K. J., & Spradlin, J. E. (1989). Conditional discrimination in mentally retarded adults: The effect of training the component simple discriminations. *Journal of the Experimental Analysis of Behavior, 52*, 1–12.

Saunders, K. J., Pilgram, C. A., & Pennypacker, H. S. (1986). Increased proficiency of search in breast self-examination. *Cancer, 58*, 2531–2537.

Savage-Rumbaugh, E. S. (1984). Verbal behavior at a procedural level in the chimpanzee. *Journal of the Experimental Analysis of Behavior, 41*, 223–250.

Savage-Rumbaugh, E. S. (1986). *Ape language: From conditioned response to symbol*. New York: Columbia University Press.

Savage-Rumbaugh, E. S., & Lewin, R. (1994). *Kanzi: The ape at the brink of the human mind*. New York: John Wiley & Sons.

Savage-Rumbaugh, E. S., Murphy, J., Sevcik, R. A., Brakke, K. E., Williams, S. L., & Rumbaugh, D. M. (1993). Language comprehension in ape and child. *Monographs of the Society for Research in Child Development, 58*, No. 233.

Savage-Rumbaugh, E. S., Shanker, S. G., & Taylor, T. J. (1998). *Apes, language, and the human mind*. New York: Oxford University Press.

Sayette, M. A., Creswell, K. G., Dimoff, J. D., Fairbairn, C. E., Cohn, J. F., Heckman, B. W. et al. (2012). Alcohol and group formation: A multimodal investigation of the effects of alcohol on emotion and social bonding. *Psychological Science, 23*, 869–878.

Schaefer, H. H., & Martin, P. L. (1966). Behavior therapy for "apathy" of hospitalized patients. *Psychological Reports, 19*, 1147–1158.

Schafer, R. J., & Moore, T. (2011). Selective attention from voluntary control of neurons in the prefrontal cortex. *Science, 332*, 1568–1571.

Scheller, R. H., & Axel, R. (1984). How genes control innate behavior. *Scientific American, 250*, 54–62.

Schlinger, H. D. (2004). The almost blank slate: Making a case for human nature. *Skeptic, 11*, 34–43.

Schlinger, H. D. (2008). Listening is behaving verbally. *The Behavior Analyst, 31*, 145–161.

Schlinger, H. D. (2009). Auditory imaging. *European Journal of Behavior Analysis, 10*, 77–85.

Schlinger, H. D. (2011). Skinner as missionary and prophet: A review of *Burrhus F. Skinner: Shaper of Behaviour. Journal of Applied Behavior Analysis, 44*, 217–225.

Schlinger, H. D., & Blakely, E. (1987). Function-altering effects of contingency-specifying stimuli. *The Behavior Analyst, 10*, 41–45.

Schlinger, H. D., Derenne, A., & Baron, A. (2008). What 50 years of research tell us about pausing under ratio schedules of reinforcement. *The Behavior Analyst, 31*, 39–60.

Schlund, M. W., Cataldo, M. F., & Hoehn-Saric, R. (2008). Neural correlates of derived relational responding on tests of stimulus equivalence. *Behavioral and Brain Functions*, doi:10.1186/1744-9081-4-6.

Schlund, M. W., Hoehn-Saric, R., & Cataldo, M. F. (2007). New knowledge derived from learned knowledge: Functional-anatomic correlates of stimulus equivalence. *Journal of the Experimental Analysis of Behavior, 87*, 287–307.

Schmidt, A. C., Hanley, G. P., & Layer, S. A. (2009). A further analysis of the value of choice: Controlling for the illusory discriminative stimuli and evaluating the effects of less preferred items. *Journal of Applied Behavior Analysis, 42*, 711–716.

Schmitt, D. R. (2001). Delayed rule following. *The Behavior Analyst, 24*, 181–189.

Schneiderman, N. (1966). Interstimulus interval function of the nictitating membrane response of the rabbit under delay versus trace conditioning. *Journal of Comparative and Physiological Psychology, 62*, 397–402.

Schoenfeld, W, N., Antonitis, J. J., & Bersh, P. J. (1950). A preliminary study of training conditions necessary for conditioned reinforcement. *Journal of Experimental Psychology, 40*, 40–45.

Schoneberger, T. (2000). A departure from cognitivism: Implications of Chomsky's second revolution in linguistics. *Analysis of Verbal Behavior, 17*, 57–73.

Schopler, E., & Mesibov, G. B. (1994). *Behavioral issues in autism.* New York: Plenum.

Schrier, A. M., & Brady, P. M. (1987). Categorization of natural stimuli by monkeys (*Macaca mulatta*): Effects of stimulus set size and modification of exemplars. *Journal of Experimental Psychology: Animal Behavior Processes, 13*, 136–143.

Schusterman, R. J., & Kastak, D. (1993). A California sea lion (*Zalophus californianus*) is capable of forming equivalence relations. *The Psychological Record, 43*, 823–839.

Schwartz, B. (1980). Development of complex stereotyped behavior in pigeons. *Journal of the Experimental Analysis of Behavior, 33*, 153–166.

Schwartz, B. (1982a). Failure to produce response variability with reinforcement. *Journal of the Experimental Analysis of Behavior, 37*, 171–181.

Schwartz, B. (1982b). Reinforcement-induced stereotypy: How not to teach people to discover rules. *Journal of Experimental Psychology: General, 111*, 23–59.

Schwartz, B. (2004). *The paradox of choice: Why more is less.* New York: HarperCollins.

Schwartz, B. & Gamzu, E. (1977). Pavlovian control of operant behavior: An analysis of autoshaping and its implication for operant conditioning. In W. K. Honig & J. E. R. Staddon (Eds.), *Handbook of operant behavior* (pp. 53–97). Englewood Cliffs, NJ: Prentice-Hall.

Schwartz, B., & Lacey, H. (1982). *Behaviorism, science, and human nature* (pp. 160–191). New York: W. W. Norton & Co.

Schwartz, B., & Williams, D. R. (1972a). The role of response reinforcer contingency in negative auto-maintenance. *Journal of the Experimental Analysis of Behavior, 18*, 351–357.

Schwartz, B., & Williams, D. R. (1972b). Two different kinds of key peck in the pigeon: Some properties of responses maintained by negative and positive response-reinforcer contingencies. *Journal of the Experimental Analysis of Behavior, 18*, 201–216.

Segal, E. F. (1962). Effects of *dl*-amphetamine under concurrent VI DRL reinforcement. *Journal of the Experimental Analysis of Behavior, 5*, 105–112.

Seligman, M. E. P. (1970). On the generality of the laws of learning. *Psychological Review, 77*, 406–418.

Seligman, M. E. P. (1975). *Helplessness: On depression, development, and death.* San Francisco, CA: Freeman.

Seligman, M. E. P., & Maier, S. F. (1967). Failure to escape traumatic shock. *Journal of Experimental Psychology, 74*, 1–9.

Sepinwall, J., & Cook, L. (1978). Behavioral pharmacology of antianxiety drugs. In L. L. Iversen, S. D. Iverson & S. H. Snyder (Eds.), *Handbook of Psychopharmacology, Volume 13* (pp. 345–393). New York: Plenum Press.

Shabani, D. B., & Fisher, W. W. (2006). Stimulus fading and differential reinforcement for the treatment of needle phobia in a youth with autism. *Journal of Applied Behavior Analysis, 39*, 449–452.

Shapiro, M. M. (1960). Respondent salivary conditioning during operant lever pressing in dogs. *Science, 132*, 619–620.

Shaver, K. G. (1985). *The attribution of blame.* New York: Springer-Verlag.

Shaw, J., Seldomridge, N., Dunkle, D., Nugent, P., Spangler, L., Bromenshenk, J. et al. (2005). Polarization lidar measurements of honey bees in flight for locating land mines. *Optics Express,13*, 5853–5863.

Shearn, D. W. (1962). Operant conditioning of heart rate. *Science, 137*, 530–531.

Sherman, J. A. (1965). Use of reinforcement and imitation to reinstate verbal behavior in mute psychotics. *Journal of Abnormal Psychology, 70*, 155–164.

Sherman, J. G., Ruskin, G., & Semb, G. B. (Eds.) (1982). *The personalized system of instruction: 48 seminal papers.* Lawrence, KS: TRI Publications.

Shermer, M. (2011). Extrasensory perception. *Scientific American, 304*, 90.

Sherrington, C. (1906) *The integrative action of the nervous system* (2nd ed. 1947). New Haven, CT: Yale University Press.

Shimp, C. P. (1969). The concurrent reinforcement of two interresponse times: The relative frequency of an interresponse time equals its relative harmonic length. *Journal of the Experimental Analysis of Behavior, 12*, 403–411.

Shimp, C. P. (1992). Computational behavior dynamics: An alternative description of Nevin (1969). *Journal of the Experimental Analysis of Behavior, 57*, 289–299.

Shizgal, P., & Arvanitogiannis, A. (2003). Gambling on dopamine. *Science, 299*, 1856–1858.

Shull, R. L. (1979). The postreinforcement pause: Some implications for the correlational law of effect. In M. D. Zeiler & P. Harzem (Eds.), *Reinforcement and the organization of behaviour* (pp. 193–221). New York: John Wiley & Sons.

Shull, R. L., & Pliskoff, S. S. (1967). Changeover delay and concurrent schedules: Some effects on relative performance measures. *Journal of the Experimental Analysis of Behavior, 10*, 517–527.

Shull, R. L., Gaynor, S. T., & Grimer, J. A. (2002). Response rate measured as engagement bouts: Resistance to extinction. *Journal of the Experimental Analysis of Behavior, 77*, 211–231.

Sidman, M. (1953). Two temporal parameters in the maintenance of avoidance behavior of the white rat. *Journal of Comparative and Physiological Psychology, 46*, 253–261.

Sidman, M. (1960). *Tactics of scientific research.* New York: Basic Books.

Sidman, M. (1962). Reduction of shock frequency as reinforcement for avoidance behavior. *Journal of the Experimental Analysis of Behavior, 5*, 247–257.

Sidman, M. (1993). Reflections on behavior analysis and coercion. *Behavior and Social Issues, 3*, 75–85.

Sidman, M. (1994). *Equivalence relations and behavior: A research story.* Boston, MA: Authors Cooperative, Inc.

Sidman, M. (2000). Equivalence relations and the reinforcement contingency. *Journal of the Experimental Analysis of Behavior, 74*, 127–146.

Sidman, M. (2001). *Coercion and its fallout.* Boston, MA: Authors Cooperative, Inc.

Sidman, M. (2006). The distinction between positive and negative reinforcement: Some additional considerations. *The Behavior Analyst, 29*, 135–139.

Sidman, M., & Cresson, O., Jr. (1973). Reading and crossmodal transfer of stimulus equivalences in severe retardation. *American Journal of Mental Deficiency, 77*, 515–523.

Sidman, M., & Tailby, W. (1982). Conditional discrimination vs. matching-to-sample: An expansion of the testing paradigm. *Journal of the Experimental Analysis of Behavior, 37*, 5–22.

Sidman, M., Brady, J. V., Boren, J. J., Conrad, D. G., & Schulman, A. (1955). Reward schedules and behavior maintained by intracranial self-stimulation. *Science, 122*, 925.

Sidman, M., Cresson, O., Jr., & Wilson-Morris, M. (1974). Acquisition of matching to sample via mediated transfer. *Journal of the Experimental Analysis of Behavior, 22*, 261–273.

Sidman M., Rauzin R., Lazar R., Cunningham, S., Tailby, W., & Carrigan, P. (1982). A search for symmetry in the conditional discriminations of rhesus monkeys, baboons, and children. *Journal of the Experimental Analysis of Behavior, 37*, 23–44.

Siegel, S. (1972). Conditioning of insulin-induced glycemia. *Journal of Comparative and Physiological Psychology, 78*, 233–241.

Siegel, S. (1975). Conditioning insulin effects. *Journal of Comparative and Physiological Psychology, 89*, 189–199.

Siegel, S. (2001). Pavlovian conditioning and drug overdose: When tolerance fails. *Addiction Research and Theory, 9*, 503–513.

Siegel, S. (2005). Drug tolerance, drug addiction, and drug anticipation. *Current Directions in Psychological Scinence, 14*, 296–300.

Siegel, S., & Domjan, M. (1971). Backward conditioning as an inhibitory procedure. *Learning and Motivation, 2*, 1–11

Siegel, S., Hinson, R. E., Krank, M. D., & McCully, J. (1982). Heroin "overdose" death: The contribution of drug-associated environmental cues. *Science, 216*, 436–437.

Sigafoos, J., Doss, S., & Reichle, J. (1989). Developing mand and tact repertoires in persons with severe developmental disabilities using graphic symbols. *Research in Developmental Disabilities, 10*, 183–200.

Sigafoos, J., Reichle, J., Doss, S., Hall, K., & Pettitt, L. (1990). Spontaneous transfer of stimulus control from tact to mand contingencies. *Research in Developmental Disabilities, 11*, 165–176.

Silva, S. P., & Lattal, K. A. (2010). Why pigeons say what they do: Reinforcer magnitude and response requirement effects on say responding in say–do correspondence. *Journal of the Experimental Analysis of Behavior, 93*, 395–413.

Silverman, K., Roll, J. M., & Higgins, S. T. (2008). Introduction to the special issue on the behavior analysis and treatment of drug addiction. *Journal of Applied Behavior Analysis, 41*, 471–480.

Simic, J., & Bucher, B. (1980). Development of spontaneous manding in nonverbal children. *Journal of Applied Behavior Analysis, 13*, 523–528.

Simon, S. J., Ayllon, T., & Milan, M. A. (1982). Behavioral compensation: Contrastlike effects in the classroom. *Behavior Modification, 6*, 407–420.

Sitharthan, G., Hough, M. J., Sitharthan, T., & Kavanagh, D. J. (2001). The Alcohol Helplessness Scale and its prediction of depression among problem drinkers. *Journal of Clinical Psychology, 57*, 1445–1457.

Skinner, B. F. (1935). Two types of conditioned reflex and a pseudo type. *Journal of General Psychology, 12*, 66–77.

Skinner, B. F. (1937). Two types of conditioned reflex: A reply to Konorski and Miller. *Journal of General Psychology, 16*, 272–279.

Skinner, B. F. (1938). *The behavior of organisms*. New York: Appleton-Century-Crofts.

Skinner, B. F. (1945). Baby in a box. *Ladies Home Journal, October issue*, 30–31, 135–136, 138.

Skinner, B. F. (1948). *Walden Two*. New York: Macmillan.

Skinner, B. F. (1950). Are theories of learning necessary? *Psychological Review, 57*, 193–216.

Skinner, B. F. (1953). *Science and human behavior*. New York: Free Press.

Skinner, B. F. (1957). *Verbal behavior*. New York: Appleton-Century-Crofts.

Skinner, B. F. (1960). Pigeons in a pelican. *American Psychologist, 15*, 28–37.

Skinner, B. F. (1968). *The technology of teaching*. New York: Appleton-Century-Crofts.

Skinner, B. F. (1969). *Contingencies of reinforcement: A theoretical analysis*. New York: Appleton-Century-Crofts.

Skinner, B. F. (1971). *Beyond freedom and dignity*. New York: Alfred A. Knopf.

Skinner, B. F. (1974). *About behaviorism.* New York: Alfred A. Knopf.

Skinner, B. F. (1976). *Particulars of my life.* New York: McGraw-Hill.

Skinner, B. F. (1978). *Reflections on behaviorism and society.* Englewood Cliffs, NJ: Prentice-Hall.

Skinner, B. F. (1979). *The shaping of a behaviorist.* New York: Alfred A. Knopf.

Skinner, B. F. (1981). Selection by consequences. *Science, 213,* 501–504.

Skinner, B. F. (1983). *A matter of consequences.* New York: Alfred A. Knopf.

Skinner, B. F. (1984a). The shame of American education. *American Psychologist, 39,* 947–954.

Skinner, B. F. (1984b). The evolution of behavior. *Journal of the Experimental Analysis of Behavior, 41,* 217–222.

Skinner, B. F. (1986). The evolution of verbal behavior. *Journal of the Experimental Analysis of Behavior, 45,* 115–122.

Skinner, B. F. (1988). An operant analysis of problem solving. In A. C. Catania & S. Harnad (Eds.), *The selection of behavior—The operant behaviorism of B. F. Skinner: Comments and consequences* (pp. 218–277). New York: Cambridge University Press.

Skinner, B. F. & Vaughan, M. E. (1983). *Enjoy old age: A program of self-management.* New York: W. W. Norton.

Smeets, P. M., Barnes-Holmes, D., & Nagle, M. (2000). Transfer and stimulus equivalence classes derived from simultaneously presented S+ and S− stimuli. *European Journal of Behavior Analysis, 1,* 33–49.

Smith, M. C., & Gormezano, I. (1965). *Conditioning of the nictitating membrane response of the rabbit as a function of backward, simultaneous, and forward CS–UCS intervals.* Paper presented at the meeting of the Psychonomic Society, Chicago, IL.

Sobsey, D. (1990). Modifying the behavior of behavior modifiers: Arguments for countercontrol against aversive procedures. In A. C. Repp & N. N. Singh (Eds.), *Perspectives on the use of nonaversive and aversive interventions for persons with developmental disabilities* (pp. 421–433). Sycamore, IL: Sycamore Publishing Co.

Solomon, P. R., Blanchard, S., Levine, E., Velazquez, E., & Groccia-Ellison, M. (1991). Attenuation of age-related deficits in humans by extension of the interstumulus interval. *Psychology of Aging, 6,* 36–42.

Solomon, R. L., & Brush, E. S. (1956). Experimentally derived conceptions of anxiety and aversion. In M. R. Jones (Ed.), *Nebraska symposium on motivation* (pp. 212–305). Lincoln, NE: University of Nebraska Press.

Sossin, W. S., Kirk, M. D., & Scheller, R. H. (1987). Peptidergic modulation of neuronal circuitry controlling feeding in *Aplysia. Journal of Neuroscience, 7,* 671–681.

Sowers-Hoag, K. M., Thyer, B. A., & Bailey, J. S. (1987). Promoting automobile safety belt use by young children. *Journal of Applied Behavior Analysis, 20,* 133–138.

Sparkes, S., Grant, V. L., & Lett, B. T. (2003). Role of conditioned taste aversion in the development of activity anorexia. *Appetite, 41,* 161–165.

Speakman, J. R. (2008). Thrifty genes for obesity, an attractive but flawed idea, and an alternative perspective: the 'drifty gene' hypothesis. *International Journal of Obesity, 32,* 1611–1617.

Spetch, M. L., & Friedman, A. (2006). Pigeons see correspondence between objects and their pictures. *Psychological Science, 17,* 966–972.

Spetch, M. L., Cheng, K., & Clifford, C. W. G. (2004). Peak shift but not range effects in recognition of faces. *Learning and Motivation, 35,* 221–241.

Spiegelman, B. (2008). The skinny fat. *The Scientist, 22,* 28. http://classic.the-scientist.com/article/display/54033/

Springer, C. R., & Pear, J. J. (2008). Performance measures in courses using computer-aided personalized system of instruction. *Computers & Education, 51,* 829–835.

Squires, N., & Fantino, E. (1971). A model for choice in simple concurrent and concurrent-chains schedules. *Journal of the Experimental Analysis of Behavior, 15,* 27–38.

Staats, A. W. (1975). *Social behaviorism.* Chicago, IL: Dorsey Press.

Staddon, J. E. R. (1977). Schedule-induced behavior. In W. K. Honig & J. E. R. Staddon (Eds.), *Handbook of operant behavior* (pp. 125–152). Englewood Cliffs, NJ: Prentice-Hall.

Staddon, J. E. R., & Simmelhag, V. L. (1971). The "superstition" experiment: A re-examination of its implications for the principles of adaptive behavior. *Psychological Review, 78,* 3–43.

Stafford, D. & Branch, M. (1998). Effects of step size and break-point criterion on progressive-ratio performance. *Journal of the Experimental Analysis of Behavior, 70*, 123–138.

Stein, L., & Belluzzi, J. D. (1988). Operant conditioning of individual neurons. In M. L. Commons, R. M. Church, J. R. Stellar, & A. R. Wagner (Eds.), *Quantitative analyses of behavior. Volume 7. Biological determinants of reinforcement and memory* (pp. 249–264). Hillsdale, NJ: Lawrence Erlbaum Associates.

Stein, L., Xue, B. G., & Belluzzi, J. D. (1994). *In vitro* reinforcement of hippocampal bursting: A search for Skinner's atoms of behavior. *Journal of the Experimental Analysis of Behavior, 61*, 155–168.

Stevens, J. R., & Stephens, D. W. (2010). The adaptive nature of impulsivity. In G. J. Madden & W. K. Bickel (Eds.), *Impulsivity: The behavioral and neurological science of discounting* (pp. 361–388). Washington, DC: American Psychological Association.

Stevenson-Hinde, J. (1983). Constraints on reinforcement. In R. A. Hinde & J. Stevenson-Hinde (Eds.), *Constraints on learning: Limitations and predispositions* (pp. 285–296). New York: Academic Press.

Stiers, M., & Silberberg, A. (1974). Lever-contact responses in rats: Automaintenance with and without a negative response-reinforcer dependency. *Journal of the Experimental Analysis of Behavior, 22*, 497–506.

Stokes, P. D. (2001). Variability, constraints, and creativity: Shedding light on Claude Monet. *American Psychologist, 36*, 355–359.

Stokes, P. D., Mechner, F., & Balsam, P. D. (1999). Effects of different acquisition procedures on response variability. *Animal Learning and Behavior, 27*, 28–41.

Stokes, T. F., & Baer, D. M. (1977). An implicit technology of generalization. *Journal of Applied Behavior Analysis, 10*, 349–367.

Stokes, T. F., Fowler, S. A., & Baer, D. M. (1978). Training preschool children to recruit natural communities of reinforcement. *Journal of Applied Behavior Analysis, 11*, 285–303.

Stonebraker, T. B., & Rilling, M. (1981). Control of delayed matching-to-sample using directed forgetting techniques. *Animal Learning and Behavior, 9*, 196–201.

Stonebraker, T. B., Rilling, M., & Kendrick, D. F. (1981). Time dependent effects of double cuing in directed forgetting. *Animal Learning and Behavior, 9*, 385–394.

Stoops, W. W. (2008). Reinforcing effects of stimulants in humans: Sensitivity of progressive-ratio schedules. *Experimental Clinical Psychopharmacology, 16*, 503–512.

Stoops, W. W., Glaser, P. E. A., Fillmore, M. T., & Rush, C. R. (2004). Reinforcing, subject-rated, performance and physiological effects of methylphenidate and d-amphetamine in stimulant-abusing humans. *Journal of Psychopharmacology, 18*, 534–543.

Storms, L. H., Boroczi, G., & Broen, W. E., Jr. (1962). Punishment inhibits an instrumental response in hooded rats. *Science, 135*, 1133–1134.

Straus, M. A. (2001). *Beating the devil out of them: Corporal punishment in American families and its effects on children* (2nd Ed.). New Brunswick, NJ: Transaction Publishers.

Stroop, J. R. (1935). Studies of interference in serial verbal reactions. *Journal of Experimental Psychology, 18*, 643–662.

Sullivan, R. M., & Hall, W. G. (1988). Reinforcers in infancy: Classical conditioning using stroking or intra-oral infusions of milk as UCS. *Developmental Psychobiology, 21*, 215–223.

Sulzer-Azaroff, B. (1986). Behavior analysis and education: Crowning achievements and crying needs. *Division 25 Recorder, 21*, 55–65.

Sun, B., & Tsai, P. S. (2011). A gonadotropin-releasing hormone-like molecule modulates the activity of diverse central neurons in a gastropod mollusk, *Aplysia californica. Frontiers in Endocrinology, 2*, 1–8.

Sunahara, D., & Pierce, W. D. (1982). The matching law and bias in a social exchange involving choice between alternatives. *Canadian Journal of Sociology, 7*, 145–165.

Sundberg, M. L. (1985). Teaching verbal behavior to pigeons. *The Analysis of Verbal Behavior, 3*, 11–17.

Sundberg, M. L. (1996). Toward granting linguistic competence to apes: A review of Savage-Rumbaugh et al.'s *Language Comprehension in Ape and Child. Journal of the Experimental Analysis of Behavior, 65*, 477–492.

Sundberg, M. L., & Michael, J. (2001). The benefits of Skinner's analysis of verbal behavior for children with autism. *Behavior Modification, 25*, 698–724.

Sundberg, M. L., & Sundberg, C. A. (2011). Intraverbal behavior and verbal conditional discriminations in typically developing children and children with autism. *The Analysis of Verbal Behavior, 27*, 23–43.

Sundberg, M. L., Endicott, K., & Eigenheer, P. (2000). Using intraverbal prompts to establish tacts for children with autism. *The Analysis of Verbal Behavior, 17*, 89–104.

Svartdal, F. (1992). Operant modulation of low-level attributes of rule-governed behavior by nonverbal contingencies. *Learning and Motivation, 22*, 406–420.

Swithers, S. E., & Davidson, T. L. (2008). A role for sweet taste: Calorie predictive relations in energy regulation by rats. *Behavioral Neuroscience, 122*, 161–173.

Swithers, S. E., Doerflinger, A., & Davidson, T. L. (2006). Consistent relationships between sensory properties of savory snack foods and calories influence food intake in rats. *International Journal of Obesity, 30*, 1685–1692.

Tait, R. W., & Saladin, M. E. (1986). Concurrent development of excitatory and inhibitory associations during backward conditioning. *Animal Learning and Behavior, 14*, 133–137.

Takamori, K., Yoshida, S., & Okuyama, S. (2001). Repeated treatment with imipramine, fluvoxamine, and tranylcypromine decreases the number of escape failures by activating dopaminergic systems in a rat learned helplessness test. *Life Sciences, 69*, 1919–1926.

Takemoto, H. (2008). Morphological analyses and 3D modeling of the tongue musculature of the chimpanzee (*Pan troglodytes*). *American Journal of Primatology, 70*, 966–975.

Tayler, C. K. & Saayman, G. S. (1973). Imitative behavior by Indian Ocean bottlenose dolphins (*Tursiops aduncus*) in captivity. *Behaviour, 44*, 286–298.

Taylor, I., & O'Reilly, M. F. (1997). Toward a functional analysis of private verbal self-regulation. *Journal of Applied Behavior Analysis, 30*, 43–58.

Taylor, S. P., & Pisano, R. (1971). Physical aggression as a function of frustration and physical attack. *Journal of Social Psychology, 84*, 261–267.

Terrace, H. S. (1963). Discrimination learning with and without "errors." *Journal of the Experimental Analysis of Behavior, 6*, 1–27.

Terrace, H. S. (1972). By-products of discrimination learning. In G. H. Bower (Ed.), *The psychology of learning and motivation. Volume 5* (pp. 195–265). New York: Academic Press.

Thomas, D. B., Gao, D. L, Ray, R. M., Wang, W. W., Allison, C. J., Chen, F. L. et al. (2002). Randomized trial of breast self-examination in Shanghai: Final results. *Journal of the National Cancer Institute, 94*, 1445–1457.

Thomas, D. R., & Setzer, J. (1972). Stimulus generalization gradients for auditory intensity in rats and guinea pigs. *Psychonomic Science, 28*, 22–24.

Thompson, R. F. & Spencer, W. A. (1966). Habituation: A model phenomenon for the study of neuronal substrates of behavior. *Psychological Review, 73*, 16–43.

Thompson, R. H., Bruzek, J., & Cotnoir-Bichelman, N. M. (2011). The role of negative reinforcement in infant caregiving: An experimental simulation. *Journal of Applied Behavior Analysis, 44*, 295–304.

Thompson, T. (2007). Relations among functional systems in behavior analysis. *Journal of the Experimental Analysis of Behavior, 87*, 423–440.

Thorndike, E. L. (1898). Animal intelligence. *Psychological Review Monograph Supplements* (Serial No. 8).

Thorndike, E. L. (1911). *Animal intelligence*. New York: Macmillan.

Thorpe, W. H. (1963). *Learning and instinct in animals*. Cambridge, MA: Harvard University Press.

Tiger, J. H., Hanley, G. P., & Hernandez, E. (2006). An evaluation of the value of choice with preschool children. *Journal of Applied Behavior Analysis, 39*, 1–16.

Tighe, T. J., & Leaton, R. N. (1976). *Habituation*. Hillsdale, NJ: Lawrence Erlbaum Associates.

Timberlake, W. (1983). Rats' responses to a moving object related to food or water: A behavior-systems analysis. *Animal Learning and Behavior, 11*, 309–320.

Timberlake, W. (1993). Behavior systems and reinforcement: An integrative approach. *Journal of the Experimental Analysis of Behavior, 60*, 105–128.

Timberlake, W., & Allison, J. (1974) Response deprivation: An empirical approach to instrumental performance. *Psychological Review, 81*, 146–164.

Timberlake, W., & Grant, D. L. (1975). Auto-shaping in rats to the presentation of another rat predicting food. *Science, 190*, 690–692.

Tinbergen, N. (1951). *The study of instinct*. Oxford: Oxford University Press.

Tinbergen, N., & Kuenen, D. J. (1957). Feeding behavior in young thrushes. In C. H. Schiller (Ed.), *Instinctive behavior: Development of a modern concept* (pp. 209–236). London: Methuen.

Tobler, P. N., Fiorillo, C. D., & Schultz, W. (2005). Adaptive coding of reward value by dopamine neurons. *Science, 307*, 1642–1645.

Todd, J. T., & Morris, E. K. (1986). The early research of John B. Watson: Before the behavioral revolution. *The Behavior Analyst, 9*, 71–88.

Tomasello, M. (2009). The question of chimpanzee culture, plus postscript (Chimpanzee culture, 2009). In K. N. Laland & B. G. Galef (Eds.), *The question of animal culture* (pp. 198–221). Cambridge, MA: Harvard University Press.

Tomasello, M., Savage-Rumbaugh, S., & Kruger, A. C. (1993). Imitative learning of actions on objects by children, chimpanzees, and enculturated chimpanzees. *Child Development, 64*, 1688–1705.

Tourinho, E. Z. (2006). Private stimuli, covert responses and private events: Conceptual remarks. *The Behavior Analyst, 29*, 13–31.

Toussaint, K. A. (2011). *Teaching tactual discrimination of Braille characters to beginning Braille readers.* Dissertation submitted to the Department of Psychology, Louisiana State University, Agricultural and Mechanical College.

Towe, A. L. (1954). A study of figural equivalence in the pigeon. *Journal of Comparative and Physiological Psychology, 47*, 283–287.

Trapp, M. A., Kottke, T. E., Viekrant, R. A., Kaur, J. S., & Sellers, T. A. (1999). The ability of trained nurses to detect lumps in a test set of silicone breast models. *Cancer, 86*, 1750–1756.

Tuckman, G. (2011). CNN: *Video: Spare the rod, spoil the child.* 15 August 2011. http://ac360.blogs.cnn.com/2011/08/15/video-spare-the-rod-spoil-the-child/

Tulving, E. (1983). *Elements of episodic memory.* New York: Oxford University Press.

Turner, N. & Horbay, R. (2004). How do slot machines and other electronic gambling machines actually work? *Journal of Gambling Issues, 11*, 1–14.

Turney, T. H. (1982). The association of visual concepts and imitative vocalization in the mynah (*Gracula religiosa*). *Bulletin of the Psychonomic Society, 19*, 59–62.

Twenge, J. M., Baumeister, R. F., Tice, D. M., & Stucke, T. S. (2001). If you can't join them, beat them: Effects of social exclusion on aggressive behavior. *Journal of Personality and Social Psychology, 81*, 1058–1069.

Twyman, J. (1996). The functional independence of impure mands and tacts of abstract stimulus properties. *The Analysis of Verbal Behavior, 13*, 1–19.

Ullstadius, E. (2000). Variability in judgment of neonatal imitation. *Journal of Reproductive and Infant Psychology, 18*, 239–247.

Ulrich, R. E., & Azrin, N. H. (1962). Reflexive fighting in response to aversive stimulation. *Journal of the Experimental Analysis of Behavior, 5*, 511–520.

Ulrich, R. E., Wolff, P. C., & Azrin, N. H. (1964). Shock as an elicitor of intra- and inter-species fighting behavior. *Animal Behaviour, 12*, 14–15.

U.S. Department of Health and Human Services, Administration for Children & Families, (2009). *Child Maltreatment 2009.* www.acf.hhs.gov/programs/cb/pubs/cm09/index.htm

Van Hest, A., van Haaren, F., & van de Poll, N. E. (1989). Operant conditioning of response variability in male and female Wistar rats. *Physiology and Behavior, 45*, 551–555.

Van Houten, R., Axelrod, S., Bailey, J. S., Favell, J. E., Foxx, R. M., Iwata, B. A. et al. (1988). The right to effective behavioral treatment. *Journal of Applied Behavior Analysis, 21*, 381–384.

Van Houten, R., Malenfant, J. E. L., Reagan, I., Sifrit, K., Compton, R., & Tenenbaum, J. (2010). Increasing seat belt use in service vehicle drivers with a gearshift delay. *Journal of Applied Behavior Analysis, 43*, 369–380.

Vargas, E. A. (1998). Verbal behavior: Implications of its mediational and relational characteristics. *Analysis of Verbal Behavior, 15*, 149–151.

Vargas, J. S. (1990). B. F. Skinner: Fact and fiction. *The International Behaviorology Association Newsletter, 2*, 8–11.

Vasquez, E. A., Denson, T. F., Pedersen, W. C., Stenstrom, D. M., & Miller, N. (2005). The moderating effect of trigger intensity on triggered displaced aggression. *Journal of Experimental Social Psychology, 41*, 61–67.

Vaughn, W., Jr. (1988). Formation of equivalence sets in pigeons. *Journal of Experimental Psychology: Animal Behavior Processes, 14*, 36–42.

Ventura, R., Morrone, C., & Puglisi-Allegra, S. (2007). Prefrontal/accumbal catecholamine system determines motivational salience attribution to both reward- and aversion-related stimuli. *Proceedings of the National Academy of Sciences of the USA, 104*, 5181–5186.

Vergoz, V., Roussel, E., Sandoz, J. C., & Giurfa, M. (2007). Aversive learning in honeybees revealed by the olfactory conditioning of the stinger extension reflex. *PLoS One, 2*, e288.

Verhave, T. (1966). The pigeon as a quality control inspector. *American Psychologist, 21*, 109–115.

Vichi, C., Andery, M. A., & Glenn, S. S. (2009). A metacontingency experiment: The effects of contingent consequences on patterns of interlocking contingencies of reinforcement. *Behavior and Social Issues, 18*, 41–57.

Villareal, J. (1967). Schedule-induced pica. *Physiology and Behavior, 6*, 577–588.

Voineagu, I., Wang, X., Johnston, P., Lowe, J. K., Tian, Y., Horvath, S. et al. (2011). Transcriptomic analysis of autistic brain reveals convergent molecular pathology. *Nature, 474*, 380–384.

Volkmar, F., Carter, A., Grossman, J., & Klin, A. (1997). Social development in autism. In D. J. Cohen & F. R.Volkmar (Eds.), *Handbook of autism and pervasive developmental disorders* (2nd Ed.) (pp. 171–194). New York: John Wiley & Sons.

Volkow, N. D., Fowler, J. S. & Wang, G.-J. (2003). The addicted human brain: Insights from imaging studies. *Journal of Clinical Investigation, 111*, 1444–1451.

Vollmer, T. R., & Hackenberg, T. D. (2001). Reinforcement contingencies and social reinforcement: Some reciprocal relations between basic and applied research. *Journal of Applied Behavior Analysis, 34*, 241–253.

Vorndran, C. M., & Lerman, D. C. (2006). Establishing and maintaining treatment effects with less intrusive consequences via a pairing procedure. *Journal of Applied Behavior Analysis, 39*, 35–48.

Voss, S. C., & Homzie, M. J. (1970). Choice as a value. *Psychological Reports, 26*, 912–914.

Vuchinich, R. E., & Simpson, C. A. (1999). Delayed reward discounting in alcohol abuse. In F. J. Chaloupka, M. Grossman, W. K. Bickel, & H. Saffer (Eds.), *The economic analysis of substance use and abuse* (pp. 103–122). Chicago: University of Chicago Press.

Wacker, D. P., Harding, J. W., Berg, W. K., Lee, J. F., Schieltz, K. M., Padilla, Y. C. et al. (2011). An evaluation of persistence of treatment effects during long-term treatment of destructive behavior. *Journal of the Experimental Analysis of Behavior, 96*, 261–282.

Wagenmakers, E. J., Wetzels, R., Borsboom, D., & van der Maas, H. (2011). Why psychologists must change the way they analyze their data: The case of psi: Comment on Bem (2011). *Journal of Personality and Social Psychology, 100*, 426–432.

Wagner, A. R., & Rescorla, R. A. (1972). Inhibition in Pavlovian conditioning: Applications of a theory. In R. A. Boakes & M. S. Halliday (Eds.), *Inhibition and learning* (pp. 301–359). London: Academic Press.

Wakefield, J. C. (2006). Is behaviorism becoming a pseudo-science? Power versus scientific rationality in the eclipse of token economies by biological psychiatry in the treatment of schizophrenia. *Behavior and Social Issues, 15*, 202–221.

Walker, S. (1987). *Animal Learning*. New York: Routledge & Kegan Paul.

Waller, M. B. (1961). Effects of chronically administered chlorpromazine on multiple-schedule performance. *Journal of the Experimental Analysis of Behavior, 4*, 351–359.

Wanchisen, B. A., Tatham, T. A., & Mooney, S. E. (1989). Variable-ratio conditioning history produces high- and low-rate fixed-interval performance in rats. *Journal of the Experimental Analysis of Behavior, 52*, 167–179.

Ward, T. A. (2006). *An experimental analysis of Harris's cultural materialism: The effects of various modes of production on metacontingencies.* Masters Thesis, Faculty of Arts, Stephen F. Austin State University.

Warden, C. J., & Jackson, T. A. (1935). Imitative behavior in the Rhesus monkeys. *Pedagogical Seminary and Journal of Genetic Psychology, 46*, 103–125.

Warden, C. J., Fjeld, H. A., & Koch, A. M. (1940). Imitative behavior in the Rhesus monkeys. *Pedagogical Seminary and Journal of Genetic Psychology, 56*, 311–322.

Warren, Z., McPheeters, M. L., Sathe, N., Foss-Feig, J. H., Glasser, A., & Veenstra-VanderWeele, J. (2011). A systematic review of early intensive intervention for autism spectrum disorders. *Pediatrics, 127*, e1303–e1311.

Wasserman, E. A. (1973). Pavlovian conditioning with heat reinforcement produces stimulus-directed pecking in chicks. *Science, 181*, 875–877.

Wasserman, E. A., & Young, M. E. (2010). Same–different discrimination: The keel and backbone of thought and reasoning. *Journal of Experimental Psychology: Animal Behavior Processes, 36*, 3–22.

Watson, J. B. (1903). *Animal education: An experimental study on the psychical development of the white rat, correlated with the growth of its nervous system.* Chicago, IL: University of Chicago Press.

Watson, J. B. (1913). Psychology as the behaviorist views it. *Psychological Review, 20*, 158–177.

Watson, J. B. (1936). John Broadus Watson. In C. Murchison (Ed.), *A history of psychology in autobiography. Volume 3* (pp. 271–281). Worcester, MA: Clark University Press.

Watson, J. B., & Rayner, R. (1920). Conditioned emotional reactions. *Journal of Experimental Child Psychology, 3*, 1–14.

Wawrzyncyck, S. (1937) Badania and parecia *Spirostomum ambiguum major. Acta Biologica Experimentalis (Warsaw), 11*, 57–77.

Wearden, J. H. (1983). Undermatching and overmatching as deviations from the matching law. *Journal of the Experimental Analysis of Behavior, 40*, 333–340.

Wearden, J. H., & Burgess, I. S. (1982). Matching since Baum (1979). *Journal of the Experimental Analysis of Behavior, 38*, 339–348.

Webbe, F. M., DeWeese, J., & Malagodi, E. F. (1978). Induced attack during multiple fixed-ratio, variable-ratio schedules of reinforcement. *Journal of the Experimental Analysis of Behavior, 20*, 219–224.

Weiner, H. (1962). Some effects of response cost upon human operant behavior. *Journal of the Experimental Analysis of Behavior, 5*, 201–208.

Weiner, H. (1969). Controlling human fixed-interval performance. *Journal of the Experimental Analysis of Behavior, 12*, 349–373.

Weiss, B., & Gott, C. T. (1972). A microanalysis of drug effects on fixed-ratio performance in pigeons. *Journal of Pharmacology and Experimental Therapeutics, 180*, 189–202.

Weissman, N. W., & Crossman, E. K. (1966). A comparison of two types of extinction following fixed-ratio training. *Journal of the Experimental Analysis of Behavior, 9*, 41–46.

West, M. J., & King, A. P. (1988). Female visual displays affect the development of male song in the cowbird. *Nature, 334*, 244–246.

West, R. P., & Young, K. R. (1992). Precision teaching. In R. P. West & L. A. Hamerlynck (Eds.), *Designs for excellence in education: The legacy of B. F. Skinner* (pp. 113–146). Longmont, CO: Sopris West, Inc.

West, R. P., Young, R., & Spooner, F. (1990). Precision teaching: An introduction. *Teaching Exceptional Children, 22*, 4–9.

Wheeler, H. (Ed.). (1973). *Beyond the punitive society.* San Francisco, CA: W. H. Freeman.

White, A. J., & Davison, M. C. (1973). Performance in concurrent fixed-interval schedules. *Journal of the Experimental Analysis of Behavior, 19*, 147–153.

White, C. T., & Schlosberg, H. (1952). Degree of conditioning of the GSR as a function of the period of delay. *Journal of Experimental Psychology, 43*, 357–362.

White, K. G. (2002). Psychophysics of remembering: The discrimination hypothesis. *Current Directions in Psychological Science, 11*, 141–145.

White, K. G., & Brown, G. S. (2011). Reversing the course of forgetting. *Journal of the Experimental Analysis of Behavior, 96*, 177–189,

White, K. G., & Wixted, J. T. (1999). Psychophysics of remembering. *Journal of the Experimental Analysis of Behavior, 71*, 91–113.

White, K. G., Parkinson, A. E., Brown, G. S., & Wixted, J. T. (2004). Local proactive interference in delayed matching to sample: The role of reinforcement. *Journal of Experimental Psychology: Animal Behavior Processes, 32*, 83–95.

White, O. R. (1986). Precision teaching—Precision learning. *Exceptional Children, 52*, 522–534.

Whiten, A., & Boesch, C. (2001). The cultures of chimpanzees. *Scientific American, 284*, 60–68.

Whiten, A., Hinde, R. A., Laland, K. N., & Stringer, C. B. (2011). Culture evolves. *Philosophical Transactions of the Royal Society B, 366*, 938–948.

Whiten, A., McGuigan, N., Marshall-Pescini, S., & Hopper. L. M. (2009). Emulation, imitation, over-imitation and the scope of culture for child and chimpanzee. *Philosophical Transactions of the Royal Society B, 364*, 2417–2428.

Wickens, T. D. (2002). *Elementary signal detection theory.* New York: Oxford University Press.

Wiesler, N. A., Hanson, R. H., Chamberlain, T. P., & Thompson, T. (1988). Stereotypic behavior of mentally retarded adults adjunctive to a positive reinforcement schedule. *Research in Developmental Disabilities, 9*, 393–403.

Wike, E. L. (1966). *Secondary reinforcement: Selected experiments.* New York: Harper & Row.

Wilcoxon, H. C., Dragoin, W. B., & Kral, P. A. (1971). Illness-induced aversions in rat and quail: Relative salience of visual and gustatory cues. *Science, 171*, 826–828.

Wilken, G. C. (1979). Whistle speech in Tlaxcala (Mexico). *Anthropos, 74*, 881–888.

Wilkes, G. (1994). *A behavior sampler.* North Bend, WA: Sunshine Books.

Williams, A. R. (1997). Under the volcano: Montserrat. *National Geographic, 192*, 59–75.

Williams, B. A. (1981). The following schedule of reinforcement as a fundamental determinant of steady-state contrast in multiple schedules. *Journal of the Experimental Analysis of Behavior, 12*, 293–310.

Williams, B. A. (1990). Pavlovian contingencies and anticipatory contrast. *Animal Learning and Behavior, 18*, 44–50.

Williams, B. A. (1992). Competition between stimulus-reinforcer contingencies and anticipatory contrast. *Journal of the Experimental Analysis of Behavior, 58*, 287–302.

Williams, B. A. (2002). Behavioral contrast redux. *Animal Learning and Behavior, 30*, 1–20.

Williams, C. D. (1959). The elimination of tantrum behavior by extinction procedures. *Journal of Abnormal and Social Psychology, 59*, 269.

Williams, D. R., & Williams, H. (1969). Automaintenance in the pigeon: Sustained pecking despite contingent non-reinforcement. *Journal of the Experimental Analysis of Behavior, 12*, 511–520.

Williams, J. L., & Lierle, D. M. (1986). Effects of stress controllability, immunization, and therapy on the subsequent defeat of colony intruders. *Animal Learning and Behavior, 14*, 305–314.

Williams, K. D., & Nida, S. A. (2011). Ostracism: Consequences and coping. *Current Directions in Psychological Science, 20*, 71–75.

Wilson, K., & Hayes, S. C. (2000). Why it is crucial to understand thinking and feeling: An analysis and application to drug abuse. *The Behavior Analyst, 23*, 25–43.

Wilson, L., & Rogers, R. W. (1975). The fire this time: Effects of race of target, insult, and potential retaliation on black aggression. *Journal of Personality and Social Psychology, 32*, 857–864.

Wing, V. C., & Shoaib, M. (2010). A second-order schedule of food reinforcement in rats to examine the role of the CB1 receptors in the reinforcement-enhancing effects of nicotine. *Addiction Biology, 15*, 380–392.

Winstanley, C. A. (2010). The neural and neurochemical basis of delay discounting. In G. J. Madden & W. K. Bickel (Eds.), *Impulsivity: The behavioral and neurological science of discounting* (pp. 95–122). Washington, DC: American Psychological Association.

Wisniewski, M. G., Church, B. A., & Mercado, E., III. (2009). Learning-related shifts in generalization gradients for complex sounds. *Learning and Behavior, 37*, 325–335.

Witoslawski, J. J., Anderson, R. B., & Hanson, H. M. (1963). Behavioral studies with a black vulture, *Coragyps atratus. Journal of the Experimental Analysis of Behavior, 6*, 605–606.

Wolfe, B. M., & Baron, R. A. (1971). Laboratory aggression related to aggression in naturalistic social situations: Effects of an aggressive model on the behavior of college students and prisoner observers. *Psychonomic Science, 24*, 193–194.

Wolfe, J. B. (1936). Effectiveness of token rewards for chimpanzees. *Comparative Psychology Monographs, 12*, 1–72.

Wyckoff, L. B., Jr. (1952). The role of observing responses in discrimination learning. Part 1. *Psychological Review, 59*, 431–442.

Wyckoff, L. B., Jr. (1969). The role of observing responses in discrimination learning. In D. P. Hendry (Ed.), *Conditioned reinforcement* (pp. 237–260). Homewood, IL: Dorsey Press.

Xue, B. G., Belluzzi, J. D., & Stein, L. (1993). *In vitro* reinforcement of hippocampal bursting activity by the cannabinoid receptor agonist CP-55,940. *Brain Research, 626*, 272–277.

Yamamoto, J., & Mochizuki, A, (1988). Acquisition and functional analysis of manding with autistic students. *Journal of Applied Behavior Analysis, 21*, 57–64.

Yamamoto, T. (2007). Brain regions responsible for the expression of conditioned taste aversion in rats. *Chemical Senses, 32*, 105–109.

Yi, J. I., Christian, L., Vittimberga, G., & Lowenkron, B. (2006). Generalized negatively reinforced manding in children with autism. *Analysis of Verbal Behavior, 22*, 21–33.

Yoon, S., & Bennett, G. M. (2000). Effects of a stimulus–stimulus pairing procedure on conditioning vocal sounds as reinforcers. *Analysis of Verbal Behavior, 17*, 75–88.

Zajonc, R. B. (1965). Social facilitation. *Science, 149*, 269–274.

Zandian, M., Ioakimidis, I., Bergh, C., & Sodersten, P. (2007). Cause and treatment of anorexia nervosa. *Physiology and Behavior, 92*, 283–290.

Zeiler, M. D. (1977). Schedules of reinforcement: The controlling variables. In W. K. Honig & J. E. R. Staddon (Eds.), *Handbook of operant behavior* (pp. 201–232). Englewood Cliffs, NJ: Prentice-Hall.

Zeiler, M. D. (1992). On immediate function. *Journal of the Experimental Analysis of Behavior, 57*, 417–427.

Zelinski, E. L., Hong, N. S., Tyndall, A.V., Halsall, B., & McDonald, R. J. (2010). Prefrontal cortical contributions during discriminative fear conditioning, extinction, and spontaneous recovery in rats. *Experimental Brain Research, 203*, 285–297.

Zentall, T. R. (2006). Imitation: Definitions, evidence and mechanisms. *Animal Cognition, 9*, 335–353.

Zentall, T. R. (2011). Social learning mechanisms: Implications for a cognitive theory of imitation. *Interaction Studies, 12*, 233–261.

Zentall, T. R., Sutton, J. E., & Sherburne, L. M. (1996). True imitative learning in pigeons. *Psychological Science, 7*, 343–346.

Zettle, R. D., & Hayes, S. C. (1982). Rule-governed behavior: A potential theoretical framework for cognitive–behavior therapy. In P. C. Kendall (Ed.), *Advances in cognitive behavioral research and therapy, Volume 1* (pp. 73–118). New York: Academic Press.

Zielinska, E. (2012). Treating fat with fat. *The Scientist, 26*, 65.

Zillmann, D. (1988). Cognition–excitation interdependencies in aggressive behavior. *Aggressive Behavior, 14*, 51–64.

Zimmerman, J., & Ferster, C. B. (1963). Intermittent punishment of S^{Δ} responding in matching-to-sample. *Journal of the Experimental Analysis of Behavior, 6*, 349–356.

Zink, C. F., Pagnoni, G., Martin-Skurski, M. E., Chappelow, J. C., & Berns, G. S. (2004). Human striatal responses to monetary reward depend on saliency. *Neuron, 42*, 509–517.

Author Index

Abbott, B. 304
Abraham, D. A. 426
Abrams, T. 60
Abramson, C. I. 239
Abramson, L. Y. 181
Abreu-Rodrigues, J. 323
Ackert, A. M. 215
Adams, C. K. 431, 432
Ader, R. 75
Afifi, T. O. 167–8
Agostino, N. R. 239
Ahearn, W. H. 378
Ainslie, G. W. 279, 280
Albanos, K. 205
Alberto, P. A. 399, 406
Albin, R. W. 179
Alciati, M. H. 430
Alcock, J. 326, 444
Aleksejev, R. M. 183
Alexander, J. H. 179
Alexander, J. L. 424–5
Alferink, L. A. 299
Allen, C. 283, 463
Allen, G. L. 315
Allen, R. 414
Allen, T. L. 430
Alling, K. 98
Allison, C. J. 430
Allison, J. 93
Alsiö, J. 274
Altemus, M. 215
Altschuler, E. L. 335
Alvarez, L. W. 440–1
Alvarez, W. 440–1
Alvord, J. R. 315
Amat, J. 181, 183
Ammar, A. 215–16
Anderson, C. A. 186
Anderson, C. D. 232
Anderson, M. J. 71
Anderson, N. D. 239
Anderson, R. B. 121
Andery, M. A. 460
Andre, J. 205
Andreatos, M. 339
Andrews, D. 406
Angeli, C. A. 58
Anger, D. 142–3
Anisfeld, M. 331, 332
Anrep, G. V. 63, 64
Antonitis, J. J. 106–7, 125, 301

Appel, J. B. 158, 160, 161
Arantes, J. 239
Arbuckle, J. L. 143
Arccdiano, F. 72
Aristotle 58
Armitage, K. B. 457
Arms, R. L. 184
Arnold, K. E. 227
Arvanitogiannis, A. 6
Arvidsson, E. 274
Arwas, S. 206
Asaro, F. 440–1
Asherson, P. 278
Ator, N. A. 97
Austin, J. 399
Autor, S. M. 298
Axel, R. 442–3
Axelrod, S. 162
Ayllon, T. 233, 315
Ayres, K. M. 424–5
Azar, B. 249
Azrin, N. H. 107, 122, 154, 157, 159, 160–1, 164, 165,
    183–4, 187, 209, 315, 402, 411

Baars, B. J. 21
Bach, H. 250
Badger, G. J. 139–41, 278, 412, 413
Badia, P. 304
Baer, D. M. 13, 20, 34, 105, 323, 324, 337–9, 340–1, 357,
    368–9, 400, 403–4, 421
Baeyens, F. 72
Bailey, J. S. 162, 372, 399, 402
Baines, C. 430
Baker, A. G. 111, 179
Baker, T. B. 73
Baldwin, J. M. 325
Ball, J. 326
Balogh, A. C. V. 233
Balow, M. 360
Balsam, P. D. 105
Bandura, A. 325, 337, 342–3, 344–5, 350
Banko, K. 90–1
Banuazizi, A. 201–2
Baratta, M. V. 181
Barbera, M. L. 422
Bard, K. 331
Barker, L. M. 206
Barksdale, D. J. 430
Barlow, G. W. 56
Barnes, C. A. 105
Barnes-Holmes, D. 323, 369, 378, 392

Subject Index

Entries in **bold** are defined in the Glossary